"I am most impressed by the high quality of the information and broad range of coverage of this text, which, while thorough and rigorous, has many appealing features and a writing style that is easy to understand and reader-friendly. I plan to use this book in my own work, as it provides an up-to-date source that helps the reader understand the importance of inclusion and social justice as well as effective instructional settings and practices for intellectually disabled students."

—James McLeskey, Professor, School of Special Education, School Psychology, and Early Childhood Studies, University of Florida

"An essential text, *Cognitive and Intellectual Disabilities* provides a complete foundation in special education, grounded in an historical perspective of pivotal events, research, and legislation that have shaped the field. The guiding questions and additional online sources will challenge readers to evaluate and apply the information presented. This book equips future teachers with the knowledge needed to effectively implement best practices for educating students with disabilities."

—Fred Spooner, Ph.D., Professor of Special Education and Child Development, University of North Carolina at Charlotte

Cognitive and Intellectual Disabilities

Second Edition

Cognitive and Intellectual Disabilities: Historical Perspectives, Current Practices, and Future Directions provides thorough coverage of the causes and characteristics of cognitive and intellectual disabilities (formerly known as mental retardation) as well as detailed discussions of the validated instructional approaches in the field today. Features include:

- A companion website that offers students and instructors learning objectives, additional activities, discussion outlines, and practice tests for each chapter of the book.
- An up-to-date volume that reflects the terminology and criteria of the DSM-V and is aligned with the current CEC standards.
- Teaching Applications: presents the strongest coverage available in any introductory text on instructional issues and applications for teaching students with cognitive and intellectual disabilities.
- A unique chapter on "Future Issues" that explores the philosophical, social, legal, medical, educational, and personal issues that professionals and people with cognitive and intellectual disabilities face.

This comprehensive and current introductory textbook is ideally suited for introductory or methods courses related to cognitive and intellectual disabilities.

Stephen B. Richards, Ed.D. is Associate Professor and Coordinator of Undergraduate Intervention Specialist Program in the Department of Teacher Education at the University of Dayton, USA.

Michael P. Brady, Ph.D. is Professor and Chair of the Department of Exceptional Student Education at Florida Atlantic University, USA.

Ronald L. Taylor was Professor of Exceptional Student Education at Florida Atlantic University, USA.

Cognitive and Intellectual Disabilities

Historical Perspectives, Current Practices, and Future Directions

Second Edition

Stephen B. Richards
Michael P. Brady
Ronald L. Taylor

Routledge
Taylor & Francis Group

NEW YORK AND LONDON

Second edition published 2015
by Routledge
711 Third Avenue, New York, NY 10017

and by Routledge
2 Park Square, Milton Park, Abingdon, Oxon OX14 4RN

Routledge is an imprint of the Taylor & Francis Group, an informa business

© 2015 Taylor & Francis

The right of Stephen B. Richards, Michael P. Brady, and Ronald L. Taylor to be identified as authors of this work has been asserted by them in accordance with sections 77 and 78 of the Copyright, Designs and Patents Act 1988.

First edition published by Pearson 2005

Library of Congress Cataloging-in-Publication Data

Richards, Steve, 1954–
[Mental retardation]
   Cognitive and intellectual disabilities : historical perspectives, current practices, and future directions / by Stephen Richards, Michael P. Brady, Ronald Taylor.
      pages cm
   Revision of: Mental retardation / Ronald L. Taylor, Stephen B. Richards, Michael P. Brady. 2005.
   Includes bibliographical references and index.
   1. Mental retardation.   I. Brady, Michael P.   II. Taylor, Ronald L., 1949–   III. Title.
   RC570.T334 2015
   616.85′88—dc23
   2014006249

ISBN: 978-0-415-83468-1 (pbk)
ISBN: 978-0-203-50825-1 (ebk)

Typeset in Minion
by Apex CoVantage, LLC

MIX
Paper from
responsible sources
FSC® C014174

Printed and bound in the United States of America by Sheridan Books, Inc. (a Sheridan Group Company).

Dedication

This text is dedicated to Dr. Ron Taylor, a friend and colleague, whose passing in 2013 was unfortunate for us and for the field of special education. He is remembered with admiration and affection by his many students and colleagues. Our love and support go out to Ron's family and we hope this text serves as some tribute to his legacy.

CONTENTS

PREFACE

This text includes 13 chapters that address historical perspectives, current practices, and future trends in the field of cognitive and intellectual disabilities (CIDs). Research from the United States and nations around the globe are cited in the various chapters. Important information, such as the definition of intellectual disabilities, is presented from the newest American Association on Intellectual and Developmental Disabilities (AAIDD) definition and manual.

Each chapter includes helpful components such as **Key Points** at the beginning of each chapter. **Research That Made a Difference** and **Events That Made a Difference** boxes inform the reader of historically important developments in the field. **Reflection** questions are inserted throughout the chapters to help the reader describe and discuss concepts and practices. The end of each chapter includes a **Summary Checklist** that focuses the reader on the important points in the chapter, including key terms that are bolded both in the chapter and in the checklist. **Discussion Questions** can be used to reflect on the chapter material as well as inspire essay questions for assessment. **Activities** that focus on exploring and applying chapter concepts and practices in real life contexts are provided, along with several **e-sources** that guide the reader to more in-depth examinations of organizations and sources of information.

Following is a brief synopsis of each chapter.

Part One: Introduction to CIDs

Chapter 1 focuses on historical perspectives from ancient times until more recent trends and practices. The reader can trace changes in how individuals have been treated, what professionals have been prominent in providing treatment, and the legal and advocacy movements that have ultimately resulted in better service delivery over time. Current perspectives are summarized as well.

Chapter 2 focuses on defining CIDs and on classification of individuals. Historical trends are included, such as the evolution of a definition that has led to the current

AAIDD definition. The current AAIDD definition and its impact are included. The historical and current trends in classification, including the personalized levels of support perspective, are discussed. Prevalence of CIDs in the United States and other geographical regions is examined.

Chapter 3 focuses on assessment for identification. Legal and ethical considerations are examined in reference to U.S. legislation. An overview of norm-referenced assessments includes concepts and practices that affect identification. Conceptual models of intelligence are included as well as commonly used intelligence tests. Adaptive behavior/skill assessment and commonly used instruments are also discussed.

Part Two: Causes of CIDs

Chapter 4 focuses on chromosomal and genetic factors. There is a brief discussion of the role of genetics in heredity followed by explanations and reviews of autosomal and sex-linked chromosomal disorders, disorders related to the number and structure of chromosomes, and disorders of multiple or unknown causes. The roles of genetic testing and genetic counseling are also discussed.

Chapter 5 focuses on environmental and psychosocial causes. These are discussed as prenatal, perinatal, and postnatal causes. Social correlates such as living in poverty are examined. Psychological correlates include factors such as child-rearing practices, abuse and neglect. Finally, both early interventions and medical interventions are discussed in relation to prevention of CIDs.

Part Three: Characteristics of CIDs

Chapter 6 focuses on cognitive and learning characteristics. Also included are discussions of attention, memory, and speech and language characteristics present among people with CIDs.

Chapter 7 focuses on educational, psychological, behavioral, and adaptive behavior characteristics. These include atypical and delayed development, skill development, psychological and behavioral strengths and challenges, and performance and acquisition deficits.

Chapter 8 focuses on societal, family, and multicultural factors. How individuals are viewed, treated, and interact with various social systems are considered. How families are affected and the impact on caregiving and caregivers are discussed. The impact of sociological and multicultural factors on individuals, families, and educators is included.

Part Four: Instructional Considerations

Chapter 9 focuses on instructional assessment. The various factors affecting instructional assessment are examined, including the multidimensional nature of instructional assessment, legal mandates, using informal assessments for decision making and progress monitoring, providing assessment accommodations, and assessing functional skill areas. Assessment in different contexts such as school and community is also discussed.

Chapter 10 focuses on instructional content. This chapter provides perspectives on what all students need to learn, what those with CIDs need to learn, the principles applied to instructional content decision making, and sources useful for planning instructional content. Information on the Common Core State Standards and Individualized Education Programs is included.

Chapter 11 focuses on instructional procedures including assumptions that guide instructional delivery, how instructional programs can be organized, how to deliver instruction, as well as evaluating instruction. Instructional strategies used in general education settings, as well as in special education and community contexts, are reviewed and explained.

Chapter 12 focuses on instructional settings. The importance of instructional setting decisions is discussed in relation to their impact on individuals within society, opportunities to learn and apply skills, how settings may change over an individual's lifetime, and how accommodations can provide for better instructional settings.

Part Five: The Future of CIDs

Chapter 13 focuses on trends in philosophical, social, legal, medical, and educational perspectives. Unique to this chapter are Research and Event boxes that suggest developments that could happen over the next decade and beyond that will have positive impacts on individuals with CIDs and on the field.

The reader should find this text easily accessible, providing historical references and research as well as current ones. Students and instructors will find the chapter end materials, the research event, and reflection features useful in understanding the concepts presented, assessing one's knowledge, and facilitating more in-depth examination of topics.

Part One

Introduction to CIDs

1

HISTORICAL CONCEPTS AND PERSPECTIVES[1]

Key Points

➤ AN EARLY DARK HISTORY—Although ancient Egypt was tolerant of individuals with cognitive/intellectual disabilities (CIDs),[2] ancient Rome and Greece often supported infanticide. Attitudes were later affected by religion and medical practices.

➤ A SHIFT TO CARE—The first half of the 19th century brought a positive approach to the treatment of individuals with CIDs. Although institutions were popular, efforts of individuals such as Itard, and his student Seguin, resulted in attempts at education.

➤ AN AGE OF CONFLICT—The mid- to late 19th century and beginning 20th century again resulted in negative stereotypes. Custodial institutions and the eugenics movement were popular.

➤ HUMANIZATION OF PEOPLE WITH CIDs—The mid- to late 20th century saw many advances in medicine and education. Deinstitutionalization and normalization were encouraged, laws were passed, and court cases supported the rights of individuals with CIDs.

➤ CURRENT PERSPECTIVES—Current and future areas that have been, and will be, addressed include legal issues, medical advances, educational considerations, and the use of terminology.

The field of CIDs has had a long, and at times, tumultuous history. The treatment of individuals with CIDs by others has progressed from kindness, to barbarism, to neglect, to enlightenment, to care, and eventually to education. More recently, the recognition and encouragement of these individuals to become self-advocates and active participants in deciding their goals and futures have been emphasized. The terms used to describe individuals with CIDs have shown a similar evolution. *Idiot, imbecile, moron,* and *feeble-minded,* although quite offensive in today's society, were terms used by scholars of the various time periods. Later terms such as *mental defective* and *mental deficiency* led the way to the use of the term *mental retardation*. The use of this term was eventually challenged and has been replaced by the term *cognitive/intellectual disability*. The term *intellectual/developmental disability* is also used by many. Interestingly, the term *mental retardation* is still used in the Individuals with Disability Education Act of 2004 (IDEA 04) although individual states were allowed to use different terms (e.g., *cognitive disability, cognitive delay, intellectual disability*). However, in 2010, President Obama signed Rosa's law, which officially changed the term *mental retardation* to *intellectual disability* so future legislation will use the latter term. Throughout the text, CID(s) will be used in reference to studies in which the term *mental retardation* was used to characterize the participant. In studies in which the terminology is less clear, the original descriptive terms will be used.

AN EARLY DARK HISTORY

The history of CIDs has been chronicled by a number of researchers for half a century (e.g., Kanner, 1964; Winzer, 1993; Scheerenberger, 1983; Trent, 1994), although the early history is not well documented and is left to many sources that have resulted in a certain degree of speculation (see Research Box 1.1). The first actual description of CIDs was probably in Thebes (in Egypt) as early as 1500 B.C. (Grossman, 1983) and is somewhat ambiguous. This discovery came about in 1862 when two medical papyri were discovered in a tomb. These documents indicated some reference to individuals with CIDs, although translation problems caused some uncertainty in their message. Another example of speculation occurring in history regards the role of St. Nicholas Thaumaturgos, who was the Bishop of Myra (an area that would now be in southern Turkey) in the fourth century A.D. He has been described as both the protector and the saint of individuals with CIDs (although that term certainly wasn't used at that date). St. Nicholas, however, has also been regarded as the patron saint of all children, of sailors, and actually of pawnbrokers (Kanner, 1964). St. Nicholas is best known today as the prototype for Santa Claus.

Ancient Egypt

Scheerenberger (1983) suggested that CID has undoubtedly been apparent since the dawn of human history. He argued that in any given society there have been individuals who are more capable and less capable than average. In ancient history,

---

1.1 RESEARCH THAT MADE A DIFFERENCE

Scheerenberger, R. (1983). *A history of mental retardation*. Baltimore: Paul H. Brookes.

Although there have been many histories of people with cognitive and intellectual disabilities compiled, Scheerenberger perhaps researched and produced the most comprehensive work on this topic. His book consists of two major parts. The first looks at the European influences beginning in prehistoric times and continuing until the 20th century. The other part focuses on the history of CIDs in the United States, beginning in the early 1600s, in what he calls the formative years that continued until the mid-1800s. He then has a chapter on Strife, Reconstruction, and the Gilded Age (Chapter 5), the Progressive Era (Chapter 6), Normalcy, Depression, and the New Deal (Chapter 7), and Conflict and Change (Chapter 8). The last chapter is an epilogue that highlighted the current status of CIDs in the early 1980s.

different societies dealt with individuals with CIDs differently. For example, ancient Egyptians valued their children and through religion and medicine, attempts were made to "cure" a variety of maladies. Priests would encourage the use of spiritual healing, and the use of amulets and incantations was widespread. Medicine was also becoming more popular. One of the previously mentioned papyri found in Thebes "represents a collection of ancient recipes for the physician covering innumerable human ailments" (Scheerenberger, 1983; p. 10). Conversely, in later years, during the rise and fall of the Greek and Roman civilizations, **infanticide** (killing an infant) became widespread.

Greek and Roman Civilizations

In Greece, children were not considered property of the parents but rather of the commonwealth (Winzer, 1993). For example, in Sparta newborn babies would be brought before a board of elders to determine their physical capability. If a child was considered to have a disability (including a CID), the child would be thrown into the river Eurotes or abandoned in the wilderness. Other forms of infanticide were also used.

On the positive side, medicine continued to make advances that led to treatment rather than torture of individuals with disabilities. Hippocrates championed the concept of humane treatment for all individuals. Unfortunately, Hippocrates and physicians for many future centuries were concerned with physical problems and pain and left problems of the mind and soul to philosophers (Scheerenberger, 1983). Both Plato and Aristotle voiced very negative attitudes about individuals with disabilities.

The era of the Roman civilization lasted from 800 B.C. until 476 A.D. Ancient Romans held similar beliefs to the Greeks about infants with disabilities. The major difference between Rome and Greece was that in Rome the child was considered a property of the parents; therefore it was their decision, particularly the father's, whether or not to reject the child at birth (Winzer, 1993). In effect, the child was the property of the father who could choose the future for the child. Because of the strong family bonds, high birth rates, and the self-sustaining nature of the family, many children with CIDs (particularly those without severe CIDs) were spared. These individuals would assist in menial tasks and manual labor. By the first century, however, Rome had become an empire and attitudes and needs changed. At this time, infanticide became widespread and continued until the fourth century, when Christianity began having a more humanitarian influence (Scheerenberger, 1983).

The Middle Ages

The Middle Ages, considered the period between the fall of Rome and the beginning of the Renaissance, was a time of religion, superstition, and fear. There were also numerous plagues and wars that affected the expected life span. Boys were considered men at age 16 and men at 25 were considered middle aged (Scheerenberger, 1983). Certain medical advances were made during the Middle Ages, however. Perhaps the most notable physician during this period was Avicenna. Avicenna's writing, which drew heavily from Hippocrates, actually described proposed treatments for conditions related to CIDs such as meningitis and hydrocephalus.

Renaissance and Reformation

During the Renaissance (starting in the 1300s) and the Reformation (which began in the 1500s), several physicians had an impact on the field of CIDs. One was Paracelsus, a Swiss physician who lived from 1493 to 1541. He was perhaps the first who distinguished between CIDs and mental illness. Two statements attributed to him are "Many are those who are ill who are not thought to be mentally sick. For as fools (simpletons, feeble-minded) are of many kinds, so also are there many kinds of crazy people not of one sort nor in one way, but in many ways of many sorts, in many patterns and forms" and "the 'feeble-minded' behaved in the 'ways of a healthy animal, but the psychopathic in the manner of an irrational animal'" (Galston, 1950, cited in Scheerenberger, 1983). Another individual who had an impact on CIDs during this time period was Felix Platter, also a Swiss physician, who lived from 1536 to 1614. In 1614, the year of his death, Platter commented:

> Now we see many (foolish or simple from the beginning) who even in infancy showed signs of simplicity in their movement and laughter, who did not pay attention easily, or who are docile and yet they do not learn. If anyone asked him to do any kind of task, they laugh and joke, they cajole and they make mischief. They take great delight and seem satisfied in the habits of these simple actions, and so they are taught in their homes.
> We have known others who are less foolish, who correctly attend to many tasks of life, who are able to perform certain skills yet they show their dullness, in that they long to be praised and at the same time they say and do foolish things.
> (Platter, 1614, pp. 35–36; cited in Scheerenberger, 1983)

The Reformation era began when Martin Luther nailed his 95 theses on church abuse to a church door in Wittenberg. Ironically, however, Martin Luther's views on CIDs were extremely negative. He made a statement in one of his *Table Talks* that the "feeble-minded were merely a mass of flesh, a *massa carnis*, with no soul. For it is in the Devil's power that he corrupts people who have reason and souls when he possesses them" (Luther, 1652, p. 387; cited in Kanner, 1964).

17th and 18th Centuries

The 17th and 18th centuries, considered the Age of Reason and Enlightenment in Europe, and the colonial period in America, resulted in many medical advances. Unfortunately, however, treatment of individuals with CIDs (particularly in the 17th century) was more inhumane. In Europe, there was an extreme dichotomy within the society. On the one hand there was lavish wealth and on the other, utter deprivation. Begging became a public nuisance; it is estimated that during the Thirty Years War more than 100,000 beggars lived in Paris alone. During this time individuals with CIDs were confined to institutions such as hospitals and prisons where the death rate often exceeded 75–80% (Hickson, Blackman, & Reis, 1995). Giordani (1961) noted that begging became so popular that professional beggars would purchase young individuals from orphanages and proceed to disable them so that they could get more money. Subsequently, when their usefulness was no longer profitable, they were left on their own and many died.

In America, this time period was influenced by religious beliefs and superstitions. Many individuals with CIDs were thought to be witches and were subjected to persecution, and perhaps even execution (Hickson et al., 1995). The best-known event was the Salem Witch Trials (see Event Box 1.1).

1.1 EVENT THAT MADE A DIFFERENCE

1692–1693—Salem Witch Trials in Salem, Massachusetts

In the years leading up to 1692, the Puritans in Colonial America were in a very anxious state. Reasons for this anxiety have been speculated and three seem to be associated: the outbreak of smallpox, the constant fear of Indian attacks, and the revocation of the Massachusetts Bay Colony Charter by Charles II. The Puritans believed that these events were God's punishment. This led to a heightened sense of superstition and the belief that some individuals were witches. Individuals who acted odd or hysterical were particularly targeted. The culmination was the Salem Witch Trials, which began in mid-1692 and continued through the beginning of 1693. Records indicate that 19 (both women and men) were hanged, one was pressed to death, and at least 13 died in prison awaiting their trial. Contrary to popular belief, burning at the stake was not the form of execution in the United States where witchcraft was considered a felony. That form of execution was used in Europe where witchcraft was considered heresy.

Source: www.salemwitchtrials.com/faqs.html

All was not negative during this time period. There were those who felt that individuals with disabilities should not only be dealt with in a humane fashion, but also that they could and should be educated. In Europe, two individuals who championed this cause in the late 18th century were Jacob Rodrigues Periere (1715–1780) and Phillipe Pinel (1745–1826). Periere was primarily interested in people who were deaf and who did not speak. He was among the first who thought that these individuals could be taught and actually developed a simple sign language system to allow communication. Although he did not work directly with individuals with CIDs, he had a significant impact on later individuals such as Itard and Seguin, who worked directly with that population (MacMillan, 1985). Pinel was a psychiatrist who was involved in a movement toward more humane treatment of individuals with mental illness (called insane at that time). He is best known for freeing the patients of the Bicetre, a male insane asylum in Paris and later the Salpetriere, a female asylum. His more humane approach has been referred to as **moral treatment** and attempted to end treatments based on the assumption of demonic possession and to begin more positive, psychologically oriented therapies. His ties to CIDs are very clear—he was the mentor of Jean Marc Gaspard Itard, considered the first individual to attempt to *educate* an individual with a CID.

> *Reflection*
>
> **What factors in history affected the different attitudes toward individuals with CIDs through the 18th century? Do you find evidence of these attitudes in today's societies?**

A SHIFT TO CARE

The first half of the 19th century finally brought a positive approach to the treatment of individuals with CIDs through the efforts of many. Medical advances were made and, perhaps more significantly, there was a realization that it was important not only to attempt educational practices but also to accept that their success might be possible.

At the same time, both Europe and the United States moved toward the use of asylums and institutions for those with disabilities, although not initially for individuals with CIDs. In fact, as early as the late 1700s, asylums and institutions for people who were blind had been developed in Europe. Unfortunately, the conditions of these institutions, particularly for those with mental illness, were often inhumane. This helped lead to laws such as the 1828 and 1844 English Lunacy Acts, which sought to improve the conditions and services of asylums. As a result, public asylums appeared after 1845 (Winzer, 1993).

In the United States, institutions were also developed for people who were blind and deaf. For example, in 1818, the New York Institution for the Deaf and Dumb was established. In 1817, the Connecticut Asylum for the Education and Instruction of Deaf and Dumb Persons was founded. The New England Asylum for the Blind was established in 1832. It wouldn't be long until this movement would also impact the field of CIDs.

There were several individuals who were influential in the movement toward both the education and the residential care of individuals with CIDs. These include Itard, Esquirol, and Guggenbuhl in Europe, Howe in the United States, and Seguin in both Europe and the United States.

Jean Marc Gaspard Itard (1774–1838)

Perhaps the most influential impact came from Jacques Marc Gaspard Itard, a French physician who was working primarily with individuals with hearing impairments when he became interested in CIDs. Itard is best known for his work with Victor, the wild boy of Aveyron (see Event Box 1.2), a "feral child" who was found living in the woods in France. Itard's work with Victor was essentially the first formal attempt of trying to educate an individual thought to have a CID. Interestingly, Philippe Pinel, Itard's mentor, was of the opinion that the boy was incurable and that no attempt at education would be successful. Itard, however, disagreed, and accepted the task of teaching Victor. Itard felt that Victor's CID was due to social and educational neglect and was, therefore, reversible. He developed five goals for Victor that focused on developing his senses, his intellect, and his emotional status. He worked with Victor for five years after which he stopped, considering his work a failure. However, Itard actually did demonstrate that education could make a difference. Victor was able to recognize objects, identify letters of the alphabet, understand the meaning of several words, and apply names to objects, among other things. After Itard's work with Victor, the French Academy of Science even lauded his accomplishments (Kanner, 1964).

1.2 EVENT THAT MADE A DIFFERENCE

1800—Itard begins his work with Victor, the wild boy of Aveyron

According to historical reports, Victor was given his name by Itard; Victor was found by three hunters in 1799 naked in the Caune Woods. They captured him and brought him to Lacaune where he stayed with an elderly widow. Victor escaped but was eventually recaptured. He was sent to an orphanage but again was successful in escaping on several occasions. Eventually he was recaptured and brought to Paris where Itard accepted the challenge to educate the "feral child."

Source: www.ling.lancs.ac.uk/monkey/ihe/linguistics/LECTURE4/4victor.htm

---

Jean Etienne Esquirol (1772–1840)

Esquirol was a French psychiatrist who is best known for his work with mentally ill patients. He was one of the earliest to actively differentiate between mental illness and CIDs. He also had specific views on CIDs, believing that they existed on a continuum (i.e., there were degrees of CIDs). He differentiated between "idiots" whose CIDs were severe, and "imbeciles," whose CIDs were not as significant. This was one of the earlier efforts in establishing *levels* of CIDs. As will be discussed in Chapter 2, this view has fallen in and out of favor by professionals over time. Like Itard, Esquirol was also a student of Pinel although Itard's and Esquirol's philosophies differed. Esquirol shared Pinel's views that individuals with CIDs could not be educated, whereas Itard disagreed with Pinel feeling that they could.

Johan Jacob Guggenbuhl (1816–1863)

Guggenbuhl was a Swiss physician who is generally credited as being the first individual to start an institution for individuals with CIDs. He was primarily interested in **cretinism,** a condition that is caused by a thyroid deficiency that results in physical deformity and CIDs. When he was 20 years old, Guggenbuhl reportedly came across "a dwarfed, crippled, cretin of stupid appearance mumbling the Lord's Prayer at a wayside cross" (Kanner, 1964; p. 17). He spoke with the man's mother and found that she could not afford to educate her son. As a result, Guggenbuhl devoted his life to the education and care of individuals with this condition. He felt that residential care was critical for these individuals. Interestingly, he found through his research that cretinism was supposedly associated with areas of low altitude (lowlands). In fact, the percentage of the population in Switzerland with cretinism was quite high. Cretinism develops later in life and is caused by a lack of iodine. It is possible that some environmental condition or diet associated with those areas resulted in more individuals with cretinism than would be expected. Subsequently, he established his institution in Abendberg, Switzerland, an area that was over 4,000 feet above sea level. Rather than simply housing the residents, Guggenbuhl encouraged proper health care, physical exercise, and a proper diet, and used medication and educational techniques such as sensory, memory, and language training (Scheerenberger, 1983). Abendberg quickly gained notoriety and was visited by professionals from all over Europe. Guggenbuhl and Abendberg had a considerable impact on the growth of institutions (discussed later in this chapter).

Unfortunately, incidents occurred that led to the eventual closing of Abendberg. Guggenbuhl became very much in demand to lecture about his techniques and successes. As a result, his stepfather took over the primary care of Abendberg and allowed the conditions to deteriorate. Perhaps more significantly, many professionals became skeptical and suspicious of Guggenbuhl's claims of curing cretinism. In 1858, the government authorized an investigation into Guggenbuhl and Abendberg. The negative report included many criticisms of both the successes of Guggenbuhl and the conditions at Abendberg. Among the accusations were that Guggenbuhl had been deceptive because only one third of the residents were actually diagnosed with cretinism, that no person with cretinism was actually cured, and that there was no medical or educational supervision at Abendberg for a number of years (Kanner, 1964). Although Abendberg was not closed until 1868, Guggenbuhl died in 1863 "scorned and labeled a swindler, quack, charlatan, embezzler, and bigot" (Scheerenberger, 1983; p. 73). Nonetheless, Kanner (1964), who studied Guggenbuhl extensively, stated "But Guggenbuhl must be acknowledged as the indisputable originator of the idea and practice of the institutional care for feebleminded individuals. The hundreds of institutions now in existence derive in direct line from the Abendberg" (p. 30). It is important to note that this statement was made in 1964; the movement toward deinstitutionalization (discussed later in this chapter) had not had its full effect as yet.

Samuel Gridley Howe (1801–1876)

Howe was primarily known for his work with individuals with visual impairments in the New England area. He founded the New England Asylum for the Blind in 1832, whose name was changed to the Perkins Institution for the Blind in 1877, and eventually the Perkins School for the Blind in 1955. He also, however, had an impact on the field of CIDs. He chaired a committee to study the issue in Massachusetts and established a wing in his institution for the experimental study of 10 children with CIDs in 1848 (MacMillan, 1985). This effort would later lead to the development of the Massachusetts School for Idiotic and Feebleminded Children in 1855.

Edouard Seguin (1812–1881)

Seguin was a student of Esquirol and was given the responsibility of supervising a large number of mentally ill patients at the Bicetre in France. In 1826, a school for children with CIDs was also started at Bicetre. In 1837, he met Itard, who quickly became his mentor. That same year, Seguin opened a private school for individuals with CIDs, where he reportedly worked with one child who made gains in a number of areas. Seguin used what was referred to as the **physiological method,** which was an extension of the work by Pinel and Itard. He later wrote a classic text that described the physiological method (see Research Box 1.2) Esquirol lauded Seguin's accomplishments, although he defended his position of incurability by suggesting that the boy must have been a "seeming idiot" (Kanner, 1964). In 1844, the Paris Academy declared that Seguin had solved the dilemma of educating this population (Kanner, 1964).

1.2 RESEARCH THAT MADE A DIFFERENCE

Seguin, E. (1866). *Idiocy and its treatment by the physiological method*. New York: William Wood.

Seguin's physiological method was an extension of some of the approaches used by Itard with Victor. It was based on the importance of training the muscular system and nervous system; sensory training, including vision, hearing, tasting and smelling; teaching general ideas; developing abstract thinking skills; and moral training. Goals progressed from the development of self-care skills to vocational skills using perception, imitation, memory, and generalization (Biasini, Grupe, Huffman, & Bray, 2002). Seguin, in describing his method, wrote "Man being a unit, is artificially analyzed, for study's sake, into his three prominent vital expressions, activity, intelligence, and will. We consider the idiot as a man infirm in the expressions of his trinity; and we understand the method of training idiots, or mankind, as the philosophical agency by which the unity of mankind can be reached as far as practicable in our day, through the trinary analysis" (Seguin, 1866, cited in Scheerenberger, 1983; p. 78). Thus, according to Seguin, the goal is to educate, in concert, the activity, intelligence, and will of man.

John Conolly, a physician from England, visited Seguin's program at the Bicetre and wrote the following about his accomplishments: "There is no case incapable of some amendment; that every case may be improved, or cured, up to a certain point is a principle of great general importance in reference to treatment" (Conolly, 1845; p. 293, cited in Trent, 1994). Word of Seguin's success in educating "idiots" quickly spread to the United States. Seguin later moved to the United States in 1850 and began having even more impact on the field of CIDs. He helped develop several institutions, including the Institution for Feeble-minded Youth in Barre, Massachusetts. He also worked at Howe's institution. In 1876, he and five others formed the Association of Medical Officers of American Institutions for Idiotic and Feebleminded Persons and Seguin was elected as the first president. This organization would later be called the American Association on Mental Deficiency and the Association on Mental Retardation, and currently the American Association on Intellectual and Developmental Disabilities. Before his death, he founded the Seguin Physiological School for Feebleminded Children with his wife. This school was designed as a day school for those children who could live at home.

Reflection

Do you think that placing individuals with CIDs in institutions during the 19th century was justified? Is it still justifiable today and if so, under what circumstances do you believe it is justifiable?

AN AGE OF CONFLICT

After Guggenbuhl's and Seguin's efforts to develop institutions that had an educational focus, the term *school,* or *training school,* often replaced the term *institution.* The goal of these training schools was to make the residents productive members of society. Hervey Wilbur opened a private school in 1848 using Seguin's educational techniques. Other schools were later opened in Pennsylvania (1852), New York (1855), and Ohio (1857). Unfortunately, bad economic times and the effects of the Civil War had a negative impact on the educational nature of the residential facilities. Employment for individuals with CIDs was difficult and there was a need to provide care for a rapidly growing population including those wounded in the war. The result was more of a custodial institution in which the residents were trained at skills to help make the institution more self-sufficient; they were not necessarily trained to develop marketable skills to return to the community. The term *school* began to disappear from the names of institutions and was once again replaced by terms such as *asylums* and *hospitals* that more accurately reflected their custodial nature. Interestingly, these institutions were initially developed to protect the individuals with CIDs from the rest of society, not the other way around. However, institutions were subject to three negative factors: isolation, enlargement, and economization, and their focus later changed from protecting atypical people from typical individuals (Wolfensberger, 1975).

In the 1880s another institutional movement evolved—the farm colony. These were designed to be self-sufficient (residents grew their own food, raised cattle for dairy products) and relieved the overcrowding of institutions in more urban, populous areas. The first farm colony was the "Howe Farm" opened in Massachusetts in 1881 (Trent, 1994).

As noted previously, there was a shift in the role of institutions to segregate and isolate individuals with CIDs who were being viewed as "a menace to society" (Lazerson,

1975). As a result, the institutions became larger, more impersonal, and greater in number. There was a steady increase in the number of public institutions throughout the first half of the 20th century. In addition, an, alarming, and certainly related movement, **eugenics**, began in the late 1800s and continued through the first part of the 1900s.

The Eugenics Movement

The concept of eugenics was introduced by Frances Galton "as a science that took into account the various factors that allegedly improve the inherent qualities of a race" (MacMillan, 1985; p. 23). This movement received support after the publication of *The Jukes: A Study in Crime, Pauperism, Disease, and Heredity* (Dugdale, 1877). Dugdale was a prison inspector in New York State who discovered six relatives who were all in jail at the same time. He traced their family histories and located 790 individuals spanning six generations. Of these, he found that 18 were brothel keepers, 128 were prostitutes, 200 were welfare cases, and 76 were criminals (Blanton, 1975). The study of the Jukes family suggested the inheritability of socially negative traits. Although, at this time, intelligence tests were not available to document the Jukes's intelligence levels, Estabook (1916) in a follow-up of Dugdale's study concluded "Not all the Jukes are criminals, but all the Jukes criminals that I have known I regard as mentally defective" and "One half of the Jukes were and are mentally defective" (Kanner, 1964; p. 128). This stereotype continued for several decades. Tredgold, a member of the British Eugenics Society, estimated that 90% of CIDs was hereditary. The most influential treatment of the subject was written by Sir Henry Goddard in 1912 (see Event Box 1.3) who traced the genealogy of the descendants of a man who had an illegitimate child with a mother with a CID as well as another child in wedlock with a mother of normal intelligence.

1.3 EVENT THAT MADE A DIFFERENCE

1912—Henry Goddard publishes his book, *The Kallikak Family: A Study in the Heredity of Feeblemindedness*.

Henry Goddard decided to study the family history of a woman he named Deborah Kallikak who lived at the Vineland Training School in New Jersey where he was serving as a psychologist. Kallikak was actually a fictional name combining the Greek terms for *good* and *bad*. Supposedly, Deborah's great-great-great grandfather was a Revolutionary War soldier who had fathered both an illegitimate child with a "feeble-minded" mother, and a child with a mother of normal intelligence whom he had married. Goddard located 480 descendants of the illegitimate child, of whom 143 had CIDs. On the basis of these numbers he concluded that CIDs were hereditary. His other conclusions were that the descendants of the illegitimate child had a high incidence of criminal behavior, alcoholism, prostitution, and other negative traits. On the other hand, the descendants of his wife with normal intelligence were highly educated and employed in a variety of professional positions. The publication of Goddard's findings reinforced the thinking at the time that individuals with CIDs were dangerous and deviant and that if they had children they would have similar traits as well. Goddard's study was later criticized as being scientifically inaccurate and invalid. For example, Smith and Wehmeyer (2012) reported that Deborah Kallikak's real name was Emma Wolverton and that despite some behavioral problems associated with her life in an institution, she was actually literate and well read.

Source: www.mnCIDs.org/parallels/four/4d/8.html

The hysteria provided by the Goddard study and other advocates of eugenics helped fuel the previously described movement toward more segregated institutions. Men and women were separated within the same institution and separate institutions were developed for women of child-bearing age to ensure that they would not get pregnant.

Another disturbing result was the use of forced sterilization. Several states passed laws allowing sterilization. Interestingly, famous Supreme Court Justice Oliver Wendell Holmes, responding to a Virginia court case, upheld that sterilization practices were constitutional. An even more radical recommendation was the use of euthanasia. Smith (1997) reported the account of a physician, Dr. Harry Haiselden, who not only allowed "defective" newborns to die but also used drugs to hasten their deaths. His practices resulted in a movie, *The Black Stork,* that encouraged the use of euthanasia. *The Black Stork* was shown in public movie houses from 1916 through the 1920s (Pernick, 1996).

The fear of individuals with CIDs became so widespread that an American Breeder's Association was established in 1907 that had a section devoted to eugenics "to control the reproduction of defective classes" (*American Breeder's Magazine,* 1909, p. 235; cited in Winzer, 1993; p. 301). Ironically, even advocates for individuals with disabilities jumped on the bandwagon. In 1915, Helen Keller wrote "It seems to me that the simplest, wisest thing to do would be to submit cases like that of the malformed idiot baby to a jury of expert physicians. . . . A mental defective . . . is almost sure to be a potential criminal. The evidence before a jury of physicians considering the case of an idiot would be exact and scientific" (Keller, 1915; p. 174; cited in Smith, 1997; p. 139). Also in 1915, Fernald presented several reasons why society's views of individuals with CIDs had changed so drastically. First, the development and widespread use of intelligence tests made it easier to identify more individuals with CIDs, particularly those who were physically less recognizable (see Chapters 2 and 3 for discussions of these topics). Second, the research of Goddard and others on the inheritability of CIDs implied that the cure was to keep individuals with CIDs from having children. Third, he argued that there was evidence that CIDs were a cause of crime and delinquency, prostitution, and illegitimacy, among other undesirable traits. Finally, Fernald noted that the prevalence of CIDs was increasing. Wolfensberger (1975) pointed out that the prevailing thought was that individuals with CIDs would produce children at a higher rate than those without CIDs, thus resulting in disproportionately higher numbers.

In the 1920s and 1930s, institutions continued to increase in number and size and decrease in quality. The Great Depression had an impact because there was a growing need to house more individuals and a subsequent lack of funding to support them, making the conditions even worse. Wolfensberger (1975) referred to the increase in institutionalization as "continuity of momentum," arguing that there was no real rationale for their growth and that they resulted in greater dehumanization of individuals with CIDs.

Reflection

Why do you think the eugenics movement was allowed to occur? Is there evidence in societies today that suggests some people are inferior and should be restricted in their freedoms?

HUMANIZATION OF PEOPLE WITH CIDs

After the first two decades of the 20th century, a number of philosophical, educational, medical, and legal factors positively affected individuals with CIDs.

1920s–1940s

Kanner (1964) referred to the time period from 1920–1940 as the "the great lull" in which the knowledge of CIDs was not really advanced and the institutions became merely housing units for the growing numbers. Scheerenberger (1983), however, suggested that there were several events during this time period that resulted in positive changes (although not necessarily on the number and focus of institutions). *Philosophically,* individuals such as Fernald and Goddard made complete turn-arounds regarding their views of individuals with CIDs. Thus, perceptions of CIDs were changed somewhat and the emphasis on eugenics was downplayed. *Politically,* with Franklin Delano Roosevelt as President of the United States, there was also a push to have more governmental support for all citizens, including those with CIDs.

Educationally, individuals such as Edgar Doll began to have an impact, noting the importance of identifying and developing adaptive skills (see Research Box 1.3).

Although special education programs had been developed for a number of years, the 1920s and 1930s began an era in which they were endorsed by many states. By 1930, 16 states had legislation supporting special education although the criteria for teaching credentials was lax (Scheerenberger, 1983). Unfortunately, those with more severe disabilities were still routinely excluded. Institutions continued to be overcrowded, with many having long waiting lists.

Advocacy groups such as the Council for Exceptional Children were founded that provided support for parents and professionals working with children with disabilities. Organizations such as the American Association on Mental Deficiency (today known as the American Association on Intellectual and Developmental Disabilities) continued to provide important information about the definition, classification, and education of individuals with CIDs (see Chapter 2 for a history of the various definitions and classification systems of CIDs). Also in the 1930s, research began to emerge showing the educational benefits of providing a stimulating environment (e.g., Skeels & Dye, 1939). *Medically,* research began to provide important discoveries about the causes and even prevention of certain biological causes of CIDs. As an example, a researcher named Folling studied 10 individuals with CIDs, many of whom were siblings, and observed that they had elevated levels of phenylpyruvic acid in their urine. This eventually led to the identification, and more important, the cause, of phenylketonuria (PKU), a metabolic disorder that today can be detected soon after birth and can be prevented. (Chapter 4 addresses many medical advances that have occurred in the past half century.)

1.3 RESEARCH THAT MADE A DIFFERENCE

Doll, E.A. (1936). Current thoughts on mental deficiency. *Proceedings and Addresses of the American Association on Mental Deficiency, 41,* 33–49.

In this publication of Doll's presidential address to the American Association on Mental Deficiency, he critically summarized the current status of the field of mental deficiency. Of particular importance were his views on social competence. Doll stated that individuals with subnormal intelligence who were socially competent could not be considered feeble-minded. Doll also argued that the amelioration of mental deficiency should be addressed through systematic treatment of social and industrial skills. In other words, the goal should be to teach them skills, including social skills that would allow them to adapt to their environment.

1940s–1950s

Philosophical/Political Climate

World War II brought about political and economic changes that had an effect on individuals with CIDs. For one thing, it resulted in a very united country in which all citizens were expected to contribute. This included enlistment opportunities, employment in defense plants, and other job opportunities to support the war effort. This was very different from the opportunities during World War I in which the prevailing attitude was that individuals with CIDs should not serve their country (Scheerenberger, 1983). This latest realization meant that individuals with CIDs needed to be taught functional skills. After the war, however, the need for such civilian manpower was not as important and individuals with CIDs once again were placed in institutions (Scheerenberger, 1983). After World War II, exposés of the horrendous conditions in institutions were published. One example was Haverman's set of photographs in 1948 that demonstrated the deplorable conditions at Litchwood Village in New York. Although in the 1950s the number of individuals living in institutions increased, so

Table 1.1 Selected Legislation of the 1950s

Year	Action	Result
1950	National Mental Health Act	Established National Institute of Mental Health providing funds for training and research
1954	Cooperative Research and Education Act	Provided funds for mental retardation research
1957	Amendment of Social Security Act	Added a clause to provide payment to "adult disabled children"
1958	Public Law 85-926	Provided funds for university-level professors to train individuals who work with individuals with mental retardation

did the numbers in advocacy organizations who felt that the majority of institutions were inappropriate. In 1959, the American Association on Mental Deficiency began studying the conditions in these facilities and, in 1964, published a report outlining specific standards that institutions needed to address. Clearly, the conditions were set for the deinstitutionalization movement to begin.

Legislation and Litigation

In the 1950s, in particular, there were a significant number of legislative acts that provided support for individuals with disabilities (see Table 1.1). Although there was limited funding from the legislation summarized in Table 1.1, it did signify an increased interest in CIDs and special education services. Parents also became greater advocates, forming the National Association of Retarded Citizens, which became a powerful lobbying group and published the "Educational Bill of Rights for the Retarded Child" in 1953 (Winzer, 1993).

Another factor that began to affect the field of CIDs was litigation. Interestingly, it was a civil rights court case that would later stimulate legal action on behalf of students with CIDs. In *Brown v. Board of Education of Topeka* (1954), the U.S. Supreme Court ruled against segregating students educationally on the basis of race. This ruling made parents question why the same principle of equal access to education did not apply to their children with CIDs as well (Heward, 2013).

Advances in Education

Special education was starting to become routine in the 1950s and the number of students served continued to increase (Winzer, 1993). However, programs for students with more severe CIDs (called trainable mental retardation at the time) were in place prior to those for students with less severe CIDs (called educable mental retardation at the time) (MacMillan, 1985). Most of these programs were segregated where the students were taught together and therefore separated from their peers without disabilities.

Universities became more involved in developing education programs that trained teachers to work with students with CIDs. This was encouraged, in part, to Public Law

85-926 that provided funds for such training. Textbooks describing specific educational techniques were incorporated into these teacher training programs. One example was *Educating the Retarded Child* (Kirk & Johnson, 1951) that was coauthored by Samuel Kirk, who was later known to coin the phrase "learning disabilities."

During the 1940s and 1950s, new information became available that impacted the field of CIDs, particularly related to environmental causes. These included greater understanding of prenatal risk factors such as the lack of maternal nutrition and the presence of maternal rubella as well as perinatal risk factors such as anoxia, or the lack of oxygen to the fetus during the birth process (Stevens, 1954). Chapter 5 includes a discussion of these and other environmental causes of CIDs.

1960s
Philosophical/Political Climate
The decade of the 1960s was marked by many turbulent events, from the Cuban Missile Crisis to the Vietnam War. It was also a time of rebellion and increased social awareness. President Kennedy, who himself had a sister with a CID, appointed the Presidential Panel on Mental Retardation. This group was responsible for recommending national policy. Its recommendations included the need for more research, increased preventive measures, stronger educational programs, increased protection of civil rights, the use of community-centered programs, and efforts to increase public awareness of CIDs. Kennedy also formed the Division of Handicapped Children and Youth and Samuel Kirk was appointed as Director. This resulted in even more special education funding.

Although the number of individuals living in state institutions hit its plateau in 1967 at almost 200,000 (Anderson, Lakin, Mangan, & Prouty, 1998), deinstitutionalization continued, fueled by the book *Christmas in Purgatory* (Blatt & Kaplan, 1966). This book included pictures and brief descriptions of the deplorable conditions at a number of institutions. "We heard a good deal of laughter but saw little cheer. There were few things to be cheerful about. . . . Even the television sets, in several of the day rooms, appeared to be co-conspirators in the crusade for gloom. These sets were not in working order. Sadly, the residents continued to sit on their benches, in neat rows, looking at the blank tubes" (p. 47). The deinstitutionalization movement was further reinforced by the introduction of the concept of **normalization** from Scandinavia, which supported the idea that individuals with CIDs should be afforded the same opportunities and conditions in life as those without disabilities (Kugel & Wolfensberger, 1969; Nirje, 1969). According to Nirje (1969), normalization referred to "making available to the mentally retarded patterns and conditions of everyday life which are as close as possible to the norms and patterns of the mainstream of society" (p. 181).

Legislation and Litigation
Legislation and litigation continued in the 1960s. The Mental Retardation Facilities and Mental Health Centers Construction Act was passed in 1963. This legislation resulted in the development of Mental Retardation Research Centers that provided support and facilities for cohesive, interdisciplinary programs for research and

research training. The primary legislation during the 1960s, however, was the passage of the Elementary and Secondary Education Act as well as a number of amendments to the law. These provided funds for disadvantaged children and children with disabilities and created the Bureau of Education for the Handicapped, a separate special education division of what is now the Office for Special Education Programs in Washington. One notable court case was *Hobson v. Hansen* (1967). This was the first case that focused on the misuse or discriminatory use of test scores to place minority students into lower educational tracks. It would be the basis for many other cases in which minority students were overrepresented in classes for students with CIDs.

Advances in Education

Although early in the decade segregated programs were still supported, different philosophical opinions began to evolve. The appropriateness of labeling children from impoverished, low socioeconomic environments as having CIDs was challenged and the effectiveness of segregated programs for these students began to be questioned. In fact, the movement against segregated educational programs has been linked to the movement against racial segregation that was present at that time (Blanton, 1975). As previously mentioned, the *Hobson v. Hansen* court case brought attention to the inappropriate labeling of minority students. One example of the movement against segregated programs and the labeling of minority students was the publication of an article entitled "Special Education for the Mildly Retarded—Is Much of It Justifiable?" in an issue of *Exceptional Children* (Dunn, 1968; see Research Box 1.4).

1.4 RESEARCH THAT MADE A DIFFERENCE

Dunn, L. (1968). Special education for the mildly retarded—Is much of it justifiable? *Exceptional Children, 35,* 5–22.

This article was written by Lloyd Dunn, who at the time was the past president of the Council for Exceptional Children. He indicated in the preface that this was to be his "swan song" for now. In it, he argued that a great disservice had been done to "socioculturally deprived children with mild learning problems who have been labeled educable mentally retarded" (p. 5). He argued against labeling these children and placing them in segregated classrooms. He pointed out that segregated special education classes and schools were a form of homogeneous grouping and tracking, which had recently come under legal fire. Interestingly, Dunn's views represented early ideas about "mainstreaming" and the integration of students with disabilities in the general education classroom.

Another area that received attention was early intervention, particularly for at-risk students from low socioeconomic environments. One implied goal of these programs was to prevent CIDs. Although there had been some small-scale programs in the 1950s, such as the Philadelphia Project and the Early Training Project, large-scale programs like Head Start represented a significant commitment to provide early intervention and prevention services to a large number of at-risk children. In the first Head Start summer program in 1965 more than a half million children were enrolled. Unfortunately, the research on the effectiveness of these programs was unclear. Specifically, research such as the Westinghouse/Ohio University study (Cicirelli, 1969) indicated that although there were gains in IQ (i.e., early intervention was effective), those gains did not maintain into the school years (i.e., prevention did not occur). As Hodges and Cooper (1981) noted, "Many scientists have concluded that Head Start was a failure while other scientists have professed that it was a success. Both the views can be found expressed in unequivocal terms" (p. 228).

1970s

Philosophical/Political Climate

The decade of the 1970s was a time when, through the courts and through the U.S. Congress, individuals with CIDs received increasing rights, mirroring the 1960s when civil rights for minority individuals were advanced. It also paralleled the Equal Rights Amendment that focused on discrimination on the basis of gender. In terms of education, the instructional programs for students with CIDs, which had previously taken place primarily in segregated classrooms, began to move toward integration into regular education classes with students without disabilities. This move largely was encouraged by federal laws and led to a period of uncertainty and cautious optimism as new territory was being explored.

In addition to legal mandates, changing philosophies also had an effect on the attempts to promote the rights of these individuals. One example was the growing emphasis on the concept of normalization, introduced in the 1960s, which became a major focus in the 1970s. Another shift in philosophy was noted by Winzer (1993). She pointed out that there was a shift in the perception of individuals with disabilities from a *qualitative* to a *quantitative* perspective. The qualitative position represented the view that individuals with disabilities were fundamentally different, learning and thinking in ways unlike those without disabilities. On the other hand, the quantitative position held that differences were a matter of degree; individuals with disabilities might make slower and more limited progress but they were not fundamentally different from their peers without disabilities.

Litigation and Legislation

As just mentioned, this decade was a time of significant litigation and major legislation that led to increased educational rights for individuals with CIDs. The decade started with two landmark court cases that dealt with the issue of exclusion of students from appropriate educational programs. In *Pennsylvania Association for Retarded Citizens (PARC) v. Commonwealth of Pennsylvania* (1972), a class action suit was filed because of the lack of educational services for students with CIDs. In the PARC case, the Court ruled that students with CIDs have the right to a free, public education. This case was closely followed by *Mills v. Board of Education of District of Columbia* (1972), which was filed on behalf of seven children who were denied educational services because of their learning and behavior problems. Again the Court supported the plaintiffs, this time requiring the school district to give all students a free, appropriate public education, regardless of their disability. This case set a precedent in that it set the stage for rights for all students with disabilities including, but not limited to, those with CIDs.

Other cases also focused on the lack of appropriate educational programs. *LeBanks v. Spears* (1973) was a Louisiana court case filed because of the state's failure to provide educational programs for a group of children with CIDs. This case resulted in the state having to provide an educational program that made students more self-sufficient and employable. It also required that educational services be offered to adults who had not received them when they were students. Another case was *Maryland Association for Retarded Citizens v. Maryland Equity* (1974). This was another suit on behalf of children with CIDs and other disabilities who were denied an appropriate education. The court again sided with the plaintiff requiring the state to provide services. The court also noted that if all students with disabilities were to receive an appropriate education, the purpose of that education needed to be redefined (Turnbull, Stowe, & Huerta, 2007). In a sense, this case began to grapple with the difficult question of what "appropriate" actually meant.

Ironically, whereas the previously discussed cases dealt with exclusion of students from receiving special education, another set of cases was filed because students were inappropriately placed into special education programs for students with CIDs. In other words, these cases were based on *discrimination*. Table 1.2 summarizes these discrimination cases filed in the 1970s.

Other court cases that directly affected individuals with CIDs, specifically related to institutionalization, were *Wyatt v. Stickney* (1972) and *Halderman v. Pennhurst* (1977). The *Wyatt* case was filed on behalf of a group of individuals living in an institution called the Partlow State School in Tuscaloosa, Alabama. The Court ruled that the constitutional rights of the residents were being violated under the Fourteenth Amendment. It resulted in a comprehensive set of standards and monitoring procedures requiring that appropriate educational programs, not just custodial

Table 1.2 1970s Court Cases Focusing on Discrimination

Case	Issue	Result
Diana v. State Board of Education (1970)	Class action suit on behalf of Spanish-speaking students labeled as having mental retardation based on IQ tests administered in English	Must determine dominant language and administer tests in that language
Guadalupe v. Tempe (1972)	Similar to *Diana* case	Similar findings plus the importance of considering adaptive behavior before labeling a student as having mental retardation
Larry P. v. Riles (1972)	The alleged cultural bias of IQ tests	Judge ruled that IQ tests are biased and could not be used to identify African-American students as having mental retardation

Table 1.3 Additional Litigation Related to Institutional Issues

Case	Issue	Result
Burham v. Georgia (1972)	Right to appropriate treatment in institutions	Institutional residents had the right to treatment but the state was not legally contradicting the *Wyatt* case
Jackson v. Indiana (1972)	Rights of an individual with mental retardation confined to an institution after committing a crime	Due process is violated if confinement is ordered that does not include treatment and efforts for rehabilitation
New York Association for Retarded Citizens v. Rockefeller (1975)*	Deplorable conditions at Willowbrook Developmental Center (after a well-publicized exposé)	Drastic reduction in the number of residents, improvement of living environment, and rights to appropriate treatment were among the results
O'Connor v. Donaldson (1975)	Involuntary institutionalization of an inmate who was neither dangerous nor in need of such care	Court ordered payment for compensatory damages and established the illegality of unnecessarily institutionalizing an individual
Youngberg v. Romeo (1982)	Rights of individuals who are involuntarily committed to institutions	Rights of these individuals are the same as those who are voluntarily committed

*Litigation actually continued in 1987 when the facility was virtually closed.

programs, be provided to the residents. It also dealt with the issue of deinstitutionalization, particularly for those individuals who could and should function in a less segregated setting. In the *Pennhurst* case, arguments were supported that institutions were inappropriate and should be replaced by community-based facilities. Although this decision was not upheld by the Supreme Court, it paved the way for the movement to less restrictive, more community-based housing options. Several other cases also dealt with the issue of institutions and the rights of individuals with CIDs (see Table 1.3).

Legislation in the 1970s was largely "rights-oriented." In 1973, the Vocational Rehabilitation Act, initially passed after World War I, was amended. Part of that amendment, Section 504, established that individuals with disabilities should have the same access to educational and employment opportunities as those without disabilities in any program receiving federal funding. Largely as a result of the previously mentioned litigation, a significant piece of legislation, Public Law 94-142 or the Education for All Handicapped Children Act, was passed in 1975 (retroactively renamed the Individuals with Disabilities Education Act—IDEA). This legislation, in fact, has probably had the most significant impact of any law on the education of individuals with disabilities, including those with CIDs. In addition to providing educational rights and safeguards for individuals with disabilities, this law also provided considerable financial support to assist in its implementation. P.L. 94-142 initially required states to comply with its mandate for students ages 3–18 by September 1978 and for students ages 3–21 by September 1980. However, the federal law did not mandate services for those ages 3–5 and 18–21 years if it was inconsistent with state law. There were six principles outlined in P.L. 94-142:

1. Zero Reject—This required that *all* students with disabilities be provided a free, appropriate public education. This was referred to as FAPE.
2. Nondiscriminatory Evaluation—This principle required, among other things, that students be tested in their dominant language, that more than one person is involved in the evaluation, and that tests that are used be valid for the intended purpose of the evaluation.
3. Individualized Education Program (IEP)—This required that all students with disabilities have a specific educational program designed to meet their individual needs. Some of the components of the IEP included the documentation of the current performance level, the annual goals, short-term objectives, services needed, and evaluation procedures and schedules for determining mastery of those goals and objectives.
4. Least Restrictive Environment (LRE)—This required that students with disabilities be taught with their peers without disabilities to the maximum extent appropriate.
5. Due Process—This provided a system of checks and balances to assure that educational decisions made about a student are fair. It protects both parents and professionals as well as the student with the disability.
6. Parental Participation—Perhaps for the first time, parents were encouraged in specific ways to participate in decisions regarding their child's educational program (e.g., attending IEP meetings and providing input as to the appropriate goals and objectives for their child).

These principles were incorporated (with additions and modifications) into the various reauthorizations of the law, including the current reauthorization—IDEA 2004.

Advances in Education

In addition to the concern about whether or not individuals with disabilities were offered appropriate educational programs, another issue had to do with the placement of students to implement their educational programs. In other words, the question asked was "What is the most appropriate setting in which students with disabilities should be taught?" Interest in this area was started at the beginning of the decade with the publication of a precedent-setting article by Evelyn Deno entitled "Special Education as Developmental Capital" (see Research Box 1.5) prior to the enactment of IDEA in 1975. Although the model she presented in the Research Box had its critics, it nonetheless helped form the basis for the least restrictive environment clause that was later incorporated into Public Law 94-142 and subsequent legislation.

1.5 RESEARCH THAT MADE A DIFFERENCE

Deno, E. (1970). Special education as developmental capital. *Exceptional Children, 37, 229–237.*

This article was written at the time in special education history when there was a push toward teaching students with disabilities in settings other than segregated classrooms. Deno felt that special education should be more flexible and adaptable and was concerned that many professionals judged its success by how many more students received special education services in one year compared to the year before. Accordingly, she developed what is known as "Deno's Cascade," a fluid model that emphasized the need for various placement options for students with disabilities. Her model had seven levels:

Level 1—Students taught in regular classrooms; able to be educated with regular education accommodations with or without support or therapies.

Level 2—Students taught in regular classroom plus supplemental instructional services.

Level 3—Students taught in part-time special class.

Level 4—Students taught in full-time special class.

Level 5—Students taught at special stations.

Level 6—Students are taught at home.

Level 7—Students are either taught in a hospital, at home, or in noneducational settings (medical and/or welfare).

Using this model, the goal would be to move the student up (toward Level 1) as much and as soon as possible (i.e., toward a less restrictive environment).

Many of the educational practices in the 1970s were a direct result of the legal mandates of Public Law 94-142. In a sense, the law sent somewhat mixed messages regarding the education of individuals with disabilities. On one hand, the concept of least restrictive environment suggested that individuals with disabilities should be taught *to the maximum extent appropriate* in settings most typical for those without disabilities, considering the individual needs of the student. On the other hand, many professionals continued to discuss the term **mainstreaming,** which actually began to be implemented in the 1960s but whose spirit was formalized with the passage of Public Law 94-142 (Skrtic, 1992). Proponents of this philosophy advocated that students with disabilities should be taught with their peers without disabilities in the general education classroom for at least part of the day. Unfortunately, the term was interpreted quite differently among professionals. Some felt that mainstreaming took place simply if students with disabilities ate lunch or rode on the bus with their peers without disabilities. Others viewed it as placement in the general education classroom for the entire day. It does appear that mainstreaming *in its initial conception* was thought to be more of an educational placement than an educational support system that would benefit the student. The concept of mainstreaming resulted in somewhat apprehensive attitudes among many professionals, particularly teachers in the general education classroom who had little or no training to work with students with disabilities.

A parallel movement, normalization, which also began in the 1960s, continued to receive considerable attention during this decade. Simply put, normalization referred to the belief that all individuals with disabilities regardless of severity were entitled "to establish and/or maintain personal behaviors which are as culturally normal as possible" (Wolfensberger, 1972; p. 28). In other words, it referred to the goal that individuals with disabilities live and be treated the same as those without disabilities and that any differences between these two groups be reduced as much as possible. Normalization can be interpreted educationally as the least restrictive environment movement. It can also be interpreted in a broader sense, particularly for older individuals with CIDs. It can refer to issues such as community living options, equal employment, and even having and raising children (Field & Sanchez, 1999). Unfortunately, the concept of normalization, although apparently straightforward, is subject to different interpretations (Hallahan, Kauffman, & Pullen, 2012). However, although difficult to define, the concept did represent a significant philosophical change in the perception of individuals with CIDs.

1980s

Philosophical/Political Climate

Politically, the 1980s represented a definite shift to more conservative policies under the presidencies of Ronald Reagan and George H. W. Bush. Among other actions, government deregulation and tax relief programs marked a significant change from the liberal policies of the 1960s and the legal proliferation of the 1970s. Even the philosophical movement known as the Regular Education Initiative (discussed later) was based, in part, on the economic premise of serving more students in a fiscally responsible manner. In a sense, much of the progress for individuals with disabilities in this decade was based on advances and clarification of philosophies and policies that had already been initiated in previous decades. However, the Americans with Disabilities Act was passed during the Bush administration in 1990.

Litigation and Legislation

Much of the litigation during the 1980s had to do with interpreting various aspects of Public Law 94-142. Many of these cases focused on individuals with a variety of disabilities including those with hearing impairments (e.g., *Hendrick Hudson Central School District v. Rowley*, 1982) and physical or health impairments (e.g., *Irving Independent School District v. Tatro*, 1984). The *Rowley* case was a very significant test of the meaning of free, appropriate public education (FAPE), and was ultimately reviewed by the U.S. Supreme Court. Although this case did not involve individuals with CIDs, it had a direct impact on all students with disabilities. The issue focused on whether Amy Rowley, a student with a hearing impairment, should be provided with a sign language interpreter as part of her educational program. Although earlier court decisions had supported her entitlement to an interpreter, the Supreme Court reversed that decision based on information that she previously had made satisfactory progress and was promoted without the benefit of an interpreter. This decision meant that *appropriate education* should not be interpreted as *optimal education*. Rather, it meant that appropriate education should result in providing the student with a reasonable opportunity to learn (Turnbull et al., 2007). In a sense, it "leveled the playing field" for those students with disabilities.

The *Tatro* case specifically dealt with the issue of entitlement of related services, an area that potentially affects all students with disabilities. The Supreme Court decision in this case ultimately required that the school district must provide the nonmedical procedure of clear, intermittent catheterization for Amber Tatro, a student with Spina Bifida who was paralyzed below the waist. The rationale was that without the procedure, Amber would not be able to attend school and thereby would be denied the rights of FAPE. Another interesting case addressing the concept of FAPE was *Timothy W. v. Rochester School District* (1988), in which a District Court judge ruled that a local school district did not have to provide services for a boy with severe, multiple disabilities (including a severe CID) because he would not benefit from the instruction. However, a U.S. Appeals Court overruled and required that all children with disabilities be provided an appropriate educational program, regardless of the severity of the disability, thus upholding the FAPE philosophy inherent in P.L. 94-142.

One broad-reaching court case that continues to be debated was *Honig v. Doe* (1988). This case dealt with the controversial issue of discipline. Essentially, the Supreme Court ruled that students cannot be excluded from FAPE if their misbehavior is determined to be related to their disability. This case and others actually led to legal policies outlined in a later reauthorization of IDEA. Depending on whether or not a student's misbehavior is a manifestation of the disability, various disciplinary options are available for the school *although complete termination of educational services is prohibited.* The *Honig* decision followed the line of reasoning of lower court decisions including *S-1 v. Turlington* (1981) (see Event Box 1.4), a case involving students with a CID (Turnbull et al., 2007). Interestingly, the most recent reauthorization of IDEA has reversed this position, making it easier to discipline students with disabilities depending on the behavior displayed (e.g., bringing drugs or weapons to school).

1.4 EVENT THAT MADE A DIFFERENCE

1981—*S-1 v. Turlington*; Court case involving disciplinary action against students with CIDs.

This Florida case was filed on behalf of seven students with CIDs who were expelled from high school in the early part of 1977–1978 and the entire 1978–1979 school year for misconduct. One of the students, referred to as S-1, requested that a determination be made as to whether or not his misconduct was due to his disability. The superintendent made the judgment that it was *not* a manifestation because the student had not been classified as having a severe emotional disturbance and therefore upheld the expulsion of the student. The situations for the other students were different than those of S-1's with some not given nor requesting such a manifestation hearing, although expulsion was still an issue.

The court found that expelling the students was a violation of the FAPE concept of P.L. 94-142. Further, the court found that since expulsion is a change of educational placement, trained specialists, not the school board, should make manifestation determination decisions. The court also clarified that misconduct might be a result of any disability, including a CID, and not just for those who have an emotional disturbance.

Other cases had to do with issues related to living facilities. In *Abrahamson v. Herschman* (1983), the school district was ordered to pay for residential placement in a private school because a child with multiple disabilities required such comprehensive training. In another, *Cleburne v. Cleburne Living Center* (1985), the Supreme Court ruled against the prevention of the establishment of community living facilities (i.e., group homes) for individuals with CIDs by using zoning ordinances.

Similar to litigation, legislation in the 1980s also was primarily related to IDEA in the form of several amendments. In 1983, Public Law 98-199 was passed that required states to address the transition needs of secondary students as they moved from school to post-school settings (e.g., independent living facilities, employment settings, post-secondary education). It also included incentives to provide services for infants and preschool children with disabilities. This was followed in 1986 by the passage of Public Law 99-457, which mandated the expansion of programs for preschool children ages 3–5 and the development of programs for infants and toddlers ages birth–2 with disabilities. This law also actively involved the parents in their child's education in the form of an Individualized Family Services Plan (IFSP). The Rehabilitation Act was also amended in 1986. The result was a set of regulations that led to programs to promote supported employment opportunities for adults with disabilities.

Advances in Education

Partially as an extension of the mainstreaming phenomenon in the 1970s, and perhaps as a reaction to the lack of consensus over its meaning (Skrtic, 1992), a major philosophical movement was proposed in the mid-1980s. At that time, Madeline Will, who was Assistant Secretary of the Office of Special Education and Rehabilitative Services from the U.S. Office of Education, made a recommendation that special education teachers and regular education teachers should combine their resources and expertise to work in the regular classroom with all students who were having difficulty in school. Will estimated that whereas only approximately 10% of the school population were receiving special education services, another 10–20% who did not qualify for special education nonetheless required additional, more intense, educational programs. By pooling the resources of both special educators and general educators, the needs of more students with educational problems could be met. This movement was known as the **Regular Education Initiative** (REI), and was implemented on a trial basis in a number of states. The REI advanced the concept of mainstreaming beyond just the physical placement of the students in the regular education classroom by focusing on ways in which the educational program could be modified to meet students' needs in that setting. Although the REI was met with mixed reviews, it did have an impact on educational practices. Among other things it resulted in more collaboration between general education and special education teachers.

The concept of normalization also evolved when Wolfensberger (1983) provided a conceptual framework and proposed a name change for the term. He wrote "the highest goal of the principle of normalization has recently been clarified to be the establishment, enhancement, or defense of the social role(s) of a person or group via the enhancement of people's social images and personal competencies. In consequence, it is proposed that normalization be henceforth called social role valorization" (p. 234). The goal of **social role valorization,** therefore, was the positive development of socially valued roles of individuals with CIDs through the enhancement of social image and the enhancement of personal competence. Importantly, Wolfensberger suggested ways in which these goals could be met by addressing variables such as physical settings, relationships and groupings, and the use of language and other symbols and images.

1990s–2000s

Philosophical/Political Climate

The principles of integration and normalization reached their pinnacle in the 1990s. Educationally, the expectation that students with CIDs should be included in the general education classroom became the norm rather than the exception. From a philosophical perspective, the history of CIDs, whose positive evolution had progressed from abuse and neglect, to kindness and care, and eventually to education and respect, ended the 20th century in a very humanistic and positive fashion. For the field of CIDs, the 1990s embraced what was referred to as the **New Paradigm.** Holburn (2000), in summarizing the various philosophies of the New Paradigm, noted that it incorporated the concepts of self-determination, consumer empowerment, and person-centered planning, all of which lead to the goal of increased decision making, personal independence, and quality of life for individuals with CIDs (these concepts are discussed in subsequent chapters). Butterworth (2002) noted that many of these values were embedded in the legislation of the 1990s such as the Americans with Disabilities Act (ADA) that emphasized the importance of individual choice and consumer control as well as nondiscrimination in employment based on disability alone (ADA is discussed in the next section).

Litigation and Legislation

The decade of the 1990s brought less litigation than the previous two, although significant legislation was passed, including two major reauthorizations of IDEA. Court cases continued to focus primarily on clarification of the various aspects of existing laws, and to reexamine previous court decisions. In *Doe v. Withers* (1993), the meaning of FAPE was again tested. In this case, the parents of a student with a learning disability filed suit against a school district, and specifically a teacher who refused to provide an accommodation noted in the student's IEP (oral rather than written exams). The plaintiff sought and received monetary compensation for this violation of the FAPE concept. The nature of related services was again tested in *Cedar Rapids Community School District v. Garret F.* (1999). This case, similar to the *Tatro* case, went to the Supreme Court, and similar to the *Tatro* decision, the ruling was that necessary related services (in this case, continuous nurse's care) must be provided by the school district unless it requires the involvement of a physician.

Another aspect of IDEA that was tested in court was the meaning of least restrictive environment. One example was *Sacramento City Board of Education v. Rachel H* (1994). This case essentially led to four questions that should be addressed when considering an appropriate educational placement for a student with a disability:

1. What will be the academic benefits for the student?
2. What will be the effect on the general education teacher?
3. What will be the effect on the general education students?
4. What will be the cost of including the student in the general education classroom?

In terms of legislation, the decade began with two significant laws passed in 1990, the Americans with Disabilities Act (ADA; Public Law 101-336) and the reauthorization of P.L. 94-142 (Public Law 101-476). ADA provided sweeping protection against discrimination of individuals with disabilities. Turnbull et al. (2007) noted that the purpose of the ADA was to provide clear, strong, consistent, and enforceable standards prohibiting discrimination against individuals, without respect to their age, nature of disability, or extent of disability. The ADA dealt with issues such as transportation accommodations, accessibility (e.g., ramps for wheelchair access into buildings), telecommunications, and the ending of employment discrimination. The ultimate goal was to provide individuals with disabilities with equal opportunities, full participation, independent living, and economic self-sufficiency.

P.L. 101-476 changed the name of P.L. 94-142 from the Education of All Handicapped Children Act to the Individuals with Disabilities Education Act (IDEA). The new law changed all references to "handicaps" to "disabilities" and emphasized the importance of "person first" terminology. Thus, instead of the phrase "mentally retarded student," the phrase "student with mental retardation" would be substituted. Other changes in IDEA that specifically related to individuals with CIDs involved career/vocational education and transition services. IDEA required that an **individualized transition program** be developed for a student by the age of 16. This document indicated how the student's educational program would specifically address the preparation of the student for life after the public school experience.

HOW ARE LAWS NUMBERED?

Public Laws are denoted by two numbers separated by a hyphen; for example, 94-142, 101-476, and 105-17. What do these numbers mean? The first number refers to the U.S. Congressional session during which the law was enacted and dates back to the 1st Federal Congress that took place between March 4, 1789 and March 3, 1791. This Congress was responsible for the Bill of Rights and the establishment of the three branches of government. Each subsequent two-year session is represented by the next sequential number. Thus the 2nd Congress was from 1791–1793, the 3rd from 1793–1795, etc. You can get a good estimate of when a law was passed by noting the number of the Congressional session. The second number refers to the Public Law number within the given Congressional session. Thus the ADA, P.L. 101-336, and IDEA, P.L. 101-476, were separate laws passed in the same congressional session.

IDEA was again reauthorized in 1997 in the form of Public Law 105-17 (also referred to as IDEA 1997). This law reflected the changing philosophies regarding the education of students with disabilities. Among other things, it increased the degree of parental participation in the educational process, required that students with disabilities participate in statewide and large-scale assessment programs, and reemphasized the importance of addressing students' transition needs (requiring that a statement of transition needs be included in the IEP by age 14). Perhaps most significantly, IDEA 1997 required that students with disabilities must have access to participation in the general education curriculum. In fact, as part of the IEP, statements must be included about how the disability affects involvement and progress in the general education curriculum, and what services are necessary to allow that involvement and progress. It also required that an explanation be provided of the extent, if any, that the student does not participate in the general education curriculum. Clearly, the spirit, if not the requirement, of educational integration was sanctioned in IDEA 1997.

The most recent reauthorization of IDEA was in 2004. This reauthorization was recommended by Congress for several reasons. They acknowledged that PL 94-142 and subsequent reauthorizations resulted in improved services for students with disabilities. However, they noted that these efforts were impeded by low expectations and the need to apply research-based methods (Taylor, Smiley, & Richards, 2009). IDEA 2004 retained most of the principles of IDEA 1997 including participation in the general education curriculum. It also dovetailed with the No Child Left Behind Act to streamline the participation in statewide assessments and provide additional assessment options based on different standards. There were some differences related to evaluation procedures and the nondiscriminatory clause of PL 94-142 was incorporated in those procedures. Basically, IDEA 2002 resulted in more emphasis on participation in both the general education curriculum and in statewide assessments.

Advances in Education

Throughout the evolution of educational desegregation, various terms and phrases have been used. As noted earlier, mainstreaming and the least restrictive environment were attempts at providing education to those with disabilities in the general education classroom (Hardman, Drew, & Egan, 2003). In the 1990s, the term **inclusion** became a popular term to refer to this concept. Unfortunately, the term is somewhat difficult to define because it is used by individuals with considerably different philosophies. To some, it is more consistent with the term *mainstreaming* as a viable, desirable educational option for students with disabilities. For others, it means that all students, regardless of the type and degree of their disabilities, should be taught exclusively in the general education classroom with their peers without disabilities. This position, known as **full inclusion,** initially began as a civil rights issue based on the argument that students with disabilities, particularly those with severe disabilities, were a minority group and that denying them access to the general education classroom was a civil rights violation (e.g., Stainback & Stainback, 1985). Other terms include **partial inclusion,** referring to the situation in which students with disabilities receive most of their instruction in the general education classroom but are taught in other instructional settings when appropriate (Hardman, Drew, & Egan, 2003).

Lewis, Doorlag, and Lewis (2011) provided a meaningful compromise among the various interpretations of inclusion when they noted their belief that all students should participate in the general education classroom but that the nature and extent of that participation be based on individual need. This position seems to be consistent with the legal requirement in IDEA 2004.

As noted previously, in addition to educational advances, much progress was made in changing societal perceptions of individuals with CIDs, providing them with the opportunity to make their own choices and to improve their quality of life. Butterworth (2002) referred to this as a shift from a service-oriented paradigm to a community supports paradigm. In the former, the goal of intervention is to change the individual; in the latter, the goal is to make a fit between the individual and his or her environment. As Butterworth noted "The New Supports Paradigm suggests that individuals should first, without restrictions, define the lifestyle they prefer and the environments they want to access. Their goals and priorities then become the basis for intensity and types of support that they need to succeed in those environments" (p. 85).

Another related area is the integration of individuals with CIDs in the community. Research has consistently shown that community-based services are superior to residential or institutional environments. Kozma, Mansell, and Beadle-Brown (2009) reported on a review of 10 years of professional literature and concluded, among other findings, that small group arrangements (e.g., group homes) are superior to segregated arrangements and despite significant improvements, people with CIDs are still one of the most disadvantaged groups in society. They did note, however, that community-based services were not particularly effective in dealing with challenging behaviors, often leading to overmedication. There have been active attempts to reduce the number of individuals with CIDs living in residential settings. Thorn, Pittman, Myers, and Slaughter (2009) argued that residential settings serve the role of segregation with no real focus on community integration. In a model designed to transition these individuals from a large residential facility to community-based living settings, they found increases in community presence, community participation, community integration, and community inclusion after the transition was made.

In fact, data regarding the increased number of individuals with CIDs living in community-based environments also has attested to this shift in philosophy. Polister, Lakin, Smith, Prouty, and Smith (2002) reported a 63% decrease in state residential housing from 1982 to 2001 and an increase in community housing during that same time period. In addition, Wagner (2002) noted that by the end of the 1990s decade eight U.S. states and the District of Columbia served individuals with CIDs without any use of state facilities. He did point out, however, that although the number of state-run institutions has decreased, the number of privately run residential facilities has increased. The need for reducing both of these types of facilities in favor of community-based residential options is discussed in Chapter 12.

Reflection

What important events occurred in the 1940s–1960s that resulted in improved attitudes toward people with CIDs? What events do you perceive occurring in today's educational settings that may influence how people with CIDs are treated?

CURRENT PERSPECTIVES

Needless to say, the 21st century holds tremendous promise for individuals with CIDs. Much of this optimism is reflected in the following statement made over 10 years ago, summarizing the progress that has been made in the field of CIDs.

> We have moved from terms like feeble-minded, idiot, imbecile, and moron, to cognitive disability. We have gone from views of deviancy and deficiency to views of natural differences and at times, even a celebration of diversity. We have seen progress from institutionalization to community living. We are moving from fear to acceptance. A vast array of potential and opportunities afforded most people with disabilities has opened a world of new life options.
>
> (Black & Salas, 2001; p. 14)

In the past decade, even more has been accomplished. Among the areas that will continue to be addressed are social issues, legal concerns, medical advances, and educational considerations. Future legislation will impact many of these issues. This includes topics such as community integration, self-determination and decision making, the criminal justice system, medical prevention, ethics, and educational reform movements.

Reflection

What two issues do you think will be the most important during the next 10 years? Do you think these issues will more likely affect educational programs, community living, employment, or other areas of life for people with CIDs?

SUMMARY CHECKLIST

✓ Terms used to denote CIDs have changed over time and continue to change

An Early Dark History

✓ Accounts of CIDs date to 1500 B.C.

✓ Early Egyptians tried to cure a number of human ailments
  ➤ **Infanticide—Killing an infant; practice was widespread in ancient Greece and Rome for infants with disabilities**

✓ During the Renaissance, physicians such as Paracelsus and Platter began to distinguish between mental retardation and mental illness

✓ Although there were medical advances in the 17th century, societal factors led to inhumane treatment of individuals with CIDs in Europe and in America

✓ In the 18th century, Periere and Pinel began advocating a more humane approach
  ➤ **Moral treatment—Approach attributed to Pinel that emphasized positive, psychologically oriented components**

A Shift to Care

✓ Jean Marc Gaspard Itard—French physician best known for his work with Victor, the wild boy of Aveyron. He believed that individuals with severe CIDs could be educated

✓ Jean Etienne Esquirol—One of the first to establish levels of CIDs; differentiated between "idiots" and "imbeciles"

✓ Johan Jacob Guggenbuhl—Credited as being the first to establish an institution for individuals with CIDs in Abendberg, Switzerland
  ➤ **Cretinism—A thyroid deficiency condition resulting in physical deformity and CIDs. This is the type of individual for whom Guggenbuhl focused his work**

✓ Samuel Gridley Howe—Began his work in the United States in the area of visual impairment but had an impact on the development of institutions for individuals with CIDs

✓ Edouard Seguin—Worked initially in France and later in the United States. He was very instrumental in developing institutions and was the first president of what is now the American Association on Intellectual and Developmental Disabilities. Itard was his mentor.

An Age of Conflict

✓ The term *training school* began to replace the term *institution* in the 19th century

✓ After the Civil War and bad economic times, institutions returned and became more custodial than educational
  ➤ **Eugenics—The attempt to improve the human species through the control of hereditary factors**

✓ Eugenics movement—Occurred primarily at the end of the 19th century and the beginning of the 20th century. Supported by separate books about two families, the Jukes and the Kallikaks, that reinforced the genetic basis for CIDs and socially negative traits

✓ The number of institutions increased and the quality decreased in the 1920s and 1930s

Humanization of People with CIDs
✓ Certain factors such as the political climate, changes in philosophy, and educational and medical advances resulted in a more positive atmosphere for change in the 1930s

1940s–1950s
✓ World War II resulted in more employment opportunities
✓ Exposés of institutions began
✓ Legislation began to foster an increased interest in CIDs
✓ *Brown v. Board of Education* ruled against racial segregation and set the stage for CID litigation
✓ Special education, although primarily involving segregated classrooms, became routine

1960s
✓ President Kennedy began many programs to assist individuals with CIDs
  ➤ **Normalization—Concept that individuals with CIDs should be given the same opportunities and conditions in life as those without disabilities**
✓ *Hobson v. Hansen*—Court case that focused on the misuse of test information with minority students; basis for similar litigation for individuals with CIDs
✓ Lloyd Dunn argued for the integration of students with mild CIDs into the regular education classroom
✓ Early intervention programs such as Head Start were implemented

1970s
✓ The 1970s was a decade of considerable litigation and significant legislation
✓ *PARC* and *Mills*—Court cases that led to requirement that no student, regardless of disability, be excluded from an appropriate public education
✓ Other court cases focused on the discriminatory use of test scores to identify students as having CIDs (Table 1.2)
✓ Litigation regarding institutions (e.g., *Wyatt* and *Pennhurst*) resulted in improved conditions and increased constitutional rights of the residents
✓ P.L. 94-142, arguably the most significant legislation regarding individuals with disabilities, was passed in 1975. This law required, among other things, an individualized education program, a free, appropriate public education, and educational placement in the least restrictive environment
  ➤ **Least restrictive environment—The educational placement that allows students, to the maximum extent possible, to be taught with their peers without disabilities**
  ➤ **Mainstreaming—Philosophy that students with disabilities be taught with their peers without disabilities in the regular education classroom for at least a part of the day**
✓ Concept of normalization was expanded

1980s

✓ The 1980s was a decade of more conservative policies

✓ Litigation focused on clarifying aspects of P.L. 94-142. The *Rowley* case helped define FAPE and the *Tatro* case examined the issue of related services

✓ *Honig v. Doe*—Supreme Court case that dealt with discipline (e.g., expulsion) of students with disabilities

✓ P.L. 94-142 had several amendments including P.L. 99-457 that expanded services to infants, toddlers, and preschoolers

> **Regular Education Initiative—A movement that proposed that special education and regular education combine their resources and expertise to work within the regular class setting with all students having difficulties**

> **Social role valorization—Term suggested by Wolfensberger to replace normalization; refers to the positive development of socially valuable roles of individuals with CIDs**

1990s–2000s

> **New Paradigm—Philosophy that incorporates self-determination, consumer empowerment, person-centered planning, and increased quality of life for individuals with CIDs**

✓ There were court cases that upheld rights provided under P.L. 94-142

✓ Americans with Disabilities Act was passed in 1990; provided strong, enforceable standards to prevent discrimination against individuals with disabilities

✓ P.L. 94-142 was reauthorized in 1990 and became the Individuals with Disabilities Education Act (IDEA); provided additional protection and services for students with disabilities

✓ IDEA was reauthorized in 1997; emphasized the need to allow students with disabilities to participate in the general education curriculum

✓ IDEA was again reauthorized in 2004 and strengthened many of the principles from IDEA 97, namely, the participation in the general education curriculum and in statewide assessments

> **Inclusion—A general term used to describe the integration of students with disabilities into the general education classroom with their peers without disabilities. Inclusion has different meanings for different individuals**

> **Full inclusion—The position that all students, regardless of the type and degree of their disabilities, should be taught exclusively in the general education classroom with their peers without disabilities**

> **Partial inclusion—The situation in which students with disabilities receive most of their instruction in the general education classroom but are taught in other instructional settings when appropriate**

✓ More movement to community supports that incorporated the philosophy of the New Paradigm

✓ Continued reduction in state-supported facilities and a subsequent increase in community-based facilities

Current Perspectives

✓ Many areas show promise for the 21st century including issues related to social, legal, medical, and educational concerns

ADDITIONAL SUGGESTIONS/RESOURCES

Discussion Questions

1. Trace the evolution of institutions for individuals with CIDs throughout history. What were three factors/events that you feel had the most impact on this movement?

2. Pick any two of the six principles outlined in P.L. 94-142 (IDEA) and discuss the effect they have had for students with CIDs.

3. In recent years, there has been what appears to be a contradiction regarding the educational placement of students with CIDs. On one hand, legal mandates require that students be taught in the least restrictive environment. On the other hand, those who support full inclusion feel that all students should be taught in the general education classroom. Discuss the pros and cons of these two positions.

Activities

1. Individuals with CIDs have been portrayed in many ways in both literature and the media (e.g., cinema, television shows). Identify an example of a negative stereotype and one that portrays the individual in a more positive light. What historical factors led to these portrayals?

2. Develop a timeline that indicates the roles the courts have played (e.g., significant litigation) in shaping the education and lives of individuals with CIDs. This can also function as a study guide for this information.

3. Read Lloyd Dunn's article "Special education for the mildly retarded—Is much of it justifiable?" (Research Box 1.4). Do you agree with his position? Why or why not?

E-sources

http://cirrie.buffalo.edu/encyclopedia/en/article/143/

This is the website for the International Encyclopedia for Rehabilitation. It includes an article called "History of Intellectual Disability" written by two authors with public health backgrounds. It includes a discussion of, among other topics, early history, segregation, eugenics, and institutionalization, legal protections and services, and deinstitutionalization and global perspectives.

www.disabilitymuseum.org/lib

This website includes an index to find articles, pamphlets, letters, book excerpts, photographs, paintings, and postcards that are part of the Disability History Museum. The museum is a searchable, theme-based digital collection of material related to disability history in the United States.

NOTES

1. Terminology used in this chapter is consistent with that used during the specific time period being discussed.
2. The acronym CID is used for cognitive/intellectual disability and CIDs is used for the plural cognitive/intellectual disabilities.

2

DEFINITION AND CLASSIFICATION OF COGNITIVE/INTELLECTUAL DISABILITIES

Key Points

➢ NAMING, DEFINING, AND CLASSIFYING COGNITIVE/INTELLECTUAL DISABILITIES (CIDS)[1]—All three processes are important when characterizing individuals with CIDs.

➢ EVOLUTION OF THE DEFINITION—Early descriptions of individuals with CIDs date back to 1500 B.C. Attempts were made to differentiate CID from mental illness and to identify possible causes.

➢ AAMD/AAMR/AAIDD DEFINITIONS—The association known by several names over the years has provided definitions since 1921, the most recent in 2010.

➢ CLASSIFICATION OF CIDs—CIDs have been classified by etiology, mental ability (IQ), educational needs, and more recently, by levels of needed supports.

➢ PREVALENCE—The number of individuals with CIDs is generally reported to be about 1% of the population but varies based on age, geographic region, socioeconomic status, and ethnic background.

As pointed out in Chapter 1, the area of CIDs has had a rich and interesting history. Both attitudes toward, and practices for, individuals with CIDs have certainly evolved over the last two centuries. With these changes in attitudes have come constant, ongoing attempts to change and improve the description and definition of what is a CID. These attempts have closely paralleled the changes in attitude and practices. Over the past decade, there has been a strong movement to eliminate the term *mental retardation,* led by many professional organizations that focus on this population. For example, the Division on Mental Retardation and Developmental Disabilities of the Council for Exceptional Children dropped the term *mental retardation* from its title in 2002 and is now called the Division on Autism and Developmental Disabilities. Similarly, the American Association on Mental Retardation (AAMR) changed its name to the American Association on Intellectual and Developmental Disabilities (AAIDD) in 2008.

NAMING, DEFINING, AND CLASSIFYING CIDS

Three issues relate to terminology and were used, in part, to change our views of mental retardation, the term used for so many years. These are naming, defining, and classifying. Luckasson and Reeve (2001) wrote an influential article discussing these issues that ultimately helped in changing the term *mental retardation* to *intellectual and developmental disabilities,* now in use by the AAIDD.

Naming

In this context, naming involves the assignment of a specific term or label to a condition or disability. As noted in the cliché, "It's all in the name," naming is very important because the specific term chosen to represent the condition can impact perceptions and attitudes about that condition. In fact, the very act of naming or labeling has been criticized by a number of professionals over the years. Historically, various researchers have reported that the label of "mental retardation" resulted in lower teacher expectations and poor self-concept for the person being labeled (e.g., Algozzine & Sutherland, 1977; Jacobs, 1978; Taylor, Smiley, & Ziegler, 1983). Another issue is that identifying an individual by a label (e.g., he is mentally retarded) provides a very narrow description and, in many ways, devalues the person. For this reason, the Individuals with Disabilities Education Act (IDEA) in 1990 required a change to "person first" terminology (e.g., he is an individual with a disability). Although the term *mental retardation* is still used in IDEA 2004, the change at least emphasizes that you are a person first and foremost. As noted in Chapter 1, future legislation will undoubtedly substitute intellectual disability or some other more appropriate term for mental retardation and IDEA does allow states to use alternative terms now.

Also as noted in Chapter 1, the historical names used for this disability such as idiot and feebleminded are viewed as very negative and inappropriate in today's society. Such terms do, however, paint a picture of how CIDs were viewed at other particular points in time. In other words, names change as perceptions and attitudes change. For example, the AAIDD was founded in 1878 as the Association of Medical Officers of American Institutions for Idiotic and Feebleminded Persons. That name changed to the American Association for the Study of the Feebleminded in 1906, then the American Association of Mental Deficiency (AAMD) in 1933. In 1987, the name was changed to the American Association on Mental Retardation (AAMR) and is now the American Association on Intellectual and Developmental Disabilities.

Choosing the name to represent a certain disability should be done so very carefully and should serve a clear purpose. The following questions were identified to consider when names or terms are being considered (Luckasson & Reeve, 2001):

- Does the term name this and nothing else?
- Does this term provide consistent nomenclature?

- Does this term facilitate communication?
- Does this term incorporate current knowledge and is it likely to incorporate future knowledge?
- Does this term meet the purposes for which it is being proposed?
- Does this term contribute positively to the portrayal of people with this disability?

(pp. 48–49)

Luckasson et al. (1992) in the AAMR *Definition and Classification Manual* commented on the naming issue. "Mental retardation is not something you have, like blue eyes or a bad heart. Nor is it something you are, like being short or thin. . . . *Mental retardation* refers to a particular state of functioning that begins in childhood and in which limitations in intelligence coexist with limitations in adaptive skills. In this sense, it is a more specific term than *developmental disability* because the level of functioning is necessarily related to an intellectual limitation" (p. 9). This statement did leave the door open for the possible use of the term *intellectual disability*. Perhaps this rationale led, in part, to the organization's current use of the term *intellectual and developmental disabilities*.

According to Webster's dictionary, defining involves "a statement of what a thing is" or "a statement of the meaning of a word, phrase, etc." Luckasson and Reeve (2001) noted that the main role of a definition is to separate something from some other (named) thing. Thus, defining CID involves a precise description of the meaning and boundaries of the term. They suggested that eight questions be asked when considering a definition:

- Does this definition indicate the boundaries of the term, that is, who or what is inside the boundaries and who or what is outside the boundaries?
- Does this definition indicate the class of things to which it belongs?
- Does this definition differentiate the term from other members of the class?
- Does this definition use words that are no more complicated than the term itself?
- Does the definition define what something is, not what it is not?
- Does this definition allow some generalizations about characteristics of the individual or group named by the term?
- Is this definition consistent with a desired theoretical framework?
- Does this definition contribute positively to the portrayal of people included in the term?

(p. 49)

Haywood (1997a) urged professionals in the field to seek new definitions, "recognizing the inadequacy of present concepts and definitions to incorporate what is known about the behavior and development of persons with mental retardation" (p. 5). Schalock (2002), in his perspective on the history and future of the mental retardation definition, identified six factors that he felt have affected and will continue to impact the conceptualization and definition of the term. Among these were the population of persons with CIDs, biochemical advances that will result in prevention and cures for certain conditions, and the demise of typological thinking. As an example of this latter point, Schalock noted that the idea of the incurability of CIDs as well as the notion that persons with CIDs are inherently different from others had been abandoned in definitions by 2002. He accurately predicted that the search for new definitions will follow three paths. First, the fundamental terms, concepts, and practices will continue to be questioned. Second, the potential conflict between the requirements of science and the needs of individuals with CIDs will need to be resolved. Finally, sensitivity to disability culture and disability pride must be instilled and the acceptance of a strong self-advocacy movement must be continued. Clearly, the issue of defining CIDs is complex and multifaceted with significant implications for those individuals who are identified as well as for those concerned with their education and welfare.

Classifying

Classifying has to do with identifying subgroups of individuals within the defined group according to certain criteria. For example, individuals could be classified according to medical diagnosis (e.g., Down syndrome), or IQ level (mild, moderate, severe, or profound), or the needed levels of support (e.g., intermittent support needed). The goal of classifying should be to provide more precision so that individuals with the same classification have similar attributes or characteristics. This, in turn, should provide information regarding funding, educational and service delivery needs. The question that must be asked is "On what basis should you classify individuals?" As will be discussed later in this chapter, for example, attempts at classifying based on *etiology* (causes) became prominent as early as the end of the 19th century (see Event Box 2.1).

2.1 EVENT THAT MADE A DIFFERENCE

1898—William W. Ireland Develops Classification System Based on Medical Causes

William W. Ireland was a physician who spent much of his career studying the diagnosis and classification of CIDs. In 1898, he published a book entitled *The Mental Affections of Children: Idiocy, Imbecility, and Insanity*. In it, he described a classification system based on etiology. He identified 10 categories: (1) Genetous, (2) Microcephalic, (3) Eclampsic, (4) Epilectic, (5) Hydrocephalic, (6) Paralytic, (7) Cretinism, (8) Traumatic, (9) Inflammatory, and (10) Idiocy by Deprivation. Ireland actually referred to many of these categories in his earlier work. For example, he refers to genetous idiocy in an article published in the *Edinburgh Medical Journal* in 1882. He stated that "Of all known diseases, perhaps idiocy is most frequently propagated by heredity" (Ireland, 1882; p. 1072). The full text of this article, "On the Diagnosis and Prognosis of Idiocy and Imbecility," is available on the website.

To complete the set of questions related to the issues of naming, defining, and classifying CIDs, Luckasson and Reeve (2001) offered the following:

- Does this classification system allow coding into groups based on some consistent and meaningful criteria?
- Does this classification system facilitate record keeping?
- Does this classification system provide consistent nomenclature?
- Does this classification system facilitate communication?
- Does this classification system allow some generalizations about the individual or the group?
- Does this classification system create a principled organizing system for incorporating new knowledge?
- Does this classification system promote planning and allocation of resources?
- Does this classification system contribute to meaningful predictions for individuals or groups?
- Is this classification system consistent with a desired theoretical framework?
- Does this classification system contribute positively to the portrayal of individuals or groups?

(p. 51)

Perhaps partially as a result of these guiding questions, the current system of classifying individuals with CIDs based on needed levels of support (discussed later in this chapter) rather than an individual's IQ level is emphasized by the AAIDD. This is a much more positive, proactive approach. However, schools may still use terms such as mild, moderate, severe, or profound that are largely linked to IQ levels. The definition of CIDs has substantively reflected and influenced change over time.

EVOLUTION OF THE DEFINITION

As chronicled in Chapter 1, efforts to describe CIDs began as early as 1500 B.C. in ancient Greece. However, it wasn't until about the 16th century that attempts were made at a definition. An example is that of Fitz-Hebert who wrote in 1534:

And he who is said to be a sot (i.e., simpleton) and idiot from his birth is such a person who cannot account or remember 20 pence, nor can he tell how old he is, etc. so as it may appear that he hath no understanding or reason of what shall be for his profit nor what for his loss

(cited in Grossman, 1983, p. 8)

19th Century

Blanton (1975) in his classic discussion of the history of CIDs (see Research Box 2.1) noted that the first clear definition was provided by the psychiatrist, Esquirol, in 1845. That definition read:

Idiocy is not a disease, but a condition in which the intellectual faculties are never manifested, or have never been developed sufficiently to enable the idiot to acquire such amount of knowledge as persons his own age and placed in similar circumstances with himself are capable of receiving.

(Esquirol, 1845; p. 446)

As noted in Chapter 1, Esquirol was one of the first persons to formally attempt to differentiate CIDs from mental illness. Many of his thoughts on the subject influenced later thinking as well. For example, he felt that a CID was not an all-or-nothing condition but rather a condition that existed on a continuum. That is, CIDs manifested in different levels of severity in the population. Esquirol also opened a school for "idiots" with Edouard Seguin. Seguin was one of the first to attribute a specific cause for CIDs.

Idiocy is a specific infirmity of the cranio-spinal axis, produced by deficiency of nutrition in utero and neo-nati. It incapacitates mostly the functions which give rise to the reflex, instinctive, and conscious phenomena of life; consequently, the idiot moves, feels, understands, wills but imperfectly; does nothing, thinks of nothing, cares for nothing (extreme cases), he is legally irresponsible; isolated, without associations; a soul shut up in imperfect organs, an innocent.

(Seguin, 1866; p. 39)

2.1 RESEARCH THAT MADE A DIFFERENCE

Blanton, R. (1975). Historical perspectives on classification of mental retardation. In N. Hobbs (Ed.), *Issues in the classification of children* (Vol. 1). San Francisco: Jossey-Bass.

This chapter in Hobb's classic text on classification traces the history of CID as well as the issue of classification. Blanton provided a good account of the mental testing movement and its role in the classification of this disability. He also included an excellent discussion of the eugenics movement and the role that Goddard played with his treatise on the Kallikak family (see Chapter 1). In addition, he addressed the controversial issue of the role of heredity vs. environment as a cause of CID in a section called "The Nature-Nurture Problem." Finally, he provided a brief discussion of special education and the training of teachers. It is interesting to see how little was really known about this important area in the 1970s. He does make, however, clear references to research (e.g., Dunn, 1968) that suggests that students with CIDs should be taught in the regular education classroom, a notion that predates the concept of inclusion by almost three decades.

Early 20th Century

In terms of the conceptual understanding and descriptions of CIDs, the 20th century began a transition, although as noted in Chapter 1, attitudes about CIDs were still very negative as evidenced by trends such as the eugenics movement. The predominant term used in the early 20th century was *mental defective* or *mental deficiency.* An early 20th century definition that was influential was proposed by Tredgold (who actually was a member of the British Eugenics Society). His definition of mental deficiency was:

> It is a state of incomplete mental development of such a kind and degree that the individual is incapable of adapting himself to the normal development of his fellows in such a way to maintain existence independently of supervision, control or external support.

> (Tredgold, 1937; p. 4)

Note that this early definition uses the phrase "incapable of adapting himself" and addresses the issues of social development and independence. These concepts had a major influence on subsequent, and even current, definitions. About the same time, the research of Edgar Doll (1941) began to impact the concept of CIDs (see Research Box 2.2), specifically the various definitions proposed by the AAMD/AAMR/AAIDD.

2.2 RESEARCH THAT MADE A DIFFERENCE

Doll, E. (1941). The essentials of an inclusive concept of mental deficiency. *American Journal of Mental Deficiency, 46,* 214–219.

In this article, published by the American Association of Mental Deficiency, Doll established six criteria for the definition of mental deficiency. Those were: (1) social incompetence, (2) mental subnormality, (3) developmental arrest, (4) obtains at maturity, (5) of constitutional origin, and (6) essentially incurable. Like Tredgold, Doll mentioned social incompetence as a specific part of the definition. In fact, Doll is perhaps best known as the author of the *Vineland Social Maturity Scale,* a widely used adaptive skills assessment in its current edition. Social maturity later evolved into what is now known as adaptive behavior, which is a critical component of current definitions. Doll also mentioned that the disability was a developmental phenomenon that occurs at maturity. Current definitions now specify that CIDs occur during the developmental period (prior to age 18). The main criterion noted by Doll that did not stand the test of time was that CID is essentially incurable. In fact, current definitions of CIDs stress just the opposite.

Reflection

Do you agree with Edgar Doll's assumption that CIDs are essentially "incurable"? Even if there is no known medical cause, can an individual's overall functioning be "cured"?

AAMD/AAMR/AAIDD DEFINITIONS

There is little doubt that the AAIDD and its predecessors (AAMD and AAMR) have been leaders in defining CIDs. These definitions were included in manuals on terminology and classification published by the organization. The first manual was published in 1921, followed by new editions every 10 or 15 years. For example, manuals followed in 1933 and 1941. In 1957, a classification manual was developed based on etiology. At that time the AAMD recommended the "development of a comprehensive manual on terminology and classification in mental retardation" (Grossman, 1983; p. 5). That recommendation led to the fifth edition (Heber, 1959) of the manual that included a dual classification system: medical and behavioral. That manual also had a significant impact on how we defined and classified CIDs. Heber suggested the use of the mean and standard deviation of an intelligence test to help determine the IQ level required for identification (see Box). Heber established the IQ cutoff at one standard deviation below average (usually 85) and introduced the requirement of a deficit in **adaptive behavior** in addition to a deficit in intelligence. Adaptive behavior is difficult to define but generally refers to a person's ability to deal effectively with personal and social demands and expectations (Taylor, Smiley, & Richards, 2009). The importance of the role of adaptive behavior in the identification of CIDs is discussed in Chapter 3. Specifically, Heber defined mental retardation as:

> subaverage general intellectual functioning that originates during the developmental period and is associated with impairment in adaptive behavior.
>
> (cited in Schalock, 2002; p. 30)

INTERPRETING SCORES FROM INTELLIGENCE TESTS

The mean represents the average score for a test whereas the standard deviation (SD) represents the variability of the test scores. Approximately 68% (2/3) of the population will score between + and − one SD from the mean. Approximately 96% will score between + and − two SDs. For example, if a test has a mean of 100 and an SD of 15, approximately 2/3 of those taking the test will score between 85–115, and 96% will score between 70–130.

The wording for this definition has remained relatively constant for over 50 years. It establishes three characteristics of CIDs: an intellectual deficit, an adaptive behavior deficit, and manifestation during the developmental period. As will be discussed, however, the **criteria** for what constitutes these characteristics have changed considerably over the years.

Heber (1961) made some minor changes to the definition but it wasn't until 1973 that a significant change in the criteria was recommended (Grossman, 1973). After considerable debate, the decision was made to lower the IQ cutoff from one SD below average to two SDs below average. Thus, individuals who previously were identified as having a CID whose IQs were between approximately 70 and 85 (termed borderline mental retardation in previous manuals) no longer were identified as having a CID after this change in definition. Grossman was concerned that the 85 IQ cutoff would lead to a very high percentage of individuals being identified. In fact, approximately 16% of the population would be expected to score below 85. Heber, however, had reasoned that having the dual requirement of IQ *and* adaptive behavior deficits would address this issue. Unfortunately, the lack of a clear understanding of the concept of adaptive behavior, how it is measured, and what constituted a deficit created problems. Grossman also added the word *significantly* before "subaverage general intellectual functioning." In fact, by changing the IQ criterion to two SDs below average, he reduced the expected percentage to meet that criterion from 16% to 2%. He also raised the age limit of the developmental period to birth to age 18 (it had previously been birth–age 16). The actual definition read:

> Mental retardation refers to significantly subaverage general intellectual functioning existing concurrently with deficits in adaptive behavior, and manifested during the developmental period.
>
> (Grossman, 1973, p. 5)

Clearly, the 1973 definition affected the makeup of those who were to be identified as having mental retardation.

The next AAMR definition was published in 1977 (Grossman, 1977). The actual definition was identical to the 1973 definition. However, another change was made in the criteria used to determine a CID. At that time, the issue of **clinical judgment** was introduced (see Box). This provided greater flexibility and changed the definition from a purely quantitative perspective. For example, it meant that in certain cases, an individual whose adaptive behavior was extremely deficient might be considered as having a CID even if his or her IQ was above 70. In fact, Grossman indicated that in rare situations a person whose IQ was as high as 80 might be considered as having a CID based on his or her adaptive behavior functioning. He also, however, acknowledged the difficulty in assessing adaptive behavior.

WHAT IS CLINICAL JUDGMENT?

AAIDD (2010) provided a definition of clinical judgment based on previous information. It indicated that it is a special type of judgment rooted in a high level of clinical expertise and experience and that emerges directly from extensive data.

The last AAMR definition for which Grossman was responsible was in 1983. Again, the general definition remained the same as the 1973 and 1977 definitions. Similar to the 1977 definition, there was encouragement to use IQ limits cautiously. In fact, significantly subaverage general intellectual functioning was defined as an "IQ of 70 or below on standardized measures of intelligence. This upper limit is intended as a guideline; it could be extended upward through IQ 75 or more, depending on the reliability of the intelligence test used" (Grossman, 1983; p. 11). This reemphasized that IQ was only one criterion for a CID and that there was no single score that could result in the diagnosis. One subtle but notable change in the 1983 *Manual* was the definition of developmental period. It was changed from birth–age 18 to conception–age 18, thus acknowledging the prenatal causes of CIDs. One interesting finding regarding the 1983 AAMR definition was reported by Denning, Chamberlain, and Polloway (2000). They surveyed all 50 states and the District of Columbia regarding the actual guidelines that were used in defining and classifying students with CIDs. They found that 44 used the actual or a modified version of the 1983 definition, even though more recent definitions were available.

Luckasson et al. (1992) developed the next AAMR definition. It retained the basic features of the previous definitions although it also specifically identified adaptive behavior areas for the first time. Perhaps the frustration of having an adaptive behavior deficit as a requirement for over 30 years (without specific criteria) led to this change. That definition read:

> *Mental retardation* refers to substantial limitations in present functioning. It is characterized by significantly subaverage intellectual functioning, existing concurrently with related limitations in two or more of the following applicable adaptive skill areas: communication, self-care, home living, social skills, community use, self-direction, health and safety, functional academics, leisure, and work. Mental retardation manifests before age 18.
>
> (p. 5)

Luckasson et al. also indicated four assumptions related to the application of the definition:

1. Consideration of cultural and linguistic diversity as well as communication and behavioral factors;
2. The existence of adaptive skill areas occurs within the context of the community environment;
3. Specific adaptive skill deficits can coexist with strengths in other adaptive skill areas; and
4. With appropriate supports over a sustained period of time, life functioning will generally improve.

The 1992 *Manual* also provided one of the most drastic changes in the conceptualization of CIDs by eliminating the mild, moderate, severe, and profound *levels of mental retardation* and replacing them with *levels of needed supports* (discussed later in this chapter; also see Event Box 2.2). Although such a change was supported and encouraged as a means of better serving students (Wehmeyer, 2003), its actual practice in the school appeared to be limited. As Denning et al. (2000) found, the majority of states still used a system based on levels of CIDs; only four states had adopted the

1992 classification system. Over the past decade, however, more and more states have moved to the newer system that uses levels of support.

2.2 EVENT THAT MADE A DIFFERENCE

1992—American Association on Mental Retardation Eliminates Levels of Retardation

In 1992, the American Association on Mental Retardation (AAMR) made a controversial move that had a significant impact. In its previous *Manuals* (e.g., Grossman, 1983), individuals could be classified based on their intellectual level. The following criteria were used: mild (IQ 50–55 to approximately 70), moderate (35–40 to 50–55), severe (20–25 to 35–40), and profound (below 20–25). Critics of this approach, however, argued that it did little to indicate the actual educational and other support needs that the individuals had. They also felt that it was emphasizing the intellectual deficits that they have. In 1992, when the AAMR revised its *Manual* (Luckasson et al., 1992), it replaced the intellectual levels with level of supports (i.e., the intensity of necessary supports). These were intermittent, limited, extensive, and pervasive. Thus, an individual was classified as having mental retardation requiring _____ supports. With this change, however, came new critics who felt that the new system did not provide enough description.

In 2002, the AAMR published the 10th edition of its manual called *Mental Retardation: Definition, Classification, and Systems of Supports* (Luckasson et al., 2002). This definition was fundamentally similar to the 1992 definition, although, once again, adaptive behavior was treated somewhat differently and the 10 adaptive skill areas were collapsed into three areas: conceptual, social, and practical. That definition read:

> Mental retardation is a disability characterized by significant limitations in both intellectual functioning and adaptive behavior as expressed in conceptual, social, and practical adaptive skills. This disability originates before age 18.
>
> (p. 1)

There were several assumptions similar to those in the 1992 definition specifically stated regarding the 2002 definition. Those were:

1. Limitations in present functioning must be considered within the context of community environments typical of the individual's age peers and culture;
2. Valid assessment considers cultural and linguistic diversity as well as differences in communication, sensory, motor, and behavioral factors;
3. Within an individual, limitations often coexist with strengths;

4. An important purpose of describing limitations is to develop a profile of needed supports; and
5. With appropriate personalized supports over a sustained period, the life functioning of the person with mental retardation generally will improve.

This definition retained the three basic components of previous definitions: a deficit in intellectual functioning, a deficit in adaptive behavior, and onset before age 18. However, the adaptive behavior areas were reduced from 10 specific skill areas to the three broader areas of conceptual, social, and practical skills. This change was made on the basis of statistical (factor analytic) research that supported the existence of these three broader areas. Further, Luckasson et al. suggested that adaptive behavior be considered in light of four dimensions: (a) intellectual abilities; (b) participation, interactions, and social roles; (c) health; and (d) context. For the first time, the *specific criterion* for an adaptive behavior deficit also was identified: "performance that is at least two standard deviations below the mean of either (a) one of the following three types of adaptive behavior: conceptual, social, or practical, or (b) an overall score on a standardized measure of conceptual, social, or practical skills" (p. 14). Table 2.1 provides a comparison of the criteria used for the three main aspects of the various AAMD/AAMR/AAIDD definitions.

In 2010, the 11th *Manual* was published by what had become the AAIDD (Schalock et al., 2010). (Henceforth, this manual will be referenced to as *AAIDD, 2010* throughout this text.) Prior to the 11th edition, Schalock et al. (2007) provided justification why the term *mental retardation* should be changed. They stated, among other things, that the term *intellectual disability* (a) aligns better with current professional practices that are focused on functional behaviors and contextual factors; (b) provides a logical basis for individualized supports provision due to its basis in a social-ecological framework; (c) is less offensive to persons with disabilities; and (d) is more consistent with international terminology. The 2010 AAIDD definition reads:

> Intellectual disability is characterized by significant limitations both in intellectual functioning and in adaptive behavior as expressed in conceptual, social, and practical adaptive skills. This disability originates before age 18.
>
> (p. 5)

The 2010 definition was unchanged in any significant way from the previous definition but for the use of the term *intellectual disability*. This definition includes five assumptions that are critical in its application:

- Limitations in present functioning includes conceptual, social or practical adaptive skills and must consider the individual's community environments that are typical of chronological and cultural peers;
- Assessment of limitations in present functioning considers cultural and linguistic diversity as well as the impact of communication, sensory, or other factors that may affect assessment outcomes or present functioning;

- Strengths exist for every individual as well as limitations;
- One important reason for identifying limitations is to plan for individual supports; and
- When appropriate individualized supports are provided across the lifespan, the individual's functioning will typically improve.

(AAIDD, 2010)

Finally, AAIDD (2010) stresses the new definition with the term *intellectual disability,* and these five assumptions, still includes anyone who is or would be diagnosed with the term *mental retardation.*

Two other organizations also have provided definitions of mental retardation and intellectual disability. The World Health Organization published the *International Statistical Classification of Diseases—10th Edition (ICD-10)* in 1993 (republished as the *ICD-10 Clinical Modification* in 2010) and the American Psychiatric Association published the *Diagnostic and Statistical Manual of Mental Disorders—5th Edition (DSM-V)* in 2013. *DSM-V* now uses the terms *intellectual disability* and *intellectual developmental disorder* rather than *mental retardation.* Similar to AAIDD, *DSM-V* emphasizes that overall functioning should be considered in diagnosis as well as intelligence testing. The *ICD-11* is currently scheduled to be published in 2015, and may

Table 2.1 Comparison of AAMD/AAMR/AAIDD Definitions

Definition	IQ Deficit	Adaptive Behavior Deficit	Developmental Period
Heber (1961)	< 85	Required, noting that it can be related to motivation, learning, and/or socialization	Before age 16
Grossman (1973)	< 70	Required, defined as effectiveness or degree with which the individual meets the standards of personal independence and social responsibility expected of his/her age and cultural group Note: General areas are identified by age groups	Before age 18
Grossman (1983)	< approximately 70	Required, defined as significant limitations in an individual's effectiveness in meeting the standards of maturation, learning, personal independence, or social responsibility that are expected for his/her age and cultural group	Before age 18
Luckasson et al. (1992)	< 70–75	Identified 10 adaptive skills areas: communication, self-care, home living, social skills, community use, self-direction, health and safety, functional academics, leisure, and work	Before age 18
Luckasson et al. (2002)	Approximately 2 standard deviations below the mean, considering the standard error of measurement	Identified three areas of adaptive behavior: conceptual, social, and practical; also identified four dimensions in which a deficit might exist	Before age 18

also include a change in terminology from mental retardation to intellectual disability or a similar term.

Reflection

Should "clinical judgment" have a place in the identification of an individual with CIDs?

CLASSIFICATION OF CIDS

In addition to the evolution of the terminology and the criteria used to define CIDs, changing views of how to classify it into meaningful categories have taken place. Currently, classification is primarily used for "funding, research, provision of services and supports, and communications about selected characteristics of persons and their environment" (AAIDD, 2010; p. 73). Perhaps one of the first attempts at classification was made by Willis in 1672. He noted "Some are unable to learn their letters but can handle mechanical arts; others who fail at this can easily comprehend agriculture; others are unfit except to eat and sleep; others merely dolts or driviling fools" (quoted in Grossman, 1983). Legal definitions also provided a basis for classification. For example, the Mental Deficiency Act of 1913 identified the following classes:

- Idiot—Unable to protect themselves from common dangers
- Imbecile—Could protect themselves from common dangers, but unable to take care of themselves
- Feeble-minded—Required care to protect themselves
- Moral Defectives—Criminal or vicious personalities

Later classification systems began to focus more and more on etiology. Blanton (1975) noted that Duncan and Millard in 1866 suggested two major classes: congenital and noncongenital. The congenital type were further identified as "profound idiots," those who could stand and walk, those able to use hands to eat and do mechanical work, and feebleminded who required supervision. Grossman (1983) also pointed out the causal orientation of many early classification systems. For example, also in 1866, Langdon Down (after whom Down syndrome was later named) provided a system that included three major categories: congenital idiocy (microcephaly, hydrocephaly, and paralysis and epilepsy), developmental idiocy due to anxiety (associated with cutting teeth or with puberty), and accidental (due to injury [mechanical] or illness). In the latter part of the 19th century, systems became even more medically oriented and focused on brain pathology and CIDs. As noted in Event Box 2.1, by 1898 more elaborate systems such as that by Ireland were being used (Blanton, 1975). MacMillan (1985) pointed out that the most complete medical classification systems appeared in the various AAMD/AAMR *Manuals.*

The current AAIDD (2010) *Manual* stresses a *multidimensional* classification system that "depicts how human functioning and the manifestation of intellectual disability involve the dynamic, reciprocal engagement among intellectual ability, adaptive behavior, health, participation, context, and individualized supports" (p. 13). The system also indicates the level of supports needed. These five dimensions are further discussed in AAIDD (2010) as:

- Intellectual ability is not merely academic skill learning, but also a broader and deeper capacity to understanding our surroundings, making sense of what is going on, and then problem solving about how to respond;
- Adaptive skill abilities and limitations should be considered in the context of typical daily routines in community environments and linked to needed supports;
- Health, including physical, mental and social well-being influence how well a person functions;
- Participation in typical activities of life (including social activities) are critical to human development; and
- Context includes the individual's personal environments, the broader neighborhood and community environments, and the cultural social, national, and geopolitical influences that affect human functioning, services, etc.

Conceptualizing cognitive and intellectual disabilities through the lens of these five dimensions helps to recognize the complexity and diversity of human development and characteristics (AAIDD, 2010).

Classification by Etiology

As noted, the AAMD/AAMR, and now the AAIDD, have led the field in developing classification systems for the causes or etiologies of CIDs. The various causes of CIDs will be discussed in depth in Chapters 4 and 5. Note that the systems include primarily medical causes, although each contains categories based on environmental causes as well.

The 1961 manual (Heber, 1961) categorized CIDs into these eight groups.

1. Infection
2. Intoxication
3. Trauma or physical agent
4. Disorder of metabolism, growth, or nutrition
5. New growths (tumors)
6. Unknown prenatal influence
7. Unknown or uncertain causes with structural reactions alone manifest
8. Uncertain (or presumed psychological) cause with functional reactions alone manifest

Grossman (1973) used more familiar terms and included 10 groups instead of 8. Those were:

1. Infections and intoxications
2. Trauma or physical agent
3. Metabolism or nutrition
4. Gross-brain disease (postnatal)
5. Unknown prenatal influence
6. Chromosomal abnormality
7. Gestational disorders
8. Psychiatric disorder
9. Environmental influences
10. Other conditions

The 1983 system (Grossman, 1983) was the same as the 1973 system except for the following changes: (a) "Chromosomal abnormalities" was changed to "Chromosomal anomalies"; (b) "Gestational disorders" was dropped and replaced with "Other conditions originating in the perinatal period"; and (c) "Psychiatric disorder" was changed to "Following psychiatric disorder (specify)." More significant changes were made in 1992 (Luckasson et al, 1992). For one thing, there was a clear delineation of pre-, peri-, and postnatal causes.

In the 2002 AAMR *Manual,* Luckasson et al. actually discuss other systems, including the previously mentioned *ICD-10* and the *DSM-IV,* as well as the ICD-9 *Clinical Modification* (Medicode, 1998) and the *International Classification of Functioning, Disability, and Health* (World Health Organization, 2001). In the chapter on etiology and prevention, Luckasson et al. (2002) describe "etiologic risk factors" as well as strategies for assessing them. These risk factors relate to pre-, peri-, and postnatal factors. The latest manual (AAIDD, 2010) also identifies etiologic risk factors. Those are provided in Table 2.2. However, AAIDD (2010) stresses that defining and classifying individuals should be linked to developing needed personal supports to improve functioning over the life span.

Table 2.2 Classification System by Etiology Proposed by Luckasson et al. (1992)

Prenatal Causes	Perinatal Causes	Postnatal Causes
Chromosomal disorders	Intrauterine disorders	Head injuries
Syndrome disorders	Neonatal disorders	Infections
Inborn errors of metabolism		Demyelinating disorders
Developmental disorders of brain formation		Degenerative disorders
Environmental influences		Seizure disorders
		Toxic-metabolic disorders
		Malnutrition
		Environmental deprivation
		Hypoconnection syndrome

Classification by Mental Ability

At the beginning of the 20th century, another factor affected classification—the development and use of intelligence tests. Perhaps the greatest influence on the area of intelligence testing was made by Alfred Binet. He was asked (along with Theodore Simon) by the Ministry of Education in France to develop a test that would differentiate individuals with and without CIDs. That test (the *Binet-Simon*) was translated into English in 1905, revised in 1908 to include the concept of mental age, and was revised again by Terman in 1916 to become the *Stanford-Binet Intelligence Scale.* This was the first instrument to use Stern's (1914) term **intelligence quotient** (Bryant, 1997). The most recent Stanford-Binet Intelligence Scale and other intelligence tests are discussed in Chapter 3. Goddard, perhaps best known for his views on the Kallikak family (see Chapter 1), developed a classification system based on the mental age score from the Binet-Simon. A person with a mental age above 12 years was considered "normal," between 8 and 12 years a "moron," between 3 and 7 years an "imbecile," and fewer than 2 years an "idiot."

There were several other advances in mental testing in the early part of the 20th century as a result of differing theories about the nature of intelligence and how it is measured (e.g., Spearman, 1927; Thurstone, 1938). However, it was David Wechsler who perhaps had the greatest influence on our current practices related to intelligence testing. He developed the *Wechsler-Bellevue Intelligence Scale* in 1939 (see Event Box 2.3). That instrument was the predecessor to the Wechsler Scales currently in use. Those are the *Wechsler Preschool and Primary Scale of Intelligence-IV (WPPSI-IV)*, the *Wechsler Intelligence Scale for Children-IV (WISC-IV)*, and the *Wechsler Adult Intelligence Scale-IV (WAIS-IV)*. The Wechsler Scales provide an IQ with a mean of 100 and a standard deviation of 15 (the *Stanford-Binet-5* also has a mean of 100 and a standard deviation of 15). As noted earlier, the mean of a test represents the average score whereas the standard deviation represents the variability of the scores. For example, approximately 68% (2/3) of the population will score between +1 and −1 standard deviation from the mean. Using the mean and standard deviation from the Wechsler Scales, approximately 68% of individuals will score between 85 and 115. Wechsler recommended the guidelines for interpreting the IQs obtained from his tests (see Table 2.3). Indirectly, Wechsler used the standard deviation as a basis for his guidelines. For example, "very superior" is two standard deviations above average whereas "mentally impaired" is two standard deviations below average. As mentioned earlier, most of the AAMD/AAMR/AAIDD definitions have used the standard deviation to help determine the level of CIDs, based on how much a person's IQ deviates from the average (see Table 2.4). The latest AAIDD definition defines significant limitations in intellectual functioning as "an IQ score that is approximately two standard deviations below the mean, considering the standard error of measurement for the specific instruments used and the instruments' strengths and limitations" (AAIDD, 2010; p. 31). This is unchanged since the Luckasson et al. (2002) interpretation.

Table 2.3 Guidelines for Interpreting IQs from the Wechsler Scales

IQ Range	Interpretation
130+	Very superior (gifted)
120–129	Superior
110–119	High average
90–109	Average
80–89	Low Average
70–79	Borderline
69 and below	Mental impairment

Table 2.4 AAMD/AAMR/AAIDD Classification Systems by Mental Ability

Author	Level (name)	Level (IQ range)*
Heber (1961)	Borderline	68–84
	Mild	52–67
	Moderate	36–51
	Severe	20–35
	Profound	< 20
Grossman (1973)	Mild	52–67
	Moderate	36–51
	Severe	20–35
	Profound	< 20
Grossman (1983)	Mild	50–55 to approx. 70
	Moderate	35–40 to 50–55
	Severe	20–25 to 35–40
	Profound	< 20–25
Luckasson et al. (1992)	Eliminated levels	< 70–75
Luckasson et al. (2002)	Retained no levels	Approximately two standard deviations below average, onsidering the standard error of measurement and the strengths and weaknesses of the specific instrument

* The Grossman (1973) *Manual* based the IQ levels on the standard deviation of the test used. These levels are based on a test with an SD of 15.

2.3 EVENT THAT MADE A DIFFERENCE

1939—David Wechsler Develops the Wechsler-Bellevue Intelligence Scale

David Wechsler was born in Romania in 1896 and moved to the United States in 1902. He eventually became the Chief Psychologist at Bellevue Psychiatric Hospital in New York City. During this time, he developed the Wechsler-Bellevue Intelligence Scale, the test that was to become the predecessor of the most widely used, current intelligence scales. Wechsler was working primarily with adults and felt that the Stanford-Binet was not appropriate for that population. He argued that the test items on the Stanford-Binet were designed for children and that there was too much emphasis on speed, which would put older adults at a disadvantage. He also felt that a single IQ was not appropriate. As a result, Wechsler introduced the addition of a verbal IQ and a performance IQ within the same test (although this feature was eliminated in the most recent Wechsler Scale; see Chapter 3).

The *ICD-10* classification system also includes guidelines based on intellectual level. The *ICD-10* identifies four levels of disability: F70 (mild, IQ 50–69), F71 (moderate, IQ 35–49), F72 (severe, IQ 20–34), and F73 (profound, IQ below 20). Two other categories are F78 (other mental retardation) and F79 (unspecified mental retardation). F78 is used when associated physical or sensory impairments make it difficult to establish the intellectual level. F79 is used when there is evidence of a CID but not enough to establish the level of functioning (such as a young child whose IQ cannot be reliably determined). Again, this system may change with the publication of the *ICD-11*. As noted previously, the *DSM-V* definition now uses the term *intellectual disability* and emphasizes present functioning.

Educational Classification

When more formal programs for students with CIDs became prominent in the schools in the 1960s, a classification based on general, educational expectations became popular. One very outdated system once commonly used was based on educational classification that used the terms *educable mental retardation (EMR), trainable mental retardation (TMR),* and *severe and profound mental retardation (SPMR).* Similar to the classification systems based on mental ability, the IQ was typically used to place a student into a specific educational category. The EMR category included individuals whose IQs ranged from approximately 50–75. The TMR category included IQ levels from about 25–50, and the SPMR category included individuals whose IQs were below approximately 25.

Some systems may still use IQ levels as the primary determinant for classification, but use the terms *mild* (IQ of 50–70), *moderate* (35–50), *severe* (20–35), and *profound* (20 and below). Historically, the reliance on IQ has been one criticism of this system because educational expectations are based on limited information. Additionally, this system implies that IQ is the most relevant (and perhaps immutable) factor in determining the level or types of supports needed.

Classification by Needed Supports

As noted previously, the 1992 AAMR *Manual* first eliminated the levels of CIDs based on IQ and replaced them with levels of needed supports; this approach subsequently was retained in the 2002 and 2010 *Manuals.* The rationale was to provide a more proactive, intervention-based system, a major departure from previous ones that classified the individual based on the intellectual level of the CID. The supports classification system focused on the individual's *needs* rather than the individual's *deficits,* with the goal of providing information that will assist in intervention planning. As mentioned earlier, when an individual is diagnosed as having a CID, the level of needed supports should be identified for the following areas: intellectual ability, adaptive behavior, participation, interactions and social roles, health, and context (environments and cultures). The following are the definitions of the four levels of support (Luckasson et al., 2002; p. 152). More information on these supports can be found in Chapter 8.

INTERMITTENT—Supports on an "as needed basis," characterized by their episodic, (person not always needing the support{s}), or short-term nature (supports needed during life-span transitions, e.g., job loss or acute medical crisis). Intermittent supports may be high or low intensity when provided.

LIMITED—An intensity of supports characterized by consistency over time, time-limited but not of an intermittent nature, may require fewer staff members and less cost than more intense levels of support (e.g., time-limited employment training or transitional support during the school-to-adult period).

EXTENSIVE—Supports characterized by regular involvement (e.g., daily) in at least some environments (such as school, work, or home) and not time-limited in nature (e.g., long-term support and long-term home living support).

PERVASIVE—Supports characterized by their constancy, high intensity, provision across environments, potentially life-sustaining nature. Pervasive supports typically involve more staff members and intrusiveness than do extensive or time-limited supports.

More recently, the AAIDD (2010) emphasized that supports should be personalized and designed to encourage improved functioning over the life span. Because how a person functions intellectually and in adaptive skill areas (conceptual, social, and practical adaptive skills) is used to identify individuals with CIDs, the "centrality of supports to understanding people with ID is evident when considering these manifestations" (p. 110). In other words, to classify an individual as having a level of CID without considering to what extent that individual has had or is receiving needed personal supports is to ignore a major facet of who that person is.

> ### Reflection
> **Is it better to classify individuals with CIDs based on the level of IQ or the level of needed supports? Why or why not?**

PREVALENCE

One important, yet surprisingly complex, issue is the determination of the number of individuals who have a CID. One reason is related to terminology. In general, two terms are often used to describe the number of individuals who have a specific condition. **Incidence** refers to the number of individuals who fall into a specific category (in this case CID) for the first time during a specific period of time. Although the period of time used to determine incidence figures varies, one year is frequently used. So, for example, incidence figures might indicate the number of individuals who are initially identified as having a CID in 2013. The other term, **prevalence,** refers to the total number of individuals who have a specific condition at a given point in time. Grossman (1983) gave a good example of why incidence and prevalence are not interchangeable. He pointed out that in underdeveloped countries the *incidence* of CIDs is high because of factors such as poor nutrition and lack of prenatal care. In other words, the number of new cases of CIDs is high. On the other hand, because of excessive infant mortality the *prevalence* rate is comparatively low. Because of the death rate, the number of individuals with CIDs at a given point in time is lower.

In general, prevalence figures are those that are more frequently reported; the number of individuals with CIDs is generally reported to be around 1% of the population. Using a national survey, Larson et al. (2001) reported the prevalence rate to be 0.78%. Based on another national study, Oswald, Coutinho, Best, and Nguyen (2001) found that 1.33% had a CID. In a recent meta-analysis of 52 international studies reporting the prevalence rates of CIDs, Maulik, Mascarenhas, Mathers, Dua, and Saxena (2011) found the rate to be 1.04%.

The percentage of students actually served in classes for CIDs has remained relatively constant. The report to Congress on the implementation of IDEA indicated that 0.9% of students aged 6 through 21 were served from 1997 to 2003. For 2004 and 2005, 0.8% were served and 0.7% were served in 2007 (U.S. Department of Education, 2008).

Prevalence figures for CIDs are affected by several variables. These include ethnic status, socioeconomic status, gender, age, geographic region, and even the effect of the judicial system. This is particularly true for mild CIDs, which constitute approximately 75%–85% of all cases of CIDs. The overrepresentation of ethnic minority students in classes for CIDs is well documented (see Chapter 8 for further discussion). For example, the *Larry P. v. Riles* court case (see Chapter 3 for more information) brought attention to the fact that African-American children were grossly overrepresented in classes for students with mild CIDs. In 2007, for example, 12.8% African-American students aged 6 through 21 were served under IDEA 2004, whereas 7.1% White students were served. One reason for this phenomenon seems to be that more minority children are referred for special education in the first place. Hosp and Reschly (2003) conducted a meta-analysis of the referral rate based on the students' racial status and found that African-Americans were significantly more referred than their White counterparts.

Gender also makes a difference. For example, the prevalence of CIDs due to Fragile X syndrome, a common genetic disorder (discussed in Chapter 4) is higher in males than in females whereas Rett syndrome (also described in Chapter 4) occurs almost exclusively in females. Gender also interacts with ethnicity to affect prevalence rates. Oswald et al. (2001) reported a range of 0.44% for Asian females to 3.15% for black males. Age is also a variable that affects prevalence. Almost 20 years ago, MacMillan, Siperstein, and Gresham (1996) pointed out, "The rate in the age range of 6–17 years (i.e., the school years) dwarfs the rates found in any other comparable age range precisely due to the detection of the mild cases by the public schools—cases that are frequently dropped from case registers upon their leaving school" (p. 366). In fact, Larson et al. (2001) found that almost four times as many individuals ages 6–17 had a CID compared to adults. The meta-analysis by Maulik et al. (2011) reinforces the fact that prevalence is affected by many variables. They reported higher rates in low- and middle-income countries and for populations of children and adolescents compared with adults.

Reflection

Why do you think the prevalence of CIDs is higher for those from low socio-economic and/or ethnic minority backgrounds?

SUMMARY CHECKLIST

Naming, Defining, and Classifying

➢ Naming—Assigning a specific term or label to a disability
➢ Defining—Providing a precise description of the meaning and boundaries of a term
➢ Classifying—Identifying subgroups of individuals within a defined group according to some criteria

Evolution of the Definition

✓ 1534 Fitz-Hebert
✓ 1845 Esquirole
✓ 1866 Seguin
✓ 1937 Tredgold
✓ 1941 Doll

AAMD/AAMR/AAIDD Definitions

✓ First *Manual* published in 1921
✓ *Manuals* followed in 1933, 1941, and 1957
✓ Heber (1959) introduced levels of CIDs based on IQ; 85 was cutoff for "borderline mental retardation"; introduced requirement of adaptive behavior deficit
  ➢ Adaptive behavior—Ability to deal effectively with personal and social demands and expectations
  ➢ Mean—The average score on a test
  ➢ Standard deviation (SD)—An indication of the variability of test scores. Approximately 68% of the population will score between + and – one SD of the average score of a test
✓ Grossman (1973) lowered the IQ cutoff from 85 (one standard deviation below average) to 70 (two standard deviations below average)

✓ Grossman (1977) introduced clinical judgment to the definition
  ➢ Clinical judgment—The use of more subjective/additional information to allow more flexibility in interpreting the definition
✓ Grossman (1983) expanded the developmental period from birth to age 18 to conception to age 18; continued recommendation of IQ as a guideline only
✓ Luckasson et al. (1992) operationally defined 10 adaptive skill areas; eliminated levels of CIDs based on IQ
✓ Luckasson et al. (2002) retained elimination of levels of CIDs; changed adaptive behavior criteria to include conceptual, social, and practical skills
✓ Schalock et al. (2010) (AAIDD, 2010) retained the 2010 definition but changed the term *mental retardation* to *intellectual and developmental disability*
✓ *ICD-10* and *DSM-V*—Two other current definitions that are sometimes used

Classification

✓ Duncan and Millard (1866) used the terms *Congenital* and *Noncongenital*
✓ Ireland (1898) proposed a more medically oriented system based primarily on biological causes

Classification by Etiology

✓ Heber (1961) identified 8 categories
✓ Grossman (1973) included 10 categories
✓ Grossman (1983) made minor changes to the 1973 system
✓ Luckasson et al. (1992) grouped etiologic risk factors based on prenatal, perinatal, and postnatal causes
✓ Luckasson et al. (2002) described "etiologic risk factors" similar to the causes listed in the 1992 *Manual*
✓ AAIDD (2010) retained the etiologic risk factors (Table 2.4)

Classification by Mental Ability

✓ Alfred Binet had perhaps the greatest influence on intelligence testing
✓ 1905—Binet-Simon Intelligence Scale translated into English
✓ 1916—Terman revises the test that becomes the Stanford-Binet Intelligence Scale
✓ Goddard develops a system based on the mental age from the Binet-Simon Intelligence Scale
✓ Wechsler develops the Wechsler-Bellevue Intelligence Scale in 1939
✓ Subsequent Wechsler Scales are the most widely used intelligence tests (WPPSI-IV, WISC-IV, WAIS-IV)
✓ *ICD-10* includes IQ guidelines
✓ AAMD/AAMR *Manuals* prior to 1992 used IQ to determine levels of CIDs
✓ AAIDD *Manuals* from 2002 onward have emphasized consideration of personal supports

Classification by Needs

✓ Educational System—Mild, IQ approximately 50–75; moderate, IQ approximately 35–50; severe, IQ approximately 20–35; and profound, IQ below 20

✓ Classification by levels of support—Luckasson et al. (1992, 2002) identified four
  levels of support: Intermittent, Limited, Extensive, and Pervasive
✓ AAIDD (2010) emphasizes that what supports that have or have not been provided are essential in understanding the disability of an individual

Prevalence

➤ **Incidence—Number of individuals who fall into a category for the first time
  during a specific time period (usually one year)**
➤ **Prevalence—Total number of individuals who have a condition at a given
  point in time**
  ✓ Prevalence estimates are about 1% of the population
  ✓ A number of variables affect prevalence including ethnic and socioeconomic
    status, gender, and age

ADDITIONAL SUGGESTIONS/RESOURCES

Discussion Questions

1. Discuss the important role that naming, defining, and classifying have in the
   field of CIDs.
2. What are the similarities and differences among the 1983, 1992, 2002 AAMR and
   AAIDD 2010 definitions and classification systems? Which do you think is more
   appropriate? Why?
3. Identify several reasons why the prevalence rate of CIDs is lower for preschool
   children and adults compared to school-aged individuals.

Activities

1. Interview a teacher, pediatrician, and a psychologist to determine their perspectives on the definition of a CID. How are they the same? How are they different?
2. Read the original "On the Diagnosis and Prognosis of Idiocy and Imbecility" (see
   Event Box 2.1 for website). How have attitudes changed since the 1880s?
3. Check with your local school district to determine what definition/classification
   system it uses for students with CIDs. Can you determine its origin based on the
   information presented in this chapter?

E-sources

www.ibis-birthdefects.org/start/mr.htm
This is the website for the International Birth Defects Information Systems. It includes
several links to websites of other organizations, including the AAIDD and the ARC. It
also has links to scholarly works like book chapters on the definition and classification
of CIDs, and selected annotated bibliographies.

http://www.aaidd.org
This website, sponsored by the American Association on Intellectual and Developmental Disabilities, provides its definition and links to frequently asked questions
about the definition and a video definition. It also provides a link to access the entire
2010 *Manual.*

http://nichcy.org/disability/specific/intellectual
This website is published by the National Information Center for Children and Youth with Disabilities. It provides 13 links about various aspects of CIDs including the IDEA definition, prevalence, and a brief case study.

NOTE

1. The acronym CID is used for cognitive/intellectual disability and CIDs is used for the plural cognitive/intellectual disabilities.

3

ASSESSMENT FOR IDENTIFICATION

Key Points

➤ LEGAL AND ETHICAL CONSIDERATIONS—Among other mandates, the Individuals with Disabilities Education Act (IDEA) provides guidelines that emphasize nondiscriminatory assessment practices.

➤ NORM-REFERENCED TESTING: AN OVERVIEW—Norm-referenced tests are used to compare an individual's performance to a specific reference group called the standardization sample. Issues such as validity and reliability are important.

➤ CONCEPTUAL MODELS OF INTELLIGENCE—Early theorists such as J. Cattell, Spearman, and Thurstone, and more recently R. Cattell, Horn, and Carroll and Das and Naglieri, influenced models of intelligence used in current intelligence tests.

➤ OVERVIEW OF INTELLIGENCE TESTING—Intelligence testing dates back to the late 19th century. Current popular intelligence tests include the *Stanford-Binet Intelligence Scale-5* and the *Wechsler Intelligence Scale for Children-IV*. Alternatives to traditional intelligence testing have been proposed.

➤ ADAPTIVE BEHAVIOR ASSESSMENT—Adaptive behavior refers to an individual's ability to deal with personal and social demands. An adaptive behavior deficit is required by the American Association on Intellectual and Developmental Disabilities for a diagnosis. Popular scales include the AAMR Adaptive Behavior Scales:2 and the Vineland Adaptive Behavior Scales-II. A related instrument is the Supports Intensity Scale.

Although some individuals, particularly those with biological causes, are identified as having cognitive/intellectual disabilities (CIDs) at birth, the majority are identified later in life. Some young children are initially identified by their parents when they begin to notice delays in their child's development. Others might be initially diagnosed by the child's pediatrician. Medical and developmental histories are sometimes used to assist in this process. Also helpful are parent interviews. One example is the omnibus interview designed to be primarily unstructured and to gather a wide range of information (Beaver & Busse, 2000).

Many children are not identified until they attend school and begin to lag behind peers. Most children with CIDs caused by nonbiological factors are identified through the use of educational and psychological assessment. Although the specific eligibility criteria for CIDs vary from state to state, most require that an individual have an intellectual deficit as well as a deficit in adaptive behavior. For school-aged students, an adverse effect on educational performance usually must be documented as well. In this chapter, both issues and specific instruments in the areas of intellectual and adaptive behavior assessment are discussed. Achievement testing is briefly addressed in Chapter 9 that focuses on assessment for instruction. Before discussing the specific types of instruments used for identification, it is first important to discuss the legal and ethical issues that impact that process and must be considered.

LEGAL AND ETHICAL CONSIDERATIONS

Mental retardation (a term still used in many states) is one of several disabilities that is identified and included in the federal legislation now known as the Individuals with Disabilities Education Act. IDEA provides very specific suggestions regarding assessment procedures, including the use of assessment information to identify individuals as having a disability. Several of these are paraphrased and discussed below.

1. *You should not use any single procedure as the sole criterion for determining whether a child has a disability.* Prior to federal legislation in the 1970s, it was common for a student to be identified as having a CID and placed in special education based solely on an IQ. Current legislation mandates that multiple sources of information be used.

2. *You should use reliable and valid instruments.* This means that the characteristics of the tests, such as their reliability and validity (discussed later in this chapter), must be considered when selecting those to use with a given child. Although test manuals provide this technical information, the characteristics and suspected disability of the child being evaluated should also be taken into account.

3. *You should ensure that tests are selected and administered so as not to be discriminatory on a racial or cultural basis.* Unfortunately, this requirement has been difficult to implement. A number of approaches have been attempted, including translating tests, using interpreters, using culture-specific tests, and even banning tests altogether (see Event Box 3.1).

4. *You should ensure that tests are administered in the language and form most likely to yield accurate information.* Many early court cases (e.g., *Diana v. State Board of Education, 1970; Guadalupe v. Tempe, 1972*) were filed on behalf of children whose dominant language was Spanish. They were placed into classes for students with CIDs based on their scores from intelligence tests administered solely in English. These cases undoubtedly helped lead to current legal requirements.

Similarly, administering a motor-oriented test to an individual with a physical disability would be inappropriate.

5. Tests should only be administered by trained and knowledgeable personnel and in accordance with instructions from the test producers. There are actually many ethical issues involved in assessment. The Standards for Educational and Psychological Testing (American Educational Research Association, 1999; this book is currently under revision) outlines the ethical considerations involved in test selection, administration, and interpretation. Obviously, having a trained and knowledgeable person involved in this process is an absolute prerequisite (Taylor, 2009).

3.1 EVENT THAT MADE A DIFFERENCE

1971—*Larry P. v. Riles* litigation was initiated

The *Larry P.* case is perhaps the best-known and most complex court case dealing with assessment issues. This was a class action suit filed in California on behalf of an African-American boy who was placed in a class for students with CIDs. The plaintiffs argued that the intelligence test used was culturally biased and, subsequently, the IQ was not an accurate representation of his abilities. The case went through several injunctions until 1977 when there was an eight-month trial. In 1979 the following decisions were made: (1) intelligence tests are biased, (2) the use of intelligence tests to classify African-American children as having mental retardation is prohibited, and (3) the overrepresentation of African-American children in classes for mild mental retardation should be eliminated. In 1986, the plaintiffs again went to court arguing that the overrepresentation had not changed significantly. The result was the complete prohibition of intelligence tests for African-American students for any reason, even with parental consent. Ironically, as a result of the *Larry P.* decision, another case, *Crawford v. Honig* (1990) was filed by African-American parents arguing that their child was being discriminated against because he could *not* be evaluated using an intelligence test.

Reflection

Do you think California was justified in banning the use of intelligence tests with African-American students? Why or why not? Do you know if your state allows the use of intelligence testing for identifying students as having CIDs?

NORM-REFERENCED TESTING: AN OVERVIEW

The types of instruments typically used to identify individuals with CIDs are called **norm-referenced tests.** A norm-referenced test is one in which a person's performance is compared to a specific reference group usually by age or grade level. This reference group is called the **standardization sample** and provides the norms on which to base the comparison. This type of test is used when you are interested in finding out how a person performs in a particular area relative to others. It is important to know the characteristics of the standardization sample since this is the group to which the individual's test performance will be compared. For example, assessing a child who is an English-language learner when that population was not included in the standardization sample would be ill-advised. Norm-referenced tests used for identification purposes should include a large, nationally representative sample that considers characteristics such as geographic region, socioeconomic status, ethnicity, gender, and so on.

Generally, the first step in scoring and interpreting norm-referenced tests is to determine the raw score(s) (sometimes referred to as the obtained score). This usually involves determining the total number of correct responses or a weighted score based on the quality of the responses. For example, the optional Picture Completion subtest from the *Wechsler Intelligence Scale for Children-IV (WISC-IV;* discussed later in this chapter) requires the student to indicate, through verbalizing or pointing, what important part is missing from a series of pictures. One point is given for a correct answer and a zero is given for an incorrect one. The raw score for this subtest would be the total number of correct answers. The Comprehension subtest from the *WISC-IV,* however, involves a series of questions (e.g., "What would you do if you found a ball that belonged to one of your friends?"). Depending on the quality of the response (based on specific criteria identified in the test manual), it is assigned a score of zero, one, or two; the raw score would be the total of these weighted scores. The raw score by itself has no real meaning; rather, it is converted into a number of **derived scores** based on the scores obtained by individuals in the standardization sample (Taylor, 2009).

Types of Scores

Several derived scores are available including age equivalents, grade equivalents, percentile ranks, and stanines, among others. These scores are *derived* from the raw score. The most appropriate derived score to use when making important educational decisions (as a rule) such as determining eligibility is the **standard score.** A standard score is a transformed raw score with the same mean and standard deviation (SD). The mean represents the average score, and the SD reflects the variability of the set of scores. When a test is normed, it is "calibrated" so that 34% of the subjects score within one SD of the mean and 14% between one to two SDs. Only 2% score between two and three standard deviations (see Figure 3.1). This means that on a norm-referenced test, approximately 68 % will score between +1 and –1 SD, and approximately 96% will score between +2 and –2 SDs (Pierangelo & Giuliani, 2009). Regardless of the instrument used most standards scores have a mean of 100 and a SD of 15, although this is not universal. Therefore, when interpreting a deviation IQ, one can assume that approximately 68% will score between 85 and 115 and approximately 96% will score between 70 and 130. This also means that only about 2% would be expected to score below 70 (Pierangelo & Giuliani, 2009). As mentioned in Chapter 2, this is one of the reasons why 70 is commonly used as an IQ cutoff for CIDs.

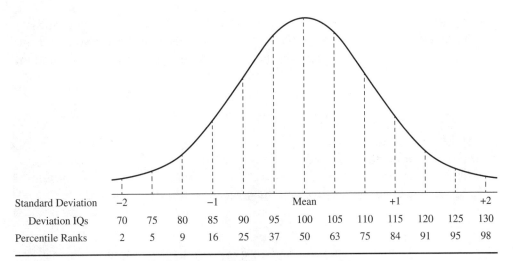

Standard Deviation	−2			−1			Mean			+1			+2
Deviation IQs	70	75	80	85	90	95	100	105	110	115	120	125	130
Percentile Ranks	2	5	9	16	25	37	50	63	75	84	91	95	98

Figure 3.1 Relationship of Various Types of Derived Scores

Technical Characteristics

It is important that a norm-referenced test have adequate technical characteristics, including validity and reliability. **Validity** refers to the extent to which a test measures what it purports to measure. In other words, does a test really measure what it claims to be measuring? There are many methods used to determine the validity of a test although a discussion of these methods is beyond the scope of this text. **Reliability** refers to a test's consistency. One type of reliability, test-retest, quantifies the extent to which results from a test remain consistent over time. It gives an indication of how closely a person would score on the same test taken after a relatively short period of time has elapsed. Again, there are a number of types of reliability and methods to determine them. Pierangelo and Guiliani (2009) include a discussion of various types of reliability and validity.

Another related term that has implications for test interpretation (particularly for identification purposes) is the **standard error of measurement** (SEM). The SEM represents an attempt to account for the variability or error involved in the administration and scoring of a test. Because no test is absolutely reliable, a person's *true score* on a test is never really known. A person's *obtained score* on a test, therefore, can be considered as an *estimate* of the true score. Using the SEM, a range can be identified that helps determine how closely an obtained score estimates the true score. Approximately 68% of the time a person's true score will fall between +1 and −1 SEM from the obtained score. Similarly, a person's true score will fall between +2 and −2 SEMs from the obtained score approximately 96% of the time (Taylor, 2009). For instance, if the SEM for a given test score was five (and the SD was also five) and a person's obtained score was 90, you would expect the true score to fall between 85 and 95 approximately 68% of the time and between 80 and 100 approximately 96% of the time. This suggests that we should interpret test scores as *bands* rather than *absolutes*. The SEM has implications in identifying CIDs. As noted in Chapter 2, definitions of CIDs often provided an IQ range such as 70–75 as the cutoff criterion, which allowed for the interpretation of the SEM. The latest AAIDD *Manual* suggests the SEM be considered when determining IQ cutoffs. Also, the criterion for an adaptive behavior deficit was established by using the SD and considering the SEM of the instrument administered.

Reflection

Why is it important to consider the standard error of measurement of a test when interpreting test scores to make eligibility decisions? What effect might the standard error of measurement have on an eligibility decision?

CONCEPTUAL MODELS OF INTELLIGENCE

Theories regarding the components of intelligence and their measurement have been proposed and debated for over 100 years. Understanding the various theories is important because many currently available intelligence tests used to help identify individuals with CIDs are based on several of these conceptual models. Specifically, James McKeen Cattell helped provide the early interest in *measuring* intelligence based on its various definitions. Others who have provided conceptual models that have influenced, directly or indirectly, many currently used intelligence tests are James Cattell, Spearman, Thurstone, Raymond Cattell, Horn, Carroll, Das, and Naglieri. Many other influential researchers have also provided definitions and theories of intelligence that have impacted the development of traditional intelligence tests or have provided the conceptualization of alternative methods of measuring intelligence (see Table 3.1)

Table 3.1 Influential Theorists and Their Contributions

Name	Seminal Work	Contributions
E.L. Thorndike	*The measurement of intelligence (1927).* New York: Bureau of Publications, Teachers College, Columbia University.	Developed a multifactor theory of intelligence that included social intelligence, concrete intelligence, and abstract intelligence
J. Piaget	*The origins of intelligence in children (1952).* New York: International University Press. (Originally published in 1936)	Best known for his four stages of development: sensorimotor, preoperational or symbolic, concrete operational, and formal operational
J. Guilford	*The nature of human intelligence (1967).* New York: McGraw-Hill.	Developed the three dimensional Structure of Intellect model that included 120 factors of intelligence
H. Gardner	*Frames of mind: The theory of multiple intelligences (1983).* New York: Basic Books.	Postulated that there are eight types of intelligences: linguistic, logical-mathematical, spatial, bodily-kinesthetic, musical, interpersonal, intrapersonal, and naturalist.
R. Sternberg	*Beyond IQ: A triarchic theory of human intelligence (1985).* New York: Cambridge University Press.	His triarchic theory views intelligence as having three components: componential, experiential, and contextual.

In the late 1800s, James McKeen Cattell made the first formal attempt to operationalize and measure intelligence, and was the first to use the term *mental test* (Anastasi & Urbina, 1997). Cattell viewed intelligence as a combination of physical, perceptual, and mental skills. As more tests and subsequent test results were made available, it was possible to analyze these to look for specific intellectual profiles that might suggest a theoretical framework for intelligence. Spearman (1927), using a statistical procedure known as factor analysis, proposed a two-factor theory of intelligence that included a general factor (g), which is present to the same degree for a person in all intellectual activities, and more specific factors (s), whose strengths are dependent on the type of intellectual activity. In a sense, the g factor is consistent with today's concept of global or general intelligence (Taylor, 2009).

Thurstone (1938; 1941), also using factor analysis, disagreed with Spearman's concept of a general factor and several specific factors. He believed that there were actually several *primary* factors (known as Primary Mental Abilities). His multiple-factor theory (Thurstone, 1947) included the following factors: (1) Verbal Comprehension, (2) Word Fluency, (3) Number Facility, (4) Spatial Visualization, (5) Associative Memory, (6) Perceptual Speed, and (7) Reasoning. Many of the intelligence tests used today include components that provide scores in areas such as these.

Thurstone's work, which downplayed the notion of general intelligence, was mirrored by Raymond Cattell, who proposed his two-factor theory of **fluid intelligence** *(Gf)* and **crystallized intelligence** *(Gc)* in 1941 and was described in detail in 1943 (Cattell, 1941; 1943). Fluid intelligence was initially defined as purely general ability whereas crystallized was defined as long-established discriminatory habits. The terms eventually evolved into more descriptive concepts. In general, *Gf* is related to abilities such as abstract thinking, drawing inferences, inductive/deductive reasoning, and using mental operations. An example of a *Gf* task follows.

EXAMPLE OF A FLUID INTELLIGENCE TASK

Identify the pattern in the following series of numbers:

3, 6, 9, 15, 24

4, 8, 12, 20, 32

Now provide the missing number in the following sequence:

5, 10, 15, 25, ___

Note: Answer is 40. The first number in the sequence is doubled; then the last two numbers are added. ($5 \times 2 = 10$; $5 + 10 = 15$; $15 + 25 = 40$)

On the other hand, *Gc* is concerned with the acquisition of knowledge (i.e., learned information). An example might be a task that measures an individual's knowledge of vocabulary words (Taylor, 2009).

Horn, one of Cattell's students, furthered the model that was later known as the Cattell-Horn model. He wrote his doctoral dissertation on the *Gf/Gc* model. With this study and subsequent research (e.g., Horn, 1965; Horn & Cattell, 1966), several other factors such as short-term memory *(Gsm)*, processing speed *(Gs)*, and visual-spatial thinking *(Gv)* were added so that it was no longer considered a dichotomous *Gf/Gc* model. Horn and Cattell actually identified eight to nine factors (Taylor, 2009).

Carroll is the latest to modify the Cattell-Horn model. Carroll was a strong supporter of the Cattell-Horn model but also believed that there was merit to Spearman's notion of general intelligence *(g)*. Carroll (1993) factor-analyzed over 450 data sets available since 1925 (Shrank, McGrew, & Woodcock, 2001). This resulted in his three-stratum model. The first stratum includes 69 narrow, specific abilities; the second includes eight broad ability factors (including *Gf* and *Gc*); and the third includes general ability *(g)*. The Cattell-Horn model and the Carroll model have been combined to form the Cattell-Horn-Carroll model.

Another individual whose concept of intelligence has had a direct impact on current testing is Das. He initially proposed that intelligence involves two primary processes (Das, 1973). The first, **simultaneous processing,** requires an individual to integrate and synthesize spatial or analogic information. An example would be the presentation of an incomplete picture to a person who would simultaneously process the parts of the picture to identify the complete picture. **Successive processing** involves the ability to arrange stimuli in sequential or serial order. Repeating a series of words or numbers read by the examiner would be examples. Das and his colleagues expanded the model by adding two more components: planning and paying attention (Taylor, 2009).

OVERVIEW OF INTELLIGENCE TESTING

As noted earlier, the term *mental test* was first used by Cattell in 1890, and he was the first to describe measures that should be included in such a test (see Research Box 3.1). However, it was the work of Alfred Binet, a French psychologist, that had the most impact on what is now termed intelligence testing (Bryant, 1997). As discussed in Chapter 2, Binet was approached by the Minister of Education in Paris to develop a test that identified slow learners. He teamed up with Theodore Simon to develop a scale in 1905 that consisted of 30 items. Examples of items on this early scale included Visual Coordination, Discrimination Between Two Weights, Repetition of a Series of Digits, and Giving Distinctions Between Abstract Terms. That scale was revised in 1908, and in 1916 his work with Terman led to the *Stanford-Binet Intelligence Scale,* which is considered the grandfather of intelligence tests (Taylor, 2009). The most recent edition is the *Stanford-Binet Intelligence Scale-Fifth Edition* (Roid, 2003).

3.1 RESEARCH THAT MADE A DIFFERENCE

Cattell, J. M. (1890). Mental tests and measurements. *Mind, 15,* 373–381.

In 1890, Cattell described an early attempt to develop an intelligence test. He proposed 10 measures that he felt reflected the underlying nature of mental testing. Those 10 measures were called (1) Dynamometer Pressure, (2) Rate of

Movement, (3) Sensation—areas, (4) Pressure Causing Pain, (5) Least Noticeable Difference in Weight, (6) Reaction Time for Sound, (7) Time for Naming
Colours, (8) Bi-section of a 50 cm. Line, (8) Judgment of 10 Seconds Time, and
(10) Number of Letters Remembered on Once Hearing. He pointed out that
these measures begin with more "bodily" measures, proceeding through psycho-
physical, to purely mental measurements. He goes on to describe the nature of
each of the 10 measures.

Interestingly, in 1917, the use of intelligence tests was extended to the military.
The *Army Alpha* and *Army Beta* tests were developed to "be used to accept or reject
recruits, classify those individuals who were accepted, assign draftees to various types
of service, and to identify potential candidates for officer training school" (Bryant,
1997; p. 19). These were actually the first examples of group-administered intelligence
tests.

In 1939, partially out of dissatisfaction with the *Stanford-Binet Intelligence Test,*
Wechsler created the *Wechsler–Bellevue Scale.* Wechsler was interested in developing
an instrument that had more use with an adult population, the group with whom
he was working most closely. This instrument was the predecessor to the current
Wechsler scales—the *Wechsler Intelligence Scale for Children-IV,* the *Wechsler Adult
Intelligence Scale-IV,* and the *Wechsler Preschool and Primary Scale of Intelligence-IV.*
His definition of intelligence was "the aggregate or global capacity of an individual
to act purposefully, to think rationally, and to deal effectively with his environment"
(Wechsler, 1958; p. 7). Although Wechsler retained the concept of global intelligence
he initially identified separate verbal and performance areas that included various
subtests that tapped very different skills.

Other instruments that have been developed and are widely used are the
Kaufman Assessment Battery for Children-II, based on the models proposed by Das
and Cattell-Horn-Carroll, and the *Woodcock-Johnson-III,* based on the Cattell-
Horn-Carroll model.

Intelligence Tests

Kaufman Assessment Battery for Children-II

The *Kaufman Assessment Battery for Children (KABC-II)* (Kaufman & Kaufman,
2004a) is designed for use with children ages 3 through 18. The instrument is based
on the Das model that includes sequential processing and simultaneous processing. It
is also based on the Cattell-Horn-Carroll model.

Sequential Processing

Number Recall—Requires the repetition of a series of verbally presented numbers
Word Order—The child must touch a series of pictures in the same sequence that is
   verbally presented by the examiner

Simultaneous Processing

Triangles—Requires the reproduction of various models using identical triangle puzzle pieces

Conceptual Thinking—Choosing from a set of four or five pictures the one that doesn't belong with the others

Block Counting—Counting partially or completely hidden blocks

Rover—Moving a toy dog on a checkerboard with obstacles to get to a bone in the fewest moves

Learning

Atlantis—Identifying objects associated with nonsense names provided by the examiner

Rebus—After learning words and concepts associated with different drawings, the student then must "read" the drawings

Planning

Pattern Reasoning—Identifying a missing stimulus from a logical, linear pattern

Story Completion—Identifying pictures that are missing in a row that tells a story

Knowledge

Riddles—Naming a concept after the examiner lists several characteristics

Verbal Knowledge—Measures receptive vocabulary and general information

Expressive Vocabulary—Choosing one of six pictures that either corresponds to a vocabulary word or answers a general information question

Summary: *Kaufman Assessment Battery for Children-II*

- *Age Level*—3 through 18 years old
- *Uses*—Two models of intelligence can be applied depending on whether the examiner wishes to include verbal ability as a cognitive skill or not, allowing for consideration of linguistic and cultural background
- *Standardization Sample*—Approximately 3,000 children from 39 states
- *Scores Yielded*—Subtest scaled scores (X = 10; SD = 3); Mental Processing Index, Fluid-Crystalized Index, Simultaneous Processing Index, Sequential Processing Index, Learning Index, Planning Index, Knowledge Index (X = 100; SD = 15) (WPS Publishing Company, n.d.; Taylor, 2009).

Stanford-Binet Intelligence Scale-Fifth Edition

The *Stanford Binet Intelligence Scale-Fifth Edition (SBIS-5)* (Roid, 2003) is the latest version of this historic test. It can be used with a wide age range beginning at age 2 and continuing through adulthood. The test yields a Full Scale, Verbal, and Nonverbal IQs and Index Scores for five factors: Fluid Reasoning, Knowledge, Quantitative Reasoning, Visual-Spatial Processing, and Working Memory. There are two special routing subtests (object series/matrices and vocabulary) that determine the developmental starting point for the 10 other subtests (see Table 3.2).

The five indexes and their accompanying subtests are:

Fluid Reasoning Index

Nonverbal Fluid Reasoning—Involves the aforementioned Object Series/Matrices activity

Verbal Fluid Reasoning—Students respond to activities in early reasoning, verbal absurdities, and verbal analogies

Knowledge Index

Nonverbal Knowledge—There are two activities involving procedural knowledge and picture absurdities

Verbal Knowledge—This is a vocabulary subtest also mentioned as one of the routing subtests

Quantitative Reasoning Index

Nonverbal Quantitative Reasoning—There are four levels of activities

Verbal Quantitative Reasoning—This subtest includes five levels of activities

Visual-Spatial Processing

Nonverbal Visual-Spatial Processing—This includes form-board and form patterns activities

Verbal Visual-Spatial Processing—This involves five levels of activity in position and direction

Working Memory Index

Nonverbal Working Memory—Delayed response and block span activities are included

Verbal Working Memory—Memory for sentences and last word activities are used (Johnson & D'Amato, 2012; Pierangelo & Giuliani, 2009; Taylor, 2009).

Table 3.2 Model Used in the *Stanford-Binet Intelligence Scale-Fifth Edition*

Factor	Nonverbal Subtests	Verbal Subtests
Fluid Reasoning	Nonverbal Fluid Reasoning	Verbal Fluid Reasoning
Knowledge	Nonverbal Knowledge	Verbal Knowledge
Quantitative Reasoning	Nonverbal Quantitative Reasoning	Verbal Quantitative Reasoning
Visual-Spatial Processing	Nonverbal Visual-Spatial Processing	Verbal Visual-Spatial Processing
Working Memory	Nonverbal Working Memory	Verbal Working Memory

Summary: *Stanford-Binet Intelligence Scale-Fifth Edition*

- *Age Level*—2 through adult
- *Uses*—Individually administered test of intelligence and cognitive abilities
- *Standardization Sample*—Nationally representative sample of almost 5,000
- *Scores Yielded*—Subtests (X = 10; SD = 3); IQs and Composite Scores (X = 100; SD = 15) (Johnson & D'Amato, 2012; Taylor, 2009).

Wechsler Intelligence Scale for Children-IV

The *Wechsler Intelligence Scale for Children-IV (WISC-IV)* (Wechsler, 2003) is one of three scales developed by Wechsler and is the most widely used intelligence test in the schools, covering the age range of 6 through 16 years, 11 months. The *WISC-IV* provides a general or full-scale IQ, as well as four index scores: Verbal Comprehension, Perceptual Reasoning, Working Memory, and Processing Speed. There are 10 subtests and five optional subtests. The subtests are described below.

Verbal Comprehension Index

Similarities—This subtest requires the child to identify the common element of two terms (e.g., a painting and a statue).
Vocabulary—Requires the student to name pictures and orally define different words
Comprehension—Measures social, moral, and ethical judgment (e.g., "What are you supposed to do if you find someone's wallet or purse in a store?")
Information and Word Reasoning are optional subtests.

Perceptual Reasoning Index

Matrix Reasoning—The student is presented a partially filled grid and must select the item that correctly completes the matrix.
Block Design—The child must reproduce certain designs using red and white blocks
Picture Concepts—From multiple rows of objects, the student must select the items that go together based on an underlying concept (e.g., animals).
Picture Completion is optional.

Working Memory Index

Letter-Number Sequencing—The student is presented a mixed series of numbers and letters and must repeat the numbers in numerical order and the letters in alphabetical order.
Digit Span—Requires the student to repeat a series of digits forward and backward.
Arithmetic is optional.

Processing Speed Index

Symbol Search—The student visually scans a group of symbols to find target symbols.
Coding—The student must copy geometric symbols that are paired with numbers in a specific time period.
Cancellation is optional. (Maller, 2012).

Summary: *Wechsler Intelligence Scale for Children-IV*

- *Age Level*—6 to 16 years old
- *Uses*—Individually administered intelligence test with more emphasis on fluid reasoning
- *Standardization Sample*—Nationally representative sample of 2,200
- *Scores Yielded*—Subtests (X = 10; SD = 3); Full Scale IQ and Composite Scores (X = 100; SD = 15) (Maller, 2012; Taylor, 2009).

Woodcock-Johnson-III Tests of Cognitive Abilities

The *Woodcock-Johnson-III—Normative Update (WJ-III-NU)* (Woodcock, McGrew, & Mather, 2007) is a comprehensive set of instruments designed to measure both general intellectual ability and specific cognitive abilities. It is designed to be used with a very broad age range (2–90+ years). The cognitive battery is designed based on the previously described Cattell-Horn-Carroll conceptual model (Riverside Publishing, n.d.). There is both a Standard Battery and an Extended Battery that can be used when further information is desired. The following is a description of the Broad Cognitive Factors and their accompanying subtests from the Standard Battery.

Comprehension—Knowledge

Verbal Comprehension—Requires identification of objects, completion of verbal analogies, and understanding of antonyms and synonyms

Long-Term Retrieval

Visual–Auditory Learning—Measures the ability to associate novel visual symbols with words and then read sentences consisting of those visual symbols

Visual–Auditory Learning–Delayed—Measures the ability to recall and relearn the visual symbols from the previous subtest after a 30-minute span

Visual-Spatial Thinking

Spatial Relations—Requires the identification of the necessary pieces to form a complete shape

Auditory Processing

Sound Blending—Involves the blending of synthesized speech sounds

Incomplete Words—Requires the identification of words in which one or more sounds is missing

Fluid Reasoning

Concept Formation—Requires categorical reasoning based on principles of logic

Processing Speed

Visual Matching—Involves locating and circling two identical numbers in a row of six numbers

Short-Term Memory

Numbers Reversed—Repeating a series of digits in reverse order
Auditory Working Memory—Involves remembering a set of words and numbers and reordering them (Taylor, 2009)

Summary: *Woodcock-Johnson-III-Normative Update* (Cognitive Battery)

- *Age Level*—2 to 90+ years old
- *Purposes*—Most useful for screenings rather than comprehensive intellectual assessment
- *Standardization Sample*—Nationally representative sample of over 8,000
- *Scores Yielded*—Subtests, cluster scores, General Cognitive Ability (X = 100; SD = 15) (Riverside Publishing, n.d.).

Intelligence Tests: Issues and Caveats

The previous discussion of the commonly used intelligence tests provides a good idea of the types of skills that are evaluated. Although there are some similarities among the instruments, there are some differences as well. This leads to an important validity question: *What are these tests actually measuring?* There is a perception, even a misperception, that intelligence tests measure "intellectual potential." This assumption has led to much of the controversy surrounding ethnic bias because it implies that lower IQs equate to lower, innate intellectual potential. These tests, however, more accurately reflect what an individual has been taught and/or material to which there has been exposure and experience (i.e., intellectual performance). Even performance on nonverbal, analytic tasks can be affected by an individual's experiences with similar tasks. Over three decades ago, Reschly (1979) warned "IQ tests measure only a portion of the competencies involved with human intelligence. . . . IQ tests do not measure innate-genetic capacity and the scores are not fixed. Some persons do exhibit significant increases or decreases in their measured IQ" (p. 24). This latter point is consistent with the AAIDD position that a CID is not necessarily a lifelong condition given appropriate personalized supports.

There are also many general concerns about using norm-referenced tests, particularly intelligence tests, to make important decisions (especially related to identification and eligibility). Pierangelo and Giuliani (2009) provide a thorough discussion of these concerns that are related to the individual being tested (examinee), the examiner, the examiner-examinee interaction, and the test itself. The AAIDD (2010) also provides practitioners with considerations for intelligence testing.

Some of the issues related to the examinee include the effect of factors such as anxiety and motivation, test wiseness, the health and emotional state of the examinee, and the type of disability that an individual might have. As an example of this latter factor, the use of an intelligence test that includes a number of motor-related items such as copying or block building would not be appropriate to use with an individual with cerebral palsy to determine an IQ that is used to assist in the identification of CIDs.

Other issues that should be considered are differences in test administration among test examiners. Even though norm-referenced tests are intended to be administered in a standardized format, there frequently are differences in administration that can result in different examinee performance (Pierangelo & Giuliani, 2009). For example, the type or amount of reinforcement or encouragement given or the degree of rapport established between the examiner and the examinee can all affect test results. Similarly, differences in the interpretation of responses are possible. Again, although criteria are provided for the scoring of specific responses, a certain degree of subjective interpretation might be necessary when an ambiguous response is given. Other concerns that have been raised are the culture and language of the examiner as well as the examinee's familiarity with the examiner. Regrettably, one factor that can affect important educational decisions relates to scoring errors. Considerable research is available indicating that errors are routinely made in scoring a test that can dramatically affect the results (Taylor, 2009).

Issues related to the tests themselves are also extremely important. The technical characteristics of an instrument must be considered when interpreting test results. Perhaps the most controversial issue related to intelligence tests themselves is their possible bias, particularly against minority ethnic groups. As noted earlier in this chapter, this potential bias has been a source of litigation, albeit with differing conclusions. There is also a large base of empirical research on test bias. Valencia and Suzuki (2001) identified 62 studies on cultural bias in testing. Not surprisingly, the vast majority of these studies (92%) were conducted in the 1970s and 1980s, the time when the discriminatory testing litigation was prominent.

One reason why there is so much confusion and debate in this area might be that there are actually several types of bias. Reschly (1979), based on an article by Flaugher (1978) in the *American Psychologist* (see Research Box 3.2), identified several types of bias that one must consider when selecting, administering, and interpreting tests. Three of the types of bias mentioned by Reschly are particularly pertinent to this discussion. These are mean difference bias, item bias, and psychometric bias.

3.2 RESEARCH THAT MADE A DIFFERENCE

Flaugher, R. (1978). The many definitions of test bias. *American Psychologist,* 33, 671–679.

This important paper focused on the various aspects of test bias. Flaugher argued that many individuals consider only one type of test bias, although it is important to keep all the various types in mind. His views on bias encompass more than simply bias in the instrument itself; rather, it involves the entire assessment process, including how we interpret and use the results of tests. He strongly asserted that one should not settle on only one operational definition of bias, and to do so only confuses the picture. The following types of bias are discussed: (1) mean difference bias, (2) test bias as overinterpretation, (3) test bias as single group or differential validity, (4) test bias as content, (5) test bias as the selection model, (6) test bias as the wrong criterion, and (7) test bias as atmosphere.

Mean difference bias is the one that receives the most attention. It addresses the question of whether groups of individuals with different characteristics (e.g., males and females, individuals from rural areas and urban areas, children of different ethnic backgrounds) score differently on the same test. Mean differences related to ethnic status have been the basis for the majority of litigation on bias and intelligence testing. It has long been reported that, as a group, children from ethnic minority backgrounds score lower than their White counterparts on traditional intelligence tests (e.g., Reschly & Ross-Reynolds, 1980; Taylor & Partenio, 1983). However, the interpretation of these differences is certainly not straightforward. One must consider variables such as educational opportunity, socioeconomic status (SES), nutrition and health, and other factors before making any judgment about the meaning of those differences. For example, Valencia and Suzuki (2001) pointed out that when SES is controlled, "the mean difference in intellectual performance between whites and minorities frequently is reduced and in some cases is negligible" (p. 143).

Item bias (similar to Flaugher's content bias) occurs when a correct response to an item might not be an appropriate response for a given child. An example might be a test item such as "Where does milk come from?" If the correct answer is "cows," then this would not be an appropriate response for a child from an urban area who might answer "the grocery store." It should be noted that the subjective determination of what items are biased against different individuals has proven to be a very unreliable process (e.g., Sandoval & Miille, 1980).

A third type of bias is *psychometric bias.* It addresses the question of whether the technical aspects of a test such as validity and reliability are similar for individuals with different characteristics. For example, does a specific test measure the same skills for Hispanic and White children (Taylor, 2009)?

Summary of Issues and Caveats

A number of issues must be addressed when using intelligence test scores (as well as other test scores) to help make decisions about identifying an individual as having a CID. Consideration of these issues is required to put test results in their proper perspective and to realize that a test score is not an absolute indication of an individual's ability in a particular area. Too often, the tests themselves have been blamed for problems such as the overidentification of minority students as having CIDs. It is necessary to recognize that a test is a tool that can be used appropriately or inappropriately. A number of variables—those related to the examiner, the examinee, and the interaction between the two—are as important as those related to the test itself. Placing too much value on the meaning of the IQ is also a potential mistake. AAIDD (2010) emphasized the following points:

- There is not a "hard and fast cutoff point/score for meeting the significant limitations in intellectual functioning criterion" (p. 35). An examiner/team should consider standard error of measurement, strengths and weaknesses of the instrument, practice effects, fatigue effects, and norms used.
- The two standard deviations below the mean criterion for IQ as the indicator of limitations in intellectual functioning is an approximate score and the decision to diagnose a CID relies on clinical judgment.

• Finally, a diagnosis of a CID is also dependent on determining deficits in adaptive skills and emergence prior to age 18 years (AAIDD, 2010).

As noted earlier, traditional intelligence tests are more accurate in measuring intellectual performance than intellectual potential. As such, they have been referred to as **static assessment procedures** because they largely measure what a child has already learned and not so much how he or she might profit from instruction. This has led to a number of techniques referred to as **dynamic assessment procedures.** These procedures usually involve interaction between the examiner and the student. The examiner is attempting to draw conclusions about how the student thinks (Pierangelo & Giuliani, 2009). In other words, the person is pretested, taught specific material or strategies, and then posttested to determine how much he or she was actually able to learn under a controlled situation. Also, dynamic assessment can be used to assess progress in learning over time (Pierangelo & Giuliani, 2009). Dynamic assessment falls under the broad general category of interactive assessment that provides a more active relationship between the examiner and the examinee than does traditional norm-referenced testing (Haywood, 1997b). Dynamic assessment procedures, however, have been questioned as instruments for identification purposes because of lack of technical characteristics (e.g., Frisby & Braden, 1992). Another point is that, by their nature, they lack a standard format that could be used to provide scores on which to make classification or eligibility decisions. Even though these alternative approaches might not replace traditional intelligence tests, they do point out the limitations of using the IQ tests, particularly when using them in an inflexible manner (Taylor, 2009).

Reflection

What factors should be considered when interpreting an IQ other than the individual's true intellectual ability? Should these factors influence decisions about eligibility for educational or other services?

ADAPTIVE BEHAVIOR ASSESSMENT

As discussed in Chapter 2, the concept of adaptive behavior has played a significant role in the history of CIDs and its impact is very evident today. As early as 1937, Tredgold suggested that adaptive behavior is an important consideration in defining mental retardation. Doll (1941) used the term *social incompetence* as one criterion for his definition of mental retardation, and was the author of the *Vineland Social Maturity Scale,* a predecessor to the *Vineland Adaptive Behavior Scales-II,* one of the most popular adaptive behavior instruments currently in use. Since 1959, an adaptive behavior deficit has been a part of the diagnostic criteria used by the AAIDD to identify student individuals with CIDs (see Event Box 3.2), although only recently has there actually been a specific criterion for what constitutes a deficit (Luckasson et al., 2002; AAIDD, 2010). However, operationalizing the definition of adaptive behavior and determining the best way to evaluate it have not been that straightforward.

3.2 EVENT THAT MADE A DIFFERENCE

1959—Heber requires a deficit in adaptive behavior as one criterion for the diagnosis of mental retardation

The American Association on Intellectual and Developmental Disabilities (then the American Association on Mental Deficiency) has been a leader in the field for over a century and has provided a manual that addresses definition and classification systems since 1921. Until 1959, the term *adaptive behavior* had not been included in the definition of mental retardation. That year, Heber, who authored the AAMD *Manual,* introduced the term and required that individuals exhibit a deficit to be considered as having mental retardation. Although no specific criterion was provided regarding what constituted an adaptive behavior deficit, it certainly had an impact on the field by drawing attention to this very important concept.

What Is Adaptive Behavior and How Is It Measured?

Adaptive behavior generally refers to an individual's ability to deal with personal and social demands. AAIDD (2010) defined it as "the collection of conceptual, practical, and social skills that have been learned and are performed by people in their everyday lives" (p. 43). One reason why it has been difficult to specifically define adaptive behavior is that it consists of different components depending on the age of the person. For example, adaptive behavior for a 3-year-old child might include motor skills, communication skills, and some independent living skills whereas adaptive behavior for a 21-year-old adult might include more social, domestic, and job-related skills. The definition of adaptive behavior must also address issues such as cultural expectations. What might be valued in one culture might be considered inappropriate in another. Also, a behavior might be within the capability of an individual, but the person might not exhibit it for cultural reasons.

After one defines adaptive behavior, it is necessary to develop instruments that accurately assess those skills. Several issues are particularly relevant for this discussion. For example, different *methods* of assessing adaptive behavior skills typically are used. Some instruments require direct observation of an individual, others involve an interview with a parent or teacher, and some can be completed by the parent or teacher independently. These different assessment modes do not always produce the same results (Pierangelo & Giuliani, 2009). In addition, there is some research that indicates that different raters (e.g., parents, teachers, and students themselves) will provide different information about the same person being rated (Bennett, Frain, Brady, Rosenberg, & Surinak, 2009; Boan & Harrison, 1997; Brady, Frain, Duffy, & Bucholz, 2010).

Another concern relates to the technical aspects of adaptive behavior instruments. As noted previously, the nature of the standardization sample is extremely important in interpreting assessment information because it describes the group to which the person's score will be compared. Adaptive behavior scales typically have used very different types of standardization samples. Some are based on national, representative samples whereas others are normed on much more restrictive populations, including some which only include individuals with CIDs. When using information for identification (eligibility) purposes, the first type of standardization sample noted above should be used. By using a large, representative sample, one will get a better picture of the level of adaptive behavior compared to a more "typical" population (i.e., detect deficits in adaptive skill areas). The following describes several frequently used adaptive behavior scales.

Adaptive Behavior Scales

AAMR Adaptive Behavior Scale: 2 (School Edition)

The *AAMR Adaptive Behavior Scale—School Edition:2 (AAMR ABS-S:2)* (Nihira, Leland, & Lambert, 1993) is used with students ages 3 to 21 years. The School Edition is actually a shorter version of another AAMR scale designed for individuals living in residential and community facilities. According to the authors, the *AAMR ABS-S:2* can be used for a variety of purposes including the identification of persons who may be in need of specialized clinical services and documentation of progress in an intervention program (Nihira et al., 1993). This and previous AAMR scales were specifically designed to address the adaptive behavior deficit component of what is now the AAIDD definition.

The *AAMR ABS-S:2* consists of two parts: Part One focuses primarily on personal independence. It includes nine domains and three factors. Part Two, which concerns the measurement of social behaviors, includes seven domains and two factors. For both parts, the information can be collected using one of two methods. *First-person assessment* is used when the evaluator is very familiar with the individual and completes the items. The other method is *third-party assessment* in which the evaluator asks an individual who is familiar with a student to assign the items to be completed. The results can be placed on a visual profile to indicate the person's strengths and weaknesses. The following are the domains included in Parts One and Two:

Part One—Note: for many of these items, behaviors are described on a dependence to independence continuum. For example, the item on bathing ranges from "Makes no attempt to wash or dry self" (scored 0) to "Prepares and completes bathing unaided" (scored 6). Obviously, the lower the score is, the more significant the adaptive behavior deficit.

Independent Functioning—Includes skills such as eating, toilet use, dressing and undressing, care of clothing, cleanliness, and other areas of independent functioning

Physical Development—Measures vision, hearing, and gross and fine motor development

Economic Activity—Includes money handling, budgeting, and shopping skills

Language Development—Measures expressive and verbal comprehension, as well as social language development skills

Numbers and Time—Understanding and manipulating numbers and time concepts

Prevocational/vocational Activity—Measures work, school, and job performance

Self-direction—Includes areas such as initiative, perseverance, and use of leisure time

Responsibility—Includes personal belongings and personal responsibility
Socialization—Includes cooperation, consideration for others, and social maturity

Part Two—Note: for each item in these domains the rater must indicate whether the student exhibits that behavior never, occasionally, or frequently, although no guidelines are provided for that determination. The following domains are included: *Social Behavior, Conformity, Trustworthiness, Stereotyped and Hyperactive Behavior, Self-abusive Behavior, Social Engagement,* and *Disturbing Interpersonal Behavior.* These domains assess areas such as threatening others, doing physical violence, resistance to instructions, lying, stealing, stereotypical behavior, sexual behavior, self-abuse, inactivity, and hypochondriacal tendencies among others (Taylor, 2009).

Summary: *AAMR Adaptive Behavior: 2 (School Edition)*

- *Age Level*—6 to 21 years old
- *Uses*—Assessing adaptive behavior deficits or lack thereof; widely available
- *Standardization Sample*—Nationally representative sample of more than 1,000 without mental retardation and 2,000 of those with mental retardation
- *Standard Scores Yielded*—Factors and domains (X = 100; SD = 15) (Harrington, 2012; Taylor, 2009).

Scales of Independent Behavior-Revised

The *Scales of Independent Behavior—Revised (SIB-R)* (Bruininks, Woodcock, Weatherman, & Hill, 1996) is designed for a very wide age range (three months to adulthood). This instrument uses a different format from others—it is actually considered a multiple-choice format. The interviewer provides a statement (e.g., "picks up and eats food such as crackers") and the rater must indicate whether the individual exhibits that behavior "never or rarely," "about one-fourth of the time," "about three-fourths of the time," or "always/almost always." It is also possible for the rater simply to read the items and complete the ratings directly on the test form. There are over 250 items that are grouped into 14 subscales and three clusters. One nice feature of the SIB-R is the availability of other components, including a screening version, a checklist, and a correlated curriculum. The following is a listing of the 14 subscales and their respective clusters. Their content is self-explanatory.

Motor Skills Cluster

Gross-motor
Fine-motor

Social Interaction and Communication Cluster

Social Interaction
Language Comprehension
Language Expression

Personal Living Skills Cluster

Eating
Toileting
Dressing
Personal Self-care
Domestic Skills

Community Living Skills Cluster

Time and Punctuality
Money and Value
Work Skills
Home/Community Orientation

Summary: *Scales of Independent Behavior-Revised*

- *Age Level*—Three months to 44 years old
- *Uses*—Comprehensive diagnostic system for adaptive behavior, problem behavior, and other areas such as language proficiency
- *Standardization Sample*—Nationally representative sample of more than 2,100
- *Standard Scores Yielded*—Subscales, clusters, Broad Independence (X = 100; SD = 15) (Maccow, 2012).

Vineland Adaptive Behavior Scales-II

The *Vineland Adaptive Behavior Scales-II (VABS-II)* (Sparrow, Cicchettim, & Balla, 2006) has a long history dating back to 1935 when Doll developed the original *Vineland Social Maturity Scale* (see Research Box 3.3). The *VABS-II* can be used with individuals from birth to age 90 and includes several components that can be used individually or in combination. One component includes two survey forms—the Survey Interview Form and the Parent/Caregiver Rating Form. There is also an Expanded Interview Form that is helpful for children ages 0–5 and adults who are low functioning and a Teacher Rating Form for ages 3–21 (Pierangelo & Giuliani, 2009).The Survey Forms are administered through the use of a semi-structured interview. This semi-structured interview is somewhat difficult to implement and considerable training is required; a video is available from the test publisher that demonstrates this procedure. For identification and eligibility purposes, the Survey Form is the most appropriate. The Parent/Caregiver Rating Form requires completion in writing using a 3-point scale. The following domains and subdomains are included.

3.3 RESEARCH THAT MADE A DIFFERENCE

Doll, E. (1935). A genetic scale of social maturity. *American Journal of Orthopsychiatry, 5,* 180–190.

This article described the initial attempts of Edgar Doll to develop a measure of social maturity based on his experience with occupational, industrial, and behavioral scales. It consisted of 117 items designed for use with infants through adults and used a reporting technique to gather the information (as opposed to direct testing and observation). It was initially administered to 15 "normal" subjects and 50 individuals with mental retardation from the Vineland Training School in New Jersey. From these data, Doll was able to determine a positive relationship between social maturity and mental age. Later that year he published another article in the *Journal of Mental Science* that provided initial information regarding the reliability and validity of the preliminary form of the *Vineland Social Maturity Scale.*

Communication—Includes receptive language, expressive language, and written language

Daily Living Skills—Includes personal skills (e.g., eating), domestic (e.g., household tasks), and community skills (e.g., use of money, job skills)

Socialization—Involves interpersonal relationships, play and leisure time, and coping skills

Motor Skills—Measures both gross motor and fine motor skills (for children 6 and under generally)

The Teacher Rating Form also includes academic and school community subdomains.

The Maladaptive Behavior Domain is optional and available only on the survey and expanded forms (not the Teacher Rating Form).

Summary: *Vineland Adaptive Behavior Scales-II*

- *Age Level*—Birth to 90 years old
- *Uses*—Assess adaptive behavior and overall self-sufficiency across the life span
- *Standardization Sample*—Nationally representative sample of more than 3,000
- *Standard Scores Yielded*—Domains (X = 100; SD = 15), subdomains (X = 16; SD = 3), and composites (X = 100; SD = 15) (Stein, 2012)

Other Instruments Associated with AAMR/AAIDD Definitions

Over the years, the concept of adaptive behavior noted in the AAMR definitions has ranged from general, more abstract guidelines, to specific adaptive skill areas, to broader areas based primarily on statistical analysis. Until recently, most adaptive behavior scales that have been developed were designed to measure the more general concept. As can be seen from the previously discussed instruments, there are many similarities in the areas or domains that are evaluated, thus reflecting the comprehensive nature of the concept. As mentioned in Chapter 2, however, Luckasson et al. (1992) operationally defined adaptive behavior as 10 specific skill areas. Those were communication, self-care, home living, social skills, community use, self-direction, health and safety, functional academics, leisure, and work. At that time, no adaptive behavior scale specifically addressed those 10 areas. As a result, an instrument was developed that provided scores in those areas. The *Adaptive Behavior Assessment System (ABAS)* (Harrison & Oakland, 2000) provides scores for the 10 areas. The ABAS also can provide scores for the three areas—conceptual, practical, and social—noted in the most recent AAIDD (2010) manual. One additional feature of the ABAS is a linking sample with the Wechsler Scales so that a person's IQ and adaptive behavior can be compared to the same standardization sample. The 2002 AAMR *Manual* also includes a table to demonstrate how the 10 adaptive skill areas can be realigned to address the new definition of adaptive behavior. Thus, the ABAS can still be used with the newest AAMR/AAIDD definition.

Supports Intensity Scale (*SIS;* Thompson et al., 2002)

The *SIS* includes the ratings of the degree of supports that an individual needs in a number of areas, including adaptive behavior. This scale is consistent with the current AAIDD emphasis on determining personal supports that an individual with a CID requires over a lifetime. Intensity is ranked on a 1–4 scale according to frequency (How often is support needed for this activity?), daily support time (On a typical day when support in this area is needed, how much time should be devoted?), and type of support (What kind of support should be provided?).

The *SIS* is an eight-page interview and profile form that evaluates support needs in 87 specific areas including life activities and behavioral and medical areas. Items are grouped into domains of Home Living, Community Living, Lifelong Learning, Employment, Health and Safety, Social Activities, and Protection and Advocacy. An example of a Home Living activity is "Preparing food"; an example of a Protection and Advocacy item is "Advocating for self." Each activity is ranked on a 1–4 scale according to frequency (How often is support needed for this activity?), daily support time (On a typical day when support in this area is needed, how much time should be devoted?), and type of support (What kind of support should be provided?). For frequency, 1 = none and 4 = hourly or more frequently; for daily support time, 1 = none and 4 = 4 hours or more. For types of support, 1 = none and 4 = full physical assistance. A support intensity level is determined based on Total Supports Need Index, a standard score based on the responses to all the items.

Summary of Issues and Caveats

While perhaps less controversial in use than intelligence testing, the AAIDD (2010) includes a number of important issues and caveats. Among these are:

- Instruments should be comprehensive measures of conceptual, social, and practical adaptive skills and applicable to the individual and population
- Instruments should include current norms for individuals with and without CIDs when the purpose is identifying an individual for services
- Based on the instrument's administration guidelines and appropriate state and professional rules, ensure the administrator is well trained
- Ensure the instrument has acceptable reliability and validity
- Ensure that any accompanying scoring software will capture/prevent any errors such as impossible answers and missing data (AAIDD, 2010).

AAIDD (2010) stressed that interpretation of adaptive skill scores take into account the standard error of measurement. Additionally, three key concepts identified include: "(a) the assessment of adaptive behavior is on the person's typical (not maximum) performance, (b) adaptive skill limitations often coexist with strengths, and (c) the person's strengths and limitations in adaptive skills should be documented within the context of community and cultural environments typical of the person's age peers and tied to the person's need for individualized supports" (p. 45).

Identification of CIDs is a multifaceted process involving selection of appropriate and technically adequate instruments, use of trained examiners and teams in administering and interpreting results, and considering many factors affecting the individual's performance. Finally, it is perhaps more important that assessments used for identification of CIDs are also effective in identifying strengths and possible individualized supports. CIDs should not be viewed within a deficit-only context, but within a context of improving skill development, opportunities for participation in the activities of life, self-determination, and satisfaction with one's quality of life.

Reflection

Why is the assessment of adaptive behavior so important? How might this type of assessment reinforce or refute the results of an IQ test?

SUMMARY CHECKLIST

✓ Most criteria for CIDs include deficits in intelligence and adaptive behavior

Legal and Ethical Considerations

✓ Don't use just one assessment procedure
✓ Use technically adequate instruments
✓ Use nondiscriminatory assessment procedures
✓ Administer tests in the most appropriate language and form
✓ Tests should be administered by trained personnel
✓ *Larry P. v. Riles*—Important California court case that resulted in the prohibition of intelligence tests with African-American students

Norm-Referenced Tests: An Overview

➢ **Norm-referenced test—A test in which a person's performance is compared to a specific reference group**
➢ **Standardization sample—The reference group that is used in a norm-referenced test**
➢ **Derived score—A converted raw score that compares an individual's performance to those in the standardization sample**
➢ **Standard score—A transformed raw score with a known mean and standard deviation**

✓ Mean—The average score
✓ Standard deviation—An indication of the variability of test scores
➢ **Validity—The degree to which a test measures what it purports to measure**
➢ **Reliability—The consistency of a test**
➢ **Standard error of measurement—The variability or error involved in a test**

Conceptual Models of Intelligence

✓ James McKeen Cattell—First person to use the term *mental test*
✓ Spearman—Viewed intelligence as consisting of a general factor (g) and several specific factors (s)
✓ Thurstone—Viewed intelligence as consisting of several primary mental abilities
✓ Raymond Cattell—Coined the terms *fluid intelligence* and *crystallized intelligence*
➢ **Fluid intelligence—Abilities such as abstract thinking, drawing inferences, and deductive/inductive reasoning**
➢ **Crystallized intelligence—Acquisition of learned information**
✓ Horn—Expanded the Cattell model to include more factors
✓ Carroll—Expanded the Cattell-Horn model
➢ **Simultaneous processing—Integrating and synthesizing spatial or analogic information**
➢ **Successive processing—Arranging stimuli in sequential or serial order**
✓ Binet—French psychologist who had a major impact on intelligence testing
✓ Wechsler—Author of several currently used intelligence tests

Intelligence Tests

✓ *Kaufman Assessment Battery for Children-II*—Based on Das's model of simultaneous and successive (sequential) processing and the Cattell-Horn-Carroll model
✓ *Stanford-Binet Intelligence Scale-5*. Latest edition of an instrument dating to the early 1900s
✓ *Wechsler Intelligence Scale for Children-IV*—Most widely used intelligence test for school-aged students
✓ *Woodcock-Johnson-III—Normative Update*—Based on the Cattell-Horn-Carroll model; also has an achievement component
✓ Intelligence tests measure intellectual performance not intellectual potential
✓ Issues related to the examinee—Factors such as anxiety, test wiseness, and disability status can affect test performance
✓ Issues related to the examiner—Factors such as test administration and interpretation differences and scoring errors can affect test results
✓ Test bias—There are many different types including mean difference, item, and psychometric
✓ AAIDD states that intelligence tests are one of only three major components of identification and many factors affect the interpretation of scores
✓ Alternatives to traditional intelligence tests—Several have been developed based on theories of individuals such as Piaget, Sternberg, and Gardner
➢ **Static assessment procedures—Measure what an individual has already learned**

> ➤ **Dynamic assessment procedures**—Use a test-train-retest format to help determine how much a person can learn information in a controlled setting

Concept of Adaptive Behavior
✓ Adaptive behavior—Has been a component of the CID definition since 1959
✓ Adaptive behavior—Is a difficult concept to operationalize

Adaptive Behavior Scales
✓ *AAMR Adaptive Behavior Scale-School Edition*—Measures both adaptive and maladaptive behavior
✓ *Scales of Independent Behavior-Revised*—Includes other components such as a screening component and a correlated curriculum
✓ *Vineland Adaptive Behavior Scales-II*—Includes a Survey Interview Form, a Parent/Caregiver Rating Form, an Expanded Interview Form, and a Teacher Rating Form
✓ The *Adaptive Behavior Assessment System* can be used for both the 2002 AAMR and the 2010 AAIDD definitions
✓ The *Supports Intensity Scale* is designed to be used to identify the appropriate level of support in the current AAIDD classification system

ADDITIONAL SUGGESTIONS/RESOURCES

Discussion Questions
1. What are some of the factors that should be considered when interpreting an IQ that has been obtained by a student?
2. Define the terms *mean, standard deviation,* and *standard error of measurement.* What role does each play in making eligibility decisions?
3. Why is adaptive behavior such a difficult concept to define? To what extent should maladaptive (i.e., behavior such as theft, vandalism, violence, etc.) be considered in determining eligibility?

Activities
1. Contact your local school district or state education agency to find out the criteria used to identify students with CIDs. What instruments are recommended?
2. Interview a school psychologist about the intelligence test that he/she recommends. What points are given for the recommendation?
3. Develop your own definition for adaptive behavior. What do you think would be the best way to assess it (e.g., interview vs. observation)?

E-sources
http://daddcec.org/Home.aspx
This website is the home for the Council for Exceptional Children's *Division on Autism and Developmental Disabilities.* It includes basic information about CID, including information for families and professionals.

http://www.aafp.org
This website of the American Academy of Family Physicians provides an article called "Identification and Evaluation of Mental Retardation" that is coauthored by three physicians. It provides general information about cognitive/intellectual disabilities and provides an illustrative case study emphasizing the importance of developmental histories. It is interesting to see the information that physicians receive about CIDs in comparison to perhaps what educators might receive.

Part Two

Causes of CIDs

4

GENETIC AND CHROMOSOMAL FACTORS

Key Points

➢ THE ROLE OF GENES AND CHROMOSOMES IN HEREDITY—Chromosomes are made up of strands of DNA; there are 22 pairs of autosomes and one pair of sex chromosomes. Genes are located on the chromosomes and dictate inherited characteristics.

➢ AUTOSOMAL GENETIC DISORDERS—These disorders can be either dominant (e.g., tuberous sclerosis and neurofibromatosis) or recessive (e.g., PKU and Tay Sachs).

➢ SEX-LINKED GENETIC DISORDERS—Fragile X is the most common, genetically inherited form of cognitive/intellectual disability (CID).[1] Other sex-linked disorders include Lesch-Nyhan and Rett syndrome.

➢ DISORDERS RELATED TO THE NUMBER OF CHROMOSOMES—These can result from nondisjunction, translocation, and mosaicism. The most common disorder is Down syndrome.

➢ DISORDERS RELATED TO THE STRUCTURE OF CHROMOSOMES—The most common cause is a deletion of part of a chromosome. For example, Prader-Willi syndrome is caused by a deletion on the long arm of chromosome 15.

➢ DISORDERS WITH MULTIPLE OR UNKNOWN CAUSES—Conditions with multiple causes include hydrocephalus and microcephalus. An example of a disorder with an unknown cause is Sturge-Weber.

➢ GENETIC TESTING AND GENETIC COUNSELING—Genetic testing procedures include amniocentesis, chorionic villus testing, and alpha fetoprotein testing.

As discussed in the next chapter, CIDs are primarily the result of environmental or unknown causes. There are, however, a number of genetic and chromosomal causes of CIDs. Over 40 years ago, the President's Commission on Mental Retardation (PCMR,

1972) made the bold challenge to reduce the incidence of CIDs 50% by the year 2000. Although that didn't happen, great gains have been made in this area, particularly related to the biological causes of CIDs. We now know much more about the genetic makeup of humans and can isolate genes that are involved with a number of disorders. Advances in research have given us much greater insight into their cause and treatment.

There are at least three reasons why understanding genetic and chromosomal disorders is important. First, there are implications for *prevention*. Through techniques such as gene therapy, the possibility exists of preventing many disorders. For example, the condition known as severe combined immunodeficiency (the so-called bubble boy disorder) has already been successfully eliminated using this technique (Warren, 2002). Another reason is related to *treatment*. For example, phenylketonuria, an inherited disorder that once resulted in a significant number of cases of CIDs, can be successfully treated. With early screening and detection, it is possible to place an individual on a specific diet after only a few days of life and avoid the serious consequences of the disorder. A third reason is *genetic counseling*. Improved diagnostic procedures have given parents increased knowledge about the nature of their unborn baby; genetic counselors can help provide information and support to those parents. In addition, prospective parents may be carriers of a gene known to be linked to a disorder. Genetic testing and subsequent counseling give the parents a better idea of the probability of having a child with the disorder.

Before discussing the specific disorders that are associated with CIDs, it is first necessary to understand the important role that genes and chromosomes play in heredity.

THE ROLE OF GENES AND CHROMOSOMES IN HEREDITY

At the time of conception, when the sperm from a male unites with the ovum from a female, a single cell called a **zygote** results. At that point, the genetic blueprint of an individual is determined. The zygote eventually duplicates itself over and over to become a living organism, complete with its unique characteristics. Genes and chromosomes play a crucial role in this development. To understand their role in the determination of those characteristics, including those associated with CIDs, it is first necessary to become familiar with their structure and function. As will be discussed, CIDs can be caused by both genetic factors and by abnormalities related to the chromosomes themselves.

Cells and Their Structure

There are two types of cells, **somatic cells** or body cells, and **germ cells** or sex cells. Each of these is involved in different types of cell divisions that will ultimately result in a human being with a unique genetic blueprint. The structure of all cells is the same (see Figure 4.1). They include a **cell membrane,** which surrounds the cell matter or **cytoplasm.** Within the cytoplasm is the **nucleus** of the cell (surrounded by the nuclear membrane). The nucleus is vital to heredity because it includes the chromosomes on

Structure of a Typical Animal Cell

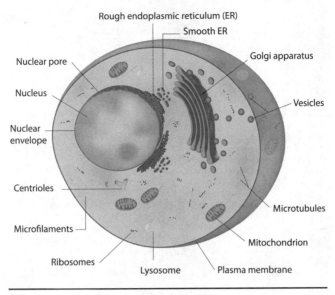

Figure 4.1 Structure of a Typical Animal Cell

which the genes are located. Chromosomes contain all the inherited material that is passed from generation to generation (Papalia & Feldman, 2011). Genes are considered the basic or smallest unit of heredity and provide a blueprint for the characteristics and functions of the human body. Genes that are responsible for specific functions or characteristics have specific locations on the chromosomes, and are the chemical determinants of heredity. This genetic blueprint is called a **genotype.** Genes and chromosomes, therefore, contain all the material necessary to determine heredity.

Composition of the Chromosomes and Genes

Chromosomes are made up of strands of **deoxyribonucleic acid (DNA).** Until 60 years ago, little was known about the structure of DNA. Watson and Crick, who won a Nobel Prize for their research, were the first to describe the composition of DNA (see Research Box 4.1). They suggested that DNA looked like a double spiral (or helix) similar to a twisting ladder consisting of several chemicals including phosphates, sugars, and nitrogenous bases (see Figure 4.2). In humans, there are four bases—**adenine (A), thymine (T), guanine (G), and cytosine (C).** Important to the function of DNA is the unique way in which these bases are joined together to form **base pairs** via a hydrogen bond. Adenine is only bonded with thymine and guanine is only bonded with cytosine. Continuing with the analogy of the ladder, the sides (or strands) would consist of the phosphates and sugars whereas the rungs would be formed by the bonding of one base on one side with its "partner" on the other side. The rungs would have four possible combinations—AT, TA, GC, or CG.

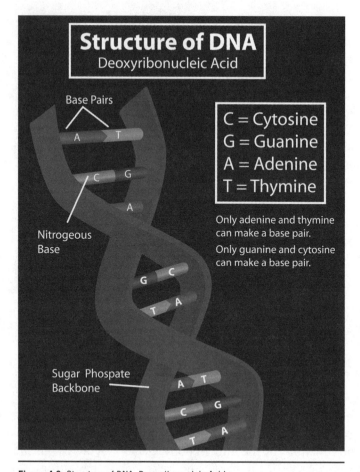

Figure 4.2 Structure of DNA: Deoxyribonucleic Acid

In other words, an adenine found on the left side will always bond with a thymine on the right, and so on. There are estimates that the human chromosomes house almost 3 billion base pairs of DNA.

4.1 RESEARCH THAT MADE A DIFFERENCE

Watson, J.D., & Crick, F.H.C. (1953). A structure for Deoxyribose Nucleic Acid. *Nature, 171,* 737.

Citing the work of Pauling (another Nobel Prize winner) and Coring as well as Fraser, who each had suggested a structure model for DNA, Watson and Crick proposed "a radically different structure." Their suggested model, discussed in this article, describes the accepted molecular structure of DNA. A prophetic statement was made by Watson and Crick in this paper regarding future practices such as cloning—"It has not escaped our notice that the specific pairing we have postulated immediately suggests a possible copying mechanism" (p. 737).

Genes, which are located on the chromosomes, actually contain thousands of base pairs. They dictate inherited characteristics through the process of synthesizing specific proteins needed by the body at various stages of development. This occurs through biochemical transmission via ribonucleic acid, which is produced by the DNA. In other words, the genes send a message about which proteins should be developed at what times. (The specific mechanism by which genes transmit their messages is beyond the scope of this discussion.)

In recent years, attempts have been made to determine the specific location of various genes (genetic mapping) and the sequencing of the base pairs. The **Human Genome Project** (see Event Box 4.1) represented over a decade of research that was involved with the mapping of over 30,000 genes and the sequencing of the over 3 billion chemical combinations that make up human DNA. Clearly, we are at the doorstep of identifying very specific genetic markers for determining human characteristics.

4.1 EVENT THAT MADE A DIFFERENCE

1990—The Human Genome Project Begins

In 1990, the U.S. Department of Energy and the National Institutes of Health began a systematic study to analyze the DNA makeup of humans. It was initially projected as a 15-year study although the U.S. government and a private agency, Celera Genomics, announced in the year 2000 that they had virtually completed the project five years ahead of schedule. The project was designed to identify the exact chromosomal location of all human genes and determine their function related to health and disease. In addition, a goal was to determine the complete sequence of the 3 billion bases in the human genome. Understanding the structure of the entire set of human genes (the genome) obviously sheds tremendous insight into the biological causes of CIDs. This information will be used to diagnose, treat, and prevent physical as well as cognitive disorders. Interestingly, but not surprisingly, a portion of the budget for the Human Genome Project was allocated to address the ethical and legal questions that might arise as a result of the information gleaned from the project. The working draft of the results from the Human Genome Project was published in 2001 in issues of *Nature* and *Science*. The Department of Energy is currently funding a follow-up project called Genomes for Life.

Number and Types of Chromosomes

Humans have 46 chromosomes that are paired together (one of each pair comes from the biological mother and the other from the biological father). Twenty-two pairs of these chromosomes are called **autosomes.** The 23rd pair are called the **sex chromosomes** and determine the gender of the offspring. Females have two X chromosomes whereas males have an X and a Y. During conception, if the male

Normal Human Karyotype

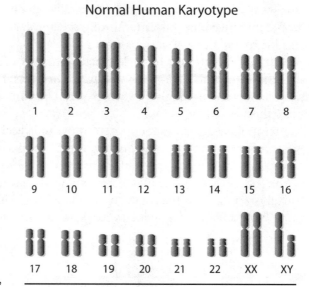

Figure 4.3 Normal Human Karyotype

provides an X chromosome that unites with an X from the female, the offspring will be female. Conversely, if the male provides a Y chromosome the offspring will be male. This process will be described later when the process of cell division is discussed. Chromosome pairs have both a numerical designation (1–23) and are grouped with a letter designation (A-G for seven groups of autosomes). Through specific chemical procedures, chromosomes can be isolated, stained, and photographed. This provides a **karyotype** that shows the magnified chromosomes placed in pairs. The autosomes are ordered according to their length (pair one the longest, pair 22 the shortest) followed by the pair of sex chromosomes (see Figure 4.3). The karyotype alone might indicate an obvious abnormality that might be associated with CIDs or other characteristics (discussed later in this chapter). Disorders resulting in CIDs can occur in problems related to either the autosomes or the sex chromosomes.

Cell Division

Genes and chromosomes also play an important part in cell division, which occurs through two processes, meiosis and mitosis. In **meiosis,** the cell division occurs within the sex cells. This process is described as reductive because the 46 chromosomes in the nucleus are halved (referred to as the haploid state). This results in the development of the sperm in males and the ova in females, each containing 23 chromosomes. Thus at conception, the offspring inherits half the chromosomes from the male and half from the female. As noted previously, for example, if the male provides the X sex chromosome the offspring will be female; if the Y chromosome is inherited the offspring will be a male. In much the same way, the genes present on the chromosomes that are inherited from the male and female can dictate other characteristics of the offspring.

In reality, approximately 75% of all genes inherited by a child will be identical to all other children. The other 25% that occur in random variations is what makes each child unique (Papalia & Feldman, 2011).

Mitosis refers to somatic cell division in which the chromosomes in the nucleus duplicate themselves before dividing. Thus, after the genetic code has been set through conception, each of the 46 chromosomes of the newly formed zygote initially will split by having the base pairs "break." This is sometimes thought of as the "unzipping" of the DNA strands. Then, each separate strand will act as a template for the development of new strands because of the need for each base (e.g., adenine) to bond with its analogous base (i.e., thymine). When the cell (called the parent cell) divides, the two new cells (called daughter cells) will contain 46 chromosomes (referred to as the diploid state). Through the processes of meiosis and mitosis, the development of a baby occurs, complete with his or her predetermined genetic makeup.

Reflection

What impact do you think the Human Genome Project will have on the field of CIDs?

AUTOSOMAL GENETIC DISORDERS

Genetic disorders can involve genes on either the 22 pair of autosomes or the one pair of sex chromosomes. Genes that produce different characteristics are referred to as **alleles;** a child will inherit one from each biological parent. In other words, the offspring will inherit one of the two alleles from each parent that are located on the parents' chromosome pairs. Assume that the two alleles are G and g. When the offspring inherits the same allele from each parent for a given characteristic, the result is a **homozygous** pairing (either GG or gg). When the offspring inherits different alleles, it is referred to as a **heterozygous** pairing (Gg).

In recent years, more information has been gathered regarding the role of genes in the inheritance of traits. Two accepted explanations for genetic inheritance are the single gene position, or the one gene–one disorder (IGOD) position, and the quantitative trait loci (QTL) position. The IGOD explanation suggests that the presence of a single gene will result in the disorder. The QTL explanation suggests that multiple genes in combination are the cause for a disorder (i.e., one isolated gene is not the cause). There is also the issue of **multifactorial transmission,** a combination of genetic and environmental factors that plays an important role in inheritance. There are some disorders related to CIDs that are considered single gene or IGOD disorders, and others that are considered QTL disorders. In addition, certain traits such as intelligence and adaptive behavior are affected by multifactorial transmission. Single gene disorders can be either **dominant** or **recessive.**

Autosomal Dominant Disorders

In an autosomal dominant disorder, if *either* of the parents passes on the allele for a given disorder, the child will have the disorder. This usually means that a child with the disorder will have one or both parents who also have the disorder. An exception would be if the condition is a result of a new mutation. In rare occasions, a child will not inherit the dominant disorder. This is referred to as **nonpenetrance.** In an autosomal dominant disorder, if an offspring receives either a homozygous (DD) or heterozygous (DU) pairing in which a dominant allele (D) is present (U stands for unaffected gene), the trait of the dominant allele will be inherited. One way to demonstrate this is by using a **Punnett Square,** named after Sir Reginald Punnett who helped establish the study of genetics at Cambridge University in the 1800s. A Punnett Square demonstrates the various genetic combinations that result from a mother and father with known allele pairs. Although it results in the probability of a given individual to inherit a disorder (or any trait), it is not an exact science. It actually only indicates the theoretical probability that a disorder will be inherited a certain percentage of the time (MacMillan, 1985). This is particularly true of heterozygous pairings.

Consider the following possible combinations that result in four children in which the father has a homozygous pair of dominant genes and the mother has a heterozygous pair. In the following examples, D stands for a dominant gene for a given disorder and U is an unaffected gene:

PUNNETT SQUARE 1

Female
D U
D DD DU

Male
 D DD DU
In this case, all four children would have the dominant gene (D) and therefore would inherit the disorder. The same would be true for a DD/UU pairing.

Now consider the case of two heterozygous parents, each with the dominant gene:

PUNNETT SQUARE 2

Female
D U
D DD DU

Male
U UD UU
In this case, three of the four children would inherit the disorder. The child with the UU combination would not have the disorder. This means that there is a 75% chance that a given child would have the disorder.

Next is an example of a heterozygous mother and a homozygous father (without the dominant gene).

PUNNETT SQUARE 3

Female
D U
U UD UU

Male
U UD UU

Here, only two children would inherit the disorder (i.e., there is a 50% chance that a given child would inherit the disorder.

Obviously, if the two parents have homozygous pairings with the dominant allele (DD), *all* children will inherit the disorder. Examples of autosomal dominant disorders that can result in a CID are tuberous sclerosis and neurofibromatosis.

Tuberous sclerosis

Tuberous sclerosis (TS) is caused by a nonworking gene located on either the ninth or the sixteenth chromosome. These genes ordinarily act to suppress the development of tumors in the body. Subsequently, the condition is characterized by tumors that can affect any number of organs, including the brain. The tumors are shaped like tubers (potatoes) and calcify (become sclerotic) with age, hence the name *tuberous sclerosis*. These tumors can lead to seizures and CIDs. Another common characteristic is the presence of skin lesions that take on several forms including red, vascular lumps on the face. Although it is an autosomal dominant disorder, the majority of cases are caused by new mutations. CIDs do not always occur, and when they do, the degree varies from mild to severe. Interestingly, the frequency of autism in individuals with TS is also quite high. Estimates are that approximately 25%–50% also have autism (Tuberous Sclerosis Alliance, 2013).

Neurofibromatosis

Like tuberous sclerosis, neurofibromatosis (NF) results in the growth of tumors. In NF, the growth of tumors can occur in either the peripheral nervous system (PNS) or the central nervous system (CNS). CIDs might or might not be present. There are two types of neurofibromatosis, NF1 and NF2. NF1 was once known as peripheral neurofibromatosis, or Von Recklinghausen disease, named after the individual who first identified it. The term *peripheral neurofibromatosis* is no longer considered appropriate, however, because CNS tumors can also occur in NF1 (National Institute of Neurological Disorders and Stroke [NINDS], 2002). NF2 was once known as central neurofibromatosis or bilateral acoustic neurofibromatosis because it was assumed that the tumors affected the auditory nerve. Evidence now exists that the tumors affect the vestibular nerve. Because of the proximity to other cranial nerves, NF2 can sometimes be life-threatening (NINDS, 2002). NF1 results in multiple tumors (neurofibromas), "café au lait" spots (light brown birth marks), lumps on the skin above the peripheral nerves, and nodules on the eyes. It can also result in macrocephaly (large head), and bone malformations. Kahl and Moore (2000) noted that the hallmarks of NF1 are cognitive implications, learning disabilities, and behavioral and emotional difficulties. NF2 results in tumors that can lead to hearing loss. A parent with NF1 or NF2 will always have a child with the same type of NF, although the severity of the characteristics can vary greatly within the same family.

A POPULAR MYTH

Most are familiar with the story of Joseph Merrick, the so-called Elephant Man. The story was based on an essay by a physician who found Merrick in a carnival and took care of him until his death. The story was later made into a motion picture that depicted Merrick as an extremely disfigured person. In 1971, a medical anthropologist made the statement that Merrick had the condition known as neurofibromatosis. This association between the visual representation of Merrick in the motion picture and the diagnosis of neu-rofibromatosis has given many a biased view of the condition. In reality, in 1996 a Canadian physician determined that Merrick actually had Proteus syndrome, not neurofibromatosis. Unfortunately, this myth has had an emotional and psychological impact on those with neurofibromatosis and their families.

Source: Kugler, M. (2014). The Elephant Man's Bones Reveal Mystery. Retrieved from http://raradiseases.about.com/cs/proteussyndrome/a/031301.htm

---

Autosomal Recessive Disorders

If an autosomal disorder is recessive in nature, *both parents must pass that particular allele to the child for him or her to inherit the disorder*. Again, using the previously presented Punnett Squares, it is possible to determine the theoretical probabilities of a child inheriting a recessive disorder. Assume in this situation that R stands for the gene for the recessive disorder and U is the unaffected gene. If both parents have heterozygous pairings (both carriers), one child would have the disorder (RR), two would be carriers (UR and RU), and one would be unaffected (UU). Accordingly, the probability would be 25% that a child would inherit the disorder, 50% that a child would be a carrier, and 25% that a child would neither have the disorder nor be a carrier. If one parent is homozygous (RR—has the disorder) and the other heterozygous (RU—is a carrier), the probability is that two children would have the disorder (RR) and two would be carriers (UR and RU). In the situation in which both parents have homozygous pairings (both have the disorder), *all* children would have the disorder. One other situation is possible. What if one parent is a carrier (heterozygous, UR) and the other is homozygous, but not with the gene for the recessive disorder (UU)? In that case, *no* children would have the condition but 50% would be carriers.

TRY IT OUT

Develop your own Punnett Squares to illustrate the various combinations described above. Does that make it easier to understand?

Many autosomal recessive disorders leading to CIDs are metabolic disorders due to enzyme deficiencies resulting in the inability to break down certain substances (e.g., proteins or sugars) in the body. This inability leads to excessive accumulation of those substances that can have devastating effects. These conditions are often referred to as **inborn errors of metabolism.** Fortunately, many of these conditions can be identified and treated early, thus avoiding at least some of the cognitive and physical consequences. These disorders are also frequently linked to ethnic background, which has important implications for genetic counseling (discussed later in this chapter). The following descriptions are provided for several metabolic disorders.

Galactosemia

Galactosemia is caused by the lack, or significant reduction, of the enzyme galactose-1-phospate uridyl transferase, which breaks down the carbohydrate (sugar) galactose. Problems occur when an individual consumes food products containing galactose or lactose (e.g., dairy products and certain legumes such as garbanzo beans). Typically, these sugars are converted to glucose for the body to use as energy but the lack of the enzyme prohibits this process from occurring. The accumulation of the galactose has serious consequences including brain damage resulting in a CID, cataracts, and the failure of organs including the liver and kidneys. Galactosemia can be identified within the first week of life using a blood test and treatment can be initiated immediately. This involves avoiding food products that include galactose and lactose. Although early treatment has been associated with a significant decrease in the characteristics, including CIDs, there is some evidence that many treated individuals with galactosemia still have lower IQs and more speech problems than the general population (Hoffmann, Wendel, Schweitzer-Krantz, 2011). There is also an invariant of galactosemia called Duarte Galactosemia. Individuals with this disorder do not show as many symptoms because there is some enzyme activity and the diet is usually not as strict.

Hurler Syndrome

Hurler syndrome is caused by the lack of an enzyme called lysosomal alpha-L-iduronase that metabolizes mucopolysaccharides (a complex carbohydrate). Subsequently, there is an accumulation in the body that affects the connective tissues, the bones and skin, and major organs including the liver and spleen that are visibly enlarged. Hurler syndrome is actually one of several syndromes that are related to problems in mucopolysaccharide metabolism. This condition was once known as "gargoylism" because of the facial features of those with the syndrome. Characteristics include severe CIDs, short stature, cloudy corneas, deafness, and distinctive facial features including large dark eyebrows, full lips, a large tongue, and a low nasal bridge.

Currently, there is no cure and it leads to early death, usually by the early teenage years. Promise has been shown, however, using stem cell transplants from bone marrow (National Institute of Mental Health, 2011).

Maple Syrup Urine Disease

Individuals with this disorder have urine that has a sweet smell like maple syrup (hence the name of the disease). It is caused by the body's inability to break down the amino acids leucine, isoleucine, and valine. The complications of Maple Syrup Urine Disease occur at various levels of severity, although even in its mildest form it can result in a CID. Other characteristics are acidosis (excessive acid in the blood), seizures, and problems with feeding and vomiting. One problem is that the presence of high levels of these amino acids has a very toxic effect, leading to brain damage. Subsequently, when the disease is detected, it is paramount to reduce these amino acid levels in the body as quickly as possible. A diet is also initiated that avoids these amino acids. An infant formula is available that makes it easier to control diet.

Tay Sachs Disease

Tay Sachs disease is primarily found among the Ashkenazi Jewish population (one of two major divisions including the Eastern European Jews). This is a severe disorder causing progressive neurological problems (including loss of motor ability, seizures, blindness, and general paralysis) and severe CIDs. Unfortunately, there is no cure and death usually occurs by age 5. It is caused by the lack of an enzyme to metabolize a lipid called Ganglioside-GM2, which eventually accumulates in the brain. In addition, cases of adult onset Tay Sachs have been reported that result in psychosis (U.S. National Library of Medicine, 2013b).

Phenylketonuria

Phenylketonuria (PKU) is a treatable condition that can be identified within the first week of life using a simple blood test that is used for routine newborn screening (see Research Box 4.2). With lab and hospital errors, however, some infants are not identified and begin to show symptoms at around 6 months of age (Waisbren, 1999). The condition results when an individual lacks the enzyme phenylalanine hydroxylase, which breaks down the amino acid phenylalanine into tyrosine. Tyrosine is further broken down into other substances including melanin (the chemical that provides skin color). As a result, individuals with PKU are light skinned. If left untreated, there is severe damage to the central nervous system, resulting in a CID.

4.2 RESEARCH THAT MADE A DIFFERENCE

Guthrie, R., & Susi, A. (1963). A simple phenylalanine method for detecting phenylketonuria in large populations of newborn infants. *Pediatrics, 32,* 338–343.

Guthrie and Susi developed a simple test using blood obtained from a heel prick in newborn infants. This was the first procedure that could accurately screen large populations of children; now it is required in all 50 states in the United States. They pointed out in their article that the test should not be done until the infant is approximately four days old because "the blood phenylalanine level is normal at birth and its rise is completely dependent upon protein intake" (p. 341). The test is now usually given after two days.

The treatment for PKU is a diet that avoids products containing phenylalanine. One controversial issue has to do with how long an individual must stay on the diet. Previously, it was thought that an individual could stop the diet once he or she entered adolescence. However, most professionals now suggest that the diet should be continued throughout adulthood. This is particularly true of women with PKU who are expecting to get pregnant; high maternal phenylalanine levels can result in serious consequences to the developing fetus (Koch, Trefz, & Waisbren, 2010). Because of the availability of early detection and diet regimens, prognosis is good, but benefits depend on the strictness of the diet. For example, Smith, Klim, and Hanley (2000) reported that individuals who were treated early did have some later cognitive problems, the degree of which was related to the phenylalanine levels in the blood at the time they were evaluated. One encouraging finding was reported by Fitzgerald et al. (2000). They found that placing previously untreated adults on the diet resulted in benefits in several areas including concentration, mood, and adaptive behavior. It also appears that even though early treatment can help avoid CIDs, treated individuals still have problems in the areas of executive mental processing, visual-spatial skills, fine-motor skills, and information processing speed (Janzen & Nguyen, 2010).

TAKE A LOOK

The next time you see a diet soda such as Diet Coke or Diet Pepsi look closely at the can or bottle. There will be a warning on it informing individuals with PKU that the drink contains phenylalanine. It is present in Aspartame, the substance used as a sweetener.

Reflection

How would you explain to parents the possible effects on a child if one parent has a specific autosomal recessive disorder and the other is a carrier of the disorder?

INHERITED SEX-LINKED DISORDERS

As noted earlier in this chapter, the 23rd pair of chromosomes determine the sex of an individual. A female will inherit an X chromosome from each parent whereas a male will inherit an X chromosome from the mother and a Y chromosome from the father. Similar to autosomal disorders, problems can arise that are related to these sex chromosomes as well, primarily with the X chromosomes. The X chromosome is much larger and contains many more genes than the Y chromosome.

The majority of genetic sex-linked disorders are recessive in nature, although dominant and recessive are determined somewhat differently than they are in autosomal disorders. In a dominant sex-linked disorder, the female who carries the gene for the disorder (nonworking gene) will have the disorder; in a recessive sex-linked disorder, the female with the nonworking gene will be a carrier (Schanen, 1997). It is rare that a female will inherit an X-linked recessive disorder. In addition, females generally do not have as severe characteristics as males. This is because females will have a working gene as well a nonworking gene. Through a process known as **lyonization,** named after geneticist Mary Lyon, only one X chromosome is randomly activated in a given cell whereas the other one is inactivated. If the working ("good") gene is activated then the nonworking ("defective") gene will not be. On the other hand, males who inherit the nonworking X chromosome only have a Y chromosome to go with it so the nonworking X chromosome will automatically be activated.

Fragile X syndrome

Fragile X syndrome is actually the most common *genetically inherited* form of CIDs. Characteristics were first noticed in 1943 and called Martin-Bell syndrome after the two individuals who made the initial identification. It wasn't until 1991 that its specific genetic cause was determined (see Research Box 4.3). Estimates vary but it appears that it occurs in approximately every 1,000–2,000 males and 2,000–4,000 females. If a female carrier passes the Fragile X chromosome to her male child, he will inherit the syndrome. On the other hand, because of the previously mentioned process of lyonization, females also will randomly receive an X chromosome with a working gene; therefore not all will inherit the disorder. Further, symptoms generally will be more severe in males than in females.

The syndrome is so named because of a noticeable pinch or weak area on the X chromosome (called a fragile site). It results from the inactivity of a gene, FMRP1, located at the fragile site that is responsible for producing a protein called FMRP (Fragile X Mental Retardation Protein). The lack of this protein results in the characteristics associated with Fragile X syndrome. FMRP deficiency in the brain cells is what leads to a CID.

The cause of Fragile X syndrome is somewhat complicated. As noted earlier in this chapter, there are various combinations of cytosine (C), guanine (G), adenine (A), and thymine (T) in human DNA. There is ordinarily a series of 6–54 specific, triplicate combinations (CGG) at the site of the FMRP1 gene. In Fragile X syndrome, however, the CGG combination goes through several more duplications, called repeats, resulting in a longer gene. This longer gene is susceptible to a chemi-cal process called methylation, which results in the inactivation of the FMRP1 gene. If the number of repeats is not too large (approximately 55–199, consid-ered a premutation), there is usually no indication that the individual has the syndrome. However, if the number of repeats is greater (>200, considered a full mutation), methylation occurs and the characteristics of the syndrome are present. One important point is that the number of repeats of the gene typically increases through succeeding generations of families; subsequently the chances of a full mutation will increase. Although there is no known cure for Fragile X syn-drome, several treatments are being pursued including gene therapy, gene repair, and psychopharmacology. The FRAXA Research Foundation (2000) identified the following treatment goals:

1. Fix the gene so that it makes normal protein,
2. Make and deliver the protein by some other means, and
3. Substitute for the function of the protein.

Males with Fragile X syndrome have several typical physical characteristics. These include large or prominent ears, enlarged testicles (macroorchidism), a long narrow face, flexibility of joints, and flat feet. Females with Fragile X syndrome typically have the large, prominent ears. Cognitive impairment is also sex-related. Most (but not all) males will have primarily mild to moderate CIDs. Females, on the other hand, are more likely to be identified as having a learning disability or mild CIDs. In addition to the cognitive deficits of individuals with Fragile X syndrome, atten-tion deficit/hyperactivity disorder, autism, and other socioemotional problems are reported as well as poor eye contact, tactile defensiveness, and impulsivity (Hager-man et al., 2009). Language delays and disorders such as repetitive speech (echolalia) and increased rate and loudness of speech (palilalia) as well as unusual hand move-ments such as hand flapping are also frequently found (Turk & Graham, 1998). One interesting characteristic that has been reported is their unusual greeting behavior. Wolff, Gardner, Paccia, and Lappan (1989) described the stereotypic pattern of gaze involvement that includes bending the entire upper body down to shake hands while looking away. This is an example of social avoidance, a core characteristic of Fragile X that has been described as autistic-like (Roberts, Weisenfeld, Hatton, Heath, & Kaufmann, 2007).

In fact, many of the characteristics of Fragile X syndrome are similar to those of autism (e.g., poor eye contact, echolalia, hand flapping). This has led many to conclude that the incidence of autism is unusually high in individuals with Fragile X syndrome or that Fragile X might actually cause autism. Using the Social Communication Ques-tionnaire, Moss, Oliver, Nelson, Richards, and Hall (2013) found that 45.6% of their Fragile X population met the cutoff for autism and 78.6% met the cutoff for autism spectrum disorder. Similarly, Hall, Lightbody, and Reiss (2008) reported that 50% of males with Fragile X that they examined met the diagnostic criteria for autism. Inter-estingly, only 20% of females met the diagnostic criteria.

4.3 RESEARCH THAT MADE A DIFFERENCE

Verkerk, A., Pieretti, M., Sutcliffe, J., Fu, Y., Kuhl, D., Pizzuti, A., . . . Warren, S. T. (1991). Identification of a gene (FMR-1) containing a CGG repeat coincident with a breakpoint cluster region exhibiting length variation of Fragile X syndrome. *Cell, 65,* 905–914.

Although the presence of a fragile site on the X chromosome was identified in 1977 (Sutherland, 1977), it wasn't until 1991 that the gene responsible for Fragile X syndrome was discovered. Verkerk et al. (1991) identified the gene and the mechanism by which it becomes activated. Prior to this discovery, chromosomal testing was used but was only helpful in identifying individuals who had the fragile site, and subsequently the syndrome itself. Individuals with Fragile X syndrome who do not have CIDs sometimes have negative results, and nonaffected carriers almost always have negative results based on chromosome testing. By isolating the specific gene, it is possible to use DNA testing, resulting in more accuracy and identifying carriers of Fragile X syndrome as well (Hagerman & Lampe, 1999). This has very important implications for genetic counseling.

Lesch-Nyhan Syndrome

Lesch-Nyhan syndrome (LNS) is a recessive disorder affecting a gene on the long arm of the X chromosome (the arms of chromosomes will be discussed later). It is an inherited disorder that occurs almost exclusively in boys. The hallmark characteristic of LNS is self-injurious behavior (head banging, self-biting, etc.) that can be quite severe and, in fact, life-threatening. Interestingly, although individuals cannot stop the self-injurious behavior themselves, they can predict it and often ask for restraints. LNS is caused by a buildup of uric acid because of an enzyme deficiency; it also can lead to problems with the kidneys and joints. Frequently, there are also swallowing and eating problems and vomiting.

Individuals with LNS have been reported to have a compulsive tendency toward aggression. In fact, Anderson and Ernst (1994), using a questionnaire with parents of children with LNS, found that aggression was as frequently reported as self-injury. There are also neurological complications such as spasticity and the presence of meaningless, repetitive behaviors. The level of CID is usually relatively severe, although it may appear more severe than it really is because of the physical and behavioral characteristics that coexist (Nyhan, 1994). There is no known cure although protective equipment frequently is used to protect against self-injury and medications are prescribed to help control the level of uric acid and some of the neurological problems.

Rett Syndrome

In 1999, researchers discovered the gene that causes Rett syndrome (RS). Mutation of that gene involving the X chromosome results in the lack of a protein, MeCP2. This protein deficiency affects the "expression" of other genes. This expression ordinarily results in the triggering of other proteins in different tissues and at different times that are essential for normal development. Subsequently, this disruption leads to a neurodevelopmental disorder. Almost all cases are thought to be due to new mutations and the chance of a family who has one child with RS to have another child with the syndrome is less than 1% (International Rett Syndrome Association [IRSA], n.d.). RS once was assumed to occur only in females, although a very few cases of males with the disorder have been reported (IRSA, n.d.; Kerr, 2002).

The characteristics of RS represent the neurodevelopmental nature of the disorder. Infants develop normally until approximately 6–18 months of age when they begin to regress, losing speech/language and motor skills. Loss of muscle tone is usually the first symptom (NINDS Rett Syndrome Fact Sheet, 2014). In addition, their head growth decelerates and they lose the ability to socially interact. Motor skill problems frequently involve the hands, resulting in nonpurposeful, repetitive hand movements such as hand wringing and clasping. Walking is also affected with a wide-based gait and occasional toe walking. Some individuals lose their ability to walk. Some individuals with RS may have seizures and curvature of the spine and might hyperventilate and hold their breath. Although intelligence is affected, it is difficult to determine a reliable estimate of the relative severity because of the significant speech and motor problems (Brown & Hoadley, 1999). There is no cure for RS and treatment is symptomatic (National Institute of Neurological Disorders and Stroke, 2002).

Reflection

Why are females with Fragile X syndrome generally less affected than males with the same disorder?

DISORDERS RELATED TO THE NUMBER OF CHROMOSOMES

Disorders resulting in CIDs can occur when an individual has too few or too many chromosomes. As noted earlier, there are usually 23 pairs of chromosomes, resulting in a total of 46. In the majority of disorders related to number of chromosomes, there will be 47 (a trisomy disorder); much more rarely there will be only 45 (a monosomy disorder). The main cause of these disorders is **nondisjunction.** In the most common type of nondisjunction, chromosomes fail to separate during meiosis so that both are passed to one daughter cell and none to the other. Other causes are the result of **translocation** and **mosaicism.** One type of translocation occurs when a portion of one chromosome fuses with a similar portion of another

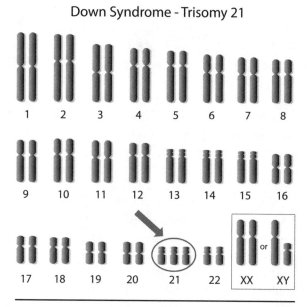

Figure 4.4 Down Syndrome—Trisomy 21

chromosome (centric-fusion translocation). This only involves chromosomes that have a certain shape—called acrocentric chromosomes (13, 14, 15, 21, and 22). Another type of translocation involves two chromosomes that exchange segments (reciprocal translocation). This is represented in Figure 4.4 In mosaicism, the failure of the chromosomes to separate usually occurs during mitosis, later in cell division. This results in some cells with 46 chromosomes and some with 47. Because there are some "normal" cells, individuals with disorders caused by mosaicism have less severe characteristics. It should be remembered that the autosome pairs are numbered according to their size. Subsequently, the lower the chromosome number, the more genetic material is likely to be affected (although some chromosomes are more "gene rich" than others). Generally, the more genetic material that is affected, the more severe the characteristics of the disorder will be. In many cases, the fetus will be miscarried if too much genetic material is involved. Disorders related to the number of chromosomes can involve either the autosomes or the sex chromosomes.

Autosomal Disorders

Down Syndrome

Down syndrome (DS) is the most common biological cause of CIDs. It was initially described in 1866 by Langdon Down, an English physician after whom the syndrome was named. It was once inappropriately referred to as mongolism because of the characteristic Asian facial features. The vast majority of cases of DS are the result of a third 21st chromosome caused by nondisjunction, although a smaller percentage are due to translocation and mosaicism. DS caused by translocation occurs when a portion of chromosome 21 is transferred to another chromosome (usually 13 or 15). In the case of DS caused by mosaicism, some cells will have an extra 21st chromosome and others will have just two chromosomes. Although DS has been associated with maternal age (higher incidence among older mothers), thus suggesting a maternal link, it is now accepted that a small percentage of DS is paternally related (Jyothy et al., 2001).

There are as many as 50 physical characteristics associated with DS, although not all individuals will have all the characteristics. Most are familiar with the common physical characteristics of DS and they have even been brought to the attention of the general public through the media. One example was the television show "Life Goes On," which told the story of Corky, a boy with DS, and his experiences trying to cope with life in high school. More recently, a cheerleader with DS appears in "Glee." The most common characteristics of DS include an upward slant of the eyes, a small nose, flattening of the back of the head, small hands and feet, thick tongue, small folds on the inner corners of the eyes (epicanthal folds), short stature, and CIDs. Cosmetic surgery has been used to change the facial features associated with DS, although the ethics of this practice has been questioned. For example, the National Down Syndrome Society (n.d.) suggested that acceptance should be encouraged from a societal perspective rather than by altering the appearance of individuals with Down syndrome.

The degree of CIDs associated with DS varies but is usually mild to moderate. In addition, these individuals are prone to have certain health problems, primarily heart defects, and are susceptible to respiratory, vision, and hearing disorders. Life expectancy is shorter than average due to heart defects and leukemia early in life and Alzheimer's and an apparent tendency toward premature aging later in life (Zigman & Lott, 2007). Advances in medical care have resulted in increases in life expectancy but lead to other medical problems of older age such as osteoporosis. As alluded to earlier, individuals with DS are more likely to get Alzheimer's disease at an early age and it is more prevalent in the DS population than in others. Chromosome 21 actually is one of several chromosomes in which gene mutations have been associated with Alzheimer's disease (van Gassen & van Broekhoven, 2000). In one study, Chapman and Hesketh (2000) found that almost half of individuals with DS over the age of 50 had characteristics of Alzheimer's disease.

Edwards Syndrome (Trisomy 18)

Edwards syndrome is caused by an additional 18th chromosome (Trisomy 18). Actually, most fetuses that have the additional chromosome will be miscarried. Similar to Down syndrome, Edwards syndrome has been associated with maternal age. The physical characteristics include microcephaly (small head), low-set malformed ears, and cleft lip/cleft palate among others. The degree of CID is quite severe and children with the syndrome are susceptible to a number of other conditions including cardiovascular and neurological problems. Because of the number of health issues, most children with this syndrome die before the age of one year.

Patau Syndrome (Trisomy 13)

As with Edwards syndrome, the majority of fetuses that have an additional 13th chromosome will be miscarried. There are numerous physical malformations associated with this syndrome including a sloping forehead, microcephaly, extra fingers and toes (syndactyly), and small or absent eyes. There is often an incomplete development of the forebrain as well as the auditory and optic nerves. The CIDs are extremely severe. Also similar to Edwards syndrome, there are numerous health problems that lead to an early death.

Sex-linked Disorders

Klinefelter Syndrome

Klinefelter syndrome (KS) occurs when a male has an extra X chromosome resulting in an XXY combination. Not all males with the extra X chromosome actually develop KS and show the symptoms. In fact, the occurrence of the extra chromosome is relatively common with some estimates as high as 1 in 500. It is also possible that more than one extra X chromosome can be found (e.g., XXXY). The characteristics of KS include hypogonadism (small testes), sterility, large breasts, and relatively tall stature. Most individuals with KS have average intelligence but a small percentage have a CID that is usually mild in severity. There is also a relatively high incidence of language-based learning problems and limitations in communication that affect social adaptation and behavior (Verri, Cremante, Clerici, Destefani, & Radicioni, 2010). It is also possible that a male can have an extra Y chromosome (XYY). This condition can also sometimes result in CIDs, although behavioral characteristics such as aggression are more prevalent. The extra Y chromosome in males has been the source of considerable controversy (see Box).

THE CRIMINAL GENE?

Misconceptions about the XYY male were widespread for a number of years and some still continue today. It was once thought that the extra Y chromosome was the "criminal gene" and that a large percentage of prisoners were XYY males. This controversy was sparked by a letter published in *Lancet* in 1968 that addressed the higher prevalence of XYY males in the prison population. The information, however, was based on a very small sample. Richard Speck, the serial killer of seven nurses, used the XYY argument in his defense, although he actually did not have the XYY combination. The misconception has also been popularized in the media. *Aliens 3* was a movie about a penal colony for men with XYY profiles. Ike (2000), in reviewing the literature, argued that the generalizations associated with XYY should be stopped.

Source: The Pathology Guy (n.d.). *XYY—Stereotype of the karyotype*. Retrieved from www.pathguy.com/xyy.htm

---

Turner Syndrome

Whereas Klinefelter syndrome affects males, Turner syndrome (TS) affects only females. In TS, the female is born with only one X chromosome resulting in an XO combination. This results in abnormal sexual development including undeveloped or missing ovaries. They also have extremely short stature, a webbed neck, problems with organs such as the kidney and heart, motor deficits, and problems with attention and visual-perceptual skills. Psychosocial problems in the areas of social adjustment and self-esteem have also been associated with TS. Intelligence is usually normal but CIDs occur in some individuals with TS. The syndrome sometimes goes undetected until the young woman fails to undergo puberty.

Pentasomy X Syndrome

In the previous discussion of Klinefelter syndrome, it was mentioned that males could actually inherit multiple X chromosomes. In Pentasomy X syndrome, females inherit three extra X chromosomes, resulting in an XXXXX combination. This is thought to be due to multiple nondisjunctions during meiosis. Characteristics include microcephaly, low-set malformed ears, curvature of the spine, webbed neck, and abnormal ovaries. CIDs and motor problems are present and delayed growth and puberty are possible. There are also other conditions in which a female might have three or four X chromosomes. In general, more X chromosomes result in more severe CIDs.

Reflection

What is your opinion about using cosmetic surgery to change the facial features of individuals with Down syndrome?

DISORDERS RELATED TO THE STRUCTURE OF CHROMOSOMES

In addition to disorders that are caused by too few or too many chromosomes, problems can occur when the structure of a chromosome is altered. The previously described process of translocation is one example of how the structure of a chromosome can be changed. The most common cause of these problems, however, is the **deletion** of a part of the chromosome. These deletions can be either large or small, and the consequences of the deletion are dependent on the amount and type of genetic material that is subsequently missing.

Identifying Locations on Chromosomes

Chromosomes are shaped in such a way that they have a long arm and a short arm. They also have a **centromere,** an area that separates the two arms. Chromosomes contain bands that can be identified through various staining techniques using high-resolution technology. There is an international system used to identify chromosome location. The long arm is designated by the small letter *q* and the short arm is designated by the small letter *p*. For example, 9q would refer to the long arm of the 9th chromosome. The bands are referred to by two-digit numbers, with the first number referring to the region on the chromosome. Therefore, 9q11 would refer to the 11th band of the long arm of chromosome 9. Subbands can also be designated after the band number. The designation 9q11.2 would refer to the 2nd subband on the 11th band of the long arm of the 9th chromosome. A deletion is designated as a negative sign (-), thus a deletion of this latter area would be 9q11.2-.

Certain disorders are associated with the deletions related to the long and short arms, particularly near the ends. It is also possible that a deletion could occur more toward the middle of a chromosome (called **interstitial**), although this is not as common. Interstitial literally means "to stand between." A discussion of several disorders caused by chromosomal deletions follow. They are presented based on the number of the chromosome (lowest number to highest number) on which the deletion occurs.

Wolf-Hirschhorn Syndrome

Wolf-Hirshhorn syndrome is the result of a partial deletion involving the short arm of the 4th chromosome (4p-). The extent of the characteristics depends on the extent of the deletion and, subsequently, the amount of genetic material that is involved. Generally, they include microcephaly, wide-spaced eyes, cleft lip/cleft palate, a broad, prominent nose, seizures, heart problems, and profound CIDs.

Cri-du-Chat Syndrome

Cri-du-Chat is translated as "cry of the cat" and the syndrome is named for the high-pitched cry that these individuals have. It is caused by a partial deletion of the short arm of the 5th chromosome (5p-); the high-pitched cry seems to be associated with the area 5p15.3. In addition to the catlike cry, these individuals have short stature, poor muscle tone (hypotonia) in childhood, low birth weight, and severe CIDs. Almost all have microcephaly and physical abnormalities such as poorly formed ears, wide-spaced eyes, and epicanthal folds.

Williams Syndrome

Williams syndrome is caused by a deletion of material on the long arm of chromosome 7 (7q11.23) that includes a gene responsible for the production of the protein elastin that provides strength and elasticity to the blood vessels. It results in characteristic "elfin-like" facial features that include a small upturned nose, wide mouth, small widely spaced teeth, full lips, small chin, and puffiness around the eyes. These individuals are impulsive and very socially outgoing and have many developmental problems. The syndrome is associated with mild to moderate CIDs; memory problems declining with age have been noted (Krinsky-McHale, Kittler, Brown, Jenkins, & Devenny, 2005). Although individuals with Williams syndrome are extremely sociable, empathic, and expressive in communication, they apparently have difficulty interpreting others' emotional expressions (Plesa-Skwerer, Faja, Schofield, Verbalis, & Tager-Flusberg, 2006). Also, even though they have relatively good structural language and concrete vocabulary abilities, they do have some difficulty with the pragmatic aspects of language (John, Rowe, Mervis, & Abbeduto, 2009).

Jacobsen Syndrome

Jacobsen syndrome is caused by a partial deletion of the long arm of chromosome 11 (11q-). It results in extremely slow growth and physical characteristics including facial malformations such as eye abnormalities. In addition to CIDs, there are also malformations of the hands and/or feet, speech and language impairments, and heart problems.

Prader-Willi Syndrome

Prader-Willi syndrome (PWS) is caused by a deletion on the long arm of chromosome 15 (15q-). Interestingly, the same bands (15q11–13) associated with PWS are also involved in Angelman syndrome (discussed next) although the two have very different characteristics. A phenomenon known as **genome imprinting** explains this difference. Genome imprinting occurs when an allele has a different effect on an offspring based on the sex of the parent. In other words, the same gene has different effects depending on its parental origin. It is now known that PWS is paternally related whereas Angelman syndrome is maternally related (Everman & Cassidy, 2000). Actually, PWS was the first human disorder associated with genome imprinting (Dykens & Cassidy, 1999).

PWS was first identified in 1956 and was called HHHO syndrome. These letters stood for the main characteristics associated with the syndrome at the time. HHHO referred to hypotonia (poor or low muscle tone), hypogonadism (small testicles), hypomentia (CID), and obesity. For 25 years, the diagnosis of PWS was made primarily on the basis of the observable characteristics, although there was some early evidence that chromosome 15 was involved in at least some of the cases (Hawkey & Smithes, 1976). In 1991, because of advances in high-resolution chromosome analysis, the 15q deletion was identified (see Event Box 4.2). In general, the HHHO characteristics are noted today, although more information is known about them and additional ones have also been associated with PWS. The hypotonia begins early in life, resulting in a condition referred to as "floppy baby." The hypotonia in infancy also results in a poor sucking reflex and, ironically, slow weight gain in the first year of life. In addition to hypogonadism, there is often cryptorchidism, in which the testes do not descend at all. The IQ levels of individuals with PWS were initially reported to be primarily in the 40–60 range (Zellweiger & Schneider, 1968). More recent information, however, indicates that most have mild CIDs (IQs 60s–70s) with about 40% having borderline CIDs and 20% having moderate CIDs (Prader-Willi Syndrome Association, 2012). There is actually a great variation in measured IQ.

The extreme obesity seen in PWS is one of its hallmark characteristics. Individuals are thought to have insatiable appetites and unusual food-related behaviors such as eating nonfood products (pica). It is also assumed that these individuals have no food preferences since they will eat virtually anything, apparently indiscriminately. Some research, however, has indicated that individuals with PWS do, in fact, have food preferences but that perhaps due to the severe restriction of food (e.g., locked refrigerators and cabinets), they eat whatever they can access (Caldwell & Taylor, 1983; Taylor & Caldwell, 1985). Another reported characteristic, food stealing, might also be related to the restrictive food environment.

Other characteristics associated with PWS are short stature, self-picking and -scratching behaviors, and impaired respiratory functioning due to the obesity that results in decreased oxygen in the lungs. This results in lethargy, sleepiness, and potential heart failure. Aggression and temper tantrums are also reported characteristics, particularly in adolescence and related to food.

4.2 EVENT THAT MADE A DIFFERENCE

1982—Chromosome Deletion in Prader-Willi Syndrome Located

In 1982, primarily because of the availability of a new process called high-resolution chromosome analysis, Ledbetter et al. were able to identify a small deletion on the 15th chromosome (15q12.) This site has now been extended to 15q11–13. The new technique magnified the bands typically seen and opened up the possibility of locating chromosomal abnormalities not found using standard karyotypes. In 1982, not all laboratories had the technology for high-resolution analysis, although it is routinely available today.

Angelman Syndrome

As in Prader-Willi syndrome, Angelman syndrome (AS) is associated with a deletion of a portion of the long arm of chromosome 15 (15.11–13q-). As mentioned, it is now known that the deletion in AS is maternally related. Williams (2010) summarized the characteristics of AS. These include developmental delay, microcephaly, seizures, speech impairment, and problems with balance and gait. Physical characteristics include a wide mouth, light skin and eyes, a protruding tongue, and a flat back of the head. Behaviorally, they commonly display oral behaviors such as tongue thrusting and excessive drooling. One unique characteristic frequently associated with AS is an unusually happy demeanor including apparently inappropriate laughing and excitable behavior such as hand flapping. Clarke and Marston (2000) found that inappropriate laughter was found in slightly more than half of the 73 individuals with AS whom they studied. Williams (2010) also reported that the laughter was heightened when adults talked to, touched, or made eye contact with the individuals with AS. Another unique characteristic is an unusual preoccupation with water and water-related activities. Ishmael, Begleiter, and Butler (2002) reported a case study of a child with AS who drowned in a shallow wading pool and warned about the need to be vigilant in this area.

Reflection

If you were a parent of a child with Prader-Willi syndrome, would you use a locked food environment? Why or why not?

DISORDERS WITH MULTIPLE OR UNKNOWN CAUSES

The previously discussed disorders have a known genetic or chromosomal cause. There are other disorders that result in CIDs for which the etiology is either unknown, or can be attributed to a variety of causes. Examples of conditions that have multiple etiologies include hydrocephaly, macrocephaly, and microcephaly, all considered cranial disorders. In fact, several of the disorders of known causes result in these conditions. An example of a disorder that has an unknown cause is Sturge-Weber syndrome.

Hydrocephaly

Hydrocephaly is sometimes incorrectly called "water on the brain." It is actually a buildup of cerebrospinal fluid (CSF) in the brain that results in an enlarged head. Ordinarily, CSF flows through the brain and the spinal cord and is then absorbed into the circulatory system. When the absorption of the CSF is blocked for some reason, it creates pressure on the brain, and subsequent destruction of brain tissue and cells. If left untreated, it can result in serious brain damage, CIDs, and ultimately death.

Hydrocephaly is associated with certain disorders such as neurofibromatosis. It can actually be caused by a number of factors, including maternal infections, trauma, structural defects, and tumors. One major cause is spina bifida, a neural tube defect that can result in a portion of the spinal cord protruding through an opening in the lower back forming a sac called a myelomeningecele.

Fortunately, there is an effective treatment for hydrocephaly involving the use of a **shunt.** This procedure involves placing a small tube under the skin that allows the CSF to bypass the normal circulatory system and channel it to other areas such as the abdominal cavity where it can be absorbed. Another available technique is called **endoscopic ventriculostomy,** in which a tiny hole is made in the ventricle of the brain and a small camera (endoscope) is inserted to view the obstruction and to allow the normal flow of CSF. It is considered a more permanent solution than the use of a shunt. Although hydrocephaly can be treated, it is important to find its cause and address any other associated medical issues.

Macrocephaly

Macrocephaly refers to a larger head than is expected for the age and sex of an individual. Technically, hydrocephaly is one cause of macrocephaly. A large head, in and of itself, is not necessarily associated with a medical condition and/or CIDs. However, it is typically a sign that there might be an identifiable cause. Two techniques that are used to investigate the possible cause of macrocephaly (as well as other cranial disorders) are magnetic resonance imaging (MRI) and computed tomography scanning (CT scanning). CT scanning is used if the involvement of the bone (skull) is suspected.

Microcephaly

Microcephaly refers to a condition in which the circumference of the head is smaller than average for a given age and sex. Similar to macrocephaly, microcephaly can occur from a variety of causes and is not necessarily associated with a medical condition or CIDs. For example, a child who is small stature and has a family history of small stature might technically have microcephaly.

As discussed, disorders such as Cri-du-Chat and Wolf-Hirshhorn frequently result in microcephaly. There is no treatment although it is important to determine if there is a specific cause that needs to be treated. These include medical disorders and maternal infections during pregnancy. Many of these causes are discussed in the next chapter.

Sturge-Weber Syndrome

To date, there is no known cause for Sturge-Weber syndrome. Its primary identifying characteristic is a purplish facial mark (called a port wine stain) that usually involves one upper eyelid and the forehead, cheek, nose, and upper lip that is caused by the overabundance of capillaries under the skin. Other characteristics are seizures that become more frequent with age, tumors, and CIDs. Hemiparesis (weakening or loss of function on one side of the body) is also found.

Reflection

Why is the phrase "water on the brain" inappropriate when used to describe individuals with hydrocephaly?

GENETIC TESTING AND GENETIC COUNSELING

With increased sophistication of diagnostic procedures, and more information about the genetic basis of many disorders, we now have more information with which to make important decisions. Several techniques are used to help determine the health status of an unborn child. For example, **alpha fetoprotein testing,** which involves a simple blood test, can be used to identify abnormal levels that have been associated with disorders such as spina bifida and Down syndrome. Also, **Bart's Test** can be used (see Box).

BART'S TEST

Bart's Test, so named after St. Bartholomew's Hospital in London where it was first used, is also referred to as the Triple test. In addition to measuring the alpha fetoprotein levels in the mother's blood, it also measures two hormones—oestriol and human chorionic gonadotropin. Abnormal levels of these hormones have also been associated with fetal problems.

Amniocentesis involves the extraction of a small amount of amniotic fluid surrounding the fetus. It is done in conjunction with ultrasound to avoid touching the fetus or the placenta. This amniotic fluid, containing fetal cells, is subsequently analyzed microscopically after a chemical treatment. This procedure does have some risks, including infection and miscarriage, which occurs in approximately 0.5%–1% of the procedures. This risk must be weighed against the information that is provided. Yet another procedure is **chorionic villus testing,** in which a small sample of placental tissue (chorionic villi) is analyzed. Similar to amniocentesis, ultrasound is used to determine fetal position. This procedure can be done earlier than amniocentesis (approximately 10–11 weeks versus 16–18 weeks) but also has a somewhat greater risk of miscarriage.

Other procedures have been developed to identify chromosomal abnormalities not detectable from a standard karyotype. One example is the **FISH technique** (Flourescent In Situ Hybridization) or chromosome painting, which results in a literal color coding of DNA sequences in the chromosomes. Another technique is **assay comparative genomic hybridization (ACGH)** that detects copy number variations (alterations of the DNA of the genome that result in the cell having an abnormal number of copies of one or more sections of DNA). Yet another technique designed to detect copy number variations is **multiplex ligation-dependent probe amplification (MLPA).**

All the above procedures are designed to give parents information about the status of their unborn child. There are other procedures, however, that can be used to provide information *prior* to pregnancy. One of these is called **carrier testing,** designed to determine whether or not parents are carriers of specific disorders. In addition, a detailed family history might provide important information for prospective parents.

The information obtained from these and other procedures is helpful in providing genetic counseling to parents and prospective parents. This includes several different facets, such as interpreting medical information, presenting probabilities of having children with a given disorder, helping them to understand the alternatives to dealing with any risks, and providing psychological and emotional support regarding decisions that are ultimately made. The role of a genetic counselor is *not* to make recommendations to parents about what they should do; rather, it is more of a nondirective role that provides information and support.

Reflection

What do you think the role of a genetic counselor should be?

SUMMARY CHECKLIST
Role of Genes and Chromosomes
- ➤ **Zygote—A single fertilized cell**
- ➤ **Somatic cell—A body cell**
- ➤ **Germ cell—A sex cell**

    ✓ Cell structure—Includes a cell membrane that surrounds the cell material (cytoplasm). The nucleus in the center of the cell houses the chromosomes

➢ **Deoxyribonucleic Acid (DNA)—Contains blueprint of life; includes phosphates, sugars, and bases**

➢ **Human Genome Project—A 10-year project that was designed to identify the exact chromosomal location of all human genes**

    ✓ There are 23 pairs of chromosomes that include all of the human genes involved in heredity

➢ **Autosomes—The first 22 pair of chromosomes**

➢ **Sex chromosomes—The 23rd pair of chromosomes; females have an XX combination, males have an XY**

➢ **Karyotype—A magnified picture of the 23 pairs of chromosomes**

➢ **Meiosis—Cell division within the sex cells**

➢ **Mitosis—Cell division in which chromosomes duplicate themselves before dividing**

Autosomal Genetic Disorders

➢ **Alleles—Genes that produce different characteristics; an offspring inherits a specific allele from each parent**

➢ **Homozygous—When an offspring inherits the same allele from both parents**

➢ **Heterozygous—When an offspring inherits a different allele from each parent**

➢ Genetic inheritance—Can occur from a single gene or from multiple genes (quantitative trait loci)

➢ **Multifactorial transmission—Interaction between genetic and environmental factors**

➢ Autosomal Dominant Disorder—When an offspring inherits a disorder if either parent has the allele for that disorder

➢ **Nonpenetrance—A rare occurrence when an offspring does not inherit a dominant disorder**

➢ **Punnett Square—A method to show various genetic combinations of offspring of parents with known allele pairs**

    ✓ Tuberous Sclerosis—An autosomal dominant disorder in which the gene responsible for inhibiting the growth of tumors is nonworking. Results in tumors in the organs, including the brain; CIDs may or may not be present and the degree of symptoms vary from person to person.

    ✓ Neurofibromatosis—An autosomal dominant disorder involving growth of tumors in the peripheral nervous system and the central nervous system. There are two types: NF1 and NF2. NF1 leads to physical malformation; CID may or may not be present and the degree of symptoms vary from person to person.

➢ **Autosomal Recessive Disorder—When an offspring inherits a disorder only when both parents have the allele for the disorder**

➢ **Inborn errors of metabolism—Autosomal recessive disorders involving a missing enzyme that normally metabolizes certain substances**

✓ Galactosemia—Autosomal recessive disorder resulting in the inability to break down the sugar galactose. Buildup of galactose can cause brain damage and organ failure. Individuals should avoid foods containing lactose and galactose.

✓ Hurler syndrome—Autosomal recessive disorder resulting in the inability to break down complex carbohydrates called mucopolysaccharides. Results in distinctive physical features and severe CIDs; death usually occurs by early teenage years.

✓ Maple Syrup Urine Disease—Autosomal recessive disorder resulting in the inability to metabolize the amino acids leucine, isoleucine, and valine. Urine has a distinctive sweet smell like maple syrup. If untreated, it results in brain damage. A diet is used that restricts those amino acids.

✓ Tay Sachs Disease—Autosomal recessive disorder found primarily in the Ashkenazi Jewish population. It is caused by the lack of an enzyme that breaks down a specific lipid, which accumulates in the brain. Serious complications result and death usually occurs at an early age.

✓ Phenylketonuria—An autosomal recessive disorder in which an enzyme is not available to metabolize the amino acid phenylalanine. PKU can be detected in the first week of life using routine blood screening. A diet is used to avoid the specific amino acid.

Sex-linked Disorders

✓ Those involving the 23rd pair of chromosomes (usually the X chromosome)

➢ **Lyonization—The process when only one X chromosome is randomly activated and the other one inactivated**

 ✓ Fragile X Syndrome—The FMR-1 gene on the X chromosome fails to produce a protein that results in CIDs. It is more prevalent in males than females and males generally have more severe characteristics. It is the most common form of an inherited CID.

 ✓ Lesch-Nyhan Disorder—Associated with a gene on the X chromosome that results in self-injurious behavior, aggression, and CIDs

 ✓ Rett Disorder– A dominant neurodevelopmental disorder involving the X chromosome that results in decelerated head growth, loss of motor and language skills, and CIDs. Occurs almost exclusively in females.

Chromosomal Abnormalities

Disorders related to the number of chromosomes—Usually occurs when there are 47 chromosomes (trisomy) rather than the normal 46; less frequently there are 45 chromosomes (monosomy)

➢ **Nondisjunction—The failure of a chromosome to divide during meiosis. It results in three chromosomes going to one daughter cell and only one chromosome going to the other daughter cell.**

➢ **Translocation—An exchange of materials between two chromosomes or the fusion of a portion of one chromosome to a similar portion of another chromosome**

➢ **Mosaicism—A situation in which some cells have 46 chromosomes and some have 47**

    ✓ Down syndrome—Most common biological cause of CIDs. It is most often caused by an extra 21st chromosome. The syndrome is associated with distinctive facial features, frequent heart and other health problems, and mild to moderate CIDs.

    ✓ Edwards syndrome—Caused by an extra 18th chromosome. It results in microcephaly (small head), health problems, and severe CIDs.

    ✓ Patau syndrome—Caused by an extra 13th chromosome. Involves numerous physical malformations and very severe CIDs resulting in an early death.

    ✓ Klinefelter syndrome—Occurs when a male has an additional X chromosome (usually an XXY combination). Not all will have CIDs; many have language-based and communication problems.

    ✓ XYY male—Sensationalized condition that was once associated with criminal behavior

    ✓ Turner syndrome—Occurs when a female has a missing X chromosome (XO). Not all will have CIDs.

    ✓ Pentasomy X—Three extra X chromosomes resulting in an XXXXX combination. In general, the more X chromosomes the more severe the CID will be.

Disorders related to the structure of the chromosomes—When the basic structure of the chromosome is altered

➢ **Deletion—When a large or small portion of the chromosome is missing**
➢ **Centromere—The area on a chromosome that separates the long arm (q) and the short arm (p)**
➢ **Interstitial—When a deletion occurs toward the middle of the chromosome**

    ✓ Wolf-Hirshhorn syndrome—Due to partial deletion of the short arm of the 4th chromosome; usually results in microcephaly and significant CIDs

    ✓ Cri-du-Chat—Literally, the cat's cry syndrome, named after characteristic high-pitch cry; due to partial deletion of the 5th chromosome. It usually results in microcephaly and significant CIDs.

    ✓ Williams syndrome—Deletion on the 7th chromosome that results in "elfin-like" facial characteristics. CIDs with relative strengths in language and interpersonal skills are involved.

    ✓ Jacobsen syndrome—Partial deletion of the long arm of the 11th chromosome. Results in slow growth and physical abnormalities in addition to CIDs.

    ✓ Prader-Willi syndrome—Partial deletion of the long arm of the 15th chromosome; characteristics include short stature, insatiable appetite and obesity, and varying degrees of cognitive problems; PWS is paternally inherited

➢ **Genome imprinting—When an allele has a different effect on an offspring based on the sex of the parent from whom it came**

    ✓ Angelman syndrome—Associated with the same portion of the 15th chromosome as PWS but is maternally inherited. Characteristics include microcephaly, seizures, and CIDs as well as behavior problems. Two unique characteristics are inappropriate laughter and preoccupation with water.

Disorders with Multiple or Unknown Causes

- ✓ Some disorders are known to have multiple causes or are presumed to have a biological cause that is not identified.
- ✓ Hydrocephalus—Buildup of cerebrospinal fluid in the brain resulting in an enlarged head
- ➤ **Shunt and endoscopic ventriculostomy—Two procedures used to divert the cerebrospinal fluid away from the brain in hydrocephaly.**
  - ✓ Macrocephaly—A larger head than is expected for age and sex; has multiple causes
  - ✓ Microcephaly—A smaller head than is expected for age and sex; has multiple causes
  - ✓ Sturge-Weber syndrome—Characteristics include a facial port wine stain, seizures, and CIDs

Genetic Testing and Genetic Counseling

- ➤ **Alpha fetoprotein screening—A maternal blood test looking for abnormal amounts of alpha fetoprotein that is associated with certain disorders**
- ➤ **Bart's Test—A maternal blood test that screens for the presence of abnormal amounts of two maternal hormones in addition to alpha fetoprotein**
- ➤ **Amniocentesis—A procedure in which a small amount of amniotic fluid is extracted; the fetal cells in the fluid are analyzed**
- ➤ **Chorionic villus sampling—A procedure in which a small amount of placental tissue is extracted; the fetal cells in the tissue are analyzed**
- ➤ **FISH technique—Fluorescent in situ hybridization; technique to assist in detecting subtle chromosomal problems**
- ➤ **Multiplex ligation-dependent probe amplification (MLPA) and assay comparative genomic hybridization (ACGH)—Techniques used to detect copy number variations (alterations of DNA resulting in abnormal number of copies of one or more sections of DNA)**
- ➤ **Carrier testing—Used to determine if parents are carriers for a given disorder**
- ➤ **Genetic counseling—Interpreting medical information and providing support for parents; informing parents of probabilities of having a child with a given disorder**

ADDITIONAL SUGGESTION/RESOURCES

Discussion Questions

1. What are autosomal dominant and recessive disorders? Demonstrate the chances of two carrier parents having a child that has the disorder or is the carrier of the disorder.
2. List and define the various types of problems (e.g., nondisjunction) that can result in the abnormal number or structure of a chromosome.
3. Down syndrome and Fragile X syndrome are the two chromosomal and genetic disorders that result in the greatest number of cases of CIDs. Discuss the causes for each of these syndromes. Why are more males than females affected by Fragile X syndrome?

Activities

1. Research the Internet for information about the Human Genome Project (see "E-sources" for an example of one such website). Develop a concept map of important discoveries.
2. Check your local community about the availability of genetic counseling services. Contact an agency to determine what services are available that provide information and parent support (see "E-sources" for a mechanism to help you).
3. Most syndromes and disorders have related organizations that provide information about the syndrome and are vehicles for parent input and parent support. Develop a directory of websites of these organizations for future use (see "E-sources" for an example).

E-sources

www.ornl.gov/hgmis

This site, furnished by the Department of Energy, provides a very thorough description of the Human Genome Project and includes links to information on research, education, medicine, and ethical, legal, and social issues. It provides access to the original papers published in *Nature* and *Science*. It also describes the DOE's newest project called the Genomic Science Program.

www.nads.org/

This is the website for the National Association for Down Syndrome, an organization founded by parents in 1961. In addition to a description about the organization and its history and goals, there are links to information about DS in general, and teens and adults with DS as well as links for available resources, and news and events. There's also information for new parents of a baby with DS, support for grandparents, and a discussion forum.

www.nsgc.org/

This is the website for the National Society of Genetic Counselors, Inc. It describes the organization and provides links to frequently asked questions, publications, how to become a genetic counselor, and a Resourcelink that allows you to find a genetic counselor in your area.

NOTE

1. The acronym CID is used for cognitive/intellectual disability and CIDs is used for the plural cognitive/intellectual disabilities.

5

ENVIRONMENTAL AND PSYCHOSOCIAL CAUSES

Key Points

- ➤ PRENATAL CAUSES—A variety of factors that occur during pregnancy, such as infections and radiation, are discussed.
- ➤ PERINATAL CAUSES—A variety of factors that occur during or shortly after the birthing process such as anoxia, prematurity, metabolic disorders, and birthing problems are examined.
- ➤ POSTNATAL CAUSES—A variety of factors that occur after birth including serious illnesses, poisoning, malnutrition, and injuries that increase the risk of CIDs are reviewed.
- ➤ SOCIAL CORRELATES—These correlates include factors such as poverty, low maternal educational levels, and the language environment that do not directly cause CIDs, but are known to increase the risk of CIDs.
- ➤ PSYCHOLOGICAL CORRELATES—These correlates include factors such as child-rearing practices, abuse and neglect that are known or suspected to increase the risk of CIDs.
- ➤ PREVENTIVE MEASURES—Primary, secondary, and tertiary measures for prevention or mediation of CIDs are available.

There are myriad causes of CIDs. Many cases are of biological origin, although in the majority of cases the cause is unknown. Instead, developmental delays are noted until a child eventually shows significant delays in many or all developmental areas (Shapiro & Batshaw, 2013). Many individuals who are eventually diagnosed with CIDs are presumed to have had at least the potential for typical growth and development that was subsequently disrupted by factors occurring pre-, peri-, or postnatally. These factors may be environmental (e.g., due to drug or alcohol abuse by the mother during pregnancy), due to social correlates (e.g., risks associated with living in poverty such as malnutrition), or due to psychological correlates (e.g., abuse and neglect). Estimates vary as to the number of individuals with CIDs whose disability is preventable, but many of the causes discussed in this chapter might at least be mediated. These causes may result in various degrees of CIDs producing individual characteristics that may influence the support needs an individual might eventually have in order to live as independently as possible (AAIDD, 2012). In many instances, these causes may result in no CID at all, or they result in other developmental disabilities (e.g., cerebral palsy, autism). Simon (2010) noted that mapping cognitive functions and their underlying substrate in the atypically developing brain is a challenge and researchers in neurocognitive functioning of individuals with CID face explaining not only how behavior and abilities may differ from typically developing peers, but also why they differ. Because precise biological origins are not easily identified in many cases, the category of CIDs could be viewed as a socially defined disability as much as a scientific/medical one (AAIDD, 2010).

The impact of the factors discussed in this chapter is perhaps less predictable than the impact of those discussed in Chapter 4. We discuss environmental pre-, peri-, and postnatal causes, then social correlates and psychological correlates. We also discuss some preventive measures.

Research Box 5.1 highlights an historical reference textbook that provides insight into the medical perspectives on the causes and nature of CIDs that emerged by the mid-20th century. Notably, there are many fewer references to social and psychological correlates than one would typically expect in a modern textbook.

5.1 RESEARCH THAT MADE A DIFFERENCE

Tredgold, R. F., & Soddy, K. (1956). *A handbook of mental deficiency*. Baltimore: Williams & Wilkins.

This text, written by two English physicians and based on compilations by Tredgold's father, Dr. A. F. Tredgold, represents an early effort at comprehensively examining CIDs. Dr. A. F. Tredgold had single-handedly compiled seven previous editions, the first being in 1908. This landmark series of texts provide international and historical perspectives on CIDs. It should be noted that CID was not the terminology used in this particular time period as suggested in the title of the book.

Environmental causes may be subdivided into those that occur prenatally (during pregnancy), perinatally (during the birth process), and postnatally (following birth). In general, the younger a child is the greater the impact of some of these factors may be. For example, malnutrition may have a more serious effect on a 6-week-old child than it might have on a 12-year-old child. Also, keeping the AAIDD definition in mind, our discussion of postnatal factors will be restricted to those occurring during the developmental period (up to age 18). Finally, although some factors (e.g., trauma to the brain) may functionally affect a person's cognitive or intellectual abilities, these factors may be associated with disabilities that are not classified as CIDs (e.g., head injury). We should distinguish here between two types of brain injury: (1) traumatic brain injury affecting an individual who has already experienced typical development, and (2) the type of brain injury that affects the onset of typical development and thus is considered a cause of CIDs.

PRENATAL CAUSES

Teratogens

Teratogens are any agents that cause a defect in a developing embryo/fetus (National Institutes of Health, http://ghr.nlm.nih.gov). These include infections, radiation, maternal malnutrition, and low birth weight (see Table 5.1). Other prenatal risk factors can include maternal age, lack of prenatal care, maternal health problems, and drug and substance abuse during pregnancy. These factors may be associated with an increased risk of developmental difficulties, but they do not necessarily lead to CIDs. This distinction is important because the presence of one or more of the prenatal factors may have significant effects on a child, or in some cases, have no discernible effect at all. These factors may lead to the development of CIDs or may at least create conditions in which CIDs may develop. As noted earlier, the causes of CIDs are not known directly in most instances of students with milder CIDs but are more often known in students with more severe CIDs.

Infections

Common infections that may lead to CIDs include toxoplasmosis, rubella, cytomegalovirus, and sexually transmitted infections. These infections may have different effects depending on when they occur during pregnancy.

Toxoplasmosis is an infection that may be carried in raw meat and cat feces (Best & Heller, 2009). It may be congenital or acquired but is most dangerous if acquired during pregnancy. The congenital infection is associated with eye and retina conditions, cerebral palsy, hydrocephaly, microcephaly, disturbances in psychomotor development, seizures, feeding difficulties, and CIDs in untreated children. There are treatments available at birth that may reduce or eliminate cognitive and neurologic effects but the research in this area is still limited (Best & Heller, 2009).

Rubella, or German measles, especially when contracted by the mother during the first trimester of pregnancy, is associated with increased risks for CIDs and other issues for the newborn including eye problems, deafness, irritability, small head size, seizures, and heart defects, among others (U.S. National Library of Medicine, 2011b). The infant contracts the rubella infection through the placenta; therefore the mother's immunization prior to pregnancy or avoidance of exposure to infected others is the best prevention (U.S. National Library of Medicine, 2011b). Since the 1960s, immunization of the population has dramatically reduced the number of cases of congenital rubella.

Sexually Transmitted Infections

Cytomegalovirus may lead to symptoms in about 1 in 10 infants who are exposed prenatally but up to 90% of infants displaying symptoms at birth will have neurological disorders (U.S. National Library of Medicine, 2011a). This virus is in the herpes virus group that also includes Epstein-Barr virus, herpes simplex virus, and varicella-zoster virus (which causes chicken pox and shingles) (Widerstrom & Nickel, 1997). Symptoms in the fetus may include enlarged liver or spleen, microcephaly, deafness, and other health issues. This virus, which is very common in the environment, may have the most likelihood of causing neurological damage in infants (U.S. National Library of Medicine, 2011a).

Syphilis is a venereal disease that when contracted by the mother can cross the placenta and infect the fetus resulting in nearly half of all infected newborns dying at or shortly after birth (U.S. National Library of Medicine, 2012b). It is treatable through administering antibiotics but an increase in the number of pregnant women with syphilis has led to an increase in infected children. If it goes untreated, the child may fail to thrive and/or exhibit a host of health-related problems that can result in neurologic disorders, facial deformities, and sensory disabilities (U.S. National Library of Medicine, 2012b).

HIV infection in pregnant women may be passed to the child and lead to future neurological damage (Merck Manual, 2003). The number of children across the globe who have contracted HIV is now at epidemic proportions (Best & Heller, 2009). In the United States, children are at greater risk of contracting HIV in utero when they live in poverty (Best & Heller, 2009).

Other sexually transmitted infections are myriad and include chlamydia, genital herpes—discussed under perinatal causes—gonorrhea, hepatitis B, and human papillomavirus (more commonly known as HPV) among others. Sexually transmitted diseases can cause premature labor and uterus infection after birth. Some are passed on to the unborn child crossing through the placenta or during delivery as the baby passes through the birth canal. Low birth weight, brain damage, sensory impairments, and health-impairing conditions are among the possible harmful outcomes to the child (U.S. Department of Health and Human Services, 2009).

According to the World Health Organization (2011b), sexually transmitted infections rank in the top five disease categories for which adults seek care in developing countries. The impact on pregnancies and neonates is staggering. Up to 25% of pregnancies associated with untreated early syphilis result in stillbirth and another 14% in neonatal death. Up to 35% of women with untreated gonorrhea will experience spontaneous abortions and premature deliveries (World Health Organization, 2011b). Although there are no specific statistics for the prevalence of intellectual disabilities, clearly these statistics indicate there is serious threat to the health, development, and well-being of children in developing countries in particular from sexually transmitted infections.

Radiation

Radiation was associated with birth defects following research conducted with survivors of the Hiroshima and Nagasaki atomic bombings (Graham & Morgan, 1997). Problems have also been found in fetuses of women who received significantly less exposure such as medical radiation, particularly if occurring during weeks 2 to 18 of pregnancy (Centers for Disease Control and Prevention, 2011). Although there can be effects from exposure of the fetus to radiation at later gestational periods, high rates of brain damage occur during this 2- to 18-week gestational period (Centers for Disease Control and Prevention, 2011).

Maternal Malnutrition During Pregnancy

Malnutrition may have detrimental effects both pre- and postnatally. Malnutrition, in combination with environmental deprivation after birth, may be the most common cause of CIDs in the world (Merck Manual, 2003). It is a major concern in developing countries where famine and hunger are more common (Merck Manual, 2003). Abu-Saad and Fraser (2010) stressed that maternal malnutrition may have at least three major adverse birth effects including low birth weight, preterm birth, and intrauterine growth restriction. In turn these birth outcomes can lead to neonatal death, short- and long-term health problems, chronic disease later in life, and disabilities.

Low birth weight is an established risk factor highly associated with poor nutrition and inadequate maternal weight gain during pregnancy (Widerstrom & Nickel, 1997). Low birth weight (which can be defined as weight below 2,500 grams) is associated with neonatal death, particularly in developing countries (Abu-Saad & Fraser, 2010). In developed and developing countries, low birth weight is strongly associated with an increased risk of long-term disability (Abu-Saad & Fraser, 2010). Similarly, intrauterine growth restriction outcomes include increased risks for neurologic disorders, learning disabilities, psychiatric disorders, and CIDs (Abu-Saad & Fraser, 2010). Horvath et al. (1993) stressed that malnutrition before and after birth can result in as much as a 40%–60% reduction in brain cells and that these individuals may never catch up to the levels of well-nourished peers. Although many variables confound research with humans (e.g., environmental factors such as infection and poverty associated with malnourishment), animal studies have demonstrated that prenatal malnourishment affects cognitive performance, emotional reactivity, and social interactions (Abu-Saad & Fraser, 2010). We will discuss nutrition and poverty and its effect on children later in the section of this chapter devoted to postnatal causes of CIDs. Several factors may be interrelated and their effects individually may be more difficult to investigate than the overall constellation of variables, especially those associated with living in poverty (Abu-Saad & Fraser, 2010).

Other Factors Affecting Prenatal Development

Some factors affect prenatal development that are not teratogens and can have varied effects on birth outcomes. Maternal age, for example, may or may not have any adverse effects. Heavy alcohol consumption during pregnancy is very likely to lead to adverse effects.

Maternal and Paternal Age

Maternal age is related to higher risk of medical problems in newborns and infants. Mothers at either extreme of child-bearing age (e.g., below 20 years of age or above 40 years of age) are associated with greater risk of birth defects (Gill, Broussard, Devine, Green, Rasmussen, & Reefhuis, 2012). Also, younger mothers are more likely to give birth prematurely (Widerstrom & Nickel, 1997). Robison and Gonzalez (1999) stressed that children born prematurely are at risk for delays in cognition, motor development, behavior, and language. Also, as discussed in Chapter 3, both maternal and paternal age has also come into focus as a possible risk factor for conditions such as Down syndrome. Yang, Wen, Leader, Chen, Lipson, and Walker (2007) found that there is an association with birth defects in general, and Down syndrome and other chromosomal disorders, in children born to fathers of advancing age (above 29 years of age). However, the association to paternal age was weaker than that of advancing maternal age (Yang et al., 2007).

Lack of Prenatal Care

Lack of prenatal care is another factor potentially affecting child outcomes. Widerstrom and Nickel (1997) suggested that inadequate prenatal care increases risk of prematurity and low birth weight as well as premature rupture of amniotic membranes (PROM). The American Congress of Obstetricians and Gynecologists (ACOG) (2012) noted U.S. infant mortality remains at nearly 7 deaths within the first year of life per 1,000. The ACOG also stressed that prenatal care is the primary means for identifying and treating problems affecting pregnancy and birth. In 2008, premature births occurred in 1 of 8 births in the United States. Preterm birth is the leading cause of newborn death and disability in the United States (ACOG, 2012).

Maternal health problems are also associated with increased risk for birth defects and subsequent developmental delays (Widerstrom & Nickel, 1997). The Centers for Disease Control and Prevention (CDC) (2012) noted that medication intake, obesity, poorly controlled diabetes, and alcohol and illegal drug exposure can lead to birth defects. About 1 in every 33 babies is born with a birth defect (CDC, 2012).

Drug and substance abuse during pregnancy represent major risk factors for embryos and fetuses. The March of Dimes (2008) estimated that 4% of pregnant women in the United States use illicit drugs during pregnancy. Exposure to drugs such as Ecstasy, methamphetamine and other amphetamines may result in reduced head circumference, low birth weight, and learning problems. Learning problems may result from in utero exposure to heroin. Other drugs (e.g., PCP) may lead to withdrawal symptoms and learning or behavioral problems in children exposed in utero (March of Dimes, 2008).

Alcohol consumption can disrupt fetal development at any stage of development, including in the earliest stages when a woman may not know she is pregnant (National Institute on Alcohol Abuse and Alcoholism, 2012). Fetal Alcohol Spectrum Disorders (FASD) include Fetal Alcohol Syndrome (FAS) (the most serious disorder), Partial Fetal Alcohol Syndrome, Alcohol-Related Birth Defects, and Alcohol-Related Neurodevelopmental Disorder. FAS may result in facial abnormalities, growth deficits both prenatally and after birth, central nervous system disorders, small brains, and other problems. FAS results from heavy drinking during pregnancy, which could be defined as consuming four or more drinks per occasion. However, smaller amounts of alcohol can also lead to the other disorders listed. Partial FAS includes most of the symptoms associated with FAS. The other disorders in the spectrum can also lead to physical abnormalities, learning and memory problems, problems in attention, understanding and following directions,

Table 5.1 Prenatal Causes for Risk of Developing Disabilities

Teratogens	Other Factors
Infections	Maternal and paternal age
Radiation	Lack of prenatal care
Maternal malnutrition	Maternal health problems
Low birth weight	Drug and substance abuse

communicating and socializing, among other issues (National Institute on Alcohol Abuse and Alcoholism, 2012). Research also suggests that children may be more significantly affected if their mothers drank and also lived in poor conditions, were of lower socioeconomic status, and experienced higher levels of stress (National Institute on Alcohol Abuse and Alcoholism, 2012).

Finally, nicotine exposure in utero can also result in premature birth, greater likelihood of a miscarriage, early detachment of the placenta, and certain birth defects such as cleft palate or cleft lip (Centers for Disease Control and Prevention, 2013). Although smoking is not directly linked to CIDs, it is worth noting that premature birth is a known risk factor for developmental delays.

Not all factors discussed are direct causes of intellectual disabilities and as noted, the direct cause is more frequently not known than known. It is probably most important to remember that as the factors discussed occur in combination, the result is an increase in fetal risk. In fact, many fetuses do experience exposure to multiple factors (e.g., nicotine and alcohol exposure in addition to poor prenatal care and low birth weight and/or premature birth). In addition to the myriad prenatal factors, there is also a variety of perinatal factors. Table 5.1 includes a summary of various prenatal causes.

Reflection

How might lifestyle choices of pregnant women affect the outcomes of their offspring? What might be some ways exposure to prenatal factors might be avoided?

PERINATAL CAUSES

Among perinatal factors are asphyxia, prematurity, low birth weight, respiratory problems, hemorrhages, jaundice, metabolic problems such as hypoglycemia, seizures, and congenital anomalies. Birthing itself can also present risk factors including multiple births, abnormal presentation, and prolapsed umbilical cord. Prematurity and low birth weight have been discussed in the previous section but will also be discussed here as they are two of the more common factors.

Anoxia and Asphyxia

Anoxia refers to a lack of oxygen to tissues which can lead to damage or death. **Asphyxia** also refers to a lack of oxygen but is generally more sudden and severe than anoxia. Lack of sufficient oxygen may become noticeable when there is a low Apgar score. Gaitatzes, Chang, and Baumgart (2013) stated that the Apgar score is derived from five measures including the newborn's color/appearance, heart rate, respirations, reflex irritability when stimulated, and muscle tone at rest. These are reflected in assessing the child's activity (a = muscle tone), pulse (p), grimace (g = reflex irritability), appearance (a = color/appearance), and respiration (r). Each measure is assigned a value from 0–2 depending on the condition of the newborn. The total score can range from 0–10 and is taken at 1 minute and 5 minutes after birth but may also be taken at 10 and 15 minutes if complications are present. Apgar scores are most useful in helping health care professionals discuss opinions of the newborn's condition and are not necessarily indicative of long-term outcomes (Gaitatzes et al., 2013). However, if a child experiences serious lack of oxygen, risk for disabilities is present.

Hypoxic Ischemic Encephalopathy (HIE) is the result of both inadequate oxygen and blood circulation to the brain (Gaitatzes et al., 2013). Newborns with HIE will display symptoms such as abnormal neurological functioning, decreased activity level, poor sucking and feeding, respiratory issues, unstable body temperature, and seizures. Children with severe cases of HIE have a higher risk of CIDs by 1–2 years of age (Gaitatzes et al., 2013).

Prematurity

As previously discussed, prematurity is a significant risk factor. Rais-Bahrami and Short (2013) stated that premature birth occurs at or before 36 weeks gestation. There are differences in physical appearance of premature infants from full-term infants, but perhaps more important are the neurological and behavioral differences. The preterm infant may display low muscle tone, behavioral passivity, and neurological disorganization. About 13% of births worldwide are premature and nearly one-half of that 13% result in neonatal neurodevelopmental disabilities (e.g., cerebral palsy) (Rais-Bahrami & Short, 2013). Also, preterm births occur twice as often in African-Americans as in Caucasians. Additionally, premature birth may lead to respiratory distress syndrome, the need for supplemental oxygen, hemorrhage in the brain, brain damage due to low oxygen or low blood flow, increased risk of hearing loss, and apnea, among other issues (Rais-Bahrami & Short, 2013).

Low Birth Weight

Low birth weight is perhaps the most "universal" risk factor because so many variables may precipitate it. It is also closely associated with preterm birth but not necessarily. Low birth weight can be defined as below 2,500 grams (5.5 pounds). Very low birth weight occurs at 1,500 grams (3.33 pounds) and extreme low birth weight less than 1,000 grams (2.25 pounds). Small for gestational age occurs when either a premature or full-term infant falls below the 10th percentile for birth weights at a particular gestational age (Rais-Bahrami & Short, 2013). Low birth weight is frequently the result of malnutrition as the result of intrauterine growth restriction. This may occur due to maternal illness, smoking, alcohol consumption, infections, malnutrition, and in some chromosomal disorders (Rais-Bahrami & Short, 2013). Small for gestational age children are at risk for neonatal complications, long-term growth issues, and developmental disabilities. Low birth weight infants have a better survival rate now but this outcome also poses increased association with neurodevelopmental disabilities. By school age, children with birth weights below 1,500 grams are at increased risk for displaying developmental disabilities (Rais-Bahrami & Short, 2013).

Metabolic Disorders

Metabolic disorders lead to increased risk of disability, although these are often treatable and/or preventable. Metabolic disorders arise from a deficiency in one of the enzymes needed to catalyze an important biochemical reaction in the cells (Batshaw & Lanpher, 2013). The brain or other organs may be damaged as a result of this failure of biochemical cellular reaction. Batshaw and Lanpher (2013) noted there are three types of inborn errors of metabolism including:

- Silent disorders such as phenylketonuria and congenital hypothyroidism which may lead to developmental disabilities over time but are not evident for a relatively long period of time;
- Disorders presenting an acute metabolic crisis that cause episodic but life-threatening symptoms such as urea cycle disorders;
- Disorders leading to progressive neurological disability such as Tay Sachs disease that cause physical and/or neurological deterioration over time.

While silent disorders and those with acute symptoms are often treatable, there has been less progress overall with progressive disorders. In some progressive or untreated disorders, a toxic accumulation of compounds or insufficient synthesis may result in various disabilities with intellectual disabilities and cerebral palsy being more common (Batshaw & Lanpher, 2013).

Hypoglycemia

Hypoglycemia or low blood sugar occurs more commonly in infants born to diabetic mothers but can also occur in infants who are small for gestational age, have intrauterine growth restriction, asphyxia, or hypoxia (Gaitatzes et al., 2013). If untreated, hypoglycemia can lead to brain damage but is generally treatable (Gaitatzes et al., 2013). When treated, the prognosis is generally determined by the condition predisposing the hypoglycemia rather than the hypoglycemia itself.

Seizures

Seizures in neonates can be clinically present (e.g., stiffening and jerking movements of the arms and legs), present but subtle (e.g., lip smacking or tongue thrusting), or be present only as abnormalities on EEGs (Gaitatzes et al., 2013). Seizures may result from low blood calcium, low blood sugar, brain injury or hemorrhage, infections, and withdrawal symptoms as the result of maternal substance abuse. If the EEG pattern does not improve and becomes more abnormal, longer-term neurological issues are at increased risk. Antiepileptic drugs may be prescribed but their use with neonates is an area of debate (Gaitatzes et al., 2013).

Congenital Anomalies/Defects

Congenital anomalies/defects may lead to a number of the conditions discussed here such as hemorrhage, hypoglycemia, and infection that may result in CIDs. Hydrocephaly is caused by excess cerebro-spinal fluid leading to brain damage. Hydrocephaly is treatable through surgery to implant shunts to divert the excess fluid to another part of the body (Yaun, Keating, & Gropman, 2013). Hydrocephaly is considered a neural tube defect as is anencephaly. In anencephaly, there is severe congenital malformation of the head and brain with no neural development above the brainstem (Liptak, 2013). Microcephaly (abnormally small head and brain size) also leads to CIDs.

Birthing Problems

Birthing problems may also lead to increased risk. Problems during delivery present additional risks and include abnormal presentation and prolapsed umbilical cord. In a small number of pregnancies, the infant presents in breech position or face first. Typically, these do not present a significant risk when identified and caesarean section delivery is performed. However, the child could have his or her oxygen supply compromised, which increases risk for other problems. Table 5.2 includes a summary of perinatal causes of CIDs.

To this point, we have discussed conditions that are generally of a physiological nature that may lead to increased risk of disability. These conditions may persist into the postnatal period. Additionally, a number of other factors associated with the postnatal period may increase a child's risk. We will distinguish between psychosocial correlates (e.g., abuse and neglect, low parental educational levels) and postnatal factors, although many authors may treat these within the same discussion.

Reflection

Worldwide, what is the impact of pre- and perinatal factors on newborns compared to the United States? How severe are the impacts in developing countries?

Table 5.2 Perinatal Causes for Risk of Developing Disabilities

Asphyxia	Prematurity	Low Birth Weight
Inborn Errors of Metabolism	Seizures	Congenital Anomalies
Birthing Problems		

POSTNATAL CAUSES

For our discussion, postnatal factors and causes will include quality of attachment, serious illnesses, poisoning, postnatal malnutrition, and accidental injuries. Again, premature birth and low birth weight place the child at risk for conditions that persist in the postnatal period that may eventually lead to developmental disabilities. Shapiro and Batshaw (2013) suggested postnatal environmental influences may affect the expression of a neurological problem, although less than half of students with milder CIDs have identifiable causes. CID prevalence tends to peak at 10–14 years of age, suggesting in many instances there may be an interaction of factors affecting growth and development (Shapiro & Batshaw, 2013).

Quality of Attachment

Quality of attachment refers to the degree to which the parents and infant develop a reciprocal relationship resulting in quality and mutually satisfying interactions. This postnatal factor differs from others discussed in this section in that it could be included later as a social correlate. However, many variables, including the child's physical status (e.g., severe physical disabilities, lengthy stays in the hospital), affect growth and development such that it is not clearly always an issue related to the social aspects of the environment.

As infants display typical newborn behaviors, parents in turn respond to the child resulting in increased interaction and mutual reinforcement. When disabilities are present (e.g., cerebral palsy), the interactions may be more challenging for parents and infants. But, other factors less obvious may affect the quality of attachment, including depression in parents, abuse and neglect, temperament, personality, level of parenting skills, social network support, the quality of a marriage, and even the ways in which families solve problems and conduct their daily routines (Martin, Brady, & Kotarba, 1992). Zajicek-Farber (2013) noted that parents with a child with a disability may experience:

- Intellectual stresses as they are required to integrate information about the child's disability, treatment, and potential effects;
- Instrumental stresses such as financing the child's needs, handling insurance issues, and managing the labor requirements for the child and other family functions;
- Emotional stresses such as handling the uncertainty of the situation and the child's future, transitions of the child (e.g., from home to school age, elementary to middle school), possible behavior problems, and isolation from others in their community.

Parental depression may also be present and can affect the quality of the attachment to the child. Depression is not unusual following a diagnosis of disability and may result in parental anger, assignment of blame, or disagreement over decisions that need to be made (Martin et al., 1992; Zajicek-Farber, 2013).

Serious Illnesses

Serious illnesses are a threat to typical development in infants and toddlers as well as to fetuses in utero. Two serious illnesses causing infection are encephalitis and meningitis. Encephalitis is a postnatal inflammation of the brain that may be caused by a variety of infectious agents (e.g., measles, pneumonia, rubella, chicken pox). CIDs may develop as the result of high and extended fever. The most common infectious agent is from herpes simplex (discussed earlier) (Baroff, 1999). Effects may be immediate or delayed for up to several years (Horvath et al., 1993).

A CURRENT EVENT

Sentinel chickens may sound like an odd term, but they serve an important function. Chickens may contract infectious agents carried by mosquitoes. In the United States and other nations, these chickens' blood is periodically checked for the presence of an infectious virus that may lead to encephalitis. Results of tests are often posted on local or regional government websites. The chickens do not typically get sick from the viruses and are subjected only to a minor pinprick type of blood drawing. In some instances, the chickens are "retired" after a period of time and returned to a farm or similar living environment.

Meningitis is an inflammation of the meninges or lining membrane of the brain and may actually occur pre-, peri-, or postnatally. Meningitis may be caused by viruses or bacteria and can result in CIDs as well as hearing loss, seizures, neuromotor problems, and speech impairments (Horvath et al., 1993).

Poisoning

Under prenatal causes of CIDs, we discussed intrauterine exposure to alcohol, cocaine, and other drugs that might affect the fetus. Following birth, poisoning by lead or mercury are concerns.

Lead is present from many sources particularly older house paints (before 1978), toys and furniture painted before 1976, toys and other items from outside the United States, and even from lead soldering in older pipes, among other sources (U.S. National Library of Medicine, 2013a). Typically, lead poisoning builds up slowly over time from repeated exposure. However, even low levels of lead exposure can affect a child's mental development. Complications from lead poisoning include behavior and attention problems, school failure, hearing problems, slowed body growth, and diminished IQ (U.S. National Library of Medicine, 2013a).

Mercury can also affect the central nervous system if ingested. It is most dangerous to unborn children but can cause brain and nervous system damage postnatally. Most often, it is ingested by eating meat from animals fed with seed grain preserved with mercury or by eating fish from waters contaminated with mercury (U.S. National Library of Medicine, 2012a). The symptoms of severe exposure to mercury are similar to the symptoms of cerebral palsy. Unfortunately, once damage has occurred, it is irreversible. While some are concerned about mercury being included in some vaccines, research indicates that childhood vaccines do not increase mercury to dangerous levels (U.S. National Library of Medicine, 2012a).

Malnutrition

Malnutrition is most devastating in its effects prenatally, but can also have substantial effects in the postnatal period. Lack of adequate nutrition may result from neglect or from living in impoverished circumstances. Maternal and child nutrition are both more prevalent in low- and middle-income countries (Black et al., 2008). Black et al. (2008) reported that about 35% of childhood deaths and 11% of global disease could be attributed to nutrition-related factors. Malnutrition effects can be reversed in many cases through an improved diet and treatment. However, severe childhood malnutrition or starvation can result in permanent physical disabilities as well as CIDs. Malnutrition may emerge in underdeveloped or developed countries. It may be present as the result of poverty, natural disasters, political upheavals, and war (U.S. National Library of Medicine, 2011c).

Injuries

Injuries may lead to CIDs. Horvath et al. (1993) noted that the two main causes are abuse (which we will discuss in a later section) and accidents, both of which are preventable. Blows to the head, penetrations of bone or foreign objects into the brain, cerebral edema (swelling), hematoma (blood accumulations), and thrombosis (clots or obstruction) may also cause brain damage (Horvath et al., 1993). However, traumatic brain injury (TBI) is a separate category under IDEA and particularly older children and adolescents may not be diagnosed as having CIDs but be diagnosed with TBI. Postnatally and through the developmental period (birth to 18 years of age) there are a number of factors that may affect growth and ultimately lead to identification of CIDs. Generally, these factors are thought of as preventable causes and factors that are amenable to early intervention, preschool, and school-age services. Also, to this point we have focused on environmental factors that may have identifiable organic outcomes such as brain damage. See Table 5.3 for a summary of postnatal causes. In the following section, we will also discuss factors that are presumed to cause CIDs but whose impact on the individual are more difficult to assess in a direct manner.

Reflection

Can you think of recent events in the United States or worldwide that may have led to malnutrition and/or starvation? Were these primarily natural disasters or man-made events (poverty, political upheaval, war)?

Table 5.3 Postnatal Causes for Risk of Developing Disabilities

Quality of attachment	Illnesses	Poisoning	Malnutrition	Injuries

PSYCHOSOCIAL FACTORS

Despite advances in understanding the human genome, genetics "clearly cannot explain the cause of [CIDs] in every case. Individuals with perfectly normal DNA still develop . . ." CIDs ". . . as the result of child abuse or extreme social deprivation" (AAIDD, 2010, p. 59). Social and/or psychological factors are not mutually exclusive; as noted earlier, other authors have categorized these factors in some other, although similar, manner. For example, the AAIDD (2010) includes social factors, behavioral factors, and educational factors (as well as biomedical factors, many of which we have discussed already).

Social correlates include socioeconomic status that includes prenatal care, poverty, and nutrition, which have been discussed also in prior sections. Other social correlates include maternal educational level and the language environment. Psychological correlates include child-rearing practices, abuse and neglect, and violence.

The term *correlates* is a useful one. The impact of these factors on human development must often be inferred rather than directly measured. These factors are often associated with or correlated with measures related to cognitive, social, motoric, and language development and school achievement. It is important to understand that many psychosocial factors may be identified in early life, but their impact is often presumed to emerge over time and in many cases not be evident until the child enters a more formal educational setting when the child's developmental progress is compared to that of peers.

Social Correlates

Social correlates to the child's environment that affect the development of disabilities include socioeconomic status, family interactions, parental absence, and parental educational level. Similar to many risk factors, these do not *necessarily* lead to CIDs. As the number of risk factors increases, however, the risk for disability also increases. It is also important to understand that these factors are amenable to mediation in many instances, and it is widely believed that at least some cases of CIDs associated with psychosocial risk factors may be preventable. AAIDD (2010) stressed that some factors may be considered intergenerational. That is, that individual and family supports can be used to prevent or reduce the effects of such social factors. Many social correlates are associated with one another. For example, children born to mothers of low socioeconomic status are at greater risk for poor prenatal and postnatal care and therefore at greater risk for development of disabilities. Although we discuss factors somewhat independently of one another, they often co-exist and their effects may be compounded accordingly.

In times past, the view of intergenerational factors and co-existing factors as "preventable" led to what today we would consider rather disturbing viewpoints as evidenced in Event Box 5.1.

5.1 EVENT THAT MADE A DIFFERENCE

1927—*Buck v. Bell* U.S. Supreme Court Case

Carrie Buck was a 17-year old-girl committed in 1924 to the Virginia Colony for Epileptics and Feebleminded. Her mother had been committed three years earlier. Carrie was pregnant, unmarried, and gave birth at the institution to a daughter. In the minds of officials, the daughter represented a third generation of imbeciles. State officials petitioned to sterilize Carrie under a Virginia statute enacted that same year. Eventually, the case reached the U.S. Supreme Court, and Justice Oliver Wendell Holmes offered his opinion:

"We have seen more than once that the public welfare may call upon the best citizens for their lives. It would be strange if it could not call upon those who already sap the strength of the state for these lesser sacrifices . . . to prevent our being swamped with incompetence. It is better for all the world, if instead of waiting to execute degenerate offspring for crime, or to let them starve for their imbecility, society can prevent those who are manifestly unfit from continuing their kind. The principle that sustains compulsory vaccination is broad enough to cover cutting Fallopian tubes. . . . Three generations of imbeciles are enough." Justice Holmes went on to state:

"this reasoning . . . fails when it is confined to the small number who are in the institutions named and not applied to the multitude" (Trent, 1994; pp. 198–199).

While we might be shocked by such opinions today, the politics of how society should best address problems associated with poverty, recurring disabilities in families, young unwed mothers, and the means to support these individuals has hardly disappeared. It was not so long ago the term *cultural, familial retardation* was commonly used to describe this phenomenon.

Low Socioeconomic Status

Low socioeconomic status (SES) is a risk factor for a multitude of developmental problems including CIDs. Historically, research examining the associations between poverty and disability suggest that 68% of students in special education live in households with incomes below $25,000 compared to 39% in the general population (Birenbaum, 2002). Although cause-effect relationships have not been established, studies also suggest that as poverty increases in the population, so does the number of children with disabilities (Birenbaum, 2002). We noted earlier in this chapter that low SES is also associated with low or no prenatal care (Child Trends Data Bank, 2012), reduced nutrition (Black et al., 2008), and increased substance abuse (National Institute on Alcohol Abuse and Alcoholism , 2012). Clearly, low SES might also contribute to poor health care in general, which may increase risk for infections and disease as well as undiagnosed chronic conditions (e.g., metabolic disorders) that can lead to development of CIDs. Similarly, low SES may lead to fewer educational services that can contribute to poor developmental outcomes. Low SES may be associated with all of these factors, but as Ramey and Ramey (1992) noted, "the actual developmental quality of the home environment can differ dramatically even among poverty-level families" (p. 337).

Low Parental Intelligence and Educational Level

Low maternal intelligence and educational level, in particular, have been linked to poor cognitive and behavioral outcomes for offspring. This association has been studied for a number of years. Feldman and Walton-Allen (1997) studied the impact of low maternal IQ and poverty on children with mothers with or without mild CIDs. These researchers found that children whose mothers had mild CIDs had lower intelligence quotients and academic achievement, and more behavior problems than children with mothers without mild CIDs, even when poverty was present for both groups. Also, the quality of the home environment and maternal social supports were lower for the group with mild CIDs. These authors suggested that being raised by a mother with mild CIDs could have effects not attributable to poverty alone (Feldman & Walton-Allen, 1997). Ramey and Ramey (1992), in their discussion of effective early intervention services, noted that the mother's level of tested intelligence was a strong predictor of risk for delayed development at age 3, although early intervention could mediate this risk. Kelley, Morisset, Barnard, and Patterson (1996) suggested that the provision of learning opportunities, responsive caregiving, and children's intelligence were interrelated with the mother's intelligence. These same authors noted that there is some debate as to whether poor outcomes might not also have some biological origins aside from the environmental factors.

More recently, Chapman, Scott, and Stanton-Chapman (2008) found that low maternal education resulted in the highest risk for a child having CIDs across a large population. Low maternal educational level, again, across a population and not for any given individual family, indicated higher risk than low birth weight. This association between maternal education and the risk of having a child with CIDs held across all levels of CIDs including those with profound levels of disability. However, it should also be noted that low maternal education is also associated with low SES and health care (Chapman et al. 2008). These same authors suggested that there may be some genetic link, but also prenatally, low maternal education may also be associated with certain risk factors. We have noted that illicit drug use and alcohol consumption during pregnancy may occur more frequently in women of low SES status, as well as poor prenatal and postnatal health care, poor nutrition, and poor living environments.

Farber (1968) discussed a classic study by Skeels and Dye concerning the role of maternal intelligence and educational level and the risks for CIDs. A portion of his discussion is summarized in Research Box 5.2.

5.2 RESEARCH THAT MADE A DIFFERENCE

Skeels, H. M., & Dye, H. B. (1939). A study of the effects of differential stimulation on mentally retarded children. *Proceedings of the American Association of Mental Deficiency, 44,* pp. 114–136.

Despite what we may think of as the risks associated with being raised by a mother with CIDs, one early research study used mothers with CIDs as caregivers. Skeels and Dye identified 13 children with CIDs, aged 7 to 30 months, who they moved from an orphanage to an institution for people with CIDs.

Older girls with disabilities were assigned as caregivers for one baby each. After 2 years, these children had a median increase in IQ of about 27 points with a range of 7–58 points change over a pretest. Twelve children with somewhat higher intelligence scores remained in the orphanage where not much attention was provided. Two years later, these children's intelligence scores had decreased by a median of 26 points. Further follow-up across the years indicated the children given care by the females in the institution were all self-supporting as adults and had completed a median of 12 years of school. Outcomes for the children left in the orphanage were substantially poorer (Farber, 1968). Although the ethics involved in this early research would be questionable today, it served as an early indicator that caregivers with low maternal intelligence and education might be adequately trained to affect intellectual growth and future adjustment in those for whom they cared. It also served to illustrate that environmental factors could influence IQ apart from genetic inheritance.

Language Environment

Language is critical in the development of young children. Tredgold and Soddy (1956) noted that speech and language impairments and delays were common among individuals with CIDs. Such delays and impairments have been evident for years. It is useful to distinguish between speech impairments and language delays or impairments. That is, one may be capable of producing speech but still have difficulty in generating, transmitting, and understanding linguistic communications. Much of our early learning is dependent on verbal mediation by caregivers (Baroff, 1999), which parents with CIDs may be less well equipped to provide. Ramey and Ramey (1992) stressed that children need a rich and responsive language environment, regardless of parental level of intelligence. They noted how important it is to "have adults provide a predictable and comprehensible communication environment, in which language is used to convey information, provide social rewards, and encourage learning of new materials and skills" (p. 343). Language is the most important early influence on the child and the communication environment may be enhanced by written materials (Ramey & Ramey, 1992).

In a study in the Netherlands, van der Schuit, Peters, Segers, van Balkom, and Verhoeven (2009) found that the home language environment of children with CIDs was different from chronological age peers without CIDs. Children with CIDs had "fewer experiences with reading, writing and drawing materials, and showed less interest in storybook reading activities. . . . During storybook reading sessions, they were less involved in story, picture and word orientation activities" (p. 1031). These same authors noted, however, that parents adapted their home language activities in part because of child variables such as cognitive and speech disabilities. Therefore, it may be that there is an interaction effect between the language development environment that families provide and the language responsiveness and initiation of activities of children with CIDs (van der Schuit et al., 2009). Also, in another study, results suggested that children with CIDs at ages 4 and 5 years were developing vocabulary at a level in pace with their mental levels, but were still significantly behind peers without disabilities in phonological working memory and syntax (van der Schuit, Segers, van Balkom, & Verhoeven, 2011).

Social factors or correlates are not clearly distinguishable from the psychological factors or correlates that follow, although it is helpful for discussion purposes to separate them. Again, these factors should be considered as ones that frequently occur in combination with one another and whose cumulative effects increase the risks for developmental disabilities.

Reflection

To what extent does society have an obligation to mediate or reduce the effects of the social correlates of CIDs? What might be the costs to society (e.g., taxation, service provision) and possible benefits (e.g., reduced needs for special education and related services; more positive school and adult outcomes)?

PSYCHOLOGICAL CORRELATES

Psychological correlates are primarily associated with the home environment (other than the language environment). These include family interactions, and abuse and neglect.

Family Interactions

Despite what one might assume given the stressors of having a child with a disability, families of children with disabilities are often quite functional, productive, happy, and well-adjusted (Martin et al., 1992). However, stress can emerge in caregivers and affect family interactions (Guralnick, 2005). Hassall, Rose, and McDonald (2005) found that when stress did occur in mothers of children with CIDs, it was more clearly associated with child behavioral issues than the child's abilities or skill levels. Stronger social support was also associated with lower levels of parental stress. The perceived helpfulness of the support received appeared more important than the range or number of supports. Martin et al. (1992) noted that many predictors of stress (e.g., severity of disability) played less of a role as a family stressor than the repetitive and mundane chores and daily routines—particularly when families lacked active problem-solving strategies to deal with basic life events.

In general, parents experienced lower stress levels when they had higher levels of parenting self-esteem and a stronger sense of internal locus of control (Hassall et al., 2005). Also, Emerson, Hatton, Llewellyn, Blacker and Graham (2006) suggested that SES was a major factor in parental stress and might, at least in part, account for an orientation that having a child with CIDs means a life of stress.

Guralnick noted that it is altogether possible that various stressors (need for information, need for financial and other resources, need to reevaluate family goals and routines, and in combination) can have a negative impact on family interactions at some point in time. Therefore, early identification of these stressors and intervention to ameliorate or reduce their effects should be part of a comprehensive approach to working with families (Guralnick, 2005). In the "Quality of Attachment" section included under "Postnatal Causes," you may also find a discussion of parent-child interactions.

Abuse and Neglect

Abuse and neglect occur in populations with and without CIDs. Historically, it has been known that infants who are abused or maltreated are less likely to form secure attachments and this pattern of maladaptation may continue leading to delayed development (Widerstrom & Nickel, 1997). Abuse may be physical, sexual, or emotional. Abuse (e.g., severe shaking of an infant) can result in injury which may affect a child's development and adjustment. Abuse can lead to a number of other possible conditions including anxiety disorders, depression, substance abuse, aggression, and a cycle of abuse that is carried on in succeeding generations. According to the Merck Manual (2012), child maltreatment in general affects males and females equally and more often involves both abuse and neglect. Maltreatment is associated with several contributing factors. Parental personality features may stem from lack of affection or warmth in childhood and abuse in their own childhood. Such parents may have unrealistic expectations of children to provide the affection the parent lacked in his or her own childhood. Loss of impulse control and frustration may occur. Drug and alcohol abuse may contribute to or cause loss of control. Children who are irritable or place greater demands on parents (including those with developmental or physical disabilities) may provoke anger or lead to less resilient emotional ties between parent and child. Isolated parents and those without support systems may feel greater stress. Physical abuse, emotional abuse, and neglect are associated with low SES and living in poverty, while sexual abuse risks increase in those with several caregivers or a caregiver who has multiple sex partners (Merck Manual, 2012). Neglect may occur by itself but often in conjunction with abuse. Neglect is more often seen among families with physical, psychological, or substance abuse problems and especially when mental disorders are present in parents (Merck Manual, 2012). The lack of physical care and/or injuries incurred from abuse can lead to retardation of growth physically, psychologically, and emotionally. Children who are born with disabilities may also create greater stress in parents and families, increasing the risk for abuse or neglect. Parents of children with CIDs need support services. Parent advocacy services and support groups are generally available in most urban and suburban areas. The E-sources at the end of this chapter include websites of support groups available to parents. Table 5.4 includes a summary of psychosocial factors.

We have discussed a variety of factors, both environmental and psychosocial, that may place a fetus, infant, or child at risk for developing CIDs. Such discussions may lead the reader to wonder how such problems may ever be overcome or mediated. In

Table 5.4 Psychosocial Factors Associated with Risk of Developing Disabilities

Social Correlates	Psychological Correlates
Low socioeconomic status	Family interactions
Nutrition and poverty	Abuse and neglect
Low maternal intelligence and educational level	
Language environment	

fact, it is important to remember that CIDs are relatively uncommon despite the many risk factors. Over time, measures have been developed to alleviate or reduce the risk of developing CIDs when such factors are present. As discussed in Chapter 4, there are a variety of procedures for fetal diagnosis of risks or existing disabilities as well as tests for metabolic disorders. In the earlier discussion in this chapter, we addressed preventive measures related to pre-, peri-, and postnatal causes (e.g., examination of Apgar scores, treatment for metabolic disorders). Next, we will focus on additional measures to prevent or reduce the risk of developing CIDs.

Reflection

What are child-rearing practices that enhance development as well as deter development?

PREVENTIVE MEASURES

For some time, professionals have agreed that CIDs are, at least in some cases, preventable. For example, Coulter (1992) addressed the need for an ecological approach to the prevention of CIDs. He stated:

> This new vision of prevention has two separate but related components: (a) an ecological understanding of the interaction between individuals and their environment, and (b) an ecological understanding of how risk factors from multiple dimensions (biomedical, social, behavioral, and educational) interact across generations to result in [CIDs]. . . . This approach will include greater attention to environmental variables that are critical modifiers of the impact of intellectual limitations on personal functioning. (p. 365)

An ecological approach that addresses those factors that arise during gestation, at birth, and immediately after birth should be used. More recently, AAIDD (2010) indicated prevention supports can be primary, secondary, or tertiary (as discussed earlier in this chapter). Additionally, AAIDD also identified how prevention supports can be conceived and developed.

Primary Prevention

Primary prevention strategies are those that actually prevent the development of a disease or condition itself (AAIDD, 2010). These could involve good prenatal and health care. Good prenatal care is probably the most fundamental preventive measure. There is considerable evidence that malnutrition during gestation, premature birth, and low birth weight are all significant risk factors. Also, substance abuse and the presence of infectious diseases are other factors that may be avoided or mediated by good prenatal care. Immunizations, safety precautions, and other strategies such as family planning, birth control, and genetic counseling are services to reduce the risk of children being born with or developing disabilities.

Secondary Prevention

Secondary prevention strategies are those that are used to prevent the emergence of disabilities when a condition exists that could lead to such (AAIDD, 2010). Good neonatal care is critical in reducing the risks of developing disabilities. Historically, it has been demonstrated that more family-centered approaches to neonatal intensive care have increased collaboration between families and professionals. In such approaches, parents remain primary caregivers. Also, more information can be provided to parents in such programs. Parents can be referred to or children's developmental progress tracked through follow-up neonatal services as well (Widerstrom, 1997). Universal screening at birth for metabolic disorders (remember, these may exist but the disabilities resulting from lack of treatment can take some time to emerge), early developmental screening along with early intervention are examples of secondary strategies (AAIDD, 2010). Low birth weight and children born prematurely have been found to be more likely to need special education services and experience developmental delays. Follow along services to ensure these children are thriving and meeting developmental milestones is also important.

Once children are home, the challenges associated with raising a child who has disabilities or is at risk become apparent. For example, premature infants may be irritable, cry much of the time, have poor sleep-wake cycles, need frequent feedings and expensive formulas, and vomit frequently, and these events can be stressors on the family. Other stressors on families raising such children have been discussed earlier. Because support systems within families may be limited or inadequate, early intervention service systems may be a critical need.

Early intervention services are now mandated by the Individuals with Disabilities Education Act. Formal service systems (either home- or center-based) and informal service systems (e.g., respite care, parent groups, and counseling) alike may differ substantially in theoretical approaches to intervention and services provided. Still, there are some elements of early intervention programs that have been researched and supported by data. Following is a description of those elements, particularly as they relate to mothers who are disadvantaged, have low educational levels, and/or have cognitive difficulties themselves. Important studies in the area of early intervention and prevention of disability were discussed by Garber (1988) (see Research Box 5.3).

5.3 RESEARCH THAT MADE A DIFFERENCE

Garber, H.L. (1988). *The Milwaukee Project. Preventing mental retardation in children at risk.* Washington, DC: American Association on Mental Retardation.

Garber (1988) reported on the Milwaukee Project, which studied whether CIDs could be prevented in children at risk. Garber stated in his epilogue:

"The Milwaukee study results suggest that the environment is not effectively mediated by the low IQ, low verbal skilled mother and that impoverished psychosocial early microenvironment in the home she creates is a major factor associated with her offspring's declining IQ performance. Through early intervention, this effect can be mitigated, thus preventing IQ declines" (p. 403). The Milwaukee Project has had its critics concerning the conclusions drawn. Zigler and Hodapp (1986) noted that there have been very limited peer-reviewed publications concerning the Milwaukee Project (one example would be Heber & Garber, 1970).

Ramey and Ramey (1992) published an article reporting on results from the Carolina Abecedarian Project, Project CARE, and the Infant Health and Development Program. These authors and colleagues found evidence "to show that without early intervention, children of low-IQ mothers are particularly at-risk for poor intellectual outcomes and that such children respond very favorably to intensive, systematic early intervention" (p. 337). These studies, among others, indicated that psychosocial factors that affect the risk for developmental disabilities could be mediated. Ramey and Ramey (1992) provided a set of suggestions for "essential daily ingredients" in the lives of young children. These included:

- Encouragement of exploration;
- Mentoring in basic skills such as labeling, sorting, sequencing, comparing, and noting means-ends relations;
- Celebration of developmental advances;
- Guided rehearsal and extension of new skills;
- Protection from inappropriate disapproval, teasing, or punishment;
- Provision of a rich and responsive language environment.

Tertiary Prevention

Finally, tertiary strategies may reduce but not necessarily eliminate the effects of a disability on the individual's functioning in school, home, and community. Physical disabilities might be prevented through treatment and screening (e.g., using physical therapy to improve ambulation and avoid need for a power-chair). Behavioral supports that reduce problem behaviors and improve other skill areas (such as vocational skills) are another example. Similarly, educational and social strategies that increase inclusion and prevent isolation and reduced overall functioning are also tertiary strategies (AAIDD, 2010).

In combination, the use of primary, secondary, and tertiary strategies can be helpful in preventing disabilities altogether, preventing their emergence over time, or prevent the most negative impacts of the disabilities. When prevention strategies are conceived in this three-level supports system model, one can discern that prevention supports are likely to be needed for families and individuals before, during, and after birth, including across environments and the life span.

In this chapter, environmental and psychosocial factors affecting the risk for developing disabilities and CIDs have been discussed along with preventive measures. In the "Additional Suggestions/Resources" and "E-sources" sections, you will find ways for exploring these topics in greater depth.

Reflection

How effective do you think early educational intervention might be in preventing CIDs?

SUMMARY CHECKLIST

- ➤ **Environmental Factors**—May occur pre-, peri-, or postnatally
- **Prenatal Causes**—Those that occur prior to birth
- ➤ **Teratogens**—Any agents that may cause a defect in a developing fetus
  - ✓ **Infections**
  - ✓ *Toxoplasmosis*—An infection carried in raw meat and cat feces
  - ✓ *Rubella*—Or German measles is an infection particularly problematic if contracted in the first trimester of pregnancy
  - ✓ *Sexually transmitted infections*
  - ✓ *HIV infection*—May be passed from mother to child and lead to future neurological damage
  - ✓ *Radiation*—Was first associated with birth defects following the bombings of Hiroshima and Nagasaki, although medical radiation exposure has been found to cause problems in fetuses, especially at an early gestational age
  - ✓ *Malnutrition*—Is a major concern in developing countries
  - ✓ *Maternal malnutrition during pregnancy*—May affect children prenatally and, in combination with environmental deprivation after birth, may be the most common cause of CIDs in the world
  - ✓ *Low birth weight*—Is an established risk factor closely associated with poor nutrition and inadequate maternal weight gain during pregnancy or may lead to being small for gestational age
- ➤ **Other factors affecting prenatal development**—Include variables other than teratogens
  - ✓ *Maternal and paternal age*—Is related to higher risk of medical problems in newborns

✓ *Maternal age*—Is the more significant single factor increasing the likelihood of preterm delivery

✓ *Paternal age*—Is also a risk factor that is discussed more in-depth in Chapter 3

✓ *Lack of prenatal care*—Is critical to normal development but may be less adequate in African-American women, indigent women, teen mothers, single women, and women with a sexually transmitted disease

✓ *Maternal health problems*—Include endocrine, cardiovascular, and rheumatological disorders as well as anemia and may predispose an infant to preterm delivery and intrauterine growth retardation

✓ *Drug and substance abuse during pregnancy*—Represent major risk factors for fetuses with the prevalence increasing and the problem found in all socioeconomic strata and races

✓ *Methamphetamines, heroin, and PCP use*—All lead to increased risks of low birth weight and other conditions

✓ *Fetal Alcohol Syndrome*—Alcohol consumption during pregnancy leads to risk of low birth weight, developmental delay, a variety of other conditions as well as fetal alcohol effects and syndrome

✓ *Nicotine use*—Can lead to increased risk of miscarriage and low birth weight

Perinatal causes—Those that occur just prior to and during birth

➢ **Anoxia and Asphyxia**—Anoxia is a lack of oxygen to the brain that can lead to brain damage or death; asphyxia is generally more sudden and severe than anoxia

✓ Apgar scores are derived from measures of a newborn's heart rate, respiratory effort, muscle tone, gag reflex, and body color. Each measure receives a score from 0–2 and overall scores below 4 five minutes after birth are associated with increased risk of disability

✓ *Hypoxic Ischemic Encephalopathy*—Results from both inadequate oxygen and blood circulation to the brain

✓ *Prematurity*—Is defined as being born before 36 weeks' gestation and is a significant risk factor for a variety of conditions

✓ *Low birth weight*—Is a weight of less than 2,500 grams or 5½ pounds at birth and is associated with a variety of conditions; very low birth weight occurs at 1,500 grams and extremely low birth weight at less than 1,000 grams

✓ *Metabolic disorders*—Include hyperbilirubinemia or jaundice, which if untreated in the newborn can result in cerebral palsy and brain damage

✓ *Hypoglycemia*—Refers to low blood sugar and can lead to brain damage if untreated

✓ *Seizures*—May lead to brain damage

✓ *Congenital anomalies/defects*—Can lead to hemorrhages, hypoglycemia, and infection

✓ *Birthing problems*—Include risks associated with multiple births, abnormal presentation such as breech birth, and prolapsed umbilical cord

Postnatal factors—Those that occur just after birth and in the first few weeks of life

➢ **Quality of attachment**—Refers to the degree to which parents and an infant develop a mutually satisfying and reciprocal relationship

✓ *Serious illnesses*—Include encephalitis (an inflammation of the brain caused by infectious agents) and meningitis (an inflammation of the meninges or lining of the brain caused by viruses or bacteria)

✓ *Poisoning*—Can be caused by heavy metals such as lead or mercury, chemical agents such as cyanide, alcohol or barbiturates, or organic agents such as herbicides and fertilizers and can lead to brain damage

✓ *Malnutrition*—Is most devastating prenatally but can lead to a reduction in brain cells if experienced during critical brain growth periods

✓ *Injuries*—Abuse and neglect can both lead to blows to the head resulting in brain damage

Psychosocial factors—May be either social or psychological and associated with physical environment, language environment, and family interactions including abuse and neglect

➢ **Social Correlates**—Include socioeconomic status, low parental intelligence and educational level, family interactions, parental absence

✓ *Low socioeconomic status (SES)*—Is a common and serious risk factor especially in combination with other environmental factors

✓ Low SES alone creates stressors in families but may not alone account for subsequent developmental problems in children

✓ Low SES may affect overall family functioning, parental ability to cope, and access to good health care and educational services, which in turn may affect overall development

✓ *Low parental intelligence and educational level*—Have been researched extensively as risk factors

✓ *Low SES and health care*—May be associated factors that influence child outcomes as a result of low parental educational level

✓ The risk associated with these factors may be mediated through early intervention

✓ *Language environment*—A rich and responsive language environment where learning is verbally mediated and communication is encouraged are critical in development

➢ **Psychological Correlates**—Include family interactions and abuse and neglect

✓ *Family interactions*—Involve complex interaction among the family members and the environment, including level of supports available for families and parental stress

✓ *Abuse and neglect*—Abuse may be emotional, sexual, or physical while neglect occurs more frequently, although not exclusively, in abusive families

✓ *Abuse*—May lead to anxiety, depression, substance abuse, aggression, and a cycle of generational abuse

✓ *Abuse*—May stem from a variety of factors with parents such as drug and alcohol abuse and parents may have unrealistic expectations of children

✓ *Neglect*—Is associated with abuse and substance abuse as well as chronic depression in the mother

✓ *Children who are born with disabilities*—May create greater stress on families

➢ **Preventive measures**—Should involve an ecological approach that addresses a host of factors; these can be primary, secondary, or tertiary measures

➢ **Primary Prevention**—Strategies that actually prevent the development of a disease or condition

  ✓ *Good prenatal care*—Is probably the most fundamental preventive measure

  ✓ *Immunizations, safety precaution, family planning, and birth control*—Are other primary support measures to avoid disease or conditions

➢ **Secondary Prevention**—Strategies that are used to prevent the emergence of disabilities when a condition exists that could lead to disabilities

  ✓ *Universal screening at birth*—Can detect metabolic and other disorders

  ✓ *Follow along services*—Are often provided for infants with low birth weight or born prematurely

  ✓ *Early intervention services*—Can be home- or center-based and have been shown to be effective in preventing disabilities

➢ **Tertiary Prevention**—Strategies that may reduce but not eliminate the effects of a disability on an individual's functioning

  ✓ *Treatment of physical disabilities, behavioral supports, educational and social strategies*—Are examples of tertiary strategies that may lessen the effects of a disability

ADDITIONAL SUGGESTIONS/RESOURCES

Discussion Questions

1. Considering the number of possible causes of CIDs discussed, why do you think so few people actually have CIDs? How do variables in developing countries impact the occurrence of CIDs?

2. To what extent does society have an obligation and interest in taking care of its disadvantaged citizens, particularly children?

3. To what extent does society have a right to intervene in the lives of citizens "for their own best interests"?

Activities

1. Contact or visit the closest neonatal intensive care unit in your area. Devise a list of questions in advance related to what types of problems newborns in the NICU present typically, when are the problems diagnosed, how are they treated, and what types of follow-up assessment and services are available to children and their caretakers.

2. Contact or visit a local early intervention services provider. Devise a list of questions in advance related to what types of problems are present in families and children that need to be addressed. What are some of the outcomes experienced at school age and do such problems go unnoticed or untreated? Do you see evidence of the "essential daily ingredients" for young children listed by Ramey and Ramey (1992)?

3. Ask a mother what if any special precautions or instructions she may have received to ensure good prenatal care. Ask the mother if there was a specific

cause of disability or at-risk factor these precautions/instructions were designed to prevent. Investigate further good prenatal care regimens for pregnant women. Compile a list as a class and compare it to those offered by medical/obstetrical or other organizations.

E Sources

www.cec.sped.org

The official website of the Council for Exceptional Children. This website has a wide variety of information for current research and publications as well as access to various "divisions," including the Division on Autism and Developmental Disabilities. This website also includes links to information concerning the Individuals with Disabilities Education Act and information for exploring the area of early intervention services.

www.fpg.unc.edu

The official website of the Frank Porter Graham Child Development Institute at the University of North Carolina at Chapel Hill. Included are links to websites for ongoing and ended research projects, including the Carolina Abecedarian Project. This website provides information about the importance and impact of early intervention programs.

www.nih.gov

The National Institutes of Health website includes links to various institutes that focus on particular types of disorders and also provides a wealth of information on prevention, treatments, and characteristics of many disorders. The NIH also provides information on variables such as hunger, and neonatal care and how these may affect children.

Part Three
Characteristics of CIDs

6

COGNITIVE AND LEARNING CHARACTERISTICS

Key Points

➢ COGNITIVE CHARACTERISTICS—Piaget's and Vygotsky's developmental perspectives are discussed along with the meanings of cognitive delays and differences.

➢ LEARNING CHARACTERISTICS—Transfer/generalization of skills, use of learning strategies, and metacognitive skills are discussed.

➢ ATTENTION—Difficulties in attending to relevant versus irrelevant stimuli and maintaining attention over time are examined.

➢ MEMORY—Problems with working and short-term memory are more common while long-term memory tends to be better. Difficulties with retrieval of information are also discussed.

➢ SPEECH AND LANGUAGE—Language delays are common along with speech disorders. Augmentative and alternative communication systems are discussed.

In Chapters 6–8, characteristics of individuals with CIDs will be examined. As appropriate, differentiation in characteristics between those with milder levels (i.e., less in need of support) versus more severe levels (i.e., more in need of support) of CIDs will be made.

It is important to understand that one may perceive CIDs as a "single" condition, but given the definition, identification procedures, and various professionals' perspectives thereof, it should be apparent that the condition has myriad effects on people. Similarly, there are many potential causal factors associated with CIDs, also leading to diverse outcomes for individuals' characteristics. While this discussion describes many possible characteristics, they may or may not be apparent in any given person. It is best to learn and understand the possible characteristics, but bear in mind each of us is unique. It is also best to think of individuals with CIDs as persons first, rather than a compilation of characteristics associated with the condition. In other words, no one wants to be thought of as a typical or stereotypical example of a condition, but rather as an individual who should be given the resources and opportunity to grow and fulfill his/her chosen destiny. Also, AAIDD (2010) stresses that systems of supports to improve overall human functioning across environments, situations, skill areas, and the life span are individualized and constructed based on need rather than a particular level or cause of CIDs.

In this chapter, we will discuss characteristics related to cognition, learning, attention, memory, and speech and language. It is worthwhile at the outset to discuss briefly our use of the terms *delay* and *difference* in human development. Remember, CID is defined as a disability emerging in the developmental period. An individual with a developmental delay may exhibit or acquire much of the same knowledge and skills as an individual without CIDs but at a slower rate and/or at a later age. For example, a child with CIDs may begin to speak later than most children or take longer to develop more complex language skills even if he/she did begin speaking at a typical age. There is considerable variance among children as to when various skills and knowledge are acquired. So, a developmental delay must be viewed in this context. A developmental difference is when an individual displays behavior that is atypical of children or adolescents. For example, an individual may display "echolalia" at school age or as an adolescent (a pattern of speech in which the individual tends to repeat what others say to him or her). Again, however, a difference must be viewed within the developmental framework. Many children repeat what is said to them as they acquire speech and language skills. Most children ultimately lose this pattern and develop more adult-like language patterns (including most children with CIDs). A difference, then, may be a behavior that is typical at some point in human development but its persistence suggests challenges beyond delayed development. Delays and differences in development are evident within the population of individuals with CIDs, although both are not necessarily evident in any particular individual. As discussed in earlier chapters, an individual must display deficiencies in adaptive skills to be considered as potentially having CIDs under the AAIDD's definition (AAIDD, 2010). However, the AAIDD stresses that characteristics once considered permanent are malleable when the appropriate individualized supports are provided.

Cognitive and learning characteristics are discussed first as these may be considered the most prominent in assessing, identifying, and defining CIDs. Additionally, much of the seminal research in the area of characteristics of individuals with CIDs was conducted in the middle period (1950s–1970s) of the twentieth century. Therefore, some references in this chapter appear dated but do represent important and enduring work.

COGNITIVE CHARACTERISTICS

The AAIDD (2010) notes that intellectual functioning must be viewed within the context of several other dimensions, including (a) adaptive behavior (conceptual, social, and practical skills); (b) participation, interactions, and social roles; (c) health (physical and mental health and etiological factors); and (d) context (environments and culture). In other words, cognitive and other characteristics must be considered to be interactive and codependent on factors among these various dimensions.

To understand cognitive and learning characteristics of individuals with CIDs (and in turn delays and differences in cognitive development), it is first necessary to gain at least a rudimentary understanding of two major theories concerning cognitive development. These two theories were developed by Piaget and Vygotsky and are constructivist in orientation. That is, each theory emphasizes that an individual constructs, through increasingly complex cognitive functions, his/her understanding of the environment, events, and interactions with others, as well as his/her own thoughts and actions.

Piaget (1952) referred to schemas or frameworks within a child's mind by which he/she can organize and interpret the input received through the senses and experience. Children's schemas are altered through assimilation (when a child learns new skills and knowledge and integrates them into existing knowledge) and accommodation (when a child adjusts thoughts and actions based on new knowledge). Piaget also identified four major stages of cognitive development. These are outlined in Research Box 6.1. Children's schemas are evident based on their stage of development and continued growth toward the next stage.

6.1 RESEARCH THAT MADE A DIFFERENCE

Piaget, J. (1952). *The origins of intelligence in children.* **New York: International Universities Press.**

Piaget outlined four major stages of development with associated characteristics. Piaget also identified substages not discussed here.

Sensorimotor Stage (Birth to 2 years of age)

The child constructs meaning of the world through sensory experiences and physical actions. Infants progress (through assimilation) from reflexive behavior and more instinctual responses toward the beginning of symbolic thinking by age 2 (e.g., words representing real objects and actions).

Preoperational Stage (2 to 7 years of age)

The child progresses in representational use of words and actions that reflect increasingly symbolic thinking. For example, the child begins to demonstrate understanding that objects can be represented in their absence, distinguishes between his/her own and others' perspectives, and wants answers to his/her questions. Children tend to be egocentric and intuitive in their thinking (they "know" but don't know how they "know" and yet are confident in their knowing).

Concrete Operational Stage (7 to 11 years)

The child reasons logically about events which are "concrete" (e.g., a child recognizes that the same amount of water is in two glasses even though one is tall and thin and the other glass is short and wide). These are operational thoughts. That is, the child realizes actions and mental representations can be reversible although abstract thinking can still be problematic. Children are able to classify objects and understand concrete relationships among objects.

Formal Operational Stage (11–15 years)

The child/adolescent (through assimilation and accommodation) is able to think more abstractly, idealistically, and logically and beyond concrete events.

Additional Source: O'Donnell, A.M., Reeve, J., & Smith, J.K. (2007). *Educational psychology: Reflection for action.* Hoboken, NJ: Wiley and Sons.

Santrock (2001) noted that critics of Piaget point out that the stages do not necessarily correspond to the emergence of skills in children. Some may occur earlier or later than Piaget suggested. Critics suggest that the stages are not as synchronous as suggested and that children are not in a particular stage but are developing skills/ knowledge from different stages at different times. Also, some suggest children can be taught to perform behaviors one would expect of children at a later stage. Finally, Santrock noted that culture and education might have greater influence on development than Piaget originally conceived. This last concept is important in understanding why Vygotsky's theories of cognitive development have been popular.

Vygotsky placed considerable emphasis on social and cultural processes in the development of the individual's mental functioning (O'Donnell et al., 2007). Mediation, often through language and discourse, is the means by which cognitive functions are modified and altered. Mediation occurs within social, historical, and cultural contexts (Daniels, 2001). Mediation (guidance and assistance) should occur within the child's **zone of proximal development.** Santrock (2001) defined this zone as the "range of tasks that are too difficult for children to master alone but that can be learned with guidance and assistance from adults or more skilled children" (p. 60). **Scaffolding** is the process of altering the level of guidance and assistance given as a child becomes increasingly effective and efficient at various skills and mental functions. Hence, dynamic assessment and the revision of the level of mediation based on a child's level of development are important processes in teaching and learning in Vygotsky's theory (Daniels, 2001).

Although other theories concerning cognitive development have been posited, Piaget's and Vygotsky's theories are widely accepted in Western culture and society (with various modifications and criticisms as already noted). These theories are relevant to our discussion in several ways. First, we have discussed the idea that cognitive development may be delayed or different. One needs a frame of reference to understand each of these potential difficulties. Second, deficits in cognitive development are an integral part of what defines CIDs so understanding what represents typical development and the processes that affect human development is useful. Finally, these theories (and others, e.g., behaviorism) help us to understand how individuals learn and develop, providing some basis for understanding the educational process by which characteristics may be established or altered. As early as the 1960s, researchers were exploring how Piaget's theories of human development might provide insight into studies related to individuals with CIDs (e.g., see Woodward, 1963). Next follows a discussion of those characteristics of individuals with CIDs that tend to indicate delays or differences in cognitive development.

Cognitive Delays

Cognitive delays are evident in individuals with CIDs. However, when we examine the concepts of delays and differences we must also consider what CIDs are. Some would argue that individuals with mild CIDs primarily display cognitive delays but not differences. Historically, Zigler (1969a) stated that the developmental delay position suggests that "if you equate on a cognitive level, there should be no differences in cognitive functioning associated with IQ" (p. 541). That is, if you compare the performance of individuals with CIDs to those of individuals of a similar mental age (not necessarily chronological age), you should obtain similar results between the two groups. Zigler further elaborated noting that, "The difference or defect position states that even when individuals are equated on general cognitive level, there would be differences in cognitive performance associated with IQ" (p. 541). Proponents of the idea that milder levels of CIDs are primarily characterized by cognitive delays would suggest that the "condition" becomes apparent when an individual has problems adapting to an environment or situation (thus displaying difficulties with adaptive behavior). In other situations in which adjustment is achieved, others may have no perception of delayed or different development. These same proponents might suggest that individuals with milder levels of CIDs learn and think in much the same way as those without CIDs, although their cognitive functions may be less efficient and sophisticated. The inefficiency or lack of sophistication is evident at some times and not at others. For example, an individual may be considered as perfectly typical within the context of the child's neighborhood, playing games and interacting with other children. This same child may display delays in learning in school when the demands for reading increase in amount and complexity. This perspective is evident in the current views of the AAIDD (2010).

However, as Zigler (1969a) suggested, others contend that cognitive differences are more evident and those differences are relatively stable (see Research Box 6.2). That is, delays may be more evident at particular times or in particular contexts than others, but individuals with CIDs will be affected in adaptation and adjustment in a variety of areas (e.g., learning, language development, self-sufficiency) as well as a variety of contexts (e.g., at school, in the community, at home), and those difficulties will maintain over time. The proponents of the idea that delays are more evident than differences in cognitive development might then argue that such children could go through Piaget's stages of development in a predictable manner but more slowly and perhaps these children would not achieve as high a level of abstract, idealistic, or logical reasoning as an individual without disabilities.

Those who might argue that *differences in cognitive development* are more evident could suggest that individuals with CIDs assimilate, accommodate, and learn differently than others. Such differences may be more evident in individuals with severe levels of CIDs or with specific etiologies. For example, problems in genetic inheritance, malnutrition, drug abuse during pregnancy, brain infections, and exposure to toxins may affect brain growth and development and the way in which the brain functions. One might be characterized as having a difference in cognitive development when the stages that typically occur in individuals without CIDs are not evident or the skills and knowledge developed in a stage are substantially reduced or the synchronicity (order of stages) is altered even in the presence of adequate mediation and support. For example, a child may not display verbal skills at all or may not attain the ability to associate letters with sounds, numbers with objects, or understand the passage of time across a day, week, or year. Still, this same child could have developed normal gross and fine motor skills for everyday life.

6.2 RESEARCH THAT MADE A DIFFERENCE

Zigler, E. (1969b). Development vs. difference theories of mental retardation and the problem of motivation. In E. Zigler & D. Balla (Eds.), *Mental retardation: The developmental difference controversy* (pp. 163–188). Hillsdale, NJ: Erlbaum.

In this chapter, Zigler examined the theories that individuals with CIDs experience primarily delays in development versus the theory that intellectual deficits create differences in the skills and attainment of individuals with CIDs compared to those without CIDs, regardless of whether they actually function at the same developmental level. Zigler discussed variables such as motivation, etiology, and the concept of mental age and how these impact each theory.

Danielsson, Henry, Messer, and Ronnberg (2012) suggested that the executive functioning of children with CIDs more closely resembled children without CIDs but with similar mental ages in certain measures (e.g., switching, fluency tasks, verbal executive-loaded working memory tasks). This same group of children with CIDs performed less well than mental age peers in other measures (e.g., inhibition, planning). The children with CIDs scored below that of chronological age peers on all executive functioning tasks. These authors suggested that children with CIDs may have a specific profile for executive functioning and that the development of different executive functioning skills may be related to children's mental and life experiences (Danielsson et al., 2012). Similarly, Lindblad, Gillberg, and Fernell (2011) found that among parents/caregivers and teachers of children with "mild mental retardation," 55%–85% reported the children had difficulties with executive functions among other skill areas.

Van Nieuwenhuijzen and Vriens (2012) found among a sample of children with mild to borderline CIDs that when these children had difficulties with emotion recognition, interpretation, working memory, and inhibition skills, they also had difficulties in social information processing and problem solving. However, these authors also suggested that when working memory and emotion recognition skills are well developed, children use more information and knowledge in a given situation and in encoding information from new social situations.

Finally, Thirion-Marissiaux and Nader-Grosbois (2008) found that children with CIDs, when matched on global developmental age with typically developing children, displayed developmental differences and similarities in global Theory of Mind belief and in some specific Theory of Mind tasks. Theory of mind, in a global sense, has to do with an individual's ability to recognize and understand his/her own beliefs, intents, desires, and so on, and that others may have mental states different from one's own (Thirion-Marissaiuax & Nader-Grosbois, 2008). For example, a typically developing child should recognize at some point in development that she/he believes an act to be unfair, but also recognize that the same act is considered fair by another (e.g., the child's parent).

Both delays and differences in cognitive skills likely exist in the overall population of individuals with CIDs. It may be most helpful to think how these characteristics affect an individual in a given situation or context and the support provided in that context. The AAIDD (2010) states that "Human functioning is typically enhanced through the use of individualized supports. [Which are] resources and strategies that aim to promote the development, education, interests, and personal well-being of a person and that enhance individual functioning" (p. 18). How one adapts and thrives can be better understood when we examine particular cognitive functions, specifically learning, attention, and memory functions, as well as speech and language development. Included in the following section is a discussion of cognitive and metacognitive processes, which are closely related to strategic learning.

Reflection

How does understanding typical development in children help to understand the characteristics of children with CIDs? How does understanding developmental delays and developmental differences help?

LEARNING CHARACTERISTICS

There are a number of areas in learning that affect individuals with CIDs. These areas are the ability to transfer and generalize knowledge and skills, and to use learning strategies. In turn, deficits in the use of learning strategies can affect cognitive and metacognitive processes as well. For the purposes of discussion, it is helpful to separate areas of development and associated characteristics to add clarity and organization. But, it is impossible in real life to separate such areas as they affect the individual. An individual with problems in learning to transfer and generalize clearly has difficulties in cognitive functioning and similarly might have deficits in attention, memory, and speech and language development. Historically, where and in what environments an individual functions successfully and unsuccessfully has long been a consideration in how society views the nature of CIDs and its consequent characteristics.

Tredgold and Soddy (1956), in their text *Mental Deficiency* wrote:

the essential characteristics of feeble-minded children have been described as *social* incapacity, or inability to adapt themselves independently to their social surroundings.

As has been pointed out, such inability is often, indeed usually, accompanied by some degree of scholastic retardation . . . the school is a more exacting environment for the child than is social life for the adult. At school, the child is required to learn new things, acquire new skills, and adjust to new attitudes, in an atmosphere of close supervision and subject to frequent tests of progress, in a way which is quite unlike that of adult life.

(p. 349)

Transfer and Generalization of Knowledge and Skills

Transfer and generalization of knowledge and skills is an area of difficulty for many individuals with CIDs. Transfer and generalization refers to one's ability to use knowledge and/or skills learned in one situation or setting and apply that same knowledge and/or those skills in the same or different ways over time, in a new setting or situation, or in the display of related knowledge and skills (Alberto & Troutman, 2013).

Across time, it has been evident that individuals with CIDs frequently have difficulty with transfer and generalization (Falvey, 1989). For example, a child may learn to use a calculator to add monetary sums (e.g., adding $1.00, $1.25, and $2.45) in her school classroom. However, on a community instructional trip to shop for groceries, she may not use the calculator to add the prices of items unless she is explicitly instructed to do so. The ability to transfer and generalize knowledge and skills has a major impact on one's ability to adapt to various environments and situations. If explicit instruction is required to apply a skill in each setting or situation in which it is used, the learning process is slowed and the complexity of the learning might be limited to those skills being explicitly taught. In our earlier discussion, we noted that according to Vygotsky's theories, learning is contextual. Problems with transfer and generalization of knowledge and skills leads to a greater need for support and guidance in various environments and makes more evident to those without disabilities the challenges faced by an individual (Luckasson et al., 2002).

Transfer and generalization also involves higher order thinking, using specific knowledge and skills in other environments and situations but using them in different ways. Calculator skills used in shopping can also be used for balancing a checking account. Individuals without CIDs would likely determine independently a variety of ways in which addition and subtraction could be used in other ways in everyday life (e.g., in using recipes, in measuring length) whereas individuals with CIDs, particularly more severe levels, might require more explicit instruction. Still, instructional technologies and emphasis on teaching toward transfer and generalization continue to increase in the literature as the difficulties in this area for people with CIDs are increasingly recognized (Alberto & Troutman, 2013).

For example, students with CIDs have been taught to generalize math skills (Calik & Kargin, 2010), grocery store purchasing skills (Hansen & Morgan, 2008), conversational skills (Hughes, Golas, Cosgriff, Brigham, Edwards, & Cashen, 2011), and to use public transportation (Mechling & O'Brien, 2010). These represent only a very few of the studies indicating that students with CIDs can be taught to generalize skills. This point is important, because these individuals do have issues with transfer and generalization, it is incumbent on support providers to specifically teach students toward generalization of knowledge and skills over time, across settings and situations, and across related skill areas.

Acquisition of and the eventual transfer and generalization of knowledge and skills (particularly academic skills) are dependent on learning strategies. That is, each individual strives to develop means or strategies by which to effectively and efficiently learn. **Learning strategies** are the methods (i.e., cognitive tools) we use to help us acquire, retain, retrieve, and eventually use knowledge. They help each of us become more self-regulated, independent learners (Polloway, Serna, Patton, & Bailey, 2013). For example, a child may be told to remember her street address. The child might naturally write the address down. But suppose it was necessary to remember the address and be able to retrieve it from memory and subsequently be able to state it and/or write it down. Most children would learn that reciting the address repeatedly and verbally rehearsing the address would be an effective means for remembering the address and retrieving it for later. Verbal rehearsal is only one of many strategies most of us use to learn, memorize, and retrieve information.

Some research suggests that individuals with CIDs can and do use learning strategies, although their strategies may be less sophisticated, they may draw from fewer strategies, and they may not transfer or generalize their use as well as their peers without disabilities. For example, performance in problem-solving and memory-related tasks can be improved through strategy instruction (Hughes & Rusch, 1989). Kwong (1998) found that adolescent individuals with mild CIDs used fewer strategies and used them less frequently than matched subjects without disabilities, although they did use strategies for memorization. It was also suggested that multiple methods of assessment including observations, self-reports, and investigator assessments were useful in determining at least the initial state of memory strategies (Kwong, 1998). Baldi (1998), in a study involving adolescents with CIDs, discovered positive trends in the ability of most of the participants with CIDs to retain sets of names in long-term memory as the result of a memory training program.

It has been suggested that while many strategies have been used successfully to improve access to the general education curriculum for students with learning disabilities, additional research is still needed in the academic content areas to validate fully their use with students with CIDs (Lee et al., 2006). These authors suggested that the use of graphic organizers, chunking, mnemonic strategies, goal-setting, and problem-solving may be useful strategies for use with students with CIDs (Lee et al., 2006). The use of strategies is also related to our attributions.

Turner (1998) found that the attributions (to what we attribute our success or failure) of African-American students with CIDs were related to memory strategy use and recall. Individuals with stronger beliefs that effort and ability were more important in succeeding obtained more positive results in strategy use and recall. Conversely, those with stronger beliefs in external factors for success (e.g., luck, powerful others, and unknown factors) tended to have less positive results for strategy use and recall. Kwong (1998), studying a small group of individuals with mild CIDs, found that the adolescents were more likely to attribute success to effort and failure to lack of ability, effort, and luck. If one has appropriate attributions as to what helps one succeed (e.g., one's best efficient and effective efforts), one is more likely to persist in attempts to learn even difficult knowledge and skills and to apply a variety of strategies in the process as needed. Those with less appropriate attributions (e.g., success is the result of luck or failure is due to one not possessing the ability to learn) may experience greater difficulty in using learning strategies, especially when tasks become increasingly difficult.

Learning strategies give us cognitive tools by which we can assimilate new information and make accommodations within present and future environments and situations. Possessing a repertoire of learning strategies is desirable because different environments and situations demand different strategies for learning.

Metacognitive processing becomes critical in an individual's management of his/her own strategic learning and adaptation. **Metacognition** has to do with an individual's ability to know about his/her own knowing or to learn about his or her own learning (Reid, 1988). For example, a student might read a portion of this chapter and recognize after some period of time that he or she had actually read the words but recalled almost nothing of what was read. Similarly, one might decide to use verbal rehearsal to memorize information needed for a test and recognize sometime during the process that the needed information was not being remembered and could not be retrieved. These are metacognitive processes at work. It should be apparent that this level of cognition is higher than using a learning strategy. Metacognition involves understanding how one's own mind works; what works best for processing, remembering, and retrieving information; and how one is progressing in learning tasks. Metacognitive abilities are processes important to individuals with CIDs as they are central to limitations such as outer-directedness and lack of strategy transfer, and central to desirable outcomes such as self-determination (Moreno & Saldana, 2005).

In general, individuals with milder levels of CIDs are able to learn strategies and use their metacognition. The more abstract the material to be learned and the performance tasks become, the greater the challenge. For individuals with more severe levels of CIDs, acquisition of learning strategies may be very challenging and their cognitive deficits may make development of metacognitive processes equally challenging. Nevertheless, Moreno and Saldana (2005) found that individuals with severe CIDs could improve metacognitive abilities and maintain those improvements over time. Also, deficits of speech and language abilities can make learning metacognitive skills more difficult, but the use of appropriately trained adults may still be able to promote limited self-regulation in some context (Moreno & Saldana, 2005).

THE RELATIONSHIP BETWEEN LEARNING STRATEGIES AND METACOGNITION

Learning Strategies

Cognitive tools that allow one to understand information, store it, and later retrieve it for application on some task

Metacognition

Cognitive awareness and understanding of how one learns—metacognitive processes involve understanding whether one is learning what one needs to learn

Cognitive processes that allow one to adapt, revise, and adjust strategies and evaluate further their effectiveness based on how the knowledge and skills must be used

The learning and cognitive characteristics of individuals with CIDs are related to how well they attend to incoming information and how well needed information is remembered. Specifically, the ability to focus attention on what is relevant to learning and one's ability to remember those relevant characteristics are critical in the processes just discussed. Many individuals with CIDs have difficulties in the areas of attention and memory.

Reflection

How might delayed learning affect a child as she/he moves from early elementary years to later elementary and middle school years? In what areas might you expect to see the achievement gap widen and how might that eventually affect adult functioning?

ATTENTION CHARACTERISTICS

Individuals with CIDs may exhibit various difficulties in attention. The two more common characteristics are related to attending to relevant versus irrelevant stimuli and maintaining attention over time. Each of these areas presents challenges and typically increasingly so as the level of disability becomes more severe.

Visual Orienting

In a study of 88 individuals with ages 4–14 years with CIDs, researchers found that the visual orienting responses (e.g., ocular movements and visual fixation) of the children indicated that children with lower IQs and Down syndrome required more time to process some visual stimuli (Boot, Pel, Evenhuis, van der Steen, 2012). Motor impairment ocular issues such as nystagmus and strabismus also affected visual orienting. Boot et al. suggested that higher visual processing dysfunctions in children with CIDs may be more prevalent than previously considered. However, more research is needed to establish any specific connections among factors such as age, IQ, gender, etiology of disability, and so on, and specific visual dysfunctions (Boot et al., 2012). Visual orienting is a basic skill in establishing and maintaining visual attention.

Relevant Versus Irrelevant Stimuli

The use of reinforcement strategies (providing incentives for correct choices and responses and withholding incentives for making incorrect choices and responses), historically and recently has been shown to increase the ability of individuals to attend to cues that lead to correct responses (Alberto & Troutman, 2013; Zeaman & House, 1963). For example, an individual might be instructed on how to safely cross streets. One important dimension to this task would be attending to a "Walk"/"Don't Walk" sign. A teacher might repeatedly point out the sign, ask the individual to verbalize which sign is on and what it means, and finally to demonstrate the safe actions suggested by the lighted sign. The individual might appear to be flawless in her choices and performance. But suppose the two signs were different colors when lit with the "Walk" sign being green and the "Don't Walk" sign being red. Later, when the teacher "tests" the individual on the task in another location, the individual's performance is diminished significantly. The teacher then realizes that both signs are the same color when lit at that corner and the individual had been attending more to the color rather than the word configurations that were lit. The teacher then realizes she must focus attention on position of the words and the configuration of the letters in addition to any color in order to ensure the student can attend to what is relevant for crossing the street at a wide variety of corners. Krupski (1977) suggested that individuals with CIDs might also attend to the person presenting a task or stimulus rather than the cues in the specific stimulus or task. An example of this might be when an individual is choosing between two choices (Walk/ Don't Walk) but actually is watching the teacher's eyes and face to obtain clues as to which choice to make rather than attending to the signs themselves. Alberto and Troutman (2013) noted that individuals can have difficulties with attending to irrelevant stimuli, but also by focusing too strongly on a single characteristic stimuli (e.g., learning a red circle is "red" results in all circles being referred to as "red").

Zeaman and House (1963) noted that attention may be focused on stronger cues at first (e.g., large written letters) and progressively transferred to weaker cues (ordinary printed letters) over time. Controlling the strength of the cue helps in directing attention and maintaining it with the typical stimulus dimensions in the environment (the ordinary letters that appear in most printed materials). Three-dimensional stimuli may also help in controlling attention (Zeaman & House, 1963). Included in Research Box 6.3 is a brief summary of Zeaman's and House's research.

6.3 RESEARCH THAT MADE A DIFFERENCE

Zeaman, D., & House, B. J. (1963). The role of attention in retardate discrimination learning. In N. R. Ellis (Ed.), *Handbook of mental deficiency*. New York: McGraw-Hill.

David Zeaman and Betty J. House reported on research they had conducted on the role of attention in discrimination learning in "retardates." In their attention theory of learning, Zeaman and House stressed that attention is limited to only one or a few, at most, of the many possible stimulus dimensions available to an individual at the moment of choice, individuals may learn to attend to or disregard aspects of a stimulus as a result of reinforcement strategies, and cues are those aspects of the stimulus to which one is attending. Zeaman and House stressed that novelty in new stimuli might increase attention and that the "secret of successful training of moderately retarded children lies in the engineering of their attention. In training tasks, which require discrimination, one should seek ways of increasing that attention value of the relevant cues" (p. 218).

Although teaching methods are not our chief concern in this chapter, this research helped to establish understanding of the abilities of individuals with CIDs to attend to task stimuli and how attention to what is important in a task or stimulus can be focused or modified to enhance learning.

Maintaining Attention

Even when an individual knows what to attend to, he/she may have difficulty in maintaining that attention over time. Richard Lavoie in his videotape, *How Difficult Can This Be? The F.A.T. City Workshop* (1989), addresses problems associated with attention. Mr. Lavoie makes an interesting and worthwhile distinction concerning attention. He notes that such terms as *distractible* and *no attention span* are often used interchangeably and therefore incorrectly. He suggests that an individual who is distractible has difficulty focusing attention on what is relevant because he/she is attending to too many stimuli or dimensions in the environment (e.g., what the teacher is wearing, pictures on the classroom walls, the sounds coming from the hall). The individual with problems in attention has difficulty maintaining his/her focus on any stimuli for a sustained period of time. Individuals with CIDs may experience both types of difficulty. Shortened attention span and distractibility are both possible characteristics found in the population.

Burack, Evans, Klaiman, and Iarocci (2001) found in their review of research on attention that the empirical evidence is not supportive of an overarching relation between attention deficits and CIDs when comparisons are made between individuals functioning at the same general mental age. In other words, although it is known that individuals with CIDs have deficits in attention, the exact nature of those deficits and their origins are still not fully clear. However, it is known generally that attention span can be increased and distractibility decreased through reinforcement strategies and controlling of task-related stimuli.

In their review of the literature, Deutsch, Dube, and McIlvane (2008) found that many individuals with CIDs do exhibit dysregulated attention, impulsivity, and behavioral impersistence. However, these same researchers noted it is currently difficult to ascertain if these attentional difficulties are the result of delayed or atypical development. Also the etiology of CIDs and its association with attention deficits remains an area of needed research (Deutsch et al., 2008). Similarly, Reilly and Holland (2013) found that the prevalence of attention-deficit /hyperactivity disorder is more prevalent among individuals with CIDs, but that how best to identify, treat the symptoms (e.g., pharmacologically), and design school supports for students are areas still lacking in sufficient research.

Serna and Carlin (2001) noted that guiding the attention of individuals with CIDs is important early in educational interventions to assist with problems with attention, focusing on relevant stimuli in a task and ultimately transfer. In general, stimulus dimensions of novelty and relevance to real life are believed to also help focus attention (Alberto & Troutman, 2013). For example, a high school student may have little attention span for and interest or success in learning map-reading skills in a geography class. However, when the map-reading skills involve learning routes through the town to be able to get to and from a job to earn money, the attention span and interest of the individual may be increased. A variety of approaches discussed later in this text are available to educators to assist in overcoming attention deficits. Once attention is maintained and focused, other characteristics may still emerge that affect adaptation.

Of importance in learning and cognitive development is the ability to remember and retrieve information. This discussion has noted that there are cognitive processing challenges, possible difficulties in learning, and potential problems in attending, all of which can inhibit one's ability to remember. Individuals with CIDs may experience some particular difficulties with memory that are characteristically common in the population. These include difficulties in working and short-term memory leading to problems with storage of information, retrieval of information, organization of information, and producing effective responses based on performance requirements.

Reflection

What are the implications of having difficulty in attending to the most relevant aspects of a task? What are the implications of a lowered ability to maintain attention in school, home, and community?

MEMORY CHARACTERISTICS

Historically, most people have assumed that individuals with CIDs have memory deficits. In fact, this is an accurate assumption with many such individuals. However, over time, research has indicated that the manner and functions of memory that may be impaired can be complex and can help in understanding how to better assist individuals in learning and overall human functioning.

Working and Short-Term Memory

Working memory can be defined as a processing resource of limited capacity that involves preserving information while simultaneously processing the same or other information (Swanson, 1999). Numminen, Service, and Ruoppila (2002) hypothesized that adults with intellectual disabilities may have performed better on some tasks than a comparison group of children (matched for intellectual levels) because of the adults' reliance on knowledge support from long-term memory. Henry and MacLean (2002) found evidence that, when compared to matched groups by chronological age and mental age, 11- to 12-year-old individuals with intellectual disabilities scored more poorly on working memory span tasks than either control group, suggesting a possible difference in cognitive functioning. Vicari (2004) also suggested that there might be qualitatively different patterns of memory functioning in individuals with Williams syndrome and Down syndrome. However, Henry and MacLean (2002) also found some evidence in their study that the group of individuals with CIDs more closely matched the performance of the mental age matched group, suggesting a more developmental perspective. Some evidence also indicated a better performance by those with CIDs than the mental age matched controls, further complicating the overall study findings (Henry & MacLean, 2002). Schuchardt, Gebhardt, and Maehler (2010) found difficulties in phonological information processing that increase as IQ decreases and that these difficulties were also apparent when compared to mental age peers.

Van der Molen, van Luit, Jongmans, and van der Molen (2007) found that individuals with mild CIDs appeared to be deficient in phonological storage and fractured executive functions specifically and that, in general, there are multiple working memory deficits. Van der Molen et al. (2007) also noted that these deficits tended to be consistent with a developmental delay rather than developmental differences. Numminen et al. (2002) also noted that past research suggested that working memory is deficient at all levels of CIDs, regardless of etiology.

Short-term memory is widely recognized as a problem area for many individuals with CIDs. Historically, the short-term memory issues of individuals with CIDs have received considerable attention in the literature. Difficulties in remembering information for the short term can include having a lack of learning strategies (Borkowski & Day, 1987) as well as attentional problems (Agran, Salzberg, & Stowitchek, 1987).

Interestingly, some feel that once information is committed sufficiently to short-term memory, long-term memory abilities are less affected by CIDs (McCartney, 1987). That is, with the successful use of various educational interventions (e.g., repeated presentations, massed trial and distributed practice, among others discussed in later chapters of this text), once material has been adequately committed in working memory, it remains stored for the long term in ways comparable to people without disabilities. Van der Molen, van Luit, van der Molen, Klugkist, and Jongmans (2010) found that with training, working memory and short-term verbal memory can be trained and improved significantly. Connors, Rosenquist, Arnett, Moore, and Hume (2008) also found that auditory verbal memory could be improved through training, although the improvements in that area did not transfer to improved sentence memory or verbal working memory. Clearly, the exact nature of why or how people with CIDs experience deficits in working and short-term memory is not fully understood.

Problems in Storage and Retrieval of Information

Problems in storage of information are characteristic of many individuals. Storage of information in both short- and long-term memories is dependent on many factors. The more challenges faced, the more difficult storage becomes. If one has difficulty in processing information cognitively, the more difficult it becomes to focus and maintain attention to what is relevant, and subsequently to use a learning strategy to ensure it is committed to short-term memory and eventually to long-term memory. Consider some point in your life when you have been studying for a test. Perhaps you are distracted by noise in the environment; perhaps you physically don't feel well; in addition, you have other things in your life that concern you and are vying for your attention. The learning is completely new to you and you are not sure how best to study it to ensure you can remember it when needed. You probably have experienced the frustration or disappointment in not learning what you or others might have expected you to learn. Although not precisely comparable to the experience of an individual with CIDs, the example serves to illustrate that getting information into storage does require adequate processing, learning strategies, attention, and memory all governed by metacognitive processes. The more energy and effort that goes into the act of learning (e.g., decoding words in a text), the more difficult it may be to achieve storage of information. For example, many individuals with CIDs have difficulty learning to read more complex materials. If the new vocabulary, complexity of the passage, and foreign nature of the information is very challenging, it is unlikely much of the information will be understood and stored for later retrieval because so much effort and attention is expended on decoding the written language. Additionally, storage also depends on the individual's ability to know where to store the information. Although this notion may seem elusive, it is important for an individual to be able to associate new learning with existing knowledge to achieve this end. For example, when one is learning the word and concept of "circle," it is typical to pair that learning with square and triangle as these are related geometric forms. Similarly, when one learns an address, that learning is often paired with a telephone number as well. Knowing what to associate new learning with in one's existing knowledge is very helpful in retention and memory. Finally, the working memory deficits of students with CIDs may be characteristic of behaviors such as failing to remember directions and task completion (Alloway, 2010).

Retrieval difficulties are also characteristic of many individuals with CIDs. For stored information to be truly useful, it should be retrievable at the needed time. A student could learn his/her address and be able to recite it upon questioning in a rote fashion. This same student should be able to give a correct address when asked to do so under normal life circumstances. Retrieval may prove to be a problem when those circumstances differ from the ones where initial and subsequent educational interventions occurred. A simple example might be as follows. A student is taught to give correct responses in a classroom when asked the question, "What is your address?" by her teacher. At another time and in another environment, someone different asks her, "Where do you live?" The student may have trouble transferring the skill to the new environment or individual or generalizing the correct response to the differently worded question. Retrieval can be aided when instruction or mediation involves varying settings and circumstances (and even the specific wording/language used) to encourage transfer/generalization (Taylor, Smiley, & Richards, 2015). Table 6.1 summarizes the factors related to memory.

Students with more severe disabilities often have multiple disabilities and therefore experience more confounding issues in the areas of cognition, learning, attention, and memory than many individuals with milder disabilities. The additional disabilities (e.g., cerebral palsy) may also tend to inhibit verbal and physical abilities

Table 6.1 Factors Related to Memory

Attention	
Attention to relevant stimuli	Maintaining attention

Memory
Short-term memory
Working memory
Long-term memory

Storage of information	Retrieval of information

needed to demonstrate levels of knowledge. In general, individuals with more severe levels of CIDs experience the same difficulties as those with mild to moderate levels but those difficulties are more pronounced. Henry and Gudjonsson (2003) found that students with moderate CIDs were less effective in recalling and retrieving eyewitness information than chronological age peers while those with mild CIDs performed more favorably in comparison to chronological peers. However, to assume individuals with severe levels of CIDs do not possess the cognitive skills to learn would be misguided. For example, Bonnaud, Jamet, Deret, and Neyt-Dumesnil (1999), in a study involving a small sample of adults with severe CIDs, found that these individuals were able to recognize faces equally as well as adults without disabilities, but those with CIDs did exhibit limited short-term memory capacity. What one likely can assume is that many skills can and will be learned but the number and variety of skills learned will not be comparable to most individuals without disabilities (Westling & Fox, 2009).

Individuals with more severe levels of CIDs often have difficulty in cognitively processing information (e.g., auditory and visual stimuli), and understanding the mediation provided (e.g., delays in language development and understanding spoken language). They also have difficulty attending to relevant stimuli and maintaining that attention (e.g., watching teacher's cues and relevant dimensions in a task) and committing to memory for later retrieval important data needed for daily life and independence (Westling & Fox, 2009). New learning and transfer and generalization of existing skills can require extensive intervention. Subsequently, much of the focus of learning for individuals with more severe levels of CIDs is on functional information and skills needed for independence as much as possible in home and community living, communication, socialization, employment, and recreation and leisure. Still, one must also be cognizant that individuals with severe levels of CIDs are not homogeneous as a population but are individuals who can vary to a wide extent on abilities and disabilities. Although individuals with more severe levels of CIDs exhibit difficulties in the more complex cognitive tasks associated with regulating one's own behavior and learning, this may be partly due to the fact that others in their environments may provide inordinate external regulation (Westling & Fox, 2009).

> *Reflection*
>
> **What are the implications of having really poor working and short-term memory skills? What are the implications as a student? As an adult living and working in the community?**

SPEECH AND LANGUAGE CHARACTERISTICS

Another area of development that impacts cognitive and social development is speech and language. The receptive understanding of language in particular and the ability to use spoken or signed language have considerable influence on an individual's ability to process and learn. Understanding typical speech and language development may be useful in understanding delays and differences that occur in individuals with CIDs. In the "E-sources" at the end of this chapter is the address for the website of the American Speech-Language-Hearing Association. This website includes summaries of typical speech and language development milestones in addition to other information useful to teachers, parents, and speech/language pathologists.

Individuals with Milder Levels of CIDs

For individuals with mild CIDs, delays in speech and particularly language development may be more evident than differences. That is, they might experience the same stages as people without CIDs but at a later age and/or slower rate (Cardoso-Martins, Mervis, & Mervis, 1985). Tager-Flusberg and Sullivan (1998) noted that while typically developing children have acquired the essential components of language by about age 4, the majority of children with CIDs are progressing down that same developmental path, having learned some words to name important people and objects in their lives and using some expressions for regulating social interactions. Bernabei, Camaioni, Paolesse, and Longobardi (2002) found that children with CIDs show gradual acquisition of communication abilities between 6 and 24 months of age. Snell and Luckasson with others (2009) stressed that social isolation and a lack of needed supports are issues that may arise with those with CIDs and higher IQs.

Fowler (1998) noted that the variability in language development among individuals with CIDs cannot be wholly explained by cognitive factors and that components of language (e.g., phonological skills, pragmatic skills) may be differentially impaired or unaffected, especially past the earliest stages of language development. More recently, Levy (2011) stressed that word decoding (essential for more advanced reading skills) is affected by phonological and auditory short-term memory skills. Vandereet, Maes, Lembrechts, and Zink (2010) found that lexical development among individuals with CIDs shows considerable heterogeneity and that prelinguistic communication skills (e.g., pointing), chronological age, cognitive skills, and vocabulary comprehension all need to be studied further as factors explaining this heterogeneity.

Speech disorders are more commonly found among individuals with CIDs than in the general population as well (Taylor et al., 2015). Speech disorders could include articulation problems (e.g., difficulty with producing certain sounds such as the "th" or "s" sounds), voice disorders (e.g., hoarse or raspy voice, unusually high-pitched or low-pitched voice, unusual volume), or fluency disorders (e.g., stuttering). Most individuals with milder levels of CIDs are able to acquire adequate speech and language to function normally in everyday life. The aforementioned issues in the home literacy environment may also affect speech development (van der Schuit et al., 2009). The delays (and perhaps deficits in acquiring more abstract and complex understanding of language) may affect children in learning to read, write, and understand information presented in school. Indeed, as noted in earlier chapters, difficulties in learning to read and write are characteristics that frequently result in children being assessed for a possible disability. Much of the learning in school is linguistically mediated. Therefore, deficits or delays in understanding higher levels of speech and language can affect significantly school functioning and ultimately others' perceptions of an individual's abilities and worth.

Byrne (2000) states:

> The one discernible property which sets human beings apart from other creatures and which seems to be relevant . . . is intelligence and what flows from its possession. . . . Human beings can place themselves in the past and in the future as having done this or that or as possibly going to do this or that. The ability so to place one's thoughts and desires is a reflection of the human being's possession of language. . . . Only by means of language, or some equivalent symbolic system, can one represent possibilities not immediately present in some stimulus. The same applies to memory. So, does the world impose a "criterion of personhood" . . . [which] places a question mark . . . over those human beings whose intellectual development is disordered or retarded, and who may . . . not acquire that sufficient grasp of language, self and the world which allows them to function as fully self-conscious, autonomous, and rational creatures.
>
> (pp. 3–5)

Obviously, speech, memory, and other language abilities have a major impact on whether a person with CIDs will require interventions. Event Box 6.1 includes information about the founding of the American Speech-Language-Hearing Association (ASHA), an organization with a deep understanding of this field.

6.1 EVENT THAT MADE A DIFFERENCE

1925—Founding of ASHA

The American Speech-Language-Hearing Association was founded in 1925. ASHA "is the national professional, scientific and credentialing organization for more than 111,000 audiologists, speech-language pathologists, and speech, language and hearing scientists." ASHA is also an advocacy organization serving people with communication disorders. Audiologists and speech-language pathologists, in particular, are often involved in providing services to individuals with CIDs who also have disabilities in speech, language, and hearing.

Source: ASHA website: www.asha.org

Individuals with More Severe Levels of CIDs

For individuals with severe disabilities, there are more delays and differences in language development found than in those with milder levels of CIDs. Individuals with severe levels of CIDs and multiple disabilities tend to exhibit speech disorders as well. Some individuals do not acquire speech and/or their disorders of speech may be so pronounced that *augmentative (aided) communication systems* (e.g., synthesized speech) or *alternative communication systems* (e.g., picture communication systems, sign language) are required. In general, augmentative systems are used to assist the individual to communicate with others in a manner similar to those without communication difficulties. For example, an individual may use assistive technology (e.g., computerized programs and devices) to produce speech or written language for others to read. Alternative systems, such as sign language or picture systems, may allow the individual to communicate, primarily but not exclusively, with those who are familiar with the system (e.g., teachers, family members). In general, the more understandable the communication system used is to others not familiar with the system (e.g., bus drivers, restaurant workers), the more desirable. Because development in speech and language can be limited to basic communicative functions such as indicating needs, wants, and emotions, emphasis on functional communication skills is common in educational programs (Westling & Fox, 2009). Augmentative and alternative communication systems should meet these basic needs. However, systems should be able to "grow" in sophistication and complexity as an individual develops, matures, and gains new knowledge and skills. Systems that allow the individual to communicate in social situations (e.g., at family gatherings, with friends) are also advantageous. The system should be designed to satisfy as wide a variety of communication needs as possible. Wilkinson and Hennig (2007) stressed that more research is necessary to evaluate the use of augmentative and communication systems for individuals with severe CIDs and that this is one of the more important directions in the field. It is also worth noting that the speech and language characteristics typically identified through standardized testing may be of limited use with individuals with CIDs (Cascella, 2006). Finally, van der Schuit, Segers, van Balkom, and Verhoeven (2011) noted that nonverbal intelligence (e.g., concept development, working memory and attention skills) are very important in ongoing language development of children with CIDs.

For those with severe disabilities and very limited communication abilities, others in the environment may need to interpret their communicative efforts. For example, seemingly maladaptive behavior such as refusals to comply with directions or physical responses indicating "leave me alone" may need to be viewed within this communicative context. Grove, Bunning, and Porter (2001) suggested there may be three perspectives by which others can better understand the communicative intent of individuals with severe disabilities. These include perceiving communication as a dynamic, coordinated, and interactive process; emphasis on relevance and the role of inference in communication; and a constructionist perspective that suggests individuals grow as communicators through the scaffolding of adults (Grove et al., 2001). The less one is capable of communicating in conventional fashion, the more necessary it becomes to interpret other behavior as serving some communicative function. That is why the use of augmentative and alternative communication systems, that increase communicative functions, make messages accessible to others, increase social interactions, and allow individuals to exert control over their lives, are critical to providing dignity and a quality of life to such individuals.

Some individuals with severe levels of CIDs exhibit unique differences in speech and language development. Echolalia was an example discussed earlier in this chapter. These individuals tend to repeat what is said to them just prior to giving their own response. For example, if someone asked such an individual, "How are you?", the individual might reply, "How are you?". Another example might be an individual who develops idiosyncratic gestures, signs, sounds, or words to meet communicative functions (e.g., someone who imitates using a steering wheel to indicate going somewhere). Such unique differences are relatively uncommon among people with CIDs in general.

It is important to remember that in human development, receptive understanding (i.e., understanding what is expressed to us by others) tends to precede expressive ability (i.e., being able to communicate to others through a language or similar symbol system), although the two abilities are interactive and mutually dependent. Individuals with CIDs may well understand much more that is said to them by others than they themselves might be able to communicate in return. Also, Roberts and Kaiser (2011) found in a meta-analysis of the literature that parent-implemented language interventions could have positive outcomes on language development. Parents could focus on socially communicative interaction, expand their use of linguistic forms, and learn how to encourage communication during everyday routines; these interventions can be effective across a range of intellectual and linguistic skills, and parent training in implementing such interventions may need as little as once per week to improve language outcomes (Roberts & Kaiser, 2011).

> *Reflection*
> **Are there technological devices or software programs you are familiar with that might be of assistance to someone with problems with speech and language? What are the implications in school, home, and community of an individual not being equipped with the ability to communicate with others?**

A FINAL NOTE

This chapter has included a discussion of characteristics found among individuals with CIDs at milder and more severe levels. At the outset, the point was made that these characteristics are not necessarily exhibited by any individual and in a few examples given, not even by many or most people with CIDs. We are unique individuals. The definition and assessment of individuals with CIDs tend to have a focus on deficits. That is, by definition, the term *CID* suggests deficits in cognitive functioning and adaptive behavior. Therefore, discussions concerning characteristics of individuals and groups of individuals tend to focus on deficits as well. People with CIDs, like everyone else, also possess strengths, both in terms of abilities and character. Many individuals with CIDs lead lives that by virtually any standards are much more successful than the lives of others with no apparent disabilities. People with CIDs have jobs, families, homes, friends, hobbies, relationships, goals, and aspirations.

In the following two chapters, we will continue to examine characteristics of individuals with CIDs as well as characteristics identified within society, families, and cultures that are associated with (but not necessarily the cause of) CIDs.

SUMMARY CHECKLIST

Cognitive Characteristics

✓ Intellectual functioning must be viewed within the context of (a) adaptive behavior, (b) participation, interactions, and social roles, (c) health, and (d) context (environment and culture)

✓ Constructivist theories of development emphasize that an individual constructs, through increasingly complex cognitive functions, his/her understanding of the environment, events, interactions with others, as well as his/her own thoughts and actions

✓ Piaget identified four major stages of development including the sensorimotor, preoperational, concrete operational, and formal operational stages

   ➢ **The zone of proximal development**—From Vygotsky's theory of development, is the range of tasks that are too difficult for a person to master alone but can be learned with guidance and assistance

✓ Scaffolding—The process of altering the level of guidance or assistance given as a child becomes increasingly effective and efficient at various skills and mental functions

✓ Developmental delay—When a person learns much of the same knowledge/skills in the same developmental sequence as those without disabilities, but at a slower rate

✓ Developmental difference—When a person displays behaviors that are atypical of children or adolescents

✓ Both cognitive delays and differences—Are evident in the population of people with CIDs

Learning Characteristics

✓ Transfer and generalization of knowledge and skill refers to the ability to use knowledge and skills in the same or different ways in a new setting or situation

✓ Transfer and generalization is a common area of difficulty often resulting in a greater need for support and guidance in various environments

   ➢ **Learning strategies**—The methods we use to help us acquire, retain, retrieve, and eventually use knowledge

✓ Some research suggests that people with CIDs can and do use learning strategies although their strategies may be less sophisticated, fewer in number, and may not be transferred/generalized as well as those used by people without disabilities

✓ Attributions—Are to what we attribute our successes and failure and are related to strategy use

> **Metacognition**—Has to do with an individual's ability to understand about his/her own knowing or to learn about his/her own learning

✓ In general, individuals with milder levels of CIDs are able to learn strategies and use their metacognition, although the more abstract the material to be learned and the performance tasks become, the greater the challenge in their learning and use

Attention Characteristics

✓ *Visual orienting*—Is an early indicator of how well children can focus their visual attention

✓ *Relevant versus irrelevant stimuli*—Many individuals with CIDs experience difficulty in attending to stimuli that are relevant to learning and ignoring or filtering out those stimuli that are not relevant

✓ *Maintaining attention*—Some people with CIDs have difficulty maintaining attention over sustained periods of time

Memory Characteristics

✓ *Working and short-term memory*—A processing resource of limited capacity that involves preserving information while simultaneously processing the same or other information; short-term memory involves the ability to store small amounts of information for a short period of time. Working memory involves the ability to take information in the short-term memory and relate it to other information.

✓ *Problems in storage and retrieval of information*—May result from lack of attention to what is relevant, short attention span, lack of learning strategies, and both short-term and long-term memory deficits; retrieval difficulties emerge when an individual has trouble remembering or applying stored information when needed

✓ Individuals with more severe levels of CIDs may have multiple disabilities and experience these problems in cognition, learning, attention, and memory to even greater degrees than those with milder levels

Speech and Language Characteristics

✓ The ability to use language is very important in developing cognition, learning, attention, and memory

✓ Language is a form of communication, whether spoken, written, or signed, that is based on a system of symbols and that can be used to produce an infinite number of messages from a finite set of symbols and rules

✓ For people with milder levels of CIDs, delays in speech and language may be more evident than differences

✓ Speech disorders are more commonly found among people with CIDs than in the general population

✓ Language use and intelligence are linked in the perception of many people

✓ For individuals with more severe levels of CIDs, differences in speech and language development are more evident than for those with milder levels
✓ Augmentative and alternative communication systems may be useful in assisting individuals with speech and language deficits
✓ Echolalia, or repeating what is said to one, is an example of such a difference

ADDITIONAL SUGGESTIONS/RESOURCES

Discussion Questions

1. What are the characteristics of individuals with CIDs that you believe most affect the ability of an individual to adapt in school? In everyday life?
2. What are some ways in which teachers and textbooks draw your attention to what is important to remember? In what ways do textbooks create distractions?
3. How does the ability to express oneself through speech and language affect the perceptions of others about one's overall cognitive abilities? If someone communicates in "simple" language, do you think of that person as less intelligent and why or why not?

Activities

1. Review texts that include information about the work of Piaget and Vygotsky as well as any other theories concerning human development (e.g., behaviorism, psychoanalytic theory). Compare and contrast these theories of development. Decide/debate as to which best "fits" your perceptions of development and the characteristics of people with CIDs.
2. Interview a local educational diagnostician or school psychologist, special education teacher, and/or parent. Ask what types of characteristics do they believe are commonly exhibited in individuals with CIDs? Ask to what extent characteristics may vary from individual to individual? Are there any characteristics that have a greater impact on the individual with CIDs than others?
3. Visit and observe in preschool and lower elementary grade levels (i.e., first and second grades) where there are children identified with having CIDs or who are in the RTI process. What characteristics did you observe, and did the children appear to be qualitatively different in characteristics than those without disabilities or who are meeting their developmental benchmarks? If so, how did they appear to be different? Did you observe characteristics indicative of delays in development?

E-sources

http://www.thearcpub.com/?source=overture
This is the national publications website for The ARC, which contains a wide variety of publications, videos, and other media available covering many aspects of CIDs.

http://www.acf.dhhs.gov/programs/pcpid
This website is for the President's Commission for People with Intellectual Disabilities. It contains information about the mission, history, and publications available from

this important advisory group to the President of the United States. It also includes links to various state organizations that address the needs of people with CIDs.

http://www.asha.org/
This is the official website of the American Speech-Language-Hearing Association. There is information available to the public as well as professionals concerning a wide variety of topics under the A–Z topics link (much of the information from the homepage appears to be primarily for speech and language professionals). Included are explanations and summaries concerning speech and language development, disorders, and information concerning treatments and intervention.

7

EDUCATIONAL, PSYCHOLOGICAL, AND BEHAVIORAL CHARACTERISTICS

Key Points

➤ EDUCATIONAL CHARACTERISTICS—Academic skills, abstract concepts, comprehension, and functional academics are all areas of concern in educational programs.

➤ PSYCHOLOGICAL CHARACTERISTICS—Atypical psychological characteristics have led to segregation. Many individuals are less well adjusted than they could be.

➤ BEHAVIORAL CHARACTERISTICS—Behavioral and psychological disorders are more common among people with CIDs than those without disabilities, although most individuals establish meaningful relationships.

➤ ADAPTIVE SKILL CHARACTERISTICS—Performance and acquisition deficits are evident, although support and education could significantly alter these characteristics in any given individual.

As in the previous chapter, one should not perceive the characteristics discussed here as independent of one another, but as interactive and mutually dependent. Also, these characteristics are present in some or many individuals, but no person is likely to possess all of them. In Chapter 6, many characteristics related to cognition and learning were examined. In this chapter, there is a focus on educational characteristics including academic skills, comprehension skills, and functional academic skills. Psychological characteristics include learned helplessness, self-concept and self-regulation, locus of control, self-determination and self-direction, motivation, and dual diagnoses with psychiatric disorders. Behavioral characteristics include issues related to behavioral disorders, stereotypical behavior and self-injurious behavior, and interpersonal relationships. Finally, in the section on adaptive skill characteristics, challenges related to leisure, work, community, and self-care and home living are discussed. As in Chapter 6, the characteristics of individuals with milder and more severe levels of CIDs will be discussed as appropriate.

EDUCATIONAL CHARACTERISTICS

The educational characteristics of individuals with CIDs vary greatly and are influenced by many factors. For example, the severity of disability influences the type of educational program that a student receives. The types of supports available in school, the home, and community may affect considerably the outcomes for individuals (AAIDD, 2010). The age of the student influences educational characteristics, as well as the physical environment, teaching content and materials, instructional approach, curricula, and use of adaptive and augmentative equipment, among a host of other factors. In later chapters, specific teaching procedures that are employed to produce the best possible outcomes are discussed. Yet, to discuss characteristics one must consider the educational process itself as this influences the individual in particular and the population in general.

Educational characteristics are affected by the cognitive and learning characteristics reviewed in Chapter 6. It is necessary in this discussion to refer to that review for understanding those characteristics that emerge during the typical formal educational years. And, as suggested in Chapter 5, these characteristics may be among the first that lead to concerns that the individual's development is delayed or different from the development of his or her peers. Because academic skill deficits often manifest early in their school careers, the need for access to the general education curriculum, as well as an adapted or modified curriculum for individuals with CIDs, also becomes manifest to many. Event Box 7.1 includes information related to an important issue concerning assessment of individuals with CIDs.

7.1 EVENT THAT MADE A DIFFERENCE

1997—IDEA mandates that students with disabilities be included in statewide assessments

The 1997 reauthorization of the IDEA included a provision that students with disabilities be included in statewide assessments. Prior, students with CIDs and other disabilities that affected cognitive functioning were sometimes excluded from such tests. IDEA intended to increase the opportunities for these students to participate in the general education curriculum and the associated assessments.

With the current emphasis on "high stakes" assessments and the emphasis on holding educators accountable for academic learning, some may question whether it is appropriate to use such measures with individuals with CIDs. Nevertheless, the passage of the No Child Left Behind Act and the 2004 reauthorization strengthened the position that all students with disabilities should be afforded access to the general education curriculum and subsequently, the Common Core State Standards, and the myriad state and district assessments of learning in that curriculum. IDEA does allow students to be alternately assessed or to be excluded from the individual outcomes of not passing state or district assessments.

Academic Skills

As noted in Chapter 6, the definition of CIDs tends to focus on deficits and challenges as well as support needs. Individuals with CIDs can and do learn academic skills. Given the difficulties that individuals with CIDs may confront, including learning abstract concepts, cognitive functioning issues, attention issues, and language development issues, many educators believe this may generate the need for being taught a modified functional academic/vocational/career curriculum at some point during the school career.

Conceptual Thinking

Concepts are "abstractions that are the result of assigning objects, people, ideas, or experiences to categories" (p. 262), which in turn can reduce the complexity of learning by providing procedures and rules to define a concept (e.g., a triangle has three sides while squares and rectangles have four sides) (O'Donnell, Reeve, & Smith, 2007). As discussed in Chapter 6, memory and retrieval of information are problem areas for many individuals with CIDs. Also, O'Donnell et al. noted that concept formation is greatly enhanced by the ability to learn critical attributes, and characteristics of the concept. Focusing and maintaining attention on relevant stimuli in a task, object, or event is, as previously stated in Chapter 6, another problem area. Subsequently, developing concepts can also prove challenging. In general, concrete concepts are more easily learned (e.g., coins and bills are both forms of money) whereas more abstract concepts are more difficult to learn (e.g., a paycheck represents money minus taxes and deductions). AAIDD (2010) gives as examples of conceptual skills: language skills, reading and writing, money, time, and number concepts.

WHY ARE CONCEPTS IMPORTANT?

Santrock (2001) made the following observations: "Imagine a world in which we had no concepts: we would see each object as unique and would not be able to make any generalizations. If we had no concepts, we would find the most trivial problems to be time-consuming and even impossible to solve. Consider the concept of a book. If a student were not aware that a book is sheets of paper of uniform sizes, all bound together along one edge, and full of printed words and pictures in some meaningful order, each time the student encountered a new book she would have to figure out what it was. In a way, then, concepts keep us from 'reinventing the wheel' each time we come across a new piece of information" (p. 291). Santrock provides simple insight into why the ability to learn concepts helps us to generalize across settings and situations and develop an increasingly sophisticated and more complex understanding of the world.

Learning abstract concepts is often dependent on the use of metacognitive skills as well as memory skills. One must be able to make connections between prior and current learning to develop more complex and abstract concepts over time. Students with CIDs do have difficulties with memory that tend to be more pronounced as intelligence scores decrease (Schuchardt, Gebhardt, & Maehler, 2010). Deficits in executive functioning may also affect the ability to learn efficiently and effectively (Danielsson, Henry, Messer, & Ronnberg, 2012).

Hayes and Conway (2000) compared 9- and 14-year-old individuals with mild intellectual disabilities to chronological and mental age matched peers on their ability to categorize. These authors suggested that if individuals with CIDs experience challenges in concept acquisition and storage, it then follows they will have difficulty in responding to novel concept (category) members. Another potential problem area for learning concepts for people with CIDs results from the fact that many concepts do not have uniquely defined rules or features (e.g., fruits, furniture, and friends are three concepts that have many exemplars that can be quite different from one another within each concept) (Hayes & Conway, 2000). Some instances of a category tend to better fit the concept than others (e.g., a dog may be a more typical example of a mammal than is a whale) further complicating the acquisition of concepts. Hayes and Conway (2000) found that compared to matched peers, children with intellectual disabilities were able to form abstract concepts about prototypical category types as did their counterparts without disabilities. The more exemplars the children were exposed to, the better they were able to abstract the prototypical features despite exemplar-specific features. On the other hand, the children with disabilities were less successful in using exemplar-specific features for categorizing. In short, the results suggested that individuals with intellectual disabilities can be expected to extract and retain prototypical information from exemplars (e.g., most mammals live on land), but to have greater difficulty in retaining atypical features (e.g., some mammals live in oceans). The use of exemplar-specific information to guide responses to whether a stimulus matched a category did not change from 9 to 14 years of age in the groups of individuals with CIDs (Hayes & Conway, 2000). This could suggest some stability in this problem area although this might be due to instructional techniques. More recently, however, Jimenez, Browder, and Courtade (2009) found that three students with moderate intellectual disabilities could be taught science concepts through a self-directed learning prompt that required both recall and application of knowledge and to generalize the use of the learning prompt to a general science class where the same materials and experiments were being used. This suggests that individuals with CIDS are capable of learning concepts given appropriate instruction.

How well individuals with CIDs are able to categorize was the focus of study in the early and mid-20th century. Research Box 7.1 illustrates this.

7.1 RESEARCH THAT MADE A DIFFERENCE

Werner, H., & Strauss, A. A. (1943). Impairment in thought processes of brain-injured children. *American Journal of Mental Deficiency, 47,* 291–295.

In this study (and others), the authors investigated the thought processes of children with known brain injuries and those with "cultural-familial mental retardation." The children were asked to sort 56 small, familiar objects into groups that went together. Those with known brain injury used more groupings and more unusual combinations of groupings than did either the group with cultural-familial CID or the group with no disabilities. The children with brain injury tended to select objects based more on unusual, accidental, or irrelevant details about the objects. These early researchers helped to establish an understanding of how concept formation can be delayed or different in individuals with CIDs as well as brain injury.

Comprehension Skills

Learning concepts, particularly atypical category members, may require explicit instruction and application of learning strategies. Diminished intellectual capabilities can lead to a deficit in the acquisition of information and skills (acquisition deficit), as well as the appropriate use of information and skills (performance deficit) (Luckasson et al. 2002). As discussed in Chapter 6, deficits in speech and language may be evident and subsequently, comprehension in language arts such as listening, reading, and written expression may be adversely affected as well. Clearly, comprehension skills are imperative in educational environments. Taylor, Smiley, and Richards (2015) noted that literacy comprehension skills are often deficient.

However, van den Bos, Nakken, Nicolay, and van Houten (2007) found that, particularly for expository texts, comprehension of adults with CIDS could be improved through strategy instruction. These same authors suggested that individuals with CIDS should be taught comprehension skills through similar long-term and reciprocal teaching strategies as are other students.

Katims (2001) noted that many educational programs do not include "meaningful" literacy instruction (i.e., engaging students with well-constructed, connected written materials with appropriate language and content). Rather, literacy skills may be more restricted to sight vocabulary, and particularly functional or "safety" word recognition and comprehension (e.g., stop, exit). In a study involving 132 individuals with mild to moderate CIDs across elementary, middle, and secondary grades, Katims (2001) found 41% achieved word recognition skills on at least the primer level. Similarly, 26% achieved an instructional level of at least primer level in reading comprehension. None achieved a level as high as sixth grade. Oral reading skills improved considerably from elementary through high school, a pattern also found in word recognition. Relative strengths were in decoding with areas of difficulty including higher-level, language-based reading comprehension skills including cause/effect relationships, inferential comprehension, and drawing conclusions. Written language skills generally improved with grade level as well. Allor, Mathes, Roberts, Cheatham, and Champlin (2010) found in a longitudinal study that students with mild to moderate CIDs made significant progress in multiple measures of reading ability as a result of daily, comprehensive reading instruction in small groups (1–4 students) for 40–50 minutes daily.

It would appear that reading and comprehension skills can be improved in individuals with CIDs given adequate support and emphasis. Deficits in overall cognitive functioning and speech and language delays and differences can complicate the process. Many professionals have stressed that a focus on learning that is functional (i.e., referenced to successful functioning in present and future environments) aids in developing academic and other skills. However, recent research suggests that students with CIDs can and do improve reading and comprehension skills over time when provided with the needed supports.

Henley, Ramsey, and Algozzine (2002) noted that students with CIDs often respond to the same instructional methods used with other students although they may require more time to achieve learning, demonstrate mastery of knowledge and skills, and generalize learning across settings and situations. Individuals with mild to moderate CIDs may acquire basic academic skills as previously discussed. Basic literacy and math computational skills, as well as adequate communication skills, are frequently learned, particularly as people progress through school. When students have acquired basic academic skills, they need to demonstrate application of those skills in a manner relevant to present and later adult functioning (Henley et al., 2002). The more emphasis on skills for present and future needs for successful living, working, and recreation, the more relevance learning may have. The more authentic to real life the materials used, the more obvious the connection to everyday functioning.

Functional Skills

As suggested by Katims (2001), "functional" learning can translate into simple, relatively unchallenging learning. Therefore, defining what is functional is important. Snell and Brown (2011) define functional skills as "those skills that, if not performed in part or full by the student, must be completed for the student by someone else. . . . What is functional for one student may not be for another, because, . . . functionality depends on individual characteristics and must be determined through ecological or environmental assessment" (p. 123). Academic skills may be included in this definition, as many individuals with CIDs need functional academics to achieve success in school and community environments.

The previous discussion has focused primarily on individuals with milder levels of CIDs. Those with more severe levels (those in need of more supports), in general, acquire less complex educational knowledge and demonstrate fewer academic skills, although academic instruction is often still relevant.

Instructional strategies are not the focus of this chapter, but it is useful to accept a philosophy that learning of concepts, comprehension skills, and functional academics are possible and important. The educational characteristics of individuals with severe disabilities, in general, can make acquisition of these skills challenging.

Individuals with severe disabilities have limited ability to synthesize information and skills in an organized, useful way and may fail to see the relationships among bits of information (Westling & Fox, 2009). Further, deficits in the ability to generalize also complicate such synthesis. Difficulties in speech and language skills, discussed in Chapter 6, can make the learning of functional academics and comprehension skills time-consuming.

Students with severe levels of CIDs have greater difficulty in learning through observation. This may be the result of deficient attending skills (Westling & Fox, 2009). Because memory and retrieval skills are problem areas, many individuals with severe disabilities need extended time with repeated practice to acquire skills. A lack of self-regulation skills (i.e., the ability to monitor one's own behavior, evaluate its correctness, and self-reinforce) also contribute to problems in developing typical skills taught in educational environments.

Still, it would be inappropriate to deny access to learning of more typical educational skills, particularly for younger children whose known abilities and disabilities may be less well established. As individuals with severe disabilities grow older, the need for learning functional skills in academics, as well as work, recreation, and home and community living may become more obvious. Finally, some individuals experience multiple disabilities (e.g., physical and health impairing disabilities) that may "mask" their true overall abilities to learn.

Educational characteristics affect how one adjusts to the school environment. In turn, how one adjusts in school affects life at home, in the community, and across the life span. Overall adjustment can affect and be affected by the psychological characteristics of the individual as well.

Reflection

Do the educational characteristics of students with CIDs justify educating them in separate classrooms? Why or why not?

PSYCHOLOGICAL CHARACTERISTICS

Psychological characteristics, as all others discussed, are not inseparable from educational, behavioral, or adaptive skill characteristics. As noted previously, these are mutually interactive areas, each influencing the other (AAIDD, 2010). In this section, we will discuss characteristics related to learned helplessness, self-concept, self-regulation, locus of control, self-determination and self-direction, and motivation. While some of these areas (e.g., self-regulation, motivation) were briefly mentioned in Chapter 6, the interdependence among these characteristics should be apparent in this discussion.

Learned Helplessness

Learned helplessness is an acquired tendency to give up easily or not to try at all when faced with new or difficult tasks. Individuals may develop learned helplessness when they no longer believe they have any control over their own learning and attribute success and failure to factors other than their own learning efforts (Taylor et al., 2015). Learned helplessness may result from repeated failure (e.g., "I can't get it so what is the use in trying?"), or from a belief that others are in control (e.g., "The teacher hates me so what is the use of trying?"), or even from having others take care of one's needs unnecessarily (e.g., "If I wait long enough, someone will come along and take care of this for me"). Regardless of the root cause(s), learned helplessness is a belief that affects an individual's adaptation from childhood into adult life. Learned helplessness may lead others to view the individual as lazy, unmotivated, or uncaring about learning. This view of self and others' view may limit the experiences of an individual to the familiar, and encourage a belief system that succeeding at new or difficult tasks is impossible. The more one has learned to be helpless, the less likely one is to have a strong self-concept.

Characteristics Related to Self-Concept

Self-concept is important in both task initiation and task completion (Varsamis & Agaliotis, 2011). How one perceives oneself is also critical to long-term development (Jones, 2012). Effective instruction may influence how one perceives oneself as one experiences success, one is more likely to exhibit or express a positive self-concept (Varsamis & Agaliotis, 2011). Jones (2012) found among adolescents that the label of disability may lead to a framework of self-concept that is associated with social exclusion or limited opportunities.

Integration within the larger community may influence self-concept. Duvdevany (2002) found that physical self-concept and satisfaction with the whole self-concept were better in individuals with intellectual disabilities who participated in integrated leisure programs as opposed to segregated ones. Hodapp and Zigler (1997) also stressed that atypical life histories (e.g., failure experiences, institutionalization) of people with CIDs tend to affect self-concept and the presence of maladaptive tendencies.

If self-concept is diminished, one may also have difficulty with self-regulation. We discussed self-regulation in Chapter 6 regarding regulation of cognitive and metacognitive processes. Here, we focus on the tendency to rely on others and to be less regulated by one's own thoughts, feelings, and actions.

Characteristics Related to Self-Regulation

Self-regulation involves the abilities to plan and manage time, attend to and concentrate on tasks, organize information strategically, establish a productive environment, and utilize resources among other skills (Santrock, 2011). In one study, researchers comparing performance of young typically developing children to those with CIDs found some differences in self-regulation. Specifically, the children with CIDs had more difficulty in identifying the objectives of tasks, lower self-regulated attention, and self-regulated requesting (Nader-Grosbois & Vieillevoye, 2012).

Santrock (2011) noted that self-regulation is frequently learned from others. We learn these increasingly complex abilities from the modeling of others. The better one is able to self-regulate, the more one is likely to gain feelings of self-efficacy. Self-efficacy results in better skill acquisition and performance, working harder, persisting longer, and higher achievement. Teachers who stress self-regulatory behavior encourage students to take responsibility for their own learning and behavior, and for succeeding as students and members of society (Santrock, 2011). For example, a student who is doing science homework needs to plan the time and organize her schedule. Next, the environment should be selected and organized such that it is conducive to completing the homework. She needs to be able to concentrate on the homework and attend to the tasks involved (e.g., reading the text, completing a worksheet). The student must then organize the information gained in a manner that makes sense for completing the homework and for current and future understanding. Finally, the student should seek help from others when she is having difficulty with some aspect of the homework. When an individual possesses all these self-regulatory abilities and uses them effectively, that person is likely to have increased self-efficacy as well. One should also learn to self-regulate emotional responses as well as task-oriented abilities.

Self-regulatory behavior may very well be amenable to improvement through teaching even among individuals with multiple disabilities and more severe levels of CIDs (Westling & Fox, 2009). Self-regulation is influenced by whether an individual perceives himself or herself to be "in charge" of his or her own life and learning. The concept of locus of control is related to self-regulation.

Characteristics Related to Locus of Control

Locus of control is one element of psychological empowerment along with self-efficacy and motivation (Shogren, Bovaird, Palmer, & Wehmeyer, 2010). Those individuals with external locus of control tend to look to others for causality for outcomes and for guidance. Those with an internal locus of control tend to rely more on self-guidance and are more likely to assume personal responsibility for outcomes. Whether one engages in tasks and activities is also thought to be influenced by whether one is extrinsically or intrinsically motivated (Woolfolk, 2013).

It is difficult to determine whether a person's behavior is extrinsically or intrinsically motivated and subsequently whether she or he has an external or internal locus of control. However, Shogren et al. (2010) obtained results that suggested that as early as age 8, people with CIDs tend to be more externally oriented than either typical students or students with learning disabilities. Shogren et al. (2010) also noted that these perceptions of external orientation tend to change little over time. Nevertheless, people with CIDs, like all of us, in all likelihood will tend to fluctuate between the two types of locus of control depending on other factors such as knowledge of the task, prior experiences with success, and supports that encourage a more intrinsic locus. It is quite typical in unfamiliar situations or settings for anyone to look for external controls to regulate behavior. For example, when a child first enters school, he or she is likely to watch other children and listen to adults to understand what is expected and how to behave. As humans, even as adults, we look for guidance when we are unsure of ourselves. Similarly, as we gain confidence, we tend to look less for those external controls and rely more on our own internal ones. Research Box 7.2 includes a description of an article focused on locus of control.

7.2 RESEARCH THAT MADE A DIFFERENCE

Lawrence, E.A., & Winschel, J.F. (1975). Locus of control: Implications for special education. *Exceptional Children, 41,* 483–490.

In this article, Lawrence and Winschel reviewed the implications of prior research with various populations concerning locus of control. They then suggested implications for students with disabilities in general and in particular, those with mild CIDs. Interestingly, one of the areas these authors address is implications for mainstreaming students with mild CIDs. Through today's lens of inclusion, some of their suggestions might be perceived differently than in 1975. The authors provide an excellent overview of the concept of locus of control and its potential implications for teachers of students with disabilities.

Shogren et al. (2010) noted that future research should examine the contribution of variables such as choice making, educational setting, instructional practices, and individual characteristics to locus of control. Locus of control is related to self-determination.

Characteristics Related to Self-Determination

Characteristics related to strategy use and metacognition can inhibit an individual's ability to be self-directed. The belief that one is accomplishing goals as a result of one's own efforts and motivation (as opposed to external rewards or locus of control) are indicators of self-determination.

Wehmeyer (2001) pointed out that development of self-determination is a process that begins in early childhood and continues through the developmental period and into adulthood. Self-determined individuals are autonomous (act according to their own preferences, interests, and abilities, independently and freely); self-regulated (make choices about how to handle situations based on the task, their abilities, and are able to make and execute a plan); psychologically empowered (act based on the belief they have the ability and skills to influence outcomes in their lives); and self-realized (use a reasonably accurate and comprehensive self-concept of themselves in devising and selecting actions) (Wehmeyer & Schwartz, 1998; Marks, 2008). The acquisition of such characteristics associated with being self-regulated, self-determined, and self-directed result from developing various skills. These skills include the ability to make choices and decisions, problem solving, goal setting and achievement, self-observation, self-instruction, self-advocacy and leadership, internal locus of control, self-efficacy and outcome expectancy, and self-awareness and self-knowledge. Sheppard and Unsworth (2011) suggested that self-determination can be improved in adolescents with intellectual and developmental disabilities through instructional procedures. Also, individuals with CIDs have indicated in at least one study the importance of supports in their lives in the expression of self-determined behavior (Shogren & Broussard, 2011). Clearly, the process of developing self-determination is a complicated one and dependent on both opportunity, capacity to learn, and appropriate scaffolding and support in that learning. Because these may be limited during the critical developmental period as well as later in life for some individuals with CIDs, self-determination may be limited.

As communication abilities decrease, difficulty in being able to express one's desires and needs to others may further inhibit development, especially for those with more severe levels of CIDs. Still, self-determination can be developed with appropriate supports. It may also be related to where an individual is supported. For example, Wehmeyer and Bolding (2001) studied self-determination in 31 adults with intellectual disabilities. They found there were significant changes in a more adaptive direction toward self-determination, autonomous functioning, and choice making following movement to less restrictive work or living environments. These authors conjectured then that self-determination might be influenced by limited opportunities for choice and decision making in more restrictive environments. More recently, Nota, Ferrari, Soresi, and Wehmeyer (2007) suggested that choice-making opportunities and to engage in self-determined behavior may better predict improved self-determination than either IQ or social skills. These authors also stressed that self-determination is a critical component in an enhanced quality of life.

Self-determination and self-direction, as well as the other psychological character-istics discussed to this point, are interfaced with motivational characteristics in people with CIDs. Here, we explore in greater detail this important characteristic.

Characteristics Related to Motivation

Motivation is typically defined as an internal state that arouses, directs, and maintains our behavior (Woolfolk, 2013). Intrinsic motivation tends to stem from such factors as curiosity and interest. Intrinsically motivated individuals also tend to seek out and conquer challenges in pursuit of interests. Those with intrinsic motivation tend to rely less on external incentives or punishments (Woolfolk, 2013). Extrinsic motivation tends to stem from an interest in the consequences of efforts (reward, punishment) and less in the nature of the task itself. All of us tend to exhibit both characteris-tics. In fact, Woolfolk pointed out that people tend to fall along a continuum of fully self-determined (very intrinsically motivated, internal locus of control) to fully deter-mined by others (very extrinsically motivated, external locus of control).

We discussed in Chapter 6 that experiences with success and failure, abilities and disabilities, and supports all influence motivational tendencies. It is quite natural for people to find one task intrinsically motivating while another may have mostly an extrinsic motivational quality. For example, a person might find taking a walk out-doors to be very intrinsically motivating while reading a textbook might require exter-nal motivation to be accomplished. We can make some generalities about people with CIDs, but as with all characteristics, their presence may or may not be evident in any individual. For example, some researchers have suggested that individuals with Down syndrome tend to exhibit task persistence (an indicator of motivation) as an individual characteristic rather than as being task specific (Gilmore & Cuskelly, 2009). Research Box 7.3 includes an article which addresses the construct of motivation as it relates to individuals with CIDs.

7.3 RESEARCH THAT MADE A DIFFERENCE

Switzky, H. (1997). Mental retardation and the neglected construct of motivation. *Education and Training in Mental Retardation, 32,* **194–196.**

This article is a brief overview of an important topic and summarizes the thoughts and research of Harvey Switzky and others over the course of many years. Following is an excerpt from this article:

"For the last twenty six years, Carl Haywood, and our students and colleagues (which I have called the Peabody-Vanderbilt Group in my writings. . . .) have a working hypothesis that mental retardation involves a motivational self-system. That is, self-regulatory influences which interact with cognitive and metacogni-tive factors resulting in a person being an inefficient learner. The evidence sug-gests in study after study that performance is a complex function of cognition and motivation. Having the right amounts and kind of motivation, which in our model we have called an intrinsic motivational orientation to problem-solving tasks, can make one a more efficient learner and leads to higher performance outcomes. Having more . . . an extrinsic motivational orientation to problem-solving tasks operates to make one a less efficient learner . . ." (p. 194).

Switzky goes on to elaborate on the "Yale Group" consisting of Edward Zigler, his students and colleagues, who also have studied motivation extensively in people with CIDs (e.g., Hodapp & Zigler, 1997).

No one could argue reasonably that developing intrinsic motivation is not desirable and helpful in becoming a self-determined and autonomous individual. What remains to be discovered is how to best facilitate that process in children with CIDs beginning at an early age, and how to fully support continued development across the life span. Again, engaging in choice making, opportunities and activities that are challenging but success is achieved, goal-setting, self-monitoring and evaluating performance, and problem solving all support development of intrinsic motivation. It is also important that those supporting individuals with CIDs do not suppose that IQ is the determinant of whether one might achieve intrinsic motivation.

A number of issues related to the development of educational and psychological characteristics have been discussed. These, in turn, are interactive with behavioral characteristics. Some would argue that problematic educational and psychological characteristics lead to behavioral issues. In the following section are discussed the relationship of CIDs to behavioral problems, dual diagnosis of CIDs and psychiatric disorders, stereotypical and self-injurious behaviors, and interpersonal relationship characteristics of people with CIDs.

> *Reflection*
> **In what activities are you intrinsically and extrinsically motivated? What influences the locus of your motivation?**

BEHAVIORAL CHARACTERISTICS

The behavioral characteristics of individuals with CIDs are as varied as those of people in general. AAIDD (2012) stresses that the presence of challenging, difficult, or dangerous behavior should lead to an analysis of a person's life experiences, current situation, personality, and health condition, toward designing some intervention. Physical and mental health may enhance or inhibit the functioning of any given individual. Additionally, contextual factors such as the environment in which the individual works, plays, lives, and so on, influence behavioral adjustment. Supports that mitigate dangers and hazards are also crucial for appropriate adjustment in life. The AAIDD (2010) stresses that difficult behavior can result from:

- Internal triggers such as pain, a seizure, sensory experiences, fear, or psychotic conditions;

- External triggers such as threats from others, environmental cues (e.g., such as uncomfortable clothes or shoes), or lack of safety (e.g., neglectful environment);
- Trauma that is physical, sexual, or post-traumatic stress disorder;
- Limited range of expression;
- Differentiation from mental illness diagnoses (an overlap of conditions and behaviors) such as syndromes (e.g., Lesch-Nyhan syndrome), learned behaviors, mannerisms (such as tics versus unconscious habit), and other disease processes (e.g., metabolic disorder, medication effects from use to control disease symptoms).

The functions of an individual's behavior are an important consideration, especially in schools when such behavior interferes with the learning of the individual or the learning of others. Why an individual behaves in a particular manner is important in understanding her/his motivations, responses to the environment, and the responses of others to her/his behavior. For example, an individual who disrupts regularly may wish to escape from or avoid work assigned in a class. However, the individual could also be communicating that she/he is unable to do the work and experiencing frustration with both the material and the demands made to learn and apply it. The function of an individual's behavior helps others to better understand the individual's needs and feelings while simultaneously providing insight into how the individual can get those needs met in more behaviorally appropriate ways. *Functional behavioral assessment* (FBA) can be useful in determining intervention programs to improve an individual's adaptation in one or more environments. Table 7.1 includes a summary of steps commonly used in FBA.

Table 7.1 Steps Commonly Used in Functional Behavioral Assessment

Step 1—Brainstorm and identify the behavior (or behaviors) of concern (e.g., disruptive behavior)—be sure to involve all stakeholders including the student as appropriate

Step 2—Assess what is occurring prior to the behavior (e.g., language arts activities begin that involve reading and written expression)

Step 3—Assess what occurs after the behavior occurs (e.g., teacher reprimands student)

Step 4—Specify the behavior of concern (e.g., talking without permission, making inappropriate noises) such that they are observable and measurable

Step 5—Assess how frequently the behavior occurs (often, one or more peers may also be assessed to determine the degree to which the student's behavior is problematic in comparison to others') (e.g., 8 occurrences per hour)

Step 6—Determine a reasonable but high expectation for improvement in the behavior based on current performance and the typical performance of peers (e.g., no more than once per hour)

Step 7—Determine intervention(s) that will encourage the desired changes (e.g., praising the student for not being disruptive rather than reprimanding him when he is disruptive; providing additional academic assistance during reading and written expression activities)

Step 8—Monitor progress by collecting data and revise plans as needed

Although these steps are student-centered, it is important to remember that functional behavior assessment occur with an ecological framework. That is, whatever problems may be occurring, teachers, peers, the school system itself, medical needs, and other variables may all affect the student. Interventions need not be exclusively student-centered, but could also involve other people and systems.

Historically, as noted in Chapter 1, people concerned with the treatment of individuals with atypical behavior have been concerned with the distinction between CIDs and mental illness (Braddock, 2002). In the following section, the overall relationship between CIDs and behavioral challenges is discussed.

The Relationship Between CIDs and Behavioral Disorders

It is generally accepted that, overall, people with CIDs exhibit more behavioral problems than those without disabilities and that this is particularly applicable to those with more severe levels of CIDs. Specific diagnosis of the origins and even type of problem (e.g., a co-occurring psychiatric disorder) can be complex and is confounded by the characteristics of more severe levels of CIDs (e.g., very limited communicative ability) (AAIDD, 2010).

First, it should be acknowledged that the study of psychiatric processes and their role in the development of CIDs has not been resolved (Myrbakk & von Tetzchner, 2008). Myrbakk and von Tetzchner suggested that some problem behaviors of individuals with CIDs may be symptoms of psychiatric disorders (albeit the symptoms may be unconventional in comparison to individuals without CIDs). Also, individuals with mild to moderate CIDs display self-injury in association with depression while those with severe CIDs display screaming and aggression in association with a broader range of events (Myrbakk & von Tetzchner, 2008). This further indicates the complexity of understanding maladaptive or problem behavior, psychological/psychiatric disorders, and behavioral responses to environmental circumstances. These factors may also overlap and interact to produce behavioral issues.

The AAIDD (2010) suggests that exceptional behavioral needs occur from:

- Externally directed destructiveness such as hurting others, theft, and damaging property;
- Self-injury, pica (eating inappropriate objects such as cigarette butts), and suicidal behavior;
- Sexual aggression, inappropriateness (e.g., touching, exposing oneself);
- Other behaviors such as tantrums, wandering off, abusing alcohol or drugs, or failing to follow mental health treatments.

Still, it would be misguided to present a portrait of people with CIDs as being simultaneously behaviorally disordered. The majority of individuals with CIDs do not present behavioral issues that warrant mental health services or intensive behavioral supports. When such problems do emerge, it is possible that a dual diagnosis of both CIDs and psychiatric disorder be made. Following is a discussion of the issues related to dual diagnosis.

Dual Diagnosis

Westling and Fox (2009) pointed out that it is important to recognize that CIDs and mental illness are different conditions. One difficulty in dual diagnosis is determining whether the problem behaviors observed are a function of intellectual disability or mental illness (Westling & Fox, 2009). Hodapp and Dykens (2009) noted that behavioral phenotypes (as might arise from genetic conditions such as Fragile X or Rett syndromes) need to be researched further.

Psychiatric disorders that may occur include a wide variety found in the 2013 release of the *Diagnostic and Statistical Manual of Mental Disorders—V* (see Box below) including schizophrenia, psychosis, bipolar disorders, major depressive disorder, obsessive-compulsive disorder, post-traumatic stress disorder, and many others including intellectual disabilities.

HOW ARE PSYCHOLOGICAL DISORDERS DIAGNOSED?

The *Diagnostic and Statistical Manual of Mental Disorders (DSM-V)* (2013) is a widely used reference guide to help determine the presence of a variety of psychological and psychiatric disorders. It is published by the American Psychiatric Association and essentially gives the diagnostic criteria for a large and varied number of disorders.

It should be clear that people with CIDs can have many of the same psychiatric disorders that those without CIDs may have. Westling and Fox (2009) stressed that most individuals with dual diagnosis have mild to moderate intellectual disabilities. Stereotypy and self-injury are more frequent among those with more severe levels of CIDs.

Destructive or Aggressive Behavior

Aggressive or destructive behavior may be indicated by screaming, crying, damaging property, attacking others, as well as noncompliance, running away when called, and other similar behavior (Westling & Fox, 2009). As noted previously, screaming and aggression tended to be associated with depression in individuals with severe disabilities in one study (Myrbakk & von Tetzchner, 2008). Tsiouris, Kim, Brown and Cohen (2011) found in one study that impulse control disorder and bipolar disorder were the psychiatric diagnoses more strongly associated with aggressive behaviors in individuals with CIDs. It is critical that whatever the underlying causes, positive behavioral supports and possibly medical/psychiatric interventions are needed to minimize or eliminate such behaviors (AAIDD, 2012; Westling & Fox, 2009). Tsiouris et al. (2011) also found that self-injury was associated with anxiety, impulse control, more severe CIDS, being younger in age, and being depressed.

Self-Injurious Behavior

Examples of self-injurious behavior include hitting one's head, falling intentionally, biting, gouging, and scratching oneself. Self-injurious behavior (SIB) tends to occur more frequently in those with severe levels of CIDs, although prevalence levels are not known (Kahng, Iwata, & Lewin, 2002). Witter and Lecavalier (2008) noted that self-injury tended to be associated with having more severe levels of CIDs. As discussed in Chapter 4, medical syndromes (e.g., Lesch-Nyhan syndrome) have also been associated with SIB. Kahng et al. (2002) conducted a quantitative analysis of research across

35 years and found 396 articles pertaining to SIB, suggesting it is a widely studied if not a well-understood phenomenon. Westling and Fox (2009) noted that pica might also be considered as self-injurious.

Kahng et al. (2002) found that most treatments included in their review were successful in reducing SIB. Among treatments, there was a rise in reinforcement strategies and a slight decrease in punishment programs over the years. Although treatment options have been investigated and found to be successful, the condition persists. This suggests that efforts might need to focus on prevention of SIB (Kahng et al., 2002). Furniss and Biswas (2012) suggested that future research should examine factors associated with SIB becoming a severe and chronic condition. While operant models (reinforcement and punishment paradigms) would appear to explain to a significant extent SIB, biological factors may also play an important role, at least in some individuals also requiring pharmacological treatment as well as behavioral interventions (Furniss & Biswas, 2012). Also, SIB is more prevalent in some syndromes (e.g., Tourette, Prader-Willi, and Lesch-Nyhan syndromes) (Muehlmann & Lewis, 2012). Individuals who exhibit SIB may have more severe CIDs and also be more likely to display stereotypic behavior.

Stereotypic Behavior

Stereotypic behavior refers to repetitive behaviors that tend to be physically harmless but nevertheless interfere with adjustment. These could include (among others) rocking motions, weaving motions of the head, and flapping of the fingers or hand but could also involve very idiosyncratic movements peculiar to the individual (Newell, 1997). It should be noted that considerable recent research on the occurrence and prevention of stereotypy is conducted with individuals on the Autism Spectrum. Also, some professionals may also refer to these behaviors as self-stimulatory behavior, although the function of self-stimulation is not always evident (Westling & Fox, 2009).

Matson, Kiely, and Bamburg (1997) found that among individuals with severe CIDs, persons with high stereotypy scores had lower adaptive behavior scores, were more limited than peers in expressing their thoughts, understanding others' speech, performing necessary daily activities for survival and well-being, keeping a safe and clean home environment, developing interpersonal relationships, and engaging in functional and enjoyable activities either alone or with others. Clearly, the effects on adaptation can be harmful even if the actual repetitive behavior is not. More recently, Joosten, Bundy, and Einfeld (2008) found in a study of 74 children that anxiety was the more likely intrinsic motivator for children with dual diagnoses, escape and obtaining tangible objects was the more likely external motivator for those with dual diagnoses, and that attention and escape were the more likely motivators for children with CIDs alone. Of some interest in this study is that sensory stimulation was not the dominant motivator, even among those children in the study diagnosed with autism (Joosten et al., 2008). However, Rojahn, Zaja, Turygin, Moore, and van Ingen (2012) found in a study of 115 adults with CIDs, that stereotypy tended to be maintained more by nonsocial, self-stimulation contingencies than was aggressive behavior. Clearly the overall root causes and understanding of stereotypy and SIB are not yet fully understood.

Stereotypic behavior is amenable to treatment. Saunders, Saunders, and Marquis (1998) found that different schedules of reinforcement and type of activity available affected the rate of stereotypical in four adolescents with CIDs. Similarly, Emerson, Hatton, Robertson, Henderson, and Cooper (1999) found that support and other forms of contact were associated with higher levels of engagement and decreased levels of stereotypy among a group of individuals with severe intellectual disabilities and sensory impairments. The literature includes many other examples of successful intervention with stereotypic behavior. Interestingly, these studies generally involve a small number of participants; that might indicate the relatively low prevalence of stereotypy in the population of individuals with CIDs. Again, positive behavior supports are important in providing a therapeutic environment and treatment of problem behaviors (AAIDD, 2012).

Interpersonal and Sexual Relationships

The characteristics of interpersonal relationships of individuals with CIDs can vary widely in scope and depth. At one end of a spectrum, some individuals with CIDs who reside and work in more restrictive settings may find that many or most of their relationships are shared with people who are paid to interact with them (e.g., physicians, teachers, residential services staff). At the other end of the spectrum, many individuals enjoy rich family relationships, build and maintain friendships, and interact with others in the broader mainstream of the community. They have relationships that vary in nature based on consumerism, education, recreation/leisure, romance, employment, and living arrangements.

Storey (1997) stressed that the quality of life of persons with CIDs is connected to the quality and extent of their social network. In general, the greater the opportunity for interacting with others and sharing common interests within a supportive environment, the more likely quality relationships are to develop. However, when people with CIDs are integrated into neighborhoods, the severity of the individuals' CIDs and the size of the group being integrated may influence the responses of those without CIDs (Dijker, van Alphen, Bos, van den Borne, & Curfs, 2011).

An extensive database exists indicating relationships can and do develop among children within inclusive educational settings, although concern persists as to the possibility of stigmatization of some individuals with CIDs. For individuals with severe levels of CIDs, the co-occurrence of behavioral disorders and other variables (e.g., reduced communicative abilities) can affect the development of relationships, especially outside the immediate circle of known others (e.g., family and teachers). Problems in relationship development may be related to intellectual and physical development, but may also be influenced by opportunities for learning, environmental support, and the attitudes of others (Westling & Fox, 2009).

Geisthardt, Brotherson, and Cook (2002) conducted a preliminary study of children with a variety of disabilities 3 to 10 years of age. These authors examined the children's friendships at home. Many of these young children spent limited time with friends or peers in the home environment. Those with behavioral and cognitive limitations experienced fewer interactions than did those children who had primarily physical limitations. Although those living in more isolated areas also tended to have fewer interactions, living in close proximity to other children did not guarantee frequent interactions (Geisthardt et al., 2002).

Miller and Chan (2008) found that social support, interpersonal skills, and leisure skills among others contributed to life satisfaction scores for people with CIDs. The results suggested that "interpersonal interactions, in particular, greatly contribute to the amount of satisfaction individuals with ID feel in their lives" (p. 1044).

However, individuals with CIDs have sometimes suffered when their behavioral characteristics have been perceived in society as undesirable or dangerous. Event Box 7.2 includes an example of how societal perceptions have adversely affected people.

7.2 EVENT THAT MADE A DIFFERENCE

1908—Segregation based on moral deficiency

In 1908, a superintendent of a children's institution stated:

"The moral instincts are almost always lacking in the mentally deficient, so even in the ordinary intercourse of home and social life they are a menace to the welfare of the community.... This unfortunate tendency, coupled with the undesirable surroundings in many of their homes and the dangers of the unrestrained play of the streets, tends to nullify any ethical lessons or impressions gained by a few hours in school. Therefore, in the interest of the public as well as for their own sakes, it is of paramount importance that atypical children be prevented from coming in contact with those of normal minds, in order that their abnormal personality may not react unfavorably upon the latter" (Trent, 1994; p. 153).

How unfortunate indeed, as we now understand that many of these same "less desirable" characteristics an individual may possess are at least partially attributable to being segregated and kept apart from others, and not provided the adequate supports for accessing the knowledge and skills gained in living in the mainstream of society.

Source: Trent (1994)

Sexual relationships are of concern both to individuals with CIDs and their caregivers. Hollomotz (2008) noted that individuals with learning difficulties may have been perceived by others as being child-like and therefore not in need of sex education. In contrast, these individuals have sometimes been perceived as sexually deviant or unable to control sexual "urges" (Hollomotz, 2008).

Unfortunately, children with CIDs are at greater risk for child and sexual abuse. Research suggests they may be up to 4 times more likely to be sexually abused as children without disabilities (Kim, 2010). This increased risk of sexual abuse may be related to:

- Their dependency and often intensive interactions (e.g., bathing, clothing) with caregivers;
- They may lack the vocabulary and language skills to adequately report abuse;

- Special education tends to teach compliant behavior and compliance can be perceived as consent;
- Poorer social skills affecting the ability to discriminate between appropriate and inappropriate behavior;
- Exclusion from sex education programs in schools or elsewhere (Kim, 2010).

Therefore, it is important that children with disabilities participate in sex education programs, but also in personal safety programs that teach self-protection skills, decision-making skills, social-sexual skills (e.g., what to say and do in social and sexual relationships), and general knowledge of sexuality (Kim, 2010).

Particularly for people living in residential settings, privacy and the right to engage in a romantic relationship may be thwarted by a lack of privacy (Hollomotz, 2008). This lack of privacy, rather than preventing sexual activity, may encourage it in public places or in rushed and unsafe behavior. The need for privacy and sexual relationships among people with CIDs remains a thorny issue over time (Hollomotz, 2008). In an exploratory study, Dukes and McGuire (2009) found that the decision-making ability of individuals could be increased through individualized sex education. These researchers also found an increase in inappropriate sexual behavior among participants as a result of sex education not being available (Dukes & McGuire, 2009). Similarly, in a preliminary study, individuals with CIDs reported a general reluctance among family members and caregivers to "acknowledge and respect the sexual rights of those with an ID" (Healy, McGuire, Evans, & Carley, 2009, p. 910). These same researchers found, however, that participants with CIDs demonstrated clear understanding of relationships (ones of trust, companionship, reciprocal nature, positive effects of self-esteem) and that they aspired to being married and having children (Healey et al., 2009).

Finally, it is important that research continue as to the impact of sexual and child abuse of individuals with CIDs and their adult behavior. There may be some concern that individuals with CIDs who experience sexual abuse may replicate acts with others because they lack the abstract thinking ability to understand the prior acts were abusive (Lindsay, Steptoe, & Haut, 2012).

In this final section, characteristics related to adaptive behavior are discussed. Adaptive behavior is a major consideration in the definition, assessment, and diagnosis of CIDs (AAIDD, 2010). Deficits in adaptive behavior affect the individual's ability to function in one or more environments and can have lifelong effects. Development of adaptive behaviors is crucial to adjusting to less restrictive environments in school and the community, maintaining safety and healthy psychological and behavioral characteristics, and building meaningful relationships to others.

Reflection

How might having a social network of family, friends, and co-workers enhance the life of an individual? How would the lack of such a network impact that life? How would you react as a member of such a social network to reports that a member with CIDs was engaged in a romantic relationship?

ADAPTIVE SKILLS CHARACTERISTICS

As was discussed in Chapter 2, adaptive behavior encompasses a wide range of behavior across many areas of human learning and functioning. Its inclusion in the AAIDD definition of CIDs indicates its importance. In 2002, Luckasson et al. expressed an increased emphasis on the *performance* of adaptive skills in addition to their *acquisition*. "Thus, it is expected that reasons for limitations in adaptive skills may include (a) not knowing how to perform the skill (acquisition deficit), (b) not knowing when to use learned skills (performance deficit), or (c) other motivational factors that can affect the expression of skills (performance deficit). When an individual has limited intellectual capacity, both acquisition and performance deficits may be attributed to mental retardation" (Luckasson et al., 2002; pp. 73–74). As noted in Chapter 2, adaptive behavior in the AAIDD definition is expressed as conceptual, social, and practical adaptive skills that have been learned by individuals to function in everyday life. Also, it is assumed that an individual with CIDs will also possess strengths along with limitations, and that strengths and weaknesses will be viewed within the context of everyday community life and experiences.

Within the AIDD 2010 definition, there are three areas of consideration. Conceptual (e.g., learning abstract concepts and comprehension skills) and social skills (e.g., behavioral issues and interpersonal relationships) have been discussed. Practical skills have also been discussed in relation to functional academics. Here we address leisure, work, and community living. Finally, we will focus on self-care and home living skills.

Major areas of adaptation for anyone are in the areas of leisure, work, and community living. These areas are connected as being major endeavors in terms of time, effort, and sources of spending and making money. For people with CIDs, the lack of supported opportunities to participate constructively in leisure and work activities can cause problems in adjustment at home, school, and in the community. Work and career opportunities have proven to be elusive for many individuals, not necessarily because of deficits in abilities, but because of poor preparation and/or attitudes of others toward the ability of individuals to be successfully employed. Research Box 7.4 illustrates the dilemma in balancing the characteristics of individuals with mild disabilities with their educational needs to generate more positive outcomes.

7.4 RESEARCH THAT MADE A DIFFERENCE

Edgar, E. (1987). Secondary programs in special education: Are many of them justifiable? *Exceptional Children, 53,* 555–561.

In 1987, Eugene Edgar sounded both an alarm and call to action to educators concerned with the post-school outcomes for individuals with CIDs and other disabilities. In his conclusions he stated: ". . . those students enrolled in secondary special education programs, large numbers—over 30%—drop out. Of those who remain in school and graduate, less than 15% obtain employment with a salary above minimum wage. For those students who do find reasonable work, factors other than the educational program seem to account for their success . . ."

Edgar concluded that such results suggested there might be a need to rethink and redesign secondary curriculum for students with disabilities toward a more functional and vocational "track." He went on to state: "With only minimal thinking about this proposal one comes inexorably to the conclusion that such a change in curriculum will result in a *separate education track*. And this track will be populated, primarily, by poor, minority, male students. What a dilemma—two *equally* appalling alternatives: integrated mainstreaming in a nonfunctional curriculum which results in horrendous outcomes (few jobs, high dropout rate) or separate, segregated programs for an already devalued group, a repugnant thought in our democratic society" (p. 560).

While outcomes have improved in some respects since Edgar wrote his article, individuals with CIDS are yet to achieve full status as citizens in terms of employment, living arrangements, and community participation.

Characteristics Related to Leisure

For individuals with CIDs, participation in leisure activities and environments foster growth, development, and wellness. Leisure environments also provide opportunities to participate in age-appropriate activities with peers without disabilities (Luckasson et al., 2002). Some individuals have robust leisure lives, while others (typically with multiple disabilities) have their leisure activities greatly inhibited. Also, leisure environments can be very supportive or unsupportive, further influencing the leisure characteristics of individuals (Luckasson et al., 2002). For example, the frequency and nature of leisure activities are affected by what is available in the environment, the ability of the individual to choose, whether they are solitary or group activities and the availability of others, costs, and availability of instruction and support as needed to enhance participation. People with CIDs participate in a wide variety of leisure activities. Devine and Lashua (2002) examined the perceptions of individuals with disabilities regarding their roles in social acceptance and leisure experiences. Interview data revealed that the adolescents and young adults did perceive that they played a role in constructing social acceptance through relationships, frequency of activity, development of friendships, and accepting differences. However, Zijlstra and Vlaskamp (2005), in a study in the Netherlands, found that for people with profound disabilities, leisure activities were often limited in both overall duration and type (e.g., listening to music, watching television), suggesting that attention to leisure activities is important.

Browder, Cooper, and Levan (1998) demonstrated that individuals with severe disabilities, with supports, do learn to express choices in leisure settings. This is particularly important as individuals with severe disabilities may resort to undesirable behavior (e.g., stereotypy) if there is a pronounced lack of support and instruction for leisure activities during unstructured times and/or in unstructured environments. O'Reilly, Lancioni, and Kierans (2000), in a study involving a small number of adults with moderate levels of CIDs, found that interventions to teach leisure social skills produced immediate positive changes in the targeted social skills and the skills generalized to other settings. Similarly, researchers in Canada found that children with intellectual disabilities were engaged in fewer social activities with peers and more social activities with adults than were typically developing peers (Solish, Perry, & Minnes, 2010). However, 80% of all the children with CIDs did report having at least one friend. It should also be noted that leisure activities (e.g., watching television) did not significantly differ between children with CIDs and typically developing peers, but that social and recreational activities did differ (Solish et al., 2010).

Constructively using one's leisure time is important for one's own sake. Work, however, remains a central defining characteristic of an individual in Western society. A frequently asked question when initially meeting someone new is "What type of work do you do?" Imagine the impact on the self if that answer was usually that you do not work.

Characteristics Related to Work

Historically, the presence of a disability has led to a lower likelihood of being employed and if employed, to substantially lower income levels (Blanck, 1998). Work environments may still be less accessible to some individuals with CIDs and subsequently, after-work socializing and recreation may also be less accessible (Dusseljee, Rijken, Cardol, Curfs, & Groenewegen, 2011). Being able to work has been considered a fundamental right of all Americans but also people around the world in general. This is expressed in Event Box 7.3.

7.3 EVENT THAT MADE A DIFFERENCE

1990—Americans with Disabilities Act is passed

In 1990, the Americans with Disabilities Act (Public Law 101-336) was passed by Congress and signed into law by President George H. W. Bush to address historical segregation and encourage integration of people with disabilities into the workforce and all public settings. The law notes that employers with 15 or more employees may not refuse to hire or promote an individual on the basis of disability when the person is otherwise qualified. The law also requires employers to make reasonable accommodations to allow an individual with disabilities to perform essential job functions.

Unfortunately, the results of the law have been mixed. Findings from 1990–1996 indicated that 47% of individuals with CIDs remained in the same type of employment category while 44% moved to more integrated employment settings. About 9% actually regressed to less integrated employment settings. In addition, in 1995, estimates were as high as 72% of all noninstitutionalized working-age individuals with disabilities were unemployed and the percentage estimates were higher for women (Blanck, 1998). However, gross income did increase for individuals investigated. Clearly, there is still much to be done to improve the employment outlook and subsequently the work characteristics of many individuals with CIDs. (See Chapter 13.)

Reported findings from the National Education Longitudinal Study-2 that included 8-year follow-ups from high school graduation indicated that about 76% of students with CIDs had been employed at some point since high school, but that only about 39% were employed at the 8-year follow-up interview (Newman et al., 2011). For students with moderate to severe CIDs, low rates of employment, post-secondary attendance, and independent living were reported (Bouck, 2012).

The educational characteristics discussed earlier are influential in the actual knowledge and skills obtained that prepare one for employment. Difficulties in learning concepts, storing and retrieving information, and developing comprehension skills are all variables that can ultimately affect workplace adjustment. Also of considerable importance are challenges in transfer and generalization of skills and the need for scaffolded-instruction (e.g., ongoing job coaching or training). As these difficulties are exacerbated, particularly for individuals with more severe levels of and multiple disabilities, the likelihood of developing and maintaining a career becomes increasingly challenging although certainly not beyond reach for many individuals. Supported employment programs, job coaching, and mandated transition planning have led to improvements in the employment outcomes and work characteristics of many individuals with severe disabilities.

As discussed in earlier sections, psychological, behavioral, and other adaptive skill characteristics also affect work characteristics. Clearly, as one is more integrated into the workforce, one is also more likely to be integrated within the community in general. In fact, employment, whether in integrated or nonintegrated settings, can be a requirement for maintaining participation in some adult service programs (e.g., living in a group home where staffing is very limited during the daytime on the assumption all who live there will be working).

Characteristics Related to Community

Just as with work characteristics, community characteristics are affected by the educational characteristics of the individual. Although community characteristics initially may seem an odd topic, it is important to remember from a historical perspective that segregation from the community in residential institutions was once common and persists today. In fact, around the world, people with CIDs are found living in a variety of settings. Some people live independently in the mainstream of communities, others in supported living arrangements (e.g., apartments with supports available to help with a variety of tasks such as cooking to budgeting), group homes, and more restrictive residential facilities, among other arrangements. The costs of such arrangements can vary widely from individual to individual and community to community, although the costs are usually greater for those with more severe levels of CIDs, those with multiple disabilities, and those with challenging behaviors (Hallam et al., 2002).

Taylor (2001) noted that given the integrated education most children with CIDs receive in present times, institutional settings are disappearing slowly from the landscape of America. Taylor stated that if deinstitutionalization is controversial among some families, "it is not because any significant number want their sons and daughters placed in institutions; it is because some do not want their children placed out of such places" (p. 28).

Despite costs or controversy, outcome characteristics associated with more integrated community living arrangements seem apparent. Kim, Larson, and Lakin (2001) reviewed 33 studies on deinstitutionalization in the United States. Overall, the findings suggested there were significant increases in overall adaptive behavior scores and there were positive findings in three studies for improvements in problem behaviors. These authors found similar improved outcomes in a review of research conducted in the United Kingdom and Ireland (Kim et al., 2001).

Although community living in general appears to lead to better adaptive behavior characteristics among those with CIDs, the level of supports available can greatly influence overall quality of life (AAIDD, 2010; Taylor, 2001). Historically, people with CIDs have tended to live at home with parents longer, to be more dependent on social service systems (although not always accessing available services), less mobile, and, as noted previously, less well integrated into the workforce (Blanck, 1998) than are those without disabilities. Although the community characteristics of persons with CIDs have seen improvement from the era when residential institutions were prevalent, the need for more supported and integrated living and community access arrangements and supports is still evident (AIDD, 2010). Because the adjustment of those with CIDs in the community is so critical, educational interventions are frequently based in the community itself, particularly as an individual approaches the age of leaving school (Westling & Fox, 2009).

Finally, Jordan and Dunlap (2001) noted that the status of adulthood will not be easily achieved by those with more severe cognitive impairments if adulthood is defined by the functioning level of the individual. In other words, performing activities associated with adulthood (rather than just physical maturation into an adult body) tend to indicate adult status in Western society. Among activities that indicate adulthood (e.g., voting, marriage) is leaving home. While cultural values and economic circumstances are important factors, leaving home is a traditional rite of adulthood that may enhance choice making and empowerment (Jordan & Dunlap, 2001). It is important, therefore, to develop support systems that encourage employment and community participation (Dusseljee et al., 2011).

Characteristics Related to Self-Care and Home Living

Hibbert, Kostinas, and Luiselli (2002) emphasized that many persons with CIDs acquire self-care skills but still need supervision and prompting in performing those same skills. With appropriate supervision and instruction, people with CIDs can improve both performance and acquisition deficits (e.g., Norman, Collins, Schuster, 2001; Saloviita & Tuulkari, 2000).

Age and type and severity of the disability may also affect self-care characteristics. Zigman, Schupf, Urv, Zigman, and Silverman (2002) found declines with age in both individuals specifically with Down syndrome and those with CIDs in general. Westling and Fox (2009) noted that research over time has indicated that those with severe disabilities are capable of learning to meet most of their self-care needs. These same authors suggested that natural environments that provide many opportunities for learning all types of adaptive behavior are preferable over more institutional settings.

Community living is important in the development of self-care and home living skills. As suggested in the AAIDD 2010 definition and the present discussion, support and opportunities to learn and perform adaptive behavior skills are critical in overcoming both acquisition and performance deficits. Still, it is likely that many individuals with CIDs and most with more severe levels will require some degree of lifelong support.

The challenge for those who offer supports is to minimize those supports to the level that allows the individual to acquire adaptive skills and perform those skills as independently as possible. Everyone needs help from employers, co-workers, teachers, friends, and family. People with CIDs are no different. For people with CIDs to have the greatest degree of empowerment and dignity, that help and all the people involved in providing help should focus on building those characteristics that lead to independence and a greater likelihood of fulfillment and a high quality of life. To focus too much on those characteristics associated with deficits would be to underestimate the potential of the individual and potentially to keep the person forever in a state of "readiness" training, waiting forever to be "ready" to learn how to make one's way in the world.

> ### Reflection
>
> **Does an individual with CIDs have the right to work and be employed even though she/he might be less productive than someone without disabilities? Does an individual with CIDs have the right to live in a neighborhood community?**

SUMMARY CHECKLIST

Educational Characteristics

Characteristics Related to Academic Skills—Under IDEA, students with disabilities should have access to the general education curriculum even if they exhibit deficits in academic skills, but they may also need access to a functional curriculum over time

Conceptual Thinking

➢ **Concepts**—Categories used to group objects, events, and characteristics on the basis of common properties

✓ The more exemplars children with intellectual disabilities are exposed to, the better they may be able to abstract the prototypical features of a concept
✓ Research into the ability of individuals with CIDs to categorize established that the ability existed and could be improved

Comprehension Skills—Diminished intellectual capabilities can lead to both acquisition and performance deficits in comprehension and other areas

✓ Literacy comprehension skills are often deficient with mathematical computational skills less affected when applied in relation to the individual's overall abilities and disabilities; literacy instruction may be inadequate for many students
✓ Listening comprehension may also be a problem area
✓ Literacy instruction for students with CIDs may lack the breadth and depth needed to develop these skills

Functional Skills—Those skills that must be performed by others if not performed by the individual with CIDs

✓ Students with CIDs may require more time to achieve mastery and transfer and generalization of knowledge and skills
✓ Problems in reading can result in an ever-increasing gap between the achievement of an individual with CIDs and those without disabilities
✓ Students with severe disabilities have greater difficulty with synthesizing information and skills in an organized and useful way
✓ Emphasis on academic skills may address those skills needed for present and future living, working, and leisure
✓ Students with severe disabilities need opportunities to learn functional academic skills

PSYCHOLOGICAL CHARACTERISTICS—The presence of atypical psychological characteristics has historically led to segregation and even persecution

✓ Learned Helplessness—An acquired tendency to give up easily or not to try when faced with new or difficult tasks
✓ Learned helplessness may result from repeated failure, a belief that others are in control, or from having others take care of one's needs unnecessarily

Characteristics Related to Self-Concept—Individuals with CIDs may differ in self-concept from those without CIDs in at least two ways

✓ Lack of ability in one area (e.g., academics) might affect self-concept in other unrelated areas (e.g., friendships)

✓ The "ideal" self-image might include lower aspirations than those of individuals without disabilities

✓ Access to community living and recreational/leisure programs may positively affect self-concept

Characteristics Related to Self-Regulation—Self-regulation involves the abilities to plan and manage time, attend to and concentrate on tasks, organize information strategically, establish a productive environment, and utilize resources

✓ Self-regulation is often learned from the modeling of others

✓ Self-regulation is amenable to change; those with self-regulatory behavior view themselves as in charge of their own lives

> **Characteristics Related to Locus of Control**—Refers to placing causality for life's outcomes and whether causality is linked to external or internal sources

✓ Those with an external locus of control tend to look to others for guidance and causality of outcomes

✓ Those with an internal locus of control tend to rely more on their own guidance and are more likely to assume personal responsibility for outcomes

✓ People with CIDs, like all of us, tend to fluctuate between having an external and internal locus of control, depending on the situation

✓ The study of locus of control and internal and external motivation lacks generality and precision, making definitive judgments about these characteristics problematic

Characteristics Related to Self-Determination and Self-Direction—Concerns an individual's ability to set goals, plan how to reach goals, monitor progress toward goals, and adjust plans accordingly

✓ People with CIDs tend to stress a need for greater control in their own lives yet experience fewer options for choice making and self-determination

✓ Self-determined individuals act according to their own preferences, interests, and abilities

✓ Becoming self-determined results from the ability to make choices and decisions

✓ As communication abilities decrease, deficits in being able to express one's thoughts, feelings, and needs may inhibit self-determination

✓ Restrictive environments may limit opportunities for choice making and self-determination

Characteristics Related to Self-Determination—Self-determination refers to the belief that one is accomplishing goals as a result of one's own efforts and motivation

✓ Self-determination is a process beginning in early childhood and continuing to adulthood

✓ Self-determined individuals are autonomous, self-regulated, able to make and execute a plan, psychologically empowered, and self-realized

✓ Self-determination may be developed in less restrictive environments

Characteristics Related to Motivation—Motivation is typically defined as an internal state that arouses, directs, and maintains one's behavior

✓ Intrinsically motivated people tend to seek out and conquer challenges in pursuit of their interests and tend to rely less on external incentives

✓ Extrinsically motivated people tend to show greater interest in the external incentives associated with completing a task than in the nature of the task itself

✓ Individuals with CIDs, like all of us, tend to follow along a continuum of self-determination of being fully self-determined to fully determined by others

✓ Individuals with CIDs may derive less pleasure in solving difficult problems and may be less likely to select difficult or new tasks to attack

✓ Engaging in choice making, challenging opportunities and activities, goal-setting, self-monitoring, self-evaluation, and problem solving encourage development of intrinsic motivation

BEHAVIORAL CHARACTERISTICS—The presence of challenging, difficult, or dangerous behavior should result in an analysis of a person's life experiences, current situation, personality, and health condition toward designing some intervention

✓ Difficult behavior can result from internal or external triggers, trauma, limited range of expression, and overlap of conditions (e.g., CIDs and mental illness), learned behaviors, mannerisms, and disease processes

Relationship Between CIDs and Behavioral Disorders—It is generally accepted people with CIDs exhibit more behavioral problems than those without disabilities

✓ Individuals with CIDs may have behavioral needs arising from destructiveness, self-injury, sexual aggression, and other behaviors such as tantrums, wandering, substance abuse, or not following mental health treatments

✓ Aggression is the behavior problem most often cited when an individual is referred for mental health services

✓ Some behavior, such as rule-breaking and noncompliance, may be the result of difficulties in processing and retrieving information, frustration, or lack of opportunities for recreation/leisure

✓ The variety of potential problem behaviors is extensive but the origins of the problems are not well known

✓ **Dual Diagnosis**—Dual diagnosis results from the presence of mental illness with CIDs and is not easily identified

✓ Stressors that affect behavioral characteristics include transitional phases, environmental stressors, parenting and social support problems, illness or disability, stigmatization, and frustration

✓ Most individuals with dual diagnosis have mild to moderate CIDs

Destructive or Aggressive Behavior—May be indicated by screaming, crying, damaging property, attacking others, as well as noncompliance

✓ Impulse control and bipolar disorder may be more closely associated with aggressive behavior

✓ Self-injury was associated with more severe CIDs

Self-Injurious Behavior—Includes behavior that results in harm to the individual and includes such behavior as hitting one's head, falling intentionally, biting, gouging, and scratching oneself

✓ SIB tends to occur more frequently among those with severe levels of CIDs

✓ SIB and stereotypy might emerge in early childhood and persist, or emerge in over- or under-stimulating conditions, or be learned behavior used to control others; it is also associated with certain syndromes

✓ Research indicates there have been many successful interventions used with SIB

Stereotypic Behavior—Refers to repetitive behaviors that tend to be physically harmless but affect adjustment

✓ Those with stereotypy may exhibit lower adaptive behavior scores, have more limited expressive abilities, less understanding of others' speech, and deficits in performing daily activities and functional skills

✓ The origins of stereotypy are not well understood and research does, at times, conflict (e.g., establishing the different functions of stereotypy)

✓ Stereotypy is amenable to treatment

Interpersonal and Sexual Relationships—Vary widely among people with CIDs

✓ Those individuals in more restrictive settings may find most relationships to be with people who are paid to interact with them

✓ Quality of life is connected to one's social network

✓ The quality of interpersonal relationships can affect both mental and physical health

✓ Intellectual and physical development, behavior problems, and communication abilities can affect relationship development

✓ Proximity to other children does not guarantee frequent social interaction

✓ Sexual relationships are of concern to individuals with CIDs and caregivers

✓ People with CIDs are more at-risk for being sexually and physically abused
✓ The right to privacy for those living in residential settings may be an issue

ADAPTIVE SKILL CHARACTERISTICS—May include deficits in acquisition and performance of adaptive behaviors

✓ It is assumed that individuals with CIDs will have significant limitations in multiple dimensions of adaptive behavior

Characteristics Related to Leisure—Participation in leisure activities and environments fosters growth, development, and wellness

✓ Individuals with CIDs participate in a wide variety of leisure activities and exhibit preferences
✓ Individuals with more severe levels of CIDs can learn to express choices in leisure settings and activities

Characteristics Related to Work—The presence of a disability leads to a lower likelihood of being employed and to substantially lower levels of income

✓ The Americans with Disabilities Act was enacted to reduce discrimination in the workplace based solely on disability and mandates employers provide reasonable accommodations
✓ Individuals with CIDs who work in integrated settings tend to have better job skills and live more independently, although income levels are still low
✓ As other areas of difficulty emerge (e.g., educational and behavioral characteristics), developing and maintaining a career becomes increasingly challenging
✓ Supported employment, job coaching, and mandated transition planning can aid in obtaining employment

Characteristics Related to Community—Historically, segregation from the community has occurred and still does occur

✓ The options and costs for living in the community vary widely although the costs are usually greater for those with more severe and multiple disabilities and for those with challenging behaviors
✓ Institutional settings are on the decrease in the United States
✓ Overall, research findings suggest positive outcomes in adaptive behavior and challenging behavior associated with integrated living arrangements
✓ In general, people with CIDs tend to live at home with parents longer, to be more dependent on social service systems, to be less mobile, and to be less well integrated in the workforce than are those without disabilities
✓ The status of adulthood is often associated in Western society with leaving home and living more independently

Characteristics Related to Self-Care and Home Living—With assistance, individuals with CIDs can improve both acquisition and performance deficits in these adaptive skill areas

- ✓ Individuals living in community settings tend to have at least as good or better adaptive behaviors than those living in institutional settings
- ✓ Individuals with severe levels of CIDs are capable of learning to meet most of their self-care needs
- ✓ The challenge for service providers is to provide needed support but still allow for maximum independence

ADDITIONAL SUGGESTIONS/RESOURCES

Discussion Questions

1. Which of the characteristics discussed do you believe would be most problematic for including an individual with CIDs into a general education setting? Into the workplace? Into the community?
2. What agencies or systems (e.g., Mental Retardation Developmental Disabilities Councils, mental health agencies) are best equipped to serve individuals with a dual diagnosis?
3. Why would the development of leisure skills be so critical in the adaptation of adults with CIDs?

Activities

1. Make a list of characteristics found in this chapter (e.g., Educational Characteristics). Interview appropriate professionals (e.g., teachers) regarding the presence or absence of the characteristics listed. Determine those that are more commonly cited by the professionals. Also, inquire as to those that are more problematic in the lives of the individuals with CIDs and for those who support them. Compare results.
2. Review the *DSM-V* criteria for various psychological/psychiatric disorders. Discuss what you think might be difficult about determining the presence of such disorders in individuals with CIDs. We have chosen not to list commercial websites in "E-sources." However, by using your web browser, you can locate websites/pages that include summaries of the *DSM-V* criteria.
3. Visit a classroom, group home, or residential facility in your community. Identify what aspects of the environment you believe might tend to encourage or inhibit self-determination and self-regulation.

E-sources

http://www.ninds.nih.gov/health_and_medical/disorders/lesch_doc.htm
This website of the National Institute of Neurological Disorders and Stroke includes material about Lesch-Nyhan syndrome as well as a wide variety of other disorders. This site should serve as a resource for research and general information.

http://www.thearc.org
This page is the website of The ARC, an advocacy organization. It includes a variety of fact sheets about intellectual disabilities, its causes, characteristics, and interventions.

http://www.bestbuddies.org
This is the homepage for Best Buddies International, Inc. This organization has chapters on many college/university campuses dedicated to encouraging friendships among those with and without intellectual and developmental disabilities. The website includes a history of the organization, its purpose, location of chapters, and other information.

8

SOCIETAL, FAMILY, AND MULTICULTURAL CHARACTERISTICS

Key Points

➤ SOCIETAL CHARACTERISTICS—Individual rights within society are considered, how individuals with CIDs interact with the justice system, and the rights of individuals to treatment over the life span are also included.
➤ FAMILY CHARACTERISTICS—Concerns of parents of children with CIDs are examined along with early childhood concerns, issues related to siblings, issues related to planning for the future, and the adult with CID as a parent and family member.
➤ MULTICULTURAL CHARACTERISTICS—Includes the importance of sociological and demographic factors in groups represented in special education and educational factors that interact with culture to affect individuals, families, and educators.

In Chapters 6 and 7 we discussed many characteristics of individuals with CIDs. In Chapter 8, we discuss characteristics from somewhat broader perspectives: societal, familial, and multicultural. We begin with societal characteristics. Within this section, we focus on perspectives of the individual's rights within society in general, within the justice system, and the right to treatment across the life span. Under family characteristics, we address parental issues and perspectives, concerns related to early childhood, siblings and other family members, planning for the future, and family issues for the individual as an adult. In the final section, multicultural characteristics, we address sociological and demographic factors and educational factors associated with schools and cultural differences, and changing demographics of the United States.

Some of these topics have been addressed in earlier chapters. For example, Chapter 5 includes information about environmental causes of CIDs related to poverty and poor health care. Chapters 5 and 6 include information about viewing an individual's strengths and support needs in context of his or her life circumstances, culture, family and community resources, and the demands of various environments. Here we will bring into focus the overall impact of CIDs on the individual and on society, the family, and cultures in general. The emphases in Chapter 8 will be less on specific individual characteristics and more on how the characteristics of people with CIDs in general interact with and impact on their place in society and society's response.

As we examine societal characteristics, we are concerned with how the individual's rights are respected and protected within the larger society. As we pointed out in Chapter 1, from a historical perspective, these rights have not always been protected.

SOCIETAL CHARACTERISTICS

In this section, we will specifically focus on three major areas with attention to legal perspectives. First, individual rights related to competence and consent will be addressed. Second, we will discuss what issues and concerns have emerged from the interactions of people with CIDs with the justice system. Finally in this section, we will discuss the rights of people with CIDs to treatment across the life span.

Individual Rights

Our purpose is not to examine all aspects of consent and competence (e.g., all the possible legal procedures) but rather how this issue impacts on individuals and society. Still, it is necessary to have a basic understanding of capacity, competence, consent, and guardianship.

O'Sullivan (1999) made the following distinctions. She noted that mental incapacity "generally means that a person has impaired or very limited ability to reason, remember, make choices, see the consequences of actions, and plan for the future. In law, it means that the person is unable to make legally binding decisions" (p. 13). She pointed out that while incompetency is frequently used interchangeably with incapacity, "incompetency suggests a more global inability" (p. 13). O'Sullivan also stressed that an individual can be competent to make some decisions (e.g., who should manage her money) but not be competent to make other decisions (e.g., to manage a bank account). In turn, one must be competent in order to give consent.

In a joint statement, The ARC and AAIDD (2009a) noted that appointing a guardian is serious for at least two reasons:

1. It limits a person's autonomy, that is, the person's choice of how to live and from whom to receive support to carry out that choice; and
2. It transfers the person's rights of autonomy to another person, a guardian.
   (www/aaidd.org)

O'Sullivan (1999) outlined several additional points in understanding competence, consent, and guardianship. She stated that "Guardianship concerns the inability of a person to give knowing consent, either totally, partially, or temporarily. **Guardianship** is a court action in which someone alleges that the person with disabilities *cannot* give consent" (p. 7). The AAIDD and The ARC emphasize that there should be a presumption of competence and that there are less intrusive alternatives to guardianship including limited guardianship, power of attorney, or advance directives. Full guardianship should be used only to the extent necessary (The ARC & AAIDD, 2009a). O'Sullivan stressed that guardianship is not to be taken lightly or simply sought because an individual turns 18 years of age and is legally an adult. Once established, guardianship is also difficult to undo and inserts oversight and court intervention into a person's life. Guardianship can vary from state to state but in general, "The guardianship of an adult is a legal procedure in which a court determines that a person has severe disabilities that impair the person's ability to make decisions, that the person is in need of, and that there is no less restrictive alternative to guardianship protection. The court appoints someone else, the guardian, to act for that person and authorizes the guardian to make decisions about her person, property, or both" (O'Sullivan, 1999; p. 8). The ARC and AAIDD (2009a) also stress that when a guardian is appointed, there should be an accompanying plan to teach and support the person to learn and use the skills needed to make decisions affecting his or her own life.

Consent, competence, and guardianship issues affect people with CIDs and society at large. Courts, legal professionals, medical professionals, advocacy organizations, educators, adult service providers in addition to families and people with CIDs may all be involved. Because these issues do have such important effects, position statements by professional organizations such as the one referenced here (The ARC and AAIDD joint statement on guardianship, 2009a) are used to provide guidelines.

Dinerstein (1999) summarized research from authors, various policy statements, and court decisions concerning consent, competence, and guardianship. Dinerstein outlined 12 major points that, in turn, we have summarized.

> American society places an emphasis on the autonomy of the individual and one's right to self-governance.
> Each citizen is presumed to be competent or to be capable of making decisions regarding his or her life.
> Giving consent presupposes that a person has capacity and information, and the consent is voluntary.
> As the importance of a decision increases (e.g., one that creates the possibility of physical harm such as a serious medical procedure), the need for formal procedures to determine capacity to give consent also increases.
> Because of cognitive, communicative, or educational capacity, persons with CIDs may not always be able to make independent decisions and give consent and therefore may need assistance.
> To maintain maximum autonomy and self-governance, when assistance is needed it should offer the least restrictive intervention for the shortest time possible.
> Anyone assisting the decision maker should consult with and seek the views of the individual with CID.
> Anyone assisting the individual should try to make decisions the person would make if competent, rather than basing decisions on what the assisting person thinks is in the best interest of the individual. The assisting person then must know the individual and what types of decisions the person has made or does make. The "best interests" basis is used if the views or desires of the individual with CID cannot be learned.

➢ Consent presupposes adequate knowledge. Those providing assistance or seeking consent must take steps to enhance the person's knowledge base and to communicate effectively. Lack of information should not be confused with an inability to make a decision.

➢ Consent must be given freely and without coercion. For those who have lived in more restrictive settings where decision making has been limited, coercion may take subtle forms and must be carefully avoided.

➢ Who should ask for consent from a person should be carefully considered, especially if the individual seeking consent is one whom the person with CID would not likely refuse a request.

➢ The need for autonomy must be balanced with the need to protect people with CIDs from exploitation or abuse.

People with CIDs may have difficulty exercising individual rights due to limitations in their own capacities and/or because of others' perceptions of deficits in those capacities. It would be wrong to assume, as The ARC and the AAIDD (2009a) asserted, that because an individual is identified as having CID, he or she should be presumed not to be capable of exercising his or her rights to give consent, vote, marry, and carry out all functions of adulthood.

Still, in some cases, exercising individual rights can come into conflict with the laws that govern society. When this occurs, the justice system may become involved. People with CIDs as a group have had a long and controversial place in the justice system.

People with CIDs and the Justice System

In recent years, the debate concerning whether individuals with CIDs should ever be executed for capital crimes has been played out in courts, legislatures, and in the media. As a result of the landmark 2002 U.S. Supreme Court case *Atkins v. Virginia*, it was banned in the United States. Event Box 8.1 includes a summary of this landmark case.

While capital punishment in general and of those with CIDs in particular is controversial, most people with CIDs interact with the justice system in much less drastic fashion. People with CIDs are more likely to be the victims of crimes than the perpetrators. The Americans with Disabilities Act is intended to ensure equal protection and equal access under the law. Still, the problems associated with how people with CIDs are treated within the justice system, as suspects and criminals, as well as witnesses and victims, remains.

8.1 EVENT THAT MADE A DIFFERENCE

2002—*Atkins v. Virginia*

The Supreme Court of the United States ruled that the death penalty was cruel and unusual punishment for criminals with CIDs. The Supreme Court overturned an earlier ruling in Virginia upholding the death penalty for Atkins relying on *Penry v. Lynaugh,* an earlier Supreme Court ruling. In writing for the majority, Justice Stevens stated: "because of their disabilities in areas of reasoning, judgment, and control of their impulses . . . they do not act with level of moral culpability that characterizes the most serious adult criminal conduct." The majority went on to suggest that the nature of intellectual disabilities could create risk to the fairness of capital punishment proceedings. Finally, Justice Stevens noted the prohibition against cruel and unusual punishment applied to offenders with intellectual disabilities "in the light of our evolving standards of decency."

> *Atkins v. Virginia*, 536 U.S. 304 (2002).

Additional source: Salekin, Olley, & Hedge (2010)

Individuals with CIDs as Suspects of Crime

In a joint statement, The ARC and the AAIDD (2008) noted that "People with intellectual and/or developmental disabilities (1) who are victims, suspects or witnesses, like other residents of the United States, have the right to justice and fair treatment" (www.aaidd.org). Moreover, The ARC and the AAIDD (2008) stressed individuals with CIDs:

- May not have their disability identified;
- May give incriminating but inaccurate statements, may try to please authorities, or be confused or misled by investigative methods;
- May be found incompetent to stand trial;
- Having been found incompetent, find themselves inappropriately placed for extensive time in an institutional setting;
- Be less able to assist their own attorney;
- Waive rights (e.g., Miranda warning) unknowingly; and
- Be denied the right to speak or testify.

It is clear that individuals with CIDs are often at greater risk for denial of justice and/or legal rights more often than those without disabilities. This risk is of importance whether an individual is a victim or suspect, or a witness to criminal activity.

Individuals with CIDs as Victims of Crime

The ARC and the AAIDD (2008) stated that individuals with CIDs are 4 to 10 times more likely to be victimized and that their cases are rarely prosecuted. Historically, Sobsey (1997) suggested several reasons why crimes against people with CIDs and other disabilities may not be prosecuted. First, such cases that occur in caregiving settings may be treated as investigations of abuse rather than in the criminal justice system. Second, prosecutors may fear that witnesses with disabilities will be excluded or not believed in court proceedings. Police may not vigorously pursue investigations because they feel the cases cannot be prosecuted. People with disabilities may not report the crimes for fear their allegations will not be acted upon. Sobsey also suggested that in some cases when convictions are achieved, lesser penalties might be applied to perpetrators who commit crimes against people with disabilities. The ARC (2006) emphasized that "Victims with disabilities must be able to file charges, report criminal activity or pursue any other legal action necessary in order to have an equal opportunity to protect themselves and protect their rights" (p. 10). Research Box 8.1 includes a very useful and enlightening document created by The ARC regarding individuals with CIDs and the justice system.

8.1 RESEARCH THAT MADE A DIFFERENCE

The ARC's Justice Advocacy Guide (2006). *An advocate's guide on assisting victims and suspects with intellectual disabilities* **(http://www.thearc.org/ document.doc?id=3669).**

This 40-page document was developed by The ARC and the National Organization for Victim Assistance. It includes five major topics including:

- Responding to victimization
- Responding to arrest
- Answers to commonly asked questions
- Justice advocacy programs within The ARC
- Other resources for victims and suspects

While the document is intended for advocates, it includes a wealth of information for anyone concerned with individuals with CIDs and their interactions with the criminal justice system. There are many suggestions for supporting and assisting people presented in a step-by-step or stages format. Because this is a web-based resource, it should be periodically updated as well.

It is also important to recognize that different states and countries have different laws affecting how the criminal justice system works and the interaction with people with CIDs. Therefore, maintaining up-to-date information is important. Also, some legal professionals do specialize in assisting individuals with disabilities (The ARC, 2006).

Individuals with CIDs as Offenders

There has been research into the experiences and outcomes for individuals with CIDs as they interact with justice systems as offenders. Salekin, Olley, and Hedge (2010) suggested that most individuals who are offenders are likely functioning in the milder levels of CID, at least based on IQ. In comparison to those with more severe disabilities, those with higher IQs may be "more vulnerable to the negative influences of typical offenders who reside in the community and, if raised in a home where one or more individuals engage in criminal behavior, they are more likely to follow this course rather than carving out a separate existence" (Salekin et al., 2010; p. 101). Of some importance when an individual with CID is arrested, comprehension of Miranda rights and competence to stand trial are two important issues to be assessed (Salekin et al., 2010).

Individuals with CIDs, as noted previously in The ARC and the AAIDD joint statement (2008), may not comprehend fully Miranda rights. Furthermore, they may change their responses or positions on waiving rights due to influences from those in authority providing friendly feedback or advice (Salekin et al., 2010). Also, Salekin et al. found in their literature review that a relatively small percentage of defendants with CIDs were found competent to stand trial. Interestingly, those with higher IQs and African-American defendants were more likely to be found competent for legal proceedings to advance. Evaluations are important to also identify any individuals who may attempt to feign a CID to avoid legal consequences (Salekin et al., 2010).

The ARC (2006) stated that individuals with CIDs are overrepresented in the U.S. and other criminal justice systems. Also, individuals are likely to need supports throughout legal proceedings although there may not be enough trained professionals (The ARC & AAIDD, 2008). People with CIDs within the juvenile justice system present additional challenges. From a historical perspective, Ransom and Chimarusti (1997) cited research suggesting that as much as 23% of the offenders in youth correction agencies had disabilities including learning disabilities, emotional disturbances, and CIDs. They also noted the application of educational programs to these youths was not consistent.

When an individual is found guilty and sentenced, The ARC and the AAIDD (2008) stress that the person:

- Be given reasonable accommodations, treatment, and education as well as community-based corrections as appropriate;
- Have trained probation and parole officers who treat them fairly based on disability and accommodations needs;
- Be exempt from the death penalty;
- Have access to expert witnesses and legal professionals experienced in working with individuals with CIDs; and
- Have their disabilities identified through state procedures that are accurate and fair.

Smith, Polloway, Patton, and Beyer (2008) stressed that while only a minority of youth with disabilities will actually encounter the justice system, it is a sufficient number to merit the attention and planning of educators. Educators should be concerned with educating students about the justice system and the implications of both victimization and as offenders. Educators can also involve school resource officers and other legal professionals in teaching and role playing. Finally, educators may need to act in the role of advocate (Smith et al., 2008).

It is apparent that interactions between individuals with CIDs and the justice system are less than optimal. Under IDEA, educational services are mandated to 21 years of age. Under the AAIDD (2010) definition of intellectual disabilities, it is recognized that many individuals will need intermittent to pervasive lifelong support. Therefore, the right to treatment across the life span is an important consideration.

Right to Treatment Across the Life Span

The right to treatment across the life span and in the community is one established in the courts; through many government programs at local, state, and federal levels; and through informal support systems such as recreational and religious organizations. Treatment across the life span is linked to self-determination and quality of life. Event Box 8.2 discusses another important court case related to treatment of adults with CIDs.

8.2 EVENT THAT MADE A DIFFERENCE

1999—U.S. Supreme Court's Olmstead Decision: *Olmstead v. L. C.,* **527 U.S. 581 (1999)**

In an important U.S. Supreme Court decision, the court asserted that exclusion of individuals from community-based services provided by a public entity on the basis of disability alone was a violation of the Americans with Disabilities Act. In this case, two women with intellectual disabilities and mental health issues were voluntarily institutionalized in Georgia. Eventually, the health care professionals caring for the women believed they could be cared for in a community-based program. The women remained institutionalized nevertheless. The court reasoned that the disabilities the women had were the reasons for them not receiving community-based programming rather than the state's claim of lack of funding. The court ruled that unnecessary institutionalization based solely on disability could be considered discrimination.

Treatment also means establishing a system of supports to provide services. The AAIDD (2010) provides principles and guidelines for establishing such supports within society. The AAIDD emphasized that supports for individuals with CIDs may be necessary across the life span. This organization noted that disability is an expression of limitations in individual functioning within a social context; it is not fixed but is fluid and changing; and a person's disability may be lessened by providing interventions and supports that address prevention, adaptive behaviors, and role status. Therefore, treatment services across the life span may be needed because of the impact of CIDs and the fluidity of that impact within various contexts (e.g., home, community, employment, age, family situation).

AAIDD (2010) includes supports of varying intensities. To identify those support needs, the AAIDD discusses a five-component process:

- Component 1 is identifying desired life experiences and goals that focus on the individual's preferences, dreams, and interests;
- Component 2 involves determining the pattern and intensity of support needs and how often and where those supports are needed to accomplish those experiences and goals from Component 1;
- Component 3 is to develop an individualized support plan that specifically notes settings, activities, and types and intensity of supports, and who will deliver the supports;
- Component 4 is to monitor progress on the implementation of the individualized support plan; and
- Component 5 is an evaluation of whether the plan is resulting in the desired experiences and goals (AAIDD, 2010).

If the evaluation of the plan indicates outcomes are not being met, then the supports planning team should revert back to Component 3 to revise the plan (AAIDD, 2010).

Finally, the AAIDD emphasizes that individuals may need services such as educational and advocacy services and may also have Individualized Education Programs or Individualized Written Rehabilitation Plans in addition to a supports plan.

Person-Centered Planning

Person-centered planning is a critical element in Component 1 of the AAIDD's suggested process for developing a supports plan. Historically, person-centered planning includes the following principles. First, the individual is the most important person in the planning process and the plans made. Second, family, friends, and significant others should be involved in the process and these personal relationships should be a major source of support for the individual. Third, the abilities, talents, and aspirations of the individual should be considered in the planning rather than focusing on disabilities. Fourth, the plan for the individual's life span and desired outcomes should not be restricted by the services currently available. Finally, a broader implementation approach could be used which focuses more on generic services that are local and informal (e.g., a church volunteer may help an individual with budgeting and shopping rather than the individual paying for formal assistance from a local agency) (Butterworth, Steere, & Whitney-Thomas, 1997).

Person-centered planning may also give the individual greater access to and choice in the services that are paid for by him or her or by government agencies (e.g., purchasing supported employment assistance as opposed to attending a sheltered workshop). Self-determination and self-regulation, as well as opportunities for making choices, are critical in person-centered planning. To exercise choice and control, an individual needs to be both self-determined and self-regulated. The more typical the education, life, and living environment for an individual, the more likely the individual will learn to be self-determined and self-regulated and will be able to participate or direct the person-centered planning process. For example, an individual who is able to participate in a meaningful way may express preference for working in a business as opposed to working in a sheltered facility and to live in an apartment alone or with a friend as opposed to a group home. The individual may direct that available funds be spent on support in a new job and rely on natural family supports for help with apartment living rather than paying for the sheltered facility or living in the group home. In a joint statement, The ARC and the AAIDD (2009) stressed that individuals with CIDs should receive the supports they need at all stages of their lives, including the resources to explore and define how they live and with whom they interact.

Factors Affecting Supports

Where one lives affects the individual's system of supports and quality of life. Kellow and Parker (2002) found that individuals living in suburban versus rural settings used about the same number of formal supports with about the same frequency. However, those in suburban settings had more informal supports and utilized informal supports more frequently. Employment opportunities in particular tended to be more limited in rural areas and were recognized as a void for those individuals who were unemployed (Kellow & Parker, 2002). Because formal sources of support can be expensive to society, their use should be effective in terms of costs and outcomes.

Braddock, Hemp, Rizzolo, Haffer, Tanis, and Wu (2011) stated that in nearly every state as of 2009, more public spending for disability services for those with CIDs focused on community-based services rather than more expensive institutional services. Approximately 75% of all individuals lived in an environment inhabited by 1–6 persons in 2009. Also as of 2009, the average cost of services for an individual living in a supported living environment was about $26,200 while those in larger state-operated institutions had an average cost of about $191,100 (Braddock et al., 2011). Clearly, living in the community is not only providing individuals with more opportunities for work, leisure, and community experiences, but it is less costly on average as well.

Funding is used to support major societal efforts such as special education, deinstitutionalization, long-term care, health care, and employment. If individuals with disabilities are to be successfully employed, live as independently as possible, enjoy leisure and social opportunities that enhance quality of life, supports must be aimed at achieving those goals with people with CIDs engaged in that process. Tremendous sums of money are spent by society in these processes. The right to treatment should mean moving toward less intensive supports over the life span. Right to treatment also suggests the full citizenship of people with CIDs within the larger society (Luckasson et al., 2002). Historically, full citizenship and the right to treatment have not always been of concern to professionals, even in the 20th century (see Event Box 8.3).

8.3 EVENT THAT MADE A DIFFERENCE

1912—A Social Darwinist Addresses the Massachusetts Medical Society

The following statements are attributed to an American social Darwinist in a 1912 address to the Massachusetts Medical Society:

> The feeble-minded are a parasitic, predatory class, never capable of self-support or of managing their own affairs. The great majority ultimately become public charges in some form. They cause unutterable sorrow at home and are a menace and danger to the community. Feeble-minded women almost invariably are immoral. . . . We have only begun to understand the importance of feeble-mindedness as a factor in the causation of pauperism, crime and other social problems. (p. 104)

Clearly, such attitudes were detrimental in establishing that treatment was necessary and effective, especially when provided in community settings.

Source: Byrne (2000).

As surely as a CID has an impact on the individual and society in general, it also has an impact on families. The characteristics of families vary considerably and so too can the potential impact of a CID on a family member. In Chapter 4, we discussed some issues related to parenting and CIDs. Here, we will focus primarily on parental issues and perspectives of parents without CIDs who have children with CIDs. We will also address concerns related to early childhood and development, siblings, and planning for the future. Finally, we will examine issues related to the family of the person with CID as an adult, including sexual issues, marriage, and child-rearing.

Reflection

What does the right to treatment across the life span mean for the individual with a CID and society? What are the implications for not providing treatments and supports? What are the costs?

FAMILY CHARACTERISTICS

Probably the single most important fact about families in the United States is to make no assumptions about what a "typical" family is or should be (Woolfolk, 2013). Parents of children with CIDs come from and with a variety of experiences and backgrounds. Families are both affected by and affect the outcomes for members with and without CIDs. Parents' input into the planning of and engagement in their child's education is mandated in the IDEA. Their concerns for and role in the family system and in the collaboration between school and family and adult service providers is a major influence on achieving successful outcomes.

Parental Issues and Concerns

Family outcomes are critical in nearly every person's life and certainly are often important in the lives of individuals with CIDs. The outcomes for families center around interactions, well-being, and supports (AAIDD, 2012). The AAIDD (2012) outlined several exemplars of a high quality of family life including among others:

- Spending time together, supporting one another, and problem solving;
- Parents help and teach their children and meet the children's needs;
- Pursue individual interests, have friends, and outside help;
- Opportunities for educational and employment growth;
- Achieve physical well-being through medical services and opportunities for leisure and recreation activities;
- Experience financial well-being through sufficient family income;
- Are involved in the community; and
- Has supports at school, home, and workplace and good relationships with service providers.

When life circumstances and other variables affect these outcomes, individuals with CIDs and their families can be negatively impacted. The presence of a CID in a family member is known (in some but not all cases) to affect the family and especially caregivers.

Family Stress

In a study in Australia, overall quality of life of families with a member with CID was assessed (Rillotta, Kirby, Shearer, & Nettlebeck, 2012). Domains assessed included family health, financial well-being, family relationships, supports from other people, support from related services, influence of values, careers, leisure, and recreation. Health, family relationships, and financial well-being were rated as more important than support from others. Family relationships, health, values, and leisure and recreation were also considered important domains for measuring their quality of family life.

Seltzer, Greenberg, Floyd, Pettee, and Hong (2001) contrasted outcomes for parents of children with a disability, parents of children with a mental health problem, and a normative comparison group at mid-life. Data were taken from a longitudinal study and involved a variety of questions. These researchers concluded that within their sample, participants were more or less on an even level at the outset but patterns of well-being and attainment diverged after age 18. Parents of a child with a developmental disability had lower rates of employment, had larger families, and less social participation than parents in the control group. These same parents were similar to the control parents in educational and marital status, physical health, and psychological well-being at mid-life.

More recently, Cramm and Nieboer (2012) found that parents' social well-being, changes in their well-being, and changes in their children's social well-being were good predictors of the quality of life of family members with CIDs. Similarly, Faust and Scior (2008) found that when a family member with CID also had mental health problems, parents described there were far-reaching negative consequences for them. Baker, Blacher, Crnic, and Edelbrock (2002) studied stress among parents of children with and without developmental delays at 3 years of age. These researchers found that the extent of a child's behavior problems was a stronger contributor to parent stress than was the child's cognitive delay. However, children with developmental delays were three to four more times more likely to have scores indicating significant problems on a parent-completed assessment of child behavior problems. Also, parents of children with delays reported greater negative impacts of the child on stress in the family and on family finances. These parents reported positive feelings about their children as well (Baker et al., 2002).

Assessing quality of life of parents, family members, and the member with a CID is important for service providers to understand the stresses and impacts on families.

As children with CIDs grow older, parents may still find themselves in the role of caregivers. Yoong and Koritsas (2012) reported that among participants in their study, caring for an adult with CID had both negative and positive effects on parents' quality of life. It is apparent from research in various countries that families can be under stress and that access to flexible supports for parents as well as the individual with CID are important to the quality of life of all (Cramm & Nieboer, 2011; Faust & Scior, 2008; Yoong & Koritsas, 2012).

It would appear that overall, parents of children with CIDs do experience and report stress related to their children, but also report positive effects from caregiving and supports from others. Results from studies also suggest that the stress levels experienced overall may not have been as great or debilitating on parents and families as might have once been conjectured. This is particularly important in that the roles of parents of children with CIDs can be many and demanding, as well as rewarding.

Early Childhood Issues and Concerns

Typically, children with more severe and/or multiple disabilities are identified early including prior to, at the time of, or shortly after birth. Families may experience a grief cycle which could include periods of shock, denial, guilt, anger, shame, depression, and acceptance. Westling and Fox (2009) cautioned, however, against expecting such cycles in most or many parents and families. These authors noted, for example, that having a child with a severe disability can include positive changes such as personal growth, improved relationships and interpersonal interaction skills, and strengthening of philosophical values (Westling & Fox, 2009).

Chapman, Scott, and Mason (2002) found that older maternal age and low maternal education were each associated with increased risk of CIDs. Overall, however, the authors found in their study of over 247,000 subjects in a 3-year birth cohort that the births associated with younger mothers with less than 12 years of education accounted for the greatest proportion of CIDs. The results suggested that this group of mothers may be particularly in need of prevention/early intervention efforts (Chapman et al., 2002).

We discussed in Chapter 4 that early intervention programs have been shown to produce desirable gains in development for young children with CIDs (or at risk for CIDs). Prevention and early intervention would appear to be a very significant issue related to early childhood. These efforts should typically be family-centered rather than just child-focused. Although stressors associated with the birth or diagnosis of a child with a CID and other disabilities are evident, these stressors have differential effects on parents, families, and the children themselves and can be mediated or alleviated for many families.

Parents of children with CIDs are major players in family adjustment, although siblings and other family members may also be affected. Siblings are not only important in the developmental years, but can become primary caregivers or guardians as parents of an individual with a CID age or pass away (Turnbull, Turnbull, Erwin, & Soodak, 2006).

Sibling Issues and Concerns

Turnbull et al. (2006) noted that research on siblings of individuals with disabilities in general has yielded mixed results concerning both how siblings are affected by the family member with a disability and how the siblings affect the family member with a disability. For example, some studies have suggested that behavior problems are more common among siblings of individuals with disabilities while other studies have found no significant relationship. Similarly, some studies indicate siblings have lower self-esteem while others have not revealed significant evidence of this (Turnbull et al., 2006).

Grissom and Borkowski (2002) studied 54 adolescents, 27 of whom had a sibling with a disability and 27 of whom did not. Between the two groups, there were no significant differences on scores of self-completed questionnaires measuring self-efficacy, peer competence, and maternal attitudes toward and modeling of prosocial and empathetic behavior. Findings also suggested that proactive interventions with families might be focused on increasing mothers' awareness of the effect they have on the siblings of the individual with a disability (Grissom & Borkowski, 2002).

Where the individual with CID lives may be influential on siblings and family members in general. Baker and Blacher (2002) reported on a study involving family members of residents in three large treatment centers in three different states. Although the majority of respondents in the study were parents, siblings did represent a minority of respondents. Overall, respondents demonstrated good adjustment following placement of the individual with a CID in the treatment center. For the most part, family members stayed involved, reported having good health, positive marital adjustment, and relatively low stress and caretaking burdens (Baker & Blacher, 2002). These findings suggested that planning for care of the individual with a CID in adulthood could have positive effects for other family members.

Seltzer, Krauss, Hong, and Orsmond (2001) reported on findings concerning siblings of individuals with CIDs and relocation. Overall, siblings worried less about the future following the family member's relocation to a residential program. Siblings also increased their level of involvement following relocation, suggesting their importance in long-term support to the family member with a CID (Seltzer et al., 2001). However, with more funding being aimed at community resources and less funding at larger treatment facilities (Braddock et al., 2011), more siblings may find themselves planning for supports in community-based living, working, and leisure environments.

Relocation of an individual with a CID to a residential program can provide some positive changes for family members. Concerns related to planning and providing for supports across the life span are embedded in the IDEA and are a major concern of many families.

EFFECTS RELATED TO SIBLINGS

The effect of and effect on siblings is dependent on many variables including family size, birth order, gender, and coping styles, among other factors. Negative outcomes for siblings could include embarrassment, guilt, isolation and loneliness, loss, resentment, increased responsibilities, and pressure to achieve. However, Turnbull and colleagues pointed out and the research reviewed here suggests positive outcomes can and do accrue as well. Among these include being helpful in promoting inclusion in school and other activities, providing information about school to parents, and ensuring opportunities and encouragement in the community.

Source: Turnbull, Turnbull, Erwin, & Soodak (2006).

Planning Issues and Concerns

Parents are concerned about the future of their children. As we have just discussed, families do experience worries and burdens over the long term regarding the supports needed by a loved one with a CID. Seltzer, Greenberg, Floyd, Pettee, and Hong (2001) suggested that positive outcomes and favorable adjustment by families as the individual with a CID grows older could be reflective of changes in legal and public policy initiatives. Again, Braddock et al. (2011) noted that public policy and funding has changed over the past decades toward favoring less restrictive living and working environments. These initiatives may have led to increases in educational and employment opportunities that make the future brighter from families' perspectives. However, in previous chapters we pointed out that the overall outcomes regarding employment of people with CIDs, as well as the achievement of more independent living arrangements, and the satisfaction of social and leisure lives, is far from optimal. For these outcomes to be achieved, planning for the transitions in the individual's and family's life cycles is crucial.

Factors Affecting Effective Planning

Turnbull, Turnbull, Erwin, and Soodak (2006) outlined several factors that can affect families' thinking and planning for the future. First, there may be fewer "norms" or desirable models of expected behavior from which to choose. Second, the rituals that earmark growth into adulthood (going to college, marriage, having children) may occur less frequently among individuals with CIDs (Jordan & Dunlap, 2001), particularly those with more severe levels. Transition planning programs in schools and in geographic areas (e.g., very rural or isolated areas) may be less effective or provide fewer options. Therefore, transition planning and programming are critical.

Blacher (2001) outlined a proposed model for successful transitions for individuals with CIDs. Important variables included in the model were individual characteristics, family well-being, family involvement, and environment and culture. Family well-being should include the individual (e.g., how much stress or anxiety is experienced) as well as parents and other family members. There can be positive impacts of transitions in life in addition to some of the more negative ones such as stress and anxiety. Individual characteristics that might affect transitions and future planning include age, gender, physical health, cognitive functioning, adaptive behavior, maladaptive behavior, and psychiatric status. Psychiatric problems, in particular, along with the presence of inappropriate behavior, can raise problems as opportunities for greater independence occur (Blacher, 2001). Difficulty with performing age-appropriate skills needed to participate in adult activities is problematic for many individuals, especially those with more severe disabilities. People with CIDs may be dependent longer on families, but can and do "move out" and develop more individual lives.

Bigby and Fyffe (2009) suggested that it is critical to provide long-term planning as well as immediate and long-term support for individuals with CIDs to achieve less restrictive and more community-based living arrangements. McFelea and Raver (2012) found among 54 primary caregivers of children living in either residential facilities or at home all rated family quality of life as exemplary, although overall ratings of family quality of life on various dimensions still favored those families where the child lived at home. Blacher (2001) noted from various studies that overall, adult transitions seemed to be better if done prior to parental death. Thus, family involvement is critical in transitions and such transitions should not necessarily translate into less involvement over time.

Overall, the role of and interaction with the family have the potential to very positively affect the adjustment of the individual with a CID. To this point, we have considered the family from the perspective of the individual with a CID being a child within the family system. In the following section, we discuss adult issues of growing into adulthood and, in particular, the role of the individual with a CID as a parent himself or herself.

Adult Issues and Concerns

It is important to remember that most individuals with CIDs have mild disabilities and may need fewer and less intensive supports throughout much of their lives compared to those with more severe disabilities. Individuals with CIDs do become parents themselves and have their own families. Turnbull et al. (2006) pointed out, however, that achieving adult status in various family functions is not always easy for an individual with disabilities.

Jordan and Dunlap (2001) stressed that adulthood is defined by culture, can vary based on stage of adulthood (i.e., young, middle-aged, or elderly adult) and often involves more underlying or hidden concepts than explicit concepts. Adulthood can be perceived as physical maturation of the body. It may be perceived as a level of functioning or competence that many individuals with more severe disabilities may never achieve. Competence is also dependent on the environment and the demands within that environment. Adulthood might also be perceived from a sociocultural perspective. In Western culture, independence, autonomy, and physical and emotional separation from parents are concepts that help define adulthood (Jordan & Dunlap, 2001). These authors summarized several issues associated with adulthood including voting, moving out, sexual consent, and marriage.

Voting is a right afforded all nonfelonious citizens regardless of IQ. Individuals with CIDs should be considered competent to vote unless otherwise found not to be so by a court. Training in exercising the right to vote should be a part of civics education for individuals with CIDs (Jordan & Dunlap, 2001).

There are also increased numbers of postsecondary programs available to individuals with CIDs on college campuses (Turnbull et al., 2006). These options could include separate classes designed just for people with disabilities, a mix of separate and integrated classes, or a support model focused on individualized preferences and supports (Turnbull et al., 2006). Grigal, Hart, and Weir (2012) found that, as of 2009, there were 149 programs for people with CIDs in 39 states in the United States. However, the programs surveyed varied considerably in the type of experiences provided (Grigal et al., 2012). It is important then, that consumers make individual and informed decisions about attendance and desired outcomes from such programs.

Moving out is a ritual often associated with adulthood although culture may influence the concept of moving out as a ritual of adulthood. Poor employment and fewer living arrangement options, as well as the need for pervasive supports, may limit the opportunities for individuals with CIDs to leave their family homes (Jordan & Dunlap, 2001). However, as discussed earlier, it may result in less stress on families if moving out occurs prior to the death of parents. Supported living programs are on the increase although not necessarily universally available (Braddock et al., 2011).

Marriage is less and less a required identifier for adulthood but still is prominent in many cultures. Capacity to make informed decisions is necessary to marry. Jordan and Dunlap (2001) stated that the issue should not be whether individuals with CIDs, including those with severe disabilities, should be allowed to marry but how to institute safeguards against exploitation within a relationship. Nevertheless, Watkins (2009) noted that 80% of women and 90% of men with CIDs never marry. Watkins also stressed that state laws governing marriage of people with CIDs can vary and that many parents of people with CIDs may not be aware of marriage rights of their adult children. People with CIDs, in general, and women in particular, may be at risk for abuse within relationships. However, they may also have more socio-sexual awareness than many may typically think they have (Healy, McGuire, Evans, & Carley, 2009).

Sexual consent is protected legally for younger individuals. The age at which society no longer deems it necessary to protect a person's ability to give consent for sex is also an indicator of adulthood. Capacity to give consent for sex is complex and influenced by place of residence, degree of autonomy, and culture, among other factors (Jordan &

Dunlap, 2001). The ARC and the AAIDD (2008) in a joint statement stressed that "Every person has the right to exercise choices regarding sexual expression and social relationships. The presence of an intellectual or developmental disability, regardless of severity, does not, in itself, justify loss of rights related to sexuality" (www.thearc.org). Kennedy and Niederbuhl (2001) examined the consensus of 305 doctoral-level members of the American Psychological Association concerning what factors should be considered in establishing sexual consent criteria. These authors noted that some states include the abilities to understand the nature of sexual conduct, possible consequences of actions, and appreciation of the moral dimensions of giving consent to sex as criteria employed. In their study, Kennedy and Niederbuhl (2001) found that the sample indicated that understanding the nature of sexual activity, understanding the consequences of sexual activity, and being able to protect oneself as the minimum criteria needed to establish consent for sexual activity. Although extensive data on the prevalence or incidence of sexual activity of individuals with CIDs are lacking, it stands to reason that increased opportunities for inclusive education, employment, recreation, and living arrangements will likely enhance the number of opportunities to be sexually active. It is also important to understand that adults with CIDs are not children and are likely to experience the same sexual feelings as do those without disabilities.

Problems associated with sexual behavior present great challenges. Children with CIDs are at risk for sexual abuse and can become sexual offenders. Among sex offenders themselves with CIDs, just over 59% of women reported having been sexually and/or physically abused themselves as children (Lindsay, Steptoe, & Haut, 2012). In another study in England, one-fifth of all referrals of abuse for people with CIDs involved sexual abuse with two-thirds of those referrals for women being sexually abused (Cambridge, Beadle-Brown, Milne, Mansell, & Whelton, 2011). Finally, if individuals are sexually active, the possibility of becoming a parent exists as well. Issues and concerns in parenting for individuals with CIDs are much the same as those without disabilities but involve other challenges as well.

Parenting Issues and Concerns

We have discussed extensively all the possible problematic characteristics and strengths that individuals with CIDs may exhibit. These problem areas can create difficulties in adapting in life. Parenting can be difficult for anyone and these problems can exacerbate those difficulties. In a joint statement, The ARC and the AAIDD (2008) stated that historically, "discrimination toward individuals with intellectual and/or developmental disabilities includes the denial of rights and opportunities to have and to raise their own children" (www.thearc.org). The ARC and the AAIDD also pointed out that research documents the ability of many parents with CIDs to raise a child successfully given the appropriate and effective supports. Unfortunately, such support programs are few in existence. In 2011, The ARC stressed that parents with CIDs may be more closely scrutinized for any evidence of abuse or neglect (www.thearc.org, 2011).

Lamont and Bromfield (2009) reviewed research studies from a number of countries, including the United States, Australia, Germany, the Netherlands, the United Kingdom, and Canada, and drew the following conclusions. In Australia, parents with CIDs represent only about 1%–2% of all parents in that country but are overrepresented in child protection and legal proceedings. Assessing parental competence is an issue, although there is a lack of universal standards for parental competence. As a result, IQ testing may be overemphasized. Similarly, there may be an assumption that any difficulty with parenting is a direct result of the CID.

Child neglect (rather than abuse) tends to be more the issue in court proceedings. However, the evidence provided documenting the neglect is often based primarily on the CID. It is unclear if parents with CIDs are more likely to neglect their children. Lamont and Bromfield (2009) also found that parents with CIDs and their children may be more vulnerable to predators who may sexually or physically abuse them. CIDs may contribute to parental stressors and other problems which can be associated with neglect and abuse. However, parents with CIDs did not appear more likely than other parents to engage in substance abuse or domestic violence, which tend to be the more common reasons for referrals to protective services (Lamont & Bromfield, 2009). These authors acknowledge that research indicates CIDs can adversely affect parenting, but "Prejudicial and incorrect beliefs that any parent with an intellectual disability will be unable to provide adequate care contributes to over-representation of children of parents with intellectual disabilities" (p. 16) in court and protective service proceedings. Finally, Lamont and Bromfield state "that diagnosis of intellectual disability is a poor indicator of risk for child abuse and neglect. Parents with an intellectual disability are not a homogeneous group" (p. 17).

Following is a collection of historical common myths and facts about parents with CIDs. As you can read, the prejudices and concerns are long-standing.

MYTHS/FACTS ABOUT PARENTS WITH CIDS

Myth: Their children will also have CIDs.

Fact: The incidence of CIDs due to organic or genetic causes was similar to that of the general population. However, children born to economically poor parents with CIDs may be at higher risk for developmental disabilities.

Myth: Parents with CIDs tend to have more children than parents without disabilities.

Fact: Parents with CIDs have about the same number of children as parents without disabilities of the same socioeconomic status.

Myth: These individuals cannot be adequate parents.

Fact: No direct relationship exists between IQ and "better" parenting; many individuals with CIDs are good parents and others are not, just as in the general population. Poor parenting may be more due to a lack of education regarding how to parent than to an inability to parent effectively.

Myth: Individuals with CIDs cannot learn to be parents.

Fact: Individuals with CIDs can learn parenting skills if provided education and adequate supports.

Source: Espe-Sherwindt and Crable (1993)

Adults with CIDs can be and are successful parents. To suggest otherwise would be misleading although it is likewise unrealistic to suggest that problems and challenges don't exist. It is true they may need various services aimed at building relationships, accessing informal and formal supports, parenting must evolve as children grow, having access to parent education, becoming involved in their child's community and school, health and nutritional care, accessing public benefits, crisis intervention, and equal protection under the law (The ARC, 2011). Obviously, parents will not need all these services but a coordinated system will increase the likelihood of desirable family outcomes. The life cycles of adulthood can be confusing and exhilarating, trying yet rewarding. Clearly, becoming a parent impacts the individual, family, and society as well. We have cited several potential impacts of culture as well in this process of growing into adulthood.

In the following section, we discuss multicultural characteristics of CIDs. These include sociological and demographic factors related to CIDs and factors associated with multiculturalism and education.

Reflection

How might parents and other family members cope with CIDs of a family member from early childhood and into adulthood? Do you believe parents who have CIDs should be more closely scrutinized for abuse or neglect of their children?

MULTICULTURAL CHARACTERISTICS

The AAIDD (2010) recognized the importance of culture in defining and understanding CIDs. Dimension V: Context is one of the critical elements in the multidimensionality of the condition. Included in the context are environmental and personal factors such as social environment, race, gender, coping styles, and social background (AAIDD, 2012).

Historically, minority populations have been overrepresented in special education programs, particularly those for individuals with mild CIDs. In Chapter 3, the need for nondiscriminatory assessment was discussed both historically and in the current context. These provisions are necessary to ensure that the historical overrepresentation that has existed is eliminated. Still, as much as we have learned about this phenomenon, the problem persists. In this section, we examine some of the factors associated with this persistent problem and how groups of people are affected among those who have been identified as having CIDs.

Sociological and Demographic Factors

Historically, the issue of overrepresentation of students from diverse backgrounds in special education programs has been known and acknowledged. The U.S. government issues technical assistance guides still today to assist states in identifying overrepresentation in programs under IDEA. From over a decade ago, Oswald and Coutinho (2001) reported on data collected by the U.S. Office of Civil Rights concerning the overrepresentation of Black and American Indian students in special education. These authors stated that across the period from 1980–1994, these groups of students continued to be overidentified as having mild CIDs although ratios compared to White students have declined over time. Conversely, Asian/Pacific Islander students were underidentified compared to White students. Policy makers, educators, and advocates among others debate the reasons for these outcomes but overrepresentation remains an issue. However, because the mechanisms affecting this phenomenon are complex and a part of social and institutional practices, research has yet to yield sufficient evidence of a primary cause for overrepresentation (Skiba, Simmons, Ritter, Gibb, Rausch, Cuadrado, & Chung, 2008). Importantly, overrepresentation is not just a special education phenomenon, but very possibly is affected by racial and ethnic disparities in the general education curriculum, classroom management, teacher quality, and resource inequities (Skiba et al., 2008). A number of variables have been identified, however, that do appear to affect individuals with CIDs in school and society.

Effects of Poverty
Historically, it has been suggested that poverty may account for the racial and ethnic disparities in the identification of individuals with CIDs for special education programs. In Chapter 4, we discussed the influence of poverty and associated factors (e.g., malnutrition) on the risks of experiencing developmental delays. Because more minority children live in poverty, subsequently, they may also be identified at higher rates than other children.

Birenbaum (2002) reviewed research from a variety of sources and suggested that there are links between poverty and childhood disability. Fujiura and Yamaki (2000) suggested that poverty was on the increase over the 1990s, that poverty had the greatest concentration in single-parent households, and that these trends were exacerbated by the presence of a child with a disability.

Effects of Race/Ethnicity
Skiba, Poloni-Staudinger, Simmons, Feggins-Azziz, and Chung (2005) reported in their study that race and poverty both did appear to predict identification for special education. This was especially true for African-American students and in the category of mild intellectual disabilities. However, poverty did not explain the racial/ethnic disparities. Rather, each made independent contributions to predicting the likelihood of identification (Skiba et al., 2005). In this same study, it was pointed out that poverty did appear to widen racial disparities in the categories of mild and moderate CIDs (Skiba et al., 2005).

Blacher (2001) suggested that culture can have a significant impact on the successful transition of adolescents into adulthood. Blacher pointed out that interpersonal supports (e.g., extended family support), service supports (e.g., programmatic options available), and socioeconomic status play important roles in successful adjustment. Other factors cited as important are acculturation for ethnic minority families and religious and cultural beliefs and practices.

In Chapter 4, we discussed how variables such as poverty, malnutrition, poor health care, and the lack of early intervention and education services can influence the risk of being identified with CIDs. Race/ethnicity and gender also appear to have some interaction effect with these and potentially many other variables, although there are differing opinions as to how this interaction occurs or even to what extent. Clearly, this is an area ripe for ongoing research and investigation.

Turnbull et al. (2006) noted that *culture* is a broad term encompassing such factors as geography, religion, sexual orientation, and disability status in addition to race/ethnicity and socioeconomic status. Families from various cultures may also have different perceptions about how problems are resolved. Families from diverse backgrounds may, in some cases, be less trustful of organizational and institutional practices due to a history of discrimination (Turnbull et al., 2006).

Greenen, Powers, and Lopez-Vasquez (2001) studied the involvement of culturally/linguistically diverse parents and that of European-American parents in their students' transition planning. The culturally/linguistically diverse parents placed significantly more importance than European-American parents on talking to their children about the transition, helping their children prepare for postsecondary education, teaching their children to care for their disability, teaching their children about their culture, and how to use transportation independently. Interestingly, these same parents reported being less involved in school-based planning. Turnbull et al. (2006) suggested that the special education processes of referral, assessment, and identification tend to be more Euro-American in orientation and ultimately special educators and the educational system must find means of collaborating within and valuing other ethnic/cultural value systems.

Educational Factors

In addition to those issues raised by Turnbull et al. (2006), a number of other factors may interact within our multicultural society to affect individuals with CIDs. We have discussed sociological and demographic trends in the identification of individuals with CIDs as well as noting the potential systemic bias that may also be an influence. Here, we examine more closely the overall interaction between race/ethnicity and the educational system.

Sullivan (2011) noted in her study of state-level data that English language learners (ELLs) were overrepresented in the category of mild CIDs. Interestingly, among those ELLs identified for special education, they were less likely than White students to be removed from general education for most of the school day (Sullivan, 2011). Sullivan also noted that educational policies may tend to focus on overrepresentation from a racial/ethnic perspective but should also consider language. While the movement toward inclusive education is discussed more extensively in Chapter 12, it is worth noting that a number of authors suggest there are flaws within the greater educational system that do not allow for adequate services in our multicultural society. School reform efforts are one way in which legislative bodies have attempted to address inequities.

Reform efforts have included the reauthorization of the IDEA. As noted previously, this federal mandate requires states to make provisions for nearly all students in special education to participate in state- and districtwide assessment programs (those with more severe disabilities may be identified for alternate assessment programs). As discussed in Chapter 3, students from diverse cultural backgrounds might not perform as well on some standardized tests as those from the majority culture. Also, as results are examined over time, one might expect the performance of individuals with CIDs to be predictably below average.

Ysseldyke and Bielinski (2002) studied how trends in statewide assessments results might be reported and reclassified. They stressed that progress for each student should be considered rather than group performance gap changes between general and special education students. In this manner, the focus would be on the individual as opposed to groups of individuals' outcomes. However, federal law does require schools to report on the achievement gap among minority groups (e.g., African-American students, Hispanic students, and students with disabilities) as concern continues for disparities in educational performance on such tests. While students with CIDs may be included in alternate assessments, their performance as a group and potentially as members of a diverse racial/ethnic group remains a priority for schools. The outcomes as the result of potentially poor test scores for individuals, districts, and states are not yet clear. It is reasonable to assume that they will spark continuing debate on reform efforts and how to ensure equitable and fair treatment of all students, regardless of background.

Another potential factor affecting the interaction between individuals from culturally diverse backgrounds and the school systems is the demographics of the teaching corps itself. There are proportionately fewer teachers of color than there are students of color.

THE TYPICAL TEACHER?

Sadker and Sadker (2003) pointed out that the typical teacher in American schools is a 44-year-old White woman who has been teaching for 16 years. Only 9% of teachers are African-American and fewer than 4% are Hispanic. Nearly 85% of teachers are White. About 75% of teachers are women, although 40% of secondary teachers are males. Conversely, about 65% of school principals and 90% of superintendents are men. The area of special education continues to be one with teacher shortages that might tend to exacerbate these gender and ethnic differences. The effects these demographics might have are not clear, although they raise concerns for some as to whether the majority of teachers are adequately prepared to teach students from diverse backgrounds.

Obiakor (2001) pointed out that the use of multicultural education in teacher training as a means of preparing teachers to work with all students is one that creates controversy. Obiakor stated that proponents of multicultural education stress it has an equalizing effect on teacher education programming whereas opponents contend it is balkanizing and divisive. Obiakor stresses there is a need to identify individuals from diverse backgrounds for teacher education programs and a need to ensure teachers are prepared to provide both quality and equality in the classroom. Similarly, professionals have advocated for more culturally responsive educational systems as a means of addressing the racial/ethnic disparities that exist in special education (Klingner, Artiles, Kozleski, Harry, Zion, Tate, Duran, & Riley, 2005).

Finally, the overall demographics of the United States are changing in such ways that the multicultural nature of our schools and how the educational system responds is also likely to change. Individuals with CIDs constitute a relatively small percentage of the overall population, yet the impact of this condition is far reaching. It impacts society, individual adjustment, family functioning, the justice system, and educational policy and reform. There are costs associated with appropriate treatment and education. Clearly, there are costs associated with lack of treatment options and neglect.

CID is a condition that is evident in all cultures, races, socioeconomic and educational strata, religions, and geographic regions. All groups in society are stakeholders in the outcomes for these individuals. As the 21st century progresses, change is certain but the direction of and the benefits of those changes are still to be realized.

Reflection

How do you think race/ethnicity affects who is identified for special education and particularly as having CIDs in your area? Do you see evidence of overrepresentation? Do you anticipate seeing cultural and linguistic diversity as an advantage instead of a risk factor in our schools?

SUMMARY CHECKLIST

Societal Characteristics

✓ Exercising individual rights often requires a person is competent and gives consent
✓ Rights may be abridged through the courts appointing a guardian
  ➢ **Guardianship is a court action in which someone alleges that a person with disabilities cannot give consent**
✓ At the age of adulthood, one is assumed to be competent to give consent; IDEA requires students be informed of their rights at this age
✓ Having CID does not necessarily translate into lack of competence and the ability to give consent
✓ People with CIDs do have interactions with the justice system
✓ They tend to be the victims of crime at a higher rate than those without disabilities
✓ Within the justice system, individuals may not be treated as competent witnesses or excluded from giving testimony
✓ Those individuals accused of crimes should have legal assistance from the outset of the process
✓ Many offenders with CIDs have experienced sexual or physical abuse themselves
✓ Treatment (or supports) may be needed over the life span
✓ The right to treatment across the life span has been legally established
✓ The AAIDD established individualized support planning
✓ Determining what type and level of supports are needed involves identifying relevant support areas, identifying relevant support activities in each area of functioning, and evaluating the level or intensity of supports
  ➢ **Person-centered planning—Includes the principles that the individual is the most important part of the planning; that family, friends, and significant others also should be involved; the abilities, talents, and aspirations of the individual should be considered rather than just the disabilities; and a broader implementation approach should be used which includes generic services that are local and informal as well as more formal services delivered through paid providers**

✓ Where children live may affect their system of supports in terms of frequency and types used

✓ Funding for services to provide treatment is more focused now on community-based supports

Family Characteristics

✓ Parents have historically been perceived as the source of a child's disability, although the actual cause is often unknown or attributable to other factors

✓ Parents of individuals with disabilities generally want to be involved in their child's education and treatment

✓ Parents can and do undergo stress related to child characteristics especially the presence of problem behavior

✓ Parents report positive feelings about their children with CIDs as well as stress associated with child-rearing

✓ Early childhood is a critical period for most families and individuals with CIDs

✓ SES, maternal stress, age, and education, early intervention services, and other factors can affect children's developmental gains and family adjustment

✓ Early intervention services should be family-centered, not just child-focused

✓ Research on siblings of individuals with CIDs has yielded mixed results concerning the effects on the siblings

✓ Siblings and other family members have reported good adjustment following placement of the individual with CID into a residential program

✓ The effects of and on siblings is influenced by many variables such as family size, birth order, gender, and coping styles

✓ Planning across the life span is a major concern for most families

✓ Planning and the outlook on the future can be affected by having fewer models of expected behavior, rituals of adulthood (e.g., marriage) may occur less frequently, and transition planning may not provide sufficient options

✓ Transition planning and programming is critical and should take into consideration individual characteristics, family well-being, family involvement, and environment and culture

✓ Defining adulthood for the individual with CID can take several forms including physical maturation and level of functioning or competence

✓ The rituals and rights of adulthood should not be denied to individuals with CIDs and their exercise should be encouraged and taught

✓ Voting—In general, people with CIDs are entitled to vote and should be educated about the process

✓ Moving out—May take longer and occur later in life but is achieved by many individuals; culture can also influence whether this represents a rite of adulthood

✓ Marriage—Is less a requirement of adulthood now but should be available; protections against abuse and exploitation are needed

✓ Sexual consent—Is a complex concept; one study suggested at a minimum an individual should understand the nature of sexual activity, be able to protect oneself

✓ Research has indicated individuals with CIDs do have socio-sexual knowledge

✓ Individuals with CIDs can become parents and have their own families

✓ Overall levels of stress and stress associated with child age and living in a crowded environment were evident in 82 mothers with CIDs

✓ Authors have noted myths exist about parents with CIDs, including they will have children who themselves have CID, more children than parents without disabilities, that they cannot be adequate parents, and they cannot learn parenting skills

✓ Supported parenting programs provide education and assistance in raising children

✓ Because CID occurs more frequently among people living in poverty, many young women may find themselves raising their children in less than optimal environments

✓ Early intervention programs can teach parenting skills and reduce the risk of abuse or neglect

Multicultural Characteristics

✓ Culture is an element of the AAIDD's Dimension V: Context which defines the multidimensionality of CIDs

✓ Context involves the immediate social setting; the neighborhood, community, or organizations providing services or supports; and cultural and social beliefs

✓ Overrepresentation of individuals from diverse racial/ethnic backgrounds remains a problem in special education

✓ Sociological and demographic factors include race/ethnicity and poverty and other associated factors

✓ African-American males in particular are overrepresented in special education

✓ Culture and associated beliefs and values can affect transitions and adjustment; research indicates parents who are culturally/linguistically diverse do report involvement in preparing their children for transitions

✓ Culture should be thought of in broad terms encompassing geography, religion, sexual orientation, and disability status

✓ Families from different cultures may have different perspectives on how to solve problems

✓ Educational factors also interact with the multicultural nature of society

✓ School reform efforts—The IDEA requires provisions be made for students with disabilities to participate in state and district assessment programs; some researchers stress the need to focus on individual progress rather than group performances over time

✓ Demographics of the teaching corps—Most teachers are White and most school administrators are males; teachers from ethnic/cultural minorities are underrepresented among the nation's teachers; multicultural education in preparing teachers is controversial but may be helpful

✓ Overall demographics of the United States—Indicate that the population is changing

✓ English language learners—ELLs present challenges and how best to educate these students generates controversy as they are also overrepresented in special education

ADDITIONAL SUGGESTIONS/RESOURCES

Discussion Questions

1. What do you believe about how individuals with CIDs are treated within society and by the justice system?
2. What challenges do you believe a person with a CID might face as a parent?
3. How might the changing demographics of the United States and other countries affect the educational system in the future?

Activities

1. Interview a local attorney, judge, or adult service provider about the issues related to guardianship. Devise questions such as: How is it decided someone with a CID may need a guardian? What does the process involve? Who can be appointed? What role should the guardian play? How is the life of the person with a CID likely to be affected?
2. Interview an individual involved in the justice system. Devise such questions as: What happens when someone with a CID is a victim of a crime? What happens when someone with a CID is accused of a crime? What happens when someone with a CID is to be a witness in someone else's trial? Does the justice system treat these individuals fairly? To what extent do you believe individuals who are incarcerated have CIDs or other disabilities (e.g., ADHD, learning disabilities)?
3. Research a local school district. Determine what the demographics are of the teachers, administrators, and students in the district. Compare the results to see if gender and ethnic/cultural differences exist among the groups. Discuss what, if any, implications there might be for individuals with CIDs from diverse family backgrounds.

E-sources

http://www.beachcenter.org/

The Beach Center "is affiliated with both the Schiefelbusch Institute for Life Span Studies (LSI) at the University of Kansas (KU) and the Department of Special Education." This website includes a wide variety of information for and about families with members with disabilities. There are many resources and fact sheets available that should be of use in understanding and developing knowledge about families.

www.tash.org

This advocacy organization is centered around individuals with more severe disabilities. It also includes, under its Advocacy and Programs link, information about including people from diverse backgrounds that, in turn, also includes links to other organizations and information concerned with diverse groups with disabilities.

http://nichcy.org/families-community

The National Dissemination Center for Children with Disabilities includes information specifically for families of children with intellectual disabilities. This includes basic information about disabilities, services available to families, as well as links to other organizations.

Part Four

Instructional Considerations

9

INSTRUCTIONAL ASSESSMENT

Key Points

- ➤ MULTIDIMENSIONAL NATURE—It is important that the age of the student and the severity of the disability be considered when planning and conducting functional educational assessments
- ➤ INFORMAL ASSESSMENT: INSTRUCTIONAL DECISION MAKING—Techniques for this purpose include criterion-referenced testing and criterion-referenced curriculum-based assessment
- ➤ INFORMAL ASSESSMENT: MONITORING PROGRESS—Techniques for this purpose include observation, portfolio assessment, and curriculum-based measurement
- ➤ ACCOMMODATIONS AND ALTERNATE ASSESSMENT—IDEA mandates that *all* students participate in statewide and district assessments or be given a more appropriate alternate assessment
- ➤ ASSESSMENT BY FUNCTIONAL SKILL AREA—Areas to be assessed could include independent living skills, communication skills, social skills, basic academic skills, prevocational/vocational skills, and community living skills

MULTIDIMENSIONAL NATURE

Assessing the educational needs of individuals with CIDs is a very complex process requiring considerable planning and coordination. Issues such as the age of the individual as well as the severity of the disability will have an impact on the assessment procedures, instruments, and techniques that are used. One very important point is that the assessment should be **functional** and **pragmatic.** That is, it should focus on the assessment of skills which, when taught, will lead to the greatest degree of independence. For example, when assessing young children or older individuals with more severe CIDs, it is appropriate to focus on independent living skills such as eating, dressing, and toileting. Assessing older individuals with CIDs will involve employability skills as well as community living skills. For some students, more traditional assessment of basic academic skill areas will be relevant. Areas that should be included in any assessment are communication and social skills. As discussed in the next chapter, these are very critical skills frequently targeted for educational programming; subsequently, assessment in these areas should not be overlooked.

In addition to identifying the skills to be evaluated, it is also important to identify the techniques and procedures used to assess those skills. Some techniques (e.g., the use of a norm-referenced test [NRT]) might be specific to the skill area selected for interest. Some NRTs, for example, are best used to provide instructional information on academic skills, whereas other NRTs are better for providing information on social skills. Other techniques used to assist in *instructional decision making* can be used in more than one functional skill area. Some can be used to gather instructional information in virtually any skill area. These include a number of informal assessment procedures including criterion-referenced testing and curriculum-based assessment. Another important aspect of instructional assessment is *progress monitoring,* or determining the effectiveness of an instructional program. Informal techniques that are useful for this purpose include observation, portfolio assessment, and curriculum-based measurement. (Chapter 11 provides more detail on progress monitoring.) In reality, many of these informal assessment procedures can be used for both instructional decision making and progress monitoring.

A final concern related to instructional assessment is the legal requirement that *all* students, including those with disabilities, be included in large-scale accountability assessments (e.g., districtwide or statewide assessment programs). This requirement has been in place as more and more educational reforms have required high-stakes testing for all students, but has recently generated serious concerns once the negative unintended consequences of this testing have shown an impact (Bouck, 2013; Brady, Duffy, Hazelkorn & Bucholz, in press). An important component of this mandate is the provision that testing accommodations be allowed for students with disabilities. Further, it requires that *alternate assessment procedures* be used when participation in the regular assessment program is inappropriate, even with accommodations.

The informal assessment procedures used for instructional decision making and monitoring progress will be discussed next, followed by information on the legal mandate to include students with disabilities in all testing programs. Finally, a discussion of the procedures relevant for specific functional skill areas will be presented.

Reflection

Why is it so important that the educational assessment of individuals with CIDs be *functional?*

INFORMAL ASSESSMENT: INSTRUCTIONAL DECISION MAKING

Criterion-Referenced Tests

Criterion-referenced tests (CRTs) are particularly helpful in providing information about which specific skill(s) should be targeted for instruction. Unlike norm-referenced tests, criterion-referenced tests do not compare an individual's performance to others. Rather, they give more specific information about what an individual does and doesn't know or can or cannot do. For example, instead of knowing that a student obtained a standard score of 67 in the Eating subdomain of the *Battelle Developmental Inventory* (norm-referenced information), you might find the following type of specific information: (1) the student can use a spoon independently, (2) the student can use a fork independently, (3) the student can use a knife for spreading but cannot use a knife for cutting (criterion-referenced information). Gronlund (1998) made other distinctions between the two types of tests. For instance, norm-referenced tests usually cover a broad range of areas with few items per area whereas criterion-referenced tests usually measure a more limited domain with numerous items per area.

Criterion-referenced tests are particularly helpful in providing specific information for educational objectives and can be either *teacher-made* or *commercially prepared.* Each type has advantages and disadvantages. A teacher-made test allows greater flexibility and can be constructed specifically for a given skill area for a particular student. On the other hand, these tests do take time to develop. Ideally, if a commercially prepared test includes the skill areas a teacher wants to assess, their use can save time. In actuality, many commercially prepared criterion-referenced tests include hundreds of skill areas (sequences) that offer a teacher a good selection. It is important, however, that this selection be made carefully and be matched to the student's needs. It should be noted that commercially prepared tests are usually referred to as criterion-referenced inventories (CRIs). Further, criterion-referenced inventories are designed to measure specific skills at certain age or grade levels. Specific examples of these inventories will follow in the section on assessment by functional skill area. Teacher-made tests will be discussed in greater depth next, since they can be developed for any skill area that is targeted.

Teacher-Made Tests

The first step in developing a teacher-made criterion-referenced test is to clearly define the skill areas to be measured. This can be accomplished by identifying the appropriate goal(s) for the individual (e.g., goals from the [IEP]). The next step is to identify specific objectives. One way to do this is by using **task analysis,** which is the identification and sequencing of behaviors that are necessary components of the skill required for an individual to complete a task (Taylor, 2009). Take, for example, an academic goal of "addition of two-digit numbers without renaming." Five objectives might be identified that are prerequisites for that goal (see Table 9.1). After identifying the objectives, the next step is to develop the test items themselves. For example, a worksheet similar to the one in Table 9.2 could be developed that would include items to correspond to each objective. The fourth step is to determine the standard of performance (the criteria for mastery). A teacher may decide that the student would need to correctly answer 90% of the problems (9 out of 10) for each objective to demonstrate mastery of that objective. Finally, the test is administered, scored, and interpreted.

Suppose the criterion-referenced test produced the following results:

Objective 1: 100%
Objective 2: 90%
Objective 3: 50%
Objective 4: 0%
Objective 5: Not administered
Goal: Not administered

Table 9.1 Objectives Based on Task Analysis

Objective 1: Given problems requiring the addition of two numbers with sums less than 10, the student will provide the correct answers.

Objective 2: Given problems requiring the addition of two, 1-digit numbers with sums greater than 10, the student will provide the correct answers.

Objective 3: Given problems requiring the addition of three, 1-digit numbers with sums less than 10, the student will provide the correct answers.

Objective 4: Given problems requiring the addition of three, 1-digit numbers with sums greater than 10, the student will provide the correct answers.

Objective 5: Given problems requiring the addition of 2-digit numbers to 1-digit numbers without renaming, the student will provide the correct answers.

Goal: Given problems requiring the addition of 2-digit numbers to 2-digit numbers without renaming, the student will provide the correct answers.

Table 9.2 Test Items Based on Objectives

Objective 1

	1.	2.	3.	4.	5.	6.	7.	8.	9.	10.
	1	2	3	4	2	5	7	1	6	5
	+5	+2	+2	+4	+1	+2	+2	+8	+2	+1

Objective 2

	1.	2.	3.	4.	5.	6.	7.	8.	9.	10.
	9	3	4	5	4	8	7	7	9	7
	+9	+8	+9	+8	+9	+4	+6	+8	+8	+9

Objective 3

	1.	2.	3.	4.	5.	6.	7.	8.	9.	10.
	1	1	2	3	4	3	3	3	2	1
	2	4	2	2	1	4	3	1	2	3
	+1	+3	+4	+1	+2	+2	+3	+3	+1	+1

Objective 4

	1.	2.	3.	4.	5.	6.	7.	8.	9.	10.
	8	6	4	5	7	9	3	2	1	5
	6	4	5	7	9	3	4	5	9	6
	+4	+5	+7	+9	+3	+2	+6	+8	+7	+4

Objective 5

	1.	2.	3.	4.	5.	6.	7.	8.	9.	10.
	92	53	40	36	62	91	54	41	13	85
	+6	+5	+9	+2	+5	+8	+4	+7	+3	+1

Goal

	1.	2.	3.	4.	5.	6.	7.	8.	9.	10.
	51	33	95	47	89	42	64	56	18	20
	+48	+26	+14	+32	+10	+37	+25	+43	+81	+69

These results indicate that the student has mastered objectives 1 and 2, is having difficulty with objective 3, and does not know how to do objective 4. Note: the items for objective 5 and the goal were not administered because the objectives are sequential and no correct answers were given for objective 4, a prerequisite for objective 5 and the goal. Therefore, practice on the addition of three 1-digit numbers with sums less than 10 should be incorporated into the teaching program and the concept of adding

2-digit numbers to 1-digit numbers would need to be taught for the student to eventually reach the goal. The information from this criterion-referenced test provides much more precise information on what to teach than results from a norm-referenced test (e.g., the student obtained a standard score of 78 in math computation). Another advantage of a teacher-made criterion-referenced test is that it can be developed for any of the skills targeted for instruction that are typically taught in a sequential order. This includes areas such as independent living skills (e.g., dressing) and home living skills (e.g., using a washing machine). In these instances, the "items" would be more performance-based that are actually observed behaviors. The previous description of the sequence of eating skills is a good example.

Curriculum-Based Assessment

In the past three decades **curriculum-based assessment** (CBA) has received considerable attention (see Research Box 9.1). Curriculum-based assessment involves the measurement of a student's performance in terms of the expected curriculum outcomes of the school (Tucker, 1985). Therefore, the content of the instrument is based on the student's curriculum. There are actually many different procedures that fall under the general category of curriculum-based assessment. Peverly and Kitzen (1998) identified five different models of CBA:

- Curriculum and instruction-based assessment;
- Curriculum-based assessment for instructional design;
- Curriculum-based evaluation;
- Criterion-referenced curriculum-based assessment; and
- Curriculum-based measurement.

The following discussion will focus on criterion-referenced curriculum-based assessment (CR-CBA). The section on progress monitoring will include a discussion on curriculum-based measurement (CBM).

9.1 RESEARCH THAT MADE A DIFFERENCE

Blankenship, C. (1985). Using curriculum-based assessment data to make instructional decisions. *Exceptional Children, 52,* 233–238.

This was one of the first articles in the professional literature that described the steps in developing and using curriculum-based assessment. It was part of a special issue of *Exceptional Children* that focused on that topic. Included in this article was information on what to tell students who are given a curriculum-based assessment, how to use curriculum-based assessment data at IEP meetings, and the essential characteristics of a curriculum-based assessment instrument. A sample curriculum-based assessment instrument was also provided.

Criterion-referenced curriculum-based assessment uses the task analytic model found in criterion-referenced tests, and relies on the content of the student's curriculum as the content of the assessment. (Use of a task analytic model for teaching is described in Chapter 11.) As a result, the steps in developing a criterion-referenced curriculum-based assessment are very similar to the steps in developing a criterion-referenced test. Those steps are:

1. Identify skill(s) to be measured;
2. Identify objectives;
3. Develop test items;
4. Determine standards of performance; and
5. Administer and interpret the curriculum-based assessment instrument.

To identify the skill areas to measure the teacher would use the appropriate portion of the student's curriculum. Typically, a chart is developed that includes the sequential skills and the page numbers in the curriculum where the skills are introduced. Essentially, the identification of the objectives has been accomplished by developing the chart of sequential skills. Frequently, three separate tests are developed that measure the same skill (Idol, Nevin, & Paolucci-Whitcomb, 1999). These can then be administered over a three-day period. The standards of performance or criteria for mastery can be identified considering the student's performance on the three tests. A summary sheet is sometimes used that includes the skills to be measured, the number of items measuring each skill, and the criteria for mastery. Table 9.3 shows a summary sheet for a math curriculum that includes the same skill areas as those found in Table 9.1. Table 9.4 shows an example of a criterion-referenced curriculum-based assessment instrument developed for that portion of the curriculum. Note that fewer items are

Table 9.3 Example of a Summary Sheet for a Criterion-Referenced CBA

Concepts	Problem Numbers	Day 1	Day 2	Day 3	Total Score	Mastery 7/9
Adds 2, 1-digit numbers (sum < 10)	1, 2, 3	/3	/3	/3	/9	/9
Adds 2, 1-digit numbers (sum > 10)	4, 5, 6	/3	/3	/3	/9	/9
Adds 3, 1-digit numbers (sum < 10)	7, 8, 9	/3	/3	/3	/9	/9
Adds 3, 1-digit numbers (sum > 10)	10, 11, 12	/3	/3	/3	/9	/9
Adds 2-digit and 1-digit numbers (no renaming)	13, 14, 15	/3	/3	/3	/9	/9
Adds 2-digit and 2-digit numbers (no renaming)	16, 17, 18	/3	/3	/3	/9	/9

Table 9.4 Example of a Portion of a Criterion-Referenced CBA

Add the following:

1.	6	2.	4	3.	5	4.	9	5.	8	6.	7
	+2		+3		+1		+4		+3		+6

7.	2	8.	3	9.	4	10.	5	11.	9	12.	8
	3		1		2		2		6		3
	+2		+1		+3		+6		+2		+4

13.	25	14.	47	15.	34	16.	51	17.	64	18.	43
	+3		+2		+5		+33		+25		+14

provided for each skill area on this instrument than for the criterion-referenced test presented earlier. This is because a criterion-referenced curriculum-based assessment instrument frequently covers a wide range of skills (depending on the portion of the curriculum used). The instrument could even be given to an entire class to determine instructional groupings.

Reflection

What are the advantages and disadvantages of teacher-developed criterion-referenced tests versus criterion-referenced curriculum-based assessment?

INFORMAL ASSESSMENT: MONITORING PROGRESS

Observation

Observation, particularly systematic observation, can provide invaluable information for making instructional decisions and provides an excellent vehicle for monitoring student progress. There are many advantages of observation—it is inexpensive; is readily accessible to teachers, parents, and other personnel; and provides the most direct measure of the individual's behavior. When using observation for progress monitoring, a four-step model is often followed. Those four steps are:

1. Carefully identify the target behavior/skill;
2. Precisely measure the target behavior/skill;
3. Systematically introduce an intervention or teaching program; and
4. Evaluate the program effectiveness (monitor progress).

Each of these steps will be described in greater detail.

Identify the Target Behavior. Identifying the target behavior essentially means determining the skill or behavior for which a teaching program or intervention will be designed and implemented. This can be accomplished through the use of the previously described criterion-referenced tests or criterion-referenced curriculum-based assessment. Observation, itself, can also be used to help determine the target behavior/skill. It is extremely important to be very specific when identifying and defining the behavior that is targeted for instruction. Terms such as *attention problem, math improvement,* and *aggression* are too general and vague to have much meaning when monitoring the actual progress toward learning a skill. These terms might be defined and measured differently by two different observers or might even result in inconsistent data collection when only one observer is used. Better examples of these three target behaviors would be "looks out of window during vocational instruction time," "correctly solves math problems requiring double-digit addition," and "hits others with fists or objects." The goal is to get consistent (reliable) information. If the target behavior is not observable and carefully defined, then this will not be possible.

Measure the Target Behavior. There are a number of recording procedures that can be used when gathering observational data (see Cooper, Heron, & Heward, 2007). One frequently used recording procedure is **event recording** (the number of behaviors that occur within a specific time period). An example would be the number of functional sight words read correctly in a 2-minute period. Another procedure is **duration recording.** This procedure involves the measurement of the amount of time a person engages in the target behavior within a specific time period. An example would be the amount of time spent in task engagement during a 20-minute employment skill activity. Task engagement would need to be carefully defined as well. These and other procedures for using observational measures to monitor student progress (latency, interval, and momentary time sampling) are summarized in Richards, Taylor, and Ramasamy (2013).

After the recording procedure has been chosen, the next step is to collect **baseline data.** These are data collected when no specific teaching procedure is underway, or when the current unsuccessful one is in effect. In a sense, these data serve like a pretest score when more traditional tests are used.

Introduce Intervention or Teaching Program. After baseline data have been collected, the teaching program can now be introduced. As the instruction is delivered, teachers also *Evaluate the Intervention or Teaching Program (Progress Monitoring).*

By using frequent teach-observation sessions, progress can be continuously monitored. The goal is to determine the effectiveness of the teaching or intervention program. If the data do not go in the desired direction, either the target behavior can be changed (e.g., if the skill/behavior chosen was too difficult for the student), or a different teaching program can be implemented. Alternatively, if the teaching program was successful, it might indicate that that approach would also be effective with other skills/behaviors. Figure 9.1 shows a flowchart of the observational model with appropriate questions to ask at each step.

IDENTIFY TARGET BEHAVIOR	→	RECORD BASELINE DATA	→	INTRODUCE TEACHING PROGRAM	→	EVALUATE TEACHING PROGRAM
Is Behavior Precise And Measurable?		Was the Appropriate Recording Procedure Used?		Was decision data-based?		Was program effective?

Figure 9.1 Steps in the Observation Model

Portfolio Assessment

In recent years, **portfolio assessment** has become very popular. It is defined as a systematic collection of student works that provide evidence of an individual's performance, progress, and achievement (Paulson, Paulson, & Meyer, 1991). For example, a portfolio in the area of reading might include classroom tests, audiotapes of the student reading, a list of leisure reading, teachers' notes, and the student's self-evaluation. The idea is to provide a snapshot of the student's actual work products. There are actually several types of portfolios. The two most commonly used are the **working portfolio** and the **show portfolio** (Farr & Tone, 1994). The working portfolio includes "typical examples" of student work whereas the show portfolio includes the best efforts of the student. Vavrus (1990) offered five questions that should be answered when developing a portfolio. Those questions are:

1. What should it look like?
2. What goes into it?
3. How and when are the entries selected?
4. How is the portfolio evaluated?
5. How is the portfolio passed on?

Each of these questions will be discussed separately.

What should it look like? Like other assessment procedures, portfolio assessment should be carefully planned prior to its implementation. One issue that should be addressed is the format of the portfolio. Some portfolios are kept in notebooks, others in expandable file folders, and others, depending on their content, on the computer. It is also important to specify the goal and target audience of the portfolio since this will dictate the types of entries that will be placed in it. For example, if it is used for parent conferences it might contain different information than if it were being used to more formally monitor progress.

What goes into it? The targeted skill of the portfolio will dictate to a large extent what types of entries are included, and could be based on the student's individualized educational program (IEP). For example, if the goal was monitoring progress of the development of an independent living skill (e.g., eating skills), entries might include observations, interviews with parents and teachers, videotapes of the student engaging in the skill, and information from a developmental checklist. On the other hand, a portfolio focusing on the development of functional writing skills might include writing samples (e.g., letters, descriptions of job skills and interests) collected over time, as well as student self-reflection on his or her writing ability. Self-evaluation or self-reflection should be a part of every student portfolio; it allows the individual to become more involved in the assessment process itself.

How and when are the entries selected? The answer to this question is largely dependent on the type of information that will be collected. Work typically completed in school might be selected every week; less frequent measures such as test results or videotapes might be collected less frequently. Vavrus (1990) suggested making a timeline that identifies the points at which the entries are selected. As much as possible, the student is also involved in the decision making on what entries should be included. Again, this makes the student a more active participant in the assessment process.

How is the portfolio evaluated? This is one of the more difficult questions to answer and has led to its less frequent use as a formal measure. McMillan (1997) identified four ways that portfolios should be evaluated. Two of these include the evaluation of individual portfolio entries and the evaluation of the overall progress toward meeting the student's goals. To identify specific entries a **rubric** is often developed. A rubric is a set of criteria that provides a description of the various levels of performance as well as a value to each of these levels. A four-point scale might be developed (1 = poor, 2 = fair, 3 = good, 4 = outstanding). For each of these levels, definitions and/or examples would be developed in relationship to the skill area measured. For the previous example of eating skills, a rubric using the four-point scale might be developed to assess the student's use of a spoon, use of a fork, and use of a knife. For the functional writing skills example, a rubric might be developed for five components (ideation, handwriting, spelling, usage, and mechanics). The definition of poor, fair, good, and outstanding performance would be developed for each of the three and five components of the two examples, respectively. With the adoption of Common Core standards, evaluation rubrics for academic curriculum are becoming increasingly available. Entries could be evaluated weekly to determine the student's progress in the various aspects of either functional or academic curriculum targets.

How is the portfolio passed on? There is an important assumption that the portfolio assessment process should be continuous. It should provide an opportunity to share information with parents and other teachers. The portfolio should stay with the student when he or she goes to a different class or is promoted to the next grade.

Curriculum-Based Measurement

Curriculum-based measurement (CBM) is considered a more formal, standardized type of curriculum-based assessment (see Research Box 9.2). Considerable research has been conducted to establish the reliability and validity of curriculum-based measurement (e.g., Fuchs & Fuchs, 2000). Shinn and Bamonto (1998) referred to curriculum-based measurement instruments as "academic thermometers" to monitor student

---

9.2 RESEARCH THAT MADE A DIFFERENCE

Deno, S. (1985). Curriculum-based measurement: The emerging alternative. *Exceptional Children, 52,* 219–232.

This was another article that appeared in the special issue of *Exceptional Children* that focused on curriculum-based assessment. Deno argued that traditional achievement tests are not always consistent with a student's curriculum objectives. Frequently, informal observation is used in its place although the reliability and validity of this approach is unknown. He suggested that curriculum-based measurement addresses both of these issues and can be used for screening, referral, IEP planning, monitoring progress, and making program outcome decisions. Other advantages of curriculum-based measurement that are discussed are its cost effectiveness and its increased sensitivity to student growth.

growth. They are essentially a set of simple, standard measures that target the basic skill areas of reading, spelling, mathematics computation, and written expression.

One of the characteristics of curriculum-based measurement procedures is the use of continuous measurement over time, where the data are graphed to determine a **trend line** or **progress line.** Using this approach, a specific goal and goal date are set for the student and the progress line is analyzed to indicate whether or not the goal date will be met. If the progress line is too *flat* a curriculum change would be recommended. If the progress line is too *steep*, it would indicate that the goal date should be changed (see Figures 9.2 and 9.3). Curriculum-based measurement is particularly helpful for monitoring a student's participation in the general education curriculum, one of the requirements of the Individuals with Disabilities Education Act.

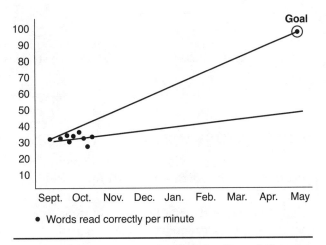

Figure 9.2 Flat Trend Line Indicating a Curriculum Change Is Necessary

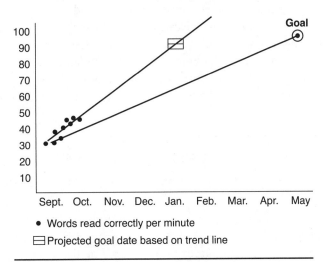

Figure 9.3 Steep Trend Line Indicating a Goal Date Change Is Necessary

As an example of the development of a curriculum-based measurement instrument in the area of spelling, Fuchs and Fuchs (2000) offered the following description:

1. Words would be chosen to represent an entire school year's spelling curriculum;
2. Twenty of those words would be randomly selected for the test;
3. The words would be dictated for 2 minutes allowing the student 10 seconds to write the correct spelling of the word; and
4. The number of correct words, or even letter sequences, would be counted and then graphed.

Using this procedure, steps 2–4 would be repeated on a daily basis until a progress line has been established.

Reflection

What type of entries might be included in a portfolio for a student with severe CIDs?

ACCOMMODATIONS AND ALTERNATE ASSESSMENT

The Individuals with Disabilities Education Act (IDEA) requires that, whenever possible, children with disabilities be included in state and district-wide assessment programs with appropriate accommodations where necessary (Bouck, 2013). Further, IDEA requires that guidelines be developed for participation of students with disabilities using alternate assessment procedures for those who cannot participate in state and districtwide programs even with accommodations (see Event Box 9.1). For example, if the assessment program focused on academic skills and the student's curriculum focused on independent living skills, an alternate assessment would be used to be more consistent with the student's goals and objectives. However, the student must still be evaluated.

If possible, however, students should be included in the same assessment program as their peers. Accommodations that might be used include increased time, revised formats (e.g., reading the items to the student instead of having the student read them), and revised response types (e.g., allowing oral instead of written responses). In general,

---

9.1 EVENT THAT MADE A DIFFERENCE

1997—Individuals with Disabilities Act mandates full participation in assessment programs

In 1997, IDEA mandated that all students, including those with disabilities, must participate in all state and districtwide assessment programs. The law also allows for appropriate testing accommodations. For those students who cannot participate even with accommodations, the state or local education agency had to develop and conduct alternate assessments by July 1, 2000. IDEA also required the states to report the number of students with disabilities participating in the regular assessment program and the number included in an alternate assessment.

the assessment accommodations that are made are often consistent with the instructional accommodations that are noted in the student's IEP (Ysseldyke et al., 2001).

If the content of the assessment program is inappropriate for a given student, an alternate assessment must be provided. The choice of this alternate assessment is usually based on the characteristics and needs of the student and the nature of the skills being measured. Many of the informal assessment procedures previously described are commonly used including observation and portfolios. The National Center on Educational Outcomes (NCEO) has been monitoring the participation of students with disabilities in assessment programs for over a decade. It reported the results of a survey on alternate assessments that are used by different states (Ysseldyke & Olsen, 1999). The top five procedures were portfolios (44%), direct observation (34%), review of progress toward goals (31%), video observation (28%), and performance assessment (23%). **Performance assessment** is defined as "a measurement approach in which individuals must perform tasks rather than just provide written or oral answers to test questions" (Wheeler & Haertel, 1993; p. 106). It focuses on the application of skills more than knowledge of information. Performance assessment has actually been used for a number of years in areas such as the performing arts (e.g., dance, chorus). As discussed later in this chapter, vocational skills could be evaluated by having students demonstrate the job requirements that they are trained to do. Unfortunately, some students have reported limitations to performance assessments, including the amount of time involved (McMillan, 1997) and the cost (Coutinho & Oswald, 2000).

Taylor (2009; p. 23) summarized the issue of testing accommodations and alternate assessments:

It is clear that states must have a clear rationale for *not* including students in assessment programs. The assumption is that they will participate unless it is not feasible to do so. Reasons for exemptions might be if the student's disability is severe enough that the assessment would not provide pertinent information on his or her progress or if the student were working toward some type of special diploma that did not include the test content in the curriculum. The law is also clear that if a student cannot participate, an alternate, more appropriate assessment must be given in its place.

Reflection

What might be some appropriate assessment accommodations for a student with CIDs who also has cerebral palsy?

ASSESSMENT BY FUNCTIONAL SKILL AREA

As discussed earlier, several informal assessment techniques and procedures can be used to provide instructional information across a variety of functional skill areas. There are also assessment procedures and instruments that address *specific* functional skill areas. For instance, many norm-referenced tests are designed to measure specific skill areas. Other norm-referenced tests include sections that address more than one skill area. In the following section, both skill-specific instruments and multiskill norm-referenced tests will be described. Examples of multiskill norm-referenced tests are the *AAMR Adaptive Behavior Scale: 2* (AAMR ABS:2), the *Scales of Independent Behavior—Revised* (SIB-R), and the *Vineland Adaptive Behavior Scales—Revised* (VABS II) described in Chapter 3. In general, results from these instruments are used more for the identification of goals rather than determination of specific objectives. An exception is the Interview Edition—Expanded Form of the *Vineland Adaptive Behavior Scales-Revised* that includes over 500 items. In addition to norm-referenced tests, commercially prepared criterion-referenced inventories and other techniques used to assess specific skill areas will be discussed in this section of the chapter. It should also be noted that the described instruments and procedures are only a representative sample of those that are available.

Independent Living Skills

Development of independent living skills is an important component of the educational program for many individuals with CIDs. Technically, all goals identified (e.g., communication goals, community living goals) should be chosen to allow the individual to become more independent. In this section, however, independent living skills are defined as the "self-help" skills that would allow individuals to take care of their basic needs (e.g., eating, dressing).

Several assessment options are available to provide information on independent living skills. As just mentioned, many adaptive behavior scales include sections that address this area. The *AAMR-Adaptive Behavior Scale: 2* has a domain called Independent Functioning that includes areas such as eating, toilet use, cleanliness, appearance, care of clothing, and dressing/undressing that can provide information on appropriate goals. Also, the *Scales of Independent Behavior-R* has a Personal Living Skills cluster that measures eating, toileting, dressing, personal self-care, and domestic skills. The *Vineland Adaptive Behavior Scales-Revised* has a domain called Daily Living Skills that measures the areas of personal, domestic, and community skills. The latter area addresses the domain of community living skills discussed later. The Interview Edition—Expanded Form of the *VABS* includes 200 items in that domain.

There are also norm-referenced developmental inventories that include these areas. One example is the *Battelle Developmental Inventory Second Edition* (BDI-2) (Newborg, Stock, Wnek, Guidubaldi, & Svinicki, 2005). The BDI-2 measures developmental skills of children from birth to age 7 years, 11 months. It involves three types of procedures for obtaining information: traditional administration, observation, and parent interview. There are also instructions included on how to determine extrapolated standard scores for individuals with more severe disabilities. This instrument has a domain called Adaptive that includes Self-Care and Personal Responsibility subdomains. The

Personal-Social domain includes Adult Interaction, Peer Interaction, and Self-Concept and Social Role. The Communication domain includes Receptive Communication and Expressive Communication. The Motor domain includes the Gross Motor, Fine Motor, and Perceptual Motor subdomains. Finally, the Cognitive domain includes Attention and Memory, Reasoning and Academic Skills, and Perception and Concepts subdomains, which includes the subdomains of Attention, Eating, Dressing, Personal Responsibility, and Toileting. Information from the BDI-2 should be used primarily for identifying goals and progress monitoring; there is also the limitation of the age range (birth–7 years, 11 months) if normative data are used (Athanasiou, 2012).

Criterion-referenced instruments can also be used to assess independent living skills. In addition to the teacher-made criterion-referenced tests previously discussed, several commercially prepared criterion-referenced inventories are available. These instruments provide sequential sets of developmental behaviors within specific skill areas. Examples of criterion-referenced inventories are the *Behavioral Characteristics Progression* (BCP) (VORT Corporation, 1973), the *Callier-Azusa Scale* (CAS) (Stillman, 1978), and the *Vulpé Assessment Battery-Revised* (VAB-R) (Vulpé, 1994). The *Behavior Characteristics Progression-Revised* has 2,300 items organized into 56 strands (skill sequences). Strands 1–22 focus on self-help skills. Booklets of instructional suggestions correlated with 1,900 of the items are also available. The *Callier-Azusa Scale* has a section called Daily Living Skills that measures dressing and undressing, personal hygiene, feeding, and toileting. Both of these instruments can be used with individuals with sensory and motor disabilities. The *Behavior Characteristics Progression-Revised* has strands designed for individuals who are blind, deaf, or have orthopedic impairments. The *Callier-Azusa Scale* includes a coding system to allow the omission of certain items that would be affected by those disabilities. The *Vulpé Assessment Battery-Revised* contains a section called Activities of Daily Living that has seven subsections: Feeding, Dressing, Social Interaction, Playing, Sleeping, Toileting, and Grooming. It also includes a unique scoring system whereby each item (skill) is scored on a 1 to 7 scale (Taylor, 2009). This scale is described below.

1—No (the individual cannot do the skill at all)
2—Attention (the individual attends to the task)
3—Physical Assistance (level of assistance necessary for individual to perform the task)
4—Social/Emotional Assistance (same as above)
5—Verbal Assistance (same as above)
6—Independent (the individual can perform the task independently)
7—Transfer (the individual can transfer the skill to a new situation)

This scoring system is particularly helpful in working with individuals with more severe disabilities. It not only indicates what skills are appropriate to teach but also the levels of support that should be incorporated into the teaching program. For instance, if the person received a score of 2 for a given skill, the immediate objective would be to "teach" to 3 for the same skill (i.e., work on getting the person to perform the skill with physical assistance). The goal would be to progress all the way to 7 (student learns the skill and can transfer it to another situation) and then begin with the next skill in the sequence.

Communication Skills

The ability to communicate is one of the most functional skills and serves many purposes in daily life. For one thing, it is the way in which an individual expresses his or her needs. Communication is also multidimensional, involving nonverbal, verbal, and/or written skills. Further, because communication is a two-way process, it involves both expressive and receptive skills. Although oral and written language are components of communication, the two terms (*language* and *communication*) are not synonymous. Many individuals with CIDs communicate without using oral or written language.

Each of the norm-referenced tests discussed in the independent living skills section also addresses the area of communication skills. The *AAMR Adaptive Behavior Scales: 2* has a domain called Language Development that measures expressive language, verbal comprehension, and social language development, although there are only 10 items in this domain. The *Scales of Independent Behavior-R* has a cluster called Social Interaction and Communication. Included in this cluster are the areas of language comprehension and language expression. Although there are only 18 items, a wide range of communication skills is measured. For example, two items in the language comprehension area are "Turns head toward speaker when name is called" and "Reads one or more articles in a regular newspaper at least weekly." Nonetheless, information from the *AAMR Adaptive Behavior Scales: 2* and the *Scales of Independent Behavior-R* should be used only to identify goals, not specific objectives. On the other hand, the Interview Edition—Expanded Form of the *Vineland Adaptive Behavior Scales-Revised* includes items measuring receptive, expressive, and written language. The *Battelle Developmental Inventory-2* also has a communication domain that measures expressive and receptive skills.

There are a number of norm-referenced tests designed to measure the various components of oral language. For example, the *Tests of Language Development—3* (Hammill & Newcomer, 1997; Newcomer & Hammill, 1997) include measures of semantics (vocabulary), syntax (sentence structure), and phonology (discrimination and articulation of speech sounds). Other tests are available that measure a single component of language. One popular instrument is the *Peabody Picture Vocabulary Test-Fourth Edition* (Dunn & Dunn, 2007), which measures receptive vocabulary. In this test an individual must identify the correct vocabulary words from four pictures that are presented on a single page (Kush, 2012). Instruments that measure written language are also available. The *Test of Written Language—3* (Hammill & Larsen, 1996) and the *Test of Written Expression* (McGhee, Bryant, Larsen, & Rivera, 1995) both measure a number of components of written language including fluency, syntax, spelling, and writing mechanics such as capitalization and punctuation skills. Interested readers are encouraged to consult Pierangelo and Giuliani (2009) for a discussion and description of oral and written language instruments and procedures.

Many criterion-referenced inventories also include skill sequences that measure communication skills. The *Vulpé Assessment Battery-Revised* has a section called Language Behaviors that includes items measuring both expressive and receptive language that cover a wide range of skills. For example, the Auditory Receptive Language subsection has items measuring such skills ranging from hearing sounds in the environment to comprehending full sentences (Graham, 2012; Taylor, 2009).

Social Skills

The development of appropriate social skills should be an integral component in educational programs designed for individuals with CIDs. Social skills encompass a number of areas such as interacting with others, cooperation, self-confidence, and personal adjustment. Early research (e.g., Domino & McGarty, 1972; Neuhaus, 1967) indicated that these skills were extremely important in predicting job success for individuals with CIDs (see Research Box 9.3).

9.3 RESEARCH THAT MADE A DIFFERENCE

Neuhaus, E. (1967). Training the mentally retarded for competitive employment. *Exceptional Children, 33,* 625–628.

In this article, Neuhaus describes a 3-year research and demonstration project designed to determine the success of employing individuals with mild CIDs (termed educable mentally retarded in 1967) in competitive jobs. A sample of individuals with CIDs was compared with a sample of individuals without disabilities. He found that the important variable in predicting job success was not so much learning the specific job skills but, rather, in developing appropriate social skills and work habits.

Across most criterion-referenced inventories, skill sequences that measure social skills are inconsistent. Typically there are few items included, and provide only a brief look at different aspects of behavior in the social domain. The *Callier-Azusa Scale,* for instance, has a domain called Social Development. The norm-referenced tests previously discussed do have domains that address the social areas but in different degrees of depth. The *AAMR Adaptive Behavior Scales: 2* has three domains: Self-Direction, Responsibility, and Socialization, although these three domains consist of only a total of 15 items. The *Scales of Independent Behavior-R* includes only one area, Social Interaction, which is part of the Social Interaction and Communication cluster. The *Interview Edition—Expanded Form of the Vineland Adaptive Behavior Scales* has 134 items measuring the subdomains of Interpersonal Relationships, Play and Leisure, and Coping Skills. The *Battelle Developmental Inventory* has a Personal/Social domain that measures the following: adult interaction, expression of feelings—affect, self-concept, peer interaction, coping, and social roles.

There are instruments that are specifically designed to measure social skills; one example is the *Social Skills Improvement Rating Scales* (SSIS) (Gresham & Elliott, 2008). The test can be used with 3- to 18-year-olds and has three forms—teacher, parents, and student. The use of this instrument allows multiple ratings of an individual's social skills including the Social Skills Scale, which assesses positive social behaviors, Behavior Problems Scale, Autism Spectrum Scale, and Academic Competence Scale (Doll & Jones, 2012). The SSIS is part of a multicomponent system to strengthen social skills and suggest interventions (Doll & Jones, 2012). Social skills are also included as areas measured by other behavior rating scales such as the *Behavior Assessment System for Children—Second Edition* (Reynolds & Kamphaus, 2004).

Basic Academic Skills

The informal procedures discussed earlier in this chapter are invaluable when assessing basic academic skills. Several norm-referenced tests are also available that measure these skills. Two examples are the *Kaufman Test of Educational Achievement—Second Edition, Comprehensive Form* (Kaufman & Kaufman, 2004b) and the *Wechsler Individual Achievement Test—Third Edition* (Pearson, 2009). These instruments are frequently used to document the extent of educational need that exists in the basic skill areas and to identify general academic goals.

Kaufman Test of Educational Achievement—Second Edition, Comprehensive Form. The *Kaufman Test of Educational Achievement—Second Edition* (KTEA-II) (Kaufman & Kaufman, 2004b) is designed for students from ages 4.6–25 years. There are two forms of the KTEA-II. One form is a comprehensive test that measures five areas; the second test is a brief form that measures three areas. The following is a description of the five composites that constitute the comprehensive form.

- *Reading Composite*—Measures Letter and Word Recognition and Reading Comprehension
- *Mathematic Composite*—Includes Math Computation and Math Concepts and Application
- *Written Language Composite*—Includes Spelling and Written Expression
- *Oral Language Composite*—Measures Listening Comprehension and Oral Expression

Summary: Kaufman Test of Educational Achievement—
Second Edition, Comprehensive Form

Age Level—4.6–25 years old

Uses—Measure achievement in reading, mathematics, written language, and oral language

Standardization Sample—Nationally representative sample of over 3,000

Standard Scores Yielded—Subtest scores, Reading and Math Composites, Total Battery (all X = 100; SD = 15) (Bonner, 2012).

Wechsler Individual Achievement Test-III. The Wechsler Individual Achievement Test-III (WIAT-III) is designed to for individuals ages 4–0 through 19–11 years. The WIAT-III includes eight composites in Oral Language, Total Reading, Basic Reading, Reading Comprehension and Fluency, Written Expression, Mathematics, Math Fluency, and Total Achievement. Each composite score is derived from a combination of 2 or more of the16 subtests which are: Listening Comprehension, Oral Expression, Early Reading Skills, Word Reading, Pseudoword Decoding, Reading Comprehension, Oral Reading Fluency, Alphabet Writing Fluency, Spelling, Sentence Composition, Essay Composition, Math Problem Solving, Numerical Operations, Math Fluency–Addition, Math Fluency–Subtraction, and Math Fluency–Multiplication (Miller, 2012).

Summary: Wechsler Individual Achievement Test-III

Age Level—4–0 years up to 19 years, 11 months old

Uses—Measures achievement in listening, speaking, reading, writing, and mathematics

Standardization Sample—Representative sample of 2,950 (grade norms) and 3,600 (age norms)

Standard Scores Yielded—Subtests and eight composites (all X = 100; SD = 15) (Miller, 2012)

Commercially Prepared Criterion-Referenced Inventories

There are also commercially prepared criterion-referenced inventories that are available that include a number of skill sequences designed for a specific age range or grade level. Albert Brigance has published several of these inventories with Curriculum Associates over the past 25 years (see Event Box 9.2). One popular instrument is the *Brigance Diagnostic Inventory of Basic Skills—Revised* (Brigance & Glascoe, 1999), which contains 154 skill assessments covering the areas of readiness, speech, listening, reading, spelling, writing, research and study skills, and mathematics. The instrument is designed to provide objectives-referenced assessment information on school-based skills for children 5–13 years of age (Cizek, 2012). Use of a portion of these skill areas might be substituted for the teacher-made test described in the previous section on teacher-made criterion-referenced tests. Another inventory is the *Brigance Inventory of Essential Skills* (Brigance, 1981). This instrument is used for assessing functional academic skills that might be appropriate for some students with CIDs. For example, this inventory includes a skill sequence related to "Functional word recognition" (e.g., warning labels) and "Completing forms" (e.g., a job application). For all the Brigance inventories, a behavioral objective is provided for each skill sequence that can be helpful in writing IEPs.

9.2 EVENT THAT MADE A DIFFERENCE

1977—Albert Brigance publishes first "Brigance Inventory"

Partially as a response to the requirement mandated in P.L. 94-142 that every student with a disability have an individualized education program (IEP), Al Brigance developed his first inventory, the *Inventory of Basic Skills*. This instrument and those that followed were designed to assist teachers to gather instructionally relevant information. One feature of the inventories was the inclusion of behavioral objectives that were associated with the test items, thus making the task of developing the IEP somewhat easier. Although his first inventory was designed primarily for students in elementary school, his later inventories cover skills from a wide age and grade range.

Vocational and Employment Skills

Employment is a crucial component in helping an individual to become independent. It is not surprising that vocational skill development is so important, particularly for older students with CIDs. The Individuals with Disabilities Education Act (IDEA) requires that all students have transition goals in their IEPs by the age of 14. It further requires that any interagency linkages must be identified by the age of 16 (or younger if determined by the IEP team). Vocational and employment skills clearly fall under this mandate. In addition, the Carl D. Perkins Vocational and Applied Technology Education Act was passed to provide increasing accessibility of vocational education services for students who receive special education services.

There are some norm-referenced tests that include domains that address this area. For example, the *AAMR Adaptive Behavior Scales: 2* has vocational activity as a test area, and the *Scales of Independent Behavior-Revised* has work skills. A third example of a formal employability evaluation is a two-instrument system called the *Job Observation and Behavior Scale* (JOBS) (Rosenberg & Brady, 2000) and the *Job Observation and Behavior Scale: Opportunity for Self-Determination (JOBS: OSD)* (Brady, Rosenberg, & Frain, 2006). Both instruments provide norms that allow comparison of work performance and support needs to other students and employees in both sheltered and supported employment settings (Brady & Rosenberg, 2002; Brady, Rosenberg & Frain, 2008). Both instruments also evaluate on-the-job performance and support needs. The majority of assessment approaches, however, are more informal in nature. These include the use of work samples, portfolio assessment, and curriculum-based vocational assessment. There are also criterion-referenced inventories that have been designed to measure vocational skills and norm-referenced tests developed to measure job-related interests.

Work samples are used to simulate tasks associated with different types of jobs and can be both commercially and locally developed (Taylor, 2009). The use of work samples allows an evaluator to determine through observation whether or not a student is able to perform the job task requirements (Thurlow & Elliot, 1998). Therefore, it is important that these work samples closely approximate the job requirements.

The technique of portfolio assessment discussed previously in this chapter also has applications for the measurement of vocational and employment skills. This is accomplished through the use of a **career portfolio.** Sarkees-Wircenski and Wircenski (1994) described the steps that were used in developing a statewide career portfolio. First, important competencies such as employability skills, work-related social skills, and job specific skills were identified. Next, these were validated by a number of professionals resulting in over 100 important competencies. Samples of work were then selected by the student and teacher for the portfolio that demonstrated their levels of performance for specific competencies. They suggested that career portfolios could be used to determine short-term and long-term instructional objectives, to formulate a job match between student competencies and job requirements, and to assist in vocational counseling. Finally, the career portfolio could be presented by the student to a prospective employer.

Curriculum-based vocational assessment uses the previously described curriculum-based assessment techniques based on the vocational curriculum chosen for a specific student. Porter and Stodden (1986) described a curriculum-based vocational assessment model that consisted of three phases. The first involves vocational courses and activities, including the readiness skills necessary for job success. The second involves the assessment of the student's performance in the vocational coursework. The third assesses work-related behaviors and skills demonstrated in the actual job placement. Ianacone and LeConte (1986; p. 117) described six key steps in developing a curriculum-based vocational assessment.

1. Identify key development personnel.
2. Conduct a comprehensive search of program models, research literature, vocational assessment instruments, and pertinent legislation.

3. Establish basic considerations for the model based on previous research; analyze and synthesize the programmatic needs.
4. Establish an operational plan to implement the process.
5. Pilot and evaluate the curriculum-based vocational assessment implementation activities.
6. Implement, evaluate, and expand options.

Several criterion-referenced inventories are available that include skills sequences that focus on vocational and employment skills. The previously described *Brigance Inventory of Essential Skills* has a set of 23 skills sequences that measure vocational areas. These include sequences such as identification of employment signs and completing applications for employment. It also has a job interview rating scale. A criterion-referenced inventory developed specifically to evaluate this area is the *Brigance Diagnostic Employability Skills Inventory* (Brigance, 1995). This instrument measures reading, listening, and speaking skills in the context of areas such as job applications, interviewing, pay and benefits, and life skills. The life skills inventory portion includes the following areas:

- Calendar and time concepts
- Simple measurements
- Money concepts
- Common signs in looking for employment
- Information signs
- Safety signs
- Directions obtained from employment forms
- Social Security card application
- Single and complex employment applications
- Completing a resume and other job-related situations (Carlson, 2012).

Another criterion-referenced inventory that is used for vocational assessment is the *Brigance Diagnostic Life Skills Inventory* (Brigance, 1994).

There are several vocational *interest* instruments available that measure an individual's interest in different occupations. These can be useful in vocational counseling and in determining what types of job skills need to be trained. Two examples are the *Gordon Occupational Checklists—2* (GOC-2) and the *Wide Range Interest—Opinion Test—Second Edition* (WRIOT2). The GOC-2 (Gordon, 1981) determines an individual's vocational preference in the areas of business, outdoor, arts, services, mechanical, and industrial. Each item is keyed to a job title and the corresponding workgroup that is listed in the U.S. Department of Labor's guide for occupational exploration. The WRIOT2 (Glutting & Wilkinson, 2003) is a reading-free instrument that uses 238 pictures to determine the student's interests in the three clusters that identify occupational preferences, interests, and matches with their "type" (e.g., investigative, artistic, enterprising) (Bugaj, 2012).

Finally, the *Job Observation and Behavior Scale* (JOBS) system actually evaluates an individual's real-life job performance. It is used to determine the quality of work performance, the types of needed supports to sustain that performance, and the student or employee's growth and development in the job over time. A unique aspect of the JOBS system is that one instrument (*JOBS*) provides information from an external evaluator's perspective (i.e., teacher, job coach, work supervisor) (Rosenberg & Brady, 2000). The second instrument (*JOBS: OSD*) provides information from the self-determined perspective of the student or employee (Brady et al., 2006). Both instruments measure three areas:

- Work-required Daily Living Activities (e.g., punctuality);
- Work-required Behavior (e.g., response to changes in routines); and
- Work-required Job Duties (e.g., follows safety procedures).

Also, both instruments assess work performance separately from the level of support needed to maintain that performance. Figure 9.4 shows the scoring criteria used to complete the *JOBS*, and a similar scoring rubric is used for *JOBS: OSD*. The JOBS system is typically used to evaluate the progress of an individual's employment skills, while monitoring comparisons to normed samples of other students and employees. Using information from both instruments also allows comparisons of work performance and support needs from two different points of view. To date, perspectives

JOBS Subscale	Quality of Performance	Type of Support
Each item is rated on performance and support need	Summarizes the student or employee's work proficiency.	Summarizes the student or employee's need for support to achieve work proficiency.
JOBS		
Work Required Daily Living Activities	5 = Superior performance	5 = No unique supervision or support needed beyond that provided to other workers
Work required Behavior	4 = Above average performance	
Work Required Job Duties	3 = Average performance	4 = Intermittent supervision is needed from a co-worker
	2 = Below average performance	3 = Intermittent supervision is needed from job coach or supervisor
	1 = Performance not acceptable for competitive employment	2 = Frequent supervision from job coach or supervisor is needed
		1 = Continuous supervision from job coach or supervisor is needed
JOBS: OSD		
Work Required Daily Living Activities	3 = Yes	3 = Can you do it by yourself?
Work Required Behavior	2 = Sometimes	2 = Can you do it with some help?
Work Required Job Duties	1 = No, not really	1 = Do you need a lot of help?

Figure 9.4 Scoring Criteria Used for JOBS and JOBS: OSD

from external evaluators (teachers, job coaches) do not correspond closely to the self-determined perspectives of the students and employees themselves (Bennett, Frain, Brady, Rosenberg, & Surinak, 2009; Brady, Frain, Duffy & Bucholz, 2010).

Community Living Skills

Goals for an individual with CIDs should transcend the school environment; they should also address the individual's functioning in the environment outside the classroom. Like the vocational and employment skills just discussed, community living skills are necessary to allow an individual to be as independent as possible. These involve areas such as transportation (e.g., using a bus) and shopping skills (e.g., using money).

Fewer instruments are available that measure this area. Adaptive behavior scales do usually address this area, although to different degrees. The *Scales of Independent Behavior-Revised* (Bruininks, Woodcock, Weatherman, and Hill, 1996) measures time and punctuality, money and value, and home/community orientation among other areas. The *AAMR Adaptive Behavior Scales: 2* has a domain called Economic Activity, although it has few items. The Daily Living Skills domain from the *Vineland Adaptive Behavior Scales* also includes items addressing community skills. An example of a criterion-referenced inventory is the previously mentioned *Brigance Diagnostic Life Skills Inventory* (Brigance, 1994), which has several skill sequences that address community living skills such as travel and transportation and money and finance.

Finally, the Supports Intensity Scale (SIS) (Thompson et al., 2002, 2004) is, according to the AAIDD (2010), the "only standardized support needs assessment currently available" (p. 114). The SIS is focused on identifying what personalized supports an individual might require to achieve or maintain his or her desired quality of life. There are 49 items related to life activities and a supplemental scale addressing self-advocacy and self-determination. There are an additional 29 nonstandardized items focused on exceptional support needs related to medical conditions and prevention of negative consequences from challenging behavioral issues (AAIDD, 2010). AAIDD points out that adaptive behavior and similar scales tend to address personal competencies. The SIS is focused on what the individual needs to participate meaningfully in daily life.

Reflection

What types of community living skills could be addressed when assessing a high school student with CIDs?

SUMMARY CHECKLIST

Multidimensional Nature

➤ **Functional assessment—Should focus on skills that lead to the greatest degree of independence**
  ✓ Age and severity level is important
  ✓ Purposes—Assessment can be used for instructional decision making and progress monitoring

Informal Assessment: Instructional Decision Making

- ➢ **Criterion-referenced tests (CRTs)—Provide specific information about what an individual does and doesn't know or can or cannot do**
  - ✓ Criterion-referenced tests can be either teacher-made or commercially prepared
  - ✓ First step in developing a criterion-referenced test is to identify skill areas to measure
- ➢ **Task analysis—Identification and sequencing of behaviors that are necessary components of skills required to complete a task; useful in developing a criterion-referenced test**
  - ✓ Other steps in developing a criterion-referenced test are developing the items themselves and determining criteria for mastery
- ➢ **Curriculum-based assessment (CBA)—The assessment of a student's performance in terms of the expected curriculum outcomes**
  - ✓ Criterion-referenced CBA (CR-CBA)—Similar to a criterion-referenced test with the student's curriculum dictating the content
  - ✓ Summary sheets—Sometimes used to organize information from a criterion-referenced curriculum-based assessment

Informal Assessment: Monitoring Progress

- ✓ Advantages of observation—Inexpensive, readily available, provides direct measurement
  - ➢ Observation for progress monitoring uses four-step model—Identify the target behavior, measure it using the appropriate recording procedure, introduce the intervention, and evaluate its effectiveness using same recording procedure
  - ➢ **Event recording—Measure of the number of behaviors that occur within a specific time frame**
  - ➢ **Duration recording—Measure of the amount of time an individual engages in a target behavior**
  - ➢ **Baseline data—Data collected before a new intervention program is introduced**
- ✓ Portfolio assessment—Systematic collection of student work that provides evidence of performance, progress, and achievement
  - ➢ **Working portfolio—Includes "typical" examples of student work**
  - ➢ **Show portfolio—Includes best examples of student work**
- ✓ Questions to ask in developing a portfolio: What should it look like? What goes in it? How and when are entries selected? How is it evaluated? How is it passed on?
  - ➢ **Rubric—Set of criteria used to provide a more objective evaluation of portfolio entries**
- ✓ Rubrics commonly used for assessing CCSS
  - ➢ **Curriculum-based measurement—A more formalized, standardized type of curriculum-based assessment**
  - ➢ **Trend line or progress line—Used in curriculum-based measurement to determine if the student is making appropriate progress toward a goal**

Accommodations and Alternate Assessment

✓ IDEA requires that all students with disabilities participate in statewide and districtwide assessment programs

✓ Appropriate testing accommodations are allowed

✓ An alternate assessment must be used if participation in the regular assessment program is inappropriate

✓ National Center on Educational Outcomes—Monitors the participation of students with disabilities in assessment programs

> **Performance assessment—Individuals perform a task instead of providing oral or written answers to questions. Sometimes used as an alternate assessment**

Assessment by Functional Skill Area

✓ Independent Living Skills (ILS)—Includes self-help skills such as eating and dressing

✓ Many adaptive behavior scales (e.g., the *Vineland Adaptive Behavior Scales*) include domains measuring independent living skills

✓ Other instruments that measure independent living skills are developmental inventories (e.g., the *Battelle*) and criterion-referenced inventories (e.g., the *Vulpé Assessment Battery-Revised*)

✓ The *Vulpé* has a unique scoring system that is helpful in evaluating skills of individuals with more severe disabilities

✓ Communication skills—Includes nonverbal, verbal, and written; also expressive and receptive skills

✓ Adaptive behavior scales and developmental/criterion-referenced inventories also include domains measuring communication skills

✓ There are specific instruments (e.g., the *Test of Language Development–3*) that measure several components of receptive/expressive language

✓ Some instruments, such as the *Peabody Picture Vocabulary Test IV,* measure primarily only one component of language

✓ Instruments are also available that measure written language skills

✓ Social skills—Involves areas such as interacting with others, cooperation, and personal adjustment

✓ Adaptive behavior scales and developmental inventories have fewer items measuring social skills

✓ Social Skills Improvement Rating System—Specifically designed to measure social skills; includes an intervention guide

✓ Basic academic skills—Appropriate for many students with CIDs

✓ Examples of two achievement tests that measure basic academic skills are the *Kaufman Test of Educational Achievement-II* and the *Wechsler Individual Achievement Test-III*

✓ Brigance inventories are a series of criterion-referenced inventories that include grade-based basic and functional academic skill sequences

✓ Vocational and employment skills—Very important for middle and secondary students

✓ IDEA requires transition goals in a student's IEP by age 14

  ➢ **Work samples—Simulated tasks used to evaluate job performance**
  ➢ **Career portfolio—Used to determine objectives, formulate a job match, and assist in vocational counseling**
  ➢ **Curriculum-based vocational assessment—A curriculum-based assessment technique using a student's vocational curriculum as the content**

✓ Brigance also has several criterion-referenced inventories designed to measure vocational skills

✓ Vocational interest inventories—Examples are the *Gordon Occupational Checklists–2* and the *Wide Range Interest and Opinion Test–II*

✓ The *Job Observation and Behavior Scale* system—Measures actual on-the-job performance and the level of support needed to sustain that performance, from an external (teacher, job coach, work supervisor) and self-determined (student, employee) perspective. JOBS system has norms for comparison to other students and employees in supported and sheltered employment.

✓ Community living skills—Important to measure skills outside the classroom environment

✓ Fewer instruments are available that measure community living skills

✓ The *Supports Intensity Scales* focuses more on what the individual needs to participate in daily life than on his or her adaptive skill achievement

ADDITIONAL SUGGESTIONS/RESOURCES

Discussion Questions

1. Compare and contrast criterion-referenced curriculum-based assessment and curriculum-based measurement.
2. Describe the four-step observational model that can be used for monitoring student progress.
3. Identify the methods and instruments that can be used to assess the area of independent skills. Do the same for vocational and employment skills.

Activities

1. Following the steps described in the first section of the chapter, develop a criterion-referenced test for the skill "subtracts two-digit numbers from three-digit numbers without renaming (borrowing)."
2. Contact your local school system to determine (a) what testing accommodations are allowed for students with disabilities, and (b) what alternate assessment procedures are being used.
3. Interview a general education teacher and a special education teacher about their views and use of portfolio assessment.

E-sources

www.psychcorp.com/

This website is home to numerous assessment instruments described in this chapter. It answers many questions that teachers and parents of students with disabilities might ask. It includes information on the types of tests that might be administered, what statewide assessments are all about, and what accommodations are allowed in testing.

www.proedinc.com

This website is from a leading publisher of standardized tests used with students with CIDs and other disabilities. Other products include books, curricular resources, and therapy materials, as well as catalog information for other companies that publish educational and psychological tests.

www.nasponline.org/publications

This website is home of the National Association of School Psychologists. It provides summaries of developments on standardized testing and excerpts of the newsletter, *Communique.*

10

INSTRUCTIONAL CONTENT

Key Points

➤ WHAT DO ALL STUDENTS NEED TO LEARN?—National school reform efforts influence decisions about what all students should learn. This raises special challenges for students with cognitive and intellectual disabilities.

➤ WHAT DO STUDENTS WITH CIDs NEED TO LEARN?—In addition to knowledge found in the general education curriculum, specific skills needed by students with CIDs include independent living skills, communication, social interactions and relations, academic skills, and transition and community living skills.

➤ PRINCIPLES FOR DECIDING INSTRUCTIONAL CONTENT—Deliberate decisions about the content of lessons includes establishing the value of the knowledge or skill, the importance of it in improving student's lives, its age-appropriateness, and the extent to which the student has an actual interest in learning the knowledge or skill.

➤ WHERE DO TEACHERS GAIN INFORMATION ABOUT INSTRUCTIONAL CONTENT?—The IEP is the formal process for determining instructional content, but additional attention is being paid to national curriculum standards. Professionals, families, and students all play an important role in this process.

WHAT DO ALL STUDENTS NEED TO LEARN?

Teachers, students, and their families are constantly asked to make decisions about what students should learn. Part of the decision making involves considering the knowledge and skills that are needed by *all* students, whether or not they have CIDs. Much of the focus on deciding what students need to learn grew out of a report published over three decades ago: *A Nation at Risk* (National Commission on Excellence in Education, 1983). This report challenged educators and the public to examine the increasing numbers of students who are unprepared for a society characterized by its increasing complexity, diversity, and reliance on technology. Since the report, school reform has been a focus of educators and the general public alike. Numerous groups have produced plans and proposals for improving America's schools, and school reform has played a major role in state and national elections. Recent federal comprehensive legislation, *No Child Left Behind* (P.L. 107-110) and the *Race to the Top* competition that followed it are intended to be the centerpiece in school reform. Reforms also have included several different sets of national goals, and proposals for such broad issues as changing the way schools are funded and organized, reductions in class size, and changes in the licensing of teachers (Bushaw & Lopez, 2012). Reform efforts also have focused on specific issues such as teaching methods that should be used for different children, and even whether too much attention is paid to some populations of children. Of the numerous lessons to take away from the national attention to reform, the fundamental message is clear:

There Is No Shortage of Voices Telling Educators What Should Be Taught in Contemporary Schools!

Academicians, state legislators, and the local citizenry all have strongly held convictions about what should be taught, to whom, and when. Although these multiple voices could create confusion, there is surprising consensus over the expectation for students. Most Americans share a common set of beliefs that students should graduate from local schools with:

- Basic mathematical competence;
- Fundamental knowledge of science and technology;
- Positive dispositions involving active citizenship;
- Literacy skills;
- Practical skills enabling students to be self-supporting after graduation;
- Problem-solving skills and skills that assist learners "learn how to learn"; and
- An understanding of the growing importance of global solutions to historically vexing problems.

These skills are considered important for all students to learn (National Education Goals Panel, 1997) and there is a continuing effort to assess the nation's progress in meeting these goals. Indeed, *No Child Left Behind* requires periodic assessment of students, schools, and states to gauge progress in achieving these national goals. Many states have adopted curriculum standards in English and Mathematics to assure these national goals are reached by all students (National Governors Association Center for Best Practices [NGACBP], 2010), but to date it is not clear whether these Common Core State Standards (CCSS) will be an expectation for all students with CIDs. The impact of *A Nation at Risk* and the Common Core State Standards is discussed further in Event Box 10.1.

10.1 EVENTS THAT MADE A DIFFERENCE

1983—U.S. Department of Education publishes its report: *A Nation at Risk*

2010—National Governors Association adopts: *Common Core State Standards*

One in a series of critiques of American education, *A Nation at Risk* sounded an alarm that rang in every state: the United States was losing a war of economic competition to countries such as Germany and Japan, in part because American students did not match the math and science outcomes of their counterparts in other developed countries. The report was the impetus for a series of school "reforms" aimed at linking curriculum to national standards. Within a decade, each state was deeply involved in developing curriculum standards and guidelines for local schools, and a host of additional federal initiatives aimed to strengthen curriculum standards, link standards from each state to one another, establish statewide student assessments to determine whether students were meeting these standards, and develop financial rewards and punishers for schools based on student test performance. Today, as a result of efforts by the National Governors Association (NGACBP, 2010), most states have adopted these Common Core State Standards (CCSS).

What impact did *A Nation at Risk* and the subsequent CCSS have for students with CIDs? The reauthorization of IDEA in 1997 included two requirements that changed the way student educational programs were implemented. *First*, local educators are required to declare the extent to which every student in special education will access the general education curriculum. Although some families and educators believe this has opened the door to more inclusive educational options, others see the reliance on the general education curriculum (e.g., math, science, and literacy) as a loss of opportunity for individualized, more functional goals. Also, increased curriculum standards go hand-in-hand with increased graduation requirements, an inherent risk for many students with disabilities. *Second*, states are required to demonstrate that students with disabilities are included in statewide assessments. Because many states now base financial rewards and punishers for schools on student test performance, these tests are often called **high-stakes tests**, and local school leaders face myriad challenges when deciding whether to include students with disabilities in these tests. Principals with an already high proportion of low-achieving students (and thus at-risk of losing funding) may view students with CIDs as too high a risk factor for a struggling school. That is, the reform movements have had many unintended consequences (Brady, Duffy, Hazelkorn, & Bucholz, 2014). The long-term effect of *A Nation at Risk* and the changes it spawned on students with CIDs is beginning to be felt in many communities throughout the nation.

Although school reform movements have had far-reaching changes for most students, many parents, advocates, and professionals have wondered how students with disabilities fit the "standards based reforms" (Shriner, 2000). Are students with

CIDs expected to achieve the same levels of academic proficiency as those who are intellectually gifted? What is a reasonable expectation of students who participate in, but do not excel or even pass, the various states' high-stakes tests (e.g., standardized tests that determine whether students will progress to another grade or school)? Goodman, Hazelkorn, Bucholz, Duffy and Kitta (2011) report an increase in drop-out rates among students with disabilities after one state increased graduation requirements in hopes of raising academic standards. Fortunately, special educators are increasingly participating in the state and national school reform agenda, and safeguards (e.g., testing accommodations) for students with CIDs are being incorporated. At a minimum, the adoption of national curriculum standards and goals means that students with CIDs will have increased access to the general education curriculum. This is a positive development since people with CIDs often have been ignored or excluded from progressive social and educational movements in the past (Polloway, Smith, Patton, & Smith, 1996). As for the student skills and educational outcomes delineated in the national goals and CCSS, many apply to students with *or* without disabilities. Although it is clear that these categories of skills do not cover every possible expectation, their mastery is considered important for participation in contemporary society. But beyond these important universal outcomes, there are other skills and knowledge needed by students with CIDs.

> *Reflection*
> **How do you think the national school reform movements will affect students with mild forms of CIDs? How will they affect students with severe CIDs?**

WHAT DO STUDENTS WITH CIDs NEED TO LEARN?

Although students with CIDs are expected to leave school with the same skills that other students obtain, they also are expected to learn more practical routines as a result of their school experience. Because students with CIDs have various challenges to learning, they also are expected to gain a set of "**critical skills**" (Gaylord-Ross & Holvoet, 1985). Critical skills for these students mirror the skills needed by all students, but their instructional programs are expected to have explicit instruction targeting these patterns and routines.

Questions about what students with CIDs should learn have not always generated productive discussion. Prior to the federal mandate to provide special education in 1975, many educators discounted the possibility of productive contributions by people with CIDs. In many local school districts, special education was not available nor was it desired by school leaders (thus necessitating federal requirements). Once federal legislation required that special education become available to all students who needed it, numerous educational advances were made in curriculum and instructional methods. This included enormous attention paid to developing **functional curriculum** (Polloway et al., 1996). Some educators created a new organization that became a focal point for research and development on functional curriculum, specifically for people with severe disabilities. The birth of what is today called TASH is found in Event Box 10.2.

10.2 EVENT THAT MADE A DIFFERENCE

1974—A new organization, AAESPH, holds its first conference to advocate for people with the most severe disabilities

Several years before the passage of P.L. 94-142 (now known as IDEA) opened American schools to all students with disabilities, a group of educators were discussing ways to make sure that children and adults with moderate to severe CIDs, multiple and physical disabilities, and behavioral disabilities such as autism would not be left out of any new efforts to include people with disabilities into public schools. With just 30 people as core members, the first annual conference of the American Association for the Education of the Severely/Profoundly Handicapped (AAESPH) was held in Kansas City, Missouri, in the fall of 1974. From the beginning, AAESPH was value-driven, and members worked hard to focus on practical training strategies, instructional methods, and interventions and services that would improve the lives of people with the most obvious disabilities. In an early keynote speech, AAESPH's president called for "the full integration into American society and the American scene" of people with severe disabilities, and to consider "the relevance of what we teach toward each individual's achievement . . . in living in his or her home community" (Haring, 1977; pp. 4–5). The first volume of the organization's journal, *AAESPH Review*, spanned eight issues, with topics including:

- Instructional procedures for teaching students to imitate
- Basic guidelines for instructional programs
- Teaching procedures to promote acquisition of complex assembly tasks
- Sample data sheets for recording and graphing student learning
- Procedures to promote functional language

and a host of other articles on life skills, vocational skills, family support, and other topics. Over the next 40 years, AAESPH (now TASH) would grow and change, but members' commitment to community values, instructional technology, and lifelong supports has remained strong. The body of knowledge and practice has grown richer as a result of the birth of AAESPH just four decades ago.

The critical skills needed by most students with CIDs may not require a completely separate curriculum. Similarly, a functional curriculum does not necessarily curtail a student's access to the general education curriculum or the CCSS. But many students with CIDs will require explicit instruction in routines that students without disabilities acquire on their own. Although these skills involve thousands of specific actions, they can be grouped into five behavioral clusters:

1. Independent Living Skills
2. Communication
3. Social interactions and relations
4. Academic Skills
5. Transition, Community Living, and Employment Skills.

Assessment and the delivery of instruction for these areas are discussed in other chapters.

Independent Living Skills

Like all other students, those with CIDs need to learn or show mastery in independent living skills, also called life skills or self-care skills. Young children with and without CIDs typically have a major proportion of their instructional programs devoted to independent living skills whereas secondary students might need less emphasis on these skills. Students with severe disabilities typically have goals that target assistance or participation in many self-care routines, while those with mild disabilities often have an expectation for independent performance. Independent living skills often fall into four broad categories including:

1. Hygiene and toileting;
2. Dressing;
3. Home living (maintaining clothes, dishes, living environment, food preparation); and
4. Personal mobility.

An important instructional distinction should be made between independent living skills that need to be *taught* versus skills that need to be *strengthened*. Younger students, or those with severe CIDs, often need direct instruction to learn the routines involved in washing their bodies, brushing their teeth, putting on clothing, and so on. Older students, or those with mild disabilities, might have these skills in their repertoires but might not *use* the skills spontaneously. They may require supports or accommodations (such as picture prompts) rather than instruction to use the skills reliably. This distinction is important for teachers when deciding what and how they will teach a student. Both instruction and supports have received a great deal of attention by educators across the past few decades. Gast, Wellons, and Collins (1994) provided excellent descriptions of direct instruction programs to teach home and community safety skills. Reamer et al. (1998) designed direct instruction procedures using video technology to help *parents* teach dressing, tooth-brushing, and self-feeding. An example of a *support* system (rather than a direct instruction approach) is the video and self-evaluation procedures used by Lasater and Brady (1995) to promote fluency in shaving, preparing lunch, doing laundry, and caring for clothes, in secondary-aged students who already had the skills in their repertoire, but who never performed them independently. Mechling (2008) reviewed a number of emerging technologies (such as iPods, PDAs, and other hand-held devices) that have incorporated prompting and video modeling systems to teach self-care skills such as food preparation. Research Box 10.1 describes an early effort that set the stage for independent living skills curriculum.

10.1 RESEARCH THAT MADE A DIFFERENCE

Lent, J. R., & McLean, B. M. (1976). The trainable retarded: The technology of teaching. In N. G. Haring & R. L. Schiefelbush (Eds.), *Teaching special children* (pp. 197–223). New York: McGraw-Hill.

In a state-run institution in Kansas, Jim Lent assembled a host of people in the early 1970s and sought the answers to two questions:

1. Could people with CIDs learn the independent skills needed to move away from institutions and into the community?
2. If so, what would the teaching procedures look like?

The result was Project MORE, a curriculum project that taught people who lived at the institution how to wash, shave, brush their teeth, and participate in a host of other life skills. Lent and his colleagues developed teaching procedures and lessons plans that showed a new generation of special educators, behavioral technologists, and human service providers that custodial care was unnecessary for many people previously thought incapable of taking care of themselves. By the early 1980s, Project MORE teaching materials were found in many schools across the nation, and had become a standard curriculum for students with CIDs.

Mobility skills, once the domain of educators of students with vision impairments and blindness, have become an increasingly important part of the curriculum for students with CIDs. During the past two decades, the focus of mobility curriculum has been expanded to a host of home and community travel skills needed by sighted learners with various types of disabilities (Westling & Fox, 2009). Many students with vision or physical disabilities are assumed to need mobility assistance. For example, students with limited vision are assumed to need instruction if they are to learn to use sighted guides, or to develop independent cane use. Other students with serious physical disabilities require instruction in using wheelchairs for mobility, or to navigate through doors using various types of walkers.

Mobility instruction is often overlooked for students with CIDs since most students typically do not require instruction to help them walk, run, climb stairs, and so on. However, if students are to participate in normalized community work, recreational, and domestic routines as adults, they must learn to become mobile within and between these environments as children. For students with mild CIDs, mobility goals often include finding locations within the community, then using whatever transportation system is available within that community to travel to and from that location. This goal may be the same for those with more severe CIDs, although the goals might also include arranging community transportation by phoning an agency appointment desk for a pick-up or drop-off reservation. For young children, mobility goals often involve learning to find one's classroom from the bus area, locating an open desk in different classes, or moving between learning centers within a classroom. Mobility goals for middle school students often involve finding (and returning from) the cafeteria, library, gym, and other classrooms. Secondary-aged students might learn to access a community work site, basketball court, hardware store, or park using public transportation. Some students have no difficulty learning a route per se, but might have tremendous difficulty if a route has a temporary detour, or is noisy or congested. For these students, the route is secondary to a more important mobility goal of safe and controlled *completion* of the route. It is important for teachers to remember that students without disabilities generally acquire these mobility goals on their own, but these goals may need to be specifically taught to some students with CIDs. **Destination, route or mobility skills, and the use of public transportation** are teachable and their mastery is critical to improvements in the quality of life for these students. These skills have been taught using a host of video and static picture prompts, video iPod technologies, and other hand-held PDAs (Cihak, Alberto, Taber-Doughty, & Gama, 2006; Kelley, Test, & Cooke, 2013; Mechling & Seid, 2011) in both individual and group instruction formats.

Communication

Communication difficulties are often targeted for heightened instructional attention for students with CIDs. The vast majority of students have the basic prerequisites for communication but have difficulties due to social, motivational, or cognitive disabilities. Other students whose families do not speak English as their first language have additional communication difficulties. The nature of communication difficulties is often quite different for students with mild CIDs than it is for students with more severe disabilities (Beirne-Smith, Ittenbach, & Patton, 2002). For students with mild CIDs, communication difficulties often result in instructional interventions targeting **speech problems** such as articulation (substitutions, omissions, distortions) and **voice problems** such as abnormal pitch or voice intensity. These students also may require interventions for **language disorders** such as delayed language and undeveloped vocabulary. Communication interventions for students with severe CIDs almost always involve more basic communication functions. Such functions may be **nonsymbolic** (e.g., changes in voice, pitch, or body tone to indicate an emotional response), symbolic but *nonverbal* (e.g., picture books or letter boards), or completely verbal in nature. Students with CIDs who do not speak English as their primary language may wrestle with speech, language, *and* communication function challenges.

When planning instructional interventions, attention often is paid to issues of *form versus function*. That is, the people planning the instruction must decide whether to improve the form (style or format) of the student's speech and language, or to strengthen a student's ability to use his or her language to influence one's surroundings (function). Instruction that targets production of a clear "s" sound would be considered an intervention for form; instruction that teaches a student to request a break from work would be considered an intervention for function. One or both might be appropriate given the needs of individual students.

Instructional techniques and teaching behaviors that optimize communication can be specialized or quite typical. Many students with CIDs benefit greatly from typical classroom instruction, and a host of naturalistic or incidental teaching approaches have been developed to teach communication skills in typical settings (Jones & Warren, 1991). Others require specifically planned and implemented instruction (Gersten & Baker, 2000; Saunders, Spooner, Browder, Wakeman, & Lee, 2013). Historically, communication interventions were thought to be the responsibility of communication specialists (speech therapists, communication disorders specialists), although best educational practices now require that teachers and communication specialists work together to determine goals and to deliver instruction. These goals and approaches incorporate many different aspects of *Universal Design for Learning* (Dettmer, Knackendoffel, & Thurston, 2013) such as promoting

- Multiple means of representation,
- Multiple means of engagement, and
- Multiple means of expression

so that students with CIDs can participate in regular and routine instructional activities. In addition, individualized interventions might include the use of picture communication systems, shared story reading, videotaped rehearsal, role-playing activities, language scripts, fluency drills, and other literacy activities (Hudson & Test, 2011; Kurth, 2013; Nietupski, Hamre-Nietupski, Curtin, & Shrikanth, 1997).

Finally, communication deficits are often the basis for severe problem behavior (Janney & Snell, 2000; Reichle & Wacker, 1993). Students unable to communicate their interests effectively frequently use problem behavior as a means of expressing frustration, discomfort, or distrust. Teachers with students whose communication deficits increase their problem behavior must establish and consistently implement a functional communication system for each learner. Much of the research on this grew from a seminal article by Carr and Durand (1985) highlighted in Research Box 10.2.

10.2 RESEARCH THAT MADE A DIFFERENCE

Carr, E., & Durand, M. (1985). Reducing behavioral problems through functional communication training. *Journal of Applied Behavioral Analysis, 18,* 111–126.

Prior to federal requirements for special education, most school-aged students with moderate to severe disabilities received no education, and many lived in institutional settings. Without education, recreational opportunities, and regular family interactions, it was common for these people to develop odd, often troubling behavior (e.g., continuous rocking, self-injury, or physical aggression). The response of professionals typically was to find ways to reduce these problem behaviors, rather than to improve the lives and skills of the people with the problem behaviors.

Carr and Durand's study was one of the early examples of an *instructional approach* to this phenomenon. By "translating" problem behavior as communication, Carr and Durand were able to develop interventions that increased individuals' communication skills. By teaching new, more socially efficient means of communicating, the *need for* the previously troubling behavior was reduced. A positive side effect was also seen; the person who previously was unable to communicate his or her thoughts and needs was now able to do so, providing an important improvement in the person's quality of life. Today, informed professionals consider the communicative intent of problem behavior as a *first* intervention option.

Social Interactions and Relations

The importance of social development in individuals with CIDs can be seen by the changes in the definition and classification system described in Chapter 2. In the American Association on Mental Retardation's (AAMR) earlier definitions, Grossman (1983) defined *adaptive behavior,* in part, by targeting deficits in social responsibility of people with CIDs. The more recent classification schemes (AAIDD, 2010; AAMR, 2002) emphasized the importance of social skills and functions even further.

Social interaction and social perception are often considered as core areas of instruction for many people with CIDs. **Social skills** are the means by which people can make connections to others, exchange information and ideas, makes their needs and desires known, and enter into (and maintain) relationships. For most persons, **social perceptions** of oneself and others provide strong motivators to communicate. Social benefits also are a strong incentive to maintain personal self-care skills or to use mobility skills. In the absence of a social motivation, the desire to learn to use these and many other skills is reduced. For many individuals with CIDs, difficulties with social interactions and perception interfere with the use of these other skills.

The specific social need of students with CIDs is influenced by numerous factors including the age of the student; the nature and degree of disability; the student's previous social experiences at school, home, and in the community; the nature and availability of social skills instruction (if any); as well as a host of personal characteristics and social cultural variables. This view contrasts sharply with historical beliefs that social outcomes were defined primarily by the *level or degree* of disability. For example, students with a history of active social skills instruction and social relationship opportunities have far greater success in school, community, and work routines than those with limited social opportunities (Carter & Hughes, 2005; Ittenbach, Bruininks, Thurlow, & McGrew, 1993). This holds true for students with mild CIDs as well as those with more severe disability.

Educational interventions that target students' social needs typically are designed to:

1. Improve social interaction skills;
2. Establish social relationships;
3. Promote self-advocacy and self-determination.

Social skills instruction for many students will be quite practical, with social skills targets designed to improve their social *initiations; responses* to others' initiations; development of continuous, enjoyable *interactions;* and dignified *terminations* of social exchanges. Students with CIDs might have difficulty making social initiations to others, or these initiations might be inappropriate to the context (e.g., initiating a physical game like *tag* to a classmate in the library). Others may not have an effective means of responding to other students' initiations, their responses might be "clumsy" (too loud, or too playful) or they might not respond at all. Sometimes, students' initiations and responses are effective, but they do not lead to a continuation of an activity. For example, two peers might greet each other, but then not have the skills to suggest or start a game. Finally, a social interaction is over when one or all participants end it. Some students have difficulty ending an activity, and instead will linger long after the enjoyment among other peers has gone. Other students might end an interaction so abruptly that the peers are offended by the termination, or believe that they did something wrong.

The research literature is replete with examples showing that these skills can be directly taught in child care settings, schools, homes, playgrounds, recreation settings, on-the-job, in community settings, and elsewhere. A now-classic example of the research on social interactions comes from the social behavior group at San Francisco State University in the 1980s and 1990s and is found in Research Box 10.3. The results of such instruction are life-changing for many students.

10.3 RESEARCH THAT MADE A DIFFERENCE

Gaylord-Ross, R., Haring, T., Breen, C., & Pitts-Conway, V. (1984). The training and generalization of social interaction skills with autistic youth. *Journal of Applied Behavior Analysis, 17,* 229–247.

Gaylord-Ross and his colleagues extended the research on social integration in two important ways. First, the study was an early investigation of a strategy that would help new skills generalize across nontraining examples. As such, it would show that social behavior could be learned and used outside of the presence of structured teaching procedures. Second, the study combined sound experimental methods into everyday, applied situations, in this case into an urban high school. The Gaylord-Ross team soon became well known for the rigor of their applied research on social behavior, and for their creativity in integrating behavioral science with positive outcomes for the participants of their research.

Unfortunately, improvements in basic social skills do not always result in meaningful social relationships. Many students benefit only when they are taught **relationship building** skills (Newton, Olson, & Horner, 1995). This includes learning more ambiguous skills such as problem solving, understanding the perspective of others, and avoiding logistical barriers in social situations (Chadsey & Sheldon, 2002). Finally, most individuals with CIDs will benefit from educational interventions that promote self-advocacy and self-determination. This involves learning skills to make informed decisions, communicate one's own needs and interests, and to take responsibility for one's personal decisions (Thoma, Nathanson, Baker, & Tamura, 2002; Wehmeyer & Schwartz, 1997). As with other social outcomes, self-determination skills have been taught successfully when students worked toward specific skills, participated in prompted and spontaneous rehearsal, engaged in role play, received performance feedback from teachers, and ultimately practiced the skill in real-life situations.

Academic Skills

Professionals and family members often struggle with the issue of how much of a student's educational program should focus on academic instruction. Some people believe that students with CIDs should be fully included in the general education curriculum. As states have moved to adopt the Common Core State Standards, two questions have emerged involving placing such a heavy academic focus on student with CIDs:

1. Can these students participate meaningfully in the CCSS?
2. What will these students miss by participating in a primarily academic curriculum?

To date there have been strong and positive indicators that students with CIDs can participate meaningfully in the Common Core. A research and development effort at the University of North Carolina–Charlotte has produced numerous encouraging studies showing that modest attention to the structure of academic lessons can result in achievement of CCSS by students with mild to severe CIDs (Browder, Spooner, Wakeman, Trela, & Baker, 2006). This team has shown that students can make impressive gains in reading, writing, and math achievement, across different content areas, consistent with the CCSS (Browder, Ahlgrim-Delzell, Spooner, Mims, & Baker, 2009; Browder, Spooner, Ahlgrim-Delzell, Harris, & Wakeman, 2008; Browder, Trela, Courtade, Jimenez, Knight, & Flowers, 2012). This follows a long line of previous research showing that the presence of CIDs does not preclude significant gains in academic achievement—if instructional materials are thoughtfully designed and carefully delivered!

The response to the second question is more complicated. Even if students can obtain meaningful gains from carefully implemented academic curriculum, many educators advocate putting more emphasis on life skills, career development, transition skills, and other components of a functional curriculum. In speaking about students with more severe disabilities, Brown (2013) points out that the current milieu of educational standards is "myopic, longitudinal and inflexible." Brown argues that the Common Core standards adopted during the reform movement focused on accountability are simply the wrong ones to use with students with severe CIDs. Brown has continually challenged the field to consider the implications of selecting one criterion over another when delivering instruction. Brown proposed an alternative set of benchmarks with more immediate impact on these students, and include:

- Avoid wasting time teaching skills that will not help these students in their current and future lives;
- Hold educators responsible for designing and delivering truly meaningful programs;
- Deliver students' educational programs in a variety of normal environments, and assess the progress being made;
- Teach students to interact well with others and expend a good work ethic;
- Teach meaningful academics that are likely to be needed to function in post-school environments;
- Teach students to function in a variety of post-school places with chronologically aged peers;
- Teach the social skills needed to interact with others in a typical array of relationships;
- Expand students' repertoires of functional skills by teaching these skills;
- Teach students to be mobile in typical community settings;
- Arrange a wide variety of normal work opportunities during the school years, and teach students to participate in these skills and settings;
- Teach students to participate in healthy and meaningful activities when they are not engaged in work tasks; and
- Teach students to function in supported living settings.

(Brady, 2013)

Fortunately, there are various models used for deciding how much of a curriculum will include academic instruction (Polloway, Serna, Patton, & Bailey, 2013). These models may be "pure" academic curricula, or they might combine the array of academic goals linked to lifelong career education outcomes (Brolin, 2004). Most of the models include the use of goal selection variables described earlier, adherence to the general education curriculum, or the development of a parallel curriculum. Any decision about academic skills will include the following variables:

1. The amount of instruction devoted to academic skills changes across grade levels;
2. The amount of academic instruction will reflect the family and student's "world view" of the student's future;
3. The content of the academic instruction has some relationship to the student's future post-secondary transition; and
4. Continued inclusion of academic instruction will be based in part on the success of previous academic instruction.

The focus of instruction for all students changes across grade levels. For example, the curriculum for young children without disabilities typically is rich with language development, socialization, and self-care activities. Academics takes on a more prominent role in the elementary years, and by high school, most students spend the majority of their school day in academic instruction (Fisher, Sax, & Pumpian, 1999). This shift is often similar for students with CIDs, but with one important difference for secondary students: as students approach high school, the curriculum often moves away from academic skills in favor of a curriculum based on career awareness, vocational skill development, and preparation for adult living (Guy, Sitlington, Larsen, & Frank, 2009).

The world views and perceived needs of families also play an important role in deciding the proportion of effort devoted to academics and other forms of instruction (Green & Shinn, 1994). Within each family structure there is a complex set of circumstances, values, needs, and history that influences the family's orientation to the future for its members (Harry, 1992; Turnbull & Turnbull, 1997). Messages based on this world view are passed among family members, often across generations. Families with a strong school and academic orientation seek greater involvement in traditional school activities (Hoover-Dempsey, Bassler, & Brissie, 1992), an emphasis that may include access to the general education curriculum and typical academics. Families with other world views (e.g., those with strong work orientations) or whose family needs require attention to more practical functions (e.g., medical issues or transition to adulthood) may minimize their academic expectations, and instead seek greater curriculum attention to social and adult living skills (Turnbull & Turnbull, 1988; 1997).

What role does previous instruction play in deciding how much of a student's educational program will target academic skills? Unlike school for the majority of students without disabilities, educational planning for students with CIDs involves a much greater degree of choice. Families, professionals, and students themselves are required to make overt decisions, on an annual basis, about educational programming. Undoubtedly, satisfaction with previous instruction influences decisions about future academic programming (Ryndak, Downing, Jacqueline, & Morrison, 1995). Given the long history of concern about the content and location of special education (Glass, 1983; Salend & Duhaney, 1999), the degree of success of a given student plays an important part in the decision making for that student's future program. Students with CIDs learn academic skills when their teachers actively engage them in instruction, use a variety of effective teaching strategies, regularly make instructional accommodations, and frequently assess the impact on their learning. These students are most likely to maintain an academic focus in future years. Students whose teachers are less actively engaged in this type of instruction are not likely to learn academic skills. It is easy for professionals to underestimate the importance of academics for students with CIDs. Many years ago one of the authors learned an embarrassing lesson about the value of academic skills, and this is shared in the Box that follows.

Although degree of academic instruction will be decided on an individual basis, there is ample evidence during the past three decades that students with CIDs can learn

---

A PERSONAL EXPERIENCE

Many years ago I had a wonderful chance to meet Tim. Tim was a teenager with Down syndrome. He had accompanied his father on a trip to a tropical island where I lived and worked, taking full advantage of the opportunity to explore an interesting geographic locale. As host, I spent several evenings entertaining Tim and his father, and soon, much to my surprise, Tim was teaching me more about intellectual disability than I ever dreamed I would learn. Tim read a lot and knew quite a bit about the islands. Casual conversation turned to substantive discussion about world events and cultural differences, but it was the card game that opened my eyes. I *thought* I let Tim win the first time, but maybe I'd lost count. When he beat me the second time, I wondered if maybe I ought to pay better attention. But when Tim beat me several times in a row, I discovered my own game strategy was faulty *and* I had miscounted the cards at least twice. I asked Tim to show me how he played his hand—but he wouldn't. Smart? You bet! Tim was smart enough to use a strategy, and smart enough not to get hustled by a guy who didn't. I had never used the words "smart" and "intellectual disability" in the same sentence before, but I do now. I also never underestimate the value of academic instruction.

Hey, Tim, want a rematch? Call me!

---

academic skills when the instruction is well planned and carefully delivered (Browder & Lalli, 1991; Browder & Xin, 1998; Conners, 1992; Nolet & Tindal, 1994). This knowledge comes with three caveats. First, as noted in Chapter 6, students with CIDs have cognitive and learning characteristics that make the acquisition of abstract academic skills inherently difficult. Second, educators will need to deliver measurably superior instruction to overcome those learning challenges. Third, there will be considerable debate about the context of that instruction. Many professionals and families will advocate that academic instruction be delivered within the context of the general education curriculum, while others will prefer that academic instruction be tied to functional, community routines. Both will likely promote effective learning for different students.

Transition, Community Living, and Employment Skills

Many students with CIDs require specific instructional planning to assist them with life transitions and with community living (Hughes & Carter, 2000; Romer & Walker, 2013). This is most common when young children go from home to school (or early intervention settings), and when students move from part-time to full-time classes (such as Kindergarten to first grade) or from segregated schools to more inclusive settings. Transition and community living skills also are needed when secondary students prepare for post-school options, including employment or post-secondary education. Transition strategies typically include planning activities for teachers, and learning targets for students. When planning transition activities, teachers focus on such variables as the social relationships and networks in the next setting, communication patterns and markers of psychological well-being in that setting, and the naturally occurring recreation opportunities there (Hughes & Carter, 2000). To prepare students for transitions, instructional interventions should promote specific skills that help students (a) make connections with future social cliques and networks, (b) enjoy the benefits of recreation and leisure, (c) participate in the normal school or work routines that characterize the next setting (Miner & Bates, 1997; Li, Bassett, & Hutchinson, 2008).

Although negotiating transitions is a logical, needed skill for students with CIDs, it remains a rarity in many school programs. Preparing for transition requires, at a minimum, active student involvement when planning in their goals and placements (Brady, Rosenberg & Frain, 2008). Unfortunately, students typically are afforded very little participation in planning their own educational programs or in participating in planning meetings (Agran, Snow, & Swaner, 1999; Wehmeyer, Agran, & Hughes, 2000). Rather, teachers, service providers, or family members make decisions involving everyday choices and instructional plans, often without seeking input of the student. As noted in Chapter 8, there are distinct advantages to bringing the individuals most affected by the decisions into the decision-making process. Participating in a planning process that affects their future enables students to gain control over many choices that affect their lives and is an important aspect of self-determination and future employment planning (Hagner, Helm, & Butterworth, 1996). Students who are preparing for transition into post-secondary life should have an opportunity to participate in the development of their transitional IEPs starting as early as age 14, and instructional opportunities to learn how to make choices should be provided across the ages. These choices include future options for community living, supported or competitive employment, and continuing education options.

Although several models exist for preparing students for transitions (Martin & Huber Marshall, 1996; Mithaug, Wehmeyer, Agran, Martin, & Palmer, 1998), most models of self-determination include the following components:

1. Self-knowledge and awareness;
2. Self-advocacy;
3. Self-efficacy and appreciation;
4. Planning and decision making;
5. Self-management, performance, and adjustment; and
6. Self-monitoring and evaluation.

Studies of these variables, individually and in a variety of combinations, have shown that including instruction in these areas results in positive post-secondary employment and community living outcomes (Carter, Austin, & Trainor, 2012; Wehmeyer & Schwartz, 1997).

> **Reflection**
>
> **How might educators arrange for individualized goals for students who spend the majority of their school day involved in academic instruction in the general education curriculum?**

PRINCIPLES FOR DECIDING INSTRUCTIONAL CONTENT

Most students with CIDs require instruction that is planned and purposeful. Teachers must make deliberate decisions when deciding what to teach if students with learning challenges are going to learn. Over two decades ago, Brown and his colleagues (Brown et al., 1979) pointed out that students who need the *most* support for learning often receive the least support.

The first step in designing meaningful instruction for these students is to establish the value of the lessons arranged for them. Brown et al. (1979) outlined a set of principles to help determine and select more important goals for students with CIDs and others with serious learning obstacles. These principles are exemplified by six guiding questions about curriculum, goals, and skills for students:

1. Will the skill help the student participate in the current or future environments?
2. Will the skill help the student gain access to a better quality of life?
3. Does the goal include skills, routines, and materials that are age-appropriate?
4. Does the goal include skills that are valued by society?
5. Will this skill assist the student to become a productive contributor to the community?
6. Does the goal reflect the student's interests and enhance the student's talents?

A curriculum principle central to these guiding questions involved the **Criterion of Ultimate Functioning** (Brown, Nietupski, & Hamre-Nietupski, 1976). This criterion, proposed for students with severe disabilities, urged teachers to select instructional goals that include important life skills. Brown and his colleagues noted that after years of instruction designed to improve students' development and growth, many students with CIDs failed to master such critical skills as feeding, dressing, mobility, and communication. As important, the skills targeted for instruction should have practical application in the various places the student currently lives, and is likely to live in the future. This established an *environmental focus* on students' curriculum. If skills did not have a likelihood of improving a student's life at home, in school, or in the community, Brown et al. argued that the skill would have a low priority for instruction (see Research Box 10.4).

10.4 RESEARCH THAT MADE A DIFFERENCE

Brown, L., Nietupski, J., & Hamre-Nietupski, S. (1976). The criterion of ultimate functioning and public school services for the severely handicapped student. In M. A. Thomas (Ed.), *Hey, don't forget about me! Education's investment in the severely, profoundly, multiply handicapped* **(pp. 2–15). Reston, VA: Council for Exceptional Children.**

Brown, Nietupski, and Hamre-Nietupski's chapter on instructional programming for students with severe disabilities proposed a curriculum principle to guide selection of instructional goals. Their *criterion of ultimate functioning* posed a simple but central question:

> *If the student could not perform the proposed skill, would another person have to do it for the student, or could the task go undone?*
>
> The impact of this goal selection criterion was dramatic. The logic of the criterion of ultimate functioning helped educators refocus their instructional decisions to target students' most important life skills, and deemphasized the assumed developmental prerequisite skills (such as bead stringing or block stacking) so often found in classes for students with CIDs, *regardless of their ages.* Using this criterion, curricula for students with CIDs and other substantial learning problems have become much more meaningful, and student learning has improved substantially.

Applying these goal selection principles to students with CIDs today, it is obvious that initial goals targeted for acquisition should include age-appropriate functional skills. These skills should help students become as independent as possible, participate in meaningful ways in routines in which they are not independent, and lead to acceptance and reinforcement in typical settings. These skills are needed by all people, not just students with CIDs. Skills such as toileting, dressing, and using utensils are prerequisite for successful independent living, and are critical in removing barriers to peer acceptance, friendship development, and community inclusion. A student who has not learned to perform these skills will require the assistance of another person (usually a family member or paid service provider) to perform the skills *for* the student.

The **Quality of Life** criterion is closely linked to the Criterion of Ultimate Functioning. Students with CIDs who rely on paid providers for their most basic daily routines will miss many opportunities for normalized interactions that improve quality of life (Romer & Walker, 2013). Selecting skills and knowledge that help individuals make choices for themselves, promote their self-determination, and otherwise participate meaningfully in the social mainstream improves the quality of life for most people.

Quality-of-life issues are considered from both an objective and subjective point of view (Crane, 2002). Objectively, there are common skills, routines, and patterns of life that improve the daily lives of most people. These skills include many of the behavioral clusters described earlier in this chapter (e.g., improving social interaction skills, traveling within one's community). For many individuals, life quality improves as they make practical gains in their independent living, mobility, communication, and social interaction skills. However, life quality is not *defined* by independence in a particular set of skills. Each individual, based on personal life satisfaction, also establishes quality of life subjectively. Choice and control are vital elements of life satisfaction, and as noted in Chapters 7 and 8, self-determination and self-regulation influence individuals' ability to practice choice and control. When deciding instructional goals for students, educational approaches that improve students' quality of life include both the skill instruction and the opportunity to promote social relationships, psychological well-being, lifestyle patterns, community participation, recreation and leisure options, self-determination, employment, and a host of other variables (Hughes & Carter, 2000; Martin & Huber Marshall, 1996).

Age appropriateness has become an important consideration since the Brown et al. (1979) challenge nearly 35 years ago. Numerous authors have observed that professionals and others in society have relegated people with CIDs into social roles as "perpetual children" (Wolfensberger, 2000). Unfortunately, many professionals use instructional materials (e.g., stuffed toys and puppets) and teach behavioral routines (e.g., singing children's songs) common to infant and toddlers to students with CIDs, regardless of their age and grade level (Brady & Cunningham, 1985). This practice has added to the perception that CID results in child-like behavioral characteristics, even though the behavior is a result of professionals' behavior (teachers who provided the toys or prompted the songs), not the disability. If students are to learn behavioral patterns that reflect their chronological age, skills and materials that reflect that age must be part of their educational programs.

Brown et al. (1979) also pointed out that if students are to learn skills and routines valued by society, goals selected for students also should reflect these social values. That is, if educators are successful in their instruction, the students' outcomes should be seen as valuable by people in typical school and community settings. Given the wide range of behavior and routines considered appropriate for adults, this criterion could be easy to accomplish. However, selecting a skill that is valued by others does not necessarily lead to a skill that would help a student become a productive contributor to the community. Brown et al. also recommended that students learn skills that *make a contribution* to society. This principle was intended to remind educators that a universal goal of American education is for all citizens to make a contribution to their neighborhoods, communities, or society. For students with CIDs, this criterion has special meaning since research on their post-school outcomes indicates that unemployment and underemployment continues to be a serious problem (Carter et al., 2012; Storey, Bates, & Hunter, 2002). Holding a job is a strong value held by most people in society; working also results in making a contribution to oneself and to a person's family.

Finally, using *student interest* as a criterion for selecting goals has at least three practical applications. First, student interest in learning is important to the motivation for learning, and is integral to students' intrinsic and personal system of personal growth and rewards. Second, student interest in learning is central to developing personal control, autonomy, preference, and choice. Often referred to as components of self-determination, these variables are often overlooked in educational programs, and are important determinants for successful post-school life (Wehmeyer, Agran, & Hughes, 2000; Wehmeyer, & Schwartz, 1997). Third, using students' self-determined input to select goals typically gives a different, and even expanded, pool of possible goals because students' perceptions of their performance and support needs often differ greatly from those of teachers, supervisors, and employers (Brady, Frain, Duffy, & Bucholz, 2010).

These criteria for deciding what to teach students differ from the criteria used for all students described at the beginning of this chapter. Rather than selecting goals based on common standards (what *all* students should learn), the different criteria proposed by educators since the Brown et al. (1976) challenge involve a far more complex series of decisions about instruction, and include other key stakeholders in students' lives. In addition to the global skills (such as mobility, social development, expressive and receptive communication skills), there are skills that many students need in *particular* school, home, and community environments. The ability to wait in line crosses community and school settings, but is seldom needed at home. Raising one's hand to ask permission to speak is required in school settings, but not in others. It is important to prioritize skills in terms of their utility to the student before teaching them. Skills that students enjoy, or have as a personal interest, are also relevant when deciding what to teach. These skills should be identified and supported so that the student has self-selected and sustaining activities. In many cases, such interests (i.e., baseball card collecting or geography information) are the basis for community involvement and friendship. Particularly when students are young, interests and skills which the family finds important or which help the student access leisure activities that the family shares help the student become more participatory in his or her family and can lead to increased reinforcement and acceptance in the student's community.

Reflection
How would you decide to structure a student's curriculum if the student, parents, and other teachers held different priorities and beliefs about what the student needs to learn?

WHERE DO TEACHERS GAIN INFORMATION ABOUT INSTRUCTIONAL CONTENT?

It can be difficult to determine the instructional program for students with CIDs, and educators should not try to do this alone. Information and the perspectives of the many persons significant to students should be gathered, and decisions about what-to-teach should be prioritized. A process that formalizes the decision making for school-aged students is the **Individualized Educational Program** or **IEP**. Although the IEP has been referred to throughout this book, the following information provides a more specific description of how the process works.

Each student who receives special education services or supports must have an IEP. The IEP is required by federal law, and each state has a process for meeting the legal requirements for all school-aged youngsters within that state. Although the IEP requirement is just one of the legal mandates governing special education, it is central to the design, delivery, and evaluation of educational programs for all students with disabilities, including those with CIDs. IEPs differ for students younger than age 5 and older than age 14, but several activities are germane to deciding what to teach a student. This includes:

1. Establishing annual goals for individual students;
2. Basing the goals on previous student performance; and
3. Gaining information about student goals on input from a team made up of educators (including those who can interpret the student's assessment results, and those who are familiar with the general education curriculum), parents, and the student.

A parallel process for infants and toddlers is the **Individualized Family Services Program** (IFSP.) Like the IEP, the IFSP is a formal process, and is used to assure that young children with CIDs and other disabilities receive the attention necessary to access supports and services relevant to their needs. The IFSP has several differences from the IEP however. Unlike the IEP, the IFSP involves families in much more of the assessment, planning, and delivery of services. Less attention is provided to achieving instructional goals for children, and more focus is provided to linking families to community services beyond the school system. A summary of IEP and IFSP differences is found in Table 10.1.

The IEP then is used as the planning mechanism for decision making. It is the document that acts as the decision-making framework for selecting the goals and skills that a student could reasonably learn within a year's time. The IEP is created with input from people who know that student best, including parents, teachers, and professionals who have worked with the student. The IEP is not a contract, but it is a formal document that guides instruction. An early examination of how the IEP works is found in Research Box 10.5.

Table 10.1 Educational Planning Differences

Planning Variable	Individualized Educational Program	Individualized Family Services Program
Age	Age 3–21	Birth–3
	(ages 3–5 require family components found in IFSP)	(ages 3–5 can be included in an IEP)
Transition	Focus on transition to adulthood; Transition plans included from age 14	Focus on transition to preschool and school
Student Involvement	Student input is encouraged	Student input is rare
Assessment Information	Present Level of Performance summarizes student functioning; description of how disability affects involvement in general education programs	Description of child's functioning and a description of family priorities, strengths, and needs
Focus of Goals	Annual student goals; description of participation in general education curriculum	Individual goals for child *and* family goals that affect the child
Coordination	No specific coordination	IFSP coordinator required

10.5 RESEARCH THAT MADE A DIFFERENCE

Goldstein, S., Strickland, B., Turnbull, A. P., & Curry, L. (1980). An observational analysis of the IEP conference. *Exceptional Children, 46,* 278–286.

The federal mandate that opened special education to all students with disabilities who needed it also required that students have Individualized Educational Programs (IEP) to guide these activities. The plan was that IEPs would be the mechanism to bring teachers, parents, and other instructional decision makers to the table to develop, *together,* educational solutions to each student's instructional needs. The Goldstein et al. study was the first empirical look to see if the promise of the federal legislation was being implemented. The results sent ripples through the field. Findings showed that parents had little input into IEPs, although student curriculum, behavior, and performance was discussed. Other relevant topics were seldom, if ever, discussed, including issues of placement, related services, future planning for students, and the actual implementation of the instruction. Even the original intent of the IEPs (brainstorming and joint input into planning) was minimized; typically a predeveloped IEP was brought to the conference to present to parents. Surprisingly, parent satisfaction was relatively high. Since the original study, other researchers have found similar results, although parent participation and satisfaction with the process has eroded over the years. The IEP process has been under federal review in recent years and a reduction in the importance of IEPs is expected in future reauthorizations of IDEA.

A great deal of assessment data is gathered on students with CIDs. Some assessment procedures are used to identify CIDs and to establish eligibility for services (see Chapter 3); other assessments (such as those in Chapter 9) have more direct impact on making instructional decisions. When IEP teams review these assessment data to make instructional decisions, the information is presented on the IEP as a Present Level of Performance. This description is intended to summarize a student's strengths and weaknesses in a skill area, thereby establishing a marker against which the student's future growth can be measured. Although formal or standardized assessments could seem overwhelming at times, assessment data become much more manageable when linked to the instructional needs on the IEP.

More informally, talking with parents and former teachers can provide a wealth of information. More than anyone else, parents know how their children function within the family structure. Skills that parents find important should take a high priority when deciding what to teach. Parents are not the only family members, however, and input from siblings can help in identifying skills that should be taught. Talking with former teachers in an informal setting also can provide useful information about what-to-teach. This includes specific information about goals and objectives in previous years (e.g., progress on reading or language arts skills), as well as a student's ability to function in the classroom. For example, information that an incoming student will transition easily given a five-minute warning, but will resist if abruptly told to move to another activity can make the difference between a successful and unsuccessful school day for a student and teacher. Chapter 9 provides specific suggestions on gathering information for instructional decision making.

Although annual planning is required for the IEP, longer-term planning (3–5 years) is very useful in selecting goals and objectives. Several long-range, person-centered planning systems have been developed and are relevant for instructional planning. These systems include instruments, procedures, and guidelines needed for family members and professionals to identify students' pragmatic needs, as well as long-term dreams of stakeholders for the student (Everson & Zhang, 2000). Systems such as PATH and MAPS (O'Brien, Pearpoint, & Kahn, 2010) include tools for promoting social connectedness, while other systems such as TEAMS (Campbell, Campbell, & Brady, 1998) hold promise for prioritizing skills most important in future environments. Although each person-centered planning tool has its own specific protocol, each follows a common process that includes:

1. Identifying key people in the student's life;
2. Identifying immediate desires and long-term dreams of the student;
3. Describing current challenges and needs that affect the student's needs and dreams;
4. Brainstorming the many resources that people in the student's life might bring to support the student;
5. Developing an action plan, timeline, and feedback loop so the plan can be implemented; and
6. Establishing a process for evaluating the effectiveness of the plan, and a means to fine tune the plan if needed.

For an educational decision model to work, it must be responsive to both the needs of the students and the unique learning characteristics that they possess. Because learning can be hard work for students, educational programs cannot be left to happenstance. Rather, education should be well planned, exquisitely designed, precisely delivered, and sensitively evaluated. Professionals and families should work jointly to select goals that would make a fundamental improvement in the lives of these students. This requires a rigorous effort in finding *potential* goals, followed by a serious effort in prioritizing them. Most students will require a combination of academic, social, communication, and community skills if schooling is to have an impact on their lives.

Reflection

How much time is reasonable for teachers and families to spend in planning and evaluating students' instructional programs? How often should this occur?

SUMMARY CHECKLIST

What Do All Students Need to Learn?

✓ *A Nation at Risk* resulted in increased attention to curriculum and accountability.

✓ Numerous groups and individuals have input into deciding educational goals.

✓ Much of the school reform movement aims to improve science, math, and literacy standards.

✓ The Common Core State Standards (CCSS) are the academic standards of choice in many states.

What Do Students with CIDs Need to Learn?

➢ **Critical skills—The skills needed to participate in daily routines**
  ✓ Many critical skills need to be taught explicitly to students with CIDs
➢ **Functional curriculum—Includes a focus on practical skills needed for everyday living**
  ✓ Independent living skills include hygiene, toileting, dressing, home living, and personal mobility
  ✓ Many independent living skills need to be specifically taught, but others need to be strengthened
➢ **Personal mobility—Includes teaching students to reach various destinations and to use various routes and public transportation when traveling**
  ✓ Communication skills are a frequent goal for students with CIDs
➢ **Speech problems—Include difficulty with articulation such as substitutions, omissions, distortions**
➢ **Voice problems—Include difficulty in pitch or voice intensity**
➢ **Language disorders—Include delayed language and underdeveloped vocabulary**
  ✓ Many students with severe CIDs have difficulty with basic communication functions
➢ **Nonsymbolic communication—Involves changes in voice, pitch, or body tone**
  ✓ Communication goals require decisions involving form versus function
  ✓ Communication training is a common intervention for students with problem behavior
  ✓ Many students with CIDs require instruction to improve their social interactions and relations
➢ **Social skills—Specific behaviors that connect people to one another**
➢ **Social perceptions—Involve understanding how people relate to one another**
  ✓ Social skills include initiations, responses to initiations, continued interactions, and terminations of social exchanges
➢ **Relationship-building skills—Involve problem solving, understanding the perspectives of others, and reading logistical barriers**
  ✓ Students with CIDs typically receive academic instruction
  ✓ Academic instruction might include access to the general education curriculum and the CCSS, or a focus on functional academics linked to career development

✓ Decisions involving the amount of academic instruction in a student's program generate a great deal of discussion among professionals and parents

✓ Many students with CIDs require instruction in transition and community living skills

Principles for Deciding Instructional Content

✓ Students with CIDs require instruction that is planned and purposeful

✓ Instructional planning requires that participants have a future, environmental focus

➢ **The Criterion of Ultimate Functioning—Asks the question: If the student could not perform the proposed skill, would another person have to do it for the student, or could the task go undone?**

➢ **The Quality of Life Criterion—Asks whether the skills taught to students would improve their life quality**

➢ **The Age Appropriateness Criterion—Requires matching the skills taught and materials used to a student's chronological age**

    ✓ Student interest is important when selecting instructional outcomes

Where Do Teachers Gain Information About Instructional Content?

➢ **Individualized Educational Program—The formal mechanism for planning an instructional program**

➢ **Individualized Family Services Program—The formal mechanism for planning programs for infants and toddlers**

    ✓ Instructional assessments yield important data when planning instructional programs

    ✓ Person-centered planning is relevant in selecting instructional goals because significant people in a student's life make statements about their long-term dreams and hopes

ADDITIONAL SUGGESTIONS/RESOURCES

Discussion Questions

1. What are some of the common skills that students *with and without* CIDs need to learn?

2. What are some of the unique skills that students with CIDs need to learn that might not be part of an instructional program for students *without* disabilities?

3. Describe at least four principles that govern educational decision making when deciding what-to-teach students with CIDs.

4. Describe the unintended consequences that might accompany a curriculum for students with CIDs that focuses only on the general education curriculum and the CCSS.

Activities

1. Examine the IEPs of two students with CIDs. How many of the goals meet the criteria established by Brown et al. (1979) as important for deciding what-to-teach?

2. Interview a student with CID to find out how much input that student had in selecting goals or objectives for his or her instructional program.

3. Observe an academic, social, and community-based lesson. Record examples of skills that are taught, and instructional materials that are used that meet and violate the principle of chronological age appropriateness.

E-sources

http://www.cast.org/library

This website is the home for the Center for Applied Special Technology (CAST), and its project, the National Center on Accessing the General Curriculum. Background on the project, issues involving the general education curriculum for students with disabilities, and information on explicit instruction, universal design for learning (UDL), differentiated instruction, and curriculum-based evaluation is found here.

http://www.corestandards.org/

This website is the home for the Common Core State Standards. Although not a site unique to cognitive and intellectual disabilities, the site provides an up-to-date summary of state-by-state progress on implementing and assessing the CCSS.

11

INSTRUCTIONAL PROCEDURES

Key Points

➢ WHAT ASSUMPTIONS GUIDE INSTRUCTIONAL DELIVERY?—Students with intellectual disabilities often benefit from typical instructional methods. However, most will also require explicit instruction, and will make substantial gains when provided with it.

➢ HOW DO TEACHERS ORGANIZE INSTRUCTIONAL PROGRAMS?— Teachers *get ready* to teach by making decisions about how their lessons will be organized, how they'll add structure to lessons, and whether their lessons will promote acquisition, fluency, or generalization.

➢ HOW IS INSTRUCTION DELIVERED?—There are a number of powerful instructional strategies that help students learn. These strategies typically involve explicit and direct instruction.

➢ HOW IS INSTRUCTIONAL PROGRESS MONITORED?—There are various strategies for assessing the impact of instruction, including procedures for evaluating accuracy, completeness, and progress. These strategies are effective only if they lead to decisions about future instruction.

WHAT ASSUMPTIONS GUIDE INSTRUCTIONAL DELIVERY?

Making decisions about *how to teach* students with CIDs requires that educators organize and deliver instructional lessons in a very effective manner. If students with CIDs are to learn, and ultimately to use the knowledge and new skills in school, family, and community settings, then teachers should organize and deliver their instruction to match the learning characteristics of students, and the learning goals of students and their families. Organization for instruction refers to the process of "getting ready" to teach. Delivering instruction involves the instructional interactions that teachers provide that produce student actions. Three common assumptions guide the delivery of instruction for students with CIDs:

1. Students with CIDs share similar patterns of schooling with most students who do not have disabilities.
2. Most students with CIDs require explicit instruction if they are to master the knowledge and skills needed for the future.
3. Students with CIDs will make remarkable learning gains when provided with powerful instruction.

As described in Chapter 10, students with CIDs share many of the common educational goals of all students. Consistent with this, many educators suggest that students with CIDs also benefit from many of the instructional procedures designed for typically developing students. For example, these students typically attend the same school settings, for approximately the same number of hours per day, days per week, weeks per year, and the same number of school years, as students who do not receive special education supports. Because of their unique learning characteristics, however (see Chapter 6), instructional procedures for many students will vary from these typical assumptions. For example, some students might not attend general education classes. Young students might have shorter school days until they learn the routines associated with full-day attendance; a few students in a school may require extended school days or years. Other students might extend their school years beyond age 18 (the typical age of graduation from high school) and remain in educational programs until they are 21. Each of these decisions, however, is made by an IEP team as an exception to the assumptions about instructional procedures for typically developing students. Each decision is governed by individual students' educational needs (Peterson et al., 2013), but often decisions are influenced by factors such as the planning and problem-solving strategies used by teachers, or even the availability of resources in a school (Blanton, Blanton, & Cross, 1994).

A second assumption that governs instructional procedures is that many students with CIDs will not learn the knowledge and skills targeted for them unless explicit instruction is provided. A common assumption in general education classes is that most students will make academic progress even if they do not receive precise instruction. This assumption has come under fire in recent years, and many of the school accountability initiatives have pointed out the need for more direct instruction in reading, science, and math (National Education Goals Panel, 1997; National Governors Association Center for Best Practices, Council of Chief State School Officers [NGACBP], 2010). However, when organizing and delivering instruction for students with CIDs, no such assumption exists. Most teachers assume just the opposite: in the absence of direct and explicit instruction, it is unlikely that students with CIDs will make meaningful gains. What constitutes direct and explicit instruction? Although there are many varieties of this approach (Gersten, Carnine, & Woodward, 1987; Wolery, Bailey, & Sugai, 1988), most systems of direct and explicit instruction have the following features:

- A clear objective is provided for the day's lesson;
- The lesson begins with an advance organizer;
- The teacher provides information and a demonstration;

- The students participate in activities that show they are learning the objective;
- The teacher fades the amount of guidance as students increase their independent practice;
- Student accuracy is strengthened; correction procedures are provided if students make errors;
- A post-organizer is used to end the lesson and prepare students for transition to the next activity; and
- Instructional materials are carefully designed to promote student engagement.

The third assumption that guides the selection of instructional procedures is the recognition that remarkable learning gains are possible when powerful instructional procedures are delivered. Few fields demonstrate this as clearly as the field of cognitive and intellectual disability. As seen in Chapter 1, access to education, rehabilitation, and other human services for people with CIDs is a relatively modern phenomenon. Even as some individuals with CIDs gained a foothold in schools during the mid-1900s, most were labeled as "un-educable" and had little hope of becoming part of any school community. However, as educators learned *how to teach* these students, assumptions involving educability changed quite dramatically.

How did the early educators of students with CIDs learn to teach? Much of the effort was through trial and error. Prior to the federal requirements for special education in 1975, there was little expectation that schools would be responsible for student learning; many students with CIDs were not even allowed to go to school. With the legal requirement for access to education, increased attention was paid to the development of teaching procedures that would work for previously excluded students. Other areas of education also paid increased attention to their instructional procedures as concerns about school outcomes in math, science, and for at-risk students were expressed. Discoveries in instructional technology were made in industry, psychology, rehabilitation, and the human services as well. Indeed, research by a psychologist with an interest in industry, Marc Gold, had a major impact on the instructional procedures used in special education. One of his studies is highlighted in Research Box 11.1.

11.1 RESEARCH THAT MADE A DIFFERENCE

Gold, M. (1976). Task analysis of a complex assembly task by the retarded blind. *Exceptional Children, 43,* 78–84.

Prior to the late 1970s, most people with moderate to severe CIDs and other obvious disabilities had little access to employment, community residences, or public education. Few educators, psychologists, or vocational professionals believed that people with severe disabilities were capable of learning the skills and life routines that would enable them to participate meaningfully in work, recreation, or community living. Marc Gold, an experimental psychologist with an interest in industrial organizational applications, held a different view. Gold believed that if people with severe disabilities did not have the skills needed for employment and community living, perhaps it was because they had never been taught! Using his background as a training psychologist, Gold embarked on a series of studies and demonstrations in which he discovered and validated teaching procedures that were powerful enough to enable people with the most severe and obvious learning and performance problems to participate in real-world employment. Gold sought out adolescents and adults with severe CIDs, vision and hearing impairments, orthopedic disabilities, and behavioral disorders. He refined teaching procedures such as task analysis, graduated guidance, and prompt fading systems. He selected jobs that had high error rates when performed by employees without disabilities, such as assembling electronic circuit boards and building braking systems for 10-speed bicycles. Finally, he taught staff trainers to interact with the new employees with dignity, encouragement, and technical precision. The result? Gold demonstrated that people with severe disabilities learned skills that were previously thought to be far beyond their abilities; they outproduced and made fewer errors than employees without disabilities. Gold went on to make tremendous contributions to the field. His application of task analysis and prompting systems helped create the teaching technology used today. As important, Gold challenged educators to accept responsibility for student learning by examining the power of their instructional procedures. Gold even challenged the very nature of our understanding of CIDs. At a time when most professionals advocated definitions based on deficits in intelligence and adaptive behavior in the people who had the condition, Gold redefined CID as *a condition that requires superior adaptive behavior and more powerful training technology on the part of professionals.* Marc Gold is one person who made a difference.

Reflection

How would you alter the way you teach students based on your familiarity with different types of teaching procedures? Do you use direct instruction procedures?

HOW DO TEACHERS ORGANIZE INSTRUCTIONAL PROGRAMS?

Organization for instruction refers to the process of "getting ready" to teach. Organizing lessons includes evaluating the strengths of the student, arranging and structuring the classroom environment, and deciding how the learning task could involve other tasks that the student will learn. Organizing involves the actions teachers take that facilitate learning. Effective teachers make three sets decisions about how they will organize instruction:

1. Delivering Isolated, Integrated, Thematic, or Unit-Based Instruction
2. Adding Physical and Personal Structure
3. Planning for Acquisition, Fluency, and Generalization

Delivering Isolated, Integrated, Thematic, or Unit-Based Instruction

When organizing a lesson teachers must ask whether the outcome of the lesson will stand alone or whether it only "makes sense" when combined with other skills (Polloway, Serna, Patton, & Bailey, 2013). For example, a student who is preparing to attend high school is unable to use a combination lock, an important skill that helps students keep their books and belongings in safe storage. The student could be taught to open or close the lock as an **isolated skill.** A teacher would organize a lesson to give direct instruction on using the lock, and this lesson could be delivered several times a day while waiting for other activities to begin or end. Isolated skill instruction has advantages including giving the teacher maximum control over the lesson, and giving opportunities to practice the lesson throughout the day. Alternately, the teacher could also organize this as an **integrated skill,** and teach lock use in the hall, at the time the student needs to exchange materials. Teaching the skill in context also has advantages. This includes linking the skill to its natural routine, a strong motivator for many students. For example, the student might have a strong motivation to practice the lesson if she can immediately use the new skill to put away heavy books or gain access to a snack stored in the locker.

For specific skills such as using a combination lock, decisions about organizing the lesson can be simple, but most students will have more complex curriculum objectives (Hudson, Browder, & Wood, 2013; Nolet & Tindal, 1993). A model often found in general education classes involves using **thematic instruction.** Rather than teaching a series of independent lessons, teachers who use thematic instruction will cross reference student outcomes to various subjects or content throughout the day (Miller, 2002). For example, if a student has a language objective of asking "WH" questions, instructional opportunities will be built in to various class activities during reading, science, or geography lessons. In addition to the natural subject area content, the student will also obtain practice opportunities by gaining instruction that embeds opportunities to practice the "WH" objective throughout the day (Hudson et al., 2013). In many schools, thematic instruction and embedded instruction have been used to reorganize the entire general education curriculum resulting in large time blocks in which students learn interrelated subjects (such as a middle school in which students study the health issues, history, and geography of a given continent). The most current extension of thematic instruction can be seen in the Core Curriculum State Standards, which includes many lessons that link mathematics and literacy instruction (NGACBP, 2010).

A fourth way to organize instruction involves using a **unit approach** (Lewis, Doorlag, & Lewis, 2011). Like thematic instruction, a unit approach also cuts across subject matter areas, but typically structures lessons around a common theme. Often the theme is derived from a current event or topic of interest. For example, a theme involving space transportation might be used as a centerpiece for teaching math, social skills, oral communication skills, and other student outcomes. The unit approach may be difficult to implement in schools that strictly follow state curriculum guidelines, but teachers often find creative ways to customize these requirements around local themes.

As noted in Chapter 6, many students with CIDs have difficulty applying what they learn to everyday routines. That is, they learn **splinter skills**—skills that are strong in some developmental areas, but not in others. When planning for instruction, it is important to decide how the lessons will be organized to avoid *further splintering*. It is also important to organize instruction so that students will use their knowledge and skills during their daily activities and routines. For example, an isolated skill lesson could result in a student learning language skills during one lesson, but then not having an instructional opportunity to *use* those same skills during other lessons and routines. To avoid this, instructional procedures should build skill practice into multiple routines, lessons, and settings (i.e., use embedded instruction). Students with significant learning problems such as CIDs require instructional procedures that actively integrate learning, where important instructional targets are built in to the student's goals and routines throughout the day. Instructional integration has become a *preferred practice* in many general education classes, and is an *evidence-based best practice* for students with CIDs (Hudson et al., 2013). For example, a student learning to use a self-control procedure involving, "Wait for 3 seconds before giving an answer" would have opportunities (and direct instruction) for that skill built in to academic classes, self-care routines, social skills lessons. Figure 11.1 presents a curriculum planning matrix form helpful for organizing integrated instruction; a sample for a secondary-aged student is provided in Figure 11.2.

Adding Physical and Personal Structure
Organizing for instruction is a challenging task for teachers because students with CIDs can be taught in the entire range of school and classroom settings. In "special education–only" classes, teachers commonly use a variety of overt and obvious organizational modifications; in general education classes, the modifications used by students must be tailored to fit within those settings.

Many of the modifications used to organize instruction for students with CIDs are similar to strategies used for students with autism (Scott, Clark, & Brady, 2000). While numerous differences exist between these disabilities, students with these conditions frequently experience attentional, organizational, and communication challenges to learning (Schopler & Mesibov, 1995). Strategies used to accommodate these learning problems often include adding **physical** or **personal structure** to the way tasks are organized (Simpson & Myles, 1998; Schopler & Mesibov, 1995). These organizational strategies typically increase structure by:

- Adding visual cues to tasks and routines,
- Developing personal schedules for individual students,
- Establishing work systems, and
- Creating work and nonwork areas in the classroom.

Curriculum Matrix

Name: _____

Activities and Subject Areas

Skill 1				
Skill 2				
Skill 3				
Skill 4				
Skill 5				
Skill 6				

Figure 11.1 Curriculum Planning Matrix

Curriculum Planning Matrix

Name: <u>Jack Albright</u>

Activities and Subject Areas

	Home Room	Science	English	Home Economics	Lunch and Recess
Skill 1 *Organize Homework and Course Assignments*	*Organize and staple homework for morning classes*	*Turn in homework when entering class*	*Place assignments in group folder*		
Skill 2 *Ask and Answer Content Questions*	*Confirm daily schedule with peers and teachers*	*Answer questions about homework content*	*Write 3 questions about English lesson*	*Ask and answer questions in peer work groups*	*Confirm lunch price at checkout counter*
Skill 3 *Use Clear Cursive Writing*	*Write daily schedule on index card*	*Write sentences onto Guided Notes handout*	*Complete 2-3 sentence journal entry*	*Write "How to" notes*	
Skill 4 *Use "Spellcheck"*			*Prepare 2-3 sentence reaction to this week's story (use "Spellcheck")*		*Use "Spellcheck" before sending e-mail*
Skill 5 *Maintain Hygiene and Personal Appearance*	*Use common restroom*		*Conduct self-check before entering class*	*Conduct self-check before entering class*	*Check clothing, teeth, and hair after lunch.*

Figure 11.2 Curriculum Planning Matrix for a Secondary-Aged Student

Although teacher assistants, paraeducators, and even student classmates can participate in instructional routines, organizing for instruction can only be done by a teacher. The origin of these teaching procedures is summarized in Event Box 11.1.

11.1 EVENT THAT MADE A DIFFERENCE

1970s—Project TEACCH was started

In the mid-1970s in North Carolina, Project TEACCH was begun to help parents and professionals find effective educational options for youngsters with autism, communication disorders, and other developmental disabilities. From its start TEACCH staff were devoted to finding or developing practical and effective ways to identify, assess, and teach students with disabilities. The project has made many contributions to the field, including:

- Publication of assessment and screening instruments;
- Validation of teaching procedures;
- Development of a consultation network; and
- Publication of curriculum materials.

Foremost among TEACCH contributions is the development of instructional procedures for organizing classrooms, curriculum, and individual students. Although many disability professionals were engaged in a search for ways to reduce behavior and control students with disabilities, TEACCH staff searched for instructional procedures that would engage students in successful learning, and make their life routines more predictable. With new skills and the ability to handle transitions, challenging behavior disappears in many students. TEACCH staff showed a generation of special education teachers how to develop work stations in classrooms, create visual structure in tasks, and promote personal schedules for students. Although much of the focus of TEACCH has targeted students with autism, its contributions have made a difference for many other students with disabilities. Four decades after its modest beginning, Project TEACCH has made a positive difference.

Adding Visual Cues and Structure

Many students (with and without CIDs) use, understand, and remember visual instructions and experiences better than information gained through auditory and other input (Schopler & Mesibov, 1995; Westling & Fox, 2009). Lessons that add visual organization or provide visual structure and cues often help students attend to the lesson. Structuring the environment and lessons by providing cues improves students' ability to move from place to place in the classroom with minimal disruption, and to be productive in the lessons or tasks in each area. Visual structure involves positioning and organizing furniture, materials, and information so that the student can successfully complete lessons and tasks *with little to no verbal information*. The use of visual structure can be applied to the entire classroom or work environment, as well as to individual tasks and lessons. The key is that a student should know what is expected by going to a learning area or by looking at a task. Scott et al. (2000) suggested that visual structure of classrooms and learning tasks should *visually* address the following student questions:

- Where should I go?
- What should I do there?
- How will I know when I'm done?
- What should I do next?
- What will happen if I do it?
- What will happen if I don't do it?
- What should I do if I don't know how to do it?

Visual structure helps students determine which stimuli in a classroom or lesson are most and least important. Visual structure is most effective when it highlights the most important information in the room (such as where to work independently versus where to work with peers) or in a task (such as where to begin, or where to place completed assignments). Visual cues such as individual student schedules, labels on areas and materials, classroom rules, and classroom schedules all help cue students. Visual cues can include both print and pictures to accommodate readers and nonreaders, but visual structure should be made interesting, informative, and age-appropriate. Visual structure in general education classes should be subtler. For example, an obvious location for independent work in a regular class might be a student's desk, whereas an individual student's daily schedule might be placed on one corner of the desk, or in a notebook. Visual structure of tasks might include an outline, an advance organizer, a transcript of the day's lecture, or a list of work to be accomplished that class period. Table 11.1 shows several examples of visual cues and structure helpful for organizing the classroom and for student lessons and activities for an elementary student.

Developing Personal Schedules for Individual Students

Another helpful application of physical and personal structure involves developing individual personal schedules for students. Personal schedules help students sequence their daily activities, and many students with disabilities can increase their levels of independence substantially when using them (MacDuff, Krantz, & McClannahan, 1993). A personal schedule uses objects, labels, or pictures to provide a visual representation of the activities or events that make up a student's day. The schedule can cover all of the day or part of the day, depending upon the student. In special education classes, students' personal schedules might be located in a common, transition area; each student begins the day by going to the common area to obtain his or her schedule. In general education classes, personal schedules are typically kept in a student's memo book, day planner, or pocket.

Many students need to be taught how to use their own personal schedules. Each unit (time period or activity) of the schedule is placed in a given order (either "left to right" or "top to bottom"). This order becomes a visual strategy that helps students

Table 11.1 Visual Cues and Structure

Classroom Settings	Lessons and Tasks
• Arrange pencils, texts, paper at work stations	• Use 3-ring binders to organize students' lessons by subject area
• Color or picture code areas in the room for independent study, group work, break	• Use laminated food cards (pictures or words) to make choices before entering cafeteria
• Post directions for task at each work station	• Provide a "Finished Box" for completed student tasks and materials
• Use boxes, lockers, folders for student belongings	• Use objects to represent scheduled activities for nonreaders
• Use tape, paint, or stick-ons to designate permanent areas (paths, personal space around desks, storage zones)	• Post sequence of students' activities on Velcro strips (pictures, words or objects)
• Use obstacles to block access (teacher storage areas, chemistry lab supplies)	• Use Day Timer or pocket calendars to prompt students to move to next activity
• Post pictures of student working in work areas, reading in quiet areas, working in groups in team areas	• Ask students to retrieve lessons and materials from preorganized file folders

understand the sequence as a common and predictable standard. Personal schedules provide visual answers to student questions of: "Where do you want me to go?" (to the designated area) and "What do I do then?" (work on the lessons that are indicated there). Personal schedules increase predictability of daily activities and reduce dependence on teachers for directions. In turn, this predictability increases task completion and accuracy, and reduces the disruptive behavior often associated with uncertainty and breaks in routine (MacDuff et al., 1993).

How common are personal schedules and what do they look like? Personal schedules are common today for many students with disabilities. First developed for students with autism, increasingly teachers discovered the value of this tool for other students as well. Students with CIDs and people with no disabilities at all have "things to do" lists and personal notebooks. Personal schedules, conceptually, are the same. A personal schedule to promote independence at home might include such tasks as "make bed, take shower, wash hair, brush teeth, dress, eat breakfast, and go to bus stop." A schedule for a general education classroom might include: "Period 1: Math, Period 2: English, Period 3: Music," and so on. Any sequence of activities can become part of a student's schedule, based on the student's need for assistance. Although some teachers intuitively plan to fade the use of personal schedules, it is not necessary to do so. Visual structure and personal schedules are examples of **permanent prompts;** if a prompt increases a student's independence, then removing it is not necessary. This is similar to not removing a wheelchair from a student who is unable to walk, or to not removing a Braille writer from a student who is blind. If a student with a CID uses a stack of pictures to stay on target during employment training, then this personal schedule should be considered a necessary assistive device.

Establishing Work Systems

Another effective way to organize lessons that came from teachers of students with autism is the use of **work systems.** Work systems establish visual clarity in tasks so that students can manage their assignments, complete the tasks accurately, and minimize their requests for assistance (Schopler & Mesibov, 1995). Like other forms of physical and personal structure, work systems use a consistent format (e.g., "left to right" and "top to bottom") so that students develop a consistent strategy for approaching any new task.

For academics, a work system might involve a list of written assignments in a labeled folder, or a prepared assignment with the problems highlighted with a yellow marker. For a self-care skill, a work system might involve a list of activities for the student to check off when completed. A *prepare for school* sequence might include activities such as "turn off the alarm, use the toilet, wash your face and body, put on your school clothes, eat breakfast, and go to the bus stop." These can be as simple as pictures or model objects on a board, or as subtle as a written list of activities, in order, in a day planner.

Creating Work and Nonwork Areas in the Classroom

Many students with CIDs have difficulty identifying cues, reading teachers' intentions, and following unstated routines (Beirne-Smith, Ittenbach, & Patton, 2002). Because school classrooms are busy and complex, the physical environment of a classroom should be structured to highlight the areas where students *should work* and *should not* work (Lewis et al., 2011). In many special education settings, classrooms are arranged into curriculum and break areas, and students rotate among these areas as they complete their lessons. In this arrangement, students work on science, math, social studies, self-care, community living, or domestic skills in specific areas of the classroom. Once a lesson is completed, the student moves to another curriculum area or to a break area (e.g., a computer, art or reading center) until it is time for the next subject lesson. Other classrooms are arranged around independent work areas, where students work in their own designated areas on specific tasks (Scheuermann & Webber, 2002). These areas often incorporate individual desks or study carrels. Once tasks are completed, students check their schedules and move to a break area. The break area may or may not have other students in it, depending on whether other students have completed their assigned tasks. The break area should have both solitary and small group leisure activities so that students have a variety of choices. After a break from class work, each student checks the class schedule or his or her personal schedule, and returns to the work area (Scheuermann & Webber, 2002). In general education classes, students often work at their desks, then, they move to a computer or reading area until the next transition. Regardless of the particular classroom arrangement, rotation between areas and lessons can be accomplished through teacher announcements, neutral cues (timers or the school bell), or through independent student scheduling.

Providing students with work and nonwork areas helps distractible students to distinguish between work and nonwork tasks, and promotes student task engagement. Work and break areas can be distinguished by using partitions and seating arrangements. For students with more distractible behavior, and in many special education classes, classrooms should also have a **transition area.** A transition area is a common location to which students go after they complete their lessons or tasks, to check their schedules, and see what activity is next. Using a transition area reduces the ambiguity that often accompanies transitions and task completion. By proceeding to a transition area after a lesson, students develop a routine of seeking out the next scheduled activity. In general education classes, students with transition difficulty can be asked to "check your schedule." If an actual place is still needed to ease transitions, that area might be in a space next to a teacher's desk or near another teacher work space.

Planning for Acquisition, Fluency, and Generalization

A final set of decisions about organizing instruction involves the type or stage of student learning that a teacher's lesson is designed for. Students progress through a series of learning stages as they move from an initial encounter with information, to independent and proficient use of the information. Although many descriptors exist for these stages of learning, most learning experts agree that learning incorporates acquisition of initial material, fluency in its use, and generalization of the new information in novel ways.

Acquisition involves initial learning of new concepts, skills, and actions. Raymond (2000) described acquisition as moving "from no skill to basic mastery." The goal of acquisition involves accuracy. This requires performance that might begin with zero accuracy and ends with an accuracy indication of 85% correct. Acquisition of new skills or knowledge often is not a steady process. Initial acquisition may be difficult if students face social stigma associated with public errors, as well as challenges to their own attributions about their ability to learn. With instruction, feedback, and time students will perform with some indication of learning, but their performance may be erratic (i.e., range from 50% to 75% accuracy). With effective teaching, students gain mastery over a lesson, although their acquisition does not imply that a teacher's lesson is over.

Students with CIDs encounter numerous challenges during acquisition. Obviously, skills and knowledge with which a student has some basic mastery *before* instruction will facilitate new learning. On the other hand, students who have not been exposed to rich and challenging learning opportunities are at a disadvantage. Second, students who have unsuccessful experiences trying to learn a skill previously may have to overcome motivational challenges before they will devote the energy necessary to try to learn the skill again. Third, students who have made some gains in learning, but never achieved a stable level of accuracy may have actually learned to perform errors! This occurs when flaws in instruction allow students to practice without supervision, allowing students to complete a lesson with errors and no feedback about the errors. More effective teaching procedures for acquisition incorporate modeling, guidance, and error analysis procedures. Additional suggestions for organizing instructional procedures to match acquisition and other stages of learning are found in Table 11.2

Fluency is a more complex level of learning. Fluency is a combination of accuracy plus speed that allows a skill to be useful in a natural environment (Binder, 1996). Building fluency is important in many academic skills. For example, many students

Table 11.2 Organizing Instruction for Acquisition, Fluency, and Generalization

Acquisition	Fluency	Generalization
• Provide frequent instruction • Increase opportunities for student engagement • Use errorless learning procedures • Use attention-getting procedures • Provide close supervision • Provide feedback on errors • Provide reinforcing feedback for accuracy	• Increase timed practice • Provide feedback only after student completes task • Encourage speed drills and "sprints" • Decrease teacher involvement during practice activities • Provide reinforcing feedback for speed as well as accuracy • Increase pretask rehearsal	• Use multiple teaching examples • Link lessons to real-world uses • Promote skill fluency • Use common materials and language in teaching and generalization settings • Teach toward the general case • Include specific generalization procedures in lessons

with CIDs demonstrate high percentages of accuracy in reading or math, but the slow speed of their performance interferes with using these skills in real-world tasks. Accuracy without normative speed prevents skills from become automatic in learners (Podell, Tournaki-Rein, & Lin, 1992; White & Haring, 1980). Fluency problems also hinder students' performance in nonacademic areas. For example, accurate but nonfluent street crossing or use of power tools would result in dangerous conditions for students and place serious limitations on their access to community living and employment.

Although some students with severe CIDs have physical or sensory problems that challenge their fluency, most students do not develop fluent responding for other reasons. Much of the curriculum designed for students with disabilities targets only basic skills, often at a rudimentary level of acquisition (Lewis et al., 2011; Polloway et al., 2013). However, teaching for fluency requires different instructional procedures than teaching for acquisition (White & Haring, 1980). For example, Scott et al. (2000) described a resurgence in a procedure called Precision Teaching that incorporates speed drills as a fluency building procedure. Other approaches include increasing the number of learning trials, distributing practice across the day, reducing the use of manipulative materials during performance, using computer-assisted instruction, and increasing behavioral rehearsal and self-modeling prior to performing the skill (Lasater & Brady, 1995; Podell et al., 1992; Raymond, 2000; Reamer, Brady, & Hawkins, 1998).

Generalization involves using a skill in novel (untaught) ways. This includes using one's knowledge and skills long after instruction is over (maintenance), applying the knowledge or skill to new people, places, or things (stimulus generalization), and adapting or changing the skill to use different forms of the behavior (response generalization). Students with CIDs often have difficulties with all three types of generalization. For example, when students learn the rules for turning singular nouns into plural nouns, that information is assumed to stay with the students to use as needed (maintenance). If a student can't retrieve that information several months after acquiring it, that student is showing evidence of a maintenance problem. An example of stimulus generalization is seen when a student learned to read the word "turtle" from a set of captioned picture cards, then reads the word "turtle" spontaneously in a book. Having learned a skill (reading the word "turtle") under one set of circumstances (captioned picture cards), the student should be able to perform that same skill under similar but not identical circumstances (a book). An example of response generalization can be seen when a student interacts in any of several ways to the social initiations of peers. She may spontaneously respond, "Hi," "Hello," "Hi there," "Whassup?" or "Sup?" when greeted by a peer. In this case, one of a series of behaviors is produced in response to an initiation by a peer. If the student has only *one way* to respond (e.g., always says, "Hi" and never varies the greeting), this is an example of a response generalization difficulty.

As noted earlier, much instruction targets only skill acquisition. Teachers may teach a skill until a student reliably demonstrates it when requested, then move on to teaching another skill. The downfall of this practice is that many students never learn skills well enough to make them permanent or functional; such skills essentially stay at the acquisition level and never become fluent nor generalizable. In teaching students with CIDs, generalization problems are common. Thus, a student may demonstrate knowledge or skills that can be shown only under very specific circumstances, with certain people, or when using specific materials. One reason for these generalization problems is that many students are never *taught* the skill past an acquisition level (Horner, Bellamy, & Colvin, 1984). A landmark article on ways to promote generalization by Stokes and Baer (1977) is highlighted in Research Box 11.2.

11.2 RESEARCH THAT MADE A DIFFERENCE

Stokes, T. F., & Baer, D. M. (1977). An implicit technology of generalization. *Journal of Applied Behavior Analysis, 10,* 349–367.

Much of the early research on how people with developmental disabilities learn identified generalization problems as an inherent characteristic of the disability. Stokes and Baer's article turned the onus for the lack of generalization around. Their paper showed that a failure to generalize was, in part, a function of the teaching interventions that were used. Stokes and Baer found that the most common strategy used in the literature was for professionals to *train and hope* that their interventions would promote durable and lasting change. In the absence of interventions that were *designed* to produce durable learning, there's little wonder that the interventions of the day produced little evidence of lasting change in people with the least sophisticated learning abilities. Train and hope indeed!

Stokes and Baer also showed that an instructional technology was emerging that showed promise for promoting generalization. While still in its infancy, it held promise for people with disabilities and professionals alike. Stokes and Baer catalogued a set of interventions that would challenge researchers and remains relevant today. These two researchers effectively "raised the bar" by signaling an expectation that to be considered "effective," an intervention should include procedures for generalized learning and change.

Effective teachers use numerous ways to teach for generalization, and the procedures continue to evolve. A common procedure is to use *lots of examples* during the initial instruction. For example, teaching students that any of 15 picture cards of saltwater fish all represent the concept of "fish" is more likely to facilitate stimulus generalization of a student's knowledge of "fish" than using just one example. A second procedure is to *link instruction to the real-world use* of the skill. For example, teaching measurement units with worksheet examples has produced learning difficulties for untold numbers of students until the instruction involved real-world applications in recipes, time and distance sporting events, and employment tasks that required use of rulers. A third set of teaching procedures includes using a set of learning materials in a lesson, and then *using the same or similar materials in a real-world situation*. For example, a high school teacher might teach a student to write an assignment using a specific format, then provide an overlay of that format for the student to take to other academic classes where the student has writing assignments. Similar to using multiple examples, some educators teach the *general case* lesson instead of a very specific instruction. For example, the objective of a lesson on using office machines involves being able to operate a wide range of copiers across various machines and employment settings. The copy machine at school might be similar to the copy machine at a jobsite, but have function buttons in a different location, and have paper loading in the front instead of the side. The copy machine at the office supply store may be different yet. Teaching to the general case involves teaching students to use different types of button layout schemes and different paper feed systems. Generalized copying skills would include using all of these machines without direct instruction on each one. Finally, another procedure that promotes generalization is to *promote skill fluency*. When students achieve high rates of speed and accuracy, they retain what they have learned, and are able to apply their learning to meet real-world requirements (Binder, 1996). If a skill is not yet mastered, generally it will not generalize. Given the acknowledged generalization problems facing students with CIDs, developing fluent performance is essential.

Reflection

How would you arrange your classes, tasks, and lessons for students to maximize the likelihood that they will have successful learning opportunities?

HOW IS INSTRUCTION DELIVERED?

Good teaching means skillful delivery of instruction. For students with CIDs, effective instructional delivery requires attention to nine issues:

1. Who delivers the instruction?
2. Where should instruction be delivered?
3. Group versus individual instruction;
4. Task analyzing instruction;
5. Using errorless teaching and match-to-sample formats;
6. Using discrete trial formats;
7. Using prompts and assistance;
8. Using naturalistic teaching procedures; and
9. The link between instruction and problem behavior.

Who Delivers Instruction?

There are many models of professional interaction. One such model involves general education teachers delivering instruction, while another model is built on instruction by special education teachers. For students with physical and communication disabilities, therapists sometimes deliver instruction; in other models, therapists assess students and devise instructional recommendations for teachers to deliver. Teacher assistants also play a role in the delivery of instruction, and in some districts family members co-teach lessons along with educators. For those who play an instructional role, therapists, assistants, parents, and other family members can be very effective. In the absence of training and instructional methods, however, these people are likely to use a "mixed bag" of techniques, some of which may have little instructional value.

For professionals and family members to participate in instruction, a system of **collaboration** and a simple progress monitoring system will help in keeping instruction on track for a learner (Dettmer, Knackendoffel, & Thurston, 2013). A collaboration system that encourages genuine consultation, exchange of information, and shared perceptions is needed if the multiple adults in schools are to form a successful team that promotes students' development (Idol, Nevin, Paolucci-Whitcomb, 1999). Four guidelines should be followed by adults who collaborate in delivering instruction (Scott et al., 2000). First, therapists, parents, and other teachers should be given the opportunity to select the instructional targets they believe they could realistically implement. Second, for any skill that the primary teacher shares responsibility for with other adults, the student should *already be making progress* on the skill so that other adults are involved in building fluency or supporting generalization rather than teaching for initial skill acquisition. Third, instruction based in community or home settings should be presented in brief segments so that these **natural environments** do not take on the characteristics of a school classroom. This allows for a clearer distinction between teaching interactions and social interactions among students, peers, and adults. It also reserves the more difficult levels of instruction for controlled classroom environments, while promoting the natural use of new skills (i.e., generalization) in community and home settings. Finally, progress on students' skills should be evaluated, using direct but simple data collection and evaluation methods.

Where Should Instruction Be Delivered?

There is no single best location for teaching. When students with CIDs work in the general education curriculum and are included in Common Core State Standards, a typical classroom with typically developing students is the setting of choice (Hudson, Browder, & Wood, 2013). When students participate in a community-based curriculum, the instructional setting includes local businesses, parks, and shopping centers (Bates, Cuvo, Miner, & Korabek, 2001). For vocational preparation, instruction is frequently delivered at a jobsite (Storey, 2002). Teachers' choices regarding the location of instruction should be influenced by the objective of the lesson, the pragmatics of gaining access to a location, and their ability to deliver effective instruction in that setting.

When teachers deliver instruction in general education classrooms, the tasks and routines can be organized and structured. Instructional materials are handy, and the setting can be rearranged as needed. Instruction delivered in community, vocational, home, or other settings often lacks this structure and flexibility. As a result, learning can be slower and more arduous for some students. On the other hand, teaching in natural environments can promote learning for many students by providing a real-world context for new skills (Storey, 2002). Although many important life skills can be integrated into students' school-based curricula, ultimately skills needed for home and community transition must be mastered in those community environments (Bambara, Koger, & Bartholomew, 2011; Patton, Cronin, & Wood, 1999). Decisions about who delivers instruction and where skills are taught should be made by teachers, family members, and other members of the IEP team who have expertise in teaching complex skills to students with CIDs.

Group versus Individual Instruction

Many teachers assume that one-to-one instruction is the primary way to provide instruction to students with disabilities. Although it is important that instruction is *individualized* for students with disabilities, this seldom means that instruction must be delivered in a one-to-one format. Students with CIDs can be successful in a variety of individual and group instructional formats, and each has advantages and disadvantages (Snell & Brown, 2011; Gaylord-Ross & Holvoet, 1985).

One-to-one instruction is desirable for *any learner on occasion*. This format gives the teacher the maximum control over the delivery of the lesson, provides an opportunity for immediate and precise reinforcement or correction of a student's participation, and helps the teacher see the options for redesigning instruction for greater learning (Alberto, Jobs, Sizemore, & Duran, 1980). This format is not necessary for many students' instructional programs, however, and often has unintended side effects if used too frequently. For many students with CIDs, these negative effects include learned helplessness, increased dependence on teacher prompts, missed opportunities to interact with peers, and increased difficulty in generalizing skills learned in one-to-one instruction (Carter, Sisco, Melekoglu, & Kurkowski, 2007; Kamps et al., 1992; Snell & Brown, 2011). Students with a history of one-to-one instruction often need direct instruction on how to interact in a group before a group instructional formats can be used effectively (Munk et al., 1998; Reid & Favell, 1984).

Group instruction formats vary widely. The number of students in a group is a function of many variables including the degree of heterogeneity among the learners, overall class size, and the ability of the teacher to provide guidance within the group (Lewis et al., 2011; Snell & Brown, 2011). There are at least three effective group instruction formats (Gaylord-Ross & Holvoet, 1985). Most general education teachers are familiar with large group formats involving **choral responding,** sometimes called **concurrent instruction** (Snell & Brown, 2011). In this format, a teacher delivers a lesson and students respond to the teacher's question or request in unison. This is a common format, but many students (with or without disabilities) do not respond to the teacher cues. However, since it is used frequently in general education classes, a student with CID who is preparing to transition into these classes will need direct instruction in how to respond to this format.

A group instruction format that involves more cooperative engagement with peers is **interactive group instruction** (Gaylord-Ross & Holvoet, 1985). An interactive group format involves a teacher cue (question or request) delivered to the group, followed by student-to-student interaction. For example, a teacher might direct the group to, "Use your rulers to draw a line on your partner's map between Denver and Boca Raton." Student participation in this group format involves (a) teacher-to-group requests, (b) peer-to-peer interactions, and (c) teacher feedback to the group *and* individual students.

A third group format described by Gaylord-Ross and Holvoet (1985) is a **one-to-one in a group** (or concurrent individualized) format. This format provides features of both individualized and small group instruction. During a lesson involving saltwater marine life, for example, a teacher might form a group of 10 students. Each student has specific objectives, many of which *differ* substantially. An objective for Jonah, a student with CID, might be to convert singular nouns (snapper, dolphin) to their plural forms (snappers, dolphins). For Marla and other students, the objective is content-related and includes defining the differences between fish and mammals. The teacher delivers cues and elicits information to and from each student individually while maintaining this group activity. This format also allows a teacher to add students to the group gradually until an individual teaching format gradually becomes group instruction (Snell & Brown, 2011).

Task Analyzing Instruction

Task analysis was discussed in Chapter 9 as an effective means of assessing instruction. In addition, task analysis is an effective procedure for *teaching* complex skills. Task analysis involves dividing a complex skill into smaller subskills. The purpose of task analyzing instruction is to allow students to focus on a small unit of instruction rather than the entire, more complex skill. Task analysis involves both a *process* and a *product* (Gold, 1976). As a process, task analysis involves a detailed description and evaluation of a complex activity. In turn, the process shows teachers how and where to divide the skill into more manageable objectives so it can be taught successfully. As a product, a task analysis results in a written sequence of skills (or lesson plan) which guides instruction.

In most instructional task analyses, each step becomes a discrete behavior that can be taught to a student. The completion of one step usually serves as the cue to perform the next step in the task analysis. There is no magic formula for developing a task analysis; the actual number of steps depends on the complexity of the skill, the current skills of the learner, and the time and skill of the teacher. A task analysis can be broad or very specific. Lewis et al. (2011) suggested that a task analysis for writing a friendly letter would include four components, each of which may incorporate multiple skills:

1. Handwriting or keyboarding;
2. Conventional spelling;
3. Using capitals and punctuation; and
4. Forming sentences and paragraphs.

Other task analyses that incorporate academic skills might be process-oriented, or include complex chains of steps. For example, Hua, Morgan, Kaldenberg, and Goo (2012) used a task analysis of a cognitive learning strategy to teach math applications to young adults with CIDs, while Browder, Trela, and Jimenez (2007) incorporated task analyses into curriculum covering Common Core literature standards for middle schoolers with CIDs. Other task analyses with narrow, specific skills might contain more steps. Gaylord-Ross and Holvoet (1985), for example, described several task analyses of social exchanges involving video games and basketball with over a dozen individual performance steps.

Prior to teaching, a task analysis should be tested and validated to establish that the plan (a) actually leads to skill completion, and (b) does so in an efficient manner. Cooper, Heron, and Heward (2007) suggested five methods for validating a task analysis:

1. Analyze the actions of people who perform the skill in a competent manner. Their sequence of steps will be a reasonable task analysis.
2. Request that people with expertise in the task specify the steps that are necessary for successful completion.
3. Request a teacher to perform the skill under typical instructional conditions. Delineate each step in the process.
4. Consider how the skill is performed in time and sequence. This "thoughtful analysis" will be a reasonable approximation of most task analyses.
5. Conceptualize the skill by the degree of difficulty of each separate task. Teach easy tasks first, and more difficult tasks later.

Many functional and independent living skills are fairly easy to task analyze, and instructional materials are commercially available. Typically, a task analysis developed for one student will have application for others, although teachers often customize the lessons to meet the needs of particular students. For example, a common task analysis for teaching students to wash and dry their hands might require a teacher to add supplemental steps so a student in a wheelchair can access the sink.

Students learn some skills better when all the parts of the skill are taught simultaneously, as a whole task. For these skills, a task analysis of the teacher's assistance is helpful. This allows the student to practice the entire skill each time it is performed. For example, when learning to use a calculator for a division problem, a student would practice each step, each time, but the level of teacher assistance would be the target of the analysis. Using a prompting hierarchy, the *condition under which the lesson is presented* would be task analyzed so that the student would perform the division steps on the calculator:

1. With spoken directions and finger-to-hand touch as assistance;
2. With spoken directions and intermittent hand shadowing as assistance;
3. With spoken directions as assistance;
4. With pointing from a distance as assistance; and ultimately
5. Without assistance.

A task analysis of teachers' prompts is frequently referred to as **graduated guidance** (Cooper et al., 2007; Snell & Brown, 2011; Westling & Fox, 2009). The task analysis can arrange for the teacher prompts to deliver the most assistance first, with a gradual increase in the power of the prompts as needed, or the least assistance first with gradual decreases in more powerful prompts as the student learns to perform the skill.

Finally, some skills overwhelm students because they are complex, or because they contain social or sensory experiences that interfere with learning. Rather than teach the entire skill each time, the student is taught only one "piece" of the whole skill at a time. As each step is mastered, another step is added to the sequence. This process of **chaining** steps together was used by Lasater and Brady (1995) when teaching a student to shave with an electric razor. To counter the disturbing effects of the sensory stimulation, the student was taught to shave only a small portion of his face at a time. As he mastered this skill, additional parts of his face were added until he could perform the entire task at once. An adapted version of the task analysis includes:

1. Shave right and left cheek;
2. Shave cheeks and chin;
3. Shave cheeks, chin, and neck;
4. Shave cheeks, chin, neck, and upper lip;
5. Shave cheeks, chin, neck, and upper lip, and trim sideburns.

Using Errorless Teaching and Match-to-Sample Formats

Young children with CIDs, students who were previously unsuccessful in their school efforts, and students who are extremely noncompliant sometimes require extraordinary efforts to encourage them to participate in instruction. If students do not respond to teachers' requests, one instructional strategy involves **errorless learning.** This procedure requires that teachers prompt and reinforce *any* student response, potentially including occasional student errors, so that the students can be brought in willingly to an instructional interaction. Accuracy of students' responses is less important than simply increasing the students' participation in an instructional interaction. Once students begin to participate actively in instruction, then the focus of instruction shifts to student accuracy of responding.

There are various procedures that reduce students' ability to make errors (Gaylord-Ross & Holvoet, 1985), but one approach involves using a **match-to-sample** teaching format (Scott et al., 2000). At its simplest, a teacher presents only one stimulus item and an identical example, then requests the student to "Show (Touch, Give, Point to . . .) me a—" (name of item). Any response by which the student indicates the matching item should be accepted and reinforced, thus building a momentum of accurate (and reinforced) responses. In subsequent lessons, the teacher gradually adds more stimuli and different types of stimuli ("distractors"). A task analysis of a lesson used to teach a student to identify a picture of a school bus is provided in the next Box.

MATCH-TO-SAMPLE FORMAT WITH ERRORLESS LEARNING

Where's the School Bus?

1. Student matches to the sample with *NO* distractors. (*Matches picture of a school bus to an identical picture.*)
2. Student matches to the sample with two *very different* distractors. (*Matches picture of a school bus to identical picture. Also present are pictures of a toilet and a Doberman.*)
3. Student matches to the sample with three *moderately different* distractors. (*Matches picture of a school bus to identical picture. Also present are pictures of a motorcycle, a camper, and a riding mower.*)
4. Student matches to the sample with four *similar* distractors. (*Matches picture of school bus to identical picture. Also present are pictures of a car, a fire truck, a city bus, and a family van.*)

Choosing the correct match thus requires the student to make finer discriminations of the item, based on how much attention and focus the student devotes to the lesson. This format begins as a genuinely errorless procedure, then progresses to a low error procedure as the student learns to participate in instruction, and then finally to a more difficult one. A match-to-sample lesson can be modified by adding or removing types and numbers of distractors. Other modifications that increase participation and accuracy include pairing photographs with object miniatures or moving from photos to line drawings to words. The task analysis changes when the objective of the lesson progresses from matching to a sample to identifying and selecting from a pool of distracters without having a "match" available.

Using Discrete Trial Formats

Discrete trial teaching formats consistently have been known for their effectiveness for teaching new skills to students with extreme attention disorders and severe intellectual disabilities. A discrete trial is a structured learning opportunity that has a specific beginning and end. A single, discrete trial consists of three elements:

Delivery of a Trial

Teacher Request	⇨ Teacher Prompt (if needed)	⇨ Student Response	⇨ Teacher	Feedback	⇨ Time between Trials		⇨ Begin Next Trial Sequence
			If Correct	If Error	Mass Practice	Distributed Practice	

Example

| "Point to the verb Mary Lou" | ⇨ Hold up reminder card: "Verb = Doing" | ⇨ Circles the verb | ⇨ "Alright!" | "Oops circle the word that shows doing" | ⇨ 3-5 seconds | 20 minutes or longer | ⇨ "Point to the verb Mary Lou" |

Figure 11.3 Delivery of a Trial

- A teacher delivers a cue or request for a student to do something;
- The teacher observes while the student responds to the request; and
- The teacher presents a reinforcer to acknowledge a correct student response, or a correction of the student's error, based on the student's performance.

Discrete trial teaching is most often used in one-to-one instruction, although it can be adapted for group instruction.

A discrete trial format is most common when teaching for new skill acquisition (Storey, 2002; Westling & Fox, 2009). With difficult skills, the teacher sometimes adds a gesture, touch prompt, or a picture to accompany the verbal request given to a student (e.g., the teacher points to the paper when delivering a verbal cue to, "Draw a circle around the right answer."). Discrete trial instruction usually requires multiple trials before the student masters the skill. These trials can be grouped together in a *massed trial format* (15–30 trials per lesson), or they might be presented in a *distributed format* where a few trials of the skill are interspersed throughout various lessons during the day (Gaylord-Ross & Holvoet, 1985; Snell & Brown, 2011). As the student demonstrates fluency in the skill, the skills can be *embedded* into various classroom and curriculum routines. Figure 11.3 presents a schematic that represents a discrete trial teaching format.

Using Prompts and Assistance

Teachers use a variety of prompts and assistance when students are learning new skills. These prompts often include physical assists, gestures, picture prompts, or verbal directions. Often these prompts are delivered in a hierarchical order; at other times they are given sporadically as a "nudge" or reminder to a student. As natural as the use of prompts seems today, they were not always considered to be powerful teaching procedures. An article describing a line of research using prompting strategies is highlighted in Research Box 11.3.

11.3 RESEARCH THAT MADE A DIFFERENCE

Strain, P. S., & Shores, R. E. (1977). Social reciprocity: A review of research and educational implications. *Exceptional Children, 43,* 526–530.

Prompt and praise. These two verbs revolutionized special education and improved the lives of hundreds of children who lived through the impact of social withdrawal. Through most of the 20th century, prevailing professional opinion held that children with CIDs, autism, and other socially disabling conditions lacked the ability to socialize with other children. Without the capacity for social development, these youngsters would not benefit from regular home, school, and community environments.

A research team in Nashville, Tennessee, challenged this thinking, and initiated a series of elegant yet powerful studies. Strain and Shores used a simple logic to guide their research: If children are never taught to interact, we'll never know if they could learn. In a research plan that would span two decades, Strain and Shores went about the business of discovering ways to teach these children basic social interaction skills. They prompted children to interact with one another, then praised them for doing so. They prompted children with disabilities to interact with children who had no disabilities, and then they praised them for doing so. They prompted children without disabilities to socialize with children who did have disabilities. Praise followed. Children with CIDs. Children with autism spectrum disorders. Children with emotional and behavior disorders. Toddlers. Elementary students. Secondary students. Adults. They faded the praise and the presence of adults as the children learned to enjoy the social interaction. They incorporated toys and games and routines found in local schools and child care centers. They tested their procedures to discover how to teach the students to generalize their new social skills beyond the experimental settings. They pushed to identify the conditions that would strengthen children's social interaction. Or weaken them.

Today, few people doubt that children and adults with CIDs and other developmental disabilities can acquire social interaction skills, and then use these skills in meaningful ways. Skills promote relationships. Relationships help people gain access to improvements in patterns and quality of life. Prompt and praise.

As described in the Task Analysis section, prompts are most effective when they are sequenced to increase or decrease their power, aligned with a student's need for assistance with performance. The **most-to-least** prompt format begins with whatever assistance is necessary to help the student respond, then gradually decreases this assistance as the student becomes more proficient (Wolery et al., 1988). A high level of assistance for a student who is learning to use a keyboard may involve hand-over-hand assistance or even a physical manipulation of the student's hand to position it correctly on the keyboard. Physical assistance might not be necessary for other students; they may only require *gestural* assistance, or pointing to the hand position on the keyboard. *Picture* prompts might include showing a picture of the student's hands in the correct keyboarding position. For this student, the least intensive prompt might be a *verbal* reminder to the student to reposition his hands.

The most-to-least prompt format has several advantages. It does not allow students to make many errors since a teacher provides assistance to promote correct responding. Students obtain many opportunities for reinforcement, since they are reinforced for any responding beyond the assistance provided by the teacher. For example, if a student is learning to use a coffee pot with gestural assistance, he will receive reinforcement for using it independently, or with verbal, gestural, or picture assistance. The format does have disadvantages. Although the format provides maximum support during acquisition, some students are likely to become prompt-dependent unless the assistance is faded as soon as possible. To counter this, some teachers use a variety of novel and subtle prompts such as *shadowing* and delivering gestures from *progressively farther distances*. To shadow, a teacher might place his hand parallel to but several inches away from the student's hand, then move in synchrony with the student as she uses the coffee pot. Shadowing is often a helpful intermediary step for moving students from physical to other prompts.

The **least-to-most** prompt format allows for more errors, but is less likely to facilitate prompt dependence. This format begins by adding only verbal assistance to the initial teacher request. The next level of assistance might involve giving the student a picture of the skill to be performed; a *gestural assist* or a *prompt to point to next step* is the next, progressively higher level of assistance. The maximum support, physical assistance, might include hand-over-hand assistance. Although this format reduces the likelihood of prompt dependence, students risk learning error patterns if they make unsupervised errors during instruction. Care is needed when using this format to ensure that errors are few and correct responses are highly reinforced.

An assumption of the prompt formats described here is that eventually, they will be removed, and the student will participate without prompts at some point. This assumption is not always valid. Many prompts are available to people without disabilities and they are not supposed to be removed over time. For example, signs reminding employees to wash their hands are posted in most public washrooms. These signs are permanent fixtures, and are used to remind employees to perform a specific behavior. Students with disabilities also benefit from permanent prompts. Although teachers assume that "artificial" cues for students will not be needed after successful instruction, such assistance need not be removed if:

1. Removal would degrade a student's performance, and
2. The prompt can be made to "blend in" to the normative social or cultural surroundings.

As noted earlier, many students use personal schedules to help them organize their daily routines, and reduce problems that accompany unpredictable changes in transitions and routines. These personal schedules can become a permanent means of promoting independence. Other permanent prompts include pictures that remind students to perform all tasks in a job sequence, or a list of the bus stops and transfers between home and work. Across the past three decades, numerous types of technology have been found to be effective as prompting systems, including audio tapes with personal messages (Alberto, Sharpton, Briggs, & Stright, 1986; Davis et al., 1992) for students to perform work and school tasks, video iPods to teach pedestrian navigation (Kelley, Test, & Cooke, 2013), and static picture guides for a host of community and home skills (Cihak, Alberto, Taber-Doughty, & Gama, 2006). These prompt systems can be used to teach new skills, promote task fluency, or to maintain and generalize existing skills. If their removal results in a deterioration of skills, teachers can leave the prompts in place, thus making them permanent.

Using Naturalistic Teaching Procedures

A number of naturalistic teaching procedures have shown their utility for students with CIDs (Chung, Carter, & Sisco, 2012). They are known by various terms including *incidental teaching, milieu teaching, mand–model,* and other names (Warren & Reichle, 1992). These naturalistic teaching procedures are valuable because they incorporate practice opportunities into naturally occurring classroom routines. The procedures were first described by Hart and Risley (1968) as a natural method of providing language instruction. The common approach across all the naturalistic teaching procedures requires that a teacher "set up" a situation in which a student can see and request a desirable object or activity. Having established this intent, the teacher then asks the student to use a form of language that the teacher has already selected as an instructional target. By using the language target, the student gains access to the object or activity. Most naturalistic teaching procedures have five elements, in sequence (Warren & Reichle, 1992):

- The teacher engineers the setting to evoke a language opportunity.
- The student initiates a communication.
- The adult requests an elaboration of the request.
- The adult reinforces the elaboration, typically by providing access to the referent indicated by the student.
- If the student does not produce the instructional target, the adult then *models* the correct behavior.

Although this instructional format appears somewhat unstructured, there is nothing "incidental" about it. The teaching opportunity is well planned, and the learning opportunity is highly structured (Ostrosky, Drasgow, & Halle, 1999). Naturalistic teaching procedures can take place in nearly any setting, but many successful demonstrations have occurred during free play or activity times. For example, a student with verbal skills may need to use the sink to wash her hands. Although she has verbal abilities, she stands next to a sink and gestures for help. The teacher, having set up the situation in advance might say, "Tell me what you need." This request may be enough of a cue so that the student then responds, "Help, please." The teacher then praises the student's speech, and quickly provides access to the sink. The language objective should be determined in advance by the teacher and IEP team.

The key to successfully using naturalistic teaching procedures involves determining in advance the objective of the lesson, and maintaining complete readiness and responsiveness by adults (Ostrosky et al., 1999). Adults must be sensitive to a student's level of language, and maintain an ongoing effort to raise the level of language for each student. At any point in time adults might find it easier to "read" the child's behavior, accept minimal communication, and then provide what the child wants (Ostrosky et al., 1999). However, this negates the effectiveness of a powerful and natural learning opportunity.

Reflection

How would you decide which type of instructional delivery format you might use for different students, at different ages, and with different instructional objectives?

The Link Between Instruction and Problem Behavior

Students with CIDs sometimes display challenges in their personal and social behavior. Some behavior is problematic because it occurs *in excess;* it occurs over such long durations, or at such high frequency, that other people will not tolerate it (e.g., repeated complaining, or perseveration on a single topic). Other behavior becomes a problem when it is missing or occurs at a lower duration or frequency than expected (e.g., difficulty initiating social contact, or infrequent use of self-control). A third type of problem involves behaviors that are displayed *out of context.* These behaviors are appropriate to some circumstances, but are a problem when displayed elsewhere (e.g., verbal protests are appropriate during debates of current events, but not during a math class). Finally, some students with severe disabilities exhibit a *preoccupation* with one or two narrow activities and do not move on to other activities. Some may exhibit stereotyped body movements such as hand flapping or rocking. These behaviors serve to isolate the student from peers, and reduce the opportunities for social relationships.

Students with CIDs who also have challenging behavior are difficult anywhere, but present additional challenges in typical classroom, community, or home environments. Problem behaviors that interfere with learning very often result in (a) providing strong negative consequences to the student, or (b) removing these students from mainstream school environments. Schloss and Smith (1998) pointed out that the typical public school response to challenging behavior relies on *discipline* rather than *instruction,* and that such discipline is generally ineffective in changing the behavior. That is, teachers typically use some form of punishment in hopes of making the student *stop* performing a problem behavior. Since these procedures do not teach the student what to do instead, the student seldom learns more productive patterns of behavior.

There are clear disadvantages to using the discipline model. First, unless a student's problem behavior is easily corrected by a brief period of discipline, teachers will find themselves spending increasingly large amounts of time and energy focusing on *management rather than instruction* (Gunter & Denny, 1998). This situation exists in many special education classrooms, and in some "low achieving" schools. As a result, students fall increasingly further behind in their academics as the school year progresses. A second disadvantage involves a basic principle of learning: a focus on discipline does not yield learning. Discipline models that target behavioral reduction do not result in the mastery of the skills needed to *replace* difficult behavior. Third, a discipline focus is based on the faulty assumption that students with CIDs willingly choose to engage in each problem behavior, and that controls provided by teachers or others are needed to prevent the display of these problems. It is increasingly clear that many students with CIDs do not have the skills needed to practice self-control *unless they are specifically taught to do so*. Finally, discipline often exacerbates challenging behavior. For example, many students engage in problem behavior to *escape* from an unpleasant class or teacher. In this situation, discipline that results in removing the student from the situation serves as a positive reinforcer for the problem behavior, and thus produces even stronger behavior problems for the future.

An Instructional Approach to Challenging Behavior

An instructional approach to problem behavior was described by Colvin and Sugai (1988). They pointed out that teachers seldom resort to punishment procedures for students' *academic errors,* but often use punishers as the first line of intervention when students' errors involve social or personal behavior. Colvin and Sugai recommended that teachers apply the same instructional model used for academic deficiencies to remediate problem behavior. This means that problem behavior would elicit *instructional interventions* from teachers rather than *management procedures*. In other words, problem behavior can best be addressed instructionally, using the same process used to teach new academic, social, motor, or independent living skills.

Applying an instructional model requires a change in thinking for many teachers. First, an instructional model equates problem behavior with behavioral *errors*. Students who produce social behavior errors should be *taught* replacement skills rather than be punished for the error (Scott et al., 2000). Second, teachers need to conduct an assessment of the errors, referred to in Chapter 7 as a functional behavioral assessment (FBA). An FBA helps teachers identify the *function* served by students' challenging behavior (Carter & Horner, 2007; O'Neill et al., 1997). Several FBA procedures are available that yield this information, and a common strategy used by many teachers involves observing immediately before and after the student produces the challenging behavior. With practice, teachers can learn to identify the conditions that typically lead to the behavior, as well as the reaction of peers and adults to its display. This information is helpful in identifying the conditions that make the problem behavior an effective tool for a student. The following Box provides an example of how an instructional approach and an FBA differs from a traditional orientation to behavior management.

AN INSTRUCTIONAL APPROACH TO PROBLEM BEHAVIOR

Henry is a 10-year-old with moderate to severe CID. Henry often whines and throws things when he is frustrated or alone. Henry's teacher has tried to eliminate his problem behavior by sending him to a "timeout area" (actually, an isolation area), and by removing his favorite books whenever he throws something. After two years, Henry still throws things. After conducting a functional assessment of behavior, Henry's teacher learned that the function of his throwing is to *gain attention*. Since Henry does not speak clearly enough to get attention from peers or adults, his teacher and a speech pathologist design a communication system consisting of picture cards and a pointer. Both adults implement a direct instruction lesson to teach Henry to use this system, and other adults also ask him to use it. As a result, Henry has learned to get the attention of an adult or peer whenever he is frustrated by a task, or has been alone for too long. His need to throw objects for attention was replaced by the use of a communication system. Henry's throwing has been eliminated. Best of all, he now communicates with numerous peers and teachers.

For Henry, a continued attempt to use discipline to eliminate his problem behavior ignored the important function served by that behavior: he threw things to communicate with others that he needed attention. An *instructional approach* to his challenging behavior resulted in teaching him a replacement skill, thus eliminating the need for him to engage in the problem behavior.

Behavior Serves a Function

All human behavior serves *some* purpose. Sometimes the purpose is obvious, but many times it is not. When teachers conduct a functional behavioral assessment, they are looking for the function or *purpose* of the problem behavior. Educators make two common mistakes when considering problem behavior. First, problem behavior is seldom *caused* by a student's disability. Behavior is the result of a complex interaction between people and their environments, not a simple result of a human condition. The second mistake involves attributing a student's problem behavior to willful and deliberate decisions to engage in that behavior. Behavioral excesses or deficits are seldom due just to a student's laziness, stubbornness, or choice to be "disobedient" (Chandler & Dahlquist, 2002). For the vast majority of students, the "disability attribution" and the "willful choice attribution" do not help educators solve these problems or help students learn and grow (Scott et al., 2000). An instructional approach to challenging behavior requires that educators understand the function served by the problem behavior. Simply stated, most human behavior, *including challenging behavior,* has one of two functions:

- To get something, or
- To escape or avoid something.

Two seminal articles on behavioral function and effective behavioral interventions are found in Research Box 11.4.

11.4 RESEARCH THAT MADE A DIFFERENCE

Iwata, B. A., Dorsey, M., Slifer, K., Bayman, K., & Richman, G. (1982). Toward a functional analysis of self injury. *Analysis and Intervention in Developmental Disabilities, 2,* 3–20.

and

Horner, R. H., Dunlap, G., Koegel, R., Carr, E., Sailor, W., Anderson, J., Albin, R., & O'Neill, R. (1990). Toward a technology of "nonaversive" behavioral support. *Journal of the Association for Persons with Severe Handicaps, 15,* 125–132.

Iwata and his colleagues set a new standard in 1982 when they published a paper that established experimentally that self-injurious behavior served a variety of functions for people with severe disabilities. While self-injury is not common, it compels a high need for immediate, continued, and effective interventions. By demonstrating that even this extreme form of challenging behavior served a lawful purpose, this team of researchers helped establish an expectation that all problem behavior should be assessed for function prior to intervention.

In less than a decade, the paper by Horner and his colleagues extended this expectation by making a challenge to professionals. If functional assessment could help establish conditions that maintain problem behavior, then professionals should build interventions that were not only effective, but that recognized the humanity of the individuals as well. Horner et al. (1990) urged teachers, psychologists, rehabilitation professionals, and others to design, deliver, and evaluate behavioral interventions that empowered people rather than merely reduced their problem behaviors.

Taken together, these two papers helped shift the state of the art and practice for interventions for people with challenging behavior.

How can problem behavior help a student "get something"? Social reinforcement is one of the most powerful consequences available to humans. This includes speaking to a student, touching a student, or nearly anything else that acknowledges the student's presence. Attention need not be *positive* to serve as a positive reinforcer; even harsh or negative attention can still act as a positive reinforcer. Frequently, disruptive behavior is maintained by the attention that a teacher or group of peers will provide. Many student fights are reinforced by the status gained by "standing up" to a bully. Other examples include class disruptions that are reinforced by the attention of cheering classmates, even if the disruption eventually results in serious trouble for the offending student. Both of these are examples of problem that is maintained by attention. Tangible items can also serve as positive reinforcers for problem behavior. By standing in a cookie aisle at a supermarket for a few minutes, it won't take long before a parent quiets a tantrumming child by breaking open a bag of cookies and giving several to the child. These tantrums result in payoff—the child gains tangible reinforcers (and probably adult attention as well). In school, cheating is often reinforced in the same manner. The student gains answers (tangible reinforcers) to tests or homework. Finally, the sensory feedback gained by a student's own behavior can be positively reinforcing. Some types of stereotypic behavior (such as rocking or making loud noises) provide self-stimulation, although it is important to note that not all stereotypic behavior is self-stimulatory. For a few students, even self-injury provides reinforcing sensory feedback. Sensory consequences are often sought out by students with disabilities, particularly if they live in environments with little other simulation or other opportunities for reinforcement.

Escape and avoidance also produces a considerable amount of challenging behavior. For many students, challenging behavior is a way of communicating dissatisfaction with the people, places, and demands of instructional tasks. Some students work to escape or avoid classroom situations because they are unable to meet the demands of classroom tasks. An historical study by Weeks and Gaylord-Ross (1981) showed that students increased their problem behavior when tasks were either too easy or too difficult, although students will also work to escape tasks that are not relevant, provide too little reinforcement, or are demeaning. The task might be a broad subject area (e.g., Language Arts) or a specific activity (e.g., journal writing during Language Arts). Some students will also engage in problem behavior to escape or avoid certain adults or classmates. This is particularly so when the adults have a history of providing discipline; escape and avoidance have long been recognized as unintended side effects of punishment. Students who learn that their problem behavior will result in being removed from an unpleasant situation will increase their problem behavior to earn the "reward" of being removed from people and activities they do not like.

Fortunately, a great deal has been learned about designing interventions for problem behavior, and the shift from management to an instructional paradigm has helped many educators rethink their actions as providing **positive behavioral support** (Bambara & Kern, 2005). An FBA will tell a teacher what function a student's problem behavior serves, and teachers can use that information to deliver supportive and instructional interventions. An effective intervention *matches the function* of the problem behavior. For example, if a student's challenging behavior is maintained by escape, the intervention should in some manner target escape. This could involve teaching the student to tolerate the situation (e.g., teach coping skills), teaching the student a more appropriate way of requesting an escape (e.g., asking for a break), or simply reducing the time spent in an arduous or unpleasant situation.

Recent advances show that a number of interventions can be designed to match the functions served by most challenging behavior (Horner & Carr, 1997), and decision-making guidelines exist to help teachers select interventions (Horner, Albin, Todd, Newton, & Sprague, 2011; Scott et al., 2000). As important, interventions to support students with problem behavior can be implemented for *individual* students, *classwide,* and even *schoolwide.* Schoolwide interventions, better known as **schoolwide positive behavior support,** have been used to solve individual student problems while creating a more positive instructional culture for learning and social support in schools (Horner et al., 2011). Interventions often include noninstructional school staff (e.g., custodians, cafeteria workers, family members) as well as teachers and therapists, and the interventions frequently target many interventions beyond the traditional curriculum. Interventions *within the curriculum* might include (a) communication training, (b) curricular revisions, (c) instructional delivery, (d) teaching prerequisite skills, (e) making reinforcement more explicit, (f) behavioral self-control, and (g) and choice making. Each of these interventions place instruction as a high priority, and each can be designed to match the behavioral functions. A set of guiding questions can assist teachers when selecting an instructional intervention:

1. Could the problem behavior be altered by teaching the student a more efficient way to *communicate?*
2. Could the problem behavior be altered if the teacher made *revisions to the curriculum and tasks?*
3. Could the problem behavior be altered by changing the way the teacher *delivers the instruction?*
4. Do *new (prerequisite) skills* need to be taught so that the student can perform a task better?
5. Could the problem behavior be altered by implementing a more explicit *reinforcement* system?
6. Could the problem behavior be altered by teaching the student to engage in behavioral self-control? This includes self-evaluation, management, and reinforcement.
7. Could the problem behavior be altered by increasing the options available or teaching the student to *make choices?*

> *Reflection*
> **Picture a classroom in which you've seen a student with CID engage in problem behavior. How did the teacher respond to it? How would you build an instructional approach that reduces this student's need for the problem behavior and a behavior management intervention?**

HOW IS INSTRUCTIONAL PROGRESS MONITORED?

As noted several times throughout this text, different assessments serve different purposes. Formal assessments of individual students (described in Chapter 3) establish eligibility for special education, while statewide or districtwide group assessments (described in Chapter 10) are tied to broad curriculum standards. Few of these procedures are helpful, however, in evaluating the effectiveness of instruction for an individual student. To monitor annual instructional progress, an overt system of assessment described in Chapter 9 (observation, portfolios, or CBM) is needed. For "real time" assessment of learning, a progress monitoring system is needed.

As shown in Chapter 9, instructional assessment based on teacher observation will determine (a) whether a student with CID is *learning* the lesson being taught, and (b) whether the student is learning it *efficiently.* Inference or indirect measures of progress are not sensitive enough to measure learning in most students with CIDs, and the formal assessment measures described in Chapter 9 effectively summarize annual performance. By contrast, to monitor progress on individual lessons, observations must be made *frequently enough* so that a teacher can determine whether his or her instruction is having an impact on student learning. What is "frequent enough"? For some lessons, daily progress monitoring is needed; for other lessons, an observation every 3–4 days provides the information. How are the results of the observations used? For many lessons, student progress will be *displayed graphically* so that teachers and family members can determine visually whether the student is actually learning the skill.

Chapter 9 presents a process for conducting observational assessments, and many standardized and curriculum-based measures exist to guide the curricular content of student IEPs. Many teachers, however, are unsure of how to monitor student progress on individual student objectives—that is, to collect useful data and what to do with the information once they collect it. To make instructional decisions, three ways to monitor student performance can be made through observations. This includes:

1. Monitoring the percentage of accuracy or completeness;
2. Monitoring the rate of progress; and
3. Monitoring progress in time intervals.

Monitoring the Percentage of Accuracy or Completeness

One of the simplest methods of evaluating progress is to **assess the percentage of accuracy or completeness of a task.** Accuracy is often recorded on tests, class assignments, and homework as percentage data. To calculate percentage of accuracy, two numbers are needed: the number of times the target skill was given, and the total number of opportunities that the skill *could have been given*. For example, during a practice job interview, a student provided 7 correct answers to 10 questions from an interviewer. The accuracy of responding to the interviewer was 7/10 or 70%. A similar calculation is needed to determine the percentage of completeness of a task. The teacher must be able to count the number of specific steps that were completed out of a total number of steps that *could have been completed*. For example, if a student completed 15 steps of a 20-step meal preparation task analysis, then the percentage of completeness was 15/20 or 75%.

Many lesson plans and IEP objectives have an *appearance* of accuracy, but the actual percentage cannot be obtained. The students will never be able to achieve their objectives because of an instructional error in setting the criterion for success. Typically this occurs when effective learning is represented by a percentage that cannot be obtained because the total number of opportunities cannot be accurately determined. For example, if a teacher establishes an objective for a student to "interact with peers 70% of the time" the student will never meet the objective because "of the time" does not delineate the number of possible opportunities to interact. This objective makes no sense. However, "responds positively to 70% of peers' social initiations" *is* a helpful use of percentage as a measure of learning. Peers provide a concrete number of social initiations; they can be counted, and the number of responses to those initiations also could be counted. Therefore, a student might respond to 8 of 10 initiations (or 80% of the initiations).

Percentage data is an appropriate measure of progress for establishing the accuracy of many academic skills (differentiate nouns from verbs), the completeness of many self-help skills (completing a task analysis for dressing into gym clothes), and for accuracy and completeness of various behavioral skills (e.g., self-management skill sequences). Assessing accuracy or completeness with percentage is particularly useful when evaluating the effectiveness of a lesson that leads to initial acquisition of new skills. A lesson that uses a discrete trial teaching format easily lends itself to measuring progress with percentage data. When teaching in a trial by trial format, the number of trials is known and the number of correct trials is also known. Each student's response to a trial is counted as correct or error. These correct responses or errors form the basis for calculating the percentage of accuracy for that session. When using percentage to monitor progress, any number of trials can be used for the calculation; however, incorrect responses will significantly affect the percentage scores when they are derived from only a few trials.

When using the percentage of accuracy or completeness to assess instructional effectiveness, the criterion for mastery of each skill should be established before teaching it. Different skills require different criteria for establishing when a skill is "accurate enough" to be considered as mastered. A job skill that involves counting coins into coin wrappers must be done at high levels of accuracy (near 100%). Putting towels on the correct shelf in a hotel laundry may not require as stringent a level of accuracy. Punctuation rules are usually considered mastered at a level near 85% correct, though safety skills (such as street crossing) obviously must have accuracy levels of 100%.

Monitoring the Rate of Progress

Evaluating a student's **rate of progress** is the most sensitive and precise method of instructional measurement. Rate is a measure of the number of times a skill occurs during a fixed period of time. For instructional purposes, a common time period often is defined as 1 minute. This provides teachers with a precise way of stating how a student performs a skill. Examples are:

- 35 words read correctly per minute;
- 1 articulation error per minute during an oral presentation;
- 17 correct keystrokes per minute during a keyboard exercise.

Assessing the rate of a student's performance is an effective way of evaluating the progress of many skills, especially skills that are performed at a student's own pace. Rate is not as effective for skills that require a teacher to question or cue the student prior to responding, since the time of responding is influenced by the teacher's instructional delivery, as well as the student's speed and accuracy. Calculating rate is simple. The number of student responses (e.g., words read correctly, articulation errors, or keystrokes) is divided by the time taken to perform all the behaviors. The product is then "translated" to the number of responses per minute (e.g., 68 correct keyboarding entries in 4 minutes is converted to 17 correct keystrokes per minute). The use of *count per minute* has become the standard convention for teachers who use rate measures to assess student progress.

Rate is a sensitive way of assessing instructional progress because it shows the *strength* of a behavior. Skills that are well developed permit faster and more accurate responding; skills that are less well developed occur at slower rates, and are usually accompanied by more errors. Assessing a student's rate of progress also allows teachers to gain insight into whether the student is gaining fluency in a skill. Fluency is a combination of skill accuracy and speed, a better indicator of learning than just accuracy. If a student's instructional objective includes *mastery* of a math operation, for example, fluency would be a good way to assess that objective. For example, a student might average two division problems correct per minute prior to instruction. An instructional objective for the student that demonstrates fluency might establish the criterion of success at 20 correct problems per minute (depending on the nature of the division). Performance gains of this magnitude are common in many instructional programs.

There are many conventions for teachers who use rate measures for instructional assessment (Cooper et al., 2007). Scott et al. (2000) provided a summary of general practices for teachers using rate for instructional assessment, and suggested (a) establishing the "natural range" of each behavior, (b) recording both correct displays of the skill and errors, (c) collecting 1-minute timings for academic skills, and (d) recording social and nonacademic skills during a "naturally occurring" time period. A system of rate conventions known as Precision Teaching is the subject of Research Box 11.5.

11.5 RESEARCH THAT MADE A DIFFERENCE

Lindsley, O.R. (1964). Direct measurement and prosthesis of retarded behavior. *Journal of Education, 147,* 62–81.

Ogden Lindsley is one of many professionals in psychology, education, medicine, and related fields who learned about cognitive and intellectual disabilities by observing people. He observed people identified as having CIDs and others who had no such label. He saw remarkable similarities in what people do, but he also observed drastic differences. When Lindsley's paper was published, it made a stir because he challenged the prevailing opinion that CID was a characteristic of people. To Lindsley, the term *retarded* served as a good descriptor of the *substandard environments* where many people lived, and was an appropriate term for the *low-quality teaching and interventions* provided to these people, but *retarded* had little value as a descriptor for people.

As Lindsley challenged professionals to shift the focus of CID from the person to the interaction between people and environments, he also urged that "precise behavioral description" become the standard for communication among professionals. To Lindsley, great strides could be made in engineering environments to promote human competence, but a common language of behavioral assessment was necessary to make these advances. Precise behavioral description involved unambiguous terms, measured movements, and timed periods of observation.

Behavior counts, movement cycles, and observation intervals became the standards of behavioral assessment, a distinct move away from the popular psychology of the times. Lindsley's use of frequency and rate would eventually evolve into a system of instruction known as Precision Teaching. Clear behavioral measurement yielded clear and effective instruction. By the end of the 1990s, Precision Teaching had become a model of precise behavioral description *and* teaching.

Monitoring Progress in Time Intervals

A method of assessing the effectiveness of a lesson that is especially teacher-friendly is to note the presence of a skill during a brief time interval. Interval systems are often used to record problem behaviors, but these assessment systems are also useful when teaching new skills. To use an **interval assessment system,** the new skill is identified and the teacher simply observes to see whether it was displayed during a predetermined interval of time. The total number of intervals of observation is used as the denominator in the calculation; the number of intervals in which the student displayed the skill serves as the numerator. This value is then converted to a percentage and usually displayed on a graph. Thus, if a student displayed positive social comments during 5 of 20 intervals during recess, her measure of positive social comments was 5/20 or 25%.

As with progress monitoring systems that use percentage or rate, the skill to be learned must be fully described so it can be easily counted and recorded. The definition of the skill must be a clear description of what the student actually does; it should have a clear beginning and end. One variation of the time interval assessment is the partial interval system. In a partial interval system, *any occurrence* of the skill during the time interval is recorded. A "Look–Record" audio tape is often used, so that a teacher observes the student for a brief period (e.g., 10 seconds) (the "Look" period). Immediately after the end of that interval, a recording period (e.g., another 10 seconds) is used by the teacher to mark whether the student's skill was observed (the "Record" period). This progress monitoring format allows the teacher time to record the presence or absence of the behavior immediately after the end of each brief interval. Time intervals are usually brief—from 6 to 30 seconds.

Using an interval system to monitor progress is easy, but teachers do need to practice before using it. Whoever observes the student must pay close attention to the student throughout the interval. Some teachers find it easiest to use interval systems when they supervise student activities, rather than deliver direct instruction. Second, scoring must be done quickly and definitively in the brief recording time available.

An example of using a time interval to monitor progress involves Gary, a student who does not participate in academic group activities with others. This is particularly troublesome for Gary since his middle school teacher uses several types of cooperative group learning formats in Science. The teacher defines "Group Participation" to include talking to the other students about the task, exchanging materials, and taking notes. He then establishes a 10-second interval observation schedule. During each 10-second interval, he observes to see if Gary participated at any time during that interval. If he did, Gary is given credit for that interval, by marking a "+" on a data sheet. If not, the interval is marked with a "−." At the end of the group activity, the teacher counts the number of intervals in which Gary participated, and divides this number by the total number of intervals that were available for him to participate. This value is then converted to a percentage. Gary, his parents, and other teachers can readily understand that he participated in the Science group during only 30% of the intervals prior to instruction, but then improved to over 75% of the intervals after three weeks of instruction. Although this assessment does not indicate how *well* Gary participated, it does show that his level of participation improved greatly.

Is Progress Monitoring of Instruction Useful?

Information on student progress should only be gathered if it helps teachers make decisions. Effective teaching requires monitoring how students respond to instruction, which, in turn, improves student progress. The information should help teachers make decisions about (a) changes needed in a lesson, (b) whether to move to the next lesson, or (c) whether to change the way the lesson is organized and presented. **Decision rules** are the guidelines that teachers use to make decisions about what to teach and how to teach it. Cipani and Spooner (1994) described numerous decision rules that help teachers use progress monitoring information to improve instruction. Typically, decision rules require that teachers look at student performance data, and then move through a sequence of questions aimed at isolating a change in the instruction. A summary of the Cipani and Spooner (1994) recommendations is found in Table 11.3.

Finally, although most systems of monitoring student progress simply describe an individual's performance on a task, information about the type and amount of instructional support that is provided also helps teachers and others make decisions about the future. This information is particularly important for students who use permanent prompts, graduated guidance, or some other type of support to perform at a given skill level. Progress monitoring procedures that target both the skill performance *and the level of support* needed to obtain that performance will help teachers make changes in their instructional programs by adding, removing, or altering the degree or type of support (Brady & Rosenberg, 2002). Given the trend to define cognitive, intellectual, and other disability, in part, by the amount and type of support needed, this will become an increasingly important part of instructional decision making.

Reflection

How much assessment should be built in to a student's instructional program? What should you do with the results of the assessment?

Table 11.3 Using Progress Monitoring to Make Teaching Decisions

Questions for Determining Learning Problems

Acquisition Problems

- Are there problems with instructional delivery?
- Are the prompts effective?
- Do the errors show any patterns?
- Is the student attending to the lesson and materials?
- Are there student characteristics that interfere with the lesson?
- Are there problems in the environment that interfere with learning?

Fluency Problems

- Are the reinforcers working?
- Are enough practice opportunities being provided?
- Are practice opportunities being interrupted by the teacher?
- Has a sufficient level of accuracy been established?

Generalization Problems

- Has a sufficient level of accuracy and fluency been established?
- Are generalization opportunities being provided?
- Has a teaching strategy been used that promotes generalization?
- Are there competing factors that decrease a student's willingness to act?

SUMMARY CHECKLIST

What Assumptions Guide Instructional Delivery?

- ✓ Students with CIDs benefit from the same patterns of schooling as students who do not have disabilities
- ✓ To master the knowledge and skills needed for the future, most students with CIDs will require explicit instruction
- ✓ Students with CIDs will make remarkable learning gains when provided with powerful instruction

How Do Teachers Organize Instructional Programs?

- ➢ **Isolated skill teaching—Requires direct instruction on discrete, specific skills**
- ➢ **Integrated skill teaching—Infuses instruction into routines and skill sequences**
- ➢ **Thematic instruction—Includes instruction on specific skills in the context of broad topics or themes**
- ➢ **Unit approach to instruction—Introduces skills and knowledge across subject matter**
- ➢ **Splinter skills—Skills that are developed in isolation**
  - ✓ Integrated instruction is a critical practice for students with CID
- ➢ **Physical and personal structure—Modifications that provide students with visual and environmental assistance**

- ✓ Visual cues and structure involves positioning and organizing materials so tasks can be completed with little to no verbal information
- ✓ Personal schedules help students sequence their daily activities
- ➤ **Permanent prompts—Include visual, auditory, or other assists that do not need to be removed**
- ➤ **Work systems—Structured and organized materials that add visual clarity to tasks**
  - ✓ Classrooms should be organized into work and nonwork areas
- ➤ **Transition area—A place for students to go after completing tasks, and before proceeding to the next one**
- ➤ **Acquisition—Involves learning new concepts, skills, and actions**
- ➤ **Fluency—The combination of accuracy and speed that allows a skill to be useful in a natural environment**
- ➤ **Generalization—Involves using a skill in new ways or under novel conditions**
  - ✓ Teachers use different instructional procedures for lessons aimed toward acquisition, fluency, or generalization

How Is Instruction Delivered?

- ➤ **Instructional collaboration—Requires teachers, families, and other professionals to exchange information about student learning and development**
- ➤ **Natural environments—Provide a real-world context for learning new skills**
  - ✓ The location of instruction should match the nature of the curriculum
  - ✓ Individualized instruction does not mean one-to-one instructional delivery
  - ✓ One-to-one instruction can assist most learners at some point when learning new skills
- ➤ **Choral responding—A delivery format that results in students giving a group, unison reply**
- ➤ **Interactive group instruction—Requires peer-to-peer engagement**
- ➤ **One-to-one in a group format—Elicits participation from individual students while maintaining a group activity**
  - ✓ Task analysis is helpful for teaching as well as assessment
  - ✓ Steps in a task analysis can be taught simultaneously, or in a sequential manner
  - ✓ Teacher assistance can be task analyzed when teaching a skill as a whole.
  - ✓ A task analysis of teachers' prompts is frequently referred to as **graduated guidance**
- ➤ **Chaining—Involves teaching each step of a skill at a time**
- ➤ **Errorless learning—Procedures that reinforce any active student efforts to participate in learning activities**
- ➤ **Match-to-sample format—Minimizes errors by providing students with an example of the desired outcome**
- ➤ **A discrete trial teaching format—A structured learning opportunity that requires an obvious student reply**
  - ✓ Teaching trials can be delivered in a massed or distributed format

➤ **A most-to-least prompt format—Begins with a maximum degree of teacher assistance, then decreases assistance as the student learns to produce the skill**
  ✓ Teacher assistance can include physical, gestural, vocal, pictorial prompts
➤ **A least-to-most prompt format—Begins with minimum teacher assistance, and increases assistance if the student does not show evidence of learning**
  ✓ Naturalistic teaching procedures incorporate instruction and practice opportunities into regularly occurring classroom activities
  ✓ Problem behavior requires an intervention when it occurs at too high or too low a frequency, when it occurs out of context, or when it becomes a preoccupation that interferes with learning
  ✓ Discipline and management procedures are often ineffective because they do not teach students what to do in place of the problem behavior
  ✓ An instructional approach treats challenging behavior as a behavioral error
  ✓ A functional behavioral assessment provides information on the purpose or function served by a student's challenging behavior
  ✓ The functions of problem behavior are that students get something they want, or get away from something they don't want
  ✓ Behavioral interventions are most likely to be effective when they match the function of the challenging behavior and teach the student a replacement skill
➤ **The shift from behavior management to an instructional paradigm has helped many educators rethink their actions as providing positive behavioral support**
➤ Positive behavior support can be implemented for *individual* students, *classwide*, and *schoolwide*

How Is Instructional Progress Monitored?
➤ **Instructional assessment procedures should help teachers make decisions about the content and delivery of their lessons**
➤ **Progress monitoring based on teacher observations is a direct means of assessing student skills' performance**
➤ **Accuracy and completion of tasks—Often monitored by calculating the percentage of responses correct**
➤ The level of accuracy needed to demonstrate mastery of a task depends on the nature of the task, and the impact of any errors on the student
➤ **Student rate of progress—The total number of times a skill occurs, during a specific period of time**
  ✓ Fluency is a strong indication of proficiency in skills and knowledge because it incorporates both accuracy and speed
➤ Rate is a precise measure of behavioral fluency
➤ **Interval monitoring system—Used to record whether a behavior occurs within a fixed period of time**
➤ **Decision rules—Guidelines teachers can use to make decisions about what to teach and how to teach it**
  ✓ Progress monitoring should include an evaluation of support needed by the student to perform at a given level

ADDITIONAL SUGGESTIONS/RESOURCES

Discussion Questions

1. Are there students or subjects in which more precise, explicit instruction would promote learning in students who *do not* experience CIDs?
2. In your own development as a teacher, which skills would you learn more effectively using isolated instructional formats? How about using integrated formats?
3. What are examples of permanent prompts used in home and community settings by people who *do not* have CIDs (including college students in teacher education programs)?

Activities

1. Examine a teacher's lesson plans for a student with CID to find out whether the student receives isolated, integrated, thematic, or unit instruction.
2. Identify examples in your own professional development of knowledge and skills that represent the acquisition level of learning. Identify examples of knowledge and skills for which you wish to build fluency.
3. Interview a teacher to find out how teachers determine the effectiveness of their instruction. Compare these beliefs to your own observations about student performance.

E-sources

http://www.mayer-johnson.com
This website is the home site for Board Maker and others of numerous applications for teachers. Board Maker has been used by many teachers to help build students' personal schedules, and for numerous examples of visual structure and picture communication symbols.

http://www.ku-crl.org
This website is the homepage for the Center for Research on Learning at the University of Kansas. Numerous applications of technology for learning are provided, including a section on e-learning. Multiple interventions for underachieving students are found here, with links to information on learning strategies.

http://www.BehaviorAdvisor.com
This is Dr. Mac's Amazing Behavior Management Advice Site. The site is loaded with tips about behavioral interventions, articles, discussion questions, data forms, tips for data collection, and information on functional behavioral assessment. Information on schoolwide practices is included. Includes a bulletin board for ongoing discussion. Poignant reminder: "Don't be a mean teacher."

12

INSTRUCTIONAL SETTINGS

Key Points

- ➤ INSTRUCTIONAL SETTINGS MATTER—Controversy and misunderstanding has surrounded instructional placements. Changes in terminology have reflected tremendous changes in philosophy about the roles of people with cognitive and intellectual disabilities in society.
- ➤ DO INSTRUCTIONAL SETTINGS AFFECT INSTRUCTION?—Instructional placements affect both teachers and students in various ways. Settings can influence what students have an opportunity to learn, and whether students use what they learn.
- ➤ INSTRUCTIONAL SETTINGS CHANGE AS PEOPLE GROW—Child-care, school, employment, and residential settings vary widely. Many infants, toddlers, school-aged children, and adults obtain the instruction and support they need in typical community settings. Others obtain services in separate, disability-only settings.
- ➤ WHAT PRINCIPLES GUIDE DECISIONS ABOUT INSTRUCTIONAL SETTINGS?—Accommodations make settings instructionally relevant. Changes and modifications to instruction improve the educational atmosphere of settings. Accommodations allow students to participate in a wider range of typical activities.

One of the more contentious issues in educating students with CIDs and other disabilities during the past three decades involves the question of where students should be educated. The range of educational placements, and the nature of instructional adaptations that are available there, have caused confusion among general and special educators alike. Although issues involving instructional content and procedures generate many questions among educators, issues involving placement have often required courts to resolve them.

INSTRUCTIONAL SETTINGS MATTER

IDEA specifies that students with disabilities must have access to an array of educational placements. This is intended to ensure that each student has an opportunity to benefit from a quality educational program, regardless of the nature and extent of the disability. The requirement for an array of settings also informs states and districts that they should make available more than a single placement option for students. Local school districts must provide educational alternatives for students with CIDs, ranging from those with the mildest forms of the condition to students with the most severe levels, including students with other handicapping conditions and complicating factors. For most students, educational settings include typical school classrooms, yet for other students instructional settings might include different, specialized locations including community job sites and residences. As with decisions involving instructional content and procedures, decisions about instructional settings must be a result of individual student problem solving.

Why settings matter has generated interest of both educational researchers and school reformers. As pointed out in Chapter 1, societies historically have not been kind to people with CIDs. The history of education has enough examples of segregation to make most educators wince. In the early 1900s, for example, local school personnel were successful in preventing a 13-year-old boy with developmental and physical disabilities from returning to a school he previously attended, because of fears that his appearance could upset teachers and other students (*Beattie v. Antigo,* 1919). In recent American history, people with CIDs had to use state and federal courts to gain access to schools, employment, and typical community settings; children with CIDs obtained guaranteed access to public schools only after federal law required it. Even today the doors of many charter and professional development schools, and even university lab schools, are not open to students with CIDs. In the past 35 years, much of the *legal focus* on instructional settings emerged from Congressional attempts to assure that students with disabilities would not become segregated in second-rate schools. During the original (1974) debates over the passage of what is now IDEA, Congressman Miller articulated Congressional preference for integrated schools by stating that the burden of proof is on "that administrator or teacher who seeks . . . to segregate [a student with disabilities] from nonhandicapped children" (Vlasak, 1980). Ultimately, that Congressional preference was codified in federal law (34 C.F.R. Sec. 300.550 [b][1]) by requiring that "to the maximum extent appropriate, handicapped children . . . are educated with children who are not handicapped."

Although children with CIDs have often been left out of the educational mainstream, *over time* educators have been successful in including them into the mainstream of public education. Indeed, Reynolds (1989) described the history of American education as one of **progressive inclusion.** Reynolds pointed out that after years of excluding certain populations of children, schools then took increasing responsibility for educating these youngsters. Reynolds observed that each generation has redefined America's schools to include children previously thought to be *outside* of society's mainstream due to prevailing social values about such demographics as race, language dominance, or ethnicity. Children with CIDs also fit this pattern of progressive inclusion. Initial efforts to include these youngsters typically resulted in separate and parallel programs for them; as society becomes more inclusive, schools then establish the expectation that these children should be part of the typical school mainstream.

The Vocabulary of Instructional Settings

Much of the confusion about instructional settings is due to the changes in vocabulary and thinking about where students should learn. The change in terminology has reflected a revolution in expectations about what constitutes a good instructional arrangement.

Prior to the mid-1970s, decisions about where students with CIDs should learn were bleak, but easy. The few school programs that were available were often located in churches, residential schools, preschools, institutions, or hospitals. Between 1945 and 1975 there was a six-fold increase in students receiving special education (Reynolds & Birch, 1982). Choices in settings, however, were few. Most special education was delivered in separate classes or schools. Public education reflected a segregated **two-box** system of schooling where students with disabilities did not mix in the general education population (Reynolds & Birch, 1982). By the mid-1960s, a cascade or **continuum** of settings emerged, in which a list of settings was identified, each more or less segregated than the previous one (Deno, 1970; Reynolds, 1989). This range of educational settings, found in Research Box 1.5 in Chapter 1, includes a mix of placements in general education classes, special education classes, and completely separate schools. Additional placements sometimes include home schooling, or institutional and hospital placements. This continuum of settings is still used in many states today.

The continuum of educational settings had utility and appeal for many educators from the mid-1960s to the mid-1970s; the passage of federal requirements for special education (P.L. 94-142) meant that over a million children with disabilities would enter schools for the first time, and educators needed a paradigm to guide their thinking about placement and instruction. However, the use of a continuum also generated considerable criticism. Some educators showed that, despite the best intentions, *most students did not actually progress through this continuum,* and as a result, many students remained in inferior and segregated placements that limited their opportunity for growth and development (Taylor, 1988). Maynard Reynolds, one of the originators of the continuum, became critical of its use by many public school systems. Reynolds pointed out that placing students with disabilities into separate settings for special education would not likely help them to develop the skills and knowledge needed in more educationally enriched environments (Reynolds, 1989). Indeed, in school settings *without* the developmentally appropriate language and social skills of typically developing peers, many students with disabilities would *probably not* develop the skills that teachers expected of them. That is, the settings would serve to minimize educational growth and opportunity among some students. Reynolds (1989) proposed that a *continuum of supports* was far more consistent with an educational model than a continuum of placements. In similar manner, Taylor extended this critique beyond school settings by examining the impact of the continuum concept in community living and employment settings, particularly for people with severe disabilities. Like Reynolds, Taylor showed that the focus on placement often has a negative impact on the very people the continuum is purported to help. A summary of Taylor's analysis is found in Research Box 12.1.

12.1 RESEARCH THAT MADE A DIFFERENCE

Taylor, S. (1988). Caught in the continuum: A critical analysis of the principle of the least restrictive environment. *Journal of the Association of Persons with Severe Handicaps, 13,* **41–53.**

When people with disabilities enter a specialized but isolated educational, residential, or vocational service system, do they gain the skills needed to progress to "less restrictive" or more culturally normal placements? Taylor synthesized the concerns of many professionals, advocates, family members, and people with disabilities, and exposed serious flaws to the continuum framework. The continuum concept falsely suggests a progression of skills in which a person becomes progressively "more ready" for typical schools, regular homes, and neighborhood community settings. In actual practice, few people with CIDs and more severe disabilities ever move from segregated, specialized programs once located there. Among Taylor's many challenges to the continuum:

- The existence of separate, disability-only settings legitimizes segregation, based only on the presence of a disability;
- Many people with disabilities (particularly those with CIDs, autism, and other severe disabilities) do not actually move along the continuum, so they never receive the dignity and benefit of more natural environments;
- People in segregated settings do not have access to relationships with typically developing individuals except as service providers;
- Separate settings are artificial by their nature and lack the diversity of natural environments; and
- Without typical models and environments, people in segregated environments are unlikely to ever gain the skills and knowledge needed to move up the continuum.

Taylor's analysis exposed the concept that a person with disabilities must "earn" the right to participate in regular school, community, and home environments as fundamentally undemocratic. In its place, Taylor advocated a *continuum of supports* designed to help each person be successful in typical community settings. The settings would remain constant (e.g., typical schools, local playgrounds, community jobsites), but the amount and type of supports (e.g., different instructional materials, a job coach) would vary depending on a person's needs. Using Taylor's continuum, no person would be turned away from a typical community setting for being "too disabled."

Other placement terminology has been equally confusing. The common vocabulary from the mid-1970s to approximately 1990 included the word *mainstreaming*. As noted in Chapter 1, mainstreaming often was used to refer to simply placing students with CIDs into general education classes. Many educators took strong stands against this idea (and practice), arguing that a student's disability did not disappear simply by being surrounded by other students who did not have disabilities. Yet the concept of mainstreaming was never intended to ignore the need for specialized instruction. In defining the practice, Reynolds and Birch (1982) described three separate levels of mainstreaming:

- **Physical Space Mainstreaming:** Typical schools in which students with and without disabilities shared common spaces; students with CIDs are at least *physically present* in typical schools. This is the most rudimentary form of integration, and is necessary to promote more natural interactions between students with and without disabilities.
- **Social Interaction Mainstreaming:** Deliberate and planned interactions are implemented so that students with and without disabilities learn to interact naturally with one another, and have the opportunity to develop social relationships. Regular and scheduled activities that include students with CIDs as well as same-aged students without disabilities during recess, club functions, and other school events are examples.
- **Instructional Mainstreaming:** This form of mainstreaming builds upon the physical and social forms to create genuine learning opportunities and provide instructional support for students without segregating them. This includes students with CIDs attending typical, grade-level academic classes with specialized instruction built in to the overall classroom lesson.

Many of the educational advances during the 1980s described in Chapter 1 included a shift in terminology, as many educators began calling for schools to become more *inclusive.* Part of this shift was an effort by professionals and advocates to give special education a more meaningful role in school reform efforts (Smith, Hunter, & Shrag, 1991). Just as important was an effort to decrease the large number of students who still received special education in segregated settings (Danielson & Bellamy, 1989). When the assistant secretary of the U.S. Department of Education published a paper calling for closer ties between general and special education (described as the Regular Education Initiative in Chapter 1), many students with CIDs gained access to a wider range of typical school and instructional settings (see Event Box 12.1).

12.1 EVENT THAT MADE A DIFFERENCE

1986—Assistant Secretary of the U.S. Department of Education challenges educators to design a general education system that accommodates all students

When Madeline Will was named as an Assistant Secretary of the U.S. Department of Education, many special educators and parents set high hopes for the future. Will was known as a strong advocate of change in education, and special education in particular. She had a history of bringing together advocates and professionals with divergent positions, gaining consensus, and forging new partnerships. As the chief federal education officer for special education and rehabilitation, and as a mother of a teenager with a developmental disability, Will faced challenges as what was then P.L. 94-142 (now IDEA) moved into its second decade.

Will published a report in *Exceptional Children* (the official journal of the Council for Exceptional Children) that reverberated throughout schools nationwide. Will's paper was a clear and unambiguous call for a more responsive general education environment as a means of reducing the reliance on separate special education settings. Will's paper was published at a time of increased discussion about whether schools should become more *inclusive,* and many in the field believed that her paper would become a clarion call for increased emphasis on general education classes as the location of choice for students with disabilities.

In the evolution of federal, state, and local education policy there has seldom been as much discussion about the position of a single education official's professional publication. Widely read and cited in the literature and in legal opinion, Will's paper ultimately became viewed as a direction for the field. She helped open the doors to typical neighborhood schools for many students with CIDs, but her position was not a mandate for states and districts. Few education officials have generated as much discussion about the direction of the field.

Like the confusion over mainstreaming, the terms *inclusion, inclusive education,* and *inclusive schools* also generated considerable debate. To many, inclusion was simply a replacement term for mainstreaming. Some educators focused on how fully inclusive a setting must be (the partial vs. full issue described in Chapter 1). To others, inclusion was a logical extension of the effort to eliminate special education *as a system of separate education.* In many ways, inclusive schools extended Reynolds and Birch's (1982) mainstreaming definition by adding a fourth level: mainstreaming of entire school systems (Brady, Hunter, & Campbell, 1997). Inclusive schools differ from mainstreaming due, in part, to the magnitude of the change needed to make school practices more effective for students with CIDs (or other learning, language, and social differences). Although mainstreaming was typically recommended for *individual* students, efforts to create inclusive schools involve support for *all* students who might be educated outside of (or are at-risk of removal from) the educational mainstream (Brady et al., 1997). In addition to students with CIDs, this includes others with obvious disabilities, at-risk learners, children from economically disadvantaged families, children of migrant workers, and students from families who do not speak English as their first language (Danielson & Bellamy, 1989; Hodgkinson, 1993; Reynolds & Wang, 1983; USDOE, 1993).

Catlett (1998) provided a snapshot of how special education for a student with CIDs might look in an inclusive school by surveying parents, teachers, principals, and other educators. Her respondents made it clear that inclusion was not a project, an effort to mainstream individual students, or a placement option for individual students. Instead, Catlett's respondents emphasized that inclusive schools were an outcome of school reform. Schools that had become inclusive operated with assumptions, policies, and practices that:

- Students attended their home schools (schools they would attend if they had no disability);
- Classification and labeling was not used for program development or placement, but existed *only* for eligibility purposes;

- Modifications to the typical school routine, activities, schedules, and curriculum could be made for any student, but for students with disabilities they must be decided upon individually and included on the IEP;
- The numbers of students with disabilities in a class or school represented a natural proportion of similar students in the district;
- Students with disabilities were regular members of general education classes with similar-aged peers, and received any special education in those classes; and
- Inclusive education was an ongoing experience. It was not sporadic or episodic.

The schools Catlett's respondents described were engaged in genuine school reform. Students with CIDs were not part of a *program* limited only to those with the mildest learning problems, nor were teachers in these schools "doing inclusion" in episodes by mixing students with and without disabilities during lunch or another token period of the day. The children, teachers, and families believed that the students who went there *belonged* there, regardless of the nature, extent, or degree of disability.

Given changes in definitions and the confusion over terminology, prospective teachers might wonder just what their roles are in deciding educational settings for students with CIDs. As noted in Chapter 1, the specific requirement in IDEA regarding educational settings calls for students to receive their educational programs in the *least restrictive environment* or *LRE*. The LRE assumption contains several requirements for educational settings:

- Students should be educated in general education settings, with peers without disabilities, to the maximum extent possible;
- Placements should be determined individually, not based on disability labels or categories;
- Placements should be determined after instructional goals and objectives are determined, so that the placement assists the student to reach those goals;
- Placement decisions should be reviewed at least annually; and
- Placements should help the student gain access to supplementary services and the general education curriculum as appropriate.

Defining "least restrictive" was a challenge from the beginning, and continues to generate considerable disagreement today. Often, the assumption is made that an educational setting that is least restrictive, by definition, is the general education environment. Some educators, however, point out that general education classes can be very harsh settings for students with disabilities (Lovitt, Plavins, & Cushing, 1999); some even suggest that general education classes might be *more* restrictive than separate disability-only settings (Braaten, Kauffman, Braaten, Polsgrove, & Nelson, 1988). This is particularly the case when:

- Students in general education classes participate in activities that set them apart from their peers;
- The instructional methods used by teachers require *public practice* of skills (and errors);

- Students with disabilities must frequently leave the class to receive specialized and supplemental education; and
- Students with more obvious disabilities are added to an existing class without preparing the classmates without disabilities.

Others point out that many students with CIDs should have access to a more functional curriculum, one not easily arranged in typical classes with a focus on the general education academic curriculum and core curriculum standards (CCSS). For these students, less restrictive instructional settings might include, for example, community settings (to learn recreational routines), neighborhoods (to learn to cross streets), or job sites (to learn and develop proficiency in work skills).

How "least restrictive" has become the standard for evaluating instructional settings is a reflection on how legal issues often replace the focus on pedagogy in education. This is not a new phenomenon, nor it confined to placement issues; Lilly (1985) pointed out that as educators increasingly take on new tasks and new populations of students, progress is often stymied by a focus on practices that comply with minimum legal standards rather than advancing best educational practices. The principle of least restriction is a concept borne of commerce and trade regulations, not of educational practices. In a case in the early 1900s involving restrictions on selling milk across county lines, a judge determined that a lack of electricity (and thus refrigeration) might well increase the amount of spoiled milk that a dairy delivered to a nearby town. The judge ruled that this spoilage would require vigilance on the part of the public (they would need to be smart shoppers when buying milk). Although the dairy would have to show how fresh the milk was, the potential for spoilage did not warrant a ban on all milk sales within the county borders. The principle: Governments may restrict business practices, but when they do so the restrictions must occur in a way that minimizes intrusion on personal liberty (i.e., assures that least amount of restriction). Applied to people with CIDs, this has been translated to mean that educational programs would be acceptable (legal) if they place minimal restrictions on individuals for whom they are designed (Turnbull, Ellis, Boggs, Brooks, & Biklen, 1981). As special education evolved, it became clear that the LRE standard on educational placement has little to do with promoting *best practices,* but sets guidelines on the extent of restrictions allowed when delivering educational programs. In many ways, this paradox is still evolving. What's best versus what's legal becomes a more complex question as *No Child Left Behind* standards yield Common Core academic requirements, which in turn affect placement decisions—all asking whether an educational program for a student is "appropriate" (Zirkel, 2013). The least restrictive environment standard that accepts restrictions as the criterion for placement exemplifies Lilly's observation that asking, "What's legal?" often replaces the more educationally relevant question of "What's best educational practice?"

Reflection

How has educational terminology added to the confusion over where students with CIDs should be educated?

DO INSTRUCTIONAL SETTINGS AFFECT INSTRUCTION?

A beginning teacher might well ask what difference does a setting make—*it is the teaching that matters!* But settings *do* matter. Settings influence the attitudes and behavior of students, their teachers, and society at large. For many decades, for example, the only settings of any type for people with moderate to severe CIDs were large residential institutions, typically run by states or religious groups (Wolfensberger, 1973). Families who could not provide care for their relatives had few other options than institutional placement. If people with CIDs who lived in the community with occasional support (e.g., a family member to buy groceries, pay rent, or make medical appointments) outlived their parents, they also might lose their freedom if institutional placement was their only option.

In institutional settings, little attention was paid to the quality of residents' lives, and staff often limited themselves to helping with only the most basic custodial routines (Wolfensberger, 1973). This also occurred in smaller "community" residences that, ironically, were intended to be alternatives to larger institutions. Brady and Cunningham (1985) documented that custodial care provided by residential staff actually hindered residents' abilities to perform the very skills they were learning in school or rehabilitation programs. Staff ignored the ability of youngsters with severe disabilities to feed themselves, communicate, and make recreational choices if they perceived that these skills *interfered with staff members' routines.* For example, staff members actually removed an adaptive communication device from one teenager's wheelchair each day so her communication attempts wouldn't interfere with staff's ability to help feed and care for her. Unfortunately, without the communication board, the girl was unable to communicate her most basic thoughts for two thirds of her day—although both she and her communication device remained quite clean. The difficult irony of these settings: in placements with large numbers of people with significant disabilities, the need to assure care and safety often overrides the intent to support individual growth and development, even in school and habilitation settings. Research Box 12.2 provides a different example of how settings have an impact on professionals and society at large.

12.2 RESEARCH THAT MADE A DIFFERENCE

Blatt, B., & Kaplan, F. (1966). Christmas in Purgatory: A photographic essay on mental retardation. Boston: Allyn & Bacon.

At a time when several exposes began to appear in newspapers and on television, two professors casually entered a state-run institution with notepads and cameras to record the everyday existence of people who lived there. The result was shocking. Blatt and Kaplan produced black-and-white photographs of wards with people crowded into barren rooms, sometimes naked, sometimes in restraints. The people confined in this setting were there only because they had cognitive and intellectual disabilities. When asked why they were not provided more "humane" treatment, workers at the institution calmly explained to the researchers that the residents would not be aware that this environment was cruel. Because they experienced CIDs, the staff considered them to be uneducable, and unable to appreciate things like privacy, social relations, cleanliness, and healthy living patterns. Institution staff (including medical doctors, psychologists, and other professionals) spoke about the residents as if they were not present, often describing demeaning life experiences in front of the people who had experienced them.

By bringing their work to the public, Blatt and Kaplan forced the issue of humane treatment into the open. Segregated from public view, demeaning conditions had become a way of life for people in this institution and others. Unwittingly, these conditions had also become the *standard expectation* of the professionals who worked there. *Christmas in Purgatory* is one of many exposés that put into motion a move toward deinstitutionalization. After nearly five decades, families and professionals still strive to create family-friendly and community-based support systems for people with CIDs.

Christmas in Purgatory is a dramatic example of how settings reflect a society's values about people with CIDs, and influence the attitudes and behavior of the people who work there. However, there are also practical instructional influences that settings have on students and teachers. Many students with CIDs, regardless of the degree of disability, need direct and powerful instruction to learn the skills needed to develop and maintain such important life skills as social interactions and relationships, communication skills, and behavioral self-control. Such instruction is more difficult and generally is less effective in settings where the classmates and peers also share these skill deficits. Placement has a major impact on the opportunities available to learn new skills, and on the development and maintenance of social relationships and other life skills (Fryxell & Kennedy, 1995).

The dilemma of teaching social interactions, communication, and self-control skills in **developmentally segregated environments** was described by Strain and Fox (1981) over 30 years ago. Students without the ability to initiate a social interaction would be taught to do so, but when the only classmates available also had social skill deficits, a student's newly learned skills received no response from peers. The result? Teachers made extraordinary efforts to teach skills that students would learn, then promptly lose because there was no opportunity to use these new skills in a frequent and meaningful way. The same dilemma faces teachers when their students learn new communication skills, life skills, and self-control routines. Although students can learn to produce various forms of a new skill (such as a request for information, or communicating some confusion over a school assignment), ultimately a skill must have practical value for students to use it in their daily lives (Scheuermann & Webber, 2002). Given the difficulty with generalization of learning described in Chapter 7, instructional settings that do not prepare students for "real-world" environments generally will not help students transfer their learning outside of the classroom setting (Bates, Cuvo, Miner, & Korabek, 2001; Cipani & Spooner, 1994).

Although numerous researchers have demonstrated that **developmentally integrated settings** enhance students' social skills and relationships (Chadsey & Shelden, 2002; Chung, Carter, & Sisco, 2012; Kennedy, Shukla, & Fryxell, 1997), an equally interesting body of research shows the impact of students with disabilities on their general education peers (Hall & McGregor, 2000; Kishi & Meyer, 1994). Two groundbreaking studies by Meyer (Voeltz, 1980; Voeltz, 1982) established that general education students were neither overly receptive nor hostile to children with disabilities (see Research Box 12.3). Without exposure, knowledge about the students and their conditions, and an opportunity to have meaningful personal interactions, general education students typically hold the same preconceived ideas about disabilities as society at large. Voeltz eloquently showed that the absence of opportunities to interact personally with children with CIDs resulted in knowledge and skill deficits in elementary-aged general education students; these deficits were only remedied by planned and frequent interactions among the students. Today, educators are mindful that disability is one of many diversity characteristics. Students will learn about CIDs and other disabilities by direct contact only if given the opportunity to do so. In the absence of opportunity, learning will be hypothetical (e.g., didactic or "textbook" learning) or influenced by prevailing familial or societal mores. Without direct personal contact, students without disabilities often develop relationships with students with CIDs that are *caregiving* in nature (helpers, tutors, assistants) (Hall & McGregor, 2000; Kishi & Meyer, 1994) or that result in being "leaders" while students with disabilities assume roles as "followers" (Siperstein & Leffert, 1997). Relationships with mutual enjoyment and friendship typically develop only after direct personal contact with students.

12.3 RESEARCH THAT MADE A DIFFERENCE

Voeltz, L. M. (1980). Children's attitudes toward handicapped peers. *American Journal on Mental Deficiency, 84,* 455–464.

Voeltz, L. M. (1982). Effects of structured interactions with severely handicapped peers on children's attitudes. *American Journal on Mental Deficiency, 86,* 380–390.

Shortly after P.L. 94-142 was passed in 1974, most states and districts were trying to determine how they would implement the LRE mandate. At issue was a basic question of whether students with moderate to severe disabilities should be located on the same school campuses as students without disabilities. Many educators feared that general education students would not accept students with CIDs or other obvious disabilities, and this would create a hostile environment. Many believed it would be better to create more special schools where students with disabilities would be protected.

Luanna Meyer (Voeltz) was one of those rare professors, completely ready to walk into public schools and chat with children about their beliefs, or teach lessons on social diversity to university students. With much speculation about what children without disabilities might think, she asked them directly. Were they afraid? No. Were they nervous? A little. Were they ready to become best friends with a student with CIDs? Probably not. Were they willing to get to know them? Mostly yes. Her research and follow-up studies showed that the single best predictor of positive relationships was actual personal contact between students. In the absence of personal interactions, the general education peers had little to go on besides what they heard from adults. When told that students with CIDs needed help, the peers might help. If told to beware of these students, the peers might avoid or target them for trouble. But when given knowledge and the opportunity to get to know individual children, how a student used a wheelchair or an augmentative communication system, or what a student did after class, the peers became willing to establish a range of typical childhood relationships. Her research showed that students *without* disabilities would gain from integrated schooling as much as students with disabilities.

If instructional settings have an impact on students' social communication and life skills, is there a similar impact on students' ability to learn academics? Many educators suggest that settings have little effect on instruction in the content areas—rather the focus should be on how teachers can best *deliver* their lessons. Indeed, the special education research is replete with studies showing effective instruction across every placement imaginable (Browder & Xin, 1998; Casto & Mastropieri, 1986; Chung & Carter, 2013; Forness, Kavale, Blum, & Lloyd, 1997; Guarlnick, 1998; Halpern, 1990; McLeskey, Landers, Williamson, & Hoppey, 2012). This research, coupled with the literature presented in Chapter 11, demonstrates that teachers have a vast array of effective instructional procedures available to them.

The issue of where this instruction should be delivered is not new. In 1968, Dunn reviewed the available literature on the effectiveness of special education and concluded that students with mild CID generally did no better in separate special education programs than they did in general education classes (see Research Box 1.4 in Chapter 1). When Dunn questioned the efficacy of separate special education programs, many educators predicted the demise of a movement that was still in its infancy. His review of existing research was not an exposé of ineffectiveness, however. Rather, Dunn showed that when students with mild CID had access to good instruction, they made gains in their academic achievement and adaptive behavior. The controversy that Dunn unleashed involved the *location* of special education; Dunn's review showed that separating students with mild CID for their instruction did not result in any greater improvement to learning than teaching these students in general education classes, findings that surprise nobody today (McLeskey et al., 2012).

Over the next two decades, numerous others compared the differences in what students with CID learn in different educational settings. The comparisons examined academic achievement, peer acceptance, self-esteem, individual academic skills, and a host of other learner variables. The settings in these studies have seldom been "pure." Comparisons of general education classes versus special education classes often do not account for class size, the effectiveness of the teachers, their use of differentiated instruction, the type or amount of support available to students, and a host of other variables known to affect learning. Under these circumstances, it is not surprising that the conclusions have been, at best, uncertain. In general there has been little evidence that separate special education placements for students with CIDs are *better than* general education placement (Carlberg & Kavale, 1980; Forness et al., 1997; McLeskey et al., 2012). Recent studies including students with severe disabilities have expanded the focus on student outcomes to include the ways teachers deliver instruction. Given the powerful role played by actual teacher behavior, Logan and Keefe (1997) compared teachers' instructional practices with students with severe disabilities in inclusive general education classes versus separate special education classes. Teachers delivered more individualized instruction, teacher attention, and subject matter to students with severe disabilities when they are in general education classes.

When considering the impact of educational placements, it might be helpful to remember the lessons learned many years before when Blatt and Kaplan (1966) published *Christmas in Purgatory:* placements affect students as well as the adults who teach them. Placements that do not reflect the natural diversity of society do not provide real-life contexts, experiences, models, and natural opportunities for learning. Yet specialized placements can be helpful to minimize instructional disorder, and to allow a targeted focus on skill acquisition. Placements also affect how adults think about their students, and their roles as professionals.

Reflection

How might educators decide whether a particular instructional setting might promote or hinder learning and development in a student?

INSTRUCTIONAL SETTINGS CHANGE AS PEOPLE GROW

Each year, states must report information about how many students receive special education to the U.S. Department of Education. This information, in turn, is reported to Congress. That information includes the numbers of students in each disability category of special education, as well as the types of educational placements in which they receive their education. Based on these data, three distinct findings have been noticeable about instructional settings (Beirne-Smith, Ittenbach, & Patton, 2002; Danielson & Bellamy, 1989; McLeskey et al., 2012).

1. There is wide variability across the states in the use of separate settings for students with CIDs; some states place students into separate settings in much greater numbers than others;
2. There is wide variability across different disability categories in the use of separate instructional settings;
3. In most states, a large proportion of students with CIDs remain in separate special education settings for the majority of their school day.

The reasons for this are as varied as the students within a district. For many students with CIDs, there are limited placement options, and in many locales, inclusive settings are still quite rare. Costs are often cited as a reason for not integrating students, although degree of integration does not have a specific cost factor. Hasazi, Liggett, and Schattman (1994) compiled information on "high users" and "low users" of separate instructional settings across schools in six states and 12 local school districts. Hasazi et al. (1994) found that financial considerations were reported to be a major factor to consider for *all* placements, not just those in integrated or inclusive schools.

Educators can also expect that instructional settings will vary for students based on their ages. Placement decisions for infants and toddlers vary greatly from those for school-aged students and young adults. Noonan and McCormick (1993) pointed out that placements for infants and toddlers typically comprise two categories: home-based placements, and center-based placements. Both categories of placements have numerous variations. For example, home-based programs for infants often minimize direct services by professionals (e.g., physical or occupational therapists) and instead provide consultations to family members who, in turn, deliver therapy. For toddlers, home-based services might include both direct services and consultation. Center-based services also take many forms. Centers may include hospital classes, private or neighborhood child care centers, Head Start classes, or preschool programs at public schools. Some center-based programs include specialized programs for children with disabilities, while others have no disability-specific affiliation.

Making placement decisions for infants and toddlers is complex and must involve problem-solving discussions with family members. Each placement has advantages and disadvantages (Beirne-Smith et al., 2002; Guarlnick, 1998). Children in home-based programs lack socialization opportunities with other children, and typically do not receive the amount of instruction and therapy available in centers. On the other hand, children in centers are exposed to a variety of illnesses, a serious matter for children with health concerns. Home-based programs have other advantages. Families often find home-based programs to be far less disruptive, and children gain supports within the context of typical family routines (Oliver & Brady, 2012). Targeting regular family routines frequently improves the patterns of family interaction as well as the targeted skill or routine. Clearly, there is no single setting that is right for all infants and toddlers with CIDs. Often families and professionals customize the supports for children and their families by designing programs that combine home- and centered-based programs, and incorporating consultation with professionals (Guarlnick, 1998).

For school-aged students, placement decisions are typically compared to the continuum of placement options described in Research Box 1.5 in Chapter 1. To make matters more complex, some students with CIDs require related services (e.g., physical therapy, speech therapy, or assistive technology), and the placement for these services also must be decided. If education is effective, students' needs, and therefore their settings, will change during a student's school years. During the early elementary years (ages 5–8), a student may need intensive intervention to build a foundation for learning. This could include specific instruction in a life skill such as dressing, tooth brushing, toileting, or intensive instruction in the use of an augmentative communication system. In many districts, teachers deliver the intensive instruction in a separate special education setting, with intermittent placement in general education Kindergarten or first grade settings for "socialization experiences." In other districts, 100% of the student's instruction will be delivered completely with general education classes, while still others will deliver instruction in full-time special education settings. During the elementary years, school is typically a time to build academic skills, and instructional settings often include typical classrooms. In many districts, the general education class is the *primary* setting for students, and they exit this class *only if* extraordinary instruction is needed. When this occurs, students might go to a special education setting just for specific instruction in a skill area, then return to the general education class.

During the middle school years, some students enter specialized vocational training programs while others remain in classes that concentrate on the general education curriculum. Students who enter vocational programs often split the day between school-based classes for academics, and other experiences that will prepare them to enter the job market upon graduation (Flexer, Simmons, Luft, & Baer, 2001). Vocational programs often involve work experiences within students' own schools, but might involve transportation to a vocational high school for part of the day. During the high school years, students also face decisions about following a vocational path or continuing in the general education curriculum (Flexer et al., 2001). For those who pursue vocational education, many students spend part of the school day off campus at a job site (e.g., at a public library). A job coach, either a teacher or a teacher assistant, will survey the site to gain information that the student will need to be successful there. The job coach also will provide the instruction and supervision for specific job tasks (e.g., using the library's cataloging system to reshelve books), as well as for related work routines (arriving on time, interacting with co-workers). In recent years job coaches have become the primary implementers of instruction for students in community-based employment settings (Bennett, Brady, Scott, Dukes, & Frain, 2010; Bucholz & Brady, 2008).

After high school, there is little agreement that settings must be instructional. Adults with CIDs may indeed wish to participate in some form of adult learning, a goal shared by many adults without disabilities. Although post-secondary options have been historically limited for adults with CIDs, some colleges are now developing post-secondary opportunities (Westling, Kelley, Cain, & Prohn, 2013). Like the alternatives in P-12 education, post-secondary options could be separate vocational or academic models for adults with CIDs, inclusive models in which students with CID enroll in classes with typical college students, or mixed models (Grigal & Hart, 2010). Post-secondary programs may be available through community colleges, vocational-technical schools, adult education programs, or other community organizations responsive to people with disabilities (Hunter & O'Brien, 2002; Webster, Clary, & Griffith, 2001). Other adults do not pursue either further education or vocational training; they may simply wish to be left alone to participate in family home businesses or personal activities (Bannerman, Sheldon, Sherman, & Harchik, 1990). Regardless of the degree of "professional programming" obtained by adults, there are two general settings in which most adults spend time: vocational and residential (see Table 12.1).

Table 12.1 Placement Considerations for Adults

Independent Options	Supported Options	Sheltered Options
	Vocational Settings	
• Competitive Jobs in the Community	• Mobile Work Crew	• Sheltered Workshop
• Vocational/Technical School	• Community Employment; Job Coach Provided by Employer	• Activity Center
• Employment by Family Members	• Community Employment; Job Coach Provided by Agency	• Not Working, Staying at Home
• Self-Employment	• Employee Assistance Programs	
	• Post-secondary Options	
	Residential Settings	
• Home Rental	• Supported Apartments	• Group Homes
• Home Purchase	• Short-Term Foster Homes	• Nursing Homes
	• Family Homes	• Institutional Living

Vocational settings for persons with CIDs typically are classified as competitive, supportive, or sheltered. Adults who have had previous success in regular community and school settings, and who have achieved both skill and confidence in a vocational trade, sometimes participate in independent, or competitive, community employment. **Competitive employment** implies that people obtain and hold jobs without the organized support of professionals paid to assist them. Many adults with CIDs do, indeed, "blend in" with their peers without disabilities and succeed in a host of jobs (Halpern, 1990). Typically, these jobs include entry-level positions in stores, the service industry, the military, and in low-paid labor positions (Pumpian, Fischer, Certo, & Smalley, 1997). Supports are limited to the naturally occurring supports provided by co-workers, family members, and employers (i.e., supports are not provided by paid staff).

JOSH'S COMPETITIVE EMPLOYMENT

Josh holds a job in the garden section of a local WalMart. He obtained the job after a neighbor who works there told his family about an opening. Josh applied on his own and after the neighbor put in a good word with the manager, Josh was hired within the week. Although Josh doesn't drive, his sister drops him off and picks him up when she passes the WalMart each day on her way to school. Josh holds a competitive, community job, and enjoys the natural support of a neighbor (in locating the job and getting hired) and his sister (with transportation).

Supported employment differs from competitive jobs in that the employee is expected to benefit from a system of supports, assistance, or accommodations. These supports may be delivered by a job coach, a teacher, a rehabilitation counselor, or by co-workers, but the supports are the result of planned actions designed to enable the individual to succeed in jobs that are in regular community settings (Storey, Bates, & Hunter, 2002). This contrasts sharply from **sheltered employment,** which involves work activities outside the social mainstream, and is a disability-only activity. The settings for these employment activities vary greatly. Competitive and supported job settings for adults with CIDs include the same community locations as the nondisabled workforce. Sheltered employment settings are frequently workshop settings reserved only for people with moderate to severe disabilities, and typically are charged with working to move employees toward more competitive or supported employment options.

GLORIA'S SUPPORTED EMPLOYMENT

As Gloria prepared to graduate from high school, a vocational rehabilitation (VR) counselor identified a garden center with an opening for a person to tend its orchid house. The VR counselor assisted Gloria with the job application, and accompanied her to the interview. At the interview it was apparent that Gloria would need some assistance in learning about the fertilizer mixes and watering schedules. The VR counselor arranged for a job coach to accompany Gloria for the first few days of employment, and teach her the fertilizing and watering routines. The job coach faded his assistance by providing occasional verbal prompts to Gloria through an electronic audio microphone that Gloria heard through a wireless ear bud. As Gloria mastered the job, the coach continued to check on her on a "drop in" basis until the company, Gloria, and her family all agreed that the supervision was no longer needed. After implementing this plan, the garden center hired Gloria. With the assistance in locating the job, preparing her to work there, and supervising her transition, Gloria is now a supported employee of the garden center.

Residential settings are similarly classified as independent community, supportive, or sheltered living. In today's complex world, few adults with CIDs live completely on their own in community neighborhoods. Similarly, few adults live in completely segregated communities, although that was common prior to the mid-1900s (Crane, 2002; Wolfensberger, 1973). By far, the majority of people with CIDs live within families (Lakin, Braddock, & Smith, 1996). Residential options outside of families include either **supporting living** or **sheltered living** arrangements. During the past four decades there has been a steady move to decrease reliance on sheltered living in institutional arrangements and nursing homes. Although those placements still exist, the sizes of these settings have decreased steadily (Conroy, 1997). Most residences for people with disabilities currently house under12 persons per residence (Lakin et al., 1996; Stancliffe, 1997). Variously known as **group homes** or community living centers, these residences are typically located in neighborhoods, often resembling the architecture of the community. Group homes frequently house 4 to 6 adults with CIDs and contain living quarters for professional staff that live there or rotate in shifts with other staff members. In contrast, supported living arrangements are not limited only to residents with disabilities. In a supported living arrangement, one or two townhomes or apartments

Table 12.2 Types of Supports in Adult Settings

Supports That Promote Community Living

Vocational Supports

- Confirm paycheck status
- Schedule vacation, time off for appointments
- Check employer satisfaction
- Prepare for changes in job tasks or work environment
- Check co-worker interactions
- Confirm privacy at workplace
- Guidance with work habits and behavior
- Assess job performance, support needs, and satisfaction
- Assess need for job coach, job restructuring, schedule modifications

Residential Supports

- Prompts to pay rent
- Assistance with medical appointments
- Confirm travel and mobility
- Check on health insurance, Social Security, Medicare, Medicaid
- Advice on laundry, shopping, meal preparation
- Confirm availability of prescriptions
- Help schedule recreation activities
- Confirm privacy at home
- Check on interactions with neighbors, roommates

---

for people with disabilities might be interspersed among numerous other units that are not set aside as disability-only residences. The character of the residence reflects the residential neighborhood. Professional staff might reside in a nearby townhome as neighbors, or they might travel to visit the residents one or more times each week.

As with school settings, community worksites and residences afford opportunities for people with CIDs to grow and to participate in the normal flow and cadence of a society. But like school settings, placement alone does not assure growth, acceptance, and participation. Continued supports and instruction are needed if adults are to participate in the full life of a community (Larson, Lakin, & Hill, 2012; Pumpian et al., 1997). Some of the supports available in community-based work and living are found in Table 12.2.

WHAT PRINCIPLES GUIDE DECISIONS ABOUT INSTRUCTIONAL SETTINGS?

Educators today have a wide variety of effective approaches for teaching students with CIDs. The curriculum design strategies, group instruction models, instructional delivery tactics, and data collection and assessment procedures described in previous chapters can be implemented across a wide range of instructional settings. In spite of this, legal challenges have addressed the fundamental issue of what services and supports are needed and where they should be delivered (Brady, McDougall, & Dennis, 1989; Osborne & Dimattia, 1994; Yell, 1998; Zirkel, 2013). Many of these legal challenges question whether special education could reasonably be provided when the programs are separated from typical peers. In an early case (*Orenich*, 1988) the court ordered school officials to take all steps needed to implement a student's IEP in a general education setting and to provide any necessary aids and services there, rather than requiring the student to move the class for these services. In a similar case (*Briggs v. Connecticut Board of Education*, 1988), the court determined that if specialized services that were provided in a separate special education program could be offered in an integrated setting, they should be.

For many educators, providing related services in separate settings seems to make sense. From a *cost of service* perspective, some educators prefer to cluster groups of students together so that service providers have access to many students in the same place. If considering cost alone, this appears to increase the efficiency of *delivering* the services. Related services include transportation, speech-language pathology, audiology services, psychological services, physical and occupational therapy, therapeutic recreation, social work, counseling services, rehabilitation counseling, and orientation and mobility. These services can be expensive. Yet, cost is not the primary factor in deciding how and where to deliver related services. One principle clearly specified in IDEA is that special education and related services should be based on student need. Decisions about related services must include considerations from a learning perspective; services, supports, and settings should be based on what students need to grow and develop. That principle was established over 30 years ago when a judge in *Roncker v. Walter* (1983) established the **principle of exportability:** given a preference in the law for students to be educated with peers without disabilities, related services and supports should generally be exported to these instructional settings rather than requiring students with disabilities to be exported to separate settings to receive these services (see Event Box 12.2).

12.2 EVENT THAT MADE A DIFFERENCE

1983—*Roncker v. Walter;* Court case establishes the principle of *exportability* in delivering specialized services

Numerous cases involving educational placements were brought to state and federal courts during the late 1970s and early 1980s. These cases sought to clarify the parameters of the term *least restrictive environment,* in particular whether school placements could be defined as least restrictive by the presence or absence of other children without disabilities. Although many cases bogged down in the technical procedures of court actions, *Roncker v. Walter* provided a clear test for determining if a placement was restrictive. Arguing that a student with severe intellectual disability would not benefit from a typical public school placement, a school district sought to place the student in a state special education school. In this setting, the district argued, the student could be provided with specialized and therapeutic services; further, the costs of the services would be cheaper in the separate school than in a typical public school. The court disagreed with the district's rationale. Although it recognized the increased difficulty in providing specialized services in typical school settings, the court reminded the district that the purpose of school for this student was to prepare him for more natural environments in the future, not for future segregated settings. The court specifically called for an increase in school activities that would promote opportunities for integration. The court added that the key to "least restrictiveness" for specialized services was a test of **exportability**: that is, could the specialized services available in a segregated setting *be reasonably exported* to an integrated school setting? The court determined that such practical questions far outweighed the more philosophical issues involving mainstreaming and integration, and influenced a host of future court cases on what constitutes the least restrictive environment.

In many cases, the courts' interpretation of LRE has differed (Osborne & Dimattia, 1994). Early court interpretations allowed placements in separate settings if educators justified those settings as a way to deliver "appropriate" education. In more recent decisions, courts allowed separate instructional settings only when students' goals could not be met in more inclusive settings. Increasingly, courts uphold the IDEA requirement that *removal* of a student from general education settings require substantial justification; more inclusive arrangements do not (*Boschwitz*, 1988). In 1994, a legal principle was established in a case referred to as *Sacramento City Unified School District v. Rachel H.* In balancing a student's need for services with the IDEA preferences for integrated settings, the court established what came to be known as the "*Rachel H. four-factor test.*" This test established the suitability of a particular placement by balancing four specific instructional issues:

1. The benefits of a general education class (with related services) compared with the benefits of separate, special education classes;
2. The nonacademic benefits of interacting with students without disabilities;
3. The effect of the student with disabilities on the teacher and other students in the classroom; and
4. The cost of the integrated programming.

The four-factor test has been helpful to professionals and families as a way to resolve disagreements about instructional settings for many students with CIDs.

In addition to the exportability test and the principles established by *Rachel H.*, perhaps the simplest principle for selecting settings involves the degree to which any placement will support or hinder an individual student's instructional needs. That is, a "curriculum orientation" should be used to select a setting that matches the student's instructional needs, objectives, and curriculum (Scott, Clark, & Brady, 2000). An effective placement is one that will assist in the delivery of instruction, and thus have a positive impact on a student's progress. For example, if an instructional objective for a student with CID includes access to the general education curriculum or improved social skills and relationships with peers who do not have disabilities, then instructional settings will likely include typical general education classes in typical schools. From a curriculum orientation, a separate special education–only setting would not allow the student to meet those objectives. If instructional objectives included specialized training for employment or community living, then a setting that supports the curriculum for that student would include community work and living placements. This principle extends to adults with CIDs as well. An adult setting is an empowering one if it contains opportunities, supports, and services needed to help an adult achieve the goal of becoming more successful in typical, local community environments.

> *Reflection*
> **How might instructional settings change as students with CIDs grow older? Would movement toward community-based settings, for example, mean movement away from inclusive education?**

Accommodations Make Settings Instructionally Relevant

Instructional accommodations can improve the quality of most educational settings. Instructional accommodations include the adaptations, adjustments, changes, and supports that help students with CIDs "work around any limitations" that may result from their disability (Beech, 1999). Accommodations may include changes to instructional format, testing format, or curriculum. Accommodations might involve changes to specific lesson formats (e.g., a written rather than oral presentation), or the use of specific technology (such as large-print books or communication devices). Accommodations for students with CIDs might range from simple alterations in scheduling, to the development of individual, personal schedules. Many individuals with CIDs need only minimal changes to benefit from typical school, community, and work settings; others may need significant accommodation (Fraser, 2013; Scott, Vitale, & Masten, 1998).

Brown and his colleagues (1979) provided an early rationale for making instructional accommodations. Brown et al. noted that a system of accommodations would make typical school and community environments more relevant to individuals with disabilities by encouraging them to participate in everyday life routines. This logic suggested that many typical, integrated instructional settings *could be made* less restrictive and more educationally relevant to students with disabilities by providing instructional accommodations. These accommodations would enable students to at least **partially participate** in a wide range of activities that occurred in general education settings. Brown et al. suggested three strategies for using accommodations to promote partial participation:

1. Change the rules and routines that govern the activity;
2. Change the materials used during the activity; and
3. Change the way the task is performed.

Numerous examples of accommodations have been identified to promote partial participation. Consider the following accommodations involving recreational activities. For example, if a 12-year-old with CIDs does not have the physical skills or stamina necessary to play a typical round of golf, a *rules and routines accommodation* might be implemented to permit the student to complete the course over two or three days. A *materials accommodation* might permit an adapted golf club, with a substantially wider handle that would help the student maintain a firm grip. An *accommodation to the way the task is performed* might allow a tee raised 18 inches off the ground to compensate for visual discrimination problems. Any of these accommodations might permit the student to partially participate in a golf event with typical peers rather than relegate the student to a disability-only recreational activity.

In addition to the accommodation strategies suggested by Brown et al. (1979), Scott et al. (1998), Beech (1999), and Fraser (2013) examined the various accommodations used in general education classes for students with disabilities. Although not limited to accommodations for students with CIDs, they paid particular attention to academic accommodations. Taken together, their recommendations for teachers included:

1. Make an explicit decision to use instructional accommodations to support students' learning.
2. Determine whether a student's need for accommodations involves typical or substantial modifications.
3. Target essential skills and knowledge in a lesson.
4. Make a decision about the duration of an accommodation. Some students may only need temporary accommodations, although others may need more permanent modifications.
5. Link accommodations to students' IEPs.
6. Explicitly assess student performance, including their continued need for the accommodations.

Table 12.3 provides a summary of typical instructional accommodations for school-aged students.

The need for support and instructional accommodations will differ substantially from one student to another, and across different instructional settings. The degree of a student's disability is not the determining factor for accommodations; rather a need for accommodations is established by identifying a student's need for instructional support, and then determining potential instructional settings in which the student would be successful if these accommodations were provided. Like other instructional variables described in this text, accommodations can enhance the growth and development of students with CIDs by opening them to rich opportunities in typical community settings.

The needs of individuals with CIDs and their families are complex and multi-faceted. The wide variation in their abilities and challenges suggests that selecting instructional settings is not always easy. The continuum described in IDEA is setting-bound, and as such requires a delineation of the *places* where a student's schooling will be carried out. However, in delineating goals and objectives, IDEA also requires that educators make program decisions about settings and supports based on those needs. A helpful continuum of support *beyond* the physical setting, full of opportunities for growth and development, is needed if settings are to become helpful rather than merely "less restrictive."

Table 12.3 Common Instructional Accommodations

Types of Accommodations	Instructional Examples
Instructional Methods	Add lesson demonstrations, increase feedback to students, provide graduated guidance, use video & audio presentations, tape textbooks, intersperse lectures with group responding, use covert coaching and prompts, apply Literacy Based Behavioral Interventions
Lesson Materials	Provide guided notes, highlight text passages, shorten assignments, allow students to use highlighters and sticky notes, use advance organizers, use calculators for routine calculations, progressively disclose materials, use lesson templates
Teach Learning Strategies	Teach study skills, use mnemonic strategies, teach note-taking, use pre-correction procedures, pre-read difficult passages, ask students to paraphrase lesson outcomes, teach students to use concept maps and flow charts
Alter Grouping	Allow peers to read passages aloud, use cooperative groups, use instructional pauses, exchange peers' lecture notes, alter peer grouping formats
Enhance Behavior	Increase instructional feedback, use goal setting, develop personal contracts, use video self-modeling, practice difficult routines prior to encountering them, use personal daily schedules, use timer to define task duration, intersperse preferred and nonpreferred activities, ask student to select sequence of activities, increase choice making
Adapt Testing	Test in small chunks, alter short and longer tests, provide study guides, test with a partner for concepts, alter verbal and written tests, obtain daily progress measures in lieu of quizzes, complete a draft prior to turning in the final assignment, take tests independently, use practice tests

Reflection

How would you decide whether accommodations and supports could be added to help students learn in a particular instructional setting?

SUMMARY CHECKLIST

Instructional Settings Matter

✓ IDEA specifies that students must have access to an array of educational placements

✓ Instructional settings can include typical school classrooms or specialized placements

✓ Historically, many instructional settings were not accessible to people with cognitive and intellectual disabilities

> **Progressive inclusion—The historical trend to include more people who were previously "outsiders" into the mainstream of society**

✓ Changes in terminology about placements have reflected a revolution in expectations about instruction

> **"Two box" system of schooling—Tendency to categorize school practices by "types" of students, resulting in segregated educational experiences for students with disabilities**

➤ **Continuum of placements—Emerged as a way of identifying a range of instructional settings**
✓ A continuum of supports is more instructionally relevant than a continuum of placements
✓ There has been continuing criticism over the continuum of placements
✓ The term *mainstreaming* often has been used erroneously to describe simply placing students with disabilities into general education classes
    ➤ **Physical Space Mainstreaming—Involved the physical presence of students with and without disabilities**
    ➤ **Social Interaction Mainstreaming—Involved deliberate and planned interactions between students with and without disabilities**
    ➤ **Instructional Mainstreaming—Provides instructional support for students without separating them from general education classes and peers**
✓ Inclusive schools are the result of school reform efforts to provide support to students without removing them from typical school settings
✓ Least Restrictive Environment (LRE) continues to be used when deciding placements so that students with disabilities will be educated with their peers without disabilities to the maximum extent possible
✓ Continuing debate over LRE involves schooling should be *least restrictive* or *most educational*

Do Instructional Settings Affect Instruction?
✓ In institutional settings, staff often provide only custodial care
✓ Instructional settings affect both adults and students in those settings
    ➤ **Developmentally integrated settings—Settings that include students with and without disabilities**
✓ Children without disabilities learn about cognitive and intellectual disabilities from direct contact with students
✓ Without the opportunity to establish typical social relationships, many children will develop "caregiving" behavior patterns instead of behavior patterns typical of peers
✓ Questions about the efficacy of separate education programs have existed for many years

Instructional Settings Change as People Grow
✓ There is wide variability in the use of separate special education settings across the states
✓ Many school districts report financial reasons influence their placement decisions
✓ Placements for infants and toddlers include home-based and center-based placements
✓ Different placements for infants and toddlers have advantages and disadvantages
✓ Specialized placements for school-aged children are often designed for community or vocational programs
✓ Adult settings include residential, post-secondary, and vocational options

> Competitive employment—Implies that people obtain and hold jobs with little organized or professional assistance
> Supported employment—Includes a system of support to enable the individual to succeed in regular community jobs
> Sheltered employment—Involves work in a disability-only adult setting
> Supported living—Includes intermittent assistance for adults in community homes
> Sheltered living—Includes a range of disability-only living arrangements

✓ Numerous legal challenges have helped define principles for deciding instructional placements

> Principle of exportability—States that services and supports should be "exported" to students in typical school environments

✓ Removal of students from typical settings requires substantial justification
✓ The "right" setting is one that helps students gain opportunities for growth and development

What Principles Guide Decisions About Instructional Settings?

✓ Accommodations Make Settings Instructionally Relevant

> Instructional accommodations—Include adaptations, adjustments, changes, and supports

✓ Accommodations include both minimal and significant changes
✓ Accommodations include changes to rules and routines, changes to materials, and changes in the way a task is performed

> Partial participation—Instructional accommodations allow students to partially participate in typical routines, activities, and settings

✓ Instructional accommodations should be linked to students' IEPs

ADDITIONAL SUGGESTIONS/RESOURCES

Discussion Questions

1. What types of instructional settings for children and adults might we see in 25 years that we do not currently have?
2. How might settings alone impede or promote academic and social development?
3. Why are some teachers eager to provide instructional accommodations to students with CIDs while others resist the idea?

Activities

1. Observe a separate special education class and a general education class in which a student with significant CIDs attends. What opportunities for learning and social development are unique to these two settings?
2. Interview two teachers to find out their perspectives on making instructional accommodations for students in their classes.
3. Observe a student in a separate special education class. Apply the four elements of the "Rachel H. test" and describe any changes you would recommend to the IEP team prior to the student's next IEP.

E-sources

http://www.lehman.cuny.edu/faculty/jfleitas/bandaides/
This website is the home of Bandaides & Blackboards, a site that provides information and links for children, teens, and adults with chronic illness. Information includes tips for students who are asked about their medical conditions at schools. Also available are links to well-designed learning pages for students in science, social studies, and current events.

http://www.thinkcollege.net
This site provides information on post-secondary options for students with cognitive and intellectual disabilities. It summarizes college initiatives in over 40 states, and provides literature and reviews of employment and academic preparation programs.

Part Five

The Future of CIDs

13

FUTURE DIRECTIONS

Key Points

➤ PHILOSOPHICAL PERSPECTIVES—The definition of Intellectual Disabilities and its growing acceptance and implications are discussed.

➤ SOCIAL PERSPECTIVES—Issues included are strategies for improving meaningful participation in everyday life and the variables affecting disproportionality of minority individuals classified.

➤ LEGAL PERSPECTIVES—The legal impact of CIDs and society's perspectives on having CIDs is considered.

➤ MEDICAL PERSPECTIVES—Psychiatric and cognitive neuroscience developments and needs are discussed along with public health issues and the need for protection of individuals as participants in medical research.

➤ EDUCATIONAL PERSPECTIVES—Three likely advances in educational approaches are presented.

In this chapter, we address some possible future directions of the field over the next decade and longer. In some instances, you will note we have cited experts in the field to document their thoughts and writings about the future. In other instances, we are projecting our own thoughts and ideas.

In the following sections, we continue to address several of the "perspectives" outlined in the first edition. We will address those concerns and initiatives that are ongoing and remain unfulfilled, as well as discuss new ones. Additionally, we have included some "Events That Will Make a Difference" as well as "Research That Will Make a Difference" boxes. These are our thoughts—our "what if" speculations—on what might be some positive outcomes for people with CIDs in the next decade and beyond.

PHILOSOPHICAL PERSPECTIVES

AAIDD has instituted the name change mentioned previously to intellectual disabilities. We include *cognitive disabilities* because this term (or similar ones such as *cognitive delay*) is used in various states as the replacement term for *mental retardation.* Ford, Acosta, and Sutcliffe (2013) reviewed and discussed the grassroots movement to replace *mental retardation* as the official terminology in U.S. legislation. As we noted in earlier chapters, Rosa's Law implemented the use of the terms *intellectual disability* and *intellectually disabled* in federal, health, and labor statutes (Ford et al., 2013). With some variation, other organizations (e.g., World Health Organization) have also implemented similar terminology. So, the grassroots movement to deemphasize and remove the stigmatizing term of *mental retardation* has been largely successful. Yet, the issues surrounding naming, classifying, and labeling are not yet put to rest.

Schalock and Luckasson (2013) outlined several important facets to using "intellectual disability" as the driving terminology for this condition, including:

- "the term should be specific, refer to a single entity, permit differentiation from other entities, and enhance communication" (p. 87);
- The term should be used by various stakeholders (consumers, families, schools, medical personnel, policy makers, lawyers, etc.) consistently;
- The term must reflect current knowledge and be encompassing enough to incorporate new knowledge;
- The term should be useful for multiple purposes such as defining, diagnosing, classifying, and planning educational and other supports; and
- Finally, the term should enhance the naming of the people it represents and communicate important values toward that group (Schalock & Luckasson, 2013).

These same authors argue that *intellectual disability,* as a term, is enjoying consensus among stakeholders because it meets these five criteria. Luckasson and Schalock (2013) stressed that, "Any choice of a naming term involves serious considerations of personal and social context, intended and received meaning, and use in terms of ownership and power" (p. 96). These same authors argued that *intellectual disability* is the most appropriate term at this time, and that other terms such as intellectual developmental disorder would "provoke unnecessary conflict and confusion in the field, create divisions within the ID community, and disrupt the emerging international consensus regarding the term *intellectual disability*" (p. 96). Thus, while there may be those who continue to argue for other terminology, it would appear that *intellectual disability* will be the term of preference for AAIDD and other organizations for the next decade at least. Whether federal and state education law, and other laws that affect people with disabilities aligns with the AAIDD term remains to be seen. Readers may also want to review Schalock and Luckasson (2013) and Luckasson and Schalock (2013) for discussions on defining, diagnosing, classifying, and planning supports for individuals with CIDs. As we discussed throughout the text, the ultimate purpose of these various functions should be to provide personalized supports that enhance or maintain meaningful work and community participation outcomes (among others) for individuals with CIDs. Finally, Luckasson and Schalock (2013) emphasized that these functions do directly impact people as to their inclusion or exclusion from programs and communities, stigmatization, benefit eligibility, and fair consideration in policy planning and implementation.

Given the changes in terminology in the condition and the organizations that advocate for people with CIDs over the years, we fully expect future changes in the decades to come. In Event Box 13.1, we take a long-term view of what might occur after families and professionals lose patience with *cognitive, intellectual, or developmental disabilities* as terms of choice.

13.1 EVENT THAT WILL MAKE A DIFFERENCE

Organizations Change the Name, Definition, and Criteria Used to Define "Intellectual Disability"

After years of criticism for using insulting or demeaning terminology to describe individuals as having cognitive, developmental, or intellectual disabilities, 10 years ago several organizations that advocated for these individuals merged into a single organization known as the **International Association for Support in Learning and Development** (IASLD). Previously known as the Division on Autism and Developmental Disability (DADD), International Association for the Scientific Study of Intellectual and Developmental Disabilities (IASSIDD), American Association on Intellectual and Developmental Disabilities (AAIDD), and several others, the IASLD released new guidelines today that define the criteria to be used to deliver services to individuals once thought to have learning and development problems due to personal disabilities. The new guidelines note that, *Individuals in need of supplemental support for learning and development are characterized as those who obtain only modest gains in both* **intellectual functioning** *and in* **adaptive behavior,** *unless their life experiences are accompanied with interventions or support. The interventions and support must meet research-based criteria for effectiveness. The condition originates* **before the age of 25.**

SOCIAL PERSPECTIVES

Social perspectives on a disability could incorporate dozens of ideas, many of which are unrelated. We have selected two topics that probe the intersection of society and the individual. Long a source of tension as humans wrestled with the roles of individuals in society, the application of these issues are made even more complex when the individuals with CIDs have a direct impact on society, and societal trends affect these individuals and their families.

Meaningful Opportunities for Participation

Rotholz (2009), as the outgoing President of the AAIDD, wrote an address entitled, "Creating the Future: Beyond Our Inheritance of the Past." Rotholz (p. 126) asked "When thinking about the supports for people with intellectual disability a key question is what is required if one is to have a meaningful and fulfilling life?" In this address, Rotholz outlined several important issues he envisioned as ongoing needs for people with CIDs and their families, as well as the professionals who work on their behalf. Among the issues discussed by Rotholz are:

- Making available more *community support opportunities* that will enhance the people with CIDs' choices in living in communities. Those living in settings with home- and community-based services and supports enjoy more options in daily activities than those in larger residential facilities. Expanding options requires the expansion of Medicaid waivers to support exercising these options. At least three-quarters of individuals with CIDs do not live in their own homes.
- Making *meaningful work options* more widely available to people with CIDs. Supported employment options (that we discuss in Chapter 12) are actually on the downtrend. Sheltered workshops (also discussed in Chapter 12) continue to exist in many communities and offer less meaningful and lower-wage jobs. A continuing problem is the bureaucracy involved in establishing more community-based employment and living options.
- People with CIDs are in need of more *positive behavior supports* including nonaversive approaches to building adaptive skills and addressing maladaptive behaviors. Rotholz noted that there are still examples of routine "coercive behavioral practices used with people who have intellectual or developmental disability" (p. 130). Rotholz also stated that widespread implementation of positive behavior supports will require "philosophical, political, and financial support from the agency leadership; competency-based training for supervisors, trainers, direct-support professionals, and behavior support plan developers; an effective process to ensure that behavior support plans are developed by people with appropriate qualifications and that they do this with the input and collaboration of those involved in providing and receiving the supports, and a quality assurance-quality improvement process . . ." (p. 130).
- *Quality of life* has been defined in various ways but, in essence, relates to enjoying everyday experiences and life (e.g., work, home life, leisure) and participating meaningfully in choosing what activities you experience and with whom you experience those activities. Rotholz pointed out that the addition of consumer satisfaction surveys and ratings of support services are current moves toward assessing quality of life derived from the supports provided. Rotholz further emphasized that state agencies need to ensure a feedback loop that regularly assesses the quality of supports provided, the satisfaction of the individual receiving the supports, the outcomes achieved, and a system that responds to that feedback in substantive ways.

Despite the many gains made in educational, work, leisure, and living options, the overall level of participation in the life of their communities of many individuals with CIDs remains well below what one might consider meaningful, much less optimal. Indeed, we acknowledge the challenge of developing and maintaining a system (private or government-sponsored) that provides services that are needed, enhances meaningful participation and quality of life, and is continuously sensitive and responsive to its own service providers and users. This challenge is further encumbered by location, funding, and myriad other variables. Nevertheless, this sensitivity and responsiveness remain major needs for innovation and renovation of support systems.

Disproportionality

For years, the overrepresentation of individuals from certain minority groups has remained an issue in identifying students under the IDEA category of mental retardation. African-American students have been at the forefront of this ongoing debate. Additionally, an increase in the number of students for whom English is a second language has resulted in concerns that they may be overrepresented in this category as well.

Gold and Richards (2012) reviewed the literature and cited a number of important questions regarding special education identification of African-American students. Among their concerns were:

- *Labeling* itself can have a discriminatory effect on the individual and on those identifying, classifying, and serving that individual. Labeling may conjure up and reinforce perceptions of the individual as "deviant."
- *Referrals* for intervention and evaluation of African-American students is often conducted by majority group members who are less familiar with the cultural, behavioral, and language norms of the minority culture group members.
- *Assessment procedures* may be culturally biased and may not include a sufficient representation of minority group members in norm samples to whom the student will be compared. Some tests may disproportionately classify African-American students as intellectually disabled. Cultural differences can influence the assessment of intelligence, achievement, and behavior.
- *Bias* may emerge among evaluation team members from the majority culture. This need not be a conscious, contrived bias, but may occur with respect to race, gender, or social status.
- *Placement decisions* may result in African-American students being perceived to have behavioral issues that are not typical among the majority culture team members and students (Gold & Richards, 2012).

Of importance as well is the potential overrepresentation of speakers of English as a second language. While some of the issues would be similar to those of African-American students (e.g., language usage, test bias, cultural differences), there are other concerns as well. Sullivan (2011) discussed a number of issues related to English Language Learners (ELLs) resulting from her research including:

- *Overrepresentation* at a state level of ELLs in special education in general and in the category of mild CID in particular.
- *Placements* among ELLs tended to indicate less time spent in the least restrictive environment (general education classroom) than with English-speaking majority peers.
- *Districts with a high proportion of teachers with ESL certification* tended to be more likely to place ELLs in the least restrictive environment (Sullivan, 2011).

It appears evident that disproportionality, at least among some minority culture groups, continues to be a problem area when identifying, classifying, and placing students with CIDs. This is a troubling problem that has not been resolved in the nearly

40 years since the passage of P.L. 94-142. Research Box 13.1 presents a possible course that may be important in resolving this problem.

13.1 RESEARCH THAT WILL MAKE A DIFFERENCE

Over time, multiple research studies have indicated the use of the Response to Intervention (RtI) process has been important in identifying students suspected of having specific learning disabilities with much less reliance on the use of norm-referenced standardized testing. Additionally, the RtI process results in better data for planning educational supports. RtI has also resulted in a reduction of students identified for special education through its early identification of problem learning areas and interventions that address those problems in the general education setting.

The success of the RtI process has been extended to and is now being targeted toward students suspected of having CIDs. In particular, it has been found that this process is instrumental in avoiding the cultural/linguistic biases that have been evident in identification, classification, and placement of students from minority groups in the category of CID. Research continues to support that the use of classroom-based observation, progress monitoring, and intervention is superior to traditional testing methods in identifying all children.

LEGAL PERSPECTIVES

The courts and legislatures have long had an impact on the field and on individuals with CIDs. Legal issues have addressed questions about how much liberty an individual might gain or lose, or how much treatment a person could expect when his or her liberties were restricted. During these queries advocates and families often considered the courts as partners, and state and local agencies have frequently sought clarifications and guidance on program requirements—and sometimes limits on what they were required to provide. At times the courts have established clear and compelling guidelines (ordering sterilization in *Buck v. Bell* in 1927; ordering active treatment programs in *Wyatt v. Stickney* in 1974). These cases and others were groundbreaking, and the courts have been change agents in many instances.

A second area where legal perspectives have driven the field involves criminal justice. The most recent major example involved a Supreme Court decision that death penalty executions of people with CIDs are unconstitutional (*Atkins v. Virginia*, 2002). A remarkably effective advocate for people with CIDs in the justice system, Perske (2000) points out the many abuses suffered by these individuals when they enter an adversarial decision-making system in which funding and intellect can rule the day. Perske identified many tragic anecdotes when people with CIDs enter the criminal justice world. In response to the question of whether a person with CID understood the consequences of the death penalty, Perske described how Ricky Rector left his pecan pie on the window sill of his jail cell when he went off to his execution. He wanted it to cool off so he could eat it when he returned. In response to whether individuals might be too socially malleable under interrogation, Perske also described any number of individuals who have agreed to false confessions as a desire to please a uniformed police officer or judge.

As in all other issues described in this book, definitional issues influence these legal perspectives as well. Olley (2013) pointed out that although the big issue in *Atkins v. Virginia* involved eliminating the death penalty as an option for individuals with CIDs, this "big issue" was established only after carefully pulling apart every definition of the term *mental retardation* in each of the 50 states. Many members of the public took the decision to be a sign of humanitarianism—an indication that societies become more humane as we reflect on our roles as citizens. Perhaps *Atkins v. Virginia* instead tells us that to prevail on big issues requires attention to the smaller details and nuances of definitions. Like so many other regulatory or legislative issues, establishing CID as a "normal" part of the human condition (i.e., a disability, not a disorder) allows us to focus on the functional effects of the condition as individuals interact with society (Ellis, 2013). That nuance summarizes our view of the legal perspective of CIDs during the next decade. We suspect that the legal challenges will not look like the landmark decisions seen in *Buck, Wyatt,* or *Atkins*. Instead, we believe the legal issues involving CIDs will be small and steady pushes by individuals with CIDs, their families, and their advocates to better define the parameters of health care, educational access, and supports for community living and employment. And at the heart of each legal and legislative issue will be efforts to define and understand what CID really means.

MEDICAL PERSPECTIVES

There is little doubt that in the decades to come, there will be medical advances in the diagnosis of conditions leading to CIDs, as well as treatments that could mediate and prevent their occurrence. Rather than focus on medical procedures, we focus on three stickier issues related to the medical care. First, we will discuss some research questions from the psychiatric and cognitive-neuroscience fields. Second, we will discuss international health care issues that continue to impact the prevalence and incidence of CIDs. Finally, we will discuss the ethics of including individuals with CIDs in medical research.

Psychiatric and Cognitive Neuroscience Issues

Hodapp and Dykens (2009) outlined five major issues and questions they believed would be important in future psychiatric research related to individuals with CIDs. The five issues included:

- How do genetics, the brain, and behavior connect? Hodapp and Dykens pointed out the need for studies of individuals with CIDs to help shed light as to what degree (and perhaps what facets) of intelligence might be a function of heredity, and whether that heredity might vary among populations (e.g., higher versus lower IQ individuals).
- How does the environment impact child outcomes? The nature versus nurture question remains to be answered in some fundamental and perhaps subtle ways. Hodapp and Dykens note that environmental variables may impact people with different genetic inheritances in different ways. Particularly for many individuals

with higher IQs, the impact of the environment and its interaction with genes remains unclear, as evidenced by the fact that one must offer a rather substantial list of "characteristics" that appear or do not appear in individuals with milder CIDs. Snell and Luckasson et al. (2009) stress that to assume an individual with a higher IQ does in fact have "milder" needs may be unfounded, and such a viewpoint lacks any specificity in achieving a meaningful support system.

- How do children with CIDs affect other family members? Hodapp and Dykens highlight the shift from the historical perspective that having a child with a CID meant trouble and heartache for families. The authors note that there can be either positive or negative effects on others in the family. What may be more important is determining and understanding what are the "active ingredients" in the child that impact families (e.g., maladaptive behavior, health problems, irritability, appearance, among others).
- What effects do gender and aging have on the occurrence of CIDs? Specifically, Hodapp and Dykens wonder if gender differences in the general population also play out in those with CIDs (e.g., the higher rate of occurrence of depression in women). Also, the authors suggest that longitudinal studies are much needed to better understand how development over time might affect individuals with known etiologies.
- How can supports and interventions be optimized? Hodapp and Dykens, like Rotholz (2009), noted that research is needed in understanding potential psychopathologies underlying "dually diagnosed" individuals (i.e., with CID and mental health issues). Indeed, in our experiences during the decade of 2000–2010, we found that there was an increase in the need for supports for dually diagnosed individuals but also the supports were often intensive and time-consuming. Further, Hodapp and Dykens stressed that interventions and supports should be culturally informed and sensitive.

In support of many of the issues identified by Hodapp and Dykens (2009), the *American Journal on Intellectual and Developmental Disabilities* published a special issue (March, 2010, vol. 115, number 2) that addressed the rewards and challenges of cognitive neuroscience studies of persons with intellectual and developmental disabilities (Simon, 2010). Simon, the guest editor, noted that this series of articles establishes "a wide range of cognitive processing underpinnings related to intellectual and developmental disabilities" (p. 82). In total, the studies address the goal of a "general aim to go further by generating causal mechanistic explanations for particular domains of impairment, and they also try to account for the etiology and developmental progression of the observed disorder. Frequently, this is done because a longer term goal is to develop therapeutic interventions" (p. 79).

Medical researchers should and will continue to investigate the genetic-cognitive-behavior-environment factors that impact the development and treatment of individuals with CIDs. This research promises to provide a more in-depth understanding of the variables that impact the overall health, well-being, and quality of life of individuals, as well as medical and other service provision.

Public Health Issues

A meta-analysis of 52 studies related to the prevalence of CIDs in developing countries is revealing (Maulik, Mascarenhas, Mathers, Dua, & Saxena, 2011). Maulik et al. (2011)

found the overall prevalence across countries to be 10.37/1,000 population. This would not be significantly different from the United States with about a 1% prevalence rate. However, Maulik et al. also found that prevalence rates varied based on the *income grouping* of the country. The rates were almost twice as high in low- and middle-income countries in comparison to high-income countries. Overall, prevalence rates were also higher in studies focused on children and adolescents in comparison to studies involving adults. While a number of variables could have affected the prevalence rates (e.g., method used to identify CIDs), there is concern that the prevalence rates were higher in the countries less fiscally equipped to manage the needs of individuals with CIDs (Maulik et al., 2011).

Similarly, Black et al. (2008) found that maternal and child malnutrition is more prevalent in low- and middle-income countries. These authors estimated that stunting, severe wasting, and intrauterine growth restriction in these countries may account for 2.2 million deaths, and 21% of disability adjusted life years for those children under 5 years of age. Vitamin, iron, and iodine deficiencies also accounted for hundreds of thousands of deaths. Suboptimal breast-feeding was estimated to be responsible for as many as 1–4 million deaths in young children (Black et al., 2008). Clearly, these results are appalling and the financial resources to mitigate these problems is more limited in lower-income countries. Among children who survive and live beyond 5 years of age, there is still a heavy burden of disease-related health and learning issues that emerge. Nutritional distribution systems will need to be studied and improved to avoid a continuance of these truly terrible trends (Black et al., 2008).

In another study, Emerson, Hatton, Llewellyn, Blacker, and Graham (2006) found that among nearly 7,000 British mothers, those with children with CIDs reported lower levels of happiness, self-esteem, and self-efficacy than did mothers of children without CIDs. However, these researchers also found that "a socially and statistically significant proportion of the increased risk of poorer well-being among mothers of children with IDs may be attributed to their increased risk of socio-economic disadvantage" (p. 862). Clearly, public health issues are a major concern for children and their families both in terms of early death, disease-related and developmental outcomes, as well as mental health outcomes.

Finally, Chapman, Scott, and Stanton-Chapman (2008) advocated for a public health approach to the study of CIDs. In their study, these authors found that socio-demographic variables played a key role for all levels of CIDs. These variables included low birth weight, and maternal educational level. Chapman et al. suggested that the field needs "a broader biosocial perspective reflecting the interactive complexity of the risk factors comprising the various etiological patterns" found to be the origins and influences of the prevalence of CIDs. Event Box 13.2 describes a possible breakthrough in this area.

13.2 EVENT THAT WILL MAKE A DIFFERENCE

The leading developed nations of the world will join hands and financial resources to assist less-developed and lower-income nations in eliminating the devastating effects of malnutrition on the world's population with a particular focus on mothers and their children. The developed nations, through the International Monetary Fund and World Bank, will establish a program to stabilize farming subsidies across many nations to increase the world's food supply, improve economic conditions in less-developed nations where agriculture is a major vocation for many citizens, and to improve nutrition distribution across the world.

Agencies such as UNICEF and the Red Cross among others will serve as nutrition distribution outlets to people suffering from malnutrition. Additionally, nations will employ their military resources to ensure distribution is quick, effective, and orderly. Finally, this program will expand to include medicines and medical supplies to mitigate or alleviate public health maladies in many countries. The final piece of the program will expand mental health services to those people where such programs are nonexistent or accessible only through extraordinary efforts or high expense.

Rights of Individuals with CIDs as Participants in Medical Research

Iacono and Carling-Jenkins (2012) reviewed the history of ethical guidelines for the inclusion of individuals with CIDs in medical research. They noted that despite resolutions such as the UN Convention on the Rights of Persons with Disabilities, many individuals are not well protected. Human rights violations continue as it appears that guidelines may have paid deference to medical professionals as arbiters of the best interests of participants in medical research. Iacono and Carling-Jenkins stress that nations need to develop stringent ethical guidelines to ensure the welfare of vulnerable groups of individuals are well protected and their human rights and dignity preserved. Such guidelines will present considerable challenge to medical researchers in the future but also should be instrumental in avoiding the abuses and exploitation that has occurred in the past (Iacono & Carling-Jenkins, 2012).

EDUCATIONAL PERSPECTIVES

Although nobody can predict with complete accuracy, it is likely that numerous breakthroughs will occur in educational approaches for people with CIDs. Based on the continuous progress made during the past 50 years, we believe that the next 25 years will bode well for people in at least the three following areas:

- Curriculum Access
- Instructional Delivery Methods
- Post-secondary Education

Curriculum Access

Entering the second decade of the 2000s it became clear that remarkable gains were going to be made in opening the general education curriculum to students with CIDs. Parallel to the curriculum opportunities that became available for students with severe disabilities starting in the 1970s, curriculum planning for students with mild to moderate CIDs became a central focus by educators searching for ways to engage them with the Common Core State Standards. Thanks to efforts by Browder, Spooner, and their students and colleagues at the University of North Carolina–Charlotte, and by the proponents of Universal Design for Learning (UDL) (see www.cast.org), the regular academic curriculum became a logical option for most students with severe CIDs.

Approaching the mid-point of the century, special and general educators will build on these successes, and there will be an acceptance that very little, if any, academic curriculum will be considered "off limits" to students because the students have intellectual disabilities. Even students with the most intensive support needs will participate in daily instruction matched to the Common Core State Standards. Improved access to academic curriculum will not solve the age-old dilemma of whether all students *should* work toward common general education standards. The curriculum tool of the future then will become an individual planning device that will help establish the extent of a student's curriculum drawn from CCSS, functional skills needed for current and next likely environments, or from other curriculum packages that promote growth in targeted areas (e.g., employment preparation). Long abandoned for its unmet potential, this "IEP-Type" planning focus will become quite sophisticated in coming generations, and will be linked to allocation of instructional resource.

Fortunately, because instruction will frequently incorporate content from the general education curriculum, most student placements will also be in regular classes. One caveat—educators and families will recognize that large numbers of students *without* disabilities are also in need of individual planning, and many need exposure and instruction to functional curriculum. No longer reserved as a special education placement, community-based instruction will help many students *without* CIDs acquire the skills they need to live, work, and play in inclusive communities. We fully expect to see research reports similar to that in Research Box 13.2.

13.2 RESEARCH THAT WILL MAKE A DIFFERENCE

Coalition for Effective Teaching Releases Results of Multiyear Study

CET researchers released the results of a 25-year study on the impact of different placements on the academic learning and social development of children in these schools. Conducted in 14 states, students rotated classroom placements between mixed-ability classes and homogeneous-ability classes. CET scientists discovered the following:

- Students with intellectual disabilities and other risk factors had the fewest gains in academic or social development variables when they spent their school years in placements with closely matched subjects.
- Students in heterogeneous classes without accommodations and supplemental instruction showed modest gains in academic achievement, and slightly stronger gains in social development.
- When placed in heterogeneous-ability classes and provided with accommodations and supplemental instruction, these students graduated with indistinguishable differences compared to students with no disabilities or risk factors.

The higher-achieving students in the study also showed the impact of placement on learning. Where students in homogeneously precocious classes made the most gains of all students in academic achievement, their social adjustment and life satisfaction ratings plummeted each year they remained in these placements.

Instructional Delivery Methods

Just as past successes in curriculum will drive future curriculum trends, the same progress validating instructional methods will continue into the future. Teachers and other "front-line" professionals who deliver the curriculum have a long, successful history discovering and refining instructional strategies for students with CIDs. Examples of this for students with intermittent supports involves the UDI lesson planning described previously, along with learning strategies, time delay, questioning strategies, and group instruction formats. For students who need more intense supports, examples include graduated prompt systems, visual strategies, and coaching feedback embedded into students' everyday routines.

These teaching strategies and formats will expand as more teachers are expected to make sure that students in their classes show academic growth. Several more generations of school reforms might bring little change for students, but the increased accountability on their teachers will force them to adopt more effective teaching procedures. Teachers several decades from now will be able to deliver instruction that draws from the best that learning theory has to offer, and all the while demonstrate the progress made by the students with direct measures and probes.

Post-secondary Education

Early efforts to provide post-secondary education to individuals with CIDs were a mishmash of programs, with little common agreement on either the purpose or potential of such efforts. Most efforts were an attempt to comply with a law designed to open higher education to people with CIDs; however, there was little consensus on what types of programs might be developed. Some programs were primarily aimed at providing opportunities for social integration with same-aged peers. Others took on the appearance of sheltered workshops, albeit surrounded by the ambiance of a modern college campus.

Like many first-generation efforts, there were many encouraging nuggets spread throughout these programs. Grigal and Hart (2010) provided glimpses into what will likely become best common practices during the next few decades. Some efforts may indeed provide support for adults with CIDs to earn bachelor's degrees, an effort assumed by campus offices for students with other disabilities that are already in place. More likely, post-secondary programs for students with CID will have the following characteristics:

- Curricula with academics needed to promote community inclusion;
- Curriculum to promote supported living;
- Curriculum to promote community employment;
- Certificate programs that are not linked to academic degree programs;
- Application and enrollment procedures that do not rely on SAT, ACT, and other "college-ready" test outcomes;
- Classes that range in credit, and semesters that range in length; and
- Tuition and fees that are self-sustaining, with options to spread multiple certificate programs across many years.

In short, adults with CIDs will have options for college programs that do not exist today. College will be a regular alternative for students when they exit high school. Adults who have not been in school for many years will still be able to look to their local colleges as a source of training and support for community-based employment and living. We anticipate reading about future college options such as the one described in Event Box 13.3.

13.3 EVENT THAT WILL MAKE A DIFFERENCE

Higher Education Coordinating Board Ends Restrictions on College Programs for Adults with Cognitive and Intellectual Disabilities

Colleges and universities will no longer be able to offer only bachelor degree programs and above to students at state-run institutions of higher education. As a result of a Supreme Court ruling, colleges and universities will now have to offer programs with tracks and certificates in functional academics, supported community living, and community employment for individuals with disabilities who are not candidates for traditional academic college degrees. A consortium of advocacy and educational organizations challenged the state's contention that it was not economically feasible to offer post-secondary opportunities to individuals with disabilities who did not pursue traditional college degrees. The coalition had presented its case successfully in lower courts, showing that access to continuing education opportunities increased employability and community participation among adults with disabilities.

SUMMARY CHECKLIST

Philosophical Perspectives

✓ Terminology continues to change, although there appears to be growing consensus for the term *intellectual disabilities* among the strongest professional and advocacy organizations

✓ Many states use a range of other terms to describe people with CIDs in programs and laws

✓ There will likely be future changes in the coming decades

Social Perspectives

✓ There continues to be a tension involving the role of society and the role of the individual with CIDs

✓ Both the individual and society affect each other in ways that are not easy to predict

✓ The level of participation by many individuals with CIDs in the life of their communities remains well below what most consider meaningful

✓ African-American students continue to be overidentified as having CIDs

✓ English Language Learners also are disproportionally identified and placed into special education programs

✓ The disproportionality phenomenon has not been resolved in spite of over 40 years of research and practice

Legal Perspectives

✓ Some legal issues will concern people with CIDs, resulting in groundbreaking events involving liberty, right to treatment, and criminal justice
✓ Legal perspectives also have driven questions involving criminal justice
✓ Legal issues in the coming decade likely will be small and steady pushes by individuals with CIDs, their families, and their advocates to define the parameters of health care, educational access, and supports for community living and employment

Medical Perspectives

✓ Psychiatric and cognitive neuroscience issues are a primary concern for many individuals with CIDs
✓ The nature versus nurture question remains to be addressed in both fundamental and subtle ways
✓ Studies of CIDs in developing countries reveal a prevalence rate similar to the United States
✓ Within developing countries, prevalence rates of CIDs are influenced by income distribution as well as traditional indicators of public health
✓ People with CIDs continue to be a vulnerable population when being recruited by medical researchers

Educational Perspectives

✓ Substantial breakthroughs have been made that open the general education curriculum and the Core Curriculum State Standards to most students with mild to moderate CIDs
✓ Progress is being made at a rapid pace that allows meaningful participation by students with severe CIDs in the CCSS
✓ Access to CCSS and other academic curriculum goals does not resolve the need to decide the ratio of academic versus functional curriculum for each individual student
✓ Teachers are able to deliver instruction based on the best that learning theory has to offer
✓ Early post-secondary education efforts for individuals with CIDs were a mishmash of programs, with little agreement on either the purpose or potential of such efforts
✓ As new options for college programs for adults with CIDs are developed, these individuals will be able to look to their local colleges as a source of training and support for community-based employment and living

ADDITIONAL SUGGESTIONS/RESOURCES

Discussion Questions

1. How might future generations redefine CID to incorporate more emphasis on the interplay between the individual and society?

2. What issues involving the role of the individual in society might be more complex for individuals with CIDs? What issues might be less complex?
3. How might income distribution patterns explain trends in the identification and treatment of CIDs in developing countries? To what extent are these reasons valid in developed countries as well?
4. Are all the next legal questions small ones? What might the next big legal or legislative issue be?

Activities

1. Identify examples of medical research in which individuals with CIDs might be over- and underrepresented in medical experimentation.
2. Develop a summary of educational issues involving children with CIDs in several different countries, with different economic, health, and educational characteristics.
3. Develop a sample curriculum for a 40-year-old man with Down syndrome applying to his local state college to better access his community.

E-source

www.cast.org
Transforming Education through Universal Design for Learning. This website is home to the educational research and development organization that works to expand learning opportunities for all individuals through Universal Design for Learning. UDL tools, lessons, readings, software, and other resources are available.

REFERENCES

Abrahamson v. Hirschman, 701 F.2d 223 (1st Cir. 1983).

Abu-Saad, K., & Fraser, D., (2010). Maternal nutrition and birth outcomes. *Epidemiologic Reviews, 32,* 5–25.

Agran, M., Salzberg, C.L., & Stowitchek, J. (1987). An analysis of the effects of a social skills training program using self-instructions on the acquisition and generalization of two social behaviors in a work setting. *Journal of the Association for Persons with Severe Handicaps, 12,* 131–139.

Agran, M., Snow, K., & Swaner, J. (1999). Teacher perceptions of self-determination: Benefits, characteristics, strategies. *Education and Training in Mental Retardation and Developmental Disabilities, 34,* 293–301.

Alberto, P., Jobs, N., Sizemore, A., & Duran, D. (1980). A comparison of individual and group instruction across response tasks. *Journal of the Association for Persons with Severe Handicaps, 5,* 285–293.

Alberto, P., Sharpton, W., Briggs, A., & Stright, M. (1986). Facilitating task acquisition through the use of a self-operated auditory prompting system. *Journal of the Association for Persons with Severe Handicaps, 11,* 85–91.

Alberto, P.A., Troutman, A.C. (2013). *Applied behavior analysis for teachers* (9th ed.). Upper Saddle River, NJ: Pearson.

Algozzine, B., & Sutherland, J. (1977). The "learning disabilities" label: An experimental analysis. *Contemporary Educational Psychology, 2*(3), 292–297.

Allor, J.H., Mathes, P.G., Roberts, J.K., Cheatham, J.P., & Champlin, T.M. (2010). Comprehensive reading instruction for students with intellectual disabilities: Findings from the first three years of a longitudinal study. *Psychology in the Schools, 47,* 445–466.

Alloway, T.P. (2010). Working memory and executive function profiles of individuals with borderline intellectual functioning. *Journal of Intellectual Disability Research, 54,* 448–456.

American Association on Intellectual and Developmental Disabilities (AAIDD). (2010). *Intellectual disability. Definition, classification, and systems of support* (11th ed.). Washington, DC: Author.

American Association on Intellectual and Developmental Disabilities (AAIDD). (2012). *User's guide. Intellectual disability. Definition, classification, and systems of support* (11th ed.). Washington, DC: Author.

American Association on Mental Retardation. (2002). *Mental retardation: Definition, classification, and systems of support.* Washington, DC: Author.

American Congress of Obstetricians and Gynecologists. (2012). *Facts are important. Prenatal care is important to healthy pregnancies.* http://www.acog.org/~/media/Departments/Government%20Relations%20 and%20Outreach/20120221FactsareImportant.pdf?dmc=1&ts=20140513T1036057451

American Educational Research Association. (1999). *Standards for educational and psychological testing.* Washington, DC: Author.

American Psychiatric Association. (2013). *Diagnostic and statistical manual of mental disorders (DSM-V)* (5th ed.). Washington, DC: Author.

Anastasi, A., & Urbina, S. (1997). *Psychological testing* (7th ed.). New York: MacMillan.

Anderson, L., & Ernst, M. (1994). Self-injury in Lesch-Nyhan disease. *Journal of Autism and Developmental Disorders, 24,* 67–81.

Anderson, L., Lakin, C., Mangan, T., & Prouty, R. (1998). State institutions: Thirty years of depopulation and closure. *Mental Retardation, 36,* 431–443.

Athanasiou, M. (2012). Review of *Battelle Developmental Inventory-Second Edition.* In *Mental measurements yearbook and tests in print.* http://web.a.ebscohost.com/ehost/detail?vid=7&sid=60a5b2d3-cff1-476d-a740-421449524053%40sessionmgr4002&hid=4209&bdata=JmxvZ2luLmFzcCZzaXRlPWVob3N0NLWx pdmU%3d#db=mmt&AN=TIP17023223. Online resource provided by the Board of Regents of the University of Nebraska and the Buros Center for Testing.

Atkins v. Virginia, 536 U.S. 304 (2002).

Baker, B.L., & Blacher, J. (2002). For better or worse? Impact of residential placement on families. *Mental Retardation, 40,* 1–13.

Baker, B.L., Blacher, J., Crnic, K.A., Edelbrock, C. (2002). Behavior problems and parenting stress in families of three-year-old children with and without developmental delays. *American Journal on Mental Retardation, 107,* 433–444.

Baldi, P.L. (1998). Encoding, metacognitive, autoattributional processes and memory in mentally retarded adolescents. *Psychological Reports, 82,* 931–945.

Bambara, L.M., & Kern, L. (2005). *Individualized supports for students with problem behaviors: Designing positive behavior plans.* New York: Guilford Press.

Bambara, L.M., Koger, F., & Bartholomew, A. (2011). Building skills for home and community. In M.E. Snell & F. Brown (Eds.), *Instruction of students with severe disabilities* (7th ed., pp. 529–568). Upper Saddle River, NJ: Pearson.

Bannerman, D.J., Sheldon, J.B., Sherman, J.A., & Harchik, A.E. (1990). Balancing the right to habilitation with the right to personal liberties: The rights of people with developmental disabilities to eat too many doughnuts and take a nap. *Journal of Applied Behavior Analysis, 23,* 79–89.

Baroff, G. (1999). *Mental retardation: Nature, cause, and management* (3rd ed.). Philadelphia: Brunner, Mazel.

Bates, P., Cuvo, T., Miner, C., & Korabek, C. (2001). Simulated and community-based instruction involving persons with mild and moderate mental retardation. *Research in Developmental Disabilities, 22,* 95–115.

Batshaw, M.L., & Lanpher, B. (2013). Inborn errors of metabolism. In M.L. Batshaw, N.J. Roizen, & G.R. Lotrecchiano (Eds.), *Children with disabilities* (7th ed., pp. 319–332). Baltimore: Paul H. Brookes.

Beattie v. Board of Education of the City of Antigo, 169 WIS. 231 (1919).

Beaver, B., & Busse, R. (2000). Informant reports: Conceptual and research bases of interviews with parents and teachers. In E. Shapiro & T. Kratochwill (Eds.), *Behavioral assessment in schools* (2nd ed., pp. 257–287). New York: Guilford Press.

Beech, M. (1999). *Accommodations: Assisting students with disabilities: A guide for educators.* Tallahassee: Florida Department of Education.

Beirne-Smith, M., Ittenbach, R., & Patton, J. (2002). *Mental retardation.* Upper Saddle River, NJ: Merrill/ Prentice Hall.

Bennett, K., Brady, M.P., Scott, J., Dukes, C., & Frain, M. (2010). Effects of covert audio coaching on the job performance of supported employees. *Focus on Autism and Other Developmental Disabilities, 25*(3), 173–185.

Bennett, K., Frain, M., Brady, M.P., Rosenberg, H., & Surinak, T. (2009). Differences between employees' & supervisors' evaluations of work performance and support needs. *Education and Training in Developmental Disabilities, 44*(4), 471–480.

Bernabei, P., Camaioni, L., Paolesse, C., & Longobardi (2002). Translated Title: The communicative-linguistic development in subjects with autism and mental retardation: A study conducted using the Communicative and Linguistic Questionnaire for the Second Year of Life. *Psicoligia Clinica dello Sviluppo, 5,* 169–188.

Best, S.J., & Heller, K.W. (2009). Congenital infectious diseases. In K.W. Heller, P.E. Forney, P.A. Alberto, S.J. Best, & M.N. Schwartzman (Eds.), *Understanding physical, sensory, and health disabilities* (2nd ed., pp. 387–398). Upper Saddle River, NJ: Pearson.

Biasini, F., Grupe, L., Huffman, L., & Bray, N. (2002). Mental retardation: A symptom and syndrome. In S. Netherton, D. Holmes, & C. Walker (Eds.), *Child and adolescent psychological disorders: A comprehensive textbook.* New York: Oxford University Press.

Bigby, C., & Fyffe, C. (2009). Position statement on housing and support for people with severe or profound intellectual disability. *Journal of Intellectual & Developmental Disability, 34,* 96–100.

Binder, C. (1996). Behavioral fluency: Evolution of a new paradigm. *The Behavior Analyst, 19,* 163–197.

Birenbaum, A. (2002). Poverty, welfare reform, and disproportionate rates of disability among children. *Mental Retardation, 40,* 212–218.

Blacher, J. (2001). Transition to adulthood: Mental retardation, families, and culture. *American Journal on Mental Retardation, 106,* 173–188.

Black, R. E., Allen, L. H., Bhutta, Z. A., Caulfed, L. E., de Onis, M., Ezzat, M., Mathers, C., & Rivera, J. (2008). Maternal and child undernutrition: Global and regional exposures and health consequences. *The Lancet, 371,* 243–260.

Black, R., & Salas, B. (2001, May 30). *Forty years of progress: Where have we been? Where are we now?* Paper presented at the Annual Meeting of the American Association on Mental Retardation, Denver, CO.

Blanck, P. D. (1998). *The Americans with Disabilities Act and the emerging workforce—Employment of people with mental retardation.* Washington, DC: American Association on Mental Retardation.

Blankenship, C. (1985). Using curriculum-based assessment data to make instructional decisions. *Exceptional Children, 52,* 233–238.

Blanton, L., Blanton, W., & Cross, L. (1994). An exploratory study of how general and special education teachers think and make instructional decisions about students with special needs. *Teacher Education and Special Education, 17,* 62–73.

Blanton, R. (1975). Historical perspectives on classification of mental retardation. In N. Hobbs (Ed.), *Issues in the classification of children* (Vol. 1, pp. 164–193). San Francisco: Jossey-Bass.

Blatt, B., & Kaplan, F. (1966). *Christmas in Purgatory: A photographic essay on mental retardation.* Boston: Allyn & Bacon.

Boan, C., & Harrison, P. (1997). Adaptive behavior assessment and individuals with mental retardation. In R. Taylor (Ed.), *Assessment of individuals with mental retardation* (pp. 33–54). San Diego: Singular Publishing Group.

Board of Education of the Henry Hudson Central School District v. Rowley, 458 U.S. 176 (1982).

Bonnaud, C., Jamet, F., Deret, D., & Neyt-Dumesnil, C. (1999). Translated Title: Recognition of human faces with adults with severe mental retardation. *Revue Francophone de la Deficience Intellectuelle, 10,* 5–17.

Bonner, M. (2012). Review of *Kaufman Test of Educational Achievement-Second Edition, Comprehensive Form.* In *Mental measurements yearbook and tests in print.* http://web.a.ebscohost.com/ehost/detail?vid=9&sid=60a5b2d3-cff1-476d-a740-421449524053%40sessionmgr4002&hid=4209&bdata=JmxvZ2luLmFzcCZzaXRlPWVob3N0 LWxpdmU%3d#db=mmt&AN=TIP07001349. Online resource provided by the Board of Regents of the University of Nebraska and the Buros Center for Testing.

Boot, F. H., Pel, J. J. M., Evenhuis, H. M., & van der Steen, J. (2012). Factors related to impaired visual orienting behavior in children with intellectual disabilities. *Research in Developmental Disabilities, 33,* 1670–1676.

Borkowski, J., & Day, I. (1987). *Cognition in special children: Comparative approaches to retardation, learning disabilities and giftedness.* Norwood, NJ: Ablex.

Boschwitz (1988). EHLR 213:215.

Bouck, E. C. (2012). Secondary students with moderate/severe intellectual disability: Considerations of curriculum and post-school outcomes for the National Longitudinal Transition Study-2. *Journal of Intellectual Disability Research, 56,* 1175–1186.

Bouck, E. C. (2013). High stakes? Considering students with mild intellectual disability in accountability systems. *Education and Training in Autism and Developmental Disabilities, 48,* 320–331.

Braaten, S., Kauffman, J., Braaten, B., Polsgrove, L., & Nelson, C. M. (1988). The regular Education Initiative: Patient medicine for behavioral disorders. *Exceptional Children, 55,* 21–27.

Braddock, D. (2002). *Disability at the dawn of the 21st century and the state of the states.* Washington, DC: American Association on Mental Retardation.

Braddock, D., Hemp, R., Rizzolo, M. C., Haffer, L., Tanis, .S., & Wu, J. (2011). *The state of the states in developmental disabilities 2011.* Boulder, CO: University of Colorado.

Brady, M. P. (2013). Plastics, standards, and the need to return to individualized planning: A commentary on "Educational Standards for Students with Significant Intellectual Disabilities." *TASH Connections, 38*(4), 20–23.

Brady, M. P., & Cunningham, J. (1985). Living and learning in segregated environments: An ethnography of normalization outcomes. *Education and Training of the Mentally Retarded, 20,* 241–252.

Brady, M. P., Duffy, M. L., Hazelkorn, M., & Bucholz, J. (2014). Policy and systems change: Planning for unintended consequences. *The Clearing House: A Journal of Educational Strategies, Issues, and Ideas 87,* 102–109.

Brady, M. P., Frain, M., Duffy, M. L., & Bucholz, J. (2010). Evaluating work performance and support needs in supported employment training programs: Correspondence between teachers' ratings and students' self ratings. *Journal of Rehabilitation, 76*(3), 24–31.

Brady, M.P., Hunter, D., & Campbell, P. (1997). Why so much confusion? Debating and creating inclusive schools. *Educational Forum, 61,* 240–246.

Brady, M.P., McDougall, D., & Dennis, H.F. (1989). The courts, schools and integration of students with severe handicaps. *Journal of Special Education, 23*(1), 43–58.

Brady, M.P., & Rosenberg, H. (2002). Job Observation and Behavior Scale: A supported employment assessment instrument. *Education and Training in Mental Retardation and Developmental Disabilities, 37,* 427–433.

Brady, M.P., Rosenberg, H., & Frain, M. (2006). *Job Observation and Behavior Scale: Opportunity for Self Determination (JOBS: OSD).* Wood Dale, IL: Stoelting.

Brady, M.P., Rosenberg, H., & Frain, M. (2008). A self-evaluation instrument for work performance and support needs. *Career Development for Exceptional Individuals, 31*(3), 175–185.

Brigance, A. (1977). *Brigance Inventory of Basic Skills.* North Billerica, MA: Curriculum Associates.

Brigance, A. (1981). *Brigance Diagnostic Inventory of Essential Skills.* North Billerica, MA: Curriculum Associates.

Brigance, A. (1994). *Brigance Diagnostic Life Skills Inventory.* North Billerica, MA: Curriculum Associates.

Brigance, A. (1995). *Brigance Diagnostic Employability Skills Inventory.* North Billerica, MA: Curriculum Associates.

Brigance, A., & Glascoe, F. (1999). *Brigance Diagnostic Inventory of Basic Skills—Revised.* North Billerica, MA: Curriculum Associates.

Briggs v. Connecticut Board of Education, et al. D. Conn (1988) EHLR 441:418.

Brolin, D.E. (2004). *Life-centered career education: A competency-based approach.* Reston, VA: Council for Exceptional Children.

Browder, D.M., Ahlgrim-Delzell, L., Spooner, F., Mims, P.J., & Baker, J. (2009). Using time delay to teach literacy to students with severe developmental disabilities. *Exceptional Children, 75,* 343–364.

Browder, D.M., Cooper, K.J., & Levan, L. (1998). Teaching adults with severe disabilities to express their choice of settings for leisure activities. *Education and Training in Mental Retardation and Developmental Disabilities, 33,* 228–238.

Browder, D.M., & Lalli, J.S. (1991). Review of research on sight word instruction. *Research in Developmental Disabilities, 12,* 203–228.

Browder, D.M., Spooner, F., Ahlgrim-Delzell, L., Harris, A., & Wakeman, S. (2008). A meta-analysis on teaching mathematics to students with significant cognitive disabilities. *Exceptional Children, 74,* 407–432.

Browder, D.M., Spooner, F., Wakeman, S., Trela, K., & Baker, J.N. (2006). Aligning instruction with academic content standards: Finding the link. *Research and Practice for Persons with Severe Disabilities, 31,* 309–321.

Browder, D.M., Trela, K., Courtade, G.R., Jimenez, B.A., Knight, V., & Flowers, C. (2012). Teaching mathematics and science standards to students with moderate and severe developmental disabilities. *Journal of Special Education, 46,* 26–35.

Browder, D.M., Trela, K., & Jimenez, B.A. (2007). Training teachers to follow a task analysis to engage middle school students with moderate and severe developmental disabilities in grade-appropriate literature. *Focus on Autism and Other Developmental Disabilities, 22,* 206–219.

Browder, D.M., & Xin, Y.P. (1998). A meta-analysis and review of sight word research and its implications for teaching functional reading to individuals with moderate to severe disabilities. *Journal of Special Education, 32,* 130–153.

Brown v. Board of Education of Topeka, Kansas, 347 U.S. 483 (1954).

Brown, L. (2013). Educational standards for students with significant intellectual disabilities. *TASH Connections, 38*(4), 7–19.

Brown, L., Branston, M.B., Hamre-Nietupski, S., Pumpian, N., Certo, N., & Gruenewald, L. (1979). A strategy for developing chronological age-appropriate and functional curricular content for severely handicapped adolescents and young adults. *Journal of Special Education, 13*(1), 81–90.

Brown, L., Nietupski, J., & Hamre-Nietupski, S. (1976). The criterion of ultimate functioning and public school services for the severely handicapped student. In M.A. Thomas (Ed.), *Hey, don't forget about me! Education's investment in the severely, profoundly, multiply handicapped* (pp. 2–15). Reston, VA: Council for Exceptional Children.

Brown, R., & Hoadley, S. (1999). Rett syndrome. In S. Goldstein & C. Reynolds (Eds.), *Handbook of neurodevelopmental and genetic disorders in children* (pp. 458–477). New York: Guilford Press.

Bruininks, R., Woodcock, R., & Weatherman, R., & Hill, B. (1996). *Scales of Independent Behavior-Revised.* Chicago: Riverside.

Bryant, B. (1997). Intelligence testing. In R. Taylor (Ed.), *Assessment of individuals with mental retardation* (pp. 13–32). San Diego: Singular Publishing Group.

Bucholz, J., & Brady, M.P. (2008). Teaching positive work behaviors with Literacy-Based Behavioral Interventions: An intervention for students and employees with developmental disabilities. *Teaching Exceptional Children, 41*(2), 50–55.

Buck v. Bell, 274 U.S. 200 (1927).

Bugaj, A.M. (2012). Review of *Wide Range Interest and Occupation Test-Second Edition*. In *Mental measurements yearbook and tests in print*. http://web.a.ebscohost.com/ehost/detail?vid=11&sid=60a5b2d3-cff1-476d-a740-421449524053%40sessionmgr4002&hid=4209&bdata=JmxvZ2luLmFzcCZzaXRlPWVVob3N0OLWxpdmU%3d#db=mmt&AN=TIP07002779. Online resource provided by the Board of Regents of the University of Nebraska and the Buros Center for Testing.

Burack, J.A., Evans, D.W., Klaiman, C., & Iarocci, G. (2001). The mysterious myth of attention deficits and other defect stories: Contemporary issues in the developmental approach to mental retardation. In L.M. Glidden (Ed.), *International review of research in mental retardation* (Vol. 24, pp. 299–320). San Diego, CA: Academic Press.

Burham v. Georgia (1972). Civil Action No. 16385.

Bushaw, W.J., & Lopez, S.J. (2012). Public education in the United States: A nation divided. The 44th Annual Phi Delta Kappa/Gallup Poll of the public's attitudes toward the public schools. *Phi Delta Kappan, 94*(1), 9–25.

Butterworth, J. (2002). From programs to support. In R. Schalock, P. Baker, & M.D. Croser (Eds.), *Embarking on a new century* (pp. 83–100). Washington, DC: American Association on Mental Retardation.

Butterworth, J., Steere, D.E., & Whitney-Thomas, J. (1997). Using person-centered planning to address personal quality of life. In R.L. Schalock (Ed.), *Quality of life, Vol. 2: Application to persons with disabilities* (pp. 5–24). Washington, DC: American Association on Mental Retardation.

Byrne, P. (2000). *Philosophical and ethical problems in mental handicap*. New York: St. Martin's Press.

Caldwell, M.L., & Taylor, R. (1983). A clinical note on food preference of individuals with Prader-Willi syndrome: The need for empirical research. *Journal of Mental Deficiency Research, 27*, 45–49.

Calik, N.C., & Kargin, T. (2010). Effectiveness of the touch math technique in teaching addition skills to students with intellectual disabilities. *International Journal of Special Education, 25*, 195–204.

Cambridge, P., Beadle-Brown, J., Milne, A., Mansell, J., & Whelton, B. (2011). Patterns of risk in adult protection referrals for sexual abuse and people with intellectual disability. *Journal of Applied Research in Intellectual Disabilities, 24*, 118–132.

Campbell, P., Campbell, C.R., &. Brady, M.P. (1998). Team Environmental Assessment Mapping System (TEAMS): A method for selecting curriculum goals for students with disabilities. *Education and Training in Mental Retardation and Developmental Disabilities, 33*, 264–272.

Cardoso-Martins, C., Mervis, C.B., & Mervis, C.A. (1985). Early vocabulary by children with Down syndrome. *American Journal of Mental Deficiency, 90*, 177–184.

Carlberg, C., & Kavale, K.A. (1980). The efficacy of special versus regular class placement for exceptional children: A meta-analysis. *Journal of Special Education, 14*, 295–309.

Carlson, J.V. (2012). Review of *Brigance Diagnostic Employability Skills Inventory*. In *Mental measurements yearbook and tests in print*. http://web.a.ebscohost.com/ehost/detail?vid=13&sid=60a5b2d3-cff1-476d-a740-421449524053%40sessionmgr4002&hid=4209&bdata=JmxvZ2luLmFzcCZzaXRlPWVVob3N0OLWxpdmU%3d#db=mmt&AN=TIP07000352. Online resource provided by the Board of Regents of the University of Nebraska and the Buros Center for Testing.

Carr, E., & Durand, M. (1985). Reducing behavioral problems through functional communication training. *Journal of Applied Behavioral Analysis, 18*, 111–126.

Carroll, J. (1993). *Human cognitive abilities: A survey of factor analytic studies*. New York: Cambridge University Press.

Carter, D.R., & Horner, R.H. (2007). Adding functional behavioral assessment to First Step to Success: A case study. *Journal of Positive Behavior Interventions, 9*, 229–238.

Carter, E.W., Austin, D., & Trainor, A.A. (2012). Predictors of postschool employment outcomes for young adults with severe disabilities. *Journal of Disability Policy Studies, 23*, 50–63.

Carter, E.W., & Hughes, C. (2005). Increasing social interaction among adolescents with intellectual disabilities and their general education peers: Effective interventions. *Research and Practice for Persons with Severe Disabilities, 30*, 179–193.

Carter, E.W., Sisco, L.G., Melekoglu, M.A., & Kurkowski, C. (2007). Peer supports as an alternative to individually assigned paraprofessionals in inclusive high school classrooms. *Research and Practice for Persons with Severe Disabilities, 32*, 213–227.

Cascella, P. W. (2006). Standardized speech-language tests and students with intellectual disability: A review of normative data. *Journal of Intellectual & Developmental Disability, 31,* 120–124.

Casto, G., & Mastropieri, M. A. (1986). The efficacy of early intervention programs: A meta-analysis. *Exceptional Children, 52,* 417–424.

Catlett, S. (1998). *Becoming an inclusive school: A predictable venture.* Unpublished doctoral dissertation, University of Houston, Houston.

Cattell, J. M. (1890). Mental tests and measurements. *Mind, 15,* 373–381.

Cattell, R. (1941). Some theoretical issues in adult intelligence testing. *Psychological Bulletin, 38,* 592.

Cattell, R. (1943). The measurement of adult intelligence. *Psychological Bulletin, 40,* 153–193.

Cedar Rapids Community School District v. Garret F., 119 S. Ct. 992 (1999).

Centers for Disease Control and Prevention. (2011). *Radiation and pregnancy: A fact sheet for the public.* Retrieved from www.cdc.gov

Centers for Disease Control and Prevention. (2012). *Preventing major birth defects associated with maternal risk factors.* Retrieved from www.cdc.gov

Centers for Disease Control and Prevention. (2013). *Tobacco use and pregnancy.* Retrieved from www.cdc.gov

Chadsey, J., & Sheldon, D. (2002). Social life. In K. Storey, P. Bates, & D. Hunter (Eds.), *The road ahead: Transition to adult life for persons with disabilities* (pp. 137–155). St. Augustine, FL: Training Resource Network.

Chandler, L. K., & Dahlquist, C. M. (2002). *Functional assessment: Strategies to prevent and remediate challenging behavior in school settings.* Upper Saddle River, NJ: Merrill/Prentice Hall.

Chapman, D. A., Scott, K. G., & Mason, C. A. (2002). Early risk factors for mental retardation: Role of maternal age and maternal education. *American Journal of Mental Retardation, 107,* 46–59.

Chapman, D. A., Scott, K. G., & Stanton-Chapman, T. L. (2008). Public health approach to the study of mental retardation. *American Journal on Intellectual and Developmental Disabilities, 113*(2), 102–116.

Chapman, R., & Hesketh, L. (2000). Behavioral phenotype of individuals with Down syndrome. *Mental Retardation and Developmental Disabilities Research Review, 6,* 84–95.

Child Trends Data Bank. (2012). *Late or no prenatal care.* Retrieved from www.childtrendsdatabank.org

Chung, Y.-C., & Carter, E. W. (2013). Promoting peer interactions in inclusive classrooms for students who use speech-generating devices. *Research and Practice for Persons with Severe Disabilities, 38,* 94–109.

Chung, Y.-C., Carter, E. W., & Sisco, L. G. (2012). A systematic review of interventions to increase peer interactions for students with complex communication challenges. *Research and Practice for Persons with Severe Disabilities, 37,* 271–287.

Cicirelli, V. (Ed.). (1969). *The impact of Head Start: An evaluation of the effects of Head Start on children's cognitive and affective development.* Washington, DC: National Bureau of Standards, Institute for Applied Technology.

Cihak, D., Alberto, P. A., Taber-Doughty, T., & Gama, R. I. (2006). A comparison of static picture prompting and video prompting simulation strategies using group instruction procedures. *Focus on Autism and Other Developmental Disabilities, 21,* 89–99.

Cipani, E. C., & Spooner, F. (1994). *Curricular and instructional approaches for persons with severe disabilities.* Boston: Allyn & Bacon.

Cizek, G. J. (2012). Review of *Brigance Diagnostic Comprehensive Inventory of Basic Skills-Revised.* In *Mental measurements yearbook and tests in print.* http://web.a.ebscohost.com/ehost/detail?vid=13&sid=60a5b2d3-cff1-476d-a740-421449524053%40sessionmgr4002&hid=4209&bdata=JmxvZ2luLmFzcCZzaXRlPWVo b3N0LWxpdmU%3d#db=mmt&AN=TIP07000351. Online resource provided by the Board of Regents of the University of Nebraska and the Buros Center for Testing.

Clarke, D., & Marston, G. (2000). Problem behaviors associated with 15q- Angelman syndrome. *American Journal on Mental Deficiency, 105,* 25–31.

Cleburne Living Center Inc. v. City of Cleburne, Texas, 735 F.2d 832 (5th Cir. 1985).

Colvin, G., & Sugai, G. (1988). Proactive strategies for managing social behavior problems: An instructional approach. *Education and Treatment of Children, 11,* 341–348.

Conners, F. A. (1992). Reading instruction for students with moderate mental retardation: Review and analysis of research. *American Journal on Mental Retardation, 96,* 577–597.

Connors, F. A., Rosenquist, C. J., Arnett, L., Moore, M. S., & Hume, L. E. (2008). Improving memory span in children with Down syndrome. *Journal of Intellectual Disability Research, 52,* 244–255.

Conolly, J. (1845). Notice of the lunatic asylums of Paris. *British and Foreign Medical Review, January,* 281–298.

Conroy, J. W. (1997). The small ICF/MR program: Dimensions of quality and cost. *Mental Retardation, 34,* 13–26.

Cooper, J. O., Heron, T. E., & Heward, W. L. (2007). *Applied behavior analysis* (2nd ed.). Columbus, OH: Merrill.

Cosmetic Surgery for People with Down Syndrome (n.d.). http://www.ndss.org/About-NDSS/Media-Kit/Position-Papers/Cosmetic-Surgery-for-Children-with-Down-Syndrome/

Coulter, D.L. (1992). An ecology of prevention for the future. *Mental Retardation, 30*(6), 363–369.

Coutinho, M.J., & Oswald, D.P. (2000). Disproportionate representation in special education: A synthesis and recommendations. *Journal of Child and Family Studies, 9,* 135–156.

Cramm, J.N., & Nieboer, A.P. (2012). Longitudinal study of parents' impact on quality of life of children and young adults with intellectual disabilities. *Journal of Applied Research in Intellectual Disabilities, 25,* 20–28.

Crane, L. (2002). *Mental Retardation: A community integration approach.* Belmont, CA: Wadsworth/Thomson Learning.

Crawford v. Honig. United States District Court. C-89-0014 DLU. (1990).

Daniels, H. (2001). *Vygotsky and pedagogy.* New York: Routledge Falmer.

Danielson, L., & Bellamy, G.T. (1989). State variation in placement of children with handicaps in segregated environments. *Exceptional Children, 55,* 448–455.

Danielsson, H., Henry, L, Messer, D., & Ronnberg, J. (2012). Strengths and weaknesses in executive functioning in children with intellectual disability. *Research in Developmental Disabilities, 33,* 600–607.

Das, J. (1973). Structure of cognitive abilities: Evidence for simultaneous and successive processing. *Journal of Educational Psychology, 65,*103–108.

Davis, C., Brady, M.P., Williams, R.E., & Burta, M. (1992). The effects of self-operated auditory prompting tapes on the performance fluency of persons with severe mental retardation. *Education and Training in Mental Retardation, 27,* 39–49.

Denning, C., Chamberlain, J., & Polloway, E. (2000). An evaluation of state guidelines for mental retardation: Focus on definition and classification practices. *Education and Training in Mental Retardation and Developmental Disabilities, 35,* 226–232.

Deno, E. (1970). Special education as developmental capital. *Exceptional Children, 37,* 229–237.

Deno, S. (1985). Curriculum-based measurement: The emerging alternative. *Exceptional Children, 52,* 219–232.

Dettmer, P., Knackendoffel, A., & Thurston, L.P. (2013). *Collaboration, consultation and teamwork for students with special needs* (7th ed.). Boston: Pearson.

Deutsch, C.K., Dube, W.V., & McIlvane, W.J. (2008). Attention deficits, attention-deficit hyperactivity disorder, and intellectual disabilities. *Developmental Disabilities Research Reviews, 14,* 285–292.

Devine, M.A., & Lashua, B. (2002). Constructing social acceptance in inclusive leisure contexts: The role of individuals with disabilities. *Therapeutic Recreation Journal, 36,* 65–83.

Diana v. State Board of Education, Civ. Act. No. C-70-37 (N.D. Cal. 1970).

Dijker, A., van Alphen, L., Bos, A., van den Borne, B., & Curfs, L. (2011). Social integration of people with intellectual disability: Insights from a social psychological research programme. *Journal of Intellectual Disability Research, 55,* 885–894.

Dinerstein, R.D. (1999) Introduction. In R.D. Dinerstein, S.S. Herr, & J.L. O'Sullivan (Eds.), *A guide to consent* (pp. 1–5). Washington, DC: American Association on Mental Retardation.

Doe v. Withers, 92-C-92 (1993).

Doll, B., & Jones, K. (2012). Review of *Social Skills Improvement System Rating Scales.* In *Mental measurements yearbook and tests in print.* http://web.a.ebscohost.com/ehost/detail?vid=15&sid=60a5b2d3-cff1-476d-a740-421449524053%40sessionmgr4002&hid=4209&bdata=JmxvZ2luLmFzcCZzaXRlPWVhob3N0LWx pdmU%3d#db=mmt&AN=TIP18193589. Online resource provided by the Board of Regents of the University of Nebraska and the Buros Center for Testing.

Doll, E. (1935). A genetic scale of social maturity. *American Journal of Orthopsychiatry, 5,* 180–190.

Doll, E.A. (1936). Current thoughts on mental deficiency. *Proceedings and Addresses of the American Association on Mental Deficiency, 41,* 33–49.

Doll, E. (1941). The essentials of an inclusive concept of mental deficiency. *American Journal of Mental Deficiency, 46,* 214–219.

Domino, G., & McGarty, M. (1972). Personal and work adjustment of young retarded women. *American Journal of Mental Deficiency, 77,* 314–321.

Dugdale, R. (1877). *The Jukes: A study in crime, pauperism, disease, and heredity.* New York: G.P. Putnam. (Reprinted by Arno Press 1970).

Dukes, E., & McGuire, B.E. (2009). Enhancing capacity to make sexuality-related decisions in people with an intellectual disability. *Journal of Intellectual Disability Research, 53,* 727–734.

Dunn, L.M. (1968). Special education for the mildly retarded: Is much of it justifiable? *Exceptional Children, 35,* 5–22.

Dunn, L., & Dunn, L. (2007). *Peabody Picture Vocabulary Test – IV.* Circle Pines, MN: American Guidance Service.

Dusseljee, J.C.E., Rijken, P.M., Cardol, M., Curfs, L.M.G., & Groenewegen, P.P. (2011). Participation in day-time activities among people with mild or moderate intellectual disability. *Journal of Intellectual Disability Research, 55,* 4–18.

Duvdevany, I. (2002). Self-concept and adaptive behaviour of people with intellectual disability in integrated and segregated recreation activities. *Journal of Intellectual Disability Research, 46,* 419–429.

Dykens, E., & Cassidy, S. (1999). Prader-Willi syndrome. In S. Goldstein & C. Reynolds (Eds.), *Handbook of neurodevelopmental and genetic disorders in children* (pp. 525–554). New York: Guilford Press.

Edgar, E. (1987). Secondary programs in special education: Are many of them justifiable? *Exceptional Children, 53,* 555–561.

Ellis, J.W. (2013). The law's understanding of intellectual disability as a disability. *Intellectual and Developmental Disabilities, 51*(2), 102–107.

Emerson, E., Hatton, C., Llewellyn, G., Blacker, J., & Graham, H. (2006). Socio-economic position, household composition, health status and indicators of the well-being of mothers of children with and without intellectual disabilities. *Journal of Intellectual Disability Research, 50,* 862–873.

Emerson, E., Hatton, C., Robertson, J., Henderson, D., & Cooper, J. (1999). A descriptive analysis of the relationships between social context, engagement, and stereotypy in residential services for people with severe and complex disabilities. *Journal of Applied Research in Intellectual Disabilities, 12,* 11–29.

Espe-Sherwindt, M., & Crable, S. (1993). Parents with mental retardation: Moving beyond the myths. *Topics in Early Childhood Special Education, 13,* 154–174.

Esquirol, J. (1845). *Mental maladies.* (E.K. Hunt, trans). Philadelphia: Lea & Blanchard.

Estabook, A. (1916). *The Jukes in 1915.* Washington, DC: Carnegie Institute.

Everman, D., & Cassidy, S. (2000). Genetics of childhood disorders: XII. Genetic imprinting: Breaking the rules. *Journal of the American Academy of Child and Adolescent Psychiatry, 39,* 386–389.

Everson, J.M., & Zhang, D. (2000). Person-centered planning: Characteristics, inhibitors, and supports. *Education and Training in Mental Retardation and Developmental Disabilities, 35,* 36–43.

Falvey, M.F. (1989). *Community based curriculum.* Baltimore: Paul H. Brookes.

Farber, B. (1968). *Mental retardation. Its social context and social consequences.* Boston: Houghton Mifflin.

Farr, R., & Tone, B. (1994). *Portfolio and performance assessment: Helping students evaluate their progress as readers and writers.* Fort Worth, TX: Harcourt Brace.

Faust, H., & Scior, K. (2008). Mental health problems in young people with intellectual disabilities: The impact on parents. *Journal of Applied Research in Intellectual Disabilities, 21,* 414–424.

Feldman, M.A., & Walton-Allen, N. (1997). Effects of maternal mental retardation and poverty on intellectual, academic, and behavioral status of school-age children. *American Journal on Mental Retardation, 101,* 352–364.

Field, M., & Sanchez, V. (1999). *Equal treatment for people with mental retardation: Having and raising children.* Cambridge, MA: Harvard University Press.

Fisher, D., Sax, C., & Pumpian, I. (1999). *Inclusive high schools: Learning from contemporary classrooms.* Baltimore: Paul H. Brookes.

Fitzgerald, B., Morgan, J., Keene, N., Rollinson, R., Hodgson, A., & Dalrymple-Smith, J. (2000). An investigation into diet treatment for adults with previously untreated phenylketonuria and severe intellectual disability. *Journal of Intellectual Disability Research, 44,* 53–59.

Flaugher, R. (1978). The many definitions of test bias. *American Psychologist, 33,* 671–679.

Flexer, R.W., Simmons, T.J., Luft, P., & Baer R.M. (Eds.). (2001). *Transition planning for secondary students with disabilities.* Columbus, OH: Merrill/Prentice Hall.

Ford, M., Acosta, A., & Sutcliffe, T.J. (2013). Beyond terminology: The policy impact of a grassroots movement. *Intellectual and Developmental Disabilities, 51*(2), 108–112.

Forness, S.R., Kavale, K.A., Blum, I.M., & Lloyd, J.W. (1997). Mega-analysis of meta-analysis: What works in special education and related services. *Teaching Exceptional Children, 29,* 4–9.

Fowler, A.E. (1998). Language in mental retardation: Associations with and dissociations from general cognition. In J.A. Burack, R.M. Hodapp et al. (Eds.), *Handbook of mental retardation and development,* pp. 290–333. New York: Cambridge University Press.

Fraser, D.W. (2013). 5 tips for creating independent activities aligned with Common Core State Standards. *Teaching Exceptional Children, 45*(6), 6–15.

FRAXA Research Foundation. (2000). *About Fragile X.* Retrieved from www.fraxa.org/html/about_treatment.htm

Frisby, C., & Braden, J. (1992). Feuerstein's dynamic assessment approach: A semantic, logical, and empirical critique. *Journal of Special Education, 26,* 281–301.

Fryxell, D., & Kennedy, C.H. (1995). Placement along the continuum of services and its impact on students' social relationships. *Journal of the Association for Persons with Severe Handicaps, 20,* 259–269.

Fuchs, L., & Fuchs, D. (2000). Analogue assessment of academic skills: Curriculum-based measurement and performance assessment. In E. Shapiro & T. Kratochwill (Eds.), *Behavioral assessment in schools* (2nd ed., pp. 168–201). New York: Guilford Press.

Fujiura, G.T., & Yamaki, K. (2000). Trends in demography of childhood poverty and disability. *Exceptional Children, 66,* 187–199.

Furniss, F., & Biswas, A.B. (2012). Recent research on aetiology, development and phenomenology of self-injurious behavior in people with intellectual disabilities: A systematic review and implications for treatment. *Journal of Intellectual Disability Research, 56,* 453–475.

Gaitatzes, C., Chang, T., & Baumgart, S. (2013). The first weeks of life. In M.L. Batshaw, N.J. Roizen, & G.R. Lotrecchiano (Eds.), *Children with disabilities* (7th ed., pp. 73–85). Baltimore: Paul H. Brookes.

Galston, I. (1950). The psychiatry of Paracelsus. *Bulletin of the History of Medicine, 24,* 205–218.

Garber, H.L. (1988). *The Milwaukee Project. Preventing mental retardation in children at risk.* Washington, DC: American Association on Mental Retardation.

Gast, D., Wellons, J., & Collins, B. (1994). Home and community safety skills. In M. Agran, N. Marchand-Martella, & R. Martella (Eds.), *Promoting health and safety: Skills for independent living* (pp. 11–32). Baltimore: Paul H. Brookes.

Gaylord-Ross, R., & Holvoet, J. (1985). *Strategies for educating students with severe handicaps.* Boston: Little, Brown.

Gaylord-Ross, R., Haring, T., Breen, C., & Pitts-Conway, V. (1984). The training and generalization of social interaction skills with autistic youth. *Journal of Applied Behavior Analysis, 17,* 229–247.

Geisthardt, C.L., Brotherson, M.J., & Cook, C.C. (2002). Friendships of children with disabilities in the home environment. *Education and Training in Mental Retardation and Developmental Disabilities, 37,* 235–252.

Gersten, R., & Baker, S. (2000). What we know about effective instructional practices for English language learners. *Exceptional Children, 66,* 454–470.

Gersten, R., Carnine, D., & Woodward, J. (1987). Direct Instruction research: The third decade. *Remedial and Special Education, 8*(6), 48–56.

Gill, S.K., Broussard, C., Devine, O., Green, R.F., Rasmussen, S.A., & Reefhuis, J. (2012). Association between maternal age and birth defects of unknown etiology: United States, 1997–2007. *Birth Defects Research Part A: Clinical and Molecular Teratology, 94,* 1010–1018. doi: 10.1002/bdra.23049

Gilmore, L., & Cuskelly, M. (2009). A longitudinal study of motivation and competence in children with Down syndrome: Early childhood to early adolescence. *Journal of Intellectual Disability Research, 53,* 484–492.

Giordani, I. (1961). *St. Vincent de Paul.* Milwaukee: Bruce Publishing Co.

Glass, G.V. (1983). Effectiveness of special education. *Policy Studies Review, 2,* 65–78.

Glutting, J.J., & Wilkinson, G.S. (2003). *Wide Range Interest and Occupation Test-Second Edition.* San Antonio, TX: Pearson.

Goddard, H. (1912). *The Kallikak Family: A Study in the Heredity of Feeblemindedness.* New York: Macmillan.

Gold, M. (1976). Task analysis of a complex assembly task by the retarded blind. *Exceptional Children, 43,* 78–84.

Gold, M.E., & Richards, H. (2012). To label or not to label: The special education question for African Americans. *Educational Foundations, 26*(1–2), 143–156.

Goldstein, S., Strickland, B., Turnbull, A.P., & Curry, L. (1980). An observational analysis of the IEP conference. *Exceptional Children, 46,* 278–286.

Goodman, J.I., Hazelkorn, M., Bucholz, J.L., Duffy, M.L., & Kitta, Y. (2011). Inclusion and graduation rates: What are the outcomes? *Journal of Disability Policy Studies, 21,* 241–252.

Gordon, L. (1981). *Gordon Occupational Checklists-2.* San Antonio, TX: Psychological Corporation.

Graham, E.M., & Morgan, M.A. (1997). Growth before birth. In M.L. Batshaw (Ed.), *Children with disabilities* (4th ed., pp. 53–69). Baltimore: Paul H. Brookes.

Graham, T. (2012). Review of *Vulpé Assessment Battery-Revised.* In *Mental measurements yearbook and tests in print.* http://web.a.ebscohost.com/ehost/detail?vid=17&sid=60a5b2d3-cff1-476d-a740-421449524053%40sessionmgr4002&hid=4209&bdata=JmxvZ2luLmFzcCZzaXRlPWVob3N0LWxpdmU%3d#db=mmt&AN=TIP07002730. Online resource provided by the Board of Regents of the University of Nebraska and the Buros Center for Testing.

Green, S. K., & Shinn, M. R. (1994). Parent attitudes about special education and reintegration: What is the role of student outcomes? *Exceptional Children, 61,* 269–281.

Greenen, S., Powers, L. E., & Lopez-Vasquez, A. (2001). Multicultural aspects of parent involvement in transition planning. *Exceptional Children, 67,* 265–282.

Gresham, F., & Elliott, S. (2008). *Social Skills Rating System.* Circle Pines, MN: American Guidance Service.

Grigal, M., & Hart, D. (2010). *Think College! Postsecondary education options for students with intellectual disabilities.* Baltimore: Paul H. Brookes.

Grigal, M., Hart, D., & Weir, C. (2012). A survey of postsecondary education programs for students with intellectual disabilities in the United States. *Journal of Policy and Practice in Intellectual Disabilities, 9,* 223–233.

Grissom, M. O'K., & Borkowski, J. G. (2002). Self-efficacy in adolescents who have siblings with or without disabilities. *American Journal on Mental Retardation, 107,* 79–90.

Gronlund, N. (1998). *How to construct achievement tests* (4th ed.). Englewood Cliffs, NJ: Prentice Hall.

Grossman, H. (Ed.). (1973). A *manual on terminology and classification in mental retardation.* Washington, DC: American Association on Mental Deficiency.

Grossman, H. (Ed.). (1977). A *manual on terminology and classification in mental retardation* (rev. ed.). Washington, DC: American Association on Mental Deficiency.

Grossman, H. J. (Ed.). (1983). *Classification in mental retardation.* Washington, DC: American Association on Mental Retardation.

Grove, N., Bunning, K., & Porter, J. (2001). Interpreting the meaning of behavior by the people with intellectual disabilities. Theoretical and methodological issues. In F. Columbus (Ed.), *Advances in psychology research* (Vol. 7, pp. 87–126). New York: NOVA Science Publishers.

Guadalupe v. Tempe Elementary School District No. 3, Civ. No. 71-435 (D. Ariz. 1972).

Guarlnick, M. (1998). Effectiveness of early intervention for vulnerable children: A developmental perspective. *American Journal on Mental Retardation, 102,* 319–345.

Gunter, P., & Denny, K. (1998). Trends and issues in research regarding academic instruction of students with emotional and behavioral disorders. *Behavioral Disorders, 24,* 44–50.

Guralnick, M. J. (2005). Early intervention for children with intellectual disabilities: Current knowledge and future prospects. *Journal of Applied Research in Intellectual Disabilities, 18,* 313–324.

Guthrie, R., & Susi, A. (1963). A simple phenylalanine method for detecting phenylketonuria in large populations of newborn infants. *Pediatrics, 32,* 338–343.

Guy, B. A., Sitlington, P. L., Larsen, M. D., & Frank, A. R. (2009). What are high schools offering as preparation for employment? *Career Development for Exceptional Individuals, 32,* 30–41.

Hagerman, R. J., Berry-Kravis, E., Kaufmann, W. E., Ono, M. Y., Tartaglia, N., Lachiewicz, A., . . . Tranfaglia, M. (2009). Advances in the treatment of Fragile X syndrome. *Pediatrics, 123*(1), 378–390. doi:10.1542/peds.2008-0317

Hagerman, R., & Lampe, M. (1999). Fragile X syndrome. In S. Goldstein & C. Reynolds (Eds.), *Handbook of neurodevelopmental and genetic disorders in children* (pp. 298–316). New York: Guilford Press.

Hagner, D., Helm, D. T., & Butterworth, J. (1996). "This is your meeting." A qualitative study of person-centered planning. *Mental Retardation, 34,* 159–171.

Halderman v. Pennhurst State School and Hospital (1977). 446 F. Supp. 1295 (E.D. Pa.).

Hall, L. J., & McGregor, J. A. (2000). A follow-up study on the peer relationships of children with disabilities in an inclusive school. *Journal of Special Education, 34,* 114–125.

Hall, S. S., Lightbody, A. A., & Reiss, A. L. (2008). Compulsive, self-injurious, and autistic behavior in children and adolescents with Fragile X syndrome. *American Journal on Mental Retardation, 113*(1), 44–53.

Hallahan, D. P., Kauffman, J. M., & Pullen, P. C. (2012). *Exceptional learners: An introduction to special education* (12th ed.). Boston: Pearson Education.

Hallam, A., Knapp, M., Jaerbrink, K., Netten, A., Emerson, E., Robertson, J., Gregory, N., . . . Durkan, J. (2002). Cost of village community, residential campus and dispersed housing provision for people with intellectual disability. *Journal of Intellectual Disability Research, 46,* 394–404.

Halpern, A. (1990). A methodological review of follow-up and follow-along studies tracking school leavers from special education. *Career Development for Exceptional Individuals, 13,* 13–27.

Hammill, D., & Larsen, S. (1996). *Test of Written Language – 3.* Austin, TX: Pro-Ed.

Hammill, D., & Newcomer, P. (1997). *Test of Language Development: 3 (Intermediate).* Austin, TX: Pro-Ed.

Hansen, D. L., & Morgan, R. L. (2008). Teaching grocery store purchasing skills to students with intellectual disabilities using a computer-based instruction program. *Education and Training in Developmental Disabilities, 43,* 431–442.

Hardman, M., Drew, C., & Egan, M. (2003). *Human exceptionality* (7th ed.). Boston: Allyn & Bacon.

Haring, N. (1977). From promise to reality. *AAESPH Review, 2*(1), 3–7.

Harrington, R. G. (2012). *Review of the AAMR Adaptive Behavior Scale:2 School Edition.* http://web.a.ebscohost.com/ehost/detail?vid=19&sid=60a5b2d3-cff1-476d-a740-421449524053%40sessionmgr4002&hid=4209&bdata=JmxvZ2luLmFzcCZzaXRlPWVVob3N0LWxpdmU%3d#db=mmt&AN=TIP07000003. Online resource provided by the Board of Regents of the University of Nebraska and the Buros Center for Testing.

Harrison, P., & Oakland, T. (2000). *Adaptive Behavior Assessment System.* San Antonio, TX: Psychological Corporation.

Harry, B. (1992). *Cultural diversity, families, and the special education system.* New York: Teachers College Press.

Hart, B. M., & Risley, T. R. (1968). Establishing the use of descriptive adjectives in the spontaneous speech of disadvantaged preschool children. *Journal of Applied Behavior Analysis, 1,* 109–120.

Hasazi, S., Liggett, K., & Schattman, K. (1994). A qualitative policy study of the least restrictive environment provision of the Individuals with Disabilities Education Act. *Exceptional Children, 60,* 491–507.

Hassall, R., Rose, J., & McDonald, J. (2005). Parenting stress in mothers of children with an intellectual disability: The effects of parental cognitions in relation to child characteristics and family support. *Journal of Intellectual Disability Research, 49,* 405–418.

Hawkey, C., & Smithes, A. (1976). The Prader-Willi syndrome with a 15/15 translocation: Case report and review of the literature. *Journal of Medical Genetics, 13,* 152–156.

Hayes, B. K., & Conway, R. N. (2000). Concept acquisition in children with mild intellectual disability: Factors affecting the abstraction of prototypical information. *Journal of Intellectual & Developmental Disability, 25,* 217–235.

Haywood, H. C. (1997a). Interactive assessment. In R. Taylor (Ed.), *Assessment of individuals with mental retardation* (pp. 103–130). San Diego: Singular Publishing Group.

Haywood, H. C. (1997b). *Global perspectives on mental retardation.* Keynote address presented at the Annual Meeting of the American Association on Mental Retardation, May 28, in New York.

Healy, E., McGuire, B. E., Evans, D. S., & Carley, S. N. (2009). Sexuality and personal relationships for people with an intellectual disability. Part 1: Service-user perspectives. *Journal of Intellectual Disability Research, 53,* 905–912.

Heber, R. (1959). A manual on terminology and classification and mental retardation. *American Journal of Mental Deficiency, 64* (Monograph suppl.).

Heber, R. (1961). Modifications in the manual on terminology and classification and mental retardation. *American Journal of Mental Deficiency, 65,* 490–500.

Heber, R., & Garber, H. (1970). An experiment in prevention of cultural-familial retardation. In D. Primrose (Ed.), *Proceedings of the International Association for the Study of Mental Deficiency* (Vol.1, pp. 34–43). Warsaw: Polish Medical Publishers.

Hendrick Hudson Central School District v. Rowley, 458 U.S. 176, 102 S. Ct. 3034, 73 L Ed. 2d 690 (1982).

Henley, M., Ramsey, R. S., & Algozzine, R. F. (2002). *Characteristics of and strategies for teaching students with mild disabilities.* Boston, MA: Allyn & Bacon.

Henry, L. A., & Gudjonsson, G. H. (2003). Eyewitness memory, suggestibility, and repeated recall sessions in children with mild and moderate intellectual disabilities. *Law and Human Behavior, 27,* 481–505.

Henry, L. A., & MacLean, M. (2002). Working memory performance in children with and without intellectual disabilities. *American Journal on Mental Retardation, 107,* 421–432.

Heward, W. (2013). *Exceptional children: An introduction to special education* (10th ed.). Upper Saddle, NJ: Merrill/Prentice Hall.

Hibbert, D., Kostinas, G., Luiselli, J. K. (2002). Improving skills performance of an adult with mental retardation through peer-mediated instructional support. *Journal of Developmental & Physical Disabilities, 14,* 119–127.

Hickson, L., Blackman, L., & Reis, E. (1995). *Mental retardation: Foundations of educational programming.* Boston: Allyn & Bacon.

Hobson v. Hansen, 269 F. Supp. 401 (D.D.C. 1967, aff'd sub norm).

Hodapp, R. M., & Dykens, E. M. (2009). Intellectual disabilities and child psychiatry: Looking to the future. *Journal of Child Psychology and Psychiatry, 50,* 99–107.

Hodapp, R. M., & Zigler, E. (1997). New issues in the developmental approach to mental retardation. In W. E. MacLean, Jr. (Ed.), *Ellis' handbook of mental deficiency, psychological theory, and research* (3rd ed., pp. 115–136). Mahwah, NJ: Lawrence Erlbaum Associates.

Hodges, W., & Cooper, M. (1981). Head Start and Follow Through: Influences on intellectual development. *Journal of Special Education, 15,* 221–238.

Hodgkinson, H. (1993). American education: The good, the bad, and the task. *Kappan, 74*(8), 619–623.

Hoffmann, B., Wendel, U., & Schweitzer-Krantz, S. (2011). Cross-sectional analysis of speech and cognitive performance in 32 patients with classic galactosemia. *Journal of Inherited Metabolic Disease, 34*(2), 421–427. doi:10.1007/s10545–011–9297–5

Holburn, S. (2000). New paradigms for some, old paradigm for others. *Mental Retardation, 38,* 530–531.

Hollomotz, A. (2008). "May we please have sex tonight?"—People with learning difficulties pursuing privacy in residential group settings. *British Journal of Learning Disabilities, 37,* 91–97.

Honig v. Doe, 108 S. Ct. 592. (1988).

Hoover-Dempsey, K., Bassler, O.C., & Brissie, J.S. (1992). Explorations in parent-school relations. *Journal of Educational Research, 85,* 287–294.

Horn, J. (1965). *Fluid and crystallized intelligence.* Unpublished doctoral dissertation, University of Illinois, Urbana–Champaign.

Horn, J., & Cattell, R. (1966). Refinement and test of the theory of fluid and crystallized intelligence. *Journal of Educational Psychology, 57,* 253 –270.

Horner, R.H., Albin, R.W., Todd, A.W., Newton, J.S., & Sprague, J.R. (2011). Designing and implementing individualized positive behavior support. In M.E. Snell & F. Brown (Eds.), *Instruction of students with severe disabilities* (7th ed., pp. 257–303). Upper Saddle River, NJ: Pearson.

Horner, R.H., Bellamy, G.T., & Colvin, G.T. (1984). Responding in the presence of nontrained stimuli: Implications of generalization error patterns. *Journal of the Association for Persons with Severe Handicaps, 9,* 287–295.

Horner, R.H., & Carr, E. (1997). Behavioral support for students with severe disabilities: Functional assessment and comprehensive intervention. *Journal of Special Education, 31,* 84–104.

Horner, R.H., Dunlap, G., Koegel, R., Carr, E., Sailor, W., Anderson, J., Albin, R., & O'Neill, R. (1990). Toward a technology of "nonaversive" behavioral support. *Journal of the Association for Persons with Severe Handicaps, 15,* 125–132.

Horvath, M., Hoernicke, P.A., & Kallam, M. (1993). *Mental retardation in perspective.* Retrieved from ERIC database. (ED355729)

Hosp, J.L., & Reschly, D.J. (2003). Referral rates for intervention or assessment: A meta-analysis of racial differences. *Journal of Special Education, 37*(2), 67–80.

Hua, Y., Morgan, B.S.T., Kaldenberg, E.R., & Goo, M. (2012). Cognitive strategy instruction for functional mathematical skill: Effects for young adults with intellectual disability. *Education and Training in Autism and Developmental Disabilities, 47,* 345–358.

Hudson, M.E., Browder, D.M., & Wood, L.A. (2013). Review of experimental research on academic learning by students with moderate and severe intellectual disabilities in general education. *Research and Practice for Persons with Severe Disabilities, 38,* 17–29.

Hudson, M.E., & Test, D.W. (2011). Evaluating the evidence base of shared story reading to promote literacy for students with extensive support needs. *Research and Practice for Persons with Severe Disabilities, 36,* 34–45.

Hughes, C., & Carter, E. (2000). *The transition handbook: Strategies high school teachers use that work!* Baltimore: Paul H. Brookes.

Hughes, C., Golas, M., Cosgriff, J., Brigham, N., Edwards, C. & Cashen, K. (2011). Effects of a social skills intervention among high school students with intellectual disabilities and autism and their general education peers. *Research and Practice for Persons with Severe Disabilities, 36,* 46–61.

Hughes, C., & Rusch, F. (1989). Teaching supported employees with severe mental retardation to solve problems. *Journal of Applied Behavior Analysis, 22,* 365–372.

Hunter, D., & O'Brien, L. (2002). Postsecondary education for students with disabilities. In K. Storey, P. Bates, & D. Hunter (Eds.), *The road ahead: Transition to adult life for persons with disabilities* (pp. 189–205). St. Augustine, FL: Training Resource Network.

Iacono, T., & Carling-Jenkins, R. (2012). The human rights context for ethical requirements for involving people with intellectual disability in medical research. *Journal of Intellectual Disability Research, 56,* 1122–1132.

Ianacone, R.N., & Leconte, P.J. (1986). Curriculum-based vocational assessment: A viable response to a school-based service delivery issue. *Career Development for Exceptional Individuals, 9,* 113–120.

Idol, L., Nevin, A., & Paolucci-Whitcomb, P. (1999). *Models of curriculum based assessment: A blueprint for learning.* Austin, TX: Pro-Ed.

Ike, N. (2000). Current thinking on XYY syndrome. *Psychiatric Annals, 30,* 91–95.

International Rett Syndrome Association. (n.d.). *About Rett Syndrome.* Retrieved from http://www.rettsyndrome.org/home

Ireland, W. (1882). On the Diagnosis and Prognosis of Idiocy and Imbecility. *Edinburgh Medical Journal,* (June), 1072–1085.

Ireland, W. (1898). *The Mental Affections of Children: Idiocy, Imbecility, and Insanity.* London: Churchill.

Irving Independent School District v. Tatro, 104 S. Ct. 3371 (1984).

Ishmael, H., Begleiter, M., & Butler, M. (2002). Drowning as a cause of death in Angelman syndrome. *American Journal on Mental Retardation, 107,* 69–70.

Ittenbach, R. F., Bruininks, R. H., Thurlow, M., & McGrew, K. (1993). Community adjustment of young adults with mental retardation: A multivariate analysis of adjustment. *Research in Developmental Disabilities, 14,* 275–290.

Iwata, B. A., Dorsey, M., Slifer, K., Bayman, K., & Richman, G. (1982). Toward a functional analysis of self injury. *Analysis and Intervention in Developmental Disabilities, 2,* 3–20.

Jackson v. Indiana (1972). (U.S. Supreme Ct., No. 70-5009), 39 Law Week 3413.

Jacobs, W. (1978). The effect of learning disability label on classroom teachers' ability objectively to observe and interpret child behaviors. *Learning Disability Quarterly, 1,* 50–55.

Janney, R., & Snell, M. (2000). *Behavioral support.* Baltimore: Paul H. Brookes.

Janzen, D., & Nguyen, M. (2010). Beyond executive function: Non-executive cognitive abilities in individuals with PKU. *Molecular Genetics and Metabolism, 99,* S47–S51.

Jimenez, B. A., Browder, D. M., & Courtade, G. R. (2009). An exploratory study of self-directed science concept learning by students with moderate intellectual disabilities. *Research & Practice for Persons with Severe Disabilities, 34,* 33–46.

John, A. E., Rowe, M. L., Mervis, C. B., & Abbeduto, L. (2009). Referential communication skills of children with Williams syndrome: Understanding when messages are not adequate. *American Journal on Intellectual and Developmental Disabilities, 114*(2), 85–99. doi:10.1352/2009.114.85–99

Johnson, J. A., & D'Amato, R. C. (2012). *Review of the Stanford-Binet Intelligence Scales-Fifth Edition.* http://web.a.ebscohost.com/ehost/detail?vid=21&sid=60a5b2d3-cff1-476d-a740-421449524053%40sessionmgr4002&hid=4209&bdata=JmxvZ2luLmFzcCZzaXRlPWVob3N0LWxpdmU%3d#db=mmt&AN=TIP07002411. Online resource provided by the Board of Regents of the University of Nebraska and the Buros Center for Testing.

Jones, H. A., & Warren, S. F. (1991). Enhancing engagement in early language teaching. *Teaching Exceptional Children, 23*(4), 48–50.

Jones, J. L. (2012). Factors associated with self-concept: Adolescents with intellectual and developmental disabilities share their perspectives. *Intellectual and Developmental Disabilities, 50,* 31–40.

Joosten, A. V., Bundy, A. C., & Einfeld, S. L. (2008). Intrinsic and extrinsic motivation for stereotypic and repetitive behavior. *Journal of Autism and Developmental Disorders, 39,* 521–531.

Jordan, B., & Dunlap, G. (2001). Construction of adulthood and disability. *Mental Retardation, 39,* 286–296.

Jyothy, A., Kumar, K. S. D., Rao, G. M., Rao, V. B., Devi, B. U., Sujatha, M., & Reddy, P. P. (2001). Parental age and the origin of extra chromosome 21 in Down syndrome. *Journal of Human Genetics, 46*(6), 347–350.

Kahl, A., & Moore, B. (2000). Behavioral phenotype of neurofibromatosis, type 1. *Mental Retardation and Developmental Disabilities Research Review, 6,* 117–124.

Kahng, S., Iwata, B. A., & Lewin, A. B. (2002). Behavioral treatment of self-injury. *American Journal on Mental Retardation, 107,* 212–221.

Kamps, D., Walker, D., Maher, J., & Rotholtz, D. (1992). Academic and environmental effects of small group arrangements in classrooms for students with autism and other developmental disabilities. *Journal of Autism and Developmental Disorders, 22,* 277–293.

Kanner, L. (1964). *A history of the care and study of the mentally retarded.* Springfield, IL: Charles C. Thomas.

Katims, D. (2001). Literacy assessment of students with mental retardation: An exploratory investigation. *Education and Training in Mental Retardation and Developmental Disabilities, 36,* 363–372.

Kaufman, A., & Kaufman, N. (2004a). *Kaufman Assessment Battery for Children-II.* Circle Pines, MN: American Guidance Service.

Kaufman, A., & Kaufman, N. (2004b). *Kaufman Test of Educational Achievement* (2nd ed.). Circle Pines, MN: American Guidance Service.

Keller, H. (1915, December 18). Physicians' juries for defective babies. *New Republic, 173,* 174.

Kelley, J. F., Morisset, C. E., Barnard, K. E., & Patterson, D. L. (1996). Risky beginnings: Low maternal intelligence as a risk factor for children's intellectual development. *Infants and Young Children, 8*(3), 11–23.

Kelley, K. R., Test, D. W., & Cooke, N. L. (2013). Effects of picture prompts delivered by a video iPod on pedestrian navigation. *Exceptional Children, 79,* 459–474.

Kellow, J. T., & Parker, R. I. (2002). Self-perceptions of adequacy of support among persons with mental retardation living in suburban versus rural communities. *Education and Training in Mental Retardation and Developmental Disabilities, 37,* 328–338.

Kennedy, C. H., & Niederbuhl, J. (2001). Establishing criteria for sexual consent capacity. *American Journal on Mental Retardation, 106,* 503–510.

Kennedy, C. H., Shukla, S., & Fryxell, D. (1997). Comparing the effects of educational placement on the social relationships of intermediate school students with severe disabilities. *Exceptional Children, 64,* 277–289.

Kerr, A. (2002). Rett syndrome: Recent progress and implications for research and clinical practice. *Journal of the Association for Persons with Severe Handicaps, 14,* 190–196.

Kim, S., Larson, S. A., & Lakin, K. C. (2001). Behavioural outcomes of deinstitutionalisation for people with intellectual disability: A review of US studies conducted between 1980 and 1999. *Journal of Intellectual Disability Research, 26,* 35–50.

Kim, Y.-R. (2010). Personal safety programs for children with intellectual disabilities. *Education and Training in Autism and Developmental Disabilities, 45,* 312–319.

Kirk, S., & Johnson, G. (1951). *Educating the retarded child.* Cambridge, MA: Houghton Mifflin.

Kishi, G., & Meyer, L. H. (1994). What children report and remember: A 6-year follow-up of the effects of social contact between peers with and without severe disabilities. *Journal of the Association for Persons with Severe Handicaps, 19,* 277–289.

Klingner, J. K., Artiles, A. J., Kozleski, E., Harry, B., Zion, S., Tate, W., Duran, G. Z., & Riley, D. (2005). Addressing the disproportionate representation of culturally and linguistically diverse students in special education through culturally responsive educational systems. *Education Policy Analysis Archives, 13,* 38. Retrieved April 25, 2014 from http://epaa.asu.edu/epaa/v13n38/.

Koch, R., Trefz, F., & Waisbren, S. (2010). Psychosocial issues and outcomes in maternal PKU. *Molecular genetics and metabolism, 99,* S68–S74. doi:10.1016/j.ymgme.2009.10.014

Kozma, A., Mansell, J., & Beadle-Brown, J. (2009). Outcomes in different residential settings for people with intellectual disability: A systematic review. *American Journal on Intellectual and Developmental Disabilities, 114*(3), 193–222.

Krinsky-McHale, S., Kittler, P., Brown, W. T., Jenkins, E. C., & Devenny, D. A. (2005). Repetition priming in adults with Williams syndrome: Age-related dissociation between implicit and explicit memory. *American Journal on Mental Retardation, 110*(6), 482–496.

Krupski, A. (1977). Role of attention in the reaction-time performance of mentally retarded adolescents. *American Journal of Mental Deficiency, 82,* 79–83.

Kugel, R. B., & Wolfensberger, W. (1969). *Changing patterns in residential services for the mentally retarded.* Washington, DC: President's Committee on Mental Retardation.

Kugler, M. (2014). The Elephant Man's Bones Reveal Mystery. Retrieved from http://rarediseases.about.com/cs/proteussyndrome/a/031301.htm

Kurth, J. A. (2013). Authentic literacy and communication in inclusive settings for students with significant disabilities. *Teaching Exceptional Children, 46*(2), 44–50.

Kush, J. C. (2012). Review of *Peabody Picture Vocabulary Test-Fourth Edition.* In *Mental measurements yearbook and tests in print.* http://web.a.ebscohost.com/ehost/detail?vid=23&sid=60a5b2d3-cff1-476d-a740-421449524053%40sessionmgr4002&hid=4209&bdata=JmxvZ2luLmFzcCZzaXRlPWVob3N0N0LWxpdmU%3d#db=mmt&AN=TIP18073480. Online resource provided by the Board of Regents of the University of Nebraska and the Buros Center for Testing.

Kwong, A. K.-W. T. (1998). Memory strategy assessment with adolescents with mild mental disabilities. *Dissertation Abstracts International Section A: Humanities & Social Sciences, 58*(10–A), 3833.

Lakin, K. C., Braddock, D., & Smith, G. (1996). Trends and milestones: Majority of MR/DD residential service recipients now in homes of 6 or fewer residents. *Mental Retardation, 34,* 198.

Lamont, A., & Bromfield, L. (2009). Parental intellectual disability and child protection: Key issues. *NCPC Issues, 31,* 11–19.

Larry P. v. Riles, 343 F. Supp 1306 (N.D. Cal. 1972).

Larson, S., Laken, C., Anderson, A., Kwak, N., Lee, J., & Anderson, D. (2001). Prevalence of mental retardation and developmental disabilities: Estimates from the 1994/1995 National Health Interview Survey Disability Supplements. *American Journal on Mental Retardation, 106,* 231–252.

Larson, S., Lakin, C., & Hill, S. (2012). Behavioral outcomes of moving from institutional to community living for people with intellectual and developmental disabilities: U.S. studies from 1977 to 2010. *Research and Practice for Persons with Severe Disabilities, 37,* 235–246.

Lasater, M., & Brady, M. P. (1995). Effects of video self-modeling and feedback on task fluency: A home based intervention. *Education and Treatment of Children, 18*, 389–407.

Lavoie, R.(1989). How difficult can this be? The F.A.T. City Workshop (dvd). http://www.ricklavoie.com/videos.html

Lawrence, E. A., & Winschel, J. F. (1975). Locus of control: Implications for special education. *Exceptional Children, 41*, 483–490.

Lazerson, M. (1975). Educational institutions and mental subnormality: Notes on writing a history. In M. Begab & S. Richardson (Eds.), *The mentally retarded and society* (pp. 33–52). Baltimore: University Park Press.

LeBanks v. Spears, 60 F.R.D. 135, 417F, Supp. 169 (E.D. La. 1973).

Ledbetter, D. H., Mascarello, J. T., Riccardi, V. M., Harper, V. D., Airhart, S. D., & Strobel, R. J. (1982). Chromosome 15 abnormalities and Prader-Willi syndrome: A follow-up report of 40 cases. *American Journal of Human Genetics, 34*(2), 278–285.

Lee, S.-H., Amos, B. A., Gragoudas, S., Lee, Y., Shogren, K. A., Theoharis, R., & Wehmeyer, M. L. (2006). Curriculum augmentation and adaptation strategies to promote access to the general curriculum for students with intellectual and developmental disabilities. *Education and Training in Developmental Disabilities, 41*, 199–212.

Lent, J. R., & McLean, B. M. (1976). The trainable retarded: The technology of teaching. In N. G. Haring & R. L. Schiefelbush (Eds.), *Teaching special children* (pp. 197–223). New York: McGraw-Hill.

Levy, Y. (2011). IQ predicts word decoding skills in populations with intellectual disabilities. *Research in Developmental Disabilities, 32*, 2267–2277.

Lewis, R. B., Doorlag, D. H., & Lewis, R. B. (2011). *Teaching students with special needs in general education classrooms* (8th ed.). Upper Saddle River, NJ: Pearson.

Li, J., Bassett, D. S., & Hutchinson, S. R. (2008). Secondary special educators' transition involvement. *Journal of Intellectual and Developmental Disabilities, 34*, 163–172.

Lilly, M. S. (1985). The next 30 years in special education. In M. P. Brady & P. Gunter (Eds.), *Integrating moderately and severely handicapped learners: Strategies that work* (pp. 295–310). Springfield, IL: Charles C. Thomas.

Lindblad, I., Gillberg, C., & Fernell, E. (2011). ADHD and other associated developmental problems in children with mild mental retardation. The use of the "Five to Thirteen" questionnaire in a population-based sample. *Research in Developmental Disabilities, 32*, 2805–2809.

Lindsay, W., Steptoe, L., & Haut, F. (2012). The sexual and physical abuse histories of offenders with intellectual disabilities. *Journal of Intellectual Disability Research, 56*, 326–331.

Lindsley, O. R. (1964). Direct measurement and prosthesis of retarded behavior. *Journal of Education, 147*, 62–81.

Liptak, G. S. (2013). Neural tube defects. In M. L. Batshaw, N. J. Roizen, & G. R. Lotrecchiano. (Eds.), *Children with disabilities* (7th ed., pp. 451–472). Baltimore: Paul H. Brookes.

Logan, K. R., & Keefe, E. B. (1997). A comparison of instructional context, teacher behavior, and engaged behavior for students with severe disabilities in general education and self contained classrooms. *Journal of the Association for Persons with Severe Handicaps, 22*, 16–27.

Lovitt, T. C., Plavins, M., & Cushing, M. (1999). What do pupils with disabilities have to say about their experience in high school? *Remedial and Special Education, 20*, 67–76.

Luckasson, R., Borthwick-Duffy, S., Buntinx, W., Coulter, D., Craig, E., Reeve, A., Schalock, R., . . . Tasse, M. (2002). *Mental retardation. Definition, classification, and systems of supports* (10th ed.). Washington, DC: American Association on Mental Retardation.

Luckasson, R., Coulter, D., Polloway, E., Reiss, S., Schalock, R., Snell, M., Spitalnik., D., & Stark, J. (1992). *Mental retardation: Definition, classification, and systems of supports* (9th ed.). Washington, DC: American Association on Mental Retardation.

Luckasson, R., & Reeve, A. (2001). Naming, defining, and classifying in mental retardation. *Mental Retardation, 39*, 47–52.

Luckasson, R., & Schalock, R. L. (2013). What's at stake in the lives of people with intellectual disability? Part II: Recommendations for naming, defining, diagnosing, classifying, and planning supports. *Intellectual and Developmental Disabilities, 51*(2), 94–101.

Luther, M. (1652). *Colloquia Mensalia.* London: William DuGard.

Maccow, G. (2012). *Review of the Scales of Independent Behavior—Revised.* Online resource provided by the Board of Regents of the University of Nebraska and the Buros Center for Testing. http://web.b.ebscohost.com/ehost/detail?vid=3&sid=2146364e-8fd3-4335-b2d1-3b7eb464a81c%40sessionmgr112&hid=118&bdata=JmxvZ2luLmFzcCZzaXRlPWVob3N0LWxpdmU%3d#db=mmt&AN=TIP07002240

MacDuff, G., Krantz, P., & McClannahan, L. (1993). Teaching children with autism to use photographic activity schedules: Maintenance and generalization of complex response chains. *Journal of Applied Behavior Analysis, 26,* 89–97.

MacMillan, D. (1985). *Mental retardation in school and society* (2nd ed.). Boston: Little, Brown.

MacMillan, D., Siperstein, G., & Gresham, F. (1996). A challenge to the viability of mild mental retardation as a diagnostic category. *Exceptional Children, 62,* 356–371.

Maller, S. J. (2012). *Review of the Wechsler Intelligence Scale for Children-Fourth Edition.* Online resource provided by the Board of Regents of the University of Nebraska and the Buros Center for Testing. http://web.b.ebscohost.com/ehost/detail?vid=5&sid=2146364e-8fd3-4335-b2d1-3b7eb464a81c%40sessio nmgr112&hid=118&bdata=JmxvZ2luLmFzcCZzaXRlPWVob3N0LWxpdmU%3d#db=mmt&AN= TIP07002749

March of Dimes. (2008). *Alcohol and drugs.* Retrieved from www.marchofdimes.com

Marks, S. U. (2008). Self-determination for students with intellectual disabilities and why I want educators to know what it means. *Phi Delta Kappan, September,* 55–58.

Martin, J. E., & Huber Marshall, L. H. (1996). Choicemaker: Infusing self-determination instruction into the IEP and transition process. In D. J. Sands & M. L. Wehmeyer (Eds.), *Self-determination across the lifespan* (pp. 215–236). Baltimore: Paul H. Brookes.

Martin, S., Brady, M. P., & Kotarba, J. (1992). Families with chronically ill young children: The unsinkable family. *Remedial and Special Education, 13*(2), 6–15.

Maryland Association for Retarded Citizens v. Maryland Equity No. 100/182/77676 (Cir. Ct. Baltimore Co. 1974).

Matson, J. L., Kiely, S. L., & Bamburg, J. W. (1997). The effect of stereotypies on adaptive skills as assessed with the DASH-II and Vineland Adaptive Behavior Scales. *Research in Developmental Disabilities, 18,* 471–476.

Maulik, P. K., Mascarenhas, M. N., Mathers, C. D., Dua, T., & Saxena, S. (2011). Prevalence of intellectual disability: A meta-analysis of population-based studies. *Research in Developmental Disabilities, 32,* 419–436.

McCartney, J. R. (1987). Mentally retarded and nonretarded subjects' long-term recognition memory. *American Journal of Mental Retardation, 92,* 312–317.

McFelea, J. T., & Raver, S. (2012). Quality of life of families with children who have severe developmental disabilities: A comparison based on child residence. *Physical Disabilities: Education and Related Services, 31*(2), 3–17.

McGhee, R., Bryant, B., Larsen, S., & Rivera, D. (1995). *Test of Written Expression.* Austin, TX: Pro-Ed.

McLeskey, J., Landers, E., Williamson, P., & Hoppey, D. (2012). Are we moving toward educating students with disabilities in less restrictive settings? *Journal of Special Education, 46,* 131–140.

McMillan, J. (1997). *Classroom assessment: Principles and practice for effective instruction.* Boston: Allyn & Bacon.

Mechling, L. C. (2008). High tech cooking: A literature review of evolving technologies for teaching a functional skill. *Education and Training in Autism and Developmental Disabilities, 43,* 474–485.

Mechling, L., & O'Brien, E. (2010). Computer-based video instruction to teach students with intellectual disabilities to use public bus transportation. *Education and Training in Autism and Developmental Disabilities, 45,* 230–241.

Mechling, L. C., & Seid, N. H. (2011). Use of hand-held personal digital assistant (PDA) to self-prompt pedestrian travel by young adults with moderate intellectual disabilities. *Education and Training in Autism and Developmental Disabilities, 46,* 220–237.

Medicode. (1998). *International classification of diseases, ninth revision, clinical modification* (6th ed.). Salt Lake City: Author.

Merck Manual. (2003). Retrieved from www.merck.com/pubs/manual/

Merck Manual. (2012). *Overview of child maltreatment.* Retrieved from www.merckmanuals.com

Miller, M. D. (2012). Review of *Wechsler Individual Achievement Test-Third Edition.* In *Mental measurements yearbook and tests in print.* http://web.a.ebscohost.com/ehost/detail?vid=25&sid=60a5b2d3-cff1-476d-a740-421449524053%40sessionmgr4002&hid=4209&bdata=JmxvZ2luLmFzcCZzaXRlPWVob 3N0LWxpdmU%3d#db=mmt&AN=TIP18013622http://web.a.ebscohost.com/ehost/detail?vid= 25&sid=60a5b2d3-cff1-476d-a740-421449524053%40sessionmgr4002&hid=4209&bdata=JmxvZ2luL mFzcCZzaXRlPWVob3N0LWxpdmU%3d#db=mmt&AN=TIP18013622. Online resource provided by the Board of Regents of the University of Nebraska and the Buros Center for Testing.

Miller, S. M., & Chan, F. (2008). Predictors of life satisfaction in individuals with intellectual disabilities. *Journal of Intellectual Disability Research, 52,* 1039–1047.

Miller, S. P. (2002). *Validated practices for teaching students with diverse needs and abilities.* Boston: Allyn & Bacon.

Mills v. Board of Education of District of Columbia, 348 F. Supp. 866 (D.D.C. 1972).

Miner, C., & Bates, P. (1997). The effect of person centered planning activities on the IEP/transition planning process. *Education and Training in Mental Retardation and Developmental Disabilities, 32,* 105–112.

Mithaug, D.E., Wehmeyer, M.L., Agran, M., Martin, J.E., & Palmer, S. (1998). The self-determined learning model of instruction. In M.L. Wehmeyer & D.J. Sands (Eds.), *Making it happen: Student involvement in education planning, decision making, and instruction* (pp. 299–328). Baltimore: Paul H. Brookes.

Moreno, J., & Saldana, D. (2005). Use of a computer-assisted program to improve metacognition in persons with severe intellectual disabilities. *Research in Developmental Disabilities, 26,* 341–357.

Moss, J., Oliver, C., Nelson, L., Richards, C., & Hall, S. (2013). Delineating the profile of autism spectrum disorder characteristics in Cornelia de Lange and Fragile X syndromes. *American Journal on Intellectual and Developmental Disabilities, 118*(1), 55–73. doi:10.1352/1944–7558–118.1.55

Muehlmann, A.M., & Lewis, M.H. (2012). Abnormal repetitive behaviours: Shared phenomenology and pathophysiology. *Journal of Intellectual Disability Research, 56,* 427–440.

Munk, D., Van Laarhoven, T., Goodman, S., & Repp, A. (1998). Small group direct instruction for students with moderate to severe disabilities. In A. Hilton & R. Ringlaben (Eds.), *Best and promising practices in developmental disabilities* (pp. 127–138). Austin, TX: Pro-Ed.

Myrbakk, E., & von Tetzchner, S. (2008). Psychiatric disorders and behavior problems in people with intellectual disability. *Research in Developmental Disabilities, 29,* 316–332.

Nader-Grosbois, N., & Vieillevoye, S. (2012). Variability of self-regulatory strategies in children with intellectual disability and typically developing children in pretend play situations. *Journal of Intellectual Disability Research, 56,* 140–156.

National Commission on Excellence in Education. (1983). *A nation at risk: The imperative for educational reform.* Washington, DC: US Government Printing Office.

National Down Syndrome Society. (2012). *Cosmetic surgery for children with Down syndrome.* Retrieved from https://www.ndss.org/About-NDSS/Media-Kit/Position-Papers/Cosmetic-Surgery-for-Children-with-Down-Syndrome/

National Education Goals Panel. (1997). *The National Education Goals report: Building a nation of learners.* Washington, DC: US Government Printing Office.

National Governors Association Center for Best Practices [NGACBP], Council of Chief State School Officers. (2010). *Common Core State Standards.* Washington, DC: Authors.

National Institute on Alcohol Abuse and Alcoholism. (2012). Retrieved from www.niaaa.nih.gov

National Institute of Mental Health. (2011). *Hurler syndrome.* Retrieved from www.ncbi.mlm.nih.gov

National Institute of Neurological Disorders and Stroke (NINDS). (2002). *Neurofibromatosis fact sheet.* Retrieved from www.ninds.nih.gov/health_and_medical/pubs/neurofibromatosis.htm#whatare

Neuhaus, E. (1967). Training the mentally retarded for competitive employment. *Exceptional Children, 33,* 625–628.

Newborg, J., Stock, J., Wnek, L., Guidubaldi, J., & Svinicki, J. (2005). *Battelle Developmental Inventory: 2 (BDI-2).* Allen, TX: DLM Teaching Resources.

Newcomer, P., & Hammill, D. (1997). *Test of Language Development: 3 (Primary).* Austin, TX: Pro-Ed.

Newell, K.M. (1997). Motor skills and mental retardation. In W.E. MacLean, Jr. (Ed.), *Ellis' handbook of mental deficiency, psychological theory, and research* (3rd ed., pp. 275–308). Mahwah, NJ: Lawrence Erlbaum Associates.

Newman, L., Wagner, M., Knokey, A.-M., Marder, C., Nagle, K., Shaver, D., Wei, X. (with Cameto, R., Contreras, E., Ferguson, K., Greene, S., & Schwarting, M.). (2011). *The post-high school outcomes of young adults with disabilities up to 8 years after high school. A report from the National Longitudinal Transition Study-2 (NLTS2)* (NCSER 2011–3005). Menlo Park, CA: SRI International. Retrieved from www.nlts2.org/reports/

Newton, J., Olson, D., & Horner, R.H. (1995). Factors contributing to the stability of social relationships between individuals with mental retardation and other community members. *Mental Retardation, 33,* 383–393.

New York Association for Retarded Citizens v. Rockefeller (1975). 72 Civil Action No. 356.

Nietupski, J., Hamre-Nietupski, S., Curtin, S., & Shrikanth, K. (1997). A review of curricular research in severe disabilities from 1976 to 1995 in six selected journals. *Journal of Special Education, 31,* 36–60.

Nihira, K., Leland, H., & Lambert, N. (1993). *AAMR Adaptive Behavior Scale: School Edition-2.* Austin, TX: Pro-Ed.

NINDS Rett Syndrome Fact Sheet (2014). http://www.ninds.nih.gov/disorders/rett/detail_rett.htm

Nirje, B. (1969). The normalization principle and its human management implications. In R.B. Kugel & W. Wolfensberger (Eds.), *Changing patterns in residential services for the mentally retarded* (pp. 179–195). Washington, DC: U.S. Government Printing Office.

Nolet, V., & Tindal, G. (1993). Special education in content area classes: Development of a model and practical procedures. *Remedial and Special Education, 14,* 36–48.

Nolet, V., & Tindal, G. (1994). Instruction and learning in middle school science classes: Implications for students with disabilities. *Journal of Special Education, 28,* 166–187.

Noonan, M.J., & McCormick, L. (1993). *Early intervention in natural environments: Methods and procedures.* Pacific Grove, CA: Brooks/Cole.

Norman, J.M., Collins, B.C., & Schuster, J.W. (2001). Using an instructional package including video technology to teach self-help skills to elementary students with mental disabilities. *Journal of Special Education Technology, 16,* 5–18.

Nota, L., Ferrari, L., Soresi, S., & Wehmeyer, M. (2007). Self-determination, social abilities and the quality of life of people with intellectual disability. *Journal of Intellectual Disability Research, 51,* 850–865.

Numminen, H., Service, E., & Ruoppila, I. (2002). Working memory, intelligence, and knowledge base in adult persons with intellectual disability. *Research in Developmental Disabilities, 23,* 105–118.

Nyhan, W. (1994). The Lesch-Nyhan disease. In T. Thompson & D. Gray (Eds.), *Destructive behavior in developmental disabilities: Diagnosis and treatment* (pp. 181–197). Thousand Oaks, CA: Sage Publications.

O'Brien, J., Pearpoint, J., & Kahn, L. (2010). *The PATH and MAPS handbook: Person-centered ways to build community.* Toronto: Inclusion Press.

O'Connor v. Donaldson (1975). 422 U.S. 563.

O'Donnell, A.M., Reeve, J., & Smith, J.K. (2007). *Educational psychology: Reflection for action.* Hoboken, NJ: Wiley & Sons.

O'Neill, R., Horner, R.H., Albin, R., Sprague, J., Storey, K., & Newton, S. (1997). *Functional assessment and program development for problem behavior: A practical handbook.* Pacific Grove, CA: Brooks/Cole.

O'Reilly, M.F., Lancioni, G.E., & Kierans, I. (2000). Teaching leisure skills to adults with moderate mental retardation: An analysis of acquisition, generalization, and maintenance. *Education and Training in Mental Retardation and Developmental Disabilities, 35,* 250–258.

O'Sullivan, J.L. (1999). Adult guardianship and alternatives. In R.D. Dinerstein, S.S. Herr, & J.L. O'Sullivan (Eds.), *A guide to consent* (pp. 7–37). Washington, DC: American Association on Mental Retardation.

Obiakor, F.E. (2001). Multicultural education: Powerful tool for preparing future general and special educators. *Teacher Education and Special Education, 24,* 241–255.

Oliver, P., & Brady, M.P. (2012). *Effects of covert audio coaching on parents' interactions with young children with autism.* Manuscript submitted for publication.

Olley, J.G. (2013). Definition of intellectual disability in criminal court cases. *Intellectual and Developmental Disabilities, 51*(2), 117–121.

Olmstead v. L.C., 527 U.S. 581 (1999).

Orenich (1988). EHLR 213:166.

Osborne, A., & Dimattia, P. (1994). The IDEA's least restrictive environment mandate: Legal implications. *Exceptional Children, 61,* 6–14.

Ostrosky, M., Drasgow, E., & Halle, J. (1999). How can I help you get what you want? A communication strategy for students with severe disabilities. *Teaching Exceptional Children, 31*(4), 56–61.

Oswald, D.P., & Coutinho, M.J. (2001). Trends in disproportionate representation in special education: Implications for multicultural education. In C.A. Utley & F.E. Obiakor (Eds.), *Special education, multicultural education, and school reform: Components of a quality education for students with mild disabilities* (pp. 53–73). Springfield, IL: Charles C. Thomas.

Oswald, D., Coutinho, M., Best, A., & Nguyen, N. (2001). Impact of sociodemographic characteristics on the identification rates of minority students as having mental retardation. *Mental Retardation, 39,* 351–367.

Papalia, D.E., & Feldman, R.D. (2011). *A child's world: Infancy through adolescence* (12th ed.). New York: McGraw-Hill.

Patton, J., Cronin, M., & Wood, S. (1999). *Infusing real-life topics into existing curricula at elementary, middle, and high school levels: Recommended procedures and instructional examples.* Austin, TX: Pro-Ed.

Paulson, F., Paulson, P., & Meyer, C. (1991). What makes a portfolio a portfolio? *Educational Leadership, 48,* 60–63.

Pearson. (2009). *Wechsler Individual Achievement Test–Third Edition.* San Antonio, TX: Pearson Assessments.

Pennsylvania Association for Retarded Children (PARC) v. Commonwealth of Pennsylvania, 334 F. Supp. 1257 (E.D. Pa. 1971), 343 F. Supp. 279 (E.D. Pa. 1972).

Pernick, M. (1996). *The black stork: Eugenics and the death of "defective" babies in American medicine and motion pictures since 1915.* New York: Oxford University Press.

Perske, R. (2000). Deception in the interrogation room: Sometimes tragic for persons with mental retardation and other developmental disabilities. *Mental Retardation, 38,* 532–537.

Peterson, L.Y., Burden, J.P., Sedaghat, J.M., Gothberg, J.E., Kohler, P.D., & Coyle, J.L. (2013). Triangulated IEP transition goals: Developing relevant and genuine annual goals. *Teaching Exceptional Children, 45*(6), 46–57.

Peverly, S., & Kitzen, K. (1998). Curriculum-based assessment of reading skills: Considerations and caveats for school psychologists. *Psychology in the Schools, 35,* 29–48.

Piaget, J. (1952). *The origins of intelligence in children.* New York: International Universities Press.

Pierangelo, R., & Giuliani, G.A. (2009). *Assessment in special education: A practical approach.* Upper Saddle River, NJ: Pearson.

Platter, F. (1614). *Observationum in hominis affectibus.* Basel, Switzerland: Lidovici, Koenig.

Plesa-Skwerer, D., Faja, S., Schofield, C., Verbalis, A., & Tager-Flusberg, H. (2006). Perceiving facial and vocal expressions of emotion in individuals with Williams syndrome. *American Journal on Mental Retardation, 111*(1), 15–26.

Podell, D.M., Tournaki-Rein, N., & Lin, A. (1992). Automatization of mathematics skills via computer assisted instruction among students with mild retardation. *Education and Training in Mental Retardation, 27,* 200–206.

Polister, B., Lakin, L., Smith, J., Prouty, R., & Smith, G. (2002). Institutional residents continue to decrease as community setting residents grow at an accelerating pace. *Mental Retardation, 40,* 488–490.

Polloway, E.A., Serna, L., Patton, J.R., & Bailey, J.W. (2013). *Strategies for teaching learners with special needs* (10th ed.). Boston: Pearson.

Polloway, E.A., Smith, J.D., Patton, J.R., & Smith, T.E.C. (1996). Historical changes in mental retardation and developmental disabilities. *Education and Training in Mental Retardation and Developmental Disabilities, 31,* 3–12.

Porter, M., & Stodden, R. (1986). A curriculum-based vocational assessment procedure: Addressing the school to work transition needs of secondary schools. *Career Development for Exceptional Individuals, 9,* 121–128.

Prader-Willi Syndrome Association (2012). *What is Prader-Willi syndrome?* Retrieved from http://www.pwsausa.org/syndrome/

President's Commission on Mental Retardation (PCMR). (1972). *Entering the era of human ecology.* Washington, DC: Department of Health Education and Welfare Publication no. (05), 72–77.

Pumpian, I., Fischer, D., Certo, N., & Smalley, K. (1997). Changing jobs: An essential part of career development. *Mental Retardation, 35,* 39–48.

Rais-Bahrami, K., & Short, B.L. (2013). Premature and small-for-dates infants. In M.L. Batshaw, N.J., Roizen, & G.R. Lotrecchiano (Eds.), *Children with disabilities* (7th ed., pp. 87–104). Baltimore: Paul H. Brookes.

Ramey, C.T., & Ramey, S.L. (1992). Effective early intervention. *Mental Retardation, 30,* 337–345.

Ransom, B.E., & Chimarusti, J. (1997). The education of juveniles in the criminal justice system: A mandate? *Impact, 10,* 24–25.

Raymond, E. (2000). *Learners with mild disabilities: A characteristics approach.* Boston: Allyn & Bacon.

Reamer, R., Brady, M.P., & Hawkins, J. (1998). The effects of video self-modeling on parents' interactions with children with developmental disabilities. *Education and Training in Mental Retardation and Developmental Disabilities, 33,* 131–143.

Reichle, J., & Wacker, D. (Eds.). (1993). *Communicative alternatives to challenging behavior.* Baltimore: Paul H. Brookes.

Reid, D.K. (1988). *Teaching the learning disabled.* Boston: Allyn & Bacon.

Reid, D., & Favell, J. (1984). Group instruction for people who have severe disabilities: A critical review. *Journal of the Association for Persons with Severe Handicaps, 9,* 167–177.

Reilly, C., & Holland, N. (2013). Symptoms of attention deficit hyperactivity disorder in children and adults with intellectual disability: A review. *Journal of Applied Research in Intellectual Disabilities, 24,* 291–309.

Reschly, D. (1979). Nonbiased assessment. In G. Phye & D. Reschly (Eds.), *School psychology: Perspectives and issues* (pp. 215–253). New York: Academic Press.

Reschly, D., & Ross-Reynolds, J. (1980). *Report: Iowa assessment project.* Unpublished manuscript, Department of Psychology, Iowa State University.

Reynolds, C., & Kamphaus, R. (1992). *Behavior Assessment System for Children*. Circle Pines, MN: American Guidance Service.

Reynolds, C. R., & Kamphaus, R. W. (2004). *Behavior Assessment for Children* (2nd ed.). San Antonio, TX: Pearson Assessments.

Reynolds, M. (1989). An historical perspective: The delivery of special education to mildly disabled and at-risk students. *Remedial and Special Education, 10*(6), 7–11.

Reynolds, M. C., & Birch, J. W. (1982). *Teaching exceptional children in all America's schools* (Rev. ed.). Reston, VA: Council for Exceptional Children.

Reynolds, M., & Wang, M. (1983). Restructuring "special" school programs: A position paper. *Policy Studies Review, 2*(1), 189–212.

Richards, S. B., Taylor, R. L., & Ramasamy, R. (2013). *Single subject research: Applications in educational and clinical settings* (2nd ed.). Belmont, CA: Wadsworth Cengage Learning.

Rillotta, F., Kirby, N., Shearer, J., & Nettlebeck, T. (2012). Family quality of life of Australian families with a member with an intellectual/developmental disability. *Journal of Intellectual Disability Research, 56,* 71–86.

Riverside Publishing (n.d.). *Overview of the Woodcock-Johnson III Normative Update Tests of Cognitive Abilities.* www.riversidepublishing.com

Roberts, M. Y., & Kaiser, A. P. (2011). The effectiveness of parent-implemented language interventions: A meta-analysis. *American Journal of Speech-Language Pathology, 20,* 180–199.

Robison, D., & Gonzalez, L. S. (1999). Children born premature: A review of linguistic and behavioral outcomes. *Infant-Toddler Intervention, 9,* 373–390.

Roid, G. (2003). *Stanford-Binet Intelligence Scale* (5th ed.). Chicago: Riverside.

Rojahn, J., Zaja, R. H., Turygin, N., Moore, L., & van Ingen, D. J. (2012). Functions of maladaptive behavior in intellectual and developmental disabilities: Behavior categories and topographies. *Research in Developmental Disabilities, 33*(6), 2020–2027.

Romer, L. T., & Walker, P. (2013). Offering person-centered supports on a daily basis: An initial appreciative inquiry into the relationship between personal assistants and those seeking support. *Research and Practice for Persons with Severe Disabilities, 38,* 186–195.

Roncker v. Walter, 700 F.2d 1058 (1983).

Rosenberg, H. & Brady, M. P. (2000). *Job Observation and Behavior Scale (JOBS): A work performance evaluation for supported and entry level employees.* Wood Dale, IL: Stoelting.

Rotholz, D. A. (2009). President's address 2008—Creating the future: Beyond our inheritance of the past. *Intellectual and Developmental Disabilities, 47*(2), 125–134.

Ryndak, D., Downing, J., Jacqueline, L., & Morrison, A. (1995). Parents' perceptions after inclusion of their children with moderate or severe disabilities. *Journal of the Association of Persons with Severe Handicaps, 20,* 147–157.

S-1 v. Turlington. EHLR 558:136 (S.D. Fla. 1981).

Sacramento City Unified School District Board of Education v. Rachel H., 14 F.3rd 1398 (9th Cir. 1994).

Sadker, M. P., & Sadker, D. M. (2003). *Teachers, schools, and society.* New York: McGraw-Hill.

Salekin, K. L., Olley, J. G., Hedge, K. A. (2010). Offenders with intellectual disability: Characteristics, prevalence, and issues in forensic assessment. *Journal of Mental Health Research in Intellectual Disabilities, 3,* 97–116.

Salend, S., & Duhaney, L. M. (1999). The impact of inclusion on students with and without disabilities and their educators. *Remedial and Special Education, 20,* 114–126.

Saloviita, T. J., & Tuulkari, M. (2000). Cognitive-behavioural treatment package for teaching grooming skills to a man with intellectual disability. *Scandinavian Journal of Behaviour Therapy, 29,* 140–147.

Sandoval, J., & Miille, M. (1980). Accuracy of judgments of WISC-R item difficulty for minority groups. *Journal of Consulting and Clinical Psychology, 48,* 249–253.

Santrock, J. W. (2001). *Educational psychology.* New York: McGraw-Hill.

Santrock, J. W. (2011). *Life span development* (13th ed.). New York: McGraw-Hill.

Sarkees-Wircenski, M., & Wircenski, J. (1994). Transition planning: Developing a career portfolio for students with disabilities. *Career Development for Exceptional Individuals, 17,* 203–214.

Saunders, A. F., Spooner, F., Browder, D., Wakeman, S., & Lee, A. (2013). Teaching the Common Core in English language arts to students with severe disabilities. *Teaching Exceptional Children, 46*(2), 22–33.

Saunders, M. D., Saunders, R. R., & Marquis, J. G. (1998). Comparison of reinforcement schedules in the reduction of stereotypy with supported routines. *Research in Developmental Disabilities, 19,* 99–122.

Schalock, R. (2002). Definitional issues. In R. Schalock, P. Baker, & D. Croser (Eds.), *Embarking on a new century* (pp. 29–49). Washington, DC: American Association on Mental Retardation.

Schalock, R. L., Borthwick-Duffy, S. A., Bradley, V. J., Buntinx, W. H., Coulter, D. L., Craig, E. M., . . . & Yeager, M. H. (2010). *Intellectual disability: Definition, classification, and systems of supports* (11th ed.). Washington, DC: American Association on Intellectual and Developmental Disabilities.

Schalock, R. L., Buntinx, W., Borthwick-Duffy, S., Luckasson, R., Snell, M., Tassé, M. J., et al. (2007). *User's guide: Mental retardation definition, classification, and systems of supports.* Washington, DC: American Association on Mental Retardation.

Schalock, R. L., & Luckasson, R. (2013). What's at stake in the lives of people with intellectual disability? Part I: The power of naming, defining, diagnosing, classifying, and planning supports. *Intellectual and Developmental Disabilities, 51*(2), 86–93.

Schanen, L. (1997). *The genetics of Rett syndrome.* Retrieved from www.Rettsyndrome.org/main/genetics_of_rett_syndrome.htm

Scheerenberger, R. (1983). *A history of mental retardation.* Baltimore: Paul H. Brookes.

Scheuermann, B., & Webber, J. (2002). *Autism: Teaching does make a difference.* Belmont, CA: Wadsworth/Thomson Learning.

Schloss, P., & Smith, M. (1998). *Applied behavior analysis in the classroom.* Boston: Allyn & Bacon.

Schopler, E., & Mesibov, G. (1995). *Learning and cognition in autism.* New York: Plenum.

Schuchardt, K., Gebhardt, M., & Maehler, C. (2010). Working memory functions in children with different degrees of intellectual disability. *Journal of Intellectual Disability Research, 54,* 346–353.

Scott, B., Vitale, M., & Masten, W. (1998). Implementing instructional adaptations for students with disabilities in inclusive classrooms: A literature review. *Remedial and Special Education, 19,* 106–119.

Scott, J., Clark, C., & Brady, M. P. (2000). *Students with autism: Characteristics and instructional programming for special educators.* San Diego: Singular Publishing Group.

Seguin, E. (1866). *Idiocy and its treatment by the physiological method.* New York: William Wood.

Seltzer, M. M., Greenberg, J. S., Floyd, F. J., Pettee, Y., & Hong, J. (2001). Life course impacts of parenting a child with a disability. *American Journal on Mental Retardation, 106,* 265–286.

Seltzer, M. M., Krauss, M. W., Hong. J., & Orsmond, G. I. (2001). Continuity or discontinuity of family involvement following residential transitions of adults who have mental retardation. *Mental Retardation, 39,* 181–194.

Serna, R. W., & Carlin, M. T. (2001). Guiding visual attention in individuals with mental retardation. In L. M. Glidden (Ed.), *International review of research in mental retardation* (Vol. 24, pp. 321–357). San Diego, CA: Academic Press.

Shapiro, B. K., & Batshaw, M. L. (2013). Developmental delay and intellectual disability. In M. L. Batshaw, N. J. Roizen, & G. R. Lotrecchiano (Eds.), *Children with disabilities* (7th ed., pp. 291–306). Baltimore: Paul H. Brookes.

Sheppard, L., & Unsworth, C. (2011). Developing skills in everyday activities and self-determination in adolescents with intellectual and developmental disabilities. *Remedial and Special Education, 32,* 392–405.

Shinn, M., & Bamonto, S. (1998). Advanced applications of curriculum-based measurement: "Big ideas" and avoiding confusion. In M. Shinn (Ed.), *Advanced applications of curriculum-based measurement* (pp. 1–31). New York: Guilford Press.

Shogren, K. A., & Broussard, R. (2011). Exploring the perceptions of self-determination of individuals with intellectual disabilities. *Intellectual and Developmental Disabilities, 49,* 86–102.

Shogren, K. A., Bovaird, J. A., Palmer, S. B., & Wehmeyer, M. L. (2010). Locus of control orientations in students with intellectual disability, learning disabilities and no disabilities: A latent growth curve analysis. *Research and Practice for Persons with Severe Disabilities, 35,* 80–92.

Shrank, F., McGrew, N., & Woodcock, R. (2001). *WJ-III technical report.* Chicago: Riverside.

Shriner, J. G. (2000). Legal perspectives on school outcome assessment for students with disabilities. *Journal of Special Education, 33,* 232–239.

Simon, T. J. (2010). Rewards and challenges of cognitive neuroscience studies of persons with intellectual and developmental disabilities. *American Journal on Intellectual and Developmental Disabilities, 115,* 79–82.

Simpson, R., & Myles, B. (Eds.). (1998). *Educating children and youth with autism.* Austin, TX: Pro-Ed.

Siperstein, G. N., & Leffert, J. S. (1997). A comparison of socially accepted and rejected children with mental retardation. *American Journal on Mental Retardation, 101,* 339–351.

Skeels, H. M., & Dye, H. B. (1939). A study of the effects of differential stimulation on mentally retarded children. *Proceedings of the American Association of Mental Deficiency, 44,* 114–136.

Skiba, R. J., Poloni-Staudinger, L., Simmons, A. B., Feggins-Azziz, L. R., & Chung, C.-G. (2005). Unproven links: Can poverty explain ethnic disproportionality in special education? *Journal of Special Education, 39*(3), 130–144.

Skiba, R. J., Simmons, A. B., Ritter, S., Gibb, A. C., Rausch, M. K., Cuadrado, J., & Chung, C.-G. (2008). Achieving equity in special education: History, status, and current challenges. *Exceptional Children, 74*, 264–288.

Skrtic, T. (1992). The special education paradox: Equity as the way to excellence. In T. Heher & T. Latus (Eds.), *Special education at the century's end* (pp. 203–272). Cambridge, MA: Harvard Educational Review.

Smith, A., Hunter, D., & Shrag, J. (1991). America 2000. An opportunity for school restructuring and inclusion. *Impact, 4*(3), 4–5.

Smith, J. D. (1997). The challenge of advocacy: The different voices of Helen Keller and Burton Blatt. *Mental Retardation, 35*, 138–140.

Smith, J. D., & Wehmeyer, M. L. (2012). Who was Deborah Kallikak? *Intellectual and Developmental Disabilities, 50*(2), 169–178.

Smith, M., Klim, P., & Hanley, W. (2000). Executive function in school-aged children with phenylketonuria. *Journal of Developmental and Physical Disabilities, 12*, 317–332.

Smith, T., Polloway, E. A., Patton, J. R., & Beyer, J. F. (2008). Individuals with intellectual and developmental disabilities in the criminal justice system and implications for transition planning. *Education and Training in Developmental Disabilities, 43*, 421–430.

Snell, M. E., & Brown, F. (2011a). *Instruction of students with severe disabilities* (7th ed.). Upper Saddle River, NJ: Pearson.

Snell, M. E., & Brown, F. (2011b). Selecting teaching strategies and arranging educational environments. In M. E. Snell & F. Brown (Eds.), *Instruction of students with severe disabilities* (7th ed., pp. 122–185). Upper Saddle River, NJ: Pearson.

Snell, M. E., & Luckasson, R. (with S. Borthwick-Duffy, V. Bradley, W. H. E. Buntinx, D. L. Coulter, E. M. Craig, S. C. Gomez, Y. Lachapelle, A. Reeve, R. L. Schalock, K. A. Shogren, S. Spreat, M. J. Tassé, J. R. Thompson, M. A. Verdugo, M. L. Wehmeyer, & M. H. Yeager) (2009). Characteristics and needs of people with intellectual disability who have higher IQs. *Intellectual and Developmental Disabilities, 47*, 220–233.

Sobsey, D. (1997). Equal protection of the law for crime victims with developmental disabilities. *Impact, 10*, 7–8.

Solish, A., Perry, A., & Minnes, P. (2010). Participation of children with and without disabilities in social, recreational and leisure activities. *Journal of Applied Research in Intellectual Disabilities, 23*, 226–236.

Sparrow, S. S., Cicchettim, D. V., & Balla, D. A. (2006). *Vineland-II*. Toronto: Pearson Canada Assessment.

Spearman, R. (1927). *The abilities of man: Their nature and measurement*. New York: Macmillan.

Stainback, S., & Stainback, W. (1985). *Integration of students with severe handicaps into regular schools*. Reston, VA: Council for Exceptional Children.

Stancliffe, R. J. (1997). Community living unit size, staff presence, and residents' choice-making. *Mental Retardation, 35*(1), 1–9.

Stein, S. (2012). *Review of the Vineland Adaptive Behavior Scales-II. Mental measurements yearbook and tests in print*. Online resource provided by the Board of Regents of the University of Nebraska and the Buros Center for Testing. http://web.b.ebscohost.com/ehost/detail?vid=7&sid=2146364e-8fd3-4335-b2d1-3b7e b464a81c%40sessionmgr112&hid=118&bdata=JmxvZ2luLmFzcCZzaXRlPWVob3N0LWxpdmU%3d#d b=mmt&AN=TIP18193482

Stern, W. (1914). The psychological methods of testing intelligence. In *Educational Psychology Monographs*. Baltimore: Warwick & York.

Stevens, G. D. (1954). Developments in the field of mental deficiency. *Exceptional Children, 21*, 58–62, 70.

Stillman, R. (1978). *Callier-Azusa Scale*. Dallas: University of Texas at Dallas Center of Communication Disorders.

Stokes, T. F., & Baer, D. M. (1977). An implicit technology of generalization. *Journal of Applied Behavior Analysis, 10*, 349–367.

Storey, K. (1997). Quality of life issues in social skills assessment of persons with disabilities. *Education and Training in Mental Retardation and Developmental Disabilities, 32*, 197–200.

Storey, K. (2002). Systematic instruction: Developing and maintaining skills that enhance community inclusion. In K. Storey, P. Bates, & D. Hunter (Eds.), *The road ahead: Transition to adult life for persons with disabilities* (pp. 47–64). St. Augustine, FL: Training Resource Network.

Storey, K., Bates, P., & Hunter, D. (2002). *The road ahead: Transition to adult life for persons with disabilities*. St. Augustine, FL: Training Resource Network.

Strain, P.S., & Fox, J.J. (1981). Peer social interactions and the modification of social withdrawal: A review and future perspective. *Journal of Pediatric Psychology, 6,* 417–433.

Strain, P.S., & Shores, R.E. (1977). Social reciprocity: A review of research and educational implications. *Exceptional Children, 43,* 526–530.

Sullivan, A.L. (2011). Disproportionality in special education identification and placement of English Language Learners. *Exceptional Children, 77,* 317–334.

Sutherland, G. (1977). Fragile sites on human chromosomes: Demonstration of their dependence on the type of tissue culture medium. *Science, 197,* 265–266.

Swanson, H.L. (1999). What develops in working memory? A lifespan perspective. *Developmental Psychology, 35,* 986–1000.

Switzky, H. (1997). Mental retardation and the neglected construct of motivation. *Education and Training in Mental Retardation, 32,* 194–196.

Tager-Flusberg, H., & Sullivan, K. (1998). Early language development in children with mental retardation. In J.A. Burack, R.M. Hodapp et al. (Eds.), *Handbook of mental retardation and development* (pp. 208–239). New York: Cambridge University Press.

Taylor, R.L. (2009). *Assessment of exceptional students: Educational and psychological procedures* (8th ed.). Upper Saddle River, NJ: Pearson/Merrill.

Taylor, R., & Caldwell, M.L. (1985). Type and strength of food preferences of individuals with Prader-Willi syndrome. *Journal of Mental Deficiency Research, 29,* 109–112.

Taylor, R., & Partenio, I. (1983). *Florida norms for the SOMPA.* Tallahassee, FL: Department of Education.

Taylor, R.L., Smiley, L.R., & Richards, S.B. (2015). *Exceptional students: Preparing teachers for the 21st century* (2nd ed.). New York: McGraw-Hill.

Taylor, R., Smiley, L., & Ziegler, E. (1983). The effects of labels and assigned attributes on teacher perceptions of academic and social behavior. *Education and Training of the Mentally Retarded, 18,* 45–51.

Taylor, S. (1988). Caught in the continuum: A critical analysis of the principle of the least restrictive environment. *Journal of the Association of Persons with Severe Handicaps, 13,* 41–53.

Taylor, S.J. (2001). The continuum and current controversies in the USA. *Journal of Intellectual Disability Research, 26,* 15–33.

The ARC. (2006). *Justice advocacy guide.* Retrieved from http://www.thearc.org/document.doc?id=3669

The ARC. (2008a). *Position statement parents with intellectual and/or developmental disabilities.* Retrieved from www.thearc.org

The ARC. (2008b). *Position statement sexuality.* Retrieved from www.thearc.org

The ARC. (2011). *Parents with intellectual disabilities.* Retrieved from www.thearc.org

The ARC & AAIDD. (2008). *Criminal justice.* Retrieved from www.thearc.org

The ARC & AAIDD. (2009a). *Guardianship.* Retrieved from www.thearc.org

The ARC & AAIDD. (2009b). *Quality of life.* Retrieved from www.thearc.org

Thirion-Marissiaux, A.-F., & Nader-Grosbois, N. (2008). Theory of mind "beliefs," developmental characteristics and social understanding in children and adolescents with intellectual disabilities. *Research in Developmental Disabilities, 29,* 547–566.

Thoma, C.A., Nathanson, R., Baker, S.R., & Tamura, R. (2002). Self determination: What do special educators know and where do they learn it? *Remedial and Special Education, 23,* 242–247.

Thompson, J., Bryant, B., Campbell, E.M., Craig, E., Hughes, C., Rotholz, D., . . . & Wehmeyer, M.L. (2004). *Supports Intensity Scale: Interview and Profile Form.* Washington, DC: American Association on Mental Retardation

Thompson, J., Craig, E., Schalock, R., Tassé, M., Bryant, B., Hughes, C., Silverman, W., . . . & Rotholz, D. (2002). *Supports Intensity Scale.* Washington, DC: American Association on Mental Retardation.

Thorn, S.H., Pittman, A., Myers, R.E., & Slaughter, C. (2009). Increasing community integration and inclusion for people with intellectual disabilities. *Research in Developmental Disabilities: A Multidisciplinary Journal, 30*(5), 891–901.

Thurlow, M., & Elliot, J. (1998). Student assessment and evaluation. In F. Rusch & J. Chadsey (Eds.), *Beyond high school: Transition from school to work* (pp. 265–296). Belmont, CA: Wadsworth.

Thurstone, L. (1938). *Primary mental abilities.* Chicago: University of Chicago Press.

Thurstone, L. (1941). *Factorial studies of intelligence.* Chicago: University of Chicago Press.

Thurstone, L. (1947). *Multiple factor analysis: A development and expansion of vectors of mind.* Chicago: University of Chicago Press.

Timothy W. v. Rochester School District, 875 F.2d 954 (1st Cir. 1988).

Tredgold, A. (1937). *A textbook of mental deficiency*. Baltimore: Wood.

Tredgold, R. F., & Soddy, K. (1956). *A handbook of mental deficiency*. Baltimore: Williams & Wilkins.

Trent, J. W., Jr. (1994). *Inventing the feeble mind. A history of mental retardation in the United States*. Berkeley: University of California Press.

Tsiouris, J. A., Kim, S. Y., Brown, W. T., & Cohen, I. L. (2011). Association of aggressive behaviours with psychiatric disorders, age, sex, and degree of intellectual disability: A large-scale survey. *Journal of Intellectual Disability Research, 55*, 636–649.

Tuberous Sclerosis Alliance (2013). *TSC and Autism Spectrum Disorders*. Retrieved from www.tsalliance.org

Tucker, J. (1985). Curriculum-based assessment: An introduction. *Exceptional Children, 52*, 199–204.

Turk, J., & Graham, P. (1998). Fragile X syndrome, autism, and autistic features. *Autism, 1*, 175–197.

Turnbull, A. P., & Turnbull, H. R. (1988). Toward great expectations for vocational opportunities: Family–professional partnerships. *Mental Retardation, 26*, 337–342.

Turnbull, A. P., & Turnbull, H. R. (1997). *Families, professionals, and exceptionality: A special partnership*. Upper Saddle River, NJ: Merrill/Prentice Hall.

Turnbull, A., Turnbull, H. R., Erwin, E., & Soodak, L. (2006). *Families, professionals, and exceptionality. Collaborating for empowerment* (5th ed.). Upper Saddle River, NJ: Pearson.

Turnbull, H. R., Ellis, J., Boggs, E., Brooks, P., & Biklen, D. (1981). *The Least Restrictive Alternative: Principles and practices*. Washington, DC: American Association on Mental Deficiency.

Turnbull, H. R., Stowe, M., & Huerta, N. (2007). *Free appropriate public education: The law and children with disabilities* (7th ed.). Denver, CO: Love Publishing.

Turner, L. (1998). Relation of attributional beliefs to memory strategy use in children and adolescents with mental retardation. *American Journal of Mental Retardation, 103*, 162–172.

U.S. Department of Education. (1993). *Reinventing Chapter 1: The current Chapter 1 program and new directions: Final report of the national assessment of the Chapter 1 program*. Washington, DC: Author. (ED 355 330).

U.S. Department of Education. (2008). *30th Annual Report to Congress on the Implementation of the Individuals with Disabilities Education Act*. Washington, DC: U.S. Government Printing Office.

U.S. Department of Health and Human Services. (2009). *Sexually transmitted infection (STI) fact sheet*. Retrieved from www.womenshealth.gov

U.S. National Library of Medicine. (2011a). *Congenital cytomegalovirus*. Retrieved from http://www.nlm.nih.gov/medlineplus/ency/article/001343.htm

U.S. National Library of Medicine. (2011b). *Congenital rubella*. Retrieved from http://www.nlm.nih.gov/medlineplus/ency/article/001658.htm

U.S. National Library of Medicine. (2011c). *Malnutrition*. Retrieved from http://www.nlm.nih.gov/medlineplus/malnutrition.html

U.S. National Library of Medicine. (2012a). *Methylmercury poisoning*. Retrieved from http://www.nlm.nih.gov/medlineplus/ency/article/001651.htm

U.S. National Library of Medicine. (2012b). *Syphilis-primary*. Retrieved from http://www.nlm.nih.gov/medlineplus/ency/article/000861.htm

U.S. National Library of Medicine. (2013a). *Lead poisoning*. Retrieved from http://www.nlm.nih.gov/medlineplus/ency/article/000861.htm

U.S. National Library of Medicine (2013b). *Tay-Sachs disease*. Retrieved from http://www.nlm.nih.gov/medlineplus/taysachsdisease.html

Valencia, R., & Suzuki, L. (2001). *Intelligence testing and minority students*. Thousand Oaks, CA: Sage Publications.

van den Bos, K. P., Nakken, H., Nicolay, P. G., & van Houten, E. J. (2007). Adults with mild intellectual disabilities: Can their reading comprehension ability be improved? *Journal of Intellectual Disability Research, 51*, 835–849.

Vandereet, J., Maes, B., Lembrechts, D., & Zink, I. (2010). Predicting expressive vocabulary acquisition in children with intellectual disabilities: A 2-year longitudinal study. *Journal of Speech, Language, and Hearing Research, 53*, 1673–1686.

Van der Molen, M. J., van Luit, J. E. H., Jongmans, M. J., & van der Molen, M. W. (2007). Verbal working memory in children with mild intellectual disabilities. *Journal of Intellectual Disability Research, 51*, 162–169.

Van der Molen, M. J., van Luit, J. E. H., van der Molen, M. W., Klugkist, I., & Jongmans, M. J. (2010). Effectiveness of a computerized working memory training in adolescents with mild to borderline intellectual disabilities. *Journal of Intellectual Disability Research, 54*, 443–447.

van der Schuit, M., Peters, M., Segers, E., van Balkom, H., & Verhoeven, L. (2009). Home literacy environment of pre-school children with intellectual disabilities. *Journal of Intellectual Disability Research, 53*, 1024–1037.

van der Schuit, M., Segers, E., van Balkom, H., & Verhoeven, L. (2011). How cognitive factors affect language development in children with intellectual disabilities. *Research in Developmental Disabilities, 32,* 1884–1894.

Van Gassen, G., & Van Broekhoven, C. (2000). Molecular genetics of Alzheimer's disease: What have we learned? *Acta Neurologica Belgica, 100,* 65–76.

Van Nieuwenhuijzen, M., & Vriens, A. (2012). (Social) cognitive skills and social information processing in children with mild to borderline intellectual disabilities. *Research in Developmental Disabilities, 33,* 426–434.

Varsamis, P., & Agaliotis, I. (2011). Profiles of self-concept, goal orientation, and self-regulation in students with physical, intellectual, and multiple disabilities: Implications for instructional support. *Research in Developmental Disabilities, 32,* 1548–1555.

Vavrus, L. (1990). Put portfolios to the test. *Instructor, 100,* 48–53.

Verkerk, A., Pieretti, M., Sutcliffe, J., Fu, Y., Kuhl, D., Pizzuti, A., Reiner, O., . . . & Warren, S. T. (1991). Identification of a gene (FMR-1) containing a CGG repeat coincident with a breakpoint cluster region exhibiting length variation of Fragile X syndrome. *Cell, 65,* 905–914.

Verri, A., Cremante, A., Clerici, F., Destefani, V., & Radicioni, A. (2010). Klinefelter's syndrome and psychoneurologic function. *MHR: Basic Science of Reproductive Medicine, 16*(6), 425–433.

Vicari, S. (2004). Memory development and intellectual disabilities. *Acta Paediatr 2004; Suppl. 445,* 60–64.

Vlasak, J. (1980). Mainstreaming handicapped children: The underlying legal concept. *Journal of School Health, May,* 285–287.

Voeltz, L. M. (1980). Children's attitudes toward handicapped peers. *American Journal on Mental Deficiency, 84,* 455–464.

Voeltz, L. M. (1982). Effects of structured interactions with severely handicapped peers on children's attitudes. *American Journal on Mental Deficiency, 86,* 380–390.

VORT Corporation. (1973). *Behavioral Characteristics Progression.* Palo Alto, CA: Author.

Vulpé, S. (1994). *Vulpé Assessment Battery-Revised.* East Aurora, NY: Slosson.

Wagner, B. (2002). The narrowing of institutions. In R. Schalock, P. Baker, & M. D. Croser (Eds.), *Embarking on a new century* (pp. 101–110). Washington, DC: American Association on Mental Retardation.

Waisbren, S. (1999). Phenylketonuria. In S. Goldstein & C. Reynolds (Eds.), *Handbook of neurodevelopmental and genetic disorders in children* (pp. 433–458). New York: Guilford Press.

Warren, S. (2002). Presidential address 2002—Genes, brains, and behavior: The road ahead. *Mental Retardation, 40,* 1–6.

Warren, S. F., & Reichle, J. (Eds.). (1992). *Causes and effects in communication and language intervention.* Baltimore: Paul H. Brookes.

Watkins, E. E. (2009). Marriage rights of individuals with intellectual disabilities. *EP Magazine,* Retrieved from www.eparent.com

Watson, J. D., & Crick, F. H. C. (1953). A structure for deoxyribose nucleic acid. *Nature, 171,* 737.

Webster, D., Clary G., & Griffith, P. (2001). Postsecondary education and career paths. In R. W. Flexer, T. J. Simmons, P. Luft, & R. M. Baer (Eds.), *Transition planning for secondary students with disabilities* (pp. 439–473). Columbus, OH: Merrill/Prentice Hall.

Wechsler, D. (1958). *The measurement and appraisal of adult intelligence.* Baltimore: Williams and Wilkins.

Wechsler, D. (2003). *Wechsler Intelligence Scale for Children-IV.* San Antonio: Psychological Corporation.

Weeks, M., & Gaylord-Ross, R. (1981). Task difficulty and aberrant behavior in severely handicapped students. *Journal of Applied Behavior Analysis, 14,* 449–463.

Wehmeyer, M. (2003). Defining mental retardation and ensuring access to the general curriculum. *Education and Training of Developmental Disabilities, 38,* 271–277.

Wehmeyer, M. L. (2001). Self-determination and mental retardation: Assembling the puzzle pieces. In H. N. Switzky (Ed.), *Personality and motivational differences in persons with mental retardation* (pp. 147–198). Mahwah, NJ: Lawrence Erlbaum Associates.

Wehmeyer, M., Agran, M., & Hughes, C. (2000). A national survey of teachers' promotion of self-determination and student-directed learning. *Journal of Special Education, 24,* 58–68.

Wehmeyer, M. L., & Bolding, N. (2001). Enhanced self-determination of adults with intellectual disability as an outcome of moving to community-based work or living environments. *Journal of Intellectual Disability Research, 45,* 371–383.

Wehmeyer, M., & Schwartz, M. (1997). Self-determination and positive adult outcomes: A follow-up study of youth with mental retardation or learning disabilities. *Exceptional Children, 63,* 245–255.

Wehmeyer, M. L., & Schwartz, M. (1998). The relationship between self-determination and quality of life for adults with mental retardation. *Education and Training in Mental Retardation, 33,* 3–12.

Werner, H., & Strauss, A. A. (1943). Impairment in thought processes of brain-injured children. *American Journal of Mental Deficiency, 47,* 291–295.

Westling, D. L., & Fox, L. (2009). *Teaching students with severe disabilities* (4th ed.). Upper Saddle River, NJ: Merrill.

Westling, D. L., Kelley, K. R., Cain, B., & Prohn, S. (2013). College students' attitudes about an inclusive postsecondary education program for individuals with intellectual disability. *Education and Training in Autism and Developmental Disabilities, 48,* 306–319.

Wheeler, P., & Haertel, G. (1993). *Resource handbook on performance assessment and measurement: A tool for students, practitioners, and policy-makers.* Berkeley, CA: Owl Press.

White, O. R., & Haring, N. (1980). *Exceptional teaching.* Columbus, OH: Merrill.

Widerstrom, A. H. (1997). Looking toward the future. In A. H. Widerstrom, B. A. Mowder, & S. R. Sandall (Eds.), *Infant development and risk* (2nd ed., pp. 335–346). Baltimore: Paul H. Brookes.

Widerstrom, A. H., & Nickel, R. E. (1997). Determinants of risk in infancy. In A. H. Widerstrom, B. A. Mowder, & S. R. Sandall (Eds.), *Infant development and risk* (2nd ed., pp. 61–88). Baltimore: Paul H. Brookes.

Wilkinson, K. M., & Hennig, S. (2007). The state of research and practice in augmentative and alternative communication for children with developmental/intellectual disabilities. *Mental Retardation and Developmental Disabilities Research Reviews, 13,* 58–69.

Will, M. (1986). Educating children with learning problems: A shared responsibility. *Exceptional Children, 52,* 411–416.

Williams, C. A. (2010). *The behavioral phenotype of the Angelman syndrome.* Gainesville, FL: Wiley-Liss Inc.

Winzer, M. (1993). *The history of special education.* Washington, DC: Gallaudet Free Press.

Witter, A. N., & Lecavalier, L. (2008). Psychopathology in children with intellectual disability: Risk markers and correlates. *Journal of Mental Health Research in Intellectual Disabilities, 1,* 75–96.

Wolery, M., Bailey, D., & Sugai, G. (1988). *Effective teaching: Principles and procedures of applied behavior analysis with exceptional students.* Boston: Allyn & Bacon.

Wolfensberger, W. (1972). *The principle of normalization in human services.* Toronto: National Institute on Mental Retardation.

Wolfensberger, W. (1973). The future of residential services for the mentally retarded. *Journal of Clinical Child Psychology, 2*(1), 19–20.

Wolfensberger, W. (1975). *The origin and nature of institutional models.* Syracuse, NY: Human Policy Press.

Wolfensberger, W. (1983). Social role valorization: A proposed new term for the principle of normalization. *Mental Retardation, 21,* 234–239.

Wolfensberger, W. (2000). A brief overview of social role valorization. *Mental Retardation, 33*(3), 163–169.

Wolff, P., Gardner, J., Paccia, J., & Lappan, J. (1989). The greeting behavior of Fragile X males. *American Journal on Mental Retardation, 93,* 406–411.

Woodcock, R., McGrew, N., & Mather, N. (2001). *Woodcock-Johnson-III.* Chicago: Riverside.

Woodcock, R., McGrew, N., & Mather, N. (2007). *Woodcock-Johnson-III* (Normative Update). Chicago: Riverside.

Woodward, M. (1963). The application of Piaget's theory to research in mental deficiency. In N. R. Ellis (Ed.), *Handbook of mental deficiency* (pp. 297–324). New York: McGraw-Hill.

Woolfolk, A. (2013). *Educational psychology* (12th ed.). Upper Saddle River, NJ: Pearson.

World Health Organization. (1993). *International statistical classification of diseases and related health problems* (10th ed.). Geneva: Author.

World Health Organization. (2001). *International classification of functioning, disability, and health (ICF).* Geneva: Author.

World Health Organization. (2011a). *International statistical classification of diseases and related health problems (ICD-10).* Geneva: Author.

World Health Organization. (2011b). *Sexually transmitted infections.* Retrieved from http://www.who.int/mediacentre/factsheets/fs110/en/

WPS Publishing Company. (n.d.). *Overview of the Kaufman Assessment Battery for Children* (2nd ed.). www.wpspublishing.com.

Wyatt v. Stickney (1974), 344 F. Supp. 387, 344 F. Supp. 373 (M.D. Ala. 1972), 334 F. Supp. 1341, 325 F. Supp. 781 (M.D. Ala. 1971), 772 aff'd sub nom. *Wyatt v. Aderholt,* 503 F.2d, 1305 (5th Cir.).

Yang, Q., Wen, S. W., Leader, A., Chen, X. K., Lipson, J., & Walker, M. (2007). Paternal age and birth defects: How strong is the association? *Human Reproduction, 22,* 696–701.

Yaun, A., Keating, R., & Gropman, A. (2013). The brain and nervous system. In M. L. Batshaw, N. J. Roizen, & G. R. Lotrecchiano (Eds.), *Children with disabilities* (7th ed., pp. 189–211). Baltimore: Paul H. Brookes.

Yell, M. (1998). *The law and special education.* Englewood Cliffs, NJ: Prentice Hall.

Yoong, A., & Koritsas, S. (2012). The impact of caring for adults with intellectual disability on the quality of life of parents. *Journal of Intellectual Disability Research, 56,* 609–619.

Youngberg v. Romeo (1982). 457 U.S. 307.

Ysseldyke, J., & Bielinski, J. (2002). Effect of different methods of reporting and reclassification on trends in test scores for students with disabilities. *Exceptional Children, 68,* 189–200.

Ysseldyke, J., & Olsen, K. (1999). Putting alternate assessments into practice: What to measure and possible sources of data. *Exceptional Children, 65,* 175–185.

Ysseldyke, J., Thurlow, M., Bielinski, J., House, A., Moody, M., & Haigh, J. (2001). The relationship between instructional and assessment accommodations in an inclusive state accountability system. *Journal of Learning Disabilities, 34,* 212–220.

Zajicek-Farber, S. (2013). Caring and coping: Helping the family of a child with a disability. In M. L. Batshaw, N. J. Roizen, & G. R. Lotrecchiano (Eds.), *Children with disabilities* (7th ed., pp. 657–672). Baltimore: Paul H. Brookes.

Zeaman, D., & House, B. J. (1963). The role of attention in retardate discrimination learning. In N. R. Ellis (Ed.), *Handbook of mental deficiency* (pp. 159–223). New York: McGraw-Hill.

Zellweiger, H., & Schneider, H. (1968). Syndrome of hypotonia–hypomentia–hypogonadism–obesity (HHHO) or Prader-Willi syndrome. *American Journal of the Diseases of Children, 115,* 588–598.

Zigler, E. (1969a). Developmental versus difference theories of mental retardation and the problem of motivation. *American Journal of Mental Deficiency, 73,* 536–556.

Zigler, E. (1969b). Development vs. difference theories of mental retardation and the problem of motivation. In E. Zigler & D. Balla (Eds.), *Mental retardation: The developmental difference controversy* (pp. 163–188). Hillsdale, NJ: Erlbaum.

Zigler, E., & Hodapp, R. M. (1986). *Understanding mental retardation.* New York: Cambridge University Press.

Zigman, W. B., & Lott, I. T. (2007). Alzheimer's disease in Down syndrome: Neurobiology and risk. *Mental Retardation and Developmental Disabilities Research Reviews, 13*(3), 237–246.

Zigman, W. B., Schupf, N., Urv, T., Zigman, A., & Silverman, W. (2002). Incidence and temporal patterns of adaptive behavior change in adults with mental retardation. *American Journal on Mental Retardation, 107,* 161–174.

Zijlstra, H. P., & Vlaskamp, C. (2005). Leisure provision for persons with profound intellectual and multiple disabilities: Quality time or killing time? *Journal of Intellectual Disability Research, 49,* 434–448.

Zirkel, P. A. (2013). Is it time for elevating the standard for FAPE under IDEA? *Exceptional Children, 79,* 497–508.

INDEX

Note: Page numbers in *italics* indicate figures and tables.